LOEB CLASSICAL LIBRARY

FOUNDED BY JAMES LOEB 1911

STRABO

IV

LCL 196

STRABO

GEOGRAPHY

BOOKS 8–9

WITH AN ENGLISH TRANSLATION BY

HORACE LEONARD JONES

HARVARD UNIVERSITY PRESS
CAMBRIDGE, MASSACHUSETTS
LONDON, ENGLAND

First published 1927

ISBN 978-0-674-99216-0

Printed on acid-free paper and bound by
The Maple-Vail Book Manufacturing Group

CONTENTS

LIST OF THE BOOKS OF THE GEOGRAPHY OF STRABO

Showing their place in the volumes of this edition and in the edition of Casaubon of 1620

LIST OF THE BOOKS

THE

GEOGRAPHY OF STRABO

BOOK VIII

ΣΤΡΑΒΩΝΟΣ ΓΕΩΓΡΑΦΙΚΩΝ

Η′

I

C 332 1. Ἐπεὶ δὲ ἐπιόντες ἀπὸ τῶν ἑσπερίων τῆς Εὐρώπης μερῶν, ὅσα τῇ θαλάττῃ περιέχεται τῇ ἐντὸς καὶ τῇ ἐκτός, τά τε βάρβαρα ἔθνη περιωδεύσαμεν πάντα ἐν αὐτῇ μέχρι τοῦ Ταναΐδος καὶ τῆς Ἑλλάδος οὐ πολὺ μέρος, τὴν Μακεδονίαν,[1] ἀποδώσομεν νυνὶ τὰ λοιπὰ τῆς Ἑλλαδικῆς γεωγραφίας. ἅπερ Ὅμηρος μὲν πρῶτος, ἔπειτα καὶ ἄλλοι πλείους ἐπραγματεύσαντο, οἱ μὲν ἰδίᾳ Λιμένας ἢ Περίπλους ἢ Περιόδους γῆς ἤ τι τοιοῦτον ἄλλο ἐπιγράψαντες, ἐν οἷς καὶ τὰ Ἑλλαδικὰ περιέχεται, οἱ δ᾽ ἐν τῇ κοινῇ τῆς ἱστορίας γραφῇ χωρὶς ἀποδείξαντες τὴν τῶν ἠπείρων τοπογραφίαν, καθάπερ Ἔφορός τε ἐποίησε καὶ Πολύβιος, ἄλλοι δ᾽ εἰς τὸν φυσικὸν τόπον καὶ τὸν μαθηματικὸν προσέλαβόν τινα καὶ τῶν τοιούτων, καθάπερ Ποσειδώνιός τε καὶ Ἵππαρχος· τὰ μὲν οὖν τῶν ἄλλων εὐδιαίτητά ἐστι, τὰ δ᾽ Ὁμήρου σκέψεως δεῖται κριτικῆς, ποιητικῶς τε λέγοντος καὶ οὐ τὰ νῦν, ἀλλὰ τὰ ἀρχαῖα, ὧν

[1] τὴν Μακεδονίαν, Casaubon, for τῆς Μακεδονίας, which latter Meineke ejects.

---

[1] The Mediterranean and Atlantic.

THE GEOGRAPHY OF STRABO

BOOK VIII

I

1. I BEGAN my description by going over all the western parts of Europe comprised between the inner and the outer sea;[1] and now that I have encompassed in my survey all the barbarian tribes in Europe as far as the Tanaïs and also a small part of Greece, Macedonia,[2] I now shall give an account of the remainder of the geography of Greece. This subject was first treated by Homer; and then, after him, by several others, some of whom have written special treatises entitled *Harbours*, or *Coasting Voyages*, or *General Descriptions of the Earth*, or the like; and in these is comprised also the description of Greece. Others have set forth the topography of the continents in separate parts of their general histories, for instance, Ephorus and Polybius. Still others have inserted certain things on this subject in their treatises on physics and mathematics, for instance, Poseidonius and Hipparchus. Now although the statements of the others are easy to pass judgment upon, yet those of Homer require critical inquiry, since he speaks poetically, and not of things as they now are, but of things as they were in antiquity, which for the most part have been

[2] See Book 7, *Frag.* 9, in Vol. III.

ὁ χρόνος ἠμαύρωκε τὰ πολλά. ὡς δ' οὖν δυνατὸν ἐγχειρητέον, ἀρξαμένοις ἀφ' ὧνπερ ἀπελίπομεν· ἐτελεύτα δ' ἡμῖν ὁ λόγος ἀπὸ μὲν τῆς ἑσπέρας καὶ τῶν ἄρκτων εἰς τὰ Ἠπειρωτικὰ ἔθνη καὶ τὰ τῶν Ἰλλυριῶν, ἀπὸ δὲ τῆς ἕω εἰς τὰ τῶν Μακεδόνων μέχρι Βυζαντίου. μετὰ μὲν οὖν τοὺς Ἠπειρώτας καὶ τοὺς Ἰλλυριοὺς τῶν Ἑλλήνων Ἀκαρνᾶνές εἰσι καὶ Αἰτωλοὶ καὶ Λοκροὶ οἱ Ὀζόλαι· πρὸς δὲ τούτοις Φωκεῖς τε καὶ Βοιωτοί· τούτοις δ' ἀντίπορθμός ἐστιν ἡ Πελοπόννησος, ἀπολαμβάνουσα μεταξὺ τὸν Κορινθιακὸν κόλπον
C 333 καὶ σχηματίζουσά τε τοῦτον καὶ σχηματιζομένη ὑπ' αὐτοῦ· μετὰ δὲ Μακεδονίαν Θετταλοὶ μέχρι Μαλιέων καὶ τὰ [1] τῶν ἄλλων τῶν ἐκτὸς Ἰσθμοῦ καὶ αὐτῶν τῶν ἐντός.

2. Ἑλλάδος μὲν οὖν [2] πολλὰ ἔθνη γεγένηται, τὰ δ' ἀνωτάτω τοσαῦτα, ὅσας καὶ διαλέκτους παρειλήφαμεν τὰς Ἑλληνίδας· τούτων δ' αὐτῶν τεσσάρων οὐσῶν, τὴν μὲν Ἰάδα τῇ παλαιᾷ Ἀτθίδι τὴν αὐτήν φαμεν (καὶ γὰρ Ἴωνες ἐκαλοῦντο οἱ τότε Ἀττικοί, καὶ ἐκεῖθέν εἰσιν οἱ τὴν Ἀσίαν ἐποικήσαντες Ἴωνες καὶ χρησάμενοι τῇ νῦν λεγομένῃ γλώττῃ Ἰάδι), τὴν δὲ Δωρίδα τῇ Αἰολίδι· πάντες γὰρ οἱ ἐκτὸς Ἰσθμοῦ πλὴν Ἀθηναίων καὶ Μεγαρέων καὶ τῶν περὶ τὸν Παρνασσὸν Δωριέων καὶ νῦν ἔτι Αἰολεῖς καλοῦνται, καὶ τοὺς Δωριέας δὲ ὀλίγους ὄντας καὶ τραχυτάτην

[1] τά, before τῶν ἄλλων, Müller-Dübner insert, following conj. of Meineke.

[2] Ἑλλάδος μὲν οὖν E, ἰδίᾳ μὲν οὖν B, ἰδοὺ μὲν οὖν C*slv*, ἐπιδονομὲν οὖν A*g*. Corais follows B, and Kramer and Müller-Dübner read τῆς Ἑλλάδος μὲν οὖν; but Meineke, *ἐπιδονο μὲν οὖν.

obscured by time. Be this as it may, as far as I can I must undertake the inquiry; and I shall begin where I left off. My account ended, on the west and the north, with the tribes of the Epeirotes and of the Illyrians, and, on the east, with those of the Macedonians as far as Byzantium. After the Epeirotes and the Illyrians, then, come the following peoples of the Greeks: the Acarnanians, the Aetolians, and the Ozolian Locrians; and, next, the Phocians and Boeotians; and opposite these, across the arm of the sea, is the Peloponnesus, which with these encloses the Corinthian Gulf, and not only shapes the gulf but also is shaped by it; and after Macedonia, the Thessalians (extending as far as the Malians) and the countries of the rest of the peoples outside the Isthmus,[1] as also of those inside.

2. There have been many tribes in Greece, but those which go back to the earliest times are only as many in number as the Greek dialects which we have learned to distinguish. But though the dialects themselves are four in number,[2] we may say that the Ionic is the same as the ancient Attic, for the Attic people of ancient times were called Ionians, and from that stock sprang those Ionians who colonised Asia and used what is now called the Ionic speech; and we may say that the Doric dialect is the same as the Aeolic, for all the Greeks outside the Isthmus, except the Athenians and the Megarians and the Dorians who live about Parnassus, are to this day still called Aeolians. And it is reasonable to suppose that the Dorians too, since they were few in number and lived in a most

[1] *i.e.* north of the Isthmus.

[2] See 14. 5. 26.

οἰκοῦντας χώραν εἰκός ἐστι τῷ ἀνεπιμίκτῳ παρατρέψαι τὴν γλῶτταν καὶ τὰ ἄλλα ἔθη[1] πρὸς τὸ μὴ ὁμογενές, ὁμογενεῖς πρότερον ὄντας. τοῦτο δ' αὐτὸ καὶ τοῖς Ἀθηναίοις συνέβη, λεπτόγεών τε καὶ τραχεῖαν οἰκοῦντας χώραν ἀπορθήτους μεῖναι[2] διὰ τοῦτο, καὶ αὐτόχθονας νομισθῆναί φησιν ὁ Θουκυδίδης, κατέχοντας τὴν αὐτὴν ἀεί, μηδενὸς ἐξελαύνοντος αὐτοὺς μηδ' ἐπιθυμοῦντος ἔχειν τὴν ἐκείνων· τοῦτο τοίνυν αὐτὸ καὶ τοῦ ἑτερογλώττου καὶ τοῦ ἑτεροεθοῦς[3] αἴτιον, ὡς εἰκός, ὑπῆρξε, καίπερ ὀλίγοις οὖσιν. οὕτω δὲ τοῦ Αἰολικοῦ πλήθους ἐπικρατοῦντος ἐν τοῖς ἐκτὸς Ἰσθμοῦ, καὶ οἱ ἐντὸς Αἰολεῖς πρότερον ἦσαν, εἶτ' ἐμίχθησαν, Ἰώνων μὲν ἐκ τῆς Ἀττικῆς τὸν Αἰγιαλὸν κατασχόντων, τῶν δ' Ἡρακλειδῶν τοὺς Δωριέας καταγαγόντων, ὑφ' ὧν τά τε Μέγαρα ᾠκίσθη καὶ πολλαὶ τῶν ἐν τῇ Πελοποννήσῳ πόλεων. οἱ μὲν οὖν Ἴωνες ἐξέπεσον πάλιν ταχέως ὑπὸ Ἀχαιῶν, Αἰολικοῦ ἔθνους· ἐλείφθη δ' ἐν τῇ Πελοποννήσῳ τὰ δύο ἔθνη, τό τε Αἰολικὸν καὶ τὸ Δωρικόν. ὅσοι μὲν οὖν ἧττον τοῖς Δωριεῦσιν ἐπεπλέκοντο (καθάπερ συνέβη τοῖς τε Ἀρκάσι καὶ τοῖς Ἠλείοις, τοῖς μὲν ὀρεινοῖς τελέως οὖσι καὶ οὐκ ἐμπεπτωκόσιν εἰς τὸν κλῆρον, τοῖς δ' ἱεροῖς νομισθεῖσι τοῦ Ὀλυμπίου Διὸς καὶ καθ'

[1] ἔθη (*n*), for ἔθνη; so the editors.

[2] μεῖναι, Müller-Dübner, for μὲν εἶναι.

[3] ἑτεροεθοῦς, Meineke, for ἑτεροεθνοῦς; see κατὰ τὰ . . . ἔθη, 14. 5. 26.

rugged country, have, because of their lack of intercourse with others, changed their speech and their other customs to the extent that they are no longer a part of the same tribe as before. And this was precisely the case with the Athenians; that is, they lived in a country that was both thin-soiled and rugged, and for this reason, according to Thucydides,[1] their country remained free from devastation, and they were regarded as an indigenous people, who always occupied the same country, since no one drove them out of their country or even desired to possess it. This, therefore, as one may suppose, was precisely the cause of their becoming different both in speech and in customs, albeit they were few in number. And just as the Aeolic element predominated in the parts outside the Isthmus, so too the people inside the Isthmus were in earlier times Aeolians; and then they became mixed with other peoples, since, in the first place, Ionians from Attica seized the Aegialus,[2] and, secondly, the Heracleidae brought back the Dorians, who founded both Megara and many of the cities of the Peloponnesus. The Ionians, however, were soon driven out again by the Achaeans, an Aeolic tribe; and so there were left in the Peloponnesus only the two tribes, the Aeolian and the Dorian. Now all the peoples who had less intercourse with the Dorians—as was the case with the Arcadians and with the Eleians, since the former were wholly mountaineers and had no share in the allotments[3] of territory, while the latter were regarded as sacred to the Olympian Zeus and hence

[1] 1. 2 and 2. 36.
[2] The Peloponnesian Achaea.
[3] Cp. 8. 5. 6.

αὑτοὺς εἰρήνην ἄγουσι πολὺν χρόνον, ἄλλως τε καὶ τοῦ Αἰολικοῦ γένους οὖσι καὶ δεδεγμένοις τὴν Ὀξύλῳ συγκατελθοῦσαν στρατιὰν περὶ τὴν τῶν Ἡρακλειδῶν κάθοδον), οὗτοι Αἰολιστὶ διελέχθησαν, οἱ δ' ἄλλοι μικτῇ τινὶ ἐχρήσαντο ἐξ ἀμφοῖν, οἱ μὲν μᾶλλον οἱ δ' ἧττον αἰολίζοντες. σχεδὸν δέ τι καὶ νῦν κατὰ πόλεις ἄλλοι ἄλλως διαλέγονται, δοκοῦσι δὲ δωρίζειν ἅπαντες διὰ τὴν
C 334 συμβᾶσαν ἐπικράτειαν. τοιαῦτα μὲν οὖν τὰ τῶν Ἑλλήνων ἔθνη καὶ οὕτως, ὡς τύπῳ εἰπεῖν, ἀφωρισμένα. λέγωμεν δὴ ἰδίᾳ[1] λαβόντες ὃν χρὴ τρόπον τῇ τάξει, περὶ αὐτῶν.

3. Ἔφορος μὲν οὖν ἀρχὴν εἶναι τῆς Ἑλλάδος τὴν Ἀκαρνανίαν φησὶν ἀπὸ τῶν ἑσπερίων μερῶν· ταύτην γὰρ συνάπτειν πρώτην τοῖς Ἠπειρωτικοῖς ἔθνεσιν. ἀλλ' ὥσπερ οὗτος τῇ παραλίᾳ μέτρῳ χρώμενος ἐντεῦθεν ποιεῖται τὴν ἀρχήν, ἡγεμονικόν τι τὴν θάλατταν κρίνων πρὸς τὰς τοπογραφίας, ἐπεὶ ἄλλως γ' ἐνεχώρει κατὰ τὴν Μακεδόνων καὶ Θετταλῶν γῆν[2] ἀρχὴν ἀποφαίνεσθαι τῆς Ἑλλάδος· οὕτω καὶ ἡμῖν προσήκει ἀκολουθοῦσι τῇ φύσει τῶν τόπων σύμβουλον ποιεῖσθαι τὴν θάλασσαν. αὕτη δ' ἐκ τοῦ Σικελικοῦ πελάγους προπεσοῦσα[3] τῇ μὲν ἀναχεῖται πρὸς τὸν Κορινθιακὸν κόλπον, τῇ δ' ἀποτελεῖ χερρόνησον μεγάλην τὴν Πελοπόννησον, ἰσθμῷ στενῷ κλειομένην. ἔστι δὲ ταῦτα[4] δύο μέγιστα συστήματα τῆς

[1] ἰδίᾳ λαβόντες, Meineke emends to διαλαβόντες.
[2] For γῆν, Meineke reads τήν.
[3] προπεσοῦσα (BE*l*), Jones, for προσπεσοῦσα.

have long lived to themselves in peace, especially because they belonged to the Aeolic stock and had admitted the army which came back with Oxylus[1] about the time of the return of the Heracleidae—these peoples, I say, spoke the Aeolic dialect, whereas the rest used a sort of mixture of the two, some leaning more to the Aeolic and some less. And, I might almost say, even now the people of each city speaks a different dialect, although, because of the predominance which has been gained by the Dorians, one and all are reputed to speak the Doric. Such, then, are the tribes of the Greeks, and such in general terms is their ethnographical division. Let me now take them separately, following the appropriate order, and tell about them.

3. Ephorus says that, if one begins with the western parts, Acarnania is the beginning of Greece; for, he adds, Acarnania is the first to border on the tribes of the Epeirotes. But just as Ephorus, using the sea-coast as his measuring-line, begins with Acarnania (for he decides in favour of the sea as a kind of guide in his description of places, because otherwise he might have represented parts that border on the land of the Macedonians and the Thessalians as the beginning), so it is proper that I too, following the natural character of the regions, should make the sea my counsellor. Now this sea, issuing forth out of the Sicilian Sea, on one side stretches to the Corinthian Gulf, and on the other forms a large peninsula, the Peloponnesus, which is closed by a narrow isthmus. Thus Greece consists of two

[1] Cp. 8. 3. 33.

---

[4] ταῦτα, Meineke emends to τά.

Ἑλλάδος, τό τε ἐντὸς Ἰσθμοῦ καὶ τὸ ἐκτὸς διὰ[1] Πυλῶν μέχρι τῆς ἐκβολῆς τοῦ Πηνειοῦ (καὶ τοῦτο δ' ἐστὶ τὸ Θετταλικόν[2]). ἔστι δὲ καὶ μεῖζον καὶ ἐπιφανέστερον τὸ ἐντὸς Ἰσθμοῦ· σχεδὸν δέ τι καὶ ἀκρόπολίς ἐστιν ἡ Πελοπόννησος τῆς συμπάσης Ἑλλάδος, χωρὶς γὰρ τῆς λαμπρότητος καὶ δυνάμεως τῶν ἐνοικησάντων ἐθνῶν αὐτὴ ἡ τῶν τόπων θέσις ὑπογράφει τὴν ἡγεμονίαν ταύτην, κόλποις τε καὶ ἄκραις πολλαῖς καί, τοῖς σημειωδεστάτοις, χερρονήσοις μεγάλαις διαπεποικιλμένη, ὧν ἐκ διαδοχῆς ἑτέρα τὴν ἑτέραν ἔχει. ἔστι δὲ πρώτη μὲν τῶν χερρονήσων ἡ Πελοπόννησος, ἰσθμῷ κλειομένη τετταράκοντα σταδίων. δευτέρα δὲ ἡ καὶ ταύτην περιέχουσα, ἧς ἰσθμός ἐστιν ὁ ἐκ Παγῶν[3] τῶν Μεγαρικῶν εἰς Νισαίαν, τὸ Μεγαρέων ἐπίνειον, ὑπερβολῇ σταδίων ἑκατὸν εἴκοσιν ἀπὸ θαλάττης ἐπὶ θάλατταν. τρίτη δ' ἡ καὶ ταύτην περιέχουσα, ἧς ἰσθμὸς ἀπὸ τοῦ μυχοῦ τοῦ Κρισαίου κόλπου μέχρι Θερμοπυλῶν, ἡ δ'[4] ἐπινοουμένη εὐθεῖα γραμμὴ ὅσον πεντακοσίων ὀκτὼ[5] σταδίων τὴν μὲν Βοιωτίαν ἅπασαν ἐντὸς ἀπολαμβάνουσα, τὴν δὲ Φωκίδα τέμνουσα λοξὴν καὶ τοὺς Ἐπικνημιδίους. τετάρτη δὲ ἡ ἀπὸ τοῦ Ἀμβρακικοῦ κόλπου διὰ τῆς Οἴτης καὶ τῆς Τραχινίας εἰς τὸν Μαλιακὸν

[1] διά, before Πυλῶν, Jones inserts. Meineke ejects Πυλῶν. For the readings of the other editors, see C. Müller, *Ind. Var. Lect.*, p. 989.

[2] Meineke ejects the words in parenthesis.

[3] Παγῶν, *Epit.* and *man. sec.* in C, for πάντων (ABCE*l*); so other editors.

[4] δ', A omits.

[5] ὀκτώ probably should be emended to εἴκοσι (κʹ) or πεντήκοντα (νʹ), as C. Müller suggests.

very large bodies of land, the part inside the Isthmus, and the part outside, which extends through Pylae[1] as far as the outlet of the Peneius (this latter is the Thessalian part of Greece);[2] but the part inside the Isthmus is both larger and more famous. I might almost say that the Peloponnesus is the acropolis of Greece as a whole;[3] for, apart from the splendour and power of the tribes that have lived in it, the very topography of Greece, diversified as it is by gulfs, many capes, and, what are the most significant, large peninsulas that follow one another in succession, suggests such hegemony for it. The first of the peninsulas is the Peloponnesus, which is closed by an isthmus forty stadia in width. The second includes the first; and its isthmus extends in width from Pagae in Megaris to Nisaea, the naval station of the Megarians, the distance across being one hundred and twenty stadia from sea to sea. The third likewise includes the second; and its isthmus extends in width from the recess of the Crisaean Gulf as far as Thermopylae—the imaginary straight line, about five hundred and eight stadia in length, enclosing within the peninsula the whole of Boeotia and cutting obliquely Phocis and the country of the Epicnemidians.[4] The fourth is the peninsula whose isthmus extends from the Ambracian Gulf through Oeta[5] and Trachinia to the Maliac

[1] Thermopylae.

[2] That is, from Pylae to the outlet of the Peneius.

[3] Groskurd, Kramer and Curtius think that something like the following has fallen out of the MSS.: "and that Greece is the acropolis of the whole world."

[4] The Epicnemidian Locrians.

[5] Now the Katavothra Mountain. It forms a boundary between the valleys of the Spercheius and Cephissus Rivers.

κόλπον καθήκοντα ἔχουσα τὸν ἰσθμὸν καὶ τὰς Θερμοπύλας, ὅσον ὀκτακοσίων ὄντα σταδίων· πλειόνων δ' ἢ χιλίων ἄλλος ἐστὶν ἀπὸ τοῦ αὐτοῦ κόλπου τοῦ Ἀμβρακικοῦ διὰ Θετταλῶν καὶ Μακεδόνων εἰς τὸν Θερμαῖον διήκων μυχόν. ὑπαγορεύει δή τινα τάξιν οὐ φαύλην ἡ τῶν χερρονήσων διαδοχή· δεῖ δ' ἀπὸ τῆς ἐλαχίστης ἄρξασθαι, ἐπιφανεστάτης δέ.

II

C 335 1. Ἔστι τοίνυν ἡ Πελοπόννησος ἐοικυῖα φύλλῳ πλατάνου τὸ σχῆμα, ἴση σχεδόν τι κατὰ μῆκος καὶ κατὰ πλάτος, ὅσον χιλίων καὶ τετρακοσίων σταδίων· τὸ μὲν ἀπὸ τῆς ἑσπέρας ἐπὶ τὴν ἕω, τοῦτο δ' ἐστὶ τὸ ἀπὸ τοῦ Χελωνάτα δι' Ὀλυμπίας καὶ τῆς Μεγαλοπολίτιδος ἐπὶ Ἰσθμόν· τὸ δ' ἀπὸ τοῦ νότου πρὸς τὴν ἄρκτον, ὅ ἐστι τὸ ἀπὸ Μαλεῶν δι' Ἀρκαδίας εἰς Αἴγιον· ἡ δὲ περίμετρος μὴ κατακολπίζοντι τετρακισχιλίων σταδίων, ὡς Πολύβιος· Ἀρτεμίδωρος δὲ καὶ τετρακοσίους προστίθησι· κατακολπίζοντι δὲ πλείους τῶν ἑξακοσίων ἐπὶ τοῖς πεντακισχιλίοις. ὁ δ' Ἰσθμὸς κατὰ τὸν διολκόν, δι' οὗ τὰ πορθμεῖα ὑπερνεωλκοῦσιν ἀπὸ τῆς ἑτέρας εἰς τὴν ἑτέραν θάλατταν,[1] εἴρηται ὅτι τετταράκοντα σταδίων ἐστίν.

[1] κατὰ . . . θάλατταν, omitted by BC*lsv*.

---

[1] Cp. 2. 1. 30.

[2] Cape Chelonatas, opposite the island Zacynthos; now Cape Tornese.

Gulf and Thermopylae—the isthmus being about eight hundred stadia in width. But there is another isthmus, more than one thousand stadia in width, extending from the same Ambracian Gulf through the countries of the Thessalians and the Macedonians to the recess of the Thermaean Gulf. So then, the succession of the peninsulas suggests a kind of order, and not a bad one, for me to follow in my description; and I should begin with the smallest, but most famous, of them.

II

1. Now the Peloponnesus is like a leaf of a plane-tree in shape,[1] its length and breadth being almost equal, that is, about fourteen hundred stadia. Its length is reckoned from the west to the east, that is, from Chelonatas[2] through Olympia and Megalopolis to the Isthmus; and its width, from the south towards the north, that is, from Maleae[3] through Arcadia to Aegium.[4] The perimeter, not following the sinuosities of the gulfs, is four thousand stadia, according to Polybius, although Artemidorus adds four hundred more;[5] but following the sinuosities of the gulfs, it is more than five thousand six hundred. The width of the Isthmus at the "Diolcus,"[6] where the ships are hauled overland from one sea to the other, is forty stadia, as I have already said.

[3] Cape Maleae.

[4] The Aegion, or Aegium, of to-day, though until recent times more generally known by its later name Vostitza.

[5] Polybius counted 8⅓ stadia to the mile (7. *Frag.* 56).

[6] Literally, "Haul-across"; the name of "the narrowest part of the Isthmus" (8. 6. 4), and probably applied to the road itself.

2. Ἔχουσι δὲ τῆς χερρονήσου ταύτης τὸ μὲν ἑσπέριον μέρος Ἠλεῖοι καὶ Μεσσήνιοι, κλυζόμενοι τῷ Σικελικῷ πελάγει· προσλαμβάνουσι δὲ καὶ τῆς ἑκατέρωθεν παραλίας, ἡ μὲν Ἠλεία πρὸς ἄρκτον ἐπιστρέφουσα καὶ τὴν ἀρχὴν τοῦ Κορινθιακοῦ κόλπου μέχρι ἄκρας Ἀράξου, καθ' ἣν ἀντίπορθμός ἐστιν ἥ τε Ἀκαρνανία καὶ αἱ προκείμεναι νῆσοι, Ζάκυνθος καὶ Κεφαλληνία καὶ Ἰθάκη καὶ Ἐχινάδες, ὧν ἐστὶ καὶ τὸ Δουλίχιον· τῆς δὲ Μεσσηνίας τὸ πλέον ἀνεῳγμένον πρὸς νότον καὶ τὸ Λιβυκὸν πέλαγος μέχρι τῶν καλουμένων Θυρίδων πλησίον Ταινάρου. ἑξῆς δὲ μετὰ μὲν τὴν Ἠλείαν ἐστὶ τὸ τῶν Ἀχαιῶν ἔθνος πρὸς ἄρκτους βλέπον καὶ τῷ Κορινθιακῷ κόλπῳ παρατεῖνον, τελευτᾷ δ' εἰς τὴν Σικυωνίαν· ἐντεῦθεν δὲ Σικυὼν καὶ Κόρινθος ἐκδέχεται μέχρι τοῦ Ἰσθμοῦ· μετὰ δὲ τὴν Μεσσηνίαν ἡ Λακωνικὴ καὶ ἡ Ἀργεία, μέχρι τοῦ Ἰσθμοῦ καὶ αὕτη. κόλποι δ' εἰσὶν ἐνταῦθα ὅ τε Μεσσηνιακὸς καὶ ὁ Λακωνικὸς καὶ τρίτος ὁ Ἀργολικός, τέταρτος δ' ὁ Ἑρμιονικὸς καὶ Σαρωνικός. οἱ δὲ Σαλαμινιακὸν καλοῦσιν· ὧν τοὺς μὲν ἡ Λιβυκή, τοὺς δ' ἡ Κρητικὴ θάλασσα πληροῖ καὶ τὸ Μυρτῷον πέλαγος· τινὲς δὲ καὶ τὸν Σαρωνικὸν πόρον ἢ[1] πέλαγος ὀνομάζουσι. μέση δ' ἐστὶν ἡ Ἀρκαδία, πᾶσιν ἐπικειμένη καὶ γειτνιῶσα τοῖς ἄλλοις ἔθνεσιν.

3. Ὁ δὲ Κορινθιακὸς κόλπος ἄρχεται μὲν ἀπὸ τῶν ἐκβολῶν τοῦ Εὐήνου (τινὲς δέ φασιν τοῦ

[1] ἤ, after πόρον, Groskurd inserts; so Meineke.

---

[1] See 8. 5. 1, and footnote.

2. The western part of this peninsula is occupied by the Eleians and the Messenians, whose countries are washed by the Sicilian Sea. In addition, they also hold a part of the sea-coast in both directions, for the Eleian country curves towards the north and the beginning of the Corinthian Gulf as far as Cape Araxus (opposite which, across the straits, lie Acarnania and the islands off its coast—Zacynthos, Cephallenia, Ithaca, and also the Echinades, among which is Dulichium), whereas the greater part of the Messenian country opens up towards the south and the Libyan Sea as far as what is called Thyrides,[1] near Taenarum. Next after the Eleian country comes the tribe of the Achaeans,[2] whose country faces towards the north and stretches along the Corinthian Gulf, ending at Sicyonia. Then come in succession Sicyon and Corinth, the territory of the latter extending as far as the Isthmus. After the Messenian country come the Laconian and the Argive, the latter also extending as far as the Isthmus. The gulfs on this coast are: first, the Messenian; second, the Laconian; third, the Argolic; fourth, the Hermionic; and fifth, the Saronic, by some called the Salaminiac. Of these gulfs the first two are filled by the Libyan Sea, and the others by the Cretan and Myrtoan Seas. Some, however, call the Saronic Gulf "Strait" or "Sea." In the interior of the peninsula is Arcadia, which touches as next-door neighbour the countries of all those other tribes.

3. The Corinthian Gulf begins, on the one side, at the outlets of the Evenus (though some say at the

[2] See 8. 7. 4, and footnote.

Ἀχελῴου τοῦ ὁρίζοντος Ἀκαρνᾶνας καὶ τοὺς
Αἰτωλούς) καὶ τοῦ Ἀράξου. ἐνταῦθα γὰρ πρῶτον ἀξιόλογον συναγωγὴν λαμβάνουσι πρὸς ἀλ-
λήλας αἱ ἑκατέρωθεν ἀκταί· προϊοῦσαι δὲ πλέον [1]
τελέως συμπίπτουσι κατὰ τὸ Ῥίον καὶ τὸ Ἀντίρριον, ὅσον δὴ πέντε σταδίων ἀπολείπουσαι
πορθμόν. ἔστι δὲ τὸ μὲν Ῥίον τῶν Ἀχαιῶν
ἀλιτενὴς ἄκρα, δρεπανοειδῆ τινὰ ἐπιστροφὴν εἰς
τὸ ἐντὸς ἔχουσα (καὶ δὴ καὶ καλεῖται Δρέπανον),
C 336 κεῖται δὲ μεταξὺ Πατρῶν καὶ Αἰγίου, Ποσειδῶνος
ἱερὸν ἔχουσα· τὸ δ' Ἀντίρριον ἐν μεθορίοις τῆς
Αἰτωλίας καὶ τῆς Λοκρίδος ἵδρυται, καλοῦσι δὲ [2]
Μολύκριον Ῥίον. εἶτ' ἐντεῦθεν διίσταται πάλιν
ἡ παραλία μετρίως ἑκατέρωθεν, προελθοῦσα δ'
εἰς τὸν Κρισαῖον κόλπον ἐνταῦθα τελευτᾷ,
κλειομένη τοῖς προσεσπερίοις τῆς Βοιωτίας
καὶ τῆς Μεγαρικῆς τέρμοσιν. ἔχει δὲ τὴν περίμετρον ὁ Κορινθιακὸς κόλπος ἀπὸ μὲν τοῦ Εὐήνου
μέχρι Ἀράξου σταδίων δισχιλίων διακοσίων
τριάκοντα· εἰ δ' ἀπὸ τοῦ Ἀχελῴου, πλεονάζοι
ἂν ἑκατόν που σταδίοις. ἀπὸ μέντοι Ἀχελῴου
ἐπὶ τὸν Εὔηνον Ἀκαρνᾶνές εἰσι, εἶθ' ἑξῆς ἐπὶ τὸ
Ἀντίρριον Αἰτωλοί, τὸ δὲ λοιπὸν μέχρι Ἰσθμοῦ

[1] Capps happily suggests that Strabo probably wrote σχεδόν instead of πλέον or that σχεδόν has fallen out of the text after πλέον.

[2] Before Μολύκριον, Meineke inserts καί.

---

[1] Cape Araxus; now Kalogria.

[2] Lit. "more completely" (see critical note).

[3] Cape "Drepanum." Strabo confuses Cape Rhium with Cape Drepanum, since the two were separated by the Bay of Panormus (see Frazer's *Pausanias*, notes on 7. 22. 10 and 7. 23. 4, and Curtius' *Peloponnesos*, I. p. 447).

outlets of the Acheloüs, the river that separates the Acarnanians and the Aetolians), and, on the other, at Araxus;[1] for here the shores on either side first draw notably nearer to one another; then in their advance they all but[2] meet at Rhium and Antirrhium, where they leave between them a strait only about five stadia in width. Rhium, belonging to the Achaeans, is a low-lying cape; it bends inwards (and it is in fact called "Sickle").[3] It lies between Patrae and Aegium, and possesses a temple of Poseidon. Antirrhium is situated on the common boundary of Aetolia and Locris; and people call it Molycrian Rhium.[4] Then, from here, the shoreline on either side again draws moderately apart, and then, advancing into the Crisaean Gulf, it comes to an end there, being shut in by the westerly limits of Boeotia and Megaris.[5] The perimeter of the Corinthian Gulf, if one measures from the Evenus to Araxus, is two thousand two hundred and thirty stadia; but if one measures from the Acheloüs, it is about a hundred stadia more. Now from the Acheloüs to the Evenus the coast is occupied by Acarnanians;[6] and thence to Antirrhium, by Aetolians; but the remaining coast, as far as the Isthmus, belongs to[7] the Phocians, the

[4] After Molycreia, a small Aetolian town near by.

[5] "Crisaean Gulf" (the Gulf of Salona of to-day) was often used in this broader sense. Cp. 8. 6. 21.

[6] Strabo thus commits himself against the assertion of others (see at the beginning of the paragraph) that the Acheloüs separates the Acarnanians and the Aetolians.

[7] The Greek for "the Locrians and" seems to have fallen out of the MSS. at this point; for Strabo has just said that "Antirrhium is on the common boundary of Aetolia and Locris" (see 9. 3. 1).

Φωκέων ἐστὶ[1] καὶ Βοιωτῶν καὶ τῆς Μεγαρίδος, στάδιοι χίλιοι ἑκατὸν εἴκοσι δυεῖν δέοντες· ἡ δὲ ἀπὸ τοῦ Ἀντιρρίου μέχρι Ἰσθμοῦ θάλαττα[2] Ἀλκυονὶς καλεῖται, μέρος οὖσα τοῦ Κρισαίου κόλπου· ἀπὸ δὲ τοῦ[3] Ἰσθμοῦ ἐπὶ τὸν Ἄραξον τριάκοντα ἐπὶ τοῖς χιλίοις.[4] ὡς μὲν δὴ τύπῳ εἰπεῖν τοιαύτη τις καὶ τοσαύτη ἡ τῆς Πελοποννήσου θέσις καὶ τῆς ἀντιπόρθμου γῆς μέχρι τοῦ μυχοῦ, τοιοῦτος δὲ καὶ ὁ μεταξὺ ἀμφοῖν κόλπος. εἶτα τὰ[5] καθ' ἕκαστα ἐροῦμεν, τὴν ἀρχὴν ἀπὸ τῆς Ἠλείας ποιησάμενοι.

III

1. Νῦν μὲν δὴ πᾶσαν Ἠλείαν ὀνομάζουσι τὴν μεταξὺ Ἀχαιῶν τε καὶ Μεσσηνίων παραλίαν, ἀνέχουσαν εἰς τὴν μεσόγαιαν τὴν πρὸς Ἀρκαδίᾳ τῇ κατὰ Φολόην καὶ Ἀζᾶνας καὶ Παρρασίους. τοῦτο δὲ τὸ παλαιὸν εἰς πλείους δυναστείας διῄρητο, εἶτ' εἰς δύο, τήν τε τῶν Ἐπειῶν καὶ τὴν ὑπὸ Νέστορι τῷ Νηλέως· καθάπερ καὶ Ὅμηρος εἴρηκε, τὴν μὲν τῶν Ἐπειῶν ὀνομάζων Ἦλιν·[6]

[1] Φωκέων ἐστὶ, Pletho, Corais, and Forbiger would emend to Λοκρῶν ἐστὶ καὶ Φωκέων.

[2] After θάλαττα Groskurd, Kramer and others believe that words like the following have fallen out: Κρισαῖος κόλπος ἐστίν· ἡ δὲ ἀπὸ Κρεούσης πόλεως θάλαττα. Meineke indicates a lacuna. There is no lacuna in the MSS.

[3] ἀπὸ δὲ τοῦ: the letters πὸ δὲ τοῦ are supplied by Kramer, there being a lacuna of five or six letters in A.

[4] χιλίοις: lacuna supplied by Corais (see C. Müller, *Ind. Var. Lect.*, p. 989).

Boeotians and Megaris—a distance of one thousand one hundred and eighteen stadia. The sea from Antirrhium as far as the Isthmus[1] is called Alcyonian, it being a part of the Crisaean Gulf. Again, from the Isthmus to Araxus the distance is one thousand and thirty stadia. Such, then, in general terms, is the position and extent of the Peloponnesus, and of the land that lies opposite to it across the arm of the sea as far as the recess; and such, too, is the character of the gulf that lies between the two bodies of land. Now I shall describe each part in detail, beginning with the Eleian country.

III

1. At the present time the whole of the seaboard that lies between the countries of the Achaeans and the Messenians, and extends inland to the Arcadian districts of Pholoë, of the Azanes, and of the Parrhasians, is called the Eleian country. But in early times this country was divided into several domains; and afterwards into two—that of the Epeians and that under the rule of Nestor the son of Neleus; just as Homer, too, states, when he calls the land of the Epeians by the name of "Elis"

[1] Some of the editors believe that words to the following effect have fallen out at this point: "is the Crisaean Gulf; but the sea from the city Creusa."

---

[5] εἶτα τά: for the different readings, see C. Müller, p. 989.
[6] Ἦλιν, Corais, for πόλιν; so Meineke and others.

ἠδὲ παρ'[1] Ἦλιδα δῖαν, ὅθι κρατέουσιν Ἐπειοί·

τὴν δ' ὑπὸ τῷ Νέστορι Πύλον, δι' ἧς τὸν Ἀλφειὸν ῥεῖν φησίν,

Ἀλφειοῦ, ὅς τ' εὐρὺ ῥέει Πυλίων διὰ γαίης.

Πύλον μὲν οὖν καὶ πόλιν οἶδεν ὁ ποιητής·

οἱ δὲ Πύλον, Νηλῆος ἐϋκτίμενον πτολίεθρον, ἷξον·

οὐ διὰ τῆς πόλεως δὲ οὐδὲ παρ' αὐτὴν ῥεῖ ὁ Ἀλφειός, ἀλλὰ παρ' αὐτὴν μὲν ἕτερος, ὃν οἱ μὲν Παμισόν, οἱ δὲ Ἄμαθον καλοῦσιν, ἀφ' οὗ καὶ ὁ Πύλος Ἠμαθόεις εἰρῆσθαι οὗτος δοκεῖ, διὰ δὲ τῆς χώρας τῆς Πυλίας ὁ Ἀλφειός.

2. Ἦλις δὲ ἡ νῦν πόλις οὔπω ἔκτιστο καθ' Ὅμηρον, ἀλλ' ἡ χώρα κωμηδὸν ᾠκεῖτο· ἐκαλεῖτο δὲ Κοίλη Ἦλις ἀπὸ τοῦ συμβεβηκότος· τοιαύτη γὰρ ἦν ἡ πλείστη καὶ ἀρίστη. ὀψὲ δέ ποτε συνῆλθον εἰς τὴν νῦν πόλιν Ἦλιν, μετὰ τὰ Περσικά, ἐκ πολλῶν δήμων. σχεδὸν δὲ καὶ τοὺς ἄλλους τόπους τοὺς κατὰ Πελοπόννησον πλὴν
C 337 ὀλίγων, οὓς κατέλεξεν ὁ ποιητής, οὐ πόλεις, ἀλλὰ χώρας ὀνομάζει,[2] συστήματα δήμων ἔχουσαν ἑκάστην πλείω, ἐξ ὧν ὕστερον αἱ γνωριζόμεναι πόλεις συνῳκίσθησαν, οἷον τῆς Ἀρκαδίας Μαντίνεια μὲν ἐκ πέντε δήμων ὑπ' Ἀργείων συνῳκίσθη, Τεγέα δ' ἐξ ἐννέα, ἐκ τοσούτων δὲ καὶ Ἡραία ὑπὸ Κλεομβρότου ἢ ὑπὸ Κλεωνύμου· ὡς δ' αὔτως

[1] ἠδὲ παρ', the editors, for τὴν δὲ παρ'.
[2] ὀνομάζει, Meineke emends to νομίζειν δεῖ; ὀνομάζων *no*.

[1] *Sc.* "the ship." [2] *Odyssey* 15. 298.

("and[1] passed goodly Elis, where the Epeians hold sway"),[2] and the land under the rule of Nestor, "Pylus," through which, he says, the Alpheius flows ("of the Alpheius, that floweth in wide stream through the land of the Pylians").[3] Of course Homer also knew of Pylus as a city ("and they reached Pylus, the well-built city of Nestor"),[4] but the Alpheius does not flow through the city, nor past it either; in fact, another river flows past it, a river which some call "Pamisus" and others "Amathus" (whence, apparently, the epithet "Emathoëis" which has been applied to this Pylus), but the Alpheius flows through the Pylian country.

2. What is now the city of Elis had not yet been founded in Homer's time; in fact, the people of the country lived only in villages. And the country was called Coelê[5] Elis from the fact in the case, for the most and best of it was "Coelê." It was only relatively late, after the Persian wars, that people came together from many communities into what is now the city of Elis. And I might almost say that, with only a few exceptions, the other Peloponnesian places named by the poet were also named by him, not as cities, but as countries, each country being composed of several communities, from which in later times the well-known cities were settled. For instance, in Arcadia, Mantineia was settled by Argive colonists from five communities; and Tegea from nine; and also Heraea from nine, either by Cleombrotus or by Cleonymus. And in

[3] *Iliad* 5. 545. [4] *Odyssey* 3. 4.

[5] Literally, "Hollow"; that is, consisting of hollows. So "Coelê Syria" (16. 2. 2), a district of Syria.

Αἴγιον ἐξ ἑπτὰ ἢ ὀκτὼ δήμων συνεπολίσθη, Πάτραι δὲ ἐξ ἑπτά, Δύμη δὲ ἐξ ὀκτώ· οὕτω δὲ καὶ ἡ Ἦλις ἐκ τῶν περιοικίδων συνεπολίσθη[1] (μία τούτων προσκτισ . . . . . . Ἀγριάδες).[2] ῥεῖ δὲ διὰ τῆς πόλεως ὁ Πηνειὸς ποταμὸς παρὰ τὸ γυμνάσιον αὐτῆς. ἔπραξάν τε τοῦτο Ἠλεῖοι χρόνοις ὕστερον πολλοῖς τῆς εἰς αὐτοὺς μεταστάσεως τῶν χωρίων τῶν ὑπὸ τῷ Νέστορι.

3. Ἦν δὲ ταῦτα ἥ τε Πισᾶτις, ἧς ἡ Ὀλυμπία μέρος, καὶ ἡ Τριφυλία καὶ ἡ τῶν Καυκώνων. Τριφύλιοι δ' ἐκλήθησαν ἀπὸ τοῦ συμβεβηκότος, ἀπὸ τοῦ τρία φῦλα συνεληλυθέναι, τό τε τῶν ἀπ' ἀρχῆς Ἐπειῶν καὶ τὸ τῶν ἐποικησάντων ὕστερον Μινυῶν καὶ τὸ τῶν ὕστατα ἐπικρατησάντων Ἠλείων· οἱ δ' ἀντὶ τῶν Μινυῶν Ἀρκάδας φασίν, ἀμφισβητήσαντας τῆς χώρας πολλάκις, ἀφ' οὗ καὶ Ἀρκαδικὸς Πύλος ἐκλήθη ὁ αὐτὸς καὶ Τριφυλιακός. Ὅμηρος δὲ ταύτην ἅπασαν τὴν χώραν μέχρι Μεσσήνης καλεῖ Πύλον ὁμωνύμως τῇ πόλει. ὅτι δὲ διώριστο ἡ Κοίλη Ἦλις ἀπὸ τῶν ὑπὸ τῷ

[1] After συνεπολίσθη Corais inserts ὀκτώ (η'); but Curtius (*Peloponnesos* ii. 99) dissents.

[2] μία τούτων προσκτισ . . . . . . Ἀγριάδες; so in A, with lacuna of six or seven letters before Ἀγριάδες. But the whole of μία . . . Ἀγριάδες is omitted by BC*lm*, with no lacuna. For the readings of *gkhi* (similar to A), see C. Müller, p. 989. Simply μία τούτων, Aldine; μία τούτων [οὖσα], Corais; Kramer follows A, supplying the lacuna thus: προσκτισ[θεισῶν]; Meineke makes no effort to supply the lacuna. Jones conjectures: μία δὲ τούτων προσεκτίσθη, Ἀνιγριάδες.

---

[1] It seems impossible to restore what Strabo wrote here. He appears to have said either (1) that Elis was the name

the same way the city Aegium was made up of seven or eight communities; the city Patrae of seven; and the city Dymê of eight. And in this way the city Elis was also made up of the communities of the surrounding country (one of these . . . the Agriades).[1] The Peneius River flows through the city past the gymnasium. And the Eleians did not make this gymnasium until a long time after the districts that were under Nestor had passed into their possession.

3. These districts were Pisatis (of which Olympia was a part), Triphylia, and the country of the Cauconians. The Triphylians[2] were so called from the fact that three tribes of people had come together in that country—that of the Epeians, who were there at the outset, and that of the Minyans, who later settled there, and that of the Eleians, who last dominated the country. But some name the Arcadians in the place of the Minyans, since the Arcadians had often disputed the possession of the country; and hence the same Pylus was called both Arcadian Pylus and Triphylian Pylus.[3] Homer calls this whole country as far as Messenê "Pylus," giving it the same name as the city. But Coelê Elis was distinct from the places subject to Nestor,

of one of the original communities and that the community of the Agriades was later added, or simply (2) that one of the communities, that of the Agriades, was later added. But the "Agriades" are otherwise unknown, and possibly, as C. Müller (*Ind. Var. Lect.*, p. 989) suggests, Strabo wrote "Anigriades"—if indeed there was such a people (see 8. 3. 19). See critical note on opposite page.

[2] "Tri," three, and "phyla," tribes.

[3] Now Kakovatos (Dr. Blegen, *Korakou*, p. 119, American School of Classical Studies, 1921).

Νέστορι τόπων, ὁ τῶν νεῶν κατάλογος δηλοῖ τοῖς τῶν ἡγεμόνων καὶ τῶν κατοικιῶν ὀνόμασι. λέγω δὲ ταῦτα, συμβάλλων τά τε νῦν καὶ τὰ ὑφ' Ὁμήρου λεγόμενα· ἀνάγκη γὰρ ἀντεξετάζεσθαι ταῦτα ἐκείνοις διὰ τὴν τοῦ ποιητοῦ δόξαν καὶ συντροφίαν πρὸς ἡμᾶς, τότε νομίζοντος ἑκάστου κατορθοῦσθαι τὴν παροῦσαν πρόθεσιν, ὅταν ᾖ μηδὲν ἀντίπιπτον τοῖς οὕτω σφόδρα πιστευθεῖσι περὶ τῶν αὐτῶν λόγοις· δεῖ δὴ τά τε ὄντα λέγειν καί, τὰ τοῦ ποιητοῦ παρατιθέντας, ἐφ' ὅσον προσήκει, προσσκοπεῖν.

4. Ἔστι δέ τις ἄκρα τῆς Ἠλείας πρόσβορρος ἀπὸ ἑξήκοντα Δύμης, Ἀχαϊκῆς πόλεως, Ἄραξος. ταύτην μὲν οὖν ἀρχὴν τίθεμεν τῆς τῶν Ἠλείων παραλίας· μετὰ δὲ ταύτην ἐστὶν ἐπὶ τὴν ἑσπέραν προϊοῦσι τὸ τῶν Ἠλείων ἐπίνειον ἡ Κυλλήνη, ἀνάβασιν ἔχουσα ἐπὶ τὴν νῦν πόλιν ἑκατὸν καὶ εἴκοσι σταδίων. μέμνηται δὲ τῆς Κυλλήνης ταύτης καὶ Ὅμηρος, λέγων Ὦτον[1] Κυλλήνιον ἀρχὸν Ἐπειῶν· οὐ γὰρ ἀπὸ τοῦ Ἀρκαδικοῦ ὄρους ὄντα ἔμελλεν ἡγεμόνα τῶν Ἐπειῶν ἀποφῆναι· ἔστι δὲ κώμη μετρία, τὸν Ἀσκληπιὸν ἔχουσα τὸν Κολώτου, θαυμαστὸν ἰδεῖν ξόανον ἐλεφάντινον. μετὰ δὲ Κυλλήνην ἀκρωτήριόν ἐστιν ὁ Χελωνάτας,
C 338 δυσμικώτατον τῆς Πελοποννήσου σημεῖον. πρόκειται δ' αὐτοῦ νησίον καὶ βραχέα ἐν μεθορίοις τῆς τε Κοίλης Ἤλιδος καὶ τῆς Πισατῶν, ὅθεν εἰς

[1] Ὦτον, Xylander, for Βοιωτῶν.

---

[1] *Iliad* 15. 518.
[2] Mt. Cyllenê, now Mt. Zyria.

as is shown in the *Catalogue of Ships* by the names of the chieftains and of their abodes. I say this because I am comparing present conditions with those described by Homer; for we must needs institute this comparison because of the fame of the poet and because of our familiarity with him from our childhood, since all of us believe that we have not successfully treated any subject which we may have in hand until there remains in our treatment nothing that conflicts with what the poet says on the same subject, such confidence do we have in his words. Accordingly, I must give conditions as they now are, and then, citing the words of the poet, in so far as they bear on the matter, take them also into consideration.

4. In the Eleian country, on the north, is a cape, Araxus, sixty stadia distant from Dymê, an Achaean city. This cape, then, I put down as the beginning of the seaboard of the Eleians. After this cape, as one proceeds towards the west, one comes to the naval station of the Eleians, Cyllenê, from which there is a road leading inland to the present city Elis, a distance of one hundred and twenty stadia. Homer, too, mentions this Cyllenê when he says, "Otus, a Cyllenian, a chief of the Epeians,"[1] for he would not have represented a chieftain of the Epeians as being from the Arcadian mountain.[2] Cyllenê is a village of moderate size; and it has the Asclepius made by Colotes—an ivory image that is wonderful to behold. After Cyllenê one comes to the promontory Chelonatas, the most westerly point of the Peloponnesus. Off Chelonatas lies an isle, and also some shallows that are on the common boundary between Coelê Elis and the country of the Pisatae;

Κεφαλληνίαν πλέοντί εἰσιν οὐ πλείους[1] στάδιοι ὀγδοήκοντα. αὐτοῦ δέ που καὶ ὁ Ἐλίσων ἢ Ἔλισα ῥεῖ ποταμὸς ἐν τῇ λεχθείσῃ μεθορίᾳ.

5. Μεταξὺ δὲ τοῦ Χελωνάτα καὶ τῆς Κυλλήνης ὅ τε Πηνειὸς ἐκδίδωσι ποταμὸς καὶ ὁ Σελλήεις ὑπὸ τοῦ ποιητοῦ λεγόμενος, ῥέων ἐκ Φολόης· ἐφ᾿ ᾧ Ἔφυρα πόλις, ἑτέρα τῆς Θεσπρωτικῆς καὶ Θετταλικῆς καὶ τῆς Κορίνθου, τετάρτη τις ἐπὶ τῇ ὁδῷ κειμένη τῇ ἐπὶ τὸν Λασίωνα,[2] ἤτοι ἡ αὐτὴ οὖσα τῇ Βοινώᾳ[3] (τὴν γὰρ Οἰνόην οὕτω καλεῖν εἰώθασιν) ἢ πλησίον ἐκείνης, διέχουσα τῆς Ἠλείων πόλεως σταδίους ἑκατὸν εἴκοσιν· ἐξ ἧς ἥ τε Τληπολέμου τοῦ Ἡρακλέους δοκεῖ λέγεσθαι μήτηρ· ἐκεῖ γὰρ μᾶλλον αἱ τοῦ Ἡρακλέους στρατεῖαι·[4]

τὴν ἄγετ᾿ ἐξ Ἐφύρης ποταμοῦ ἄπο Σελλήεντος·

πρὸς ἐκείναις δὲ[5] οὐδεὶς ποταμὸς Σελλήεις· καὶ ὁ τοῦ Μέγητος θώραξ,[6]

τόν ποτε Φυλεὺς
ἤγαγεν ἐξ Ἐφύρης ποταμοῦ ἄπο Σελλήεντος·

ἐξ ἧς καὶ τὰ φάρμακα τὰ ἀνδροφόνα. εἰς Ἔφυραν γὰρ ἀφῖχθαί φησι τὸν Ὀδυσσέα[7]

φάρμακον ἀνδροφόνον διζήμενον, ὄφρα οἱ εἴη
ἰοὺς χρίεσθαι·

[1] ε[ἰσιν οὐ πλεί]ους: lacuna of about nine letters in A supplied by Kramer; so Meineke.

[2] ἐπὶ τὸν Λασίωνα, Müller-Dübner, for ἐπιθαλασσίωνα (see C. Müller, *Ind. Var. Lect.*, p. 990).

[3] Βοινώᾳ, Corais, for Βοιωνώᾳ; so Meineke.

[4] ἐκεῖ . . . στρατεῖαι, Meineke transposes to position after Σελλήεντος.

[5] δέ, Meineke emends to τε.

[6] θώραξ, Meineke inserts.

and from here the voyage to Cephallenia is not more than eighty stadia. Somewhere in this neighbourhood, on the aforesaid boundary-line, there also flows the River Elison or Elisa.

5. It is between Chelonatas and Cyllenê that the River Peneius empties; as also the River Sellëeis, which is mentioned by the poet and flows out of Pholoê. On the Sellëeis is situated a city Ephyra, which is to be distinguished from the Thesprotian, Thessalian, and Corinthian Ephyras;[1] it is a fourth Ephyra, and is situated on the road that leads to Lasion, being either the same city as Boenoa (for thus Oenoê is usually called), or else near that city, at a distance of one hundred and twenty stadia from the city of the Eleians. This, apparently, is the Ephyra which Homer calls the home of the mother of Tlepolemus the son of Heracles (for the expeditions of Heracles were in this region rather than in any of the other three) when he says, "whom he had brought out of Ephyra, from the River Sellëeis";[2] and there is no River Sellëeis near the other Ephyras. Again, he says of the corselet of Meges: "this corselet Phyleus once brought out of Ephyra, from the River Sellëeis."[3] And thirdly, the man-slaying drugs: for Homer says that Odysseus came to Ephyra "in search of a man-slaying drug, that he might have wherewithal to smear his arrows";[4] and

[1] The site of the Corinthian Ephyra is probably to be identified with that of the prehistoric Korakou (Dr. Blegen, *op. cit.*, p. 54).

[2] *Iliad* 2. 659. The mother of Tlepolemus was Astyocheia.

[3] *Iliad* 15. 530.

[4] *Odyssey* 1. 261 (Athenê speaking).

[7] Meineke inserts ἡ Ἀθηνᾶ after Ὀδυσσέα.

καὶ τὸν Τηλέμαχον οἱ μνηστῆρες·

> ἠὲ καὶ εἰς Ἐφύρης ἐθέλει πίειραν ἄρουραν
> ἐλθεῖν, ὄφρ' ἔνθεν θυμοφθόρα φάρμακ' ἐνείκῃ.

καὶ γὰρ τὴν Αὐγέου θυγατέρα τοῦ τῶν Ἐπειῶν βασιλέως ὁ Νέστωρ ἐν τῇ διηγήσει τοῦ πρὸς αὐτοὺς πολέμου φαρμακίδα εἰσάγει,

> πρῶτος ἐγὼν ἕλον ἄνδρα, φήσας,[1]
> Μούλιον αἰχμητήν, γαμβρὸς δ' ἦν Αὐγείαο,
> πρεσβυτάτην δὲ θύγατρ' εἶχεν,
> ἣ τόσα φάρμακα ᾔδη, ὅσα τρέφει εὐρεῖα χθών.

ἔστι δὲ καὶ περὶ Σικυῶνα Σελλήεις ποταμὸς καὶ Ἔφυρα πλησίον κώμη, καὶ ἐν τῇ Ἀγραίᾳ τῆς Αἰτωλίας Ἔφυρα κώμη, οἱ δ' ἀπ' αὐτῆς Ἔφυροι· καὶ ἄλλοι οἱ Περραιβῶν πρὸς Μακεδονίᾳ, οἱ[2] Κραννώνιοι, καὶ οἱ Θεσπρωτικοὶ οἱ ἐκ Κιχύρου τῆς πρότερον Ἐφύρας.

6. Ἀπολλόδωρος δὲ διδάσκων, ὃν τρόπον ὁ ποιητὴς εἴωθε διαστέλλεσθαι τὰς ὁμωνυμίας, οἷον ἐπὶ τοῦ Ὀρχομενοῦ τὸν μὲν Ἀρκαδικὸν πολύμηλον καλῶν, τὸν δὲ Βοιωτιακὸν Μινύειον, καὶ Σάμον Θρηικίην συντιθεὶς

C 339 μεσσηγύς τε Σάμοιο καὶ Ἴμβρου,

ἵνα χωρίσῃ ἀπὸ τῆς Ἰωνικῆς, οὕτω φησὶ καὶ τὴν Θεσπρωτικὴν Ἔφυραν διαστέλλεσθαι τῷ τε τηλόθεν καὶ τῷ

ποταμοῦ ἄπο Σελλήεντος.

[1] ἄνδρα, repeated after φήσας, Meineke deletes.
[2] καί, before οἱ, Meineke deletes.

in speaking of Telemachus the wooers say: "or else he means to go to the fertile soil of Ephyra, that from there he may bring deadly drugs";[1] for Nestor, in his narrative of his war against the Epeians, introduces the daughter of Augeas, the king of the Epeians, as a mixer of drugs: "I was the first that slew a man, even the spearman Mulius; he was a son-in-law of Augeias, having married his eldest daughter, and she knew all drugs that are nourished by the wide earth."[2] But there is another River Sellëeis near Sicyon, and near the river a village Ephyra. And in the Agraean district of Aetolia there is a village Ephyra; its inhabitants are called Ephyri. And there are still other Ephyri, I mean the branch of the Perrhaebians who live near Macedonia (the Crannonians),[3] as also those Thesprotian Ephyri of Cichyrus,[4] which in earlier times was called Ephyra.

6. Apollodorus, in teaching us how the poet is wont to distinguish between places of the same name, says that as the poet, in the case of Orchomenus, for instance, refers to the Arcadian Orchomenus as "abounding in flocks"[5] and to the Boeotian Orchomenus as "Minyeian,"[6] and refers to Samos as the Thracian Samos[7] by connecting it with a neighbouring island,[8] "betwixt Samos and Imbros,"[9] in order to distinguish it from Ionian Samos—so too, Apollodorus says, the poet distinguishes the Thesprotian Ephyra both by the word "distant" and by the phrase "from the River Sellëeis."[10] In this, however,

[1] *Odyssey* 2. 328.
[2] *Iliad* 11. 738.
[3] See 7. *Frag.* 16.
[4] See 7. 7. 5.
[5] *Iliad* 2. 605.
[6] *Iliad* 2. 511.
[7] Samothrace.
[8] See 10. 2. 17.
[9] *Iliad* 24. 78.
[10] *Iliad* 2. 659. Cp. 7. 7. 10.

ταῦτα δ' οὐχ ὁμολογεῖ τοῖς ὑπὸ τοῦ Σκηψίου Δημητρίου λεγομένοις, παρ' οὗ μεταφέρει τὰ πλεῖστα. ἐκεῖνος γὰρ οὔ φησιν εἶναι Σελλήεντα ἐν Θεσπρωτοῖς ποταμόν, ἀλλ' ἐν τῇ Ἠλείᾳ παρὰ τὴν ἐκεῖ Ἔφυραν, ὡς προείπομεν. τοῦτό τε οὖν εἴρηκε σκέψεως δεόμενον καὶ περὶ τῆς Οἰχαλίας, ὅτι φησίν, οὐ μιᾶς οὔσης, μίαν εἶναι πόλιν Εὐρύτου Οἰχαλιῆος, τὴν Θετταλικήν, ἐφ' ἧς φησίν·

οἵ τ' ἔχον Οἰχαλίην, πόλιν Εὐρύτου Οἰχαλιῆος.

τίς οὖν ἐστίν, ἐξ ἧς ὁρμηθέντα αἱ Μοῦσαι κατὰ Δώριον

ἀντόμεναι Θάμυριν τὸν Θρήικα παῦσαν ἀοιδῆς;

φησὶ γάρ·

Οἰχαλίηθεν ἰόντα παρ' Εὐρύτου Οἰχαλιῆος.[1]

εἰ μὲν γὰρ ἦν[2] Θετταλική, οὐκ εὖ πάλιν ὁ Σκήψιος, Ἀρκαδικήν τινα λέγων, ἣν νῦν Ἀνδανίαν καλοῦσιν· εἰ δ' οὗτος εὖ, καὶ ἡ Ἀρκαδικὴ πόλις Εὐρύτου εἴρηται, ὥστ' οὐ μία μόνον· ἐκεῖνος δὲ μίαν φησί.

7. Μεταξὺ δὲ τῆς τοῦ Πηνειοῦ καὶ τοῦ Σελλήεντος ἐκβολῆς Πύλος ᾠκεῖτο κατὰ τὸ Σκόλλιον, οὐχ ἡ τοῦ Νέστορος πόλις, ἀλλ' ἑτέρα τις, ᾗ[3] πρὸς τὸν Ἀλφειὸν οὐδέν ἐστι κοινώνημα, οὐδὲ πρὸς τὸν Παμισόν, εἴτε Ἄμαθον χρὴ καλεῖν. βιάζονται δ' ἔνιοι μνηστευόμενοι τὴν Νέστορος

[1] φησὶ . . . Οἰχαλιῆος, Meineke ejects.
[2] ἦν, Meineke emends to ᾖ, perhaps rightly.
[3] ᾗ, Penzel, for ἡ; ἧς (*Acghno*).

[1] "Scepsis," the Greek word here translated "perception," seems to be a pun on (Demetrius of) "Scepsis."

Apollodorus is not in agreement with what Demetrius of Scepsis says, from whom he borrows most of his material; for Demetrius says that there is no River Sellëeis among the Thesprotians, but says that it is in the Eleian country and flows past the Ephyra there, as I have said before. In this statement, therefore, Apollodorus was in want of perception;[1] as also in his statement concerning Oechalia, because, although Oechalia is the name of not merely one city, he says that there is only one city of Eurytus the Oechalian, namely, the Thessalian Oechalia, in reference to which Homer says: "Those that held Oechalia, city of Eurytus the Oechalian."[2] What Oechalia, pray, was it from which Thamyris had set out when, near Dorium, the Muses "met Thamyris the Thracian and put a stop to his singing"?[3] For Homer adds: "as he was on his way from Oechalia, from Eurytus the Oechalian."[4] For if it was the Thessalian Oechalia, Demetrius of Scepsis is wrong again when he says that it was a certain Arcadian Oechalia, which is now called Andania; but if Demetrius is right, Arcadian Oechalia was also called "city of Eurytus," and therefore there was not merely one Oechalia; but Apollodorus says that there was one only.

7. It was between the outlets of the Peneius and the Sellëeis, near the Scollium,[5] that Pylus was situated; not the city of Nestor, but another Pylus which has nothing in common with the Alpheius, nor with the Pamisus (or Amathus, if we should call it that). Yet there are some who do violence to Homer's words, seeking to win for themselves

[2] *Iliad* 2. 730. [3] *Iliad* 2. 595. [4] *Iliad* 2. 596.

[5] Scollis Mountain (see 8. 3. 10); now Santameriotiko.

δόξαν καὶ τὴν εὐγένειαν· τριῶν γὰρ Πύλων ἱστορουμένων ἐν Πελοποννήσῳ (καθότι καὶ τὸ ἔπος εἴρηται τουτί,

> ἔστι Πύλος πρὸ Πύλοιο· Πύλος γέ μέν ἐστι
> καὶ ἄλλος),

τούτου τε καὶ τοῦ Λεπρεατικοῦ τοῦ ἐν τῇ Τριφυλίᾳ καὶ τῇ Πισάτιδι, τρίτου δὲ τοῦ Μεσσηνιακοῦ τοῦ κατὰ Κορυφάσιον, ἕκαστοι τὸν παρά σφισιν ἠμαθόεντα πειρῶνται δεικνύναι, καὶ τὴν τοῦ Νέστορος πατρίδα τοῦτον ἀποφαίνουσιν. οἱ μὲν οὖν πολλοὶ τῶν νεωτέρων[1] καὶ συγγραφέων καὶ ποιητῶν Μεσσήνιόν φασι τὸν Νέστορα, τῷ σωζομένῳ μέχρι εἰς αὐτοὺς προστιθέμενοι· οἱ δ' Ὁμηρικώτεροι, τοῖς ἔπεσιν ἀκολοθοῦντες, τοῦτον εἶναί φασι τὸν τοῦ Νέστορος Πύλον, οὗ τὴν χώραν διέξεισιν ὁ Ἀλφειός· διέξεισι δὲ τὴν Πισᾶτιν καὶ τὴν Τριφυλίαν. οἱ δ' οὖν ἐκ τῆς Κοίλης Ἤλιδος καὶ τοιαύτην φιλοτιμίαν προσετίθεσαν τῷ παρ' αὐτοῖς Πύλῳ καὶ γνωρίσματα,
C 340 δεικνύντες Γέρηνον τόπον καὶ Γέροντα ποταμὸν καὶ ἄλλον Γεράνιον, εἶτ' ἀπὸ τούτων ἐπιθέτως Γερήνιον εἰρῆσθαι πιστούμενοι τὸν Νέστορα. τοῦτο δὲ ταὐτὸ καὶ οἱ Μεσσήνιοι πεποιήκασι, καὶ πιθανώτεροί γε φαίνονται· μᾶλλον γὰρ γνώριμά φασιν εἶναι τὰ παρ' ἐκείνοις Γέρηνα,

[1] νεωτέρων, Corais, for ἑτέρων; so the later editors.

---

[1] A proverb. See Stephanus Byz. *s.v.* Κορυφάσιον, and Eustathius on *Od.* 1. 93.

the fame and noble lineage of Nestor; for, since history mentions three Pyluses in the Peloponnesus (as is stated in this verse: "There is a Pylus in front of Pylus; yea, and there is still another Pylus"),[1] the Pylus in question, the Lepreatic Pylus in Triphylia and Pisatis, and a third, the Messenian Pylus near Coryphasium,[2] the inhabitants of each try to show that the Pylus in their own country is "emathoëis"[3] and declare that it is the native place of Nestor. However, most of the more recent writers, both historians and poets, say that Nestor was a Messenian, thus adding their support to the Pylus which has been preserved down to their own times. But the writers who follow the words of Homer more closely say that the Pylus of Nestor is the Pylus through whose territory the Alpheius flows. And the Alpheius flows through Pisatis and Triphylia. However, the writers from Coelê Elis have not only supported their own Pylus with a similar zeal, but have also attached to it tokens of recognition,[4] pointing out a place called Gerenus, a river called Geron, and another river called Geranius, and then confidently asserting that Homer's epithet for Nestor, "Gerenian," was derived from these. But the Messenians have done the self-same thing, and their argument appears at least more plausible; for they say that their own Gerena is better known, and that

[2] Gosselin identifies Coryphasium with the Navarino of to-day. So Frazer, note on Pausanias 4. 36 1.

[3] The Homeric epithet of Pylus, translated "sandy"; but see 8. 3. 14.

[4] As mothers who exposed their infants hung tokens about their necks, hoping that thus their parentage would be discovered.

συνοικουμένην ποτὲ εὖ. τοιαῦτα μὲν τὰ περὶ τὴν Κοίλην Ἦλιν ὑπάρχοντα νυνί.

8. Ὁ δὲ ποιητὴς εἰς τέτταρα μέρη διελὼν τήνδε τὴν χώραν, τέτταρας δὲ καὶ τοὺς ἡγεμόνας εἰπών, οὐ σαφῶς εἴρηκεν·

> οἱ δ' ἄρα Βουπράσιόν τε καὶ Ἤλιδα δῖαν ἔναιον,
> ὅσσον ἔφ' Ὑρμίνη καὶ Μύρσινος ἐσχατιόωσα
> πέτρη τ' Ὠλενίη καὶ Ἀλείσιον ἐντὸς ἐέργει.
> τῶν αὖ τέσσαρες ἀρχοὶ ἔσαν, δέκα δ' ἀνδρὶ ἑκάστῳ
> νῆες ἕποντο θοαί· πολέες δ' ἔμβαινον Ἐπειοί.

τῷ μὲν γὰρ Ἐπειοὺς ἀμφοτέρους προσαγορεύειν τούς τε Βουπρασιεῖς καὶ τοὺς Ἠλείους, Ἠλείους δὲ μηκέτι καλεῖν τοὺς Βουπρασιεῖς, οὐ τὴν Ἠλείαν δόξειεν ἂν εἰς τέσσαρα μέρη διαιρεῖν, ἀλλὰ τὴν τῶν Ἐπειῶν, ἣν εἰς δύο μέρη διεῖλε πρότερον· οὐδ' ἂν μέρος εἴη τῆς Ἤλιδος τὸ Βουπράσιον, ἀλλὰ τῶν Ἐπειῶν μᾶλλον. ὅτι γὰρ Ἐπειοὺς καλεῖ τοὺς Βουπρασίους, δῆλον·

> ὡς ὁπότε κρείοντ' Ἀμαρυγκέα θάπτον Ἐπειοὶ Βουπρασίῳ.

τὸ δὲ Βουπράσιον εἶναί τινα χώραν τῆς Ἠλείας κατοικίαν ἔχουσαν ὁμώνυμον νυνὶ φαίνεται, τῆς Ἤλιδος ὂν μέρος καὶ τοῦτο.[1] πάλιν δὲ τῷ

[1] τὸ δὲ Βουπράσιον . . . τοῦτο, Meineke relegates to the foot of the page. οὐκ, before ἔχουσαν, *Blu* omit. δέ, after νυνί, BE*knou* insert.

---

[1] *Iliad* 2. 615. Homer seems to speak of the four last-named places as the four corners of Coelê Elis (Leaf, *The*

it was once a populous place. Such, then, is the present state of affairs as regards Coelê Elis.

8. But when the poet divides this country into four parts and also speaks of the leaders as four in number, his statement is not clear: "And they too that inhabited both Buprasium and goodly Elis, so much thereof as is enclosed by Hyrminê and Myrsinus on the borders, and by the Olenian Rock and Aleisium,—of these men, I say, there were four leaders, and ten swift ships followed each leader, and many Epeians embarked thereon."[1] For when he speaks of both the Buprasians and the Eleians as Epeians, but without going on and calling the Buprasians Eleians, it would seem that he is not dividing the Eleian country into four parts, but rather the country of the Epeians, which he had already divided into only two parts; and thus Buprasium would not be a part of Elis but rather of the country of the Epeians. For it is clear that he calls the Buprasians Epeians; "as when the Epeians were burying lord Amarynces at Buprasium."[2] But Buprasium now appears to have been a territory of the Eleian country, having in it a settlement of the same name, which was also a part of Elis.[3] And

Iliad, vol. i, p. 72). Elsewhere (11. 756) he refers to "Buprasium, rich in wheat," "the Olenian Rock" and "the hill called the hill of Aleisium" as landmarks of the country.

[2] *Iliad* 23. 630.

[3] Most of the editors regard this sentence as a gloss. Moreover, serious discrepancies in the readings of the MSS. render the meaning doubtful (see critical note on opposite page). For instance, all but three MSS. read "*no* settlement of the same name." But see Curtius, *Peloponnesos*, vol. II, p. 36; also *Etym. Mag.* and Hesych. *s.v.* Βουπράσιον.

συγκαταριθμεῖσθαι Βουπράσιόν τε καὶ Ἦλιδα δῖαν λέγοντα, εἶτ' εἰς τέσσαρας διαιρεῖν μερίδας, ὡς ἂν κοινῷ δοκεῖ τῷ τε Βουπρασίῳ καὶ τῇ Ἤλιδι αὐτὰς ὑποτάττειν. ἦν δ', ὡς ἔοικε, κατοικία τῆς Ἠλείας τὸ Βουπράσιον ἀξιόλογος, ἣ νῦν οὐκέτ' ἐστίν· ἡ δὲ χώρα καλεῖται μόνον οὕτως ἡ ἐπὶ τῆς ὁδοῦ τῆς ἐπὶ Δύμην ἐξ Ἤλιδος τῆς νῦν πόλεως.[1] ὑπολάβοι δ' ἄν τις καὶ ὑπεροχήν τινα ἔχειν τότε τὸ Βουπράσιον παρὰ τὴν Ἦλιν, ὥσπερ καὶ οἱ Ἐπειοὶ παρὰ τούτους· ὕστερον δ' ἀντ' Ἐπειῶν Ἠλεῖοι ἐκλήθησαν. καὶ τὸ Βουπράσιον μὲν δὴ μέρος ἦν τῆς Ἤλιδος, ποιητικῷ δέ τινι σχήματι συγκαταλέγειν τὸ μέρος τῷ ὅλῳ φασὶ τὸν Ὅμηρον, ὡς τὸ

ἀν' Ἑλλάδα καὶ μέσον Ἄργος,

καὶ

ἀν' Ἑλλάδα τε Φθίην τε,

καὶ

Κουρῆτές τ' ἐμάχοντο καὶ Αἰτωλοί,

καὶ

οἱ δ' ἐκ Δουλιχίοιο Ἐχινάων θ' ἱεράων·

καὶ γὰρ τὸ Δουλίχιον τῶν Ἐχινάδων. χρῶνται δὲ καὶ οἱ νεώτεροι· Ἱππῶναξ μέν·

Κυπρίων βέκος φαγοῦσι καὶ Ἀμαθουσίων πυρόν·

Κύπριοι γὰρ καὶ οἱ Ἀμαθούσιοι· καὶ Ἀλκμὰν δέ·

C 341 Κύπρον ἱμερτὰν λιποῖσα καὶ Πάφον περιρρύταν·

καὶ Αἰσχύλος·[2]

[1] ἡ δὲ χώρα . . . πόλεως, B omits.

again, when he names the two together, saying "both Buprasium and goodly Elis," and then divides the country into four parts, it seems as though he is classifying the four parts under the general designation "both Buprasium and goodly Elis." It seems likely that at one time there was a considerable settlement by the name of Buprasium in the Eleian country which is no longer in existence (indeed, only that territory which is on the road that leads to Dymê from the present city of Elis is now so called); and one might suppose that at that time Buprasium had a certain pre-eminence as compared with Elis, just as the Epeians had in comparison with the Eleians; but later on the people were called Eleians instead of Epeians. And though Buprasium was a part of Elis, they say that Homer, by a sort of poetic figure, names the part with the whole, as for instance when he says: "throughout Hellas and mid-Argos," [1] and "throughout Hellas and Phthia," [2] and "the Curetes fought and the Aetolians," [3] and "the men of Dulichium and the holy Echinades," [4] for Dulichium is one of the Echinades. And more recent poets also use this figure; for instance, Hipponax, when he says: "to those who have eaten the bread of the Cyprians and the wheaten bread of the Amathusians," [5] for the Amathusians are also Cyprians; and Alcman, when he says: "when she had left lovely Cypros and sea-girt Paphos"; [6] and Aeschylus,[7] when he

[1] *Odyssey* 1. 344.
[2] *Odyssey* 11. 496.
[3] *Iliad* 9. 529.
[4] *Iliad* 2. 625.
[5] *Frag.* 82 (Bergk).
[6] *Frag.* 21 (Bergk).
[7] Meineke (*Vind. Strab.* p. 103) thinks Strabo wrote "Archilochus," not "Aeschylus."

---

[2] For Αἰσχύλος Meineke (*Vind. Strab.*) proposes Ἀρχίλοχος.

Κύπρου Πάφου τ' ἔχουσα πάντα κλῆρον.

εἰ δ' οὐκ εἴρηκεν Ἠλείους[1] τοὺς Βουπρασίους, οὐδ' ἄλλα πολλὰ τῶν ὄντων, φήσομεν· ἀλλὰ τοῦτ' οὐκ ἔστιν ἀπόδειξις τοῦ μὴ εἶναι, ἀλλὰ τοῦ μὴ εἰπεῖν μόνον.

9. Ἑκαταῖος δ' ὁ Μιλήσιος ἑτέρους λέγει τῶν Ἠλείων τοὺς Ἐπειούς· τῷ γοῦν Ἡρακλεῖ συστρατεῦσαι τοὺς Ἐπειοὺς ἐπὶ Αὐγέαν καὶ συνανελεῖν αὐτῷ τόν τε Αὐγέαν καὶ τὴν Ἦλιν· φησὶ δὲ καὶ τὴν Δύμην Ἐπειίδα καὶ Ἀχαιίδα. πολλὰ μὲν οὖν καὶ μὴ ὄντα λέγουσιν οἱ ἀρχαῖοι συγγραφεῖς, συντεθραμμένοι τῷ ψεύδει διὰ τὰς μυθογραφίας· διὰ δὲ τοῦτο καὶ οὐχ ὁμολογοῦσι πρὸς ἀλλήλους περὶ τῶν αὐτῶν. οὐ μέντοι ἄπιστον, οὐδ' εἴ ποτε διάφοροι τοῖς Ἠλείοις ὄντες οἱ Ἐπειοὶ καὶ ἑτεροεθνεῖς εἰς ταὐτὸ συνήρχοντο κατ' ἐπικράτειαν καὶ κοινὴν ἔνεμον τὴν[2] πολιτείαν· ἐπεκράτουν δὲ καὶ μέχρι Δύμης. ὁ μὲν γὰρ ποιητὴς οὐκ ὠνόμακε τὴν Δύμην· οὐκ ἀπεικὸς δ' ἐστί, τότε μὲν αὐτὴν ὑπὸ τοῖς Ἐπειοῖς ὑπάρξαι, ὕστερον δὲ τοῖς Ἴωσιν, ἢ μηδ' ἐκείνοις, ἀλλὰ τοῖς τὴν ἐκείνων χώραν κατασχοῦσιν Ἀχαιοῖς. τῶν δὲ τεττάρων μερίδων, ὧν ἐντός ἐστι καὶ τὸ Βουπράσιον, ἡ μὲν Ὑρμίνη καὶ ἡ Μύρσινος τῆς Ἠλείας ἐστίν, αἱ λοιπαὶ δὲ ἐπὶ τῶν ὅρων ἤδη τῆς Πισάτιδος, ὥς οἴονταί τινες.

10. Ὑρμίνη μὲν οὖν πολίχνιον ἦν, νῦν δ' οὐκ ἔστιν, ἀλλ' ἀκρωτήριον πλησίον Κυλλήνης ὀρεινόν

[1] Ἠλείους, Corais, for Ἐπείους; so the later editors.
[2] ἔνεμον τὴν (*Acghno*); ἐνέμοντο (the other MSS.).

[1] *Frag.* 463 (Nauck).

says: "since thou dost possess the whole of Cypros and Paphos as thine allotment."[1] But if Homer nowhere calls the Buprasians Eleians, I will say that there are many other facts also that he does not mention; yet this is no proof that they are not facts, but merely that he has not mentioned them.

9. But Hecataeus of Miletus says that the Epeians are a different people from the Eleians; that, at any rate, the Epeians joined Heracles in his expedition against Augeas and helped him to destroy both Augeas and Elis. And he says, further, that Dymê is an Epeian and an Achaean city. However, the early historians say many things that are not true, because they were accustomed to falsehoods on account of the use of myths in their writings; and on this account, too, they do not agree with one another concerning the same things. Yet it is not incredible that the Epeians, even if they were once at variance with the Eleians and belonged to a different race, later became united with the Eleians as the result of prevailing over them, and with them formed one common state; and that they prevailed even as far as Dymê. For although the poet has not named Dymê, it is not unreasonable to suppose that in his time Dymê belonged to the Epeians, and later to the Ionians, or, if not to them, at all events to the Achaeans who took possession of their country. Of the four parts, inside which Buprasium is situated, only Hyrminê and Myrsinus belong to the Eleian country, whereas the remaining two are already on the frontiers of Pisatis, as some writers think.

10. Now Hyrminê was a small town. It is no longer in existence, but near Cyllenê there is a

ἐστι, καλούμενον Ὁρμίνα ἢ Ὕρμινα· Μύρσινος δὲ τὸ νῦν Μυρτούντιον, ἐπὶ θάλατταν καθήκουσα κατὰ τὴν ἐκ Δύμης εἰς Ἦλιν ὁδὸν κατοικία, στάδια τῆς Ἠλείων πόλεως διέχουσα ἑβδομήκοντα. πέτρην δ' Ὠλενίην εἰκάζουσι τὴν νῦν Σκόλλιν· ἀνάγκη γὰρ εἰκότα λέγειν, καὶ τῶν τόπων καὶ τῶν ὀνομάτων μεταβεβλημένων, ἐκείνου τε μὴ σφόδρα ἐπὶ πολλῶν σαφηνίζοντος· ἔστι δ' ὄρος πετρῶδες κοινὸν Δυμαίων τε καὶ Τριταιέων καὶ Ἠλείων, ἐχόμενον ἑτέρου τινὸς Ἀρκαδικοῦ ὄρους Λαμπείας, ὃ τῆς Ἤλιδος μὲν διέστηκεν ἑκατὸν καὶ τριάκοντα σταδίους, Τριταίας δὲ ἑκατόν, καὶ Δύμης[1] τοὺς ἴσους, Ἀχαϊκῶν πόλεων. τὸ δ' Ἀλείσιόν ἐστι τὸ νῦν Ἀλεσιαῖον, χώρα περὶ τὴν Ἀμφιδολίδα, ἐν ᾗ καὶ κατὰ μῆνα ἀγορὰν συνάγουσιν οἱ περίοικοι· κεῖται δὲ ἐπὶ τῆς ὀρεινῆς ὁδοῦ, τῆς ἐξ Ἤλιδος εἰς Ὀλυμπίαν· πρότερον δ' ἦν πόλις τῆς Πισάτιδος, ἄλλοτ' ἄλλως τῶν ὅρων ἐπαλλαττόντων διὰ τὰς τῶν ἡγεμόνων μεταβολάς· τὸ δ' Ἀλείσιον καὶ Ἀλεισίου κολώνην ὁ ποιητὴς καλεῖ, ὅταν φῇ·

C 342 μέσφ' ἐπὶ Βουπρασίου πολυπύρου βήσαμεν ἵππους
πέτρης τ' Ὠλενίης, καὶ Ἀλεισίου ἔνθα κολώνη κέκληται·

ὑπερβατῶς γὰρ δεῖ δέξασθαι, ἴσον τῷ καὶ ἔνθ'

[1] καὶ Δύμης, Xylander inserts, and so the later editors. καὶ ἐκ Δύμης δέ (*hi*).

---

[1] Santameriotiko Mountain.

mountain promontory called Hormina or Hyrmina. Myrsinus is the present Myrtuntium, a settlement that extends down to the sea, and is situated on the road which runs from Dymê into Elis, and is seventy stadia distant from the city of the Eleians. The Olenian Rock is surmised to be what is now called Scollis;[1] for we are obliged to state what is merely probable, because both the places and the names have undergone changes, and because in many cases the poet does not make himself very clear. Scollis is a rocky mountain common to the territories of the Dymaeans, the Tritaeans, and the Eleians, and borders on another Arcadian mountain called Lampeia,[2] which is one hundred and thirty stadia distant from Elis, one hundred from Tritaea, and the same from Dymê; the last two are Achaean cities. Aleisium is the present Alesiaeum, a territory in the neighbourhood of Amphidolis,[3] in which the people of the surrounding country hold a monthly market. It is situated on the mountain-road that runs from Elis to Olympia. In earlier times it was a city of Pisatis, for the boundaries have varied at different times on account of the change of rulers. The poet also calls Aleisium "Hill of Aleisium," when he says: "until we caused our horses to set foot on Buprasium, rich in wheat, and on the Olenian Rock, and of Aleisium where is the place called Hill"[4] (we must interpret the words as a case of hyperbaton, that is, as equivalent to "and

[2] Now Astras, apparently. See C. Müller, *Ind. Var. Lect.*, p. 990.

[3] Amphidolis, or Amphidolia, was an Eleian territory north of Olympia.

[4] *Iliad* 11. 756.

Ἀλεισίου κολώνη κέκληται· ἔνιοι δὲ καὶ ποταμὸν δεικνύουσιν Ἀλείσιον.

11. Λεγομένων δέ τινων ἐν τῇ Τριφυλίᾳ Καυκώνων πρὸς τῇ Μεσσηνίᾳ, λεγομένης δὲ καὶ τῆς Δύμης Καυκωνίδος ὑπό τινων, ὄντος δὲ καὶ ποταμοῦ ἐν τῇ Δυμαίᾳ μεταξὺ Δύμης καὶ Τριταίας, ὃς καλεῖται Καύκων θηλυκῶς,[1] ζητοῦσι περὶ τῶν Καυκώνων,[2] μὴ διττοὶ λέγονται, οἱ μὲν περὶ τὴν Τριφυλίαν, οἱ δὲ περὶ Δύμην καὶ Ἦλιν καὶ τὸν Καύκωνα· ἐμβάλλει δ' οὗτος εἰς ἕτερον, ὃς Τευθέας[3] ἀρσενικῶς καλεῖται, ὁμώνυμος πολίχνῃ τινὶ τῶν εἰς τὴν Δύμην συνῳκισμένων, πλὴν ὅτι χωρὶς τοῦ σίγμα Τευθέα λέγεται θηλυκῶς αὕτη, ἐκτεινόντων τὴν ἐσχάτην συλλαβήν, ὅπου τὸ τῆς Νεμυδίας[4] Ἀρτέμιδος ἱερόν. ὁ δὲ Τευθέας[5] εἰς τὸν Ἀχελῷον ἐμβάλλει τὸν κατὰ Δύμην ῥέοντα, ὁμώνυμον τῷ κατὰ Ἀκαρνανίαν, καλούμενον καὶ Πεῖρον. τοῦ δ' Ἡσιόδου εἰπόντος,

ᾤκεε δ' Ὠλενίην πέτρην ποταμοῖο παρ' ὄχθας
εὐρείος Πείροιο,

μεταγράφουσί τινες Πιέροιο,[6] οὐκ εὖ. περὶ δὲ τῶν Καυκώνων ζητοῦσι, φασίν,[7] ὅτι τῆς Ἀθηνᾶς

[1] θηλυκῶς is suspected by Corais, Kramer, and Müller-Dübner, and ejected by Meineke. But Eustathius retains the word in two quotations (notes on *Il.* 2. 607 and *Od.* 3. 367).

[2] ὡς, before μή, Pletho omits ; so Corais and Meineke.

[3] Τευθέας (B) ; Τευθέας (*Acghno*).

[4] Νεμιδίας (*bknou*, perhaps rightly) ; Νεμεαίας, Lobeck *ad Phryn.* p. 557 ; Νεμαίας, Corais.

[5] Τευθόας A.

[6] Πιέροιο, Jones, for Πώροιο (see Pausanias 7. 22).

where is the place called Hill of Aleisium"). Some writers point also to a river Aleisius.

11. Since certain people in Triphylia near Messenia are called Cauconians, and since Dymê also is called Cauconian by some writers, and since in the Dymaean territory between Dymê and Tritaea there is also a river which is called Caucon, in the feminine gender, writers raise the question whether there are not two different sets of Cauconians, one in the region of Triphylia, and the other in the region of Dymê, Elis, and the River Caucon. This river empties into another river which is called Teutheas, in the masculine gender; Teutheas has the same name as one of the little towns which were incorporated into Dymê, except that the name of this town, "Teuthea," is in the feminine gender, and is spelled without the *s* and with the last syllable long. In this town is the temple of the Nemydian[1] Artemis. The Teutheas empties into the Acheloüs which flows by Dyme[2] and has the same name as the Acarnanian river. It is also called the "Peirus"; by Hesiod, for instance, when he says: "he dwelt on the Olenian Rock along the banks of a river, wide Peirus."[3] Some change the reading to "Pierus," wrongly. They raise that question about the Cauconians, they say, because,

[1] "Nemydian" is otherwise unknown; perhaps "Nemidian" or "Nemeaean."

[2] Cp. 10. 2. 1.

[3] *Frag.* 74 (98).

[7] The whole passage περὶ δὲ . . . φησίν (τισίν B*klu*) . . . ἀτὰρ ἠῶθεν . . . τυχόν, according to Kramer, crept in from the margin. Meineke ejects it. Jones emends φησίν to φασίν and retains the passage.

τῆς τῷ Μέντορι ὡμοιωμένης ἐν τῇ Ὀδυσσείᾳ εἰπούσης πρὸς τὸν Νέστορα,

> ἀτὰρ ἠῶθεν μετὰ Καύκωνας μεγαθύμους
> εἶμ', ἔνθα χρεῖός μοι ὀφείλεται· οὔ τι νέον γε
> οὐδ' ὀλίγον. σὺ δὲ τοῦτον, ἐπεὶ τεὸν ἵκετο δῶμα,
> πέμψον σὺν διφρῷ τε καὶ υἱέϊ· δὸς δέ οἱ ἵππους,

δοκεῖ σημαίνεσθαι χώρα τις ἐν τῇ τῶν Ἐπειῶν, ἣν οἱ Καύκωνες εἶχον, ἕτεροι ὄντες τῶν ἐν τῇ Τριφυλίᾳ, ἐπεκτείνοντες καὶ μέχρι τῆς Δυμαίας τυχόν. οὔτε γὰρ τὴν Δύμην, ὁπόθεν Καυκωνίδα εἰρῆσθαι συμβέβηκε, παραλιπεῖν ἄξιον, οὔτε τὸν ποταμόν, ὁπόθεν Καύκων εἴρηται, διὰ τὸ τοὺς Καύκωνας παρέχειν ζήτησιν, οἵτινές ποτέ εἰσιν, ὅπου φησὶν ἡ Ἀθηνᾶ βαδίζειν κατὰ τὴν τοῦ χρέους κομιδήν. εἰ γὰρ δὴ δεχοίμεθα τοὺς ἐν τῇ Τριφυλίᾳ λέγεσθαι τοὺς περὶ Λέπρεον,[1] οὐκ οἶδ' ὅπως πιθανὸς ἔσται ὁ λόγος· διὸ καὶ γράφουσί τινες·

> ἔνθα χρεῖός μοι ὀφείλεται Ἤλιδι δίῃ,
> οὐκ ὀλίγον.

σαφεστέραν δ' ἕξει τὴν ἐπίσκεψιν τοῦτο, ἐπειδὰν τὴν ἑξῆς χώραν περιοδεύσωμεν τήν τε Πισᾶτιν καὶ τὴν Τριφυλίαν μέχρι τῆς τῶν Μεσσηνίων μεθορίας.

12. Μετὰ δὲ τὸν Χελωνάταν ὁ τῶν Πισατῶν ἐστὶν αἰγιαλὸς πολύς· εἶτ' ἄκρα Φειά· ἦν δὲ καὶ πολίχνη·

> Φειᾶς πὰρ τείχεσσιν, Ἰαρδάνου ἀμφὶ ῥέεθρα·

when Athenê in the guise of Mentor, in the *Odyssey*, says to Nestor, "but in the morning I will go to the great-hearted Cauconians, where a debt is due me, in no way new or small. But do thou send this man on his way with a chariot and with thy son, since he has come to thy house, and give him horses,"[1] the poet seems to designate a certain territory in the country of the Epeians which was held by the Cauconians, these Cauconians being a different set from those in Triphylia and perhaps extending as far as the territory of Dymê. Indeed, one should not fail to inquire both into the origin of the epithet of Dymê, "Cauconian," and into the origin of the name of the river "Caucon," because the question who those Cauconians were to whom Athenê says she is going in order to recover the debt offers a problem; for if we should interpret the poet as meaning the Cauconians in Triphylia near Lepreum, I do not see how his account can be plausible. Hence some read: "where a debt is due me in goodly Elis, no small one."[2] But this question will be investigated with clearer results when I describe the country that comes next after this, I mean Pisatis and Triphylia as far as the borders of the country of the Messenians.[3]

12. After Chelonatas comes the long sea-shore of the Pisatans; and then Cape Pheia. And there was also a small town called Pheia: "beside the walls of Pheia, about the streams of Iardanus,"[4]

[1] *Odyssey* 3. 366. [2] Cp. *Iliad* 11. 698.
[3] 8. 3. 17. [4] *Iliad* 7. 135.

---

[1] Λέπρεον, Corais, Kramer, and Müller-Dübner, for Λέπριον; Λέπρειον, Meineke.

C 343 ἔστι γὰρ καὶ ποτάμιον πλησίον. ἔνιοι δ' ἀρχὴν τῆς Πισάτιδος τὴν Φειάν φασι· πρόκειται δὲ καὶ ταύτης νησίον καὶ λιμήν, ἔνθεν εἰς Ὀλυμπίαν τὸ ἐγγυτάτω [1] ἐκ θαλάττης [2] στάδιοι ἑκατὸν εἴκοσιν. εἶτ' ἄλλη ἄκρα Ἰχθὺς [3] ἐπὶ πολὺ προὔχουσα ἐπὶ τὴν δύσιν, καθάπερ ὁ Χελωνάτας, ἀφ' ἧς πάλιν [4] ἐπὶ τὴν Κεφαλληνίαν στάδιοι ἑκατὸν εἴκοσιν. εἶθ' ὁ Ἀλφειὸς ἐκδίδωσι, διέχων τοῦ Χελωνάτα σταδίους διακοσίους ὀγδοήκοντα, Ἀράξου δὲ πεντακοσίους τετταράκοντα πέντε. ῥεῖ δ' ἐκ τῶν αὐτῶν τόπων, ἐξ ὧν καὶ ὁ Εὐρώτας· καλεῖται δὲ Ἀσέα, κώμη τῆς Μεγαλοπολίτιδος, πλησίον ἀλλήλων ἔχουσα δύο πηγάς, ἐξ ὧν ῥέουσιν οἱ λεχθέντες ποταμοί· δύντες δ' ὑπὸ γῆς ἐπὶ συχνοὺς σταδίους ἀνατέλλουσι πάλιν, εἶθ' ὁ μὲν εἰς Λακωνικήν, ὁ δ' εἰς τὴν Πισᾶτιν κατάγεται. ὁ μὲν οὖν Εὐρώτας, κατὰ τὴν ἀρχὴν τῆς Βλεμινάτιδος ἀναδείξας τὸ ῥεῖθρον, παρ' αὐτὴν τὴν Σπάρτην ῥυεὶς καὶ διεξιὼν αὐλῶνά τινα μακρὸν κατὰ τὸ Ἕλος, οὗ μέμνηται καὶ ὁ ποιητής, ἐκδίδωσι μεταξὺ Γυθίου, τοῦ τῆς Σπάρτης ἐπινείου, καὶ Ἀκραίων. ὁ δ' Ἀλφειός, παραλαβὼν τόν τε Λάδωνα [5] καὶ τὸν Ἐρύμανθον καὶ ἄλλους ἀσημοτέρους, διὰ τῆς Φρίξης καὶ Πισάτιδος καὶ Τριφυλίας ἐνεχθείς, παρ' αὐτὴν τὴν Ὀλυμπίαν ἐπὶ θάλατταν τὴν Σικελικὴν ἐκπίπτει μεταξὺ

[1] τὸ ἐγγυτάτω, B and *Epit.*, for τῷ ἐγγυτάτῳ; so Meineke.
[2] ἐστί, before στάδιοι, Corais omits; εἰσί, Meineke.
[3] Ἰχθύς, Palmer, for εὐθύς. αὖθις, Corais.

for there is also a small river near by. According to some, Pheia is the beginning of Pisatis. Off Pheia lie a little island and a harbour, from which the nearest distance from the sea to Olympia is one hundred and twenty stadia. Then comes another cape, Ichthys, which, like Chelonatas, projects for a considerable distance towards the west; and from it the distance to Cephallenia is again one hundred and twenty stadia. Then comes the mouth of the Alpheius, which is distant two hundred and eighty stadia from Chelonatas, and five hundred and forty-five from Araxus. It flows from the same regions as the Eurotas, that is, from a place called Asea, a village in the territory of Megalopolis, where there are two springs near one another from which the rivers in question flow. They sink and flow beneath the earth for many stadia[1] and then rise again; and then they flow down, one into Laconia and the other into Pisatis. The stream of the Eurotas reappears where the district called Bleminatis begins, and then flows past Sparta itself, traverses a long glen near Helus (a place mentioned by the poet),[2] and empties between Gythium, the naval station of Sparta, and Acraea. But the Alpheius, after receiving the waters of the Ladon, the Erymanthus, and other rivers of less significance, flows through Phrixa, Pisatis, and Triphylia past Olympia itself to the Sicilian Sea, into which it empties between

[1] According to Polybius (16. 17), *ten* stadia.
[2] *Iliad* 2. 584.

---

[4] πάλιν, omitted by BE*klu*.
[5] For Κελάδοντα (MSS.) Palmer conjectures Λάδωνα, C. Müller approving.

Φειᾶς τε καὶ Ἐπιταλίου.[1] πρὸς δὲ τῇ ἐκβολῇ τὸ τῆς Ἀλφειονίας Ἀρτέμιδος ἢ Ἀλφειούσης ἄλσος ἐστί (λέγεται γὰρ ἀμφοτέρως), ἀπέχον τῆς Ὀλυμπίας εἰς ὀγδοήκοντα σταδίους. ταύτῃ δὲ τῇ θεῷ καὶ ἐν Ὀλυμπίᾳ κατ' ἔτος συντελεῖται πανήγυρις, καθάπερ καὶ τῇ Ἐλαφίᾳ καὶ τῇ Δαφνίᾳ. μεστὴ δ' ἐστὶν ἡ γῆ πᾶσα Ἀρτεμισίων τε καὶ Ἀφροδισίων καὶ Νυμφαίων ἐν ἄλσεσιν ἀνθέων πλέῳς[2] τὸ πολὺ διὰ τὴν εὐυδρίαν, συχνὰ δὲ καὶ Ἑρμεῖα ἐν ταῖς ὁδοῖς, Ποσείδια δ' ἐπὶ ταῖς ἀκταῖς. ἐν δὲ τῷ τῆς Ἀλφειονίας ἱερῷ γραφαὶ Κλεάνθους τε καὶ Ἀρήγοντος, ἀνδρῶν Κορινθίων, τοῦ μὲν Τροίας ἅλωσις καὶ Ἀθηνᾶς γοναί, τοῦ δ' Ἄρτεμις ἀναφερομένη ἐπὶ γρυπός, σφόδρα εὐδόκιμοι.

13. Εἶτα τὸ διεῖργον ὄρος τῆς Τριφυλίας τὴν Μακιστίαν ἀπὸ τῆς Πισάτιδος· εἶτ' ἄλλος ποταμὸς Χαλκὶς καὶ κρήνη Κρουνοὶ καὶ κατοικία Χαλκίς, καὶ τὸ Σαμικὸν μετὰ ταῦτα, ὅπου τὸ μάλιστα τιμώμενον τοῦ Σαμίου Ποσειδῶνος ἱερόν· ἔστι δ' ἄλσος ἀγριελαιῶν πλέων· ἐπεμελοῦντο δ' αὐτοῦ Μακίστιοι· οὗτοι δὲ καὶ τὴν ἐκεχειρίαν ἐπήγγελλον, ἣν καλοῦσι Σάμιον·[3] συντελοῦσι δ' εἰς τὸ ἱερὸν πάντες Τριφύλιοι.

14. Κατὰ ταῦτα δέ πως τὰ ἱερὰ ὑπέρκειται τῆς θαλάττης ἐν τριάκοντα ἢ μικρῷ πλείοσι σταδίοις ὁ Τριφυλιακὸς Πύλος καὶ Λεπρεατικός,

[1] Ἐπιταλίου, Tzschucke, for Ἐπιτάνου (*Acgh*), Ἐπιτάνης (B), Πιτάνης (*klno*); so Kramer and the later editors.

[2] ἀνθέων πλέῳς, Meineke, and Müller-Dübner, for ἀνθέων ὡς; for other emendations, see C. Müller, *Ind. Var. Lect.*, p. 991.

Pheia and Epitalium. Near the outlet of the river is the sacred precinct of Artemis Alpheionia or Alpheiusa (for the epithet is spelled both ways), which is about eighty stadia distant from Olympia. An annual festival is also celebrated at Olympia in honour of this goddess as well as in honour of Artemis Elaphia and Artemis Daphnia. The whole country is full of temples of Artemis, Aphroditê, and the Nymphs, being situated in sacred precincts that are generally full of flowers because of the abundance of water. And there are also numerous shrines of Hermes on the road-sides, and temples of Poseidon on the capes. In the temple of Artemis Alpheionia are very famous paintings by two Corinthians, Cleanthes and Aregon: by Cleanthes the "Capture of Troy" and the "Birth of Athenê," and by Aregon the "Artemis Borne Aloft on a Griffin."

13. Then comes the mountain of Triphylia that separates Macistia from Pisatis; then another river called Chalcis, and a spring called Cruni, and a settlement called Chalcis, and, after these, Samicum, where is the most highly revered temple of the Samian Poseidon. About the temple is a sacred precinct full of wild olive-trees. The people of Macistum used to have charge over it; and it was they, too, who used to proclaim the armistice-day called "Samian." But all the Triphylians contribute to the maintenance of the temple.

14. In the general neighbourhood of these temples, above the sea, at a distance of thirty stadia or slightly more, is situated the Triphylian Pylus, also called the

---

[3] Σάμιον, Corais, for Σάμιοι; so the later editors.

C 344 ὃν καλεῖ ὁ ποιητὴς ἠμαθόεντα καὶ παραδίδωσι τοῦ Νέστορος πατρίδα, ὡς ἄν τις ἐκ τῶν ἐπῶν τῶν Ὁμήρου τεκμαίροιτο· εἴτε τοῦ παραρρέοντος ποταμοῦ πρὸς ἄρκτον Ἀμάθου καλουμένου πρότερον, ὃς νῦν Μάμαος καὶ Ἀρκαδικὸς[1] καλεῖται, ὥστ' ἐντεῦθεν ἠμαθόεντα κεκλῆσθαι· εἴτε τούτου μὲν Παμισοῦ καλουμένου ὁμωνύμως τοῖς ἐν τῇ Μεσσηνίᾳ δυσί, τῆς δὲ πόλεως ἄδηλον ἐχούσης τὴν ἐτυμολογίαν τοῦ ἐπιθέτου· καὶ γὰρ τὸ ἀμαθώδη τὸν ποταμὸν ἢ τὴν χώραν εἶναι ψεῦδός φασι. καὶ τὸ τῆς Σκιλλουντίας δὲ Ἀθηνᾶς ἱερὸν τὸ περὶ Σκιλλοῦντα τῶν ἐπιφανῶν ἐστίν, Ὀλυμπίας πλησίον κατὰ τὸν Φέλλωνα.[2] πρὸς ἕω δ' ἐστὶν ὄρος τοῦ Πύλου πλησίον ἐπώνυμον Μίνθης, ἣν μυθεύουσι παλλακὴν τοῦ Ἅδου γενομένην πατηθεῖσαν[3] ὑπὸ τῆς Κόρης εἰς τὴν κηπαίαν μίνθην μεταβαλεῖν, ἥν τινες ἡδύοσμον καλοῦσι. καὶ δὴ καὶ τέμενός ἐστιν Ἅδου πρὸς τῷ ὄρει, τιμώμενον καὶ ὑπὸ Μακιστίων, καὶ Δήμητρος ἄλσος ὑπερκείμενον τοῦ Πυλιακοῦ πεδίου. τὸ δὲ πεδίον εὔγεών ἐστι τοῦτο, τῇ θαλάττῃ δὲ συνάψαν, παρατείνει παρ' ἅπαν τὸ μεταξὺ τοῦ τε Σαμικοῦ καὶ ποταμοῦ Νέδας διάστημα. θινώδης δὲ καὶ στενός ἐστιν ὁ τῆς θαλάττης αἰγιαλός, ὥστ' οὐκ ἂν ἀπογνοίη τις ἐντεῦθεν ἠμαθόεντα ὠνομάσθαι τὸν Πύλον.

[1] καὶ Ἀρκαδικός, C. Müller would transpose to a position after Λεπρεατικός (above); cp. 8. 3. 3 and 8. 3. 26.

[2] The words καὶ τὸ τῆς . . . Φέλλωνα are transposed by Groskurd, Meineke, and others to a position after Τριφύλιοι (at end of § 13). Meineke emends Φέλλωνα to φελλῶνα (*stony ground*); C. Müller (*Philologus* 34. 79) conjectures Ἀπέλλωνα, or Φλέγωνα, and Krüger Φολόην.

Lepreatic Pylus, which Homer calls "emathöeis"[1] and transmits to posterity as the fatherland of Nestor, as one might infer from his words, whether it be that the river that flows past Pylus towards the north (now called Mamaüs, or Arcadicus) was called Amathus in earlier times, so that Pylus got its epithet "emathöeis" from "Amathus," or that this river was called Pamisus, the same as two rivers in Messenia, and that the derivation of the epithet of the city is uncertain; for it is false, they say, that either the river or the country about it is "amathodes."[2] And also the temple of Athenê Scilluntia at Scillus, in the neighbourhood of Olympia near Phellon,[3] is one of the famous temples. Near Pylus, towards the east, is a mountain named after Minthê, who, according to myth, became the concubine of Hades, was trampled under foot by Corê, and was transformed into garden-mint, the plant which some call Hedyosmos.[4] Furthermore, near the mountain is a precinct sacred to Hades, which is revered by the Macistians too,[5] and also a grove sacred to Demeter, which is situated above the Pylian plain. This plain is fertile; it borders on the sea and stretches along the whole distance between Samicum and the River Neda. But the shore of the sea is narrow and sandy, so that one could not refuse to believe that Pylus got its epithet "emathöeis" therefrom.

[1] Now interpreted as meaning "sandy." [2] "Sandy."
[3] Phellon, whether town, river, or mountain, is otherwise unknown. [4] "Sweet-smelling" (mint).
[5] As well as by the Pylians.

---

[3] πατηθεῖσαν, Corais (from conjecture of Sevin), for ἀπατηθεῖσαν; so Meineke, Forbiger, and others.

15. Πρὸς ἄρκτον δ' ὅμορα ἦν τῷ Πύλῳ δύο πολείδια Τριφυλιακά, Ὕπανα καὶ Τυμπανέαι,[1] ὧν τὸ μὲν εἰς Ἦλιν συνῳκίσθη, τὸ δ' ἔμεινε. καὶ ποταμοὶ δὲ δύο ἐγγὺς ῥέουσιν, ὅ τε Δαλίων[2] καὶ ὁ Ἀχέρων, ἐμβάλλοντες εἰς τὸν Ἀλφειόν. ὁ δὲ Ἀχέρων κατὰ τὴν πρὸς τὸν Ἅδην οἰκειότητα ὠνόμασται· ἐκτετίμηται γὰρ δὴ σφόδρα τά τε τῆς Δήμητρος καὶ τῆς Κόρης ἱερὰ ἐνταῦθα καὶ τὰ τοῦ Ἅδου, τάχα διὰ τὰς ὑπεναντιότητας, ὥς φησιν ὁ Σκήψιος Δημήτριος. καὶ γὰρ εὔκαρπός ἐστι καὶ ἐρυσίβην γεννᾷ καὶ θρύον ἡ Τριφυλία· διόπερ ἀντὶ μεγάλης φορᾶς πυκνὰς ἀφορίας γίνεσθαι συμβαίνει κατὰ τοὺς τόπους.

16. Τοῦ δὲ Πύλου πρὸς νότον ἐστὶ τὸ Λέπρεον. ἦν δὲ καὶ αὕτη ἡ[3] πόλις ὑπὲρ τῆς θαλάττης ἐν τεσσαράκοντα σταδίοις· μεταξὺ δὲ τοῦ Λεπρέου καὶ τοῦ Ἀννίου[4] τὸ ἱερὸν τοῦ Σαμίου Ποσειδῶνός ἐστιν, ἑκατὸν σταδίους ἑκατέρου[5] διέχον. τοῦτο δ' ἐστὶ τὸ ἱερόν, ἐν ᾧ καταληφθῆναί φησιν ὁ ποιητὴς ὑπὸ Τηλεμάχου τὴν θυσίαν συντελοῦντας τοὺς Πυλίους·

οἱ δὲ Πύλον, Νηλῆος ἐϋκτίμενον πτολίεθρον
ἶξον· τοὶ δ' ἐπὶ θινὶ θαλάσσης ἱερὰ ῥέζον
ταύρους παμμέλανας Ἐνοσίχθονι κυανοχαίτῃ.

C 345 πάρεστι μὲν γὰρ τῷ ποιητῇ καὶ πλάττειν τὰ μὴ ὄντα, ὅταν δ' ᾖ δυνατὸν ἐφαρμόττειν τοῖς οὖσι

[1] Τυμπανέαι, Corais, Kramer, Meineke, for Ἐπάνη (B), Ὕπανα (B *man. sec.*), Τυπάνσαι (*Abgh*). But Τυπανέαι might be the correct reading (see C. Müller, *Ind. Var. Lect.*, p. 991).

[2] Δαλίων: cp. Διάγων in Pausanias 6. 21. 4, which appears to be the same river.

[3] ἡ, after αὕτη, Groskurd inserts; so the later editors.

15. Towards the north, on the borders of Pylus, were two little Triphylian cities, Hypana and Tympaneae; the former of these was incorporated into Elis, whereas the latter remained as it was. And further, two rivers flow near these places, the Dalion and the Acheron, both of them emptying into the Alpheius. The Acheron has been so named by virtue of its close relation to Hades; for, as we know, not only the temples of Demeter and Corê have been held in very high honour there, but also those of Hades, perhaps because of "the contrariness of the soil," to use the phrase of Demetrius of Scepsis. For while Triphylia brings forth good fruit, it breeds red-rust and produces rush; and therefore in this region it is often the case that instead of a large crop there is no crop at all.

16. To the south of Pylus is Lepreum. This city, too, was situated above the sea, at a distance of forty stadia; and between Lepreum and the Annius[1] is the temple of the Samian Poseidon, at a distance of one hundred stadia from each. This is the temple at which the poet says Telemachus found the Pylians performing the sacrifice: "And they came to Pylus, the well-built city of Neleus; and the people were doing sacrifice on the sea-shore, slaying bulls that were black all over, to the dark-haired Earth-shaker."[2] Now it is indeed allowable for the poet even to fabricate what is not true, but when practicable he

[1] "Annius" (otherwise unknown) seems to be a corruption of "Anigrus" (*cp.* 8. 3 19 and Pausanias 5. 5. 5); but according to Kramer, "Alpheius."

[2] *Odyssey* 3. 4.

---

[4] Ἀννίου, Corais (following conj. of Xylander) emends to Ἀνίγρου, but Kramer conjectures Ἀλφειοῦ.

[5] ἑκατέρου, Corais, for ἑκάτερον; so the later editors.

τὰ ἔπη καὶ σώζειν τὴν διήγησιν, τὸ δ' ἀπέχεσθαι προσῆκε μᾶλλον. χώραν δ' εἶχον εὐδαίμονα οἱ Λεπρεᾶται·[1] τούτοις δ' ὅμοροι Κυπαρισσιεῖς. ἄμφω δὲ τὰ χωρία ταῦτα Καύκωνες κατεῖχον, καὶ τὸν Μάκιστον δέ, ὅν τινες Πλατανιστοῦντα καλοῦσιν. ὁμώνυμον τῇ χώρᾳ δ' ἐστὶ τὸ πόλισμα. φασὶ δ' ἐν τῇ Λεπρεάτιδι καὶ Καύκωνος εἶναι μνῆμα, εἴτ' ἀρχηγέτου τινός, εἴτ' ἄλλως ὁμωνύμου τῷ ἔθνει.

17. Πλείους δ' εἰσὶ λόγοι περὶ τῶν Καυκώνων· καὶ γὰρ Ἀρκαδικὸν ἔθνος φασί, καθάπερ τὸ Πελασγικόν, καὶ πλανητικὸν ἄλλως, ὥσπερ ἐκεῖνο. ἱστορεῖ γοῦν ὁ ποιητὴς καὶ τοῖς Τρωσὶν ἀφιγμένους συμμάχους, πόθεν δ', οὐ λέγει· δοκοῦσι δ' ἐκ Παφλαγονίας· ἐκεῖ γὰρ ὀνομάζουσι Καυκωνιάτας τινὰς Μαριανδυνοῖς ὁμόρους, οἳ καὶ αὐτοὶ Παφλαγόνες εἰσί. μνησθησόμεθα δ' αὐτῶν ἐπὶ πλέον, ὅταν εἰς ἐκεῖνον περιστῇ τὸν τόπον ἡ γραφή. νυνὶ δὲ περὶ τῶν ἐν τῇ Τριφυλίᾳ Καυκώνων ἔτι καὶ ταῦτα προσιστορητέον. οἱ μὲν γὰρ καὶ ὅλην τὴν νῦν Ἠλείαν, ἀπὸ τῆς Μεσσηνίας μέχρι Δύμης, Καυκωνίαν λεχθῆναί φασιν· Ἀντίμαχος γοῦν καὶ Ἐπειοὺς καὶ Καύκωνας ἅπαντας προσαγορεύει. τινὲς δὲ ὅλην μὲν μὴ κατασχεῖν αὐτούς, δίχα δὲ μεμερισμένους οἰκεῖν, τοὺς μὲν πρὸς τῇ Μεσσηνίᾳ κατὰ τὴν Τριφυλίαν, τοὺς δὲ πρὸς τῇ Δύμῃ κατὰ τὴν Βουπρασίδα καὶ τὴν Κοίλην Ἦλιν· Ἀριστοτέλης

[1] Λεπρεᾶται, Pletho, for Τεγεᾶται; so the editors.

---

[1] *Iliad* 20. 329. [2] 12. 3. 5.

should adapt his words to what is true and preserve his narrative; but the more appropriate thing was to abstain from what was not true. The Lepreatans held a fertile territory; and that of the Cyparissians bordered on it. Both these districts were taken and held by the Cauconians; and so was the Macistus (by some called Platanistus). The name of the town is the same as that of the territory. It is said that there is a tomb of Caucon in the territory of Lepreum—whether Caucon was a progenitor of the tribe or one who for some other reason had the same name as the tribe.

17. There are several accounts of the Cauconians; for it is said that, like the Pelasgians, they were an Arcadian tribe, and, again like the Pelasgians, that they were a wandering tribe. At any rate, the poet [1] tells us that they came to Troy as allies of the Trojans. But he does not say whence they come, though they seem to have come from Paphlagonia; for in Paphlagonia there is a people called Cauconiatae whose territory borders on that of the Mariandyni, who are themselves Paphlagonians. But I shall speak of them at greater length when I come to my description of that region.[2] At present I must add the following to my account of the Cauconians in Triphylia. Some say that the whole of what is now called Eleia, from Messenia as far as Dymê, was called Cauconia. Antimachus, at any rate, calls all the inhabitants both Epeians and Cauconians. Others, however, say that the Cauconians did not occupy the whole of Eleia, but lived there in two separate divisions, one division in Triphylia near Messenia, and the other in Buprasis and Coelê Elis near Dymê. And Aristotle has knowledge of their

δ' ἐνταῦθα μάλιστα οἶδεν ἱδρυμένους αὐτούς. καὶ δὴ τοῖς ὑφ' Ὁμήρου λεγομένοις ὁμολογεῖ μᾶλλον ἡ ὑστάτη ἀπόφασις, τό τε ζητούμενον πρότερον λαμβάνει λύσιν. ὁ μὲν γὰρ Νέστωρ ὑπόκειται τὸν Τριφυλιακὸν οἰκῶν Πύλον τά τε πρὸς νότον καὶ τὰ ἑωθινά (ταῦτα δ' ἐστὶ τὰ συγκυροῦντα πρὸς τὴν Μεσσηνίαν καὶ τὴν Λακωνικήν)[1] ὑπ' ἐκείνῳ ἐστίν, ἔχουσι δ' οἱ Καύκωνες, ὥστε τοῖς ἀπὸ τοῦ Πύλου βαδίζουσιν εἰς Λακεδαίμονα ἀνάγκη διὰ Καυκώνων εἶναι τὴν ὁδόν. τὸ δὲ ἱερὸν τοῦ Σαμίου Ποσειδῶνος καὶ ὁ κατ' αὐτὸ ὅρμος, εἰς ὃν κατήχθη Τηλέμαχος, πρὸς δύσιν καὶ πρὸς ἄρκτον ἀπονεύει. εἰ μὲν τοίνυν οἱ Καύκωνες ἐνταῦθα μόνον οἰκοῦσιν, οὐ σώζεται τῷ ποιητῇ ὁ λόγος. κελεύει γὰρ ἡ μὲν Ἀθηνᾶ[2] κατὰ τὸν Σωτάδη[3] τῷ Νέστορι, τὸν μὲν Τηλέμαχον εἰς τὴν Λακεδαίμονα πέμψαι σὺν δίφρῳ τε καὶ υἱέϊ εἰς τὰ πρὸς ἕω μέρη· αὐτὴ δ' ἐπὶ ναῦν βαδιεῖσθαι νυκτερεύσουσά φησιν ἐπὶ τὴν δύσιν καὶ εἰς τοὐπίσω·

ἀτὰρ ἠῶθεν μετὰ Καύκωνας μεγαθύμους

πορεύεσθαι ἐπὶ τὸ χρέος πάλιν εἰς τοὔμπροσθεν. τίς οὖν ὁ τρόπος; παρῆν γὰρ τῷ Νέστορι λέγειν·
C 346 ἀλλ' οἵ γε Καύκωνες ὑπ' ἐμοί εἰσι καὶ πρὸ ὁδοῦ τοῖς εἰς Λακεδαίμονα βαδίζουσιν· ὥστε τί οὐ συνοδεύεις τοῖς περὶ Τηλέμαχον, ἀλλ' ἀναχωρεῖς εἰς τοὐπίσω; ἅμα δ' οἰκεῖον ἦν τῷ βαδίζοντι ἐπὶ

[1] ἅ, before ὑπ' ἐκείνῳ, Meineke and others delete.
[2] For μὲν Ἀθηνᾶ, Madvig conjectures Μεντοραθηνᾶ.
[3] τὸν Σωτάδη (*Bkl*, Ald.); Ὀδύσσειαν (marg. B, *man. sec.* and marg. *n*.).

having been established at this latter place especially.[1] And in fact the last view agrees better with what Homer says, and furnishes a solution of the question asked above,[2] for in this view it is assumed that Nestor lived in the Triphylian Pylus, and that the parts towards the south and east (that is, the parts that are contiguous to Messenia and the Laconian country) were subject to him; and these parts were held by the Cauconians, so that if one went by land from Pylus to Lacedaemon his journey necessarily must have been made through the territory of the Cauconians; and yet the temple of the Samian Poseidon and the mooring-place near it, where Telemachus landed, lie off towards the north-west. So then, if the Cauconians live only here, the account of the poet is not conserved; for instance, Athenê, according to Sotades, bids Nestor to send Telemachus to Lacedaemon "with chariot and son" to the parts that lie towards the east, and yet she says that she herself will go to the ship to spend the night, towards the west, and back the same way she came, and she goes on to say that "in the morning" she will go "amongst the great-hearted Cauconians"[3] to collect a debt, that is, she will go forward again. How, pray? For Nestor might have said: "But the Cauconians are my subjects and live near the road that people travel to Lacedaemon. Why, therefore, do you not travel with Telemachus and his companions instead of going back the same way you came?" And at the same time it would have been

[1] The extant works of Aristotle contain no reference to the Cauconians.

[2] 8. 3. 11.

[3] *Od.* 3. 366.

χρέους κομιδήν, οὐκ ὀλίγου, ὥς φησι, πρὸς ἀνθρώπους ὑπὸ τῷ Νέστορι ὄντας, αἰτήσασθαί τινα παρ' αὐτοῦ βοήθειαν, εἴ τι ἀγνωμονοῖτο (ὥσπερ εἴωθε) περὶ τὸ συμβόλαιον· οὐ γέγονε δὲ τοῦτο. εἰ μὲν τοίνυν ἐνταῦθα μόνον οἰκοῖεν οἱ Καύκωνες, ταῦτ' ἂν συμβαίνοι τὰ ἄτοπα· μεμερισμένων δέ τινων καὶ εἰς τοὺς πρὸς Δύμῃ τόπους τῆς Ἠλείας, ἐκεῖσε ἂν εἴη λέγουσα τὴν ἔφοδον ἡ Ἀθηνᾶ, καὶ οὐκ ἂν ἔτι οὔθ' ἡ εἰς τὴν ναῦν κατάβασις ἔχοι τι ἀπεμφαῖνον, οὔθ' ὁ τῆς συνοδίας ἀποσπασμός, εἰς τἀναντία τῆς ὁδοῦ οὔσης. παραπλησίως δ' ἂν καὶ τὰ περὶ τοῦ Πύλου διαπορούμενα τύχοι τῆς προσηκούσης διαίτης, ἐπελθοῦσι μικρὸν ἔτι τῆς χωρογραφίας μέχρι τοῦ Πύλου τοῦ Μεσσηνιακοῦ.

18. Ἐλέγοντο δὲ Παρωρεᾶταί[1] τινες τῶν ἐν τῇ Τριφυλίᾳ κατέχοντες ὄρη περὶ τὸ Λέπρεον καὶ τὸ Μάκιστον καθήκοντα ἐπὶ θάλατταν πλησίον[2] τοῦ Σαμιακοῦ Ποσειδίου.

19. Ὑπὸ τούτοις ἐστὶν ἐν τῇ παραλίᾳ δύο ἄντρα, τὸ μὲν νυμφῶν Ἀνιγριάδων, τὸ δέ, ἐν ᾧ τὰ περὶ τὰς Ἀτλαντίδας καὶ τὴν Δαρδάνου γένεσιν. ἐνταῦθα δὲ καὶ τὰ ἄλση, τό τε Ἰωναῖον[3] καὶ τὸ Εὐρυκύδειον.[4] τὸ μὲν οὖν Σαμικόν ἐστιν ἔρυμα, πρότερον δὲ καὶ πόλις Σάμος προσαγορευομένη

[1] Παρωρεᾶται, Tzschucke from conj. of Casaubon (see Herod. 4. 148), for Παρωνάται (*Acgh*), Παρονάται (*Bkno*); so the later editors.

[2] μέχρι (*Bl*).

[3] For Ἰωναῖον Xylander conj. Διωναῖον; Ἐνδυμιωναῖον, Tzschucke, Corais, Groskurd, because Eurycyda was the daughter of Endymion (Pausanias 5. 1. 4).

proper for one who was going to people subject to Nestor to collect a debt—"no small debt," as she says—to request aid from Nestor, if there should be any unfairness (as is usually the case) in connection with the contract; but this she did not do. If, then, the Cauconians lived only there, the result would be absurd; but if some of the Cauconians had been separated from the rest and had gone to the regions near Dymê in Eleia, then Athenê would be speaking of her journey thither, and there would no longer be anything incongruous either in her going down to the ship or in her withdrawing from the company of travellers, because their roads lay in opposite directions. And similarly, too, the puzzling questions raised in regard to Pylus may find an appropriate solution when, a little further on in my chorography, I reach the Messenian Pylus.

18. A part of the inhabitants of Triphylia were called Paroreatae; they occupied mountains, in the neighbourhood of Lepreum and Macistum, that reach down to the sea near the Samian Poseidium.[1]

19. At the base of these mountains, on the seaboard, are two caves. One is the cave of the nymphs called Anigriades; the other is the scene of the stories of the daughters of Atlas[2] and of the birth of Dardanus. And here, too, are the sacred precincts called the Ionaeum and the Eurycydeium. Samicum[3] is now only a fortress, though formerly there was also a city which was called Samus, perhaps

[1] See 8. 3. 20.

[2] The seven Pleiades.

[3] Cp. Pausanias' account of Samicum, Arenê, and the Anigrus (5. 5. 6 and 5. 6. 1–2).

---

[4] After Εὐρυκύδειον Meineke indicates a lacuna.

διὰ τὸ ὕψος ἴσως, ἐπειδὴ σάμους ἐκάλουν τὰ ὕψη· τάχα δὲ τῆς Ἀρήνης ἀκρόπολις ἦν τοῦτο, ἧς ἐν τῷ Καταλόγῳ μέμνηται ὁ ποιητής·

οἳ δὲ Πύλον τ' ἐνέμοντο καὶ Ἀρήνην ἐρατεινήν.

οὐδαμοῦ γὰρ σαφῶς εὑρίσκοντες ἐνταῦθα μάλιστα εἰκάζουσι τὴν Ἀρήνην, ὅπου καὶ ὁ παρακείμενος Ἄνιγρος ποταμός, καλούμενος πρότερον Μινύειος, δίδωσιν οὐ μικρὸν σημεῖον· λέγει γὰρ ὁ ποιητής·

ἔστι δέ τις ποταμὸς Μινυήιος εἰς ἅλα βάλλων
ἐγγύθεν Ἀρήνης.

πρὸς γὰρ δὴ τῷ ἄντρῳ τῶν Ἀνιγριάδων νυμφῶν ἐστὶ πηγή, ὑφ' ἧς ἕλειον καὶ τιφῶδες[1] τὸ ὑποπίπτον γίνεται χωρίον· ὑποδέχεται δὲ τὸ πλεῖστον τοῦ ὕδατος ὁ Ἄνιγρος, βαθὺς καὶ ὕπτιος ὤν, ὥστε λιμνάζειν· θινώδης δ' ὢν ὁ τόπος ἐξ εἴκοσι σταδίων βαρεῖαν ὀσμὴν[2] παρέχει, καὶ τοὺς ἰχθῦς ἀβρώτους ποιεῖ. μυθεύουσι δ' οἱ μὲν ἀπὸ τοῦ τῶν τετρωμένων Κενταύρων τινὰς ἐνταῦθ' ἀπονίψασθαι τὸν ἐκ τῆς Ὕδρας ἰόν, οἱ δ' ἀπὸ τοῦ Μελάμποδα τοῖς ὕδασι τούτοις καθαρσίοις χρήσασθαι πρὸς τὸν
C 347 τῶν Προιτίδων καθαρμόν· ἀλφοὺς δὲ καὶ λεύκας καὶ λειχῆνας ἰᾶται τὸ ἐντεῦθεν λουτρόν. φασὶ δὲ καὶ τὸν Ἀλφειὸν ἀπὸ τῆς τῶν ἀλφῶν θεραπείας οὕτως ὠνομάσθαι. ἐπεὶ οὖν ἥ τε ὑπτιότης τοῦ Ἀνίγρου[3] καὶ αἱ ἀνακοπαὶ τῆς θαλάττης μονὴν

[1] τιφῶδες, Corais from conj. of Casaubon, for τειφώδης (Acg), τυφώδης (Bl, Ald.); so later editors in general.

[2] βαρεῖαν ὀσμήν, Corais from conj. of Casaubon, for βαθεῖαν ὄχθην; cp. Pausanias 5. 5. 5.

[3] Ἀνίγρου (B *man. sec.*), Pletho, for ἄντρου (other MSS.); so the other editors.

because of its lofty situation; for they used to call lofty places "Samoi." And perhaps Samicum was the acropolis of Arenê, which the poet mentions in the *Catalogue*: "And those who dwelt in Pylus and lovely Arenê."[1] For while they cannot with certainty discover Arenê anywhere, they prefer to conjecture that this is its site; and the neighbouring River Anigrus, formerly called Minyeius, gives no slight indication of the truth of the conjecture, for the poet says: "And there is a River Minyeius which falls into the sea near Arenê."[2] For near the cave of the nymphs called Anigriades is a spring which makes the region that lies below it swampy and marshy. The greater part of the water is received by the Anigrus, a river so deep and so sluggish that it forms a marsh; and since the region is muddy, it emits an offensive odour for a distance of twenty stadia, and makes the fish unfit to eat.[3] In the mythical accounts, however, this is attributed by some writers to the fact that certain of the Centaurs here washed off the poison they got from the Hydra, and by others to the fact that Melampus used these cleansing waters for the purification of the Proetides.[4] The bathing-water from here cures leprosy, elephantiasis, and scabies. It is said, also, that the Alpheius was so named from its being a cure for leprosy. At any rate, since both the sluggishness of the Anigrus and the back-wash from the sea give

[1] *Iliad* 2. 591. [2] *Iliad* 11. 722.

[3] For a fuller account see Pausanias 5. 5. 5; also Frazer's note, vol. III. p. 478.

[4] According to Pausanias (5.5.5), "some attribute the peculiarity of the river to the fact that the *objects used in the purification* of the Proetides were flung into it."

μᾶλλον ἢ ῥύσιν παρέχουσι τοῖς ὕδασι, Μινυήιόν[1] φασιν εἰρῆσθαι πρότερον, παρατρέψαι δέ τινας τοὔνομα καὶ ἀντ' αὐτοῦ ποιῆσαι Μιντήιον.[2] ἔχει δ' ἡ ἐτυμότης καὶ ἄλλας ἀφορμάς, εἴτ' ἀπὸ τῶν μετὰ Χλωρίδος τῆς Νέστορος μητρὸς ἐλθόντων ἐξ Ὀρχομενοῦ τοῦ Μινυείου, εἴτε[3] Μινυῶν, οἳ τῶν Ἀργοναυτῶν ἀπόγονοι ὄντες ἐκ Λήμνου μὲν εἰς Λακεδαίμονα ἐξέπεσον, ἐντεῦθεν δ' εἰς τὴν Τριφυλίαν, καὶ ᾤκησαν περὶ τὴν Ἀρήνην ἐν τῇ χώρᾳ τῇ νῦν Ὑπαισίᾳ καλουμένῃ, οὐκ ἐχούσῃ οὐκέτι τὰ τῶν Μινυῶν κτίσματα· ὧν τινὲς μετὰ Θήρα τοῦ Αὐτεσίωνος (ἦν δ' οὗτος Πολυνείκους ἀπόγονος) πλεύσαντες εἰς τὴν μεταξὺ Κυρηναίας καὶ τῆς Κρήτης νῆσον,

Καλλίστην τὸ πάροιθε, τὸ δ' ὕστερον οὔνομα Θήρην,

ὥς φησι Καλλίμαχος, ἔκτισαν την μητρόπολιν τῆς Κυρήνης Θήραν, ὁμώνυμον δ' ἐπέδειξαν[4] τῇ πόλει καὶ τὴν νῆσον.

20. Μεταξὺ δὲ τοῦ Ἀνίγρου καὶ τοῦ ὄρους, ἐξ οὗ ῥεῖ, ὁ τοῦ Ἰαρδάνου λειμὼν δείκνυται καὶ τάφος καὶ Ἀχαιαί, εἰσὶ δὲ πέτραι ἀπότομοι τοῦ αὐτοῦ ὄρους, ὑπὲρ ὧν ἡ Σάμος, ὡς ἔφαμεν, γέγονε πόλις· οὐ πάνυ δὲ ὑπὸ τῶν τοὺς περίπλους γραψάντων ἡ Σάμος μνημονεύεται, τάχα μέν γε διὰ τὸ πάλαι κατεσπάσθαι, τάχα δὲ καὶ διὰ τὴν θέσιν· τὸ μὲν γὰρ Ποσείδιόν ἐστιν ἄλσος, ὡς

[1] For Μινυήιον (the Homeric spelling, *Il.* 11. 722), Corais conj. Μιμνυήιον or Μενυήιον, and Meineke Ἐλινυήιον.

[2] Μιντήιον (A*gh*), Μεντήιον (*i*), Μιντήριον (*bkno*), Corais emends to Μινυήιον; so the later editors, but the change is purely conjectural.

fixity rather than current to its waters, it was called the "Minyeius" in earlier times, so it is said, though some have perverted the name and made it "Minteius"[1] instead. But the word has other sources of derivation, either from the people who went forth with Chloris, the mother of Nestor, from the Minyeian Orchomenus, or from the Minyans, who, being descendants of the Argonauts, were first driven out of Lemnos into Lacedaemon, and thence into Triphylia, and took up their abode about Arenê in the country which is now called Hypaesia, though it no longer has the settlements of the Minyans. Some of these Minyans sailed with Theras, the son of Autesion, who was a descendant of Polyneices, to the island[2] which is situated between Cyrenaea and Crete ("Callistê its earlier name, but Thera its later," as Callimachus[3] says), and founded Thera, the mother-city of Cyrenê, and designated the island by the same name as the city.

20. Between the Anigrus and the mountain from which it flows are to be seen the meadow and tomb of Iardanus, and also the Achaeae, which are abrupt cliffs of that same mountain above which, as I was saying,[4] the city Samus was situated. However, Samus is not mentioned at all by the writers of the *Circumnavigations*—perhaps because it had long since been torn down and perhaps also because of its position; for the Poseidium is a sacred precinct, as

[1] Thus connecting the name with the verb μένειν ("remain," "tarry"). Strabo probably wrote "Menteius" or "Menyeius," not "Minteius."
[2] Cp. 1. 3. 16. [3] *Frag.* 112 (Schneider). [4] 8. 3. 19.

---

[3] εἴτε, before Μινυῶν, Kramer inserts; so the later editors.
[4] ἐπέδειξαν, Meineke emends to ἀπέδειξαν.

εἴρηται, πρὸς τῇ θαλάττῃ· ὑπέρκειται δ' αὐτοῦ λόφος ὑψηλός, ἐπίπροσθεν ὢν τοῦ νῦν Σαμικοῦ, ἐφ' οὗ ἦν ἡ Σάμος, ὥστ' ἐκ θαλάττης μὴ ὁρᾶσθαι. καὶ πεδίον δ' αὐτόθι καλεῖται Σαμικόν· ἐξ οὗ πλέον ἄν τις τεκμαίροιτο ὑπάρξαι ποτὲ πόλιν τὴν Σάμον. καὶ ἡ Ῥαδινὴ δέ,[1] ἣν Στησίχορος ποιῆσαι δοκεῖ, ἧς ἀρχή·

> Ἄγε, Μοῦσα λίγει', ἄρξον ἀοιδᾶς, Ἐρατώ, νόμους[2]
> Σαμίων περὶ παίδων ἐρατᾷ φθεγγομένα λύρᾳ,

ἐντεῦθεν λέγει τοὺς παῖδας. ἐκδοθεῖσαν γὰρ τὴν Ῥαδινὴν εἰς Κόρινθον τυράννῳ φησὶν ἐκ τῆς Σάμου πλεῦσαι πνέοντος Ζεφύρου, οὐ δήπουθεν τῆς Ἰωνικῆς Σάμου· τῷ δ' αὐτῷ ἀνέμῳ καὶ ἀρχιθέωρον εἰς Δελφοὺς τὸν ἀδελφὸν αὐτῆς ἐλθεῖν, καὶ τὸν ἀνεψιὸν ἐρῶντα αὐτῆς ἅρματι εἰς Κόρινθον ἐξορμῆσαι παρ' αὐτήν· ὅ τε τύραννος, κτείνας ἀμφοτέρους, ἅρματι ἀποπέμπει τὰ σώματα, μεταγνοὺς δ' ἀνακαλεῖ καὶ θάπτει.

C 348 21. Ἀπὸ δὲ τοῦ Πύλου τούτου καὶ τοῦ Λεπρέου[3] τετρακοσίων που σταδίων ἐστὶ διάστημα ἐπὶ τὴν Μεσσηνιακὴν Πύλον καὶ τὸ Κορυφάσιον, ἐπὶ θαλάττῃ κείμενα φρούρια, καὶ τὴν παρακειμένην Σφαγίαν νῆσον, ἀπὸ δὲ Ἀλφειοῦ ἑπτακοσίων πεντήκοντα, ἀπὸ δὲ τοῦ Χελωνάτα χιλίων τριάκοντα. ἐν δὲ τῷ μεταξὺ τό τε τοῦ Μακιστίου Ἡρακλέους ἱερόν ἐστι καὶ ὁ Ἀκίδων ποταμός. ῥεῖ δὲ παρὰ τάφον Ἰαρδάνου καὶ Χάαν πόλιν

[1] εἰς, before ἥν, Tzschucke deletes; so the editors.
[2] Ἐρατώ, νόμους, Meineke for ἐρατῶν ὕμνους; so the later editors.
[3] Λεπρίου (Abcg).

I have said,[1] near the sea, and above it is situated a lofty hill which is in front of the Samicum of to-day, on the site of which Samus once stood, and therefore Samus was not visible from the sea. Here, too, is a plain called Samicum; and from this one might get more conclusive proof that there was once a city called Samus. And further, the poem entitled *Rhadinê* (of which Stesichorus is reputed to be the author), which begins, "Come, thou clear-voiced Muse, Erato, begin thy song, voicing to the tune of thy lovely lyre the strain of the children of Samus,"[2] refers to the children of the Samus in question; for Rhadinê, who had been betrothed to a tyrant of Corinth, the author says, set sail from Samus (not meaning, of course, the Ionian Samus) while the west wind was blowing, and with the same wind her brother, he adds, went to Delphi as chief of an embassy; and her cousin, who was in love with her, set out for Corinth in his chariot to visit her. And the tyrant killed them both and sent their bodies away on a chariot, but repented, recalled the chariot, and buried their bodies.

21. From this Pylus and Lepreum to the Messenian Pylus and Coryphasium (a fortress situated on the sea) and to the adjacent island Sphagia,[3] the distance is about four hundred stadia; from the Alpheius seven hundred and fifty; and from Chelonatas one thousand and thirty. In the intervening space are both the temple of the Macistian Heracles and the Acidon River. The Acidon flows past the tomb of Iardanus and past Chaa—a city that was

[1] 8. 3.13. [2] *Frag.* 44 (Bergk).
[3] Also called Sphacteria (see 8. 4. 2).

ποτὲ ὑπάρξασαν πλησίον Λεπρέου, ὅπου καὶ τὸ πεδίον τὸ Αἰπάσιον. περὶ ταύτης δὲ τῆς Χάας γενέσθαι φασὶν ἔνιοι τὸν πόλεμον τοῖς Ἀρκάσι πρὸς τοὺς Πυλίους, ὃν ἔφρασεν Ὅμηρος, καὶ δεῖν οἴονται γράφειν·

ἡβῷμ', ὡς ὅτ' ἐπ' ὠκυρόῳ Ἀκίδοντι[1] μάχοντο
ἀγρόμενοι Πύλιοί τε καὶ Ἀρκάδες
Χάας[2] πὰρ τείχεσσιν·

οὐ Κελάδοντι, οὐδὲ Φειᾶς· τῷ γὰρ τάφῳ τοῦ Ἰαρδάνου τοῦτον πλησιάζειν καὶ τοῖς Ἀρκάσι τὸν τόπον μᾶλλον ἢ ἐκεῖνον.

22. Κυπαρισσία[3] τέ ἐστιν ἐπὶ τῇ θαλάττῃ τῇ Τριφυλιακῇ καὶ Πύργοι καὶ ὁ Ἀκίδων ποταμὸς καὶ Νέδα. νυνὶ μὲν οὖν τῇ Τριφυλίᾳ πρὸς τὴν Μεσσηνίαν ὅριόν ἐστι τὸ τῆς Νέδας ῥεῦμα λάβρον ἐκ τοῦ Λυκαίου κατιόν, Ἀρκαδικοῦ ὄρους, ἐκ πηγῆς, ἣν ἀναρρῆξαι τεκοῦσαν τὸν Δία μυθεύεται Ῥέαν νίπτρων χάριν· ῥεῖ δὲ παρὰ Φιγαλίαν, καθ' ὃ γειτνιῶσι Πυργῖται, Τριφυλίων ἔσχατοι, Κυπαρισσεῦσι, πρώτοις Μεσσηνίων· τὸ δὲ παλαιὸν ἄλλως διώριστο, ὥς καί τινας τῶν πέραν τῆς Νέδας ὑπὸ τῷ Νέστορι εἶναι, τόν τε Κυπαρισσήεντα καὶ ἄλλα τινὰ ἐπέκεινα, καθάπερ καὶ τὴν θάλατταν τὴν Πυλίαν ὁ ποιητὴς ἐπεκτείνει μέχρι

[1] Ἀκίδοντι, Meineke, for Κέλαδοντι; so most editors.
[2] Χάας, Casaubon, for Φείας; so most editors.
[3] Κυπαρισσία, Tzschucke, for Κυπαρισῖνα (*Ag*), Κυπαρισσίνα (*bhkno*); so the editors.

once in existence near Lepreum, where is also the Aepasian Plain. It was for the possession of this Chaa, some say, that the war between the Arcadians and Pylians, of which Homer tells us, arose in a dispute; and they think that one should write, "Would that I were in the bloom of my youth, as when the Pylians and the Arcadians gathered together and fought at the swift-flowing Acidon, beside the walls of Chaa"—instead of "Celadon" and "Pheia";[1] for this region, they say, is nearer than the other to the tomb of Iardanus and to the country of the Arcadians.

22. Cyparissia is on the Triphylian Sea, and so are Pyrgi, and the Acidon and Neda Rivers.[2] At the present time the stream of the Neda is the boundary between Triphylia and Messenia (an impetuous stream that comes down from Lycaeus, an Arcadian mountain, out of a spring, which, according to the myth, Rhea, after she had given birth to Zeus, caused to break forth in order to have water to bathe in); and it flows past Phigalia, opposite the place where the Pyrgetans, last of the Triphylians, border on the Cyparissians, first of the Messenians; but in the early times the division between the two countries was different, so that some of the territories across the Neda were subject to Nestor—not only Cyparissëeis, but also some other parts on the far side. Just so, too, the poet prolongs the Pylian Sea as far as the seven cities

[1] "Celadon" and "Pheia" are the readings of the Homeric text (*Iliad* 7. 133). After the words "beside the walls of Pheia" Homer adds the words "about the streams of Iardanus."

[2] As often, Strabo means the *mouths* of the rivers.

τῶν ἑπτὰ πόλεων, ὧν ὑπέσχετο Ἀγαμέμνων τῷ Ἀχιλλεῖ·

πᾶσαι δ' ἐγγὺς ἁλὸς νέαται Πύλου ἠμαθόεντος.

τοῦτο γὰρ ἴσον τῷ ἐγγὺς ἁλὸς τῆς Πυλίας.

23. Ἐφεξῆς δ' οὖν τῷ Κυπαρισσήεντι ἐπὶ τὴν Μεσσηνιακὴν Πύλον παραπλέοντι καὶ τὸ Κορυφάσιον ἥ τε Ἐρανά [1] ἐστιν, ἥν τινες οὐκ εὖ Ἀρήνην νομίζουσιν κεκλῆσθαι πρότερον ὁμωνύμως τῇ Πυλιακῇ, καὶ ἡ ἄκρα [2] Πλαταμώδης, ἀφ' ἧς ἐπὶ τὸ Κορυφάσιον καὶ τὴν νῦν καλουμένην Πύλον ἑκατόν [3] εἰσι στάδιοι. ἔστι δὲ καὶ νησίον [4] καὶ πολίχνιον ἐν αὐτῷ ὁμώνυμον Πρωτή. οὐκ ἂν δ' ἐξητάζομεν ἴσως ἐπὶ τοσοῦτον τὰ παλαιά, ἀλλ' ἤρκει λέγειν ὡς ἔχει νῦν ἕκαστα, εἰ μή τις ἦν ἐκ παίδων ἡμῖν παραδεδομένη φήμη περὶ τούτων· ἄλλων δ' ἄλλα εἰπόντων, ἀνάγκη διαιτᾶν. πιστεύονται δ' ὡς ἐπὶ τὸ πολὺ οἱ ἐνδοξότατοί τε καὶ πρεσβύτατοι καὶ κατ' ἐμπειρίαν πρῶτοι· Ὁμήρου δ' εἰς ταῦτα ὑπερβεβλημένου πάντας,
C 349 ἀνάγκη συνεπισκοπεῖν καὶ τὰ ὑπ' ἐκείνου λεχθέντα καὶ συγκρούειν πρὸς τὰ νῦν, καθάπερ καὶ μικρὸν ἔμπροσθεν ἔφαμεν.

24. Περὶ μὲν οὖν τῆς Κοίλης Ἤλιδος καὶ τοῦ Βουπρασίου τὰ λεχθέντα ὑφ' Ὁμήρου προ-

[1] Ἐρανα, Xylander, for Ἐρενα; so the later editors.
[2] καὶ ἡ ἄκρα, lacuna of about ten letters supplied by Groskurd; and so most later editors. But *Bkno* have ἔστι δὲ καί.

which Agamemnon promised to Achilles: "and all are situated near the sea of sandy Pylus";[1] for this phrase is equivalent to "near the Pylian Sea."

23. Be that as it may, next in order after sailing past Cyparissëeis towards the Messenian Pylus and Coryphasium one comes to Erana, which some wrongly think was in earlier times called Arenê, by the same name as the Pylian Arenê, and also to Cape Platamodes, from which the distance to Coryphasium and to what is now called Pylus is one hundred stadia. Here, too, is a small island, Protê, and on it a town of the same name. Perhaps I would not be examining at such length things that are ancient, and would be content merely to tell in detail how things now are, if there were not connected with these matters legends that have been taught us from boyhood; and since different men say different things, I must act as arbiter. In general, it is the most famous, the oldest, and the most experienced men who are believed; and since it is Homer who has surpassed all others in these respects, I must likewise both inquire into his words and compare them with things as they now are, as I was saying a little while ago.[2]

24. I have already[3] inquired into Homer's words concerning Coelê Elis and Buprasium. Concerning

[1] This line from the *Iliad* (9. 153), though wrongly translated above, is translated as Strabo interpreted it. He, like Aristarchus, took νέαται as a *verb* meaning "are situated," but as elsewhere in the *Iliad* (*e.g.* 11. 712) it is an *adjective* meaning "last."

[2] 8. 3. 3. [3] 8. 3. 8.

---

[3] εἴκοσι is inserted by *nokt.*

[4] καὶ νησίον, Curtius, for κενήριον; so the editors.

επέσκεπται ἡμῖν. περὶ δὲ τῆς ὑπὸ τῷ Νέστορι οὕτω φησίν·

οἳ δὲ Πύλον τ' ἐνέμοντο καὶ Ἀρήνην ἐρατεινὴν
καὶ Θρύον, Ἀλφειοῖο πόρον, καὶ ἐΰκτιτον Αἶπυ
καὶ Κυπαρισσήεντα καὶ Ἀμφιγένειαν ἔναιον
καὶ Πτελεὸν καὶ Ἕλος καὶ Δώριον, ἔνθα τε Μοῦσαι
ἀντόμεναι Θάμυριν τὸν Θρήικα παῦσαν ἀοιδῆς,
Οἰχαλίηθεν ἰόντα παρ' Εὐρύτου Οἰχαλιῆος.

Πύλος μὲν οὖν ἐστί, περὶ ἧς ἡ ζήτησις· αὐτίκα δ' ἐπισκεψόμεθα περὶ αὐτῆς. περὶ δὲ τῆς Ἀρήνης εἴρηται· ἣν δὲ λέγει νῦν Θρύον, ἐν ἄλλοις καλεῖ Θρυόεσσαν·

ἔστι δέ τις Θρυόεσσα πόλις, αἰπεῖα κολώνη,
τηλοῦ ἐπ' Ἀλφειῷ·

Ἀλφειοῦ δὲ πόρον φησίν, ὅτι πεζῇ περατὸς εἶναι δοκεῖ κατὰ τοῦτον τὸν τόπον· καλεῖται δὲ νῦν Ἐπιτάλιον, τῆς Μακιστίας χωρίον· τὸ εὔκτιτον δ' Αἶπυ ἔνιοι μὲν ζητοῦσι πότερον ποτέρου ἐπίθετον, καὶ τίς ἡ πόλις, καὶ εἰ αἱ νῦν Μαργάλαι[1] τῆς Ἀμφιδολίας·[2] αὗται μὲν οὖν οὐ φυσικὸν ἔρυμα, ἕτερον δὲ δείκνυται φυσικὸν ἐν τῇ Μακιστίᾳ. ὁ μὲν οὖν τοῦθ' ὑπονοῶν φράζεσθαι ὄνομά φησι τῆς πόλεως τὸ Αἶπυ ἀπὸ τοῦ συμβεβηκότος φυσικῶς, ὡς Ἕλος καὶ Αἰγιαλὸν καὶ ἄλλα πλείω· ὁ δὲ τὴν Μαργάλαν τοὔμπαλιν ἴσως. Θρύον δὲ

[1] Μαργάλαι may be incorrectly spelled by the MSS. It seems to be the same place as Μαργάναι in Diodorus Siculus 15. 77 and Μάργαια in Stephanus Byzantinus.

[2] Ἀμφιδολίας, Tzschucke from conj. Wesseling, for Ἀμφιπολίας; so the editors.

the country that was subject to Nestor, Homer speaks as follows: "And those who dwelt in Pylus and lovely Arenê and Thryum, fording-place of the Alpheius, and well-built Aepy, and also those who were inhabitants of Cyparissëeis and Amphigeneia and Pteleus and Helus and Dorium, at which place the Muses met Thamyris the Thracian, and put a stop to his singing while he was on his way from Oechalia from Eurytus the Oechalian."[1] It is Pylus, then, with which our investigation is concerned, and about it we shall make inquiry presently. About Arenê I have already spoken.[2] The city which the poet now calls Thryum he elsewhere calls Thryoessa: "There is a certain city, Thryoessa, a steep hill, far away on the Alpheius."[3] He calls it "fording-place of the Alpheius" because the river could be crossed on foot, as it seems, at this place. But it is now called Epitalium (a small place in Macistia). As for "well-built Aepy," some raise the question which of the two words is the epithet and which is the city, and whether it is the Margalae of to-day, in Amphidolia. Now Margalae is not a natural stronghold, but another place is pointed out which is a natural stronghold, in Macistia. The man, therefore, who suspects that the latter place is meant by Homer calls the name of the city "Aepy"[4] from what is actually the case in nature (compare Helus,[5] Aegialus,[6] and several other names of places); whereas the man who suspects that "Margala" is meant does the reverse perhaps.[7]

[1] *Iliad* 2. 591. [2] § 19 above. [3] *Iliad* 11. 711.
[4] "Sheer," "steep." [5] "Marsh." [6] "Shore."
[7] That is, calls it "Euctitum" ("Well-built"), making the other word the epithet.

καὶ Θρυόεσσαν τὸ Ἐπιτάλιόν φασιν ὅτι πᾶσα μὲν αὕτη ἡ χώρα θρυώδης, μάλιστα δ' οἱ ποταμοί· ἐπὶ πλέον δὲ διαφαίνεται τοῦτο κατὰ τοὺς περατοὺς τοῦ ῥείθρου τόπους. τάχα δέ φασι Θρύον μὲν εἰρῆσθαι τὸν πόρον, εὔκτιτον δ' Αἶπυ τὸ Ἐπιτάλιον· ἔστι γὰρ ἐρυμνὸν φύσει· καὶ γὰρ ἐν ἄλλοις αἰπεῖαν κολώνην λέγει·

ἔστι δέ τις Θρυόεσσα πόλις, αἰπεῖα κολώνη,
τηλοῦ ἐπ' Ἀλφειῷ, πυμάτη Πύλου ἠμαθόεντος.

25. Ὁ δὲ Κυπαρισσήεις ἐστὶ μὲν περὶ τὴν πρότερον[1] Μακιστίαν, ἡνίκα καὶ πέραν τῆς Νέδας ἔτι ἦν Μακιστία, ἀλλ' οὐκ οἰκεῖται, ὡς οὐδὲ τὸ Μάκιστον· ἄλλη δ' ἐστὶν ἡ Μεσσηνιακὴ Κυπαρισσία· ὁμωνύμως[2] μὲν οὖν[3] ὁμοίως δὲ νῦν κἀκείνη λέγεται Κυπαρισσία ἑνικῶς τε καὶ θηλυκῶς, ὁ δὲ ποταμὸς Κυπαρισσήεις. καὶ Ἀμφιγένεια δὲ τῆς Μακιστίας ἐστὶ περὶ τὸν Ὑψόεντα, ὅπου τὸ τῆς Λητοῦς ἱερόν. τὸ δὲ Πτελεὸν κτίσμα μὲν γέγονε τῶν ἐκ Πτελεοῦ τοῦ Θετταλικοῦ ἐποικησάντων· λέγεται γὰρ κἀκεῖ

C 350 ἀγχίαλόν τ' Ἀντρῶνα ἰδὲ Πτελεὸν λεχεποίην·

ἔστι δὲ δρυμῶδες χωρίον ἀοίκητον, Πτελεάσιον[4] καλούμενον. Ἕλος δ' οἱ μὲν περὶ τὸν Ἀλφειὸν χώραν τινά φασιν, οἱ δὲ καὶ πόλιν, ὡς τὴν Λακωνικήν·

Ἕλος τ', ἔφαλον πτολίεθρον·

[1] προτέραν (Acghino).   [2] ὁμώνυμος B; so Meineke.
[3] οὖν is doubtful (see Müller, *Ind. Var. Lect.*, p. 992). Meineke reads οὐ.
[4] Πτελεάσιον, Meineke, for Πτελεάσιμον; so the later editors.

Thryum,[1] or Thryoessa, they say, is Epitalium, because the whole of this country is full of rushes, particularly the rivers; and this is still more conspicuous at the fordable places of the stream. But perhaps, they say, Homer called the ford "Thryum" and called Epitalium "well-built Aepy"; for Epitalium is fortified by nature. And in fact he speaks of a "steep hill" in other places: "There is a certain city, Thryoessa, a steep hill, far away on the Alpheius, last city of sandy Pylus."[2]

25. Cyparissëeis is in the neighbourhood of the Macistia of earlier times (when Macistia still extended across the Neda), but it is no longer inhabited, as is also the case with Macistum. But there is another, the Messenian Cyparissia; it, too, is now called by the same name as the Macistian and in like manner, namely, Cyparissia, in the singular number and in the feminine gender,[3] whereas only the river is now called Cyparissëeis. And Amphigeneia, also, is in Macistia, in the neighbourhood of the Hypsöeis River, where is the temple of Leto. Pteleum was a settlement of the colony from the Thessalian Pteleum, for, as Homer tells us, there was a Pteleum in Thessaly too: "and Antrum, near the sea, and grassy Pteleum";[4] but now it is a woody, uninhabited place, and is called Pteleasium. As for Helus, some call it a territory in the neighbourhood of the Alpheius, while others go on to call it a city, as they do the Laconian Helus: "and Helus, a city near the sea";[5] but

[1] "Rush."

[2] *Iliad* 11. 711.

[3] That is, not Cyparissiae (plural), or Cyparissëeis (masculine).

[4] *Iliad* 2. 697.

[5] *Iliad* 2. 584.

οἱ δὲ περὶ τὸ Ἀλώριον ἕλος, οὗ τὸ τῆς Ἑλείας[1] Ἀρτέμιδος ἱερόν, τῆς ὑπὸ τοῖς Ἀρκάσιν· ἐκεῖνοι γὰρ ἔσχον τὴν ἱερωσύνην. Δώριον δ' οἱ μὲν ὄρος, οἱ δὲ πεδίον[2] φασίν· οὐδὲν δὲ νῦν δείκνυται· ὅμως δ' ἔνιοι τὴν νῦν Ὄλουριν ἢ Ὄλουραν ἐν τῷ καλουμένῳ Αὐλῶνι τῆς Μεσσηνίας κειμένην Δώριον λέγουσιν. αὐτοῦ δέ που καὶ ἡ Οἰχαλία ἐστὶν ἡ τοῦ Εὐρύτου, ἡ νῦν Ἀνδανία, πολίχνιον Ἀρκαδικόν, ὁμώνυμον τῷ Θετταλικῷ καὶ τῷ Εὐβοϊκῷ· ὅθεν φησὶν ὁ ποιητὴς ἐς τὸ Δώριον ἀφικόμενον Θάμυριν τὸν Θρᾷκα ὑπὸ Μουσῶν ἀφαιρεθῆναι τὴν μουσικήν.

26. Ἐκ δὴ τούτων δῆλον, ὡς ἐφ' ἑκάτερα τοῦ Ἀλφειοῦ ἡ ὑπὸ Νέστορι χώρα ἐστίν, ἣν πᾶσαν ὀνομάζει Πυλίων γῆν· οὐδαμοῦ δὲ ὁ Ἀλφειὸς οὔτε τῆς Μεσσηνίας ἐφάπτεται οὔτε τῆς Κοίλης Ἤλιδος. ἐν ταύτῃ γὰρ τῇ χώρᾳ ἐστὶν ἡ πατρὶς τοῦ Νέστορος, ἥν φαμεν Τριφυλιακὸν Πύλον καὶ Ἀρκαδικὸν καὶ Λεπρεατικόν. καὶ γὰρ δὴ οἱ μὲν ἄλλοι Πύλοι ἐπὶ θαλάττῃ δείκνυνται, οὗτος δὲ πλείους ἢ τριάκοντα σταδίους ὑπὲρ αὐτῆς, ὅπερ καὶ ἐκ τῶν ἐπῶν δῆλον. ἐπί τε γὰρ τοὺς Τηλεμάχου ἑταίρους ἄγγελος πέμπεται πρὸς τὸ πλοῖον, καλῶν ἐπὶ ξενίαν, ὅ τε Τηλέμαχος κατὰ τὴν ἐκ Σπάρτης ἐπάνοδον τὸν Πεισίστρατον οὐκ ἐᾷ πρὸς τὴν πόλιν ἐλαύνειν, ἀλλὰ παρατρέψαντα ἐπὶ τὴν[3] ναῦν σπεύδειν, ὡς οὐ τὴν αὐτὴν οὖσαν ἐπὶ

[1] Ἑλείας, Corais, for Ἠλείας; so the later editors.

[2] After πεδίον, Meineke unwarrantedly inserts οἱ δὲ πολίδιον.

others call it a marsh,[1] the marsh in the neighbourhood of Alorium, where is the temple of the Heleian Artemis, whose worship was under the management of the Arcadians, for this people had the priesthood. As for Dorium, some call it a mountain, while others call it a plain, but nothing is now to be seen; and yet by some the Aluris of to-day, or Alura, situated in what is called the Aulon of Messenia, is called Dorium. And somewhere in this region is also the Oechalia of Eurytus (the Andania of to-day, a small Arcadian town, with the same name as the towns in Thessaly and Euboea), whence, according to the poet, Thamyris the Thracian came to Dorium and was deprived of the art of singing.

26. From these facts, then, it is clear that the country subject to Nestor, all of which the poet calls "land of the Pylians," extends on each side of the Alpheius; but the Alpheius nowhere touches either Messenia or Coelê Elis. For the fatherland of Nestor is in this country which we call Triphylian, or Arcadian, or Leprean, Pylus. And the truth is that, whereas the other places called Pylus are to be seen on the sea, this Pylus is more than thirty stadia above the sea—a fact that is also clear from the verses of Homer, for, in the first place, a messenger is sent to the boat after the companions of Telemachus to invite them to an entertainment, and, secondly, Telemachus on his return from Sparta does not permit Peisistratus to drive to the city, but urges him to turn aside towards the ship, knowing that the road towards the city is not the same

[1] "Helus" means "marsh."

---

[3] τήν, before πόλιν, the editors insert.

τὴν πόλιν καὶ τὸν ὅρμον. ὅ τε ἀπόπλους τοῦ Τηλεμάχου οὕτως ἂν οἰκείως λέγοιτο·

βὰν δὲ παρὰ Κρουνοὺς καὶ Χαλκίδα καλλιρέεθρον.
δύσετό[1] τ' ἠέλιος, σκιόωντό τε πᾶσαι ἀγυιαί·
ἡ δὲ Φεὰς ἐπέβαλλεν, ἀγαλλομένη Διὸς οὔρῳ,
ἠδὲ παρ' Ἦλιδα δῖαν, ὅθι κρατέουσιν Ἐπειοί.

μέχρι μὲν δὴ δεῦρο πρὸς τὴν ἄρκτον ὁ πλοῦς· ἐντεῦθεν δ' ἐπὶ τὸ πρὸς ἕω μέρος ἐπιστρέφει. παρίησι δὲ τὸν εὐθὺν πλοῦν ἡ ναῦς καὶ τὸν ἐξ ἀρχῆς εἰς Ἰθάκην διὰ τὸ τοὺς μνηστῆρας ἐκεῖ τὴν ἐνέδραν θέσθαι

ἐν πορθμῷ Ἰθάκης τε Σάμοιό τε·

ἔνθεν δ' αὖ νήσοισιν ἐπιπροέηκε θοῇσι.

C 351 θοὰς δὲ εἴρηκε τὰς ὀξείας· τῶν Ἐχινάδων δ' εἰσὶν αὗται, πλησιάζουσαι τῇ ἀρχῇ τοῦ Κορινθιακοῦ κόλπου καὶ ταῖς ἐκβολαῖς τοῦ Ἀχελῴου. παραλλάξας δὲ τὴν Ἰθάκην, ὥστε κατὰ νότου[2] γενέσθαι, κάμπτει πάλιν πρὸς τὸν οἰκεῖον δρόμον τὸν μεταξὺ τῆς Ἀκαρνανίας καὶ τῆς Ἰθάκης, καὶ κατὰ θάτερα μέρη τῆς νήσου ποιεῖται τὴν καταγωγήν, οὐ κατὰ τὸν πορθμὸν τὸν Κεφαλληνιακόν, ὃν ἐφρούρουν οἱ μνηστῆρες.

27. Εἰ γοῦν[3] τὸν Ἠλιακὸν[4] Πύλον εἶναί τις τὸν

[1] δύετο (*Aghino*); so Meineke.
[2] νότου, the reading of the MSS., Jones restores; Corais and the later editors emend to νώτου.
[3] εἶτ' οὖν (*Acghino*), for εἰ γοῦν.
[4] Ἠλειακόν (*Bl*).

---

[1] A spring (8. 3. 13).

as that towards the place of anchorage. And thus the return voyage of Telemachus might be spoken of appropriately in these words: "And they went past Cruni[1] and fair-flowing Chalcis.[2] And the sun set and all the ways grew dark; and the ship, rejoicing in the breeze of Zeus, drew near to Phea, and on past goodly Elis, where the Epeians hold sway."[3] Thus far, then, the voyage is towards the north, but thence it bends in the direction of the east. That is, the ship abandons the voyage that was set out upon at first and that led straight to Ithaca, because there the wooers had set the ambush "in the strait between Ithaca and Samos."[4] "And thence again he steered for the islands that are thoai";[5] but by "thoai" the poet means the islands that are "pointed."[6] These belong to the Echinades group and are near the beginning of the Corinthian Gulf and the outlets of the Acheloüs. Again, after passing by Ithaca far enough to put it south of him, Telemachus turns round towards the proper course between Acarnania and Ithaca and makes his landing on the other side of the island—not at the Cephallenian strait which was being guarded by the wooers.[7]

27. At any rate, if one should conceive the notion

[2] "Chalcis" was the name of both the "settlement" (8. 3. 13) and the river.

[3] *Odyssey* 15. 295. [4] *Odyssey* 4. 671.

[5] *Odyssey* 15. 299.

[6] Not "swift," the usual meaning given to θοαί. Thus Strabo connects the adjective with θοόω (see *Odyssey* 9. 327).

[7] In this sentence Strabo seems to identify Homer's Ithaca with what we now call Ithaca, or Thiaka; but in 1. 2. 20 (see footnote 2), 1. 2. 28, and 10. 2. 12 he seems to identify it with Leucas.

Νέστορος ἐπινοήσειεν, οὐκ ἂν οἰκείως λέγοιτο ἡ ἐντεῦθεν ἀναχθεῖσα ναῦς παρὰ Κρουνοὺς ἐνεχθῆναι καὶ Χαλκίδα μέχρι δύσεως, εἶτα Φεαῖς ἐπιβάλλειν[1] νύκτωρ, καὶ τότε τὴν Ἠλείαν παραπλεῖν· οὗτοι γὰρ οἱ τόποι πρὸς νότον τῆς Ἠλείας εἰσί, πρῶται μὲν αἱ Φεαί, εἶθ' ἡ Χαλκίς, εἶθ' οἱ Κρουνοί, εἶθ' ὁ Πύλος ὁ Τριφυλιακὸς καὶ τὸ Σαμικόν. τῷ μὲν οὖν πρὸς νότον πλέοντι ἐκ τοῦ Ἠλιακοῦ Πύλου οὗτος ἂν ὁ πλοῦς εἴη· τῷ δὲ πρὸς ἄρκτον, ὅπου ἐστὶν ἡ Ἰθάκη, ταῦτα μὲν πάντα ὀπίσω λείπεται, αὐτὴ δ' ἡ Ἠλεία παραπλευστέα ἦν, καὶ πρὸ δύσεώς γε· ὁ δέ φησι μετὰ δύσιν. καὶ μὴν εἰ καὶ πάλιν ὑπόθοιτό τις τὸν Μεσσηνιακὸν Πύλον καὶ τὸ Κορυφάσιον ἀρχὴν τοῦ παρὰ Νέστορος πλοῦ, πολὺ ἂν εἴη τὸ διάστημα καὶ πλείονος[2] χρόνου. αὐτὸ γοῦν τὸ ἐπὶ τὸν Τριφυλιακὸν Πύλον καὶ τὸ Σαμιακὸν Ποσείδιον τετρακοσίων ἐστὶ σταδίων· καὶ ὁ παράπλους οὐ[3] παρὰ Κρουνοὺς καὶ Χαλκίδα καὶ Φεάν, ἀδόξων[4] ποταμῶν ὀνόματα, μᾶλλον δὲ ὀχετῶν, ἀλλὰ παρὰ τὴν Νέδαν πρῶτον, εἶτ' Ἀκίδωνα, εἶτα τὸν Ἀλφειὸν καὶ τόπους τούτων τοὺς μεταξύ· ὕστερον δ', εἰ ἄρα, κἀκείνων ἐχρῆν μνησθῆναι· καὶ γὰρ παρ' ἐκείνοις ὑπῆρχεν ὁ πλοῦς.

28. Καὶ μὴν ἥ γε τοῦ Νέστορος διήγησις, ἣν διατίθεται πρὸς Πάτροκλον περὶ τοῦ γενομένου τοῖς Πυλίοις πρὸς Ἠλείους πολέμου, συνηγορεῖ τοῖς ὑφ' ἡμῶν ἐπιχειρουμένοις, ἐὰν σκοπῇ τις τὰ ἔπη. φησὶ γὰρ ἐν αὐτοῖς, ὅτι[5] πορθήσαντος

[1] ἐπιβαλεῖν (B*kl*); so the editors before Kramer.
[2] πλείονος (B*kl*) for πλέονος.
[3] οὐ, before παρά, the editors insert.

that the Eleian Pylus is the Pylus of Nestor, the poet could not appropriately say that the ship, after putting to sea from there, was carried past Cruni and Chalcis before sunset, then drew near to Phea by night, and then sailed past Eleia; for these places are to the south of Eleia: first, Phea, then Chalcis, then Cruni, and then the Triphylian Pylus and Samicum. This, then, would be the voyage for one who is sailing towards the south from Eleian Pylus, whereas one who is sailing towards the north, where Ithaca is, leaves all these parts behind him, and also must sail past Eleia itself—and that before sunset, though the poet says after sunset. And further, if one should go on to make a second supposition, that the Messenian Pylus and Coryphasium are the beginning of the voyage from Nestor's, the distance would be considerable and would require more time. At any rate, merely the distance to Triphylian Pylus and the Samian Poseidium is four hundred stadia; and the first part of the coasting-voyage is not "past Cruni and Chalcis" and Phea (names of obscure rivers, or rather creeks), but past the Neda; then past the Acidon; and then past the Alpheius and the intervening places. And on this supposition those other places should have been mentioned later, for the voyage was indeed made past them too.

28. Furthermore, the detailed account which Nestor recites to Patroclus concerning the war that took place between the Pylians and the Eleians pleads for what I have been trying to prove, if one observes the verses of the poet. For in them the

[4] Before ποταμῶν Corais inserts τόπων καί; perhaps rightly.
[5] ἔτι (*Achino*), for ὅτι.

Ἡρακλέους τὴν Πυλίαν, ὥστε τὴν νεότητα ἐκλειφθῆναι πᾶσαν, δώδεκα δὲ[1] παίδων ὄντων τῷ Νηλεῖ μόνον αὐτῷ περιγενέσθαι τὸν Νέστορα, νέον τελέως, καταφρονήσαντες δ' οἱ Ἐπειοὶ τοῦ Νηλέως διὰ γῆρας καὶ ἐρημίαν ὑπερηφάνως καὶ ὑβριστικῶς ἐχρῶντο τοῖς Πυλίοις. ἀντὶ τούτων οὖν ὁ Νέστωρ συναγαγὼν τοὺς οἰκείους, ὅσους οἷός τε ἦν, ἐπελθεῖν φησὶν ἐπὶ τὴν Ἠλείαν, καὶ περιελάσαι παμπόλλην λείαν,

> πεντήκοντα βοῶν ἀγέλας, τόσα πώεα οἰῶν,
> τόσσα συῶν συβόσια,

τοσαῦτα δὲ καὶ αἰπόλια· ἵππους δὲ ξανθὰς ἑκατὸν καὶ πεντήκοντα, ὑποπώλους τὰς πλείστας.

C 352 καὶ τὰ μὲν ἠλασάμεσθα Πύλον (φησὶ) Νηλήιον εἴσω,
> ἐννύχιοι προτὶ ἄστυ,

ὡς μεθ' ἡμέραν μὲν τῆς λεηλασίας γενομένης καὶ τῆς τροπῆς τῶν ἐκβοηθησάντων, ὅτε κτανεῖν λέγει τὸν Ἰτυμονέα, νύκτωρ δὲ τῆς ἀφόδου γενομένης, ὥστ' ἐννυχίους πρὸς τῷ ἄστει γενέσθαι· περὶ δὲ τὴν διανομὴν καὶ θυσίαν ὄντων, οἱ Ἐπειοὶ τῇ τρίτῃ τῶν ἡμερῶν, κατὰ πλῆθος ἀθροισθέντες πεζοί τε καὶ ἱππεῖς, ἀντεπεξῆλθον καὶ τὸ Θρύον ἐπὶ τῷ Ἀλφειῷ κείμενον περιεστρατοπέδευσαν. αἰσθόμενοι δ' εὐθὺς οἱ Πύλιοι βοηθεῖν ὥρμησαν· νυκτερεύσαντες δὲ περὶ τὸν Μινυήιον ποταμὸν ἐγγύθεν Ἀρήνης, ἐντεῦθεν ἔνδιοι πρὸς τὸν Ἀλφειὸν

[1] δέ, Jones, for δή.

---

[1] *Iliad* 11. 691. [2] *Iliad* 11. 670.

poet says that, since Heracles had ravaged the Pylian country to the extent that all the youth were slain [1] and that of all the twelve sons of Neleus only Nestor, then in his earliest youth,[2] had been left,[3] and since the Epeians had conceived a contempt for Neleus because of his old age and lack of defenders, they began to treat the Pylians in an arrogant and wanton manner. So, in return for this treatment, Nestor gathered together all he could of the people of his home-land, made an attack, he says, upon Eleia, and herded together very much booty, "fifty herds of cattle, and as many flocks of sheep, and as many droves of swine," [4] and also as many herds of goats, and one hundred and fifty sorrel mares, most of them with foals beneath them. "And these," he says, "we drove within Neleian Pylus, to the city, in the night," [5] meaning, first, that it was in the day-time that the driving away of the booty and the rout of those who came to the rescue took place (when he says he killed Itymoneus), and, secondly, that it was in the night-time that the return took place, so that it was night when they arrived at the city. And while the Pylians were busied with the distribution of the booty and with offering sacrifice, the Epeians, on the third day,[6] after assembling in numbers, both footmen and horsemen, came forth in their turn against the Pylians and encamped around Thryum, which is situated on the Alpheius River. And when the Pylians learned this, they forthwith set out to the rescue; they passed the night in the neighbourhood of the Minyeius River near Arenê, and thence arrived at the Alpheius "in open sky,"

[3] *Iliad* 11. 691.
[4] *Iliad* 11. 678.
[5] *Iliad* 11. 682.
[6] *Iliad* 11. 707.

ἀφικνοῦνται· τοῦτο δ' ἐστὶ κατὰ μεσημβρίαν· θύσαντες δὲ τοῖς θεοῖς καὶ νυκτερεύσαντες ἐπὶ τῷ ποταμῷ συμβάλλουσιν εἰς μάχην εὐθὺς ἕωθεν· λαμπρᾶς δὲ τῆς τροπῆς γενομένης, οὐκ ἐπαύσαντο διώκοντές τε καὶ κτείνοντες, πρὶν Βουπρασίου ἐπέβησαν

πέτρης τ' Ὠλενίης καὶ Ἀλεισίου ἔνθα κολώνη
κέκληται, ὅθεν αὖτις ἀπέτραπε λαὸν Ἀθήνη·

καὶ ὑποβάς·

αὐτὰρ Ἀχαιοὶ
ἂψ ἀπὸ Βουπρασίοιο Πύλονδ' ἔχον ὠκέας ἵππους.

29. Ἐκ τούτων δὴ πῶς ἂν ἢ τὸν Ἠλιακὸν Πύλον ὑπολάβοι τις ἢ τὸν Μεσσηνιακὸν λέγεσθαι; τὸν μὲν Ἠλιακόν, ὅτι, τούτου πορθουμένου, συνεπορθεῖτο καὶ ἡ τῶν Ἐπειῶν ὑπὸ τοῦ Ἡρακλέους· αὕτη δ' ἐστὶν ἡ Ἠλεία. πῶς οὖν ἤμελλον οἱ συμπεπορθημένοι καὶ ὁμόφυλοι τοιαύτην ὑπερηφανίαν καὶ ὕβριν κτήσασθαι κατὰ τῶν συναδικηθέντων; πῶς δ' ἂν τὴν οἰκείαν κατέτρεχον καὶ ἐλεηλάτουν; πῶς δ' ἂν ἅμα καὶ Αὐγέας ἦρχε τῶν αὐτῶν καὶ Νηλεύς, ἐχθροὶ ὄντες ἀλλήλων; εἴγε τῷ Νηλεῖ

χρεῖος μέγ' ὀφείλετ' ἐν Ἤλιδι δίῃ,
τέσσαρες ἀθλοφόροι ἵπποι αὐτοῖσιν ὄχεσφιν,
ἐλθόντες μετ' ἄεθλα· περὶ τρίποδος γὰρ ἔμελλον
θεύσεσθαι· τοὺς δ' αὖθι ἄναξ ἀνδρῶν Αὐγείας
κάσχεθε, τὸν δ' ἐλατῆρ' ἀφίει·

εἰ δ' ἐνταῦθα ᾤκει ὁ Νηλεύς, ἐνταῦθα καὶ ὁ

that is, at midday. And after they offered sacrifice to the gods and passed the night near the river, they joined battle at early dawn; and after the rout took place, they did not stop pursuing and slaying the enemy until they set foot on Buprasium "and on the Olenian Rock and where is the place called Hill of Aleisium,[1] whence Athenê turned the people back again";[2] and a little further on the poet says: "But the Achaeans drove back their swift horses from Buprasium to Pylus."[3]

29. From all this, then, how could one suppose that either the Eleian or Messenian Pylus is meant? Not the Eleian Pylus, because, if this Pylus was being ravaged by Heracles, the country of the Epeians was being ravaged by him at the same time; but this is the Eleian country. How, pray, could a people whose country had been ravaged at the same time and were of the same stock, have acquired such arrogance and wantonness towards a people who had been wronged at the same time? And how could they overrun and plunder their own homeland? And how could both Augeas and Neleus be rulers of the same people at the same time if they were personal enemies? If to Neleus "a great debt was owing in goodly Elis. Four horses, prize-winners, with their chariots, had come to win prizes and were to run for a tripod; but these Augeas, lord of men, detained there, though he sent away the driver."[4] And if this is where Neleus

[1] Cp. 8. 3. 10.
[2] *Iliad* 11. 757.
[3] *Iliad* 11. 759.
[4] *Iliad* 11. 698.

Νέστωρ ὑπῆρχε.[1] πῶς οὖν τῶν μεν Ἠλείων καὶ Βουπρασίων

> τέσσαρες ἀρχοὶ ἔσαν, δέκα δ' ἀνδρὶ ἑκάστῳ
> νῆες ἕποντο θοαί, πολέες δ' ἔμβαινον Ἐπειοί·

εἰς τέτταρα δὲ καὶ ἡ χώρα διῄρητο, ὧν οὐδενὸς ἐπῆρχεν ὁ Νέστωρ,

> οἳ δὲ Πύλον τ' ἐνέμοντο καὶ Ἀρήνην ἐρατεινὴν

καὶ τὰ ἑξῆς τὰ μέχρι Μεσσήνης; οἱ δὲ δὴ ἀντεπεξιόντες Ἐπειοὶ τοῖς Πυλίοις πῶς ἐπὶ τὸν Ἀλφειὸν ἐξορμῶσι καὶ τὸ Θρύον; πῶς δ', ἐκεῖ τῆς μάχης γενομένης, τρεφθέντες ἐπὶ Βουπρασίου
C 353 φεύγουσι; πάλιν δ', εἰ τὸν Μεσσηνιακὸν Πύλον ἐπόρθησεν ὁ Ἡρακλῆς, πῶς οἱ τοσοῦτον ἀφεστῶτες ὕβριζον εἰς αὐτούς, καὶ ἐν συμβολαίοις ἦσαν πολλοῖς, καὶ ταῦτ' ἀπεστέρουν χρεοκοποῦντες, ὥστε διὰ ταῦτα συμβῆναι τὸν πόλεμον; πῶς δὲ ἐπὶ τὴν λεηλασίαν ἐξιὼν Νέστωρ, τοσαύτην περιελάσας λείαν συῶν τε καὶ προβάτων, ὧν οὐδὲν ὠκυπορεῖν οὐδὲ μακροπορεῖν δύναται, πλειόνων ἢ χιλίων σταδίων ὁδὸν διήνυσεν εἰς τὴν πρὸς τῷ Κορυφασίῳ Πύλον; οἱ δὲ τρίτῳ ἤματι πάντες ἐπὶ τὴν Θρυόεσσαν καὶ τὸν ποταμὸν τὸν Ἀλφειὸν ἥκουσι, πολιορκήσοντες τὸ φρούριον· πῶς δὲ ταῦτα τὰ χωρία προσήκοντα ἦν τοῖς ἐν τῇ Μεσσηνίᾳ δυναστεύουσιν, ἐχόντων Καυκώνων καὶ Τριφυλίων καὶ Πισατῶν; τὰ δὲ Γέρηνα ἢ τὴν Γερηνίαν (ἀμφοτέρως γὰρ λέγεται) τάχα μὲν ἐπίτηδες ὠνόμασάν τινες· δύναται δὲ καὶ κατὰ

[1] ὑπῆρχε, Corais emends to ἐπῆρχε; so Meineke.

lived, Nestor too must have lived there. How, pray, could the poet say of the Eleians and the Buprasians, "there were four rulers of them, and ten swift ships followed each man, and many Epeians embarked"?[1] And the country, too, was divided into four parts; yet Nestor ruled over no one of these, but over them "that dwelt in Pylus and in lovely Arenê,"[2] and over the places that come after these as far as Messenê. Again, how could the Epeians, who in their turn went forth to attack the Pylians, set out for the Alpheius and Thryum? And how, after the battle took place there, after they were routed, could they flee towards Buprasium? And again, if it was the Messenian Pylus which Heracles had ravaged, how could a people so far distant as the Epeians act wantonly towards them, and how could the Epeians have been involved in numerous contracts with them and have defaulted these by cancelling them, so that the war resulted on that account? And how could Nestor, when he went forth to plunder the country, when he herded together so much booty consisting of both swine and cattle, none of which could travel fast or far, have accomplished a journey of more than one thousand stadia to that Pylus which is near Coryphasium? Yet on the third day they all[3] came to Thryoessa and the River Alpheius to besiege the stronghold! And how could these places belong to those who were in power in Messenia, when they were held by Cauconians and Triphylians and Pisatans? And as for Gerena, or Gerenia (for the word is spelled both ways), perhaps some people named it that to suit a purpose, though it is also possible that

[1] *Iliad* 2. 618.
[2] *Iliad* 2. 591.
[3] The Epeians.

τύχην οὕτως ὠνομάσθαι τὸ χωρίον. τὸ δ' ὅλον, τῆς Μεσσηνίας ὑπὸ Μενελάῳ τεταγμένης, ὑφ' ᾧ καὶ ἡ Λακωνικὴ ἐτέτακτο (ὡς δῆλον ἔσται καὶ ἐκ τῶν ὕστερον), καὶ τοῦ μὲν Παμισοῦ ῥέοντος διὰ ταύτης καὶ τοῦ Νέδωνος,[1] 'Αλφειοῦ δ' οὐδαμῶς,

ὅς τ' εὐρὺ ῥέει Πυλίων διὰ γαίης,

ἧς ἐπῆρχεν ὁ Νέστωρ, τίς ἂν γένοιτο πιθανὸς λόγος, εἰς τὴν ἀλλοτρίαν ἀρχὴν ἐκβιβάζων τὸν ἄνδρα, ἀφαιρούμενος δὲ τὰς συγκαταλεγείσας αὐτῷ πόλεις, πάνθ' ὑπ' ἐκείνῳ ποιῶν;

30. Λοιπὸν δ' ἐστὶν εἰπεῖν περὶ τῆς 'Ολυμπίας καὶ τῆς εἰς τοὺς 'Ηλείους ἁπάντων μεταπτώσεως. ἔστι δ' ἐν τῇ Πισάτιδι τὸ ἱερόν, σταδίους τῆς Ἤλιδος ἐλάττους ἢ τριακοσίους διέχον· πρόκειται δ' ἄλσος ἀγριελαίων, ἐν ᾧ τὸ στάδιον. παραρρεῖ δ' ὁ 'Αλφειός, ἐκ τῆς 'Αρκαδίας ῥέων εἰς τὴν Τριφυλιακὴν θάλατταν μεταξὺ δύσεως καὶ μεσημβρίας. τὴν δ' ἐπιφάνειαν ἔσχεν ἐξ ἀρχῆς μὲν διὰ τὸ μαντεῖον τοῦ 'Ολυμπίου Διός· ἐκείνου δ' ἐκλειφθέντος, οὐδὲν ἧττον συνέμεινεν ἡ δόξα τοῦ ἱεροῦ, καὶ τὴν αὔξησιν, ὅσην ἴσμεν, ἔλαβε διά τε τὴν πανήγυριν καὶ τὸν ἀγῶνα τὸν 'Ολυμπιακόν, στεφανίτην τε καὶ ἱερὸν νομισθέντα τῶν πάντων. ἐκοσμήθη δ' ἐκ τοῦ πλήθους τῶν ἀναθημάτων, ἅπερ ἐκ πάσης ἀνετίθετο τῆς 'Ελλάδος· ὧν ἦν καὶ ὁ χρυσοῦς σφυρήλατος

[1] Νέδωνος, Casaubon, for Μέδωνος; so the later editors.

---

[1] See 8. 3. 7.

[2] In the Homeric Catalogue, Strabo means. See 8. 5. 8, and the *Iliad* 2. 581–586.

the place was by chance so named.[1] And, in general, since Messenia was classified [2] as subject to Menelaüs, as was also the Laconian country (as will be clear from what I shall say later),[3] and since the Pamisus and the Nedon flow through Messenia, whereas the Alpheius nowhere touches it (the Alpheius "that floweth in broad stream through the land of the Pylians," [4] over which Nestor ruled), what plausibility could there be in an account which lands Nestor in a foreign realm and robs him of the cities that are attributed to him in the *Catalogue*,[5] and thus makes everything subject to Menelaüs?

30. It remains for me to tell about Olympia, and how everything fell into the hands of the Eleians. The temple is in Pisatis, less than three hundred stadia distant from Elis. In front of the temple is situated a grove of wild olive-trees, and the stadium is in this grove. Past the temple flows the Alpheius, which, rising in Arcadia, flows between the west and the south into the Triphylian Sea. At the outset the temple got fame on account of the oracle of the Olympian Zeus; and yet, after the oracle failed to respond, the glory of the temple persisted none the less, and it received all that increase of fame of which we know, on account both of the festal assembly and of the Olympian Games, in which the prize was a crown and which were regarded as sacred, the greatest games in the world. The temple was adorned by its numerous offerings, which were dedicated there from all parts of Greece. Among these was the Zeus of beaten gold dedicated by

[3] 8. 5. 8. [4] *Iliad* 5. 545.
[5] *Iliad* 2. 591–602.

Ζεύς, ἀνάθημα Κυψέλου, τοῦ Κορινθίων τυράννου. μέγιστον δὲ τούτων ὑπῆρξε τὸ τοῦ Διὸς ξόανον, ὃ ἐποίει Φειδίας Χαρμίδου Ἀθηναῖος ἐλεφάντινον, τηλικοῦτον τὸ μέγεθος, ὡς, καίπερ μεγίστου ὄντος τοῦ νεώ, δοκεῖν ἀστοχῆσαι τῆς συμμετρίας τὸν τεχνίτην, καθήμενον ποιήσαντα, ἁπτόμενον δὲ σχεδόν τι τῇ κορυφῇ τῆς ὀροφῆς, ὥστ' ἔμφασιν ποιεῖν, ἐὰν ὀρθὸς γένηται δια-
C 354 ναστάς, ἀποστεγάσειν τὸν νεών. ἀνέγραψαν δέ τινες τὰ μέτρα τοῦ ξοάνου, καὶ Καλλίμαχος ἐν ἰάμβῳ τινὶ ἐξεῖπε. πολλὰ δὲ συνέπραξε τῷ Φειδίᾳ Πάναινος ὁ ζωγράφος, ἀδελφιδοῦς ὢν αὐτοῦ καὶ συνεργολάβος, πρὸς[1] τὴν τοῦ ξοάνου διὰ τῶν χρωμάτων κόσμησιν, καὶ μάλιστα τῆς ἐσθῆτος. δείκνυνται δὲ καὶ γραφαὶ πολλαί τε καὶ θαυμασταὶ περὶ τὸ ἱερόν, ἐκείνου ἔργα. ἀπομνημονεύουσι δὲ τοῦ Φειδίου, διότι πρὸς τὸν Πάναινον εἶπε πυνθανόμενον, πρὸς τί παράδειγμα μέλλοι ποιήσειν τὴν εἰκόνα τοῦ Διός, ὅτι πρὸς τὴν Ὁμήρου δι' ἐπῶν ἐκτεθεῖσαν τούτων·

ἦ καὶ κυανέῃσιν ἐπ' ὀφρύσι νεῦσε Κρονίων·
ἀμβρόσιαι δ' ἄρα χαῖται ἐπερρώσαντο ἄνακτος
κρατὸς ἀπ' ἀθανάτοιο, μέγαν δ' ἐλέλιξεν
Ὄλυμπον.

εἰρῆσθαι γὰρ μάλα δοκεῖ καλῶς, ἔκ τε τῶν ἄλλων καὶ τῶν ὀφρύων, ὅτι προκαλεῖται τὴν διάνοιαν ὁ ποιητὴς ἀναζωγραφεῖν μέγαν τινὰ τύπον καὶ μεγάλην δυναμιν ἀξίαν τοῦ Διός, καθάπερ καὶ

Cypselus the tyrant of Corinth. But the greatest of these was the image of Zeus made by Pheidias of Athens, son of Charmides; it was made of ivory, and it was so large that, although the temple was very large, the artist is thought to have missed the proper symmetry, for he showed Zeus seated but almost touching the roof with his head, thus making the impression that if Zeus arose and stood erect he would unroof the temple. Certain writers have recorded the measurements of the image, and Callimachus has set them forth in an iambic poem. Panaenus the painter, who was the nephew and collaborator of Pheidias, helped him greatly in decorating the image, particularly the garments, with colours. And many wonderful paintings, works of Panaenus, are also to be seen round the temple. It is related of Pheidias that, when Panaenus asked him after what model he was going to make the likeness of Zeus, he replied that he was going to make it after the likeness set forth by Homer in these words: "Cronion spake, and nodded assent with his dark brows, and then the ambrosial locks flowed streaming from the lord's immortal head, and he caused great Olympus to quake."[1] A noble description indeed, as appears not only from the "brows" but from the other details in the passage, because the poet provokes our imagination to conceive the picture of a mighty personage and a mighty power worthy of a Zeus, just as he does in the

[1] *Iliad* 1. 528.

---

[1] τε, before τήν, Corais omits.

ἐπὶ τῆς Ἥρας, ἅμα φυλάττων τὸ ἐφ' ἑκατέρῳ πρέπον· ἔφη μὲν γάρ,[1]

σείσατο[2] δ' εἰνὶ θρόνῳ, ἐλέλιξε δὲ μακρὸν Ὄλυμπον.

τὸ δ' ἐπ' ἐκείνης συμβὰν ὅλῃ κινηθείσῃ, τοῦτ' ἐπὶ τοῦ Διὸς ἀπαντῆσαι ταῖς ὀφρύσι μόνον νεύσαντος, συμπαθούσης δέ τι καὶ τῆς κόμης· κομψῶς δ' εἴρηται καὶ τὸ ὁ τὰς τῶν θεῶν εἰκόνας ἢ μόνος ἰδὼν ἢ μόνος δείξας.[3] ἄξιοι δὲ μάλιστα τὴν αἰτίαν ἔχειν τῆς περὶ τὸ Ὀλυμπίασιν ἱερὸν μεγαλοπρεπείας τε καὶ τιμῆς Ἠλεῖοι. κατὰ μὲν γὰρ τὰ Τρωικὰ καὶ ἔτι πρὸ τούτων οὐκ ηὐτύχουν, ὑπό τε τῶν Πυλίων ταπεινωθέντες καὶ ὑφ' Ἡρακλέους ὕστερον, ἡνίκα Αὐγέας ὁ βασιλεύων αὐτῶν κατελύθη. σημεῖον δέ· εἰς γὰρ τὴν Τροίαν ἐκεῖνοι μὲν τετταράκοντα ναῦς ἔστειλαν, Πύλιοι δὲ καὶ Νέστωρ ἐνενήκοντα. ὕστερον δέ, μετὰ τὴν τῶν Ἡρακλειδῶν κάθοδον, συνέβη τἀναντία. Αἰτωλοὶ γὰρ συγκατελθόντες τοῖς Ἡρακλείδαις μετὰ Ὀξύλου καὶ συνοικήσαντες Ἐπειοῖς κατὰ συγγένειαν παλαιὰν ηὔξησαν τὴν Κοίλην Ἦλιν καὶ τῆς τε Πισάτιδος ἀφείλοντο πολλήν, καὶ Ὀλυμπία ὑπ' ἐκείνοις ἐγένετο· καὶ δὴ καὶ ὁ ἀγὼν εὕρεμά ἐστιν ἐκείνων ὁ Ὀλυμπιακός, καὶ τὰς Ὀλυμπιάδας τὰς πρώτας ἐκεῖνοι συνετέλουν. ἐᾶσαι γὰρ δεῖ τὰ παλαιὰ καὶ περὶ τῆς κτίσεως
C 355 τοῦ ἱεροῦ καὶ περὶ τῆς θέσεως τοῦ ἀγῶνος, τῶν

[1] ἔφη μὲν γάρ, Meineke, for ἔφη μὲν γάρ φησι (*Acghi*), ἔφηγάρ (*Blk*), φησὶ γάρ (*no*).

[2] σείσατο, *Epitome* and *man. sec.* A, for εἴσατο; so the editors.

case of Hera, at the same time preserving what is appropriate in each; for of Hera he says, "she shook herself upon the throne, and caused lofty Olympus to quake."[1] What in her case occurred when she moved her whole body, resulted in the case of Zeus when he merely "nodded with his brows," although his hair too was somewhat affected at the same time. This, too, is a graceful saying about the poet, that "he alone has seen, or else he alone has shown, the likenesses of the gods." The Eleians above all others are to be credited both with the magnificence of the temple at Olympia and with the honour in which it was held. In the times of the Trojan war, it is true, or even before those times, they were not a prosperous people, since they had been humbled by the Pylians, and also, later on, by Heracles when Augeas their king was overthrown. The evidence is this: The Eleians sent only forty ships to Troy, whereas the Pylians and Nestor sent ninety. But later on, after the return of the Heracleidae, the contrary was the case, for the Aetolians, having returned with the Heracleidae under the leadership of Oxylus, and on the strength of ancient kinship having taken up their abode with the Epeians, enlarged Coelê Elis, and not only seized much of Pisatis but also got Olympia under their power. What is more, the Olympian Games are an invention of theirs; and it was they who celebrated the first Olympiads, for one should disregard the ancient stories both of the founding of the temple and of the establishment of the games—

[1] *Iliad* 8. 199.

[a] εἰρῆσθαι . . . δείξας, Kramer and later editors suspect: Meineke ejects.

μὲν ἕνα τῶν Ἰδαίων Δακτύλων Ἡρακλέα λεγόντων ἀρχηγέτην τούτων, τῶν δὲ τὸν Ἀλκμήνης καὶ Διός, ὃν καὶ ἀγωνίσασθαι πρῶτον καὶ νικῆσαι· τὰ γὰρ τοιαῦτα πολλαχῶς λέγεται, καὶ οὐ πάνυ πιστεύεται. ἐγγυτέρω δὲ πίστεως, ὅτι μέχρι τῆς ἕκτης καὶ εἰκοστῆς Ὀλυμπιάδος ἀπὸ τῆς πρώτης, ἐν ᾗ Κόροιβος ἐνίκα στάδιον Ἠλεῖος, τὴν προστασίαν εἶχον τοῦ τε ἱεροῦ καὶ τοῦ ἀγῶνος Ἠλεῖοι. κατὰ δὲ τὰ Τρωικὰ ἢ οὐκ ἦν ἀγὼν στεφανίτης ἢ οὐκ ἔνδοξος, οὔθ' οὗτος οὔτ' ἄλλος οὐδεὶς τῶν νῦν ἐνδόξων· οὔτε[1] μέμνηται τούτων Ὅμηρος οὐδενός, ἀλλ' ἑτέρων τινῶν ἐπιταφίων. καίτοι δοκεῖ τισὶ τοῦ Ὀλυμπιακοῦ μεμνῆσθαι, ὅταν φῇ τὸν Αὐγέαν ἀποστερῆσαι τέσσαρας ἀθλοφόρους ἵππους, ἐλθόντας μετ' ἄεθλα· φασὶ δὲ τοὺς Πισάτας μὴ μετασχεῖν τοῦ Τρωικοῦ πολέμου, ἱεροὺς νομισθέντας τοῦ Διός. ἀλλ' οὔθ' ἡ Πισᾶτις ὑπὸ Αὐγέᾳ τόθ' ὑπῆρχεν, ἐν ᾗ ἐστὶ καὶ ἡ Ὀλυμπία, ἀλλ' ἡ Ἠλεία μόνον· οὔτ' ἐν Ἠλείᾳ συνετελέσθη ὁ Ὀλυμπιακὸς ἀγὼν οὐδ' ἅπαξ, ἀλλ' ἀεὶ ἐν Ὀλυμπίᾳ. ὁ δὲ νῦν παρατεθεὶς ἐν Ἤλιδι φαίνεται γενόμενος, ἐν ᾗ καὶ τὸ χρέος ὠφείλετο·

καὶ γὰρ τῷ χρεῖος[2] ὀφείλετ' ἐν Ἤλιδι δίῃ,
τέσσαρες ἀθλοφόροι ἵπποι.

καὶ οὗτος μὲν οὐ στεφανίτης (περὶ τρίποδος γὰρ

[1] οὔτε, Meineke emends to οὐδέ.
[2] Corais and Meineke insert μέγ' after χρεῖος.

some alleging that it was Heracles, one of the Idaean Dactyli,[1] who was the originator of both, and others, that it was Heracles the son of Alcmenê and Zeus, who also was the first to contend in the games and win the victory; for such stories are told in many ways, and no faith at all is to be put in them. It is nearer the truth to say that from the first Olympiad, in which the Eleian Coroebus won the stadium-race, until the twenty-sixth Olympiad, the Eleians had charge both of the temple and of the games. But in the times of the Trojan War, either there were no games in which the prize was a crown or else they were not famous, neither the Olympian nor any other of those that are now famous.[2] In the first place, Homer does not mention any of these, though he mentions another kind—funeral games.[3] And yet some think that he mentions the Olympian Games when he says that Augeas deprived the driver of "four horses, prize-winners, that had come to win prizes."[4] And they say that the Pisatans took no part in the Trojan War because they were regarded as sacred to Zeus. But neither was the Pisatis in which Olympia is situated subject to Augeas at that time, but only the Eleian country, nor were the Olympian Games celebrated even once in Eleia, but always in Olympia. And the games which I have just cited from Homer clearly took place in Elis, where the debt was owing: "for a debt was owing to him in goodly Elis, four horses, prize-winners."[5] And these were not games in which the prize was a crown (for the horses were

[1] See 10. 3. 22.
[2] The Pythian, Nemean, and Isthmian Games.
[3] *Iliad* 23. 255 ff. [4] See 8. 3. 29. [5] *Iliad* 11. 698.

ἔμελλον θεύσεσθαι), ἐκεῖνος δέ. μετὰ δὲ τὴν ἕκτην καὶ εἰκοστὴν Ὀλυμπιάδα οἱ Πισᾶται τὴν οἰκείαν ἀπολαβόντες αὐτοὶ συνετέλουν, τὸν ἀγῶνα ὁρῶντες εὐδοκιμοῦντα· χρόνοις δ' ὕστερον μεταπεσούσης πάλιν τῆς Πισάτιδος εἰς τοὺς Ἠλείους, μετέπεσεν εἰς αὐτοὺς πάλιν καὶ ἡ ἀγωνοθεσία. συνέπραξαν δὲ καὶ οἱ Λακεδαιμόνιοι μετὰ τὴν ἐσχάτην κατάλυσιν τῶν Μεσσηνίων συμμαχήσασιν αὐτοῖς τἀναντία τῶν Νέστορος ἀπογόνων καὶ τῶν Ἀρκάδων, συμπολεμησάντων τοῖς Μεσσηνίοις· καὶ ἐπὶ τοσοῦτόν γε συνέπραξαν, ὥστε τὴν χώραν ἅπασαν τὴν μέχρι Μεσσήνης Ἠλείαν ῥηθῆναι καὶ διαμεῖναι μέχρι νῦν, Πισατῶν δὲ καὶ Τριφυλίων καὶ Καυκώνων μηδ' ὄνομα λειφθῆναι. καὶ αὐτὸν δὲ τὸν Πύλον τὸν ἠμαθόεντα εἰς τὸ Λέπρεον συνῴκισαν, χαριζόμενοι τοῖς Λεπρεάταις κρατήσασι[1] πολέμῳ, καὶ ἄλλας πολλὰς τῶν κατοικιῶν κατέσπασαν, ὅσας θ' ἑώρων αὐτοπραγεῖν ἐθελούσας, καὶ φόρους ἐπράξαντο.

31. Διωνομάσθη δὲ πλεῖστον[2] ἡ Πισᾶτις τὸ μὲν πρῶτον διὰ τοὺς ἡγεμόνας δυνηθέντας πλεῖσ-
C 356 τον, Οἰνόμαόν τε καὶ Πέλοπα, τὸν ἐκεῖνον διαδεξάμενον, καὶ τοὺς παῖδας αὐτοῦ πολλοὺς γενο-

[1] κρατήσασι πολέμῳ, Corais and Groskurd emend to οὐ κοινωνήσασι τοῦ πολέμου, following conj. of Pletho.
[2] πλεῖστον, Meineke omits.

---

[1] So, according to Thucydides (5. 34), the Lacedaemonians settled certain Helots in Lepreum in 421 B.C.
[2] Strabo seems to mean that the Lepreatans "had prevailed in a war" over the other Triphylian cities that had sided with the Pisatae in their war against the Eleians. Several of the editors (see critical note above, on this page), citing

to run for a tripod), as was the case at Olympia. After the twenty-sixth Olympiad, when they had got back their home-land, the Pisatans themselves went to celebrating the games because they saw that these were held in high esteem. But in later times Pisatis again fell into the power of the Eleians, and thus again the direction of the games fell to them. The Lacedaemonians also, after the last defeat of the Messenians, co-operated with the Eleians, who had been their allies in battle, whereas the Arcadians and the descendants of Nestor had done the opposite, having joined with the Messenians in war. And the Lacedaemonians co-operated with them so effectually that the whole country as far as Messenê came to be called Eleia, and the name has persisted to this day, whereas, of the Pisatans, the Triphylians, and the Cauconians, not even a name has survived. Further, the Eleians settled the inhabitants of "sandy Pylus" itself in Lepreum,[1] to gratify the Lepreatans, who had been victorious in a war,[2] and they broke up many other settlements,[3] and also exacted tribute of as many as they saw inclined to act independently.

31. Pisatis first became widely famous on account of its rulers, who were most powerful: they were Oenomaüs, and Pelops who succeeded him, and the

Pausanias 6. 22. 4, emend the text to read, "had taken no part in the war," *i.e.* on the side of the Pisatae against the Eleians; C. Müller, citing Pausanias 4. 15. 8, emends to read, "had taken the field with them (the Eleians) in the war." But neither emendation seems warranted by the citations, or by any other evidence yet found by the present translator.

[3] For example, Macistus. According to Herodotus (4. 148), this occurred "in my own time." But see Pausanias 6. 22. 4, and Frazer's note thereon, Vol. IV., p. 97.

μένους· καὶ ὁ Σαλμωνεὺς δ' ἐνταῦθα βασιλεῦσαι λέγεται· εἰς γοῦν ὀκτὼ πόλεις μεριζομένης τῆς Πισάτιδος, μία τούτων λέγεται καὶ ἡ Σαλμώνη. διὰ ταῦτά τε δὴ καὶ[1] τὸ ἱερὸν τὸ Ὀλυμπίασι διατεθρύληται σφόδρα ἡ χώρα. δεῖ δὲ τῶν παλαιῶν ἱστοριῶν ἀκούειν οὕτως, ὡς μὴ ὁμολογουμένων σφόδρα· οἱ γὰρ νεώτεροι πολλὰ καινὰ[2] νομίζουσιν,[3] ὥστε καὶ τἀναντία λέγειν, οἷον τὸν μὲν Αὐγέαν τῆς Πισάτιδος ἄρξαι, τὸν δ' Οἰνόμαον καὶ τὸν Σαλμωνέα τῆς Ἠλείας· ἔνιοι δ' εἰς ταὐτὸ συνάγουσι τὰ ἔθνη. δεῖ δὲ τοῖς ὁμολογουμένοις ὡς ἐπὶ πολὺ ἀκολουθεῖν· ἐπεὶ οὐδὲ τοὔνομα τὴν Πισᾶτιν ἐτυμολογοῦσιν ὁμοίως· οἱ μὲν γὰρ ἀπὸ Πίσης ὁμωνύμου τῇ κρήνῃ πόλεως, τὴν δὲ κρήνην Πίσαν εἰρῆσθαι, οἷον πίστραν, ὅπερ ἐστὶ ποτίστρα· τὴν δὲ πόλιν ἱδρυμένην ἐφ' ὕψους δεικνύουσι μεταξὺ δυεῖν ὀροῖν, Ὄσσης καὶ Ὀλύμπου, ὁμωνύμων τοῖς ἐν Θετταλίᾳ. τινὲς δὲ πόλιν μὲν οὐδεμίαν γεγονέναι Πίσαν φασίν· εἶναι γὰρ ἂν μίαν τῶν ὀκτώ· κρήνην δὲ μόνην, ἣν νῦν καλεῖσθαι Βίσαν,[4] Κικυσίου πλησίον, πόλεως μεγίστης τῶν ὀκτώ· Στησίχορον δὲ καλεῖν πόλιν τὴν χώραν Πίσαν λεγομένην, ὡς ὁ ποιητὴς τὴν Λέσβον Μάκαρος πόλιν, Εὐριπίδης δ' ἐν Ἴωνι·

Εὔβοι' Ἀθήναις ἐστί τις γείτων πόλις·

[1] Before τὸ ἱερόν Meineke inserts διά.
[2] καινά, conj. of Edward Capps, for καί.
[3] νομίζουσιν, Meineke (following conj. of Casaubon) emends to καινίζουσιν, omitting the preceding καί.

numerous sons of the latter. And Salmoneus,[1] too, is said to have reigned there; at any rate, one of the eight cities into which Pisatis is divided is called Salmonê. So for these reasons, as well as on account of the temple at Olympia, the country has gained wide repute. But one should listen to the old accounts with reserve, knowing that they are not very commonly accepted; for the later writers hold new views about many things and even tell the opposite of the old accounts, as when they say that Augeas ruled over Pisatis, but Oenomaüs and Salmoneus over Eleia; and some writers combine the two tribes into one. But in general one should follow only what is commonly accepted. Indeed, the writers do not even agree as to the derivation of the name Pisatis; for some derive it from a city Pisa, which bears the same name as the spring; the spring, they say, was called "Pisa," the equivalent of "pistra," that is "potistra";[2] and they point out the site of the city on a lofty place between Ossa and Olympus, two mountains that bear the same name as those in Thessaly. But some say that there was no city by the name of Pisa (for if there had been, it would have been one of the eight cities), but only a spring, now called Bisa, near Cicysium, the largest of the eight cities; and Stesichorus, they explain, uses the term "city" for the territory called Pisa, just as Homer calls Lesbos the "city of Macar";[3] so Euripides in his *Ion*,[4] "there is Euboea, a neighbouring city to

[1] *Odyssey* 11. 236.
[2] Both words mean "drinking-trough."
[3] *Iliad* 24. 544. [4] *Frag.* 294 (Nauck).

---

[4] Βίσαν, the editors, for Βῆσαν (MSS.), Βῖσσαν (*Epit.*).

καὶ ἐν Ῥαδαμάνθυι·

οἳ γῆν ἔχουσ' Εὐβοΐδα πρόσχωρον πόλιν·

Σοφοκλῆς δ' ἐν Μυσοῖς·

Ἀσία μὲν ἡ σύμπασα κλῄζεται, ξένε,
πόλις δὲ Μυσῶν Μυσία προσήγορος.

32. Ἡ δὲ Σαλμώνη πλησίον ἐστὶ τῆς ὁμωνύμου κρήνης, ἐξ ἧς ῥεῖ ὁ Ἐνιπεύς· ἐμβάλλει δ' εἰς τὸν Ἀλφειόν, καλεῖται δὲ νῦν Βαρνίχιος·[1] τούτου δ' ἐρασθῆναι τὴν Τυρώ φασιν,

ἣ ποταμοῦ ἠράσσατ' Ἐνιπῆος θείοιο.

ἐνταῦθα γὰρ βασιλεῦσαι τὸν πατέρα αὐτῆς τὸν Σαλμωνέα, καθάπερ καὶ Εὐριπίδης ἐν Αἰόλῳ φησί· τὸν δ' ἐν τῇ Θετταλίᾳ ἔνιοι[2] Ἐνισέα γράφουσιν, ὃς ἀπὸ τῆς Ὄθρυος ῥέων δέχεται τὸν Ἀπιδανὸν κατενεχθέντα ἐκ Φαρσάλου.[3] ἐγγὺς δὲ τῆς Σαλμώνης Ἡράκλεια, καὶ αὕτη μία τῶν ὀκτώ, διέχουσα περὶ τεσσαράκοντα σταδίους τῆς Ὀλυμπίας, κειμένη δὲ παρὰ τὸν Κυθήριον ποταμόν, οὗ τὸ τῶν Ἰωνιάδων νυμφῶν ἱερόν, τῶν πεπιστευμένων θεραπεύειν νόσους τοῖς ὕδασι.

[1] καλεῖται . . . Βαρνίχιος, Kramer and others suspect; Meineke ejects.
[2] ἔνιοι, before Ἐνισέα, Jones inserts.
[3] τὸν δ' ἐν . . . Φαρσάλου, Meineke ejects.

---

[1] *Frag.* 658 (Nauck). [2] *Frag.* 377 (Nauck).

Athens"; and in his *Rhadamanthys*,[1] "who hold the Euboean land, a neighbouring city"; and Sophocles in his *Mysians*,[2] "The whole country, stranger, is called Asia, but the city of the Mysians is called Mysia."

32. Salmonê is situated near the spring of that name from which flows the Enipeus River. The river empties into the Alpheius, and is now called the Barnichius.[3] It is said that Tyro fell in love with Enipeus: "She loved a river, the divine Enipeus."[4] For there, it is said, her father Salmoneus reigned, just as Euripides also says in his *Aeolus*.[5] Some write the name of the river in Thessaly "Eniseus"; it flows from Mount Othrys, and receives the Apidanus, which flows down out of Pharsalus.[6] Near Salmonê is Heracleia, which is also one of the eight cities; it is about forty stadia distant from Olympia and is situated on the Cytherius River, where is the temple of the Ioniades Nymphs, who have been believed to cure diseases

[3] Meineke, following Kramer, ejects the words "and it . . . Barnichius" on the assumption that "Barnichius" is a word of Slavic origin. [4] *Odyssey* 11. 238.

[5] See *Frag.* 14 (Nauck), and the note.

[6] In 9. 5. 6 Strabo spells the name of the river in Thessaly "Enipeus," not "Eniseus"; and says that "it flows from Mt. Othrys past Pharsalus and then turns aside into the Apidanus." Hence some of the editors, including Meineke, regarding the two statements as contradictory, eject the words "The name . . . Pharsalus." But the two passages can easily be reconciled, for (1) "flows out of" (Pharsalus), as often, means "flows out of *the territory* of," which was true of the Apidanus; and (2) in 9. 5. 6 Strabo means that the Enipeus "flows past Old Pharsalus," which was true, and (3) the apparent conflict as to which of the two rivers was tributary is immaterial, since either might be so considered.

παρὰ δὲ τὴν Ὀλυμπίαν ἐστὶ καὶ ἡ Ἅρπινα,[1] καὶ
C 357 αὕτη τῶν ὀκτώ, δι᾽ ἧς ῥεῖ ποταμὸς Παρθενίας, ὡς εἰς Φηραίαν[2] ἀνιόντων·[3] ἡ δὲ Φηραία ἐστὶ τῆς Ἀρκαδίας· ὑπερκεῖται δὲ τῆς Δυμαίας καὶ Βουπρασίου καὶ Ἤλιδος· ἅπερ ἐστὶ πρὸς ἄρκτον τῇ Πισάτιδι.[4] αὐτοῦ δ᾽ ἔστι καὶ τὸ Κικύσιον τῶν ὀκτὼ καὶ τὸ Δυσπόντιον κατὰ τὴν ὁδὸν τὴν ἐξ Ἤλιδος εἰς Ὀλυμπίαν ἐν πεδίῳ κείμενον· ἐξηλείφθη[5] δέ, καὶ ἀπῆραν οἱ πλείους εἰς Ἐπίδαμνον καὶ Ἀπολλωνίαν· καὶ ἡ Φολόη δ᾽ ὑπέρκειται τῆς Ὀλυμπίας ἐγγυτάτω, ὄρος Ἀρκαδικόν, ὥστε τὰς ὑπωρείας τῆς Πισάτιδος εἶναι. καὶ πᾶσα δ᾽ ἡ Πισᾶτις καὶ τῆς Τριφυλίας τὰ πλεῖστα ὁμορεῖ τῇ Ἀρκαδίᾳ· διὰ δὲ τοῦτο καὶ Ἀρκαδικὰ εἶναι δοκεῖ τὰ πλεῖστα τῶν Πυλιακῶν ἐν Καταλόγῳ φραζομένων χωρίων· οὐ μέντοι φασὶν οἱ ἔμπειροι· τὸν γὰρ Ἐρύμανθον[6] εἶναι τὸν ὁρίζοντα τὴν Ἀρκαδίαν, τῶν εἰς Ἀλφειὸν ἐμπιπτόντων ποταμῶν, ἔξω δ᾽ ἐκείνου τὰ χωρία ἱδρῦσθαι ταῦτα.

33. Ἔφορος δέ φησιν Αἰτωλὸν ἐκπεσόντα ὑπὸ

[1] Ἄρπινα, Tzschucke, for Ἔπινα (ABchiklno), Αἴπινα (A *man. sec.*); so the editors.
[2] Φηραίαν, Meineke emends to Ἡραίαν.
[3] ἀνιόντων (Acghno), for ἰόντων, Jones restores.
[4] ἡ δὲ Φηραία . . . Πισάτιδι, Meineke ejects.
[5] ἐξηλείφθη, Meineke emends to ἐξελείφθη.
[6] Ἐρύμανθον, Palmer, for Ἀμάρυνθον; so the editors.

---

[1] According to Pausanias (6. 22. 7), with the waters of a spring that flowed into the Cytherus (note the spelling).
[2] On Arpina and its site, see Frazer's *Pausanias*, 4. 94 ff., and Pauly-Wissowa, *s.v.* "Harpina."
[3] Strabo means "through *the territory* of which."
[4] On the Parthenias (now the Bakireika), see Frazer, *l.c.*

with their waters.[1] Near Olympia is Arpina,[2] also one of the eight cities, through which [3] flows the River Parthenias,[4] on the road that leads up to Pheraea. Pheraea is in Arcadia, and it is situated above Dymaea and Buprasium and Elis, that is, to the north of Pisatis.[5] Here, too, is Cicysium, one of the eight cities; and also Dyspontium, which is situated in a plain and on the road that leads from Elis to Olympia; but it was destroyed, and most of its inhabitants emigrated to Epidamnus and Apollonia. Pholoê, an Arcadian mountain, is also situated above Olympia, and very close to it, so that its foot-hills are in Pisatis. Both the whole of Pisatis and most parts of Triphylia border on Arcadia; and on this account most of the Pylian districts mentioned in the *Catalogue*[6] are thought to be Arcadian; the well-informed, however, deny this, for they say that the Erymanthus, one of the rivers that empty into the Alpheius, forms a boundary of Arcadia and that the districts in question are situated outside that river.[7]

33. Ephorus says that Aetolus, after he had been

[5] The words "and it is situated . . . Pisatis" would seem to apply to the Achaean Pharae, not to some Arcadian city; and in that case, apparently, either Strabo has blundered or the words are an interpolation. Meineke ejects the words "Pheraea is . . . Pisatis" and emends "Pheraea" to "Heraea"; but Polybius (4. 77) mentions a "Pharaea" (note the spelling) in the same region to which Strabo refers, and obviously both writers have in mind the same city. The city is otherwise unknown and therefore the correct spelling is doubtful. See Bölte in Pauly-Wissowa (*s.v.* "Harpina"), who, however, wrongly quotes "Pharaea" as the spelling found in the MSS. of Strabo.

[6] *Iliad* 2. 591.

[7] *i.e.* on the seaward side.

Σαλμωνέως, τοῦ βασιλέως Ἐπειῶν τε καὶ Πισατῶν, ἐκ τῆς Ἠλείας εἰς τὴν Αἰτωλίαν, ὀνομάσαι τε ἀφ' αὑτοῦ τὴν χώραν καὶ συνοικίσαι τὰς αὐτόθι πόλεις· τούτου δ' ἀπόγονον ὑπάρξαντα Ὄξυλον φίλον τοῖς περὶ Τήμενον Ἡρακλείδαις ἡγήσασθαί τε τὴν ὁδὸν κατιοῦσιν εἰς τὴν Πελοπόννησον καὶ μερίσαι τὴν πολεμίαν αὐτοῖς χώραν καὶ τἆλλα ὑποθέσθαι τὰ περὶ τὴν κατάκτησιν τῆς χώρας, ἀντὶ δὲ τούτων λαβεῖν χάριν τὴν εἰς τὴν Ἠλείαν κάθοδον, προγονικὴν οὖσαν, κατελθεῖν δὲ ἀθροίσαντα στρατιὰν ἐκ τῆς Αἰτωλίας ἐπὶ τοὺς κατέχοντας Ἐπειοὺς τὴν Ἦλιν· ἀπαντησάντων δὲ τῶν Ἐπειῶν μεθ' ὅπλων, ἐπειδὴ ἀντίπαλοι ἦσαν αἱ δυνάμεις, εἰς μονομαχίαν προελθεῖν κατὰ ἔθος τι παλαιὸν τῶν Ἑλλήνων Πυραίχμην Αἰτωλὸν Δέγμενόν τ' Ἐπειόν, τὸν μὲν Δέγμενον μετὰ τόξου ψιλόν, ὡς περιεσόμενον ῥᾳδίως ὁπλίτου διὰ τῆς ἑκηβολίας, τὸν δὲ μετὰ σφενδόνης καὶ πήρας λίθων, ἐπειδὴ κατέμαθε τὸν δόλον· τυχεῖν δὲ νεωστὶ ὑπὸ τῶν Αἰτωλῶν εὑρημένον τὸ τῆς σφενδόνης εἶδος· μακροβολωτέρας δ' οὔσης τῆς σφενδόνης, πεσεῖν τὸν Δέγμενον, καὶ κατασχεῖν τοὺς Αἰτωλοὺς τὴν γῆν, ἐκβαλόντας τοὺς Ἐπειούς· παραλαβεῖν δὲ καὶ τὴν ἐπιμέλειαν τοῦ ἱεροῦ τοῦ Ὀλυμπίασιν, ἣν εἶχον οἱ Ἀχαιοί· διὰ δὲ τὴν τοῦ Ὀξύλου φιλίαν πρὸς τοὺς Ἡρακλείδας συνομολογηθῆναι ῥᾳδίως ἐκ πάντων μεθ' ὅρκου
C 358 τὴν Ἠλείαν ἱερὰν εἶναι τοῦ Διός, τὸν δ' ἐπιόντα

driven by Salmoneus, the king of the Epeians and the Pisatans, out of Eleia into Aetolia, named the country after himself and also united the cities there under one metropolis; and Oxylus, a descendant of Aetolus and a friend of Temenus and the Heracleidae who accompanied him, acted as their guide on their way back to the Peloponnesus, and apportioned among them that part of the country which was hostile to them, and in general made suggestions regarding the conquest of the country; and in return for all this he received as a favour the permission to return to Eleia, his ancestral land; and he collected an army and returned from Aetolia to attack the Epeians who were in possession of Elis; but when the Epeians met them with arms,[1] and it was found that the two forces were evenly matched, Pyraechmes the Aetolian and Degmenus the Epeian, in accordance with an ancient custom of the Greeks, advanced to single combat. Degmenus was lightly armed with a bow, thinking that he would easily overcome a heavy-armed opponent at long range, but Pyraechmes armed himself with a sling and a bag of stones, after he had noticed his opponent's ruse (as it happened, the sling had only recently been invented by the Aetolians); and since the sling had longer range, Degmenus fell, and the Aetolians drove out the Epeians and took possession of the land; and they also assumed the superintendence, then in the hands of the Achaeans, of the temple at Olympia; and because of the friendship of Oxylus with the Heracleidae, a sworn agreement was promptly made by all that Eleia should be sacred to Zeus, and that

[1] Cp. 8. 3. 30.

ἐπὶ τὴν χώραν ταύτην μεθ᾽ ὅπλων ἐναγῆ εἶναι, ὡς δ᾽ αὔτως ἐναγῆ καὶ τὸν μὴ ἐπαμύνοντα εἰς δύναμιν· ἐκ δὲ τούτου καὶ τοὺς κτίσαντας τὴν Ἠλείων πόλιν ὕστερον ἀτείχιστον ἐᾶσαι, καὶ τοὺς δι᾽ αὐτῆς τῆς χώρας ἰόντας στρατοπέδῳ, τὰ ὅπλα παραδόντας, ἀπολαμβάνειν μετὰ τὴν ἐκ τῶν ὅρων ἔκβασιν· Ἴφιτόν τε θεῖναι τὸν Ὀλυμπικὸν ἀγῶνα, ἱερῶν ὄντων τῶν Ἠλείων. ἐκ δὴ τῶν τοιούτων αὔξησιν λαβεῖν τοὺς ἀνθρώπους· τῶν γὰρ ἄλλων πολεμούντων ἀεὶ πρὸς ἀλλήλους, μόνοις ὑπάρξαι πολλὴν εἰρήνην, οὐκ αὐτοῖς μόνον, ἀλλὰ καὶ τοῖς ξένοις, ὥστε καὶ εὐανδρῆσαι μάλιστα πάντων παρὰ τοῦτο. Φείδωνα δὲ τὸν Ἀργεῖον, δέκατον μὲν ὄντα ἀπὸ Τημένου, δυνάμει δ᾽ ὑπερβεβλημένον τοὺς κατ᾽ αὐτόν, ἀφ᾽ ἧς τήν τε λῆξιν ὅλην ἀνέλαβε τὴν Τημένου διεσπασμένην εἰς πλείω μέρη, καὶ μέτρα ἐξεῦρε τὰ Φειδώνια καλούμενα καὶ σταθμοὺς καὶ νόμισμα κεχαραγμένον τό τε ἄλλο καὶ τὸ ἀργυροῦν, πρὸς τούτοις ἐπιθέσθαι καὶ ταῖς ὑφ᾽ Ἡρακλέους αἱρεθείσαις πόλεσι καὶ τοὺς ἀγῶνας ἀξιοῦν τιθέναι αὐτὸν οὓς ἐκεῖνος ἔθηκε· τούτων δὲ εἶναι καὶ τὸν Ὀλυμπικόν· καὶ δὴ βιασάμενον ἐπελθόντα θεῖναι αὐτόν, οὔτε τῶν Ἠλείων ἐχόντων ὅπλα, ὥστε κωλύειν, διὰ τὴν εἰρήνην, τῶν τε ἄλλων κρατουμένων τῇ δυναστείᾳ· οὐ μὴν τούς γε Ἠλείους ἀναγράψαι τὴν θέσιν ταύτην, ἀλλὰ καὶ ὅπλα κτήσασθαι διὰ τοῦτο καὶ ἀρξαμένους ἐπικουρεῖν σφίσιν αὐτοῖς· συμπράττειν δὲ

[1] According to Pausanias (5. 8. 2) the games were discontinued after the reign of Oxylus and "renewed" by Iphitus.

[2] So Herodotus 6. 127.

whoever invaded that country with arms should be under a curse, and that whoever did not defend it to the extent of his power should be likewise under a curse; consequently those who later founded the city of the Eleians left it without a wall, and those who go through the country itself with an army give up their arms and then get them back again after they have passed out of its borders; and Iphitus celebrated [1] the Olympian Games, the Eleians now being a sacred people; for these reasons the people flourished, for whereas the other peoples were always at war with one another, the Eleians alone had profound peace, not only they, but their alien residents as well, and so for this reason their country became the most populous of all; but Pheidon the Argive, who was the tenth in descent from Temenus and surpassed all men of his time in ability (whereby he not only recovered the whole inheritance of Temenus, which had been broken up into several parts, but also invented the measures called "Pheidonian," [2] and weights, and coinage struck from silver and other metals)—Pheidon, I say, in addition to all this, also attacked the cities that had been captured previously by Heracles, and claimed for himself the right to celebrate all the games that Heracles had instituted. And he said that the Olympian Games were among these; and so he forcibly invaded Eleia and celebrated the games himself, the Eleians, because of the peace, having no arms wherewith to resist him, and all the others being under his domination; however, the Eleians did not record this celebration in their public register, but because of his action they also procured arms and began to defend themselves; and the

καὶ Λακεδαιμονίους, εἴτε φθονήσαντας τῇ διὰ τὴν εἰρήνην εὐτυχίᾳ, εἴτε καὶ συνεργοὺς ἕξειν νομίσαντας πρὸς τὸ καταλῦσαι τὸν Φείδωνα, ἀφῃρημένον αὐτοὺς τὴν ἡγεμονίαν τῶν Πελοποννησίων, ἣν ἐκεῖνοι προεκέκτηντο· καὶ δὴ καὶ συγκαταλῦσαι τὸν Φείδωνα· τοὺς δὲ συγκατασκευάσαι τοῖς Ἠλείοις τήν τε Πισᾶτιν καὶ τὴν Τριφυλίαν. ὁ δὲ παράπλους ἅπας ὁ τῆς νῦν Ἠλείας μὴ κατακολπίζοντι χιλίων ὁμοῦ καὶ διακοσίων[1] ἐστὶ σταδίων. ταῦτα μὲν περὶ τῆς Ἠλείας.

IV

1. Ἡ δὲ Μεσσηνία συνεχής ἐστι τῇ Ἠλείᾳ, περινεύουσα τὸ πλέον ἐπὶ τὸν νότον καὶ τὸ Λιβυκὸν πέλαγος. αὕτη δ' ἐπὶ μὲν τῶν Τρωικῶν ὑπὸ Μενελάῳ ἐτέτακτο, μέρος οὖσα τῆς Λακωνικῆς, ἐκαλεῖτο δ' ἡ χώρα Μεσσήνη· τὴν δὲ νῦν ὀνομαζομένην πόλιν Μεσσήνην, ἧς ἀκρόπολις ἡ
C 359 Ἰθώμη ὑπῆρξεν, οὔπω συνέβαινεν ἐκτίσθαι· μετὰ δὲ τὴν Μενελάου τελευτήν, ἐξασθενησάντων τῶν διαδεξαμένων τὴν Λακωνικήν, οἱ Νηλεῖδαι τῆς Μεσσηνίας ἐπῆρχον. καὶ δὴ κατὰ τὴν τῶν Ἡρακλειδῶν κάθοδον καὶ τὸν τότε γενηθέντα μερισμὸν

[1] For χιλίων . . . διακοσίων (χιλ . . . σ'), C. Müller conjectures ἑξακόσιοι . . . ἑβδομήκοντα (χ' . . . ο').

---

[1] The correct distance from Cape Araxus, which was in Eleia (8. 3. 4), to the Neda River is about 700 stadia. And C. Müller seems to be right in emending the 1200 to 670,

Lacedaemonians co-operated with them, either because they envied them the prosperity which they had enjoyed on account of the peace, or because they thought that they would have them as allies in destroying the power of Pheidon, for he had deprived them of the hegemony over the Peloponnesus which they had formerly held; and the Eleians did help them to destroy the power of Pheidon, and the Lacedaemonians helped the Eleians to bring both Pisatis and Triphylia under their sway. The length of the voyage along the coast of the Eleia of to-day, not counting the sinuosities of the gulfs, is, all told, twelve hundred stadia.[1] So much for Eleia.

IV

1. Messenia borders on Eleia; and for the most part it inclines round towards the south and the Libyan Sea. Now in the time of the Trojan War this country was classed as subject to Menelaüs, since it was a part of Laconia, and it was called Messenê, but the city now named Messenê, whose acropolis was Ithomê, had not yet been founded;[2] but after the death of Menelaüs, when those who succeeded to the government of Laconia had become enfeebled, the Neleidae began to rule over Messenia. And indeed at the time of the return of the Heracleidae and of the division of the country

since 670 corresponds closely to other measurements given by Strabo (8. 2. 1, 8. 3. 12, 21). See also Curtius, *Peloponnesos*, vol. ii, p. 93.

[2] The city was founded by Epameinondas in 369 B.C. (Diod. Sic. 15. 66).

τῆς χώρας ἣν Μέλανθος βασιλεὺς τῶν Μεσσηνίων καθ' αὑτοὺς τασσομένων, πρότερον δ' ὑπήκοοι ἦσαν τοῦ Μενελάου. σημεῖον δέ· ἐκ γὰρ τοῦ Μεσσηνιακοῦ κόλπου καὶ τοῦ συνεχοῦς Ἀσιναίου λεγομένου ἀπὸ τῆς Μεσσηνιακῆς Ἀσίνης αἱ ἑπτὰ ἦσαν πόλεις, ἃς ὑπέσχετο δώσειν ὁ Ἀγαμέμνων τῷ Ἀχιλλεῖ,

Καρδαμύλην Ἐνόπην τε καὶ Ἱρὴν ποιήεσσαν
Φηράς τε ζαθέας ἠδ' Ἄνθειαν βαθύλειμον
καλήν τ' Αἴπειαν καὶ Πήδασον ἀμπελόεσσαν,

οὐκ ἂν τάς γε μὴ προσηκούσας μήτ' αὐτῷ μήτε τῷ ἀδελφῷ ὑποσχόμενος. ἐκ δὲ τῶν Φηρῶν καὶ συστρατεύσαντας τῷ Μενελάῳ δηλοῖ ὁ ποιητής, τὸν δὲ Οἴτυλον [1] καὶ συγκαταλέγει τῷ Λακωνικῷ καταλόγῳ, ἱδρυμένον ἐν τῷ Μεσσηνιακῷ κόλπῳ. ἔστι δ' ἡ Μεσσήνη μετὰ Τριφυλίαν· κοινὴ δ' ἐστὶν ἀμφοῖν ἄκρα, μεθ' ἣν ἡ Κυπαρισσία καὶ τὸ Κορυφάσιον·[2] ὑπέρκειται δ' ὄρος ἐν ἑπτὰ σταδίοις τὸ Αἰγαλέον τούτου τε καὶ τῆς θαλάττης.

2. Ἡ μὲν οὖν παλαιὰ Πύλος ἡ Μεσσηνιακὴ ὑπὸ τῷ Αἰγαλέῳ πόλις ἦν, κατεσπασμένης δὲ ταύτης ἐπὶ τῷ Κορυφασίῳ τινὲς αὐτῶν ᾤκησαν· προσέκτισαν δ' αὐτὴν Ἀθηναῖοι τὸ δεύτερον ἐπὶ

[1] Οἴτυλον, Kramer inserts (space for six or seven letters in A).

[2] Jones exchanges the positions of τὸ Κορυφάσιον and ἡ Κυπαρισσία. Meineke omits καὶ ἡ Κυπαρισσία.

which then took place, Melanthus was king of the Messenians, who were an autonomous people, although formerly they had been subject to Menelaüs. An indication of this is as follows: The seven cities which Agamemnon promised to give to Achilles were on the Messenian Gulf and the adjacent Asinaean Gulf, so called after the Messenian Asinê;[1] these cities were "Cardamylê and Enopê and grassy Hirê and sacred Pherae and deep-meadowed Antheia and beautiful Aepeia and vine-clad Pedasus";[2] and surely Agamemnon would not have promised cities that belonged neither to himself nor to his brother. And the poet makes it clear that men from Pherae[3] did accompany Menelaüs on the expedition; and in the Laconian Catalogue he includes Oetylus,[4] which is situated on the Messenian Gulf. Messenê[5] comes after Triphylia; and there is a cape which is common to both;[6] and after this cape come Cyparissia and Coryphasium. Above Coryphasium and the sea, at a distance of seven stadia, lies a mountain, Aegaleum.

2. Now the ancient Messenian Pylus was a city at the foot of Aegaleum; but after this city was torn down some of its inhabitants took up their abode on Cape Coryphasium; and when the Athenians

[1] Now the city Koron, or Koroni. See Frazer's note on Pausanias 2. 36. 4, 4. 34. 9.

[2] *Iliad* 9. 150.

[3] *Iliad* 2. 582, where Homer's word is "Pharis."

[4] *Iliad* 2. 585; now called Vitylo.

[5] The *country* Messenia is meant, not the *city* Messenê.

[6] In Strabo's time the Neda River was the boundary between Triphylia and Messenia (8. 3. 22), but in the present passage he must be referring to some cape on the "ancient boundary" (8. 3. 22).

Σικελίαν πλέοντες μετ' Εὐρυμέδοντος καὶ[1] Στρατοκλέους,[2] ἐπιτείχισμα τοῖς Λακεδαιμονίοις. αὐτοῦ δ' ἐστὶ καὶ ἡ Κυπαρισσία ἡ Μεσσηνιακὴ καὶ ἡ Πρωτὴ νῆσος[3] καὶ ἡ προκειμένη[4] πλησίον τοῦ Πύλου Σφαγία νῆσος, ἡ δ' αὐτὴ καὶ Σφακτηρία λεγομένη, περὶ ἣν ἀπέβαλον ζωγρίᾳ Λακεδαιμόνιοι τριακοσίους ἐξ ἑαυτῶν ἄνδρας ὑπ' Ἀθηναίων ἐκπολιορκηθέντας. κατὰ δὲ τὴν παραλίαν ταύτην[5] τῶν Κυπαρισσίων πελάγιαι πρόκεινται δύο νῆσοι προσαγορευόμεναι Στροφάδες, τετρακοσίους ἀπέχουσαι μάλιστά πως τῆς ἠπείρου σταδίους ἐν τῷ Λιβυκῷ καὶ μεσημβρινῷ πελάγει. φησὶ δὲ Θουκυδίδης ναύσταθμον ὑπάρξαι τῶν Μεσσηνίων ταύτην τὴν Πύλον. διέχει δὲ Σπάρτης τετρακοσίους.

3. Ἑξῆς δ' ἐστὶ Μεθώνη· ταύτην δ' εἶναί φασι τὴν ὑπὸ τοῦ ποιητοῦ Πήδασον προσαγορευομένην μίαν τῶν ἑπτά, ὧν ὑπέσχετο τῷ Ἀχιλλεῖ ὁ Ἀγαμέμνων· ἐνταῦθα Ἀγρίππας τὸν τῶν Μαυρουσίων βασιλέα τῆς Ἀντωνίου στάσεως ὄντα Βόγον κατὰ τὸν πόλεμον τὸν Ἀκτιακὸν διέφθειρε, λαβὼν ἐξ ἐπίπλου τὸ χωρίον.

[1] For καί Wesseling conj. ἐπί; and so Meineke reads.

[2] For Στρατοκλέους Palmer conj. Σοφοκλέους; and so Corais and others read. See footnote on opposite page.

[3] Πρωτὴ νῆσος, Jones inserts from conj. of Kramer (space for about ten letters in A).

[4] προκειμένη, Corais, for προσκειμένη; so Meineke.

[5] αἱ, after ταύτην, the editors omit.

---

[1] But according to Diodorus Siculus (12. 60) Stratocles was *archon* at the time of this expedition (425 B.C.); and according to Thucydides (4. 3), it was Eurymedon and Sophocles who made the expedition. Hence some emend "and Strat-

under the leadership of Eurymedon and Stratocles[1] were sailing on the second expedition to Sicily, they reconstructed the city as a fortress against the Lacedaemonians. Here, too, is the Messenian Cyparissia, and the island called Protê, and the island called Sphagia that lies off the coast near Pylus (the same is also called Sphacteria), on which the Lacedaemonians lost by capture three hundred of their own men, who were besieged and forced to surrender by the Athenians.[2] Opposite this sea-coast of the Cyparissians, out in the high sea, lie two islands called Strophades; and they are distant, I should say, about four hundred stadia from the mainland, in the Libyan and Southern Sea. Thucydides[3] says that this Pylus was the naval station of the Messenians. It is four hundred[4] stadia distant from Sparta.

3. Next comes Methonê. This, they say, is what the poet calls Pedasus,[5] one of the seven cities which Agamemnon promised to Achilles. It was here that Agrippa, during the war of Actium,[6] after he had taken the place by an attack from the sea, put to death Bogus, the king of the Maurusians, who belonged to the faction of Antony.

ocles" to "in the archonship of Stratocles," while others emend "Stratocles" to "Sophocles." It seems certain that Strabo wrote the word "Sophocles," for he was following the account of Thucydides, as his later specific quotation from that account shows; and therefore the present translator conjectures that Strabo wrote "Eurymedon and Sophocles, in the archonship of Stratocles," and that the intervening words were inadvertently omitted by the copyist.

[2] For a full account, see Thucydides, 4. 3 ff.

[3] 4. 3.

[4] Thucydides says "*about* four hundred."

[5] *Iliad* 9. 152, 294. So Pausanias (4. 35. 1).

[6] 31 B.C.

4. Τῇ δὲ Μεθώνῃ συνεχής ἐστιν ὁ Ἀκρίτας, ἀρχὴ τοῦ Μεσσηνιακοῦ κόλπου· καλοῦσι δ' αὐτὸν
C 360 καὶ Ἀσιναῖον ἀπὸ Ἀσίνης, πολίχνης πρώτης ἐν τῷ κόλπῳ, ὁμωνύμου τῇ Ἑρμιονικῇ. αὕτη μὲν οὖν ἡ ἀρχὴ πρὸς δύσιν τοῦ κόλπου ἐστί, πρὸς ἕω δὲ αἱ καλούμεναι Θυρίδες, ὅμοροι τῇ νῦν Λακωνικῇ τῇ κατὰ Κυναίθιον[1] καὶ Ταίναρον. μεταξὺ δὲ ἀπὸ τῶν Θυρίδων ἀρξαμένοις Οἴτυλός[2] ἐστι· καλεῖται δ' ὑπό τινων Βαίτυλος·[3] εἶτα Λεῦκτρον, τῶν ἐν τῇ Βοιωτίᾳ Λεύκτρων ἄποικος, εἶτ' ἐπὶ πέτρας ἐρυμνῆς ἵδρυται Καρδαμύλη, εἶτα Φηραί,[4] ὅμορος Θουρίᾳ καὶ Γερήνοις,[5] ἀφ' οὗ τόπου Γερήνιον τὸν Νέστορα κληθῆναί φασι διὰ τὸ ἐνταῦθα σωθῆναι αὐτόν, ὡς προειρήκαμεν. δείκνυται δ' ἐν τῇ Γερηνίᾳ Τρικκαίου ἱερὸν Ἀσκληπιοῦ, ἀφίδρυμα τοῦ ἐν τῇ Θετταλικῇ Τρίκκῃ. οἰκίσαι δὲ λέγεται Πέλοψ τό τε Λεῦκτρον καὶ Χαράδραν καὶ Θαλάμους,[6] τοὺς νῦν Βοιωτοὺς καλουμένους, τὴν ἀδελφὴν Νιόβην ἐκδοὺς Ἀμφίονι καὶ ἐκ τῆς Βοιωτίας ἀγόμενός[7] τινας. παρὰ δὲ Φηρὰς Νέδων ἐκβάλλει, ῥέων

[1] Κυναίθιον, Xylander, for Κυναίδιον (see Dionys. Hal. *Antiq. Rom.* 1. 50); so most editors.

[2] Οἴτυλος, the editors, for ὁ Πύλος.

[3] Βαίτυλος, Meineke emends to Βοίτυλος; Kramer prefers Βείτυλος.

[4] See footnote on Φηρῶν in next §.

[5] Γερηνίοις (*Acghinok*).

[6] Θαλάμους, Corais and Meineke emend to Θαλάμας (as spelled by other Greek writers).

4. Adjacent to Methonê[1] is Acritas,[2] which is the beginning of the Messenian Gulf. But this is also called the Asinaean Gulf, from Asinê, which is the first town on the gulf and bears the same name as the Hermionic town.[3] Asinê, then, is the beginning of the gulf on the west, while the beginning on the east is formed by a place called Thyrides,[4] which borders on that part of the Laconia of to-day which is near Cynaethius and Taenarum.[5] Between Asinê and Thyrides, beginning at Thyrides, one comes to Oetylus (by some called Baetylus[6]); then to Leuctrum, a colony of the Leuctri in Boeotia; then to Cardamylê, which is situated on a rock fortified by nature; then to Pherae,[7] which borders on Thuria and Gerena, the place from which Nestor got his epithet "Gerenian," it is said, because his life was saved there, as I have said before.[8] In Gerenia is to be seen a temple of Triccaean Asclepius, a reproduction of the one in the Thessalian Tricca. It is said that Pelops, after he had given his sister Niobê in marriage to Amphion, founded Leuctrum, Charadra, and Thalami (now called Boeoti), bringing with him certain colonists from Boeotia. Near Pherae is the mouth of the Nedon River; it flows through

[1] Strabo means the territory of Methonê (as often).

[2] Now Cape Gallo.

[3] The Hermionic Asinê was in Argolis, south-east of Nauplia (see Pauly-Wissowa, *s.v.* "Asinê").

[4] See foot-note on "Thyrides," 8. 5. 1.

[5] See Map IX in Curtius' *Peloponnesos* at the end of vol. ii.

[6] Or "Boetylus" (see critical note on opposite page).

[7] Now Kalamata.

[8] 8. 3. 28.

---

[7] ἀγόμενος, Meineke emends to ἀγαγόμενος.

διὰ τῆς Λακωνικῆς, ἕτερος ὢν τῆς Νέδας· ἔχει δ' ἱερὸν ἐπίσημον τῆς Ἀθηνᾶς Νεδουσίας· καὶ ἐν Ποιαέσσῃ[1] δ' ἐστὶν Ἀθηνᾶς Νεδουσίας ἱερόν, ἐπώνυμον τόπου τινὸς Νέδοντος, ἐξ οὗ φασὶν οἰκίσαι Τήλεκλον Ποιάεσσαν[2] καὶ Ἐχειὰς καὶ Τράγιον.[3]

5. Τῶν δὲ προταθεισῶν ἑπτὰ πόλεων τῷ Ἀχιλλεῖ περὶ μὲν Καρδαμύλης καὶ Φηρῶν[4] εἰρήκαμεν καὶ Πηδάσου. Ἐνόπην δὲ οἱ μὲν τὰ Πέλλανά[5] φασιν, οἱ δὲ τόπον τινὰ περὶ Καρδαμύλην, οἱ δὲ τὴν Γερηνίαν· τὴν δὲ Ἱρὴν κατὰ τὸ ὄρος δεικνύουσι τὸ κατὰ τὴν Μεγαλόπολιν τῆς Ἀρκαδίας ὡς ἐπὶ τὴν Ἀνδανίαν ἰόντων, ἣν ἔφαμεν Οἰχαλίαν ὑπὸ τοῦ ποιητοῦ κεκλῆσθαι, οἱ δὲ τὴν νῦν Μεσόλαν οὕτω καλεῖσθαί φασι, καθήκουσαν εἰς τὸν μεταξὺ κόλπον τοῦ Ταϋγέτου καὶ τῆς Μεσσηνίας. ἡ δ' Αἴπεια νῦν Θουρία καλεῖται, ἣν ἔφαμεν ὅμορον Φαραῖς·[6] ἵδρυται δ' ἐπὶ λόφου ὑψηλοῦ, ἀφ' οὗ καὶ τοὔνομα. ἀπὸ δὲ τῆς Θουρίας καὶ ὁ Θουριάτης κόλπος, ἐν ᾧ

[1] Ποιηέσσῃ (Bkno). [2] Ποιήεσσαν (bno).

[3] The words καὶ . . . Τράγιον are suspected by Meineke.

[4] Φηρῶν, not Φαρῶν (the Doric spelling), is the spelling used in Homer; and so read the MSS. of Strabo in this case, but in subsequent uses the MSS., though variant, favour the Doric spelling.

[5] Πέλλανα, Kramer, for Πέλαννα A, Πέλανα Bl; so the later editors. [6] See footnote 4 on Φηρῶν (above).

---

[1] "It" can hardly refer to Pherae, for Pausanias appears not to have seen, or known of, a temple of Athena there. Hence Strabo seems to mean that there was such a temple somewhere else, on the banks of the river Nedon (now River of Kalamata). The site of the temple is as yet unknown (see Curtius, *Peloponnesos* ii., p. 159).

Laconia and is a different river from the Neda. It[1] has a notable temple of Athena Nedusia. In Poeäessa,[2] also, there is a temple of Athena Nedusia, named after some place called Nedon, from which Teleclus is said to have colonised Poeäessa and Echeiae[3] and Tragium.

5. Of the seven cities[4] which Agamemnon tendered to Achilles, I have already spoken about Cardamylê and Pherae and Pedasus. As for Enopê,[5] some say that it is Pellana,[6] others that it is some place near Cardamylê, and others that it is Gerenia. As for Hirê, it is pointed out near the mountain that is near Megalopolis in Arcadia, on the road that leads to Andania, the city which, as I have said,[7] the poet called Oechalia; but others say that what is now Mesola,[8] which extends to the gulf between Taÿgetus and Messenia, is called Hirê. And Aepeia is now called Thuria, which, as I have said,[9] borders on Pharae; it is situated on a lofty hill, and hence the name.[10] From Thuria is derived the name of the Thuriates Gulf, on which there was but one

[2] "Poeäessa" is otherwise unknown. Some of the MSS. spell the name "Poeëessa," in which case Strabo might be referring to the "Poeëessa" in the island of Ceos: "Near Poeëessa, between the temple" (of Sminthian Apollo) "and the ruins of Poeëessa, is the temple of Nedusian Athena, which was founded by Nestor when he was on his return from Troy" (10. 5. 6). But it seems more likely that the three places here mentioned as colonised by Teleclus were all somewhere in Messenia.

[3] Otherwise unknown.

[4] For their position see Map V in Curtius' *Peloponnesos*, end of vol. ii.

[5] *Iliad* 9. 150.

[6] Also spelled Pellenê; now Zugra.

[7] 8. 3. 25.

[8] See 8. 4. 7.

[9] 8. 4. 4.

[10] "Aepeia" being the feminine form of the Greek adjective "aepys," meaning "sheer," "lofty."

πόλις μία[1] ἦν, Ῥίον τοὔνομα, ἀπεναντίον Γαινάρου. Ἄνθειαν δὲ οἱ μὲν αὐτὴν τὴν Θουρίαν φασίν, Αἴπειαν δὲ τὴν Μεθώνην· οἱ δὲ τὴν μεταξὺ Ἀσίνην,[2] τῶν Μεσσηνίων πόλεων οἰκειότατα βαθύλειμον λεχθεῖσαν, ἧς πρὸς θαλάττῃ πόλις Κορώνη· καὶ ταύτην δέ τινες Πήδασον λεχθῆναί φασιν ὑπὸ τοῦ ποιητοῦ.

πᾶσαι δ' ἐγγὺς ἁλός,

C 361 Καρδαμύλη μὲν ἐπ' αὐτῇ, Φαραὶ[3] δ' ἀπὸ πέντε σταδίων, ὕφορμον ἔχουσα θερινόν, αἱ δ' ἄλλαι ἀνωμάλοις κέχρηνται τοῖς ἀπὸ θαλάττης διαστήμασι.

6. Πλησίον δὲ τῆς Κορώνης κατὰ μέσον πως τὸν κόλπον ὁ Παμισὸς ποταμὸς ἐκβάλλει, ταύτην μὲν ἐν δεξιᾷ ἔχων καὶ τὰς ἑξῆς, ὧν εἰσὶν ἔσχαται πρὸς δύσιν Πύλος καὶ Κυπαρισσία· μέση δὲ τούτων Ἔρανα (ἣν οὐκ εὖ τινὲς Ἀρήνην εἶναι[4] νενομίκασι πρότερον), Θουρίαν δὲ καὶ Φαρὰς ἐν ἀριστερᾷ. μέγιστος δ' ἐστὶ ποταμῶν τῶν ἐντὸς Ἰσθμοῦ, καίπερ οὐ πλείους ἢ ἑκατὸν σταδίους ἐκ τῶν πηγῶν ῥυεὶς δαψιλὴς τῷ ὕδατι διὰ τοῦ Μεσσηνιακοῦ πεδίου καὶ τῆς Μακαρίας καλουμένης· ἀφέστηκέ τε τῆς νῦν Μεσσηνίων πόλεως ὁ ποταμὸς σταδίους[5] πεντήκοντα. ἔστι δὲ καὶ

[1] πόλις μία, Corais and Meineke emend to πόλισμα, perhaps rightly.

[2] Ἀσίνην, Corais, for Ἀσίνης; so the later editors.

[3] See footnote 4, p. 114, on Φηρῶν.

[4] εἶναι (*bno*), supplying lacuna of about five letters in A; καλεῖσθαι (*h man. sec.* and *i*).

city, Rhium[1] by name, opposite Taenarum. And as for Antheia, some say that it is Thuria itself, and that Aepeia is Methonê; but others say that of all the Messenian cities the epithet "deep-meadowed"[2] was most appropriately applied to the intervening Asinê, in whose territory on the sea is a city called Coronê;[3] moreover, according to some writers, it was Coronê that the poet called Pedasus. "And all are close to the salt sea,"[4] Cardamylê on it, Pharae only five stadia distant (with an anchoring place in summer), while the others are at varying distances from the sea.

6. It is near Coronê, at about the centre of the gulf, that the river Pamisus empties. The river has on its right Coronê and the cities that come in order after it (of these latter the farthermost towards the west are Pylus and Cyparissia, and between these is Erana, which some have wrongly thought to be the Arenê of earlier time),[5] and it has Thuria and Pharae on its left. It is the largest of the rivers inside the Isthmus, although it is no more than a hundred stadia in length from its sources, from which it flows with an abundance of water through the Messenian plain, that is, through Macaria, as it is called. The river stands at a distance of fifty[6] stadia from the present city of the Messenians. There is also another

[1] See 8. 4. 7.

[2] "Deep-meadowed Antheia," *Iliad* 9. 151.

[3] Now Petalidi. Pausanias (4. 36. 3) identifies Coronê with Homer's Aepeia.

[4] *Iliad* 9. 153.

[5] See 8. 3. 23.

[6] The MSS. read "two hundred and fifty."

---

[5] διακοσίους (σ′) καί, before πεντήκοντα, Meineke and others omit.

ἄλλος Παμισὸς χαραδρώδης, μικρός, περὶ Λεῦκτρον ῥέων τὸ Λακωνικόν, περὶ οὗ κρίσιν ἔσχον Μεσσήνιοι πρὸς Λακεδαιμονίους ἐπὶ Φιλίππου· τὸν δὲ Παμισόν, ὃν Ἄμαθόν τινες ὠνόμασαν,[1] προειρήκαμεν.

7. Ἔφορος δὲ τὸν Κρεσφόντην, ἐπειδὴ εἷλε Μεσσήνην, διελεῖν φησὶν εἰς πέντε πόλεις αὐτήν, ὥστε Στενύκλαρον μὲν ἐν τῷ μέσῳ τῆς χώρας ταύτης κειμένην ἀποδεῖξαι βασίλειον αὑτῷ, εἰς δὲ τὰς ἄλλας[2] βασιλέας[3] πέμψαι Πύλον καὶ Ῥίον καὶ Μεσόλαν καὶ[4] Ὑαμεῖτιν ποιήσαντα ἰσονόμους πάντας τοῖς Δωριεῦσι τοὺς Μεσσηνίους· ἀγανακτούντων δὲ τῶν Δωριέων, μεταγνόντα μόνον τὸν Στενύκλαρον νομίσαι πόλιν, εἰς τοῦτον δὲ καὶ τοὺς Δωριέας συναγαγεῖν πάντας.

8. Ἡ δὲ Μεσσηνίων πόλις ἔοικε Κορίνθῳ· ὑπέρκειται γὰρ τῆς πόλεως ἑκατέρας ὄρος ὑψηλὸν καὶ ἀπότομον, τείχει κοινῷ περιειλημμένον, ὥστ' ἀκροπόλει χρῆσθαι, τὸ μὲν καλούμενον Ἰθώμη, τὸ δὲ Ἀκροκόρινθος· ὥστ' οἰκείως δοκεῖ Δημήτριος ὁ Φάριος[5] πρὸς Φίλιππον εἰπεῖν τὸν Δημητρίου, παρακελευόμενος[6] τούτων ἔχεσθαι τῶν πόλεων ἀμφοῖν ἐπιθυμοῦντα τῆς Πελοποννήσου· τῶν κεράτων γὰρ ἀμφοῖν,[7] ἔφη, καθέξεις

[1] ὡς, before προειρήκαμεν, Kramer and Meineke omit.

[2] εἰς δὲ τὰς ἄλλας, Kramer, supplying lacuna of about twelve letters in A (see same phrase in 8. 5. 4); so Meineke.

[3] βασιλέας, Meineke, from conj. of Kramer, for βασιλείας (cp. βασιλέας in 8. 5. 4).

[4] καὶ Μεσόλαν καί, Meineke, supplying lacuna of about twelve letters in A. For a long reading in B and also two marginal notes, see C. Müller, *Ind. Var. Lect.*, p. 994.

[5] Φάριος, correction in *n*, for Φαληρεύς; so the editors.

Pamisus, a small torrential stream, which flows near the Laconian Leuctrum; and it was over Leuctrum that the Messenians got into a dispute with the Lacedaemonians in the time of Philip. Of the Pamisus which some called the Amathus I have already spoken.[1]

7. According to Ephorus: When Cresphontes took Messenia, he divided it into five cities; and so, since Stenyclarus was situated in the centre of this country, he designated it as a royal residence for himself, while as for the others—Pylus, Rhium, Mesola, and Hyameitis—he sent kings to them, after conferring on all the Messenians equal rights with the Dorians; but since this irritated the Dorians, he changed his mind, gave sanction to Stenyclarus alone as a city, and also gathered into it all the Dorians.

8. The city of the Messenians is similar to Corinth; for above either city lies a high and precipitous mountain that is enclosed by a common[2] wall, so that it is used as an acropolis, the one mountain being called Ithomê and the other Acrocorinthus. And so Demetrius of Pharos seems to have spoken aptly to Philip[3] the son of Demetrius when he advised him to lay hold of both these cities if he coveted the Peloponnesus,[4] "for if you hold both horns," he

[1] 8. 3. 1.
[2] *i.e.* common to the lower city and the acropolis.
[3] Philip V—reigned 220 to 178 B.C.
[4] This same Demetrius was commissioned by Philip V to take Ithomê but was killed in the attack (see Polybius 3. 19. 7. 11).

---

[6] παρακελευόμενος, Xylander, for παρακελευόμενον.
[7] After ἀμφοῖν, Xylander and others insert κρατήσας. Meineke emends ἀμφοῖν to κρατῶν (cp. Polybius 7. 11).

τὴν βοῦν, κέρατα μὲν λέγων τὴν Ἰθώμην καὶ τὸν Ἀκροκόρινθον, βοῦν δὲ τὴν Πελοπόννησον. καὶ δὴ διὰ τὴν εὐκαιρίαν ταύτην ἀμφήριστοι γεγόνασιν αἱ πόλεις αὗται. Κόρινθον μὲν οὖν κατέσκαψαν Ῥωμαῖοι[1] καὶ ἀνέστησαν πάλιν· Μεσσήνην δὲ ἀνεῖλον μὲν Λακεδαιμόνιοι, πάλιν δ' ἀνέλαβον Θηβαῖοι καὶ μετὰ ταῦτα Φίλιππος Ἀμύντου· αἱ δ' ἀκροπόλεις ἀοίκητοι διέμειναν.

C 362 9. Τὸ δ' ἐν Λίμναις τῆς Ἀρτέμιδος ἱερόν, ἐφ' ᾧ Μεσσήνιοι περὶ τὰς παρθένους ὑβρίσαι δοκοῦσι τὰς ἀφιγμένας ἐπὶ τὴν θυσίαν, ἐν μεθορίοις ἐστὶ τῆς τε Λακωνικῆς καὶ τῆς Μεσσηνίας, ὅπου κοινὴν συνετέλουν πανήγυριν καὶ θυσίαν ἀμφότεροι· μετὰ δὲ τὴν ὕβριν οὐ διδόντων δίκας τῶν Μεσσηνίων, συστῆναί φασι τὸν πόλεμον. ἀπὸ δὲ τῶν Λιμνῶν τούτων καὶ τὸ ἐν τῇ Σπάρτῃ Λιμναῖον εἴρηται τῆς Ἀρτέμιδος ἱερόν.

10. Πλεονάκις δ' ἐπολέμησαν διὰ τὰς ἀποστάσεις τῶν Μεσσηνίων. τὴν μὲν οὖν πρώτην κατάκτησιν αὐτῶν φησὶ Τυρταῖος ἐν τοῖς ποιήμασι κατὰ τοὺς τῶν πατέρων πατέρας γενέσθαι· τὴν δὲ δευτέραν, καθ' ἣν ἑλόμενοι συμμάχους Ἀργείους τε καὶ Ἠλείους[2] καὶ Πισάτας καὶ Ἀρκάδας[3] ἀπέστησαν, Ἀρκάδων μὲν Ἀριστοκράτην τὸν Ὀρχομενοῦ βασιλέα παρεχομένων

[1] Ῥωμαῖοι, Xylander inserts; so the later editors.

[2] Ἠλείους, Meineke emends to Ἀρκάδας, following conj. of Kramer; but according to Pausanias (4. 15. 4) both "the Eleians and Arcadians were with the Messenians."

[3] καὶ Ἀρκάδας, after Πισάτας, Jones inserts (see Pausanias 4. 15. 4 and 4. 17. 2).

said, "you will hold down the cow," meaning by "horns" Ithomê and Acrocorinthus, and by "cow" the Peloponnesus. And indeed it is because of their advantageous position that these cities have been objects of contention. Corinth was destroyed and rebuilt again by the Romans;[1] and Messenê was destroyed by the Lacedaemonians but restored by the Thebans and afterward by Philip the son of Amyntas. The citadels, however, remained uninhabited.

9. The temple of Artemis at Limnae, at which the Messenians are reputed to have outraged the maidens who had come to the sacrifice,[2] is on the boundaries between Laconia and Messenia, where both peoples held assemblies and offered sacrifice in common; and they say that it was after the outraging of the maidens, when the Messenians refused to give satisfaction for the act, that the war took place. And it is after this Limnae, also, that the Limnaeum, the temple of Artemis in Sparta, has been named.

10. Often, however, they went to war on account of the revolts of the Messenians. Tyrtaeus says in his poems that the first conquest of Messenia took place in the time of his fathers' fathers; the second, at the time when the Messenians chose the Argives, Eleians, Pisatans, and Arcadians as allies and revolted—the Arcadians furnishing Aristocrates[3] the king of Orchomenus as general and the Pisatae

[1] Leucius Mummius (cp 8. 6. 23) the consul captured Corinth and destroyed it by fire in 146 B.C.; but it was rebuilt again by Augustus.

[2] Cp. 6. 1. 6.

[3] On the perfidy of Aristocrates, see Pausanias 4. 17. 4.

στρατηγον, Πισατῶν δὲ Πανταλέοντα τὸν Ὀμφαλίωνος· ἡνίκα φησὶν αὐτὸς στρατηγῆσαι τὸν πόλεμον τοῖς Λακεδαιμονίοις,[1] καὶ γὰρ εἶναί φησιν ἐκεῖθεν ἐν τῇ ἐλεγείᾳ, ἣν ἐπιγράφουσιν Εὐνομίαν·

> αὐτὸς γὰρ Κρονίων, καλλιστεφάνου πόσις Ἥρης,
> Ζεὺς Ἡρακλείδαις τήνδε δέδωκε πόλιν·
> οἷσιν ἅμα προλιπόντες Ἐρινεὸν ἠνεμόεντα,
> εὐρεῖαν Πέλοπος νῆσον ἀφικόμεθα.

ὥστ᾽ ἢ ταῦτα ἠκύρωται τὰ ἐλεγεῖα, ἢ Φιλοχόρῳ ἀπιστητέον τῷ φήσαντι Ἀθηναῖόν τε καὶ Ἀφιδναῖον, καὶ Καλλισθένει καὶ ἄλλοις πλείοσι τοῖς εἰποῦσιν ἐξ Ἀθηνῶν ἀφικέσθαι, δεηθέντων Λακεδαιμονίων κατὰ χρησμόν, ὃς ἐπέταττε παρ᾽ Ἀθηναίων λαβεῖν ἡγεμόνα. ἐπὶ μὲν οὖν τοῦ Τυρταίου ὁ δεύτερος ὑπῆρξε πόλεμος· τρίτον δὲ καὶ τέταρτον συστῆναί φασιν, ἐν ᾧ κατελύθησαν οἱ Μεσσήνιοι. ὁ δὲ πᾶς παράπλους ὁ Μεσσηνιακὸς στάδιοι ὀκτακόσιοί που κατακολπίζοντι.

11. Ἀλλὰ γὰρ εἰς πλείω λόγον τοῦ μετρίου προΐμεν, ἀκολουθοῦντες τῷ πλήθει τῶν ἱστορουμένων περὶ χώρας ἐκλελειμμένης τῆς πλείστης· ὅπου γε καὶ ἡ Λακωνικὴ λιπανδρεῖ, κρινομένη πρὸς τὴν παλαιὰν εὐανδρίαν. ἔξω γὰρ τῆς

[1] After Λακεδαιμονίοις, Corais inserts ἐλθὼν ἐξ Ἐρινεοῦ; so Meineke and others. But see Bergk, *Poet. Lyr. Graec.* 2. p. 8, footnote on *Frag.* 2.

furnishing Pantaleon the son of Omphalion; at this time, he says, he himself was the Lacedaemonian general in the war,[1] for in his elegy entitled *Eunomia* he says that he came from there: "For the son of Cronus, spouse of Hera of the beautiful crown, Zeus himself, hath given this city to the Heracleidae, in company with whom I left windy Erineus, and came to the broad island of Pelops."[2] Therefore either these verses of the elegy must be denied authority or we must discredit Philochorus,[3] who says that Tyrtaeus was an Athenian from the deme of Aphidnae, and also Callisthenes and several other writers, who say that he came from Athens when the Lacedaemonians asked for him in accordance with an oracle which bade them to get a commander from the Athenians. So the second war was in the time of Tyrtaeus; but also a third and fourth war took place, they say, in which the Messenians were defeated.[4] The voyage round the coast of Messenia, following the sinuosities of the gulfs, is, all told, about eight hundred stadia in length.

11. However, I am overstepping the bounds of moderation in recounting the numerous stories told about a country the most of which is now deserted; in fact, Laconia too is now short of population as compared with its large population in olden times,

[1] *Frag.* 8 (Bergk).

[2] *Frag.* 2 (Bergk). Erineus was an important city in the district of Doris (see 9. 4. 10 and 10. 4. 6). Thucydides (1. 107) calls Doris the "mother-city of the Lacedaemonians."

[3] Among other works Philochorus was the author of an *Atthis*, a history of Attica in seventeen books from the earliest times to 261 B.C. Only fragments are extant.

[4] Diodorus Siculus (15. 66) mentions only three Messenian wars.

Σπάρτης αἱ λοιπαὶ πολίχναι τινές εἰσι περὶ τριάκοντα τὸν ἀριθμόν· τὸ δὲ παλαιὸν ἑκατόμπολίν φασιν αὐτὴν καλεῖσθαι, καὶ τὰ ἑκατόμβαια διὰ τοῦτο θύεσθαι παρ' αὐτοῖς κατ' ἔτος.

V

1. Ἔστι δ' οὖν μετὰ τὸν Μεσσηνιακὸν κόλπον
ὁ Λακωνικὸς μεταξὺ Ταινάρου καὶ Μαλεῶν,
ἐκκλίνων μικρὸν ἀπὸ μεσημβρίας πρὸς ἕω· διέχουσι δὲ σταδίους ἑκατὸν τριάκοντα αἱ Θυρίδες
τοῦ Ταινάρου ἐν τῷ Μεσσηνιακῷ οὖσαι κόλπῳ,
ῥοώδης κρημνός. τούτων δ' ὑπέρκειται τὸ Ταΰγε-
C 363 τον· ἔστι δ' ὄρος μικρὸν ὑπὲρ τῆς θαλάττης
ὑψηλόν τε καὶ ὄρθιον, συνάπτον κατὰ τὰ προσ-
άρκτια μέρη ταῖς Ἀρκαδικαῖς ὑπωρείαις, ὥστε
καταλείπεσθαι μεταξὺ αὐλῶνα, καθ' ὃν ἡ Μεσσηνία συνεχής ἐστι τῇ Λακωνικῇ. ὑποπέπτωκε
δὲ τῷ Ταϋγέτῳ ἡ Σπάρτη ἐν μεσογαίᾳ καὶ
Ἀμύκλαι, οὗ τὸ τοῦ Ἀπόλλωνος ἱερόν, καὶ ἡ
Φᾶρις. ἔστι μὲν οὖν ἐν κοιλοτέρῳ χωρίῳ τὸ
τῆς πόλεως ἔδαφος, καίπερ ἀπολάμβανον ὄρη
μεταξύ· ἀλλ' οὐδέν γε μέρος αὐτοῦ λιμνάζει, τὸ
δὲ παλαιὸν ἐλίμναζε τὸ προάστειον, καὶ ἐκάλουν
αὐτὸ Λίμνας, καὶ τὸ τοῦ Διονύσου ἱερὸν ἐν
Λίμναις ἐφ' ὑγροῦ βεβηκὸς ἐτύγχανε· νῦν δ' ἐπὶ

---

[1] Now Cape Matapan. [2] Now Cape Malea.

[3] Literally, "Windows"; now called Kavo Grosso, a peninsular promontory about six miles in circumference, with precipitous cliffs that are riddled with caverns (Frazer, *Pausanias* 3, p. 399, and Curtius, *Peloponnesos* 2, p. 281).

[4] For a description of this temple, see Pausanias 3 18 9 ff.

for outside of Sparta the remaining towns are only about thirty in number, whereas in olden times it was called, they say, "country of the hundred cities"; and it was on this account, they say, that they held annual festivals in which one hundred cattle were sacrificed.

V

1. Be this as it may, after the Messenian Gulf comes the Laconian Gulf, lying between Taenarum[1] and Maleae,[2] which bends slightly from the south towards the east; and Thyrides,[3] a precipitous rock exposed to the currents of the sea, is in the Messenian Gulf at a distance of one hundred and thirty stadia from Taenarum. Above Thyrides lies Taÿgetus; it is a lofty and steep mountain, only a short distance from the sea, and it connects in its northerly parts with the foothills of the Arcadian mountains in such a way that a glen is left in between, where Messenia borders on Laconia. Below Taÿgetus, in the interior, lies Sparta, and also Amyclae, where is the temple of Apollo,[4] and Pharis. Now the site of Sparta is in a rather hollow district,[5] although it includes mountains within its limits; yet no part of it is marshy, though in olden times the suburban part was marshy, and this part they called Limnae;[6] and the temple of Dionysus in Limnae[7] stood on wet ground, though now its

[5] Hence Homer's "Hollow Lacedaemon" (*Odyssey* 4. 1).

[6] "Marshes."

[7] Bölte (*Mitteilungen d. Kaiserl. deutsch. Arch. Inst. Athen. Abt.* vol. 34, p. 388) shows that Tozer (*Selections*, note on p. 212) was right in identifying this "temple of Dionysus in Limnae" with the Lenaeum at Athens, where the Lenaean festival was called the "festival in Limnae."

ξηροῦ τὴν ἵδρυσιν ἔχει. ἐν δὲ τῷ κόλπῳ τῆς παραλίας τὸ μὲν Ταίναρον ἀκτή ἐστιν ἐκκειμένη, τὸ ἱερὸν ἔχουσα τοῦ Ποσειδῶνος ἐν ἄλσει ἱδρυμένον· πλησίον δ' ἐστὶν ἄντρον, δι' οὗ τὸν Κέρβερον ἀναχθῆναι μυθεύουσιν ὑφ' Ἡρακλέους ἐξ ᾅδου. ἐντεῦθεν δ' εἰς μὲν Φυκοῦντα ἄκραν τῆς Κυρηναίας πρὸς νότον δίαρμά ἐστι σταδίων τρισχιλίων· εἰς δὲ Πάχυνον πρὸς δύσιν, τὸ τῆς Σικελίας ἀκρωτήριον, τετρακισχιλίων ἑξακοσίων, τινὲς δὲ τετρακισχιλίων φασίν· εἰς δὲ Μαλέας πρὸς ἕω ἑξακοσίων ἑβδομήκοντα κατακολπίζοντι· εἰς δὲ Ὄνου γνάθον, ταπεινὴν χερρόνησον ἐνδοτέρω τῶν Μαλεῶν, πεντακοσίων εἴκοσι (πρόκειται δὲ κατὰ τούτου Κύθηρα ἐν τεσσαράκοντα σταδίοις, νῆσος εὐλίμενος, πόλιν ἔχουσα ὁμώνυμον, ἣν ἔσχεν Εὐρυκλῆς ἐν μέρει κτήσεως ἰδίας, ὁ καθ' ἡμᾶς τῶν Λακεδαιμονίων ἡγεμών· περίκειται δὲ νησίδια πλείω, τὰ μὲν ἐγγύς, τὰ δὲ καὶ μικρὸν ἀπωτέρω)· εἰς δὲ Κώρυκον, ἄκραν τῆς Κρήτης, ἐγγυτάτω πλοῦς ἐστὶ σταδίων ἑπτακοσίων.[1]

2. Μετὰ δὲ Ταίναρον πλέοντι ἐπὶ τὴν Ὄνου γνάθον καὶ Μαλέας Ψαμαθοῦς[2] ἐστὶ πόλις· εἶτ' Ἀσίνη καὶ Γύθειον, τὸ τῆς Σπάρτης ἐπίνειον, ἐν διακοσίοις καὶ τετταράκοντα σταδίοις ἱδρυμένον· ἔχει δ', ὥς φασι, τὸ ναύσταθμον ὀρυκτόν· εἶθ' ὁ

[1] ἑπτακοσίων, Jones, for πεντήκοντα with σ′ (διακοσίων) inserted above the π by first hand in A. Groskurd, Meineke, and others read ἑπτακοσίων πεντήκοντα (σ′ν′). Seven hundred is the correct measurement on Kiépert's Wall Map, and is the same figure given by Strabo in 10. 4. 5, where Meineke properly inserts ἐπὶ Ταίναρον (not Μαλέαν, Groskurd and others) in the lacuna after Κιμάρου.

[2] Ψαμαθοῦς, the editors in general, for Ἀμαθοῦς.

foundations rest on dry ground. In the bend of the seaboard one comes, first, to a headland that projects into the sea, Taenarum, with its temple of Poseidon situated in a grove; and secondly, near by, to the cavern[1] through which, according to the myth-writers, Cerberus was brought up from Hades by Heracles. From here the passage towards the south across the sea to Phycus,[2] a cape in Cyrenaea, is three thousand stadia; and the passage towards the west to Pachynus,[3] the promontory of Sicily, is four thousand six hundred, though some say four thousand; and towards the east to Maleae, following the sinuosities of the gulfs, six hundred and seventy; and to Onugnathus,[4] a low-lying peninsula somewhat this side of Maleae, five hundred and twenty; off Onugnathus and opposite it, at a distance of forty stadia, lies Cythera, an island with a good harbour, containing a city of the same name, which Eurycles, the ruler of the Lacedaemonians in our times, seized as his private property; and round it lie several small islands, some near it and others slightly farther away; and to Corycus,[5] a cape in Crete, the shortest voyage is seven hundred stadia.[6]

2. After Taenarum, on the voyage to Onugnathus and Maleae, one comes to the city Psamathus; then to Asinê, and to Gythium, the seaport of Sparta, situated at a distance of two hundred and forty stadia from Sparta. The roadstead of the seaport was dug by the hand of man, so it is said. Then

[1] The "Taenarias fauces" of Vergil (*Georgics* 4. 467).

[2] Now Ras-al-Razat.

[3] Now Cape Passero.

[4] Literally, "Ass's-jaw"; now Cape Elaphonisi.

[5] To be identified with Cimarus (10. 4. 5); see Murray's *Small Classical Atlas* (1904, Map 11). The cape is now called Garabusa.

[6] From Cape Taenarum.

Εὐρώτας ἐκδίδωσι μεταξὺ Γυθείου καὶ Ἀκραίων·[1] τέως μὲν οὖν ὁ πλοῦς ἐστὶ παρ' αἰγιαλὸν ὅσον διακοσίων καὶ τεσσαράκοντα σταδίων· εἶθ' ἑλῶδες ὑπέρκειται χωρίον καὶ κώμη Ἕλος· πρότερον δ' ἦν πόλις, καθάπερ καὶ Ὅμηρός φησιν·

> οἵ τ' ἄρ' Ἀμύκλας εἶχον Ἕλος τ', ἔφαλον πτολίεθρον·

κτίσμα δ' Ἑλίου φασὶ τοῦ Περσέως. ἔστι δὲ καὶ πεδίον καλούμενον Λεύκη· εἶτα πόλις ἐπὶ χερρονήσου ἱδρυμένη Κυπαρισσία, λιμένα ἔχουσα·
C 364 εἶτα ἡ Ὄνου γνάθος, λιμένα ἔχουσα· εἶτα Βοία πόλις· εἶτα Μαλέαι· στάδιοι δ' εἰς αὐτὰς ἀπὸ τῆς Ὄνου γνάθου πεντήκοντα καὶ ἑκατόν· ἔστι δὲ καὶ Ἀσωπὸς πόλις ἐν τῇ Λακωνικῇ.

3. Τῶν δ' ὑφ' Ὁμήρου καταλεγομένων τὴν μὲν Μέσσην οὐδαμοῦ δείκνυσθαί φασι· Μεσσόαν δ' οὐ τῆς χώρας εἶναι μέρος, ἀλλὰ[2] τῆς Σπάρτης, καθάπερ καὶ τὸ Λιμναῖον κατὰ τὸν . . . κα.[3] ἔνιοι δὲ κατὰ ἀποκοπὴν δέχονται τὴν Μεσσήνην·

[1] Ἀκραίων, the editors in general, for Ἀκταίων (ABE*cghino*).

[2] ἀλλά, Corais inserts; so the later editors.

[3] The words Μεσσόαν . . . κα are omitted by BE*lt* and Pletho. But *t* has the words as far as τόν; and so *g*, which leaves a lacuna after τόν. In A about four letters between τόν and κα have perished with the margin; hence the same lacuna in *cghno*. Meineke, Müller-Dübner and others write Θόρνακα, but Kramer writes Θρᾷκα. Capps, citing 8. 5. 1, suspects that Strabo wrote καθὼς προείρηκα.

---

[1] "Helus" means "Marsh." [2] *Iliad* 2. 584.

[3] This plain extends north-east from Cyparissia.

[4] Between Acraeae and Cyparissia. Now in ruins near Xyli.

one comes to the Eurotas, which empties between Gythium and Acraea. Now for a time the voyage is along the shore, for about two hundred and forty stadia; then comes a marshy district situated above the gulf, and also a village called Helus.[1] In earlier times Helus was a city, just as Homer says: "And they that held Amyclae, and Helus, a city by the sea."[2] It is said to have been founded by Helius, a son of Perseus. And one comes also to a plain called Leucê;[3] then to a city Cyparissia, which is situated on a peninsula and has a harbour; then to Onugnathus, which has a harbour; then to the city Boea; and then to Maleae. And the distance from Onugnathus to Maleae is one hundred and fifty stadia; and there is also a city Asopus[4] in Laconia.

3. They say that one of the places mentioned in Homer's *Catalogue*,[5] Messê, is nowhere to be seen; and that Messoa was not a part of the country but of Sparta, as was the case with Limnaeum[6] . . .[7] But some take "Messê" as an apocopated form of

[5] *Iliad* 2. 484–877.

[6] "Limnae or Limnaeum, Cynosura, Messoa, and Pitanê, seem to have been the quarters or wards of Sparta, the inhabitants of each quarter forming a local tribe" (Frazer's *Pausanias*, note on 16. 9, Vol. III, p. 341).

[7] Three or four Greek letters are missing. Meineke's conjecture yields "near Thornax," which, according to Stephanus Byzantinus, was a mountain in Laconia. But as yet such a mountain has not been identified, and on still other grounds the conjecture is doubtful (cp. the note on 10. 8, "Thornax," in Frazer's *Pausanias*, Vol. III, p. 322). Kramer's tempting conjecture yields "according to the Thracian," *i.e.* Dionysius the Thracian, who wrote *Commentaries* on Homer; but it is doubtful whether Strabo would have referred to him merely by his surname (cp. the full name in 14. 2. 13).

εἴρηται γὰρ ὅτι καὶ αὐτὴ μέρος ἦν τῆς Λακωνικῆς· παραδείγμασι δὲ χρῶνται τοῦ μὲν ποιητοῦ τῷ κρῖ καὶ δῶ καὶ μάψ, καὶ ἔτι·

ἥρως[1] δ' Αὐτομέδων τε καὶ Ἄλκιμος,

ἀντὶ τοῦ Ἀλκιμέδων· Ἡσιόδου δέ, ὅτι τὸ βριθὺ καὶ βριαρὸν βρῖ λέγει· Σοφοκλῆς δὲ καὶ Ἴων τὸ ῥᾴδιον, ῥᾷ· Ἐπίχαρμος δὲ τὸ λίαν λῖ· Συρακὼ δὲ τὰς Συρακούσας· παρ' Ἐμπεδοκλεῖ δέ,

μία γίνεται ἀμφοτέρων ὄψ,

ἡ ὄψις· καὶ παρ' Ἀντιμάχῳ·

Δήμητρός τοι Ἐλευσινίης ἱερὴ ὄψ·

καὶ τὸ ἄλφιτον ἄλφι· Εὐφορίων δὲ καὶ τὸν ἧλον λέγει ἧλ· παρὰ Φιλήτᾳ δέ·

δμωίδες εἰς ταλάρους λευκὸν ἄγουσιν ἔρι·[2]
εἰς ἄνεμον δὲ τὰ πηδά,

τὰ πηδάλια Ἄρατός φησι· Δωδὼ δὲ τὴν Δωδώνην Σιμμίας. τῶν δ' ἄλλων τῶν ὑπὸ τοῦ ποιητοῦ κατωνομασμένων τὰ μὲν ἀνῄρηται, τῶν δ' ἴχνη λείπεται, τὰ δὲ μετωνόμασται, καθάπερ αἱ Αὐγειαὶ Αἰγαιαί· αἱ[3] γὰρ ἐν τῇ Λοκρίδι οὐδ' ὅλως περίεισι. τὴν δὲ Λᾶν οἱ Διόσκουροί ποτε ἐκ πολιορκίας

[1] But the MSS. of Homer (*Il.* 19. 392) read ἵππους, not ἥρως.

[2] After ἔρι Corais inserts τὸ ἔριον; so Meineke and Müller-Dübner.

[3] αἱ, before γάρ, Corais inserts in a lacuna of about four letters; A, *man. sec.*, inserts οὐ, and so read *cghino*.

---

[1] 8. 3. 29, 8. 4. 1.

"Messenê," for, as I have said,[1] Messenê too was a part of Laconia. As examples of apocopê from the poet himself, writers cite "krī," "dō," and "maps,"[2] and also the passage "the heroes Automedon and Alcimus,"[3] for "Alcimedon"; then from Hesiod, who uses "brī" for "brithu" or "briaron"; and Sophocles and Ion, "rha" for "rhadion"; and Epicharmus, "li" for "lian," and "Syracō" for "Syracuse"; and in Empedocles,[4] "ops" for "opsis": "the 'ops'[5] of both becomes one"; and in Antimachus, "the sacred 'ops' of the Eleusinian Demeter," and "alphi" for "alphiton"; and Euphorion even uses "hēl" for "hēlos"; and in Philetas, "eri" for "erion": "maidservants bring white 'eri'[6] and put it in baskets"; and Aratus says "pēda" for "pēdalia": "the 'pēda'[7] towards the wind"; and Simmias, "Dodo" for "Dodona." As for the rest of the places listed by the poet, some have been destroyed; of others traces are still left; and of others the names have been changed, for example, Augeiae[8] to Aegaeae;[9] for the Augeiae in Locris[10] no longer exists at all. As for Las, the story goes, the Dioscuri[11] once captured it

[2] For "krithē," "dōma," "mapsidion," Aristotle (*Poet.* 1458 A) quotes the same examples.

[3] *Iliad* 19. 392 (but see critical note on opposite page).

[4] *Frag.* 88 (Diels). Aristotle (*l.c.*) quotes the same example.

[5] "Vision."

[6] For "erion," "wool."

[7] "Rudders."

[8] *Iliad* 2. 583.

[9] That is, the Laconian (not the Locrian) Augeiae, which was thirty stadia from Gytheium (Pausanias 3. 21. 6), near the Limni of to-day.

[10] *Iliad* 2. 532.

[11] Castor and Pollux.

ἑλεῖν ἱστοροῦνται, ἀφ' οὗ δὴ Λαπέρσαι προσηγορεύθησαν, καὶ Σοφοκλῆς λέγει που·

νὴ τὼ Λαπέρσα, νὴ τὸν Εὐρώταν τρίτον,
νὴ τοὺς ἐν Ἄργει καὶ κατὰ Σπάρτην θεούς.[1]

4. Φησὶ δ' Ἔφορος τοὺς κατασχόντας τὴν Λακωνικὴν Ἡρακλείδας, Εὐρυσθένη τε καὶ Προκλῆ, διελεῖν εἰς ἓξ μέρη καὶ πολίσαι τὴν χώραν· μίαν μὲν οὖν τῶν μερίδων, τὰς Ἀμύκλας, ἐξαίρετον δοῦναι τῷ προδόντι αὐτοῖς τὴν Λακωνικὴν καὶ πείσαντι τὸν κατέχοντα αὐτὴν ἀπελθεῖν ὑπόσπονδον μετὰ τῶν Ἀχαιῶν εἰς τὴν Ἰωνίαν· τὴν δὲ Σπάρτην βασίλειον ἀποφῆναι σφίσιν αὐτοῖς· εἰς δὲ τὰς ἄλλας πέμψαι βασιλέας, ἐπιτρέψαντας δέχεσθαι συνοίκους τοὺς βουλομένους τῶν ξένων, διὰ τὴν λειπανδρίαν· χρῆσθαι δὲ Λαῒ μὲν ναυστάθμῳ διὰ τὸ εὐλίμενον,[2] Αἴγυι[3] δὲ πρὸς τοὺς πολεμίους ὁρμητηρίῳ, καὶ[4] γὰρ ὁμορεῖν τοῖς κύκλῳ, Φάριδι[5] δὲ ὡς γαζοφυλακίῳ[6] ἀπὸ τῶν ἐκτὸς[7] ἀσφάλειαν ἐχούσῃ τ . . .[8] ὑπα-

[1] The words καὶ Σοφοκλῆς . . . θεούς, Meineke ejects.

[2] A has να . . . λίμενον with space for about fifteen letters; for λίμενον *bno* have εὐλίμενον. The above restoration of the text follows Curtius (*Peloponnesos* ii, p. 309); so Meineke, and Müller-Dübner.

[3] Αἴγυι, the editors, following O. Müller, for Αἴτυι.

[4] A has πολε . . . γὰρ κτλ. with space for about fifteen letters; whence πολεμι in *gi*, πολεμίους in *h*. The above is the restoration of Curtius (*l.c.*); so Müller-Dübner; and Meineke (except πολέμους instead of πολεμίους). But see C. Müller, *Ind. Var. Lect.* p. 995.

[5] Φάριδι, Meineke, for Φερέα *bnc*, Φεραίᾳ (other MSS.). Others read Φαραίᾳ.

[6] A has δ . . . ἀπὸ κτλ., with space for about fifteen letters. Jones restores as above (cp. γαζοφυλακίῳ in 7. 6. 1);

by siege, and it was from this fact that they got the appellation "Lapersae."[1] And Sophocles says, "by the two Lapersae, I swear, by Eurotas third, by the gods in Argos and about Sparta."[2]

4. According to Ephorus: Eurysthenes and Procles, the Heracleidae, took possession of Laconia,[3] divided the country into six parts, and founded cities;[4] now one of the divisions, Amyclae, they selected and gave to the man[5] who had betrayed Laconia to them and who had persuaded the ruler who was in possession of it to accept their terms and emigrate with the Achaeans to Ionia; Sparta they designated as a royal residence for themselves; to the other divisions they sent kings, and because of the sparsity of the population gave them permission to receive as fellow-inhabitants any strangers who wished the privilege; and they used Las as a naval station because of its good harbour, and Aegys[6] as a base of operations against their enemies (for its territory[7] bordered on those of the surrounding peoples) and Pharis as a treasury, because it afforded security against outsiders; . . . but

[1] "Sackers of Las." [2] *Frag.* 871 (Nauck).

[3] Tradition places the Dorian Conquest as far back as 1104 B.C.

[4] Cp. 8. 5. 5. [5] Philonomus (§ 5 following).

[6] Aegys was situated in north-western Laconia near the source of the Eurotas.

[7] Its territory included Carystus (10. 1. 6.)

Curtius, δὲ ταμιείῳ πλείστην; Müller-Dübner, δὲ ὡς ταμιείῳ; Meineke, δὲ ἀρχείῳ πλείστην.

[7] ἐκτός, Meineke emends to ἐντός.

[8] After the letter τ A leaves a space for about fifteen letters; and restoration seems hopeless, though Curtius proposes Βοιαῖς δ' ἐμπορίῳ.

κούοντας δ' ἅπαντας τοὺς περιοίκους Σπαρτιατῶν
C 365 ὅμως ἰσονόμους εἶναι, μετέχοντας καὶ πολιτείας καὶ ἀρχείων· καλεῖσθαι δὲ Εἵλωτας·[1] Ἆγιν δὲ τὸν Εὐρυσθένους ἀφελέσθαι τὴν ἰσοτιμίαν καὶ συντελεῖν προστάξαι τῇ Σπάρτῃ· τοὺς μὲν οὖν ἄλλους ὑπακοῦσαι, τοὺς δ' Ἑλείους, τοὺς ἔχοντας τὸ Ἕλος, ποιησαμένους ἀπόστασιν κατὰ κράτος ἁλῶναι πολέμῳ καὶ κριθῆναι δούλους ἐπὶ τακτοῖς τισίν, ὥστε τὸν ἔχοντα μήτ' ἐλευθεροῦν ἐξεῖναι μήτε πωλεῖν ἔξω τῶν ὅρων τούτους· τοῦτον δὲ λεχθῆναι τὸν πρὸς τοὺς Εἵλωτας πόλεμον. σχεδὸν δέ τι καὶ τὴν εἱλωτείαν τὴν ὕστερον συμμείνασαν μέχρι τῆς Ῥωμαίων ἐπικρατείας οἱ περὶ Ἆγιν εἰσὶν οἱ καταδείξαντες· τρόπον γάρ τινα δημοσίους δούλους εἶχον οἱ Λακεδαιμόνιοι τούτους, κατοικίας τινὰς αὐτοῖς ἀποδείξαντες καὶ λειτουργίας ἰδίας.

5. Περὶ δὲ τῆς Λακώνων πολιτείας καὶ τῶν γενομένων παρ' αὐτοῖς μεταβολῶν τὰ μὲν πολλὰ παρείη τις ἂν διὰ τὸ γνώριμον, τινῶν δ' ἄξιον ἴσως μνησθῆναι. Ἀχαιοὺς γὰρ τοὺς Φθιώτας φασὶ συγκατελθόντας Πέλοπι εἰς τὴν Πελοπόννησον οἰκῆσαι τὴν Λακωνικήν, τοσοῦτον δ' ἀρετῇ διενεγκεῖν, ὥστε τὴν Πελοπόννησον, ἐκ πολλῶν ἤδη χρόνων Ἄργος λεγομένην, τότε Ἀχαϊκὸν Ἄργος λεχθῆναι, καὶ οὐ μόνον γε τὴν

[1] The words καλεῖσθαι δὲ Εἵλωτας, Meineke transposes to a position after Ἕλος.

though the neighbouring peoples, one and all, were subject to the Spartiatae, still they had equal rights, sharing both in the rights of citizenship and in the offices of state, and they were called Helots;[1] but Agis, the son of Eurysthenes, deprived them of the equality of rights and ordered them to pay tribute to Sparta; now all obeyed except the Heleians, the occupants of Helus, who, because they revolted, were forcibly reduced in a war, and were condemned to slavery, with the express reservation that no slaveholder should be permitted either to set them free or to sell them outside the borders of the country; and this war was called the War against the Helots. One may almost say that it was Agis and his associates who introduced the whole system of Helot-slavery that persisted until the supremacy of the Romans; for the Lacedaemonians held the Helots as state-slaves in a way, having assigned to them certain settlements to live in and special services to perform.

5. Concerning the government of the Laconians and the changes that took place among them, one might omit most things as well known, but there are certain things which it is perhaps worth while to mention. For instance, they say that the Achaeans of Phthiotis came down with Pelops into the Peloponnesus, took up their abode in Laconia, and so far excelled in bravery that the Peloponnesus, which now for many ages had been called Argos, came to be called Achaean Argos, and the name was applied not only in a general way to the

[1] Meineke and Forbiger transfer "and they were called Helots" to a position after "Helus" (following).

Πελοπόννησον, ἀλλὰ καὶ ἰδίως τὴν Λακωνικὴν οὕτω προσαγορευθῆναι· τὸ γοῦν τοῦ ποιητοῦ,

> ποῦ Μενέλαος ἔην;
> ἦ οὐκ Ἄργεος ἦεν Ἀχαιικοῦ;

δέχονταί τινες οὕτως· ἦ οὐκ ἦν ἐν τῇ Λακωνικῇ; κατὰ δὲ τὴν τῶν Ἡρακλειδῶν κάθοδον, Φιλονόμου προδόντος τὴν χώραν τοῖς Δωριεῦσι, μετανέστησαν ἐκ τῆς Λακωνικῆς εἰς τὴν τῶν Ἰώνων, τὴν καὶ νῦν Ἀχαΐαν καλουμένην· ἐροῦμεν δὲ περὶ αὐτῶν ἐν τοῖς Ἀχαϊκοῖς. οἱ δὲ κατασχόντες τὴν Λακωνικὴν[1] κατ' ἀρχὰς μὲν ἐσωφρόνουν, ἐπεὶ δ' οὖν Λυκούργῳ τὴν πολιτείαν ἐπέτρεψαν, τοσοῦτον ὑπερεβάλοντο τοὺς ἄλλους, ὥστε μόνοι τῶν Ἑλλήνων καὶ γῆς καὶ θαλάττης ἐπῆρξαν, διετέλεσάν τε ἄρχοντες τῶν Ἑλλήνων, ἕως ἀφείλοντο αὐτοὺς τὴν ἡγεμονίαν Θηβαῖοι, καὶ μετ' ἐκείνους εὐθὺς Μακεδόνες. οὐ μὴν τελέως γε οὐδὲ τούτοις εἶξαν, ἀλλὰ φυλάττοντες τὴν αὐτονομίαν ἔριν εἶχον περὶ πρωτείων ἀεὶ πρός τε τοὺς ἄλλους Ἕλληνας καὶ πρὸς τοὺς τῶν Μακεδόνων βασιλέας· καταλυθέντων δὲ τούτων ὑπὸ Ῥωμαίων, μικρὰ μέν τινα προσέκρουσαν τοῖς πεμπομένοις ὑπὸ Ῥωμαίων στρατηγοῖς, τυραννούμενοι τότε καὶ πολιτευόμενοι μοχθηρῶς· ἀναλαβόντες δὲ σφᾶς ἐτιμήθησαν διαφερόντως καὶ ἔμειναν ἐλεύθεροι, πλὴν τῶν φιλικῶν λειτουργιῶν ἄλλο συντελοῦντες
C 366 οὐδέν. νεωστὶ δ' Εὐρυκλῆς αὐτοὺς ἐτάραξε, δόξας ἀποχρήσασθαι τῇ Καίσαρος φιλίᾳ πέρα τοῦ

[1] καί, before κατ', Meineke omits.

---

[1] *Odyssey* 3. 249.

Peloponnesus, but also in a specific way to Laconia; at any rate, the words of the poet, "Where was Menelaüs?[1] or was he not in Achaean Argos?"[2] are interpreted by some thus: "or was he not in Laconia?" And at the time of the return of the Heracleidae, when Philonomus betrayed the country to the Dorians, the Achaeans emigrated from Laconia to the country of the Ionians, the country that still to-day is called Achaea. But I shall speak of them in my description of Achaea.[3] Now the new possessors of Laconia restrained themselves at first, but after they turned over the government to Lycurgus they so far surpassed the rest that they alone of the Greeks ruled over both land and sea, and they continued ruling the Greeks until they were deprived of their hegemony, first by the Thebans, and immediately after them by the Macedonians. However, they did not wholly yield even to the Macedonians, but, preserving their autonomy, always kept up a struggle for the primacy both with the rest of the Greeks and with the kings of the Macedonians. And when the Macedonians had been overthrown by the Romans, the Lacedaemonians committed some slight offences against the praetors who were sent by the Romans, because at that time they were under the rule of tyrants and had a wretched government; but when they had recovered themselves, they were held in particular honour, and remained free, contributing to Rome nothing else but friendly services. But recently Eurycles has stirred up trouble among them, having apparently abused the friendship of Caesar

[2] *Odyssey* 3. 251.

[3] 8. 7. 1.

μετρίου πρὸς τὴν ἐπιστασίαν αὐτῶν, ἐπαύσατο δ' ἡ ταραχὴ[1] ταχέως, ἐκείνου μὲν παραχωρήσαντος εἰς τὸ χρεών, τοῦ δ' υἱοῦ τὴν φιλίαν ἀπεστραμμένου τὴν τοιαύτην πᾶσαν· συνέβη δὲ καὶ τοὺς Ἐλευθερολάκωνας λαβεῖν τινὰ τάξιν πολιτείας, ἐπειδὴ Ῥωμαίοις προσέθεντο πρῶτοι οἱ περίοικοι, τυραννουμένης τῆς Σπάρτης, οἵ τε ἄλλοι καὶ οἱ Εἵλωτες. Ἑλλάνικος μὲν οὖν Εὐρυσθένη καὶ Προκλέα φησὶ διατάξαι τὴν πολιτείαν, Ἔφορος δ' ἐπιτιμᾷ, φήσας Λυκούργου μὲν αὐτὸν μηδαμοῦ μεμνῆσθαι, τὰ δ' ἐκείνου ἔργα τοῖς μὴ προσήκουσιν ἀνατιθέναι· μόνῳ γοῦν Λυκούργῳ ἱερὸν ἱδρῦσθαι καὶ θύεσθαι κατ' ἔτος, ἐκείνοις δέ, καίπερ οἰκισταῖς γενομένοις, μηδὲ τοῦτο δεδόσθαι, ὥστε τοὺς ἀπ' αὐτῶν τοὺς μὲν Εὐρυσθενίδας,

[1] ταραχή, Corais, for ἀρχή.

---

[1] Eurycles likewise abused the friendship of Herod the Great and others (Josephus, *Antiq. Jud.* 16. 10 and *Bell. Jud.* 1. 26. 1–5).

[2] Others interpret the clause to mean simply "he died," but the Greek certainly alludes to his banishment by Caesar

unduly in order to maintain his authority over his subjects; but the trouble [1] quickly came to an end, Eurycles retiring to his fate,[2] and his son [3] being averse to any friendship of this kind.[4] And it also came to pass that the Eleuthero-Lacones [5] got a kind of republican constitution, since the Perioeci [6] and also the Helots, at the time when Sparta was under the rule of tyrants, were the first to attach themselves to the Romans. Now Hellanicus says that Eurysthenes and Procles drew up the constitution; [7] but Ephorus censures Hellanicus, saying that he has nowhere mentioned Lycurgus and that he ascribes the work of Lycurgus to persons who had nothing to do with it. At any rate, Ephorus continues, it is to Lycurgus alone that a temple has been erected and that annual sacrifices are offered, whereas Eurysthenes and Procles, although they were the founders, have not even been accorded the honour of having their respective descendants

(Josephus, *Bell. Jud.* 1. 26. 4 and Plutarch, *Apophth.* 208 A), after which nothing further is known of him (see Pauly-Wissowa, *s.v.* "Eurykles").

[3] Gaius Julius, apparently named after Julius Caesar. In an inscription found on Cape Taenarum by Falconer he was extolled as the special benefactor of the Eleuthero-Lacones.

[4] *i.e.* disloyalty to Caesar.

[5] That is, "Free Laconians." Augustus released them from their subjection to the Lacedaemonians, and hence the name. At first they had twenty-four cities, but in the time of Pausanias only eighteen. For the names see Pausanias, 3. 21. 6.

[6] "Perioeci" means literally "people living round (a town)," but it came to be the regular word for a class of *dependent* neighbours. They were not citizens, though not state-slaves as were the Helots.

[7] Strabo now means the *Spartan* constitution.

τοὺς δὲ Προκλείδας[1] καλεῖσθαι, ἀλλὰ τοὺς μὲν Ἀγίδας ἀπὸ Ἄγιδος τοῦ Εὐρυσθένους, τοὺς δ' Εὐρυπωντίδας ἀπὸ Εὐρυπῶντος τοῦ Προκλέους, τοὺς μὲν γὰρ βασιλεῦσαι[2] δικαίως, τοὺς δέ, δεξαμένους ἐπήλυδας ἀνθρώπους, δι' ἐκείνων δυναστεῦσαι· ὅθεν οὐδ' ἀρχηγέτας νομισθῆναι, ὅπερ πᾶσιν ἀποδίδοται οἰκισταῖς. Παυσανίαν τε τῶν Εὐρυπωντιδῶν ἐκπεσόντα ἔχθει[3] τῆς ἑτέρας οἰκίας ἐν τῇ φυγῇ συντάξαι λόγον περὶ τῶν Λυκούργου νόμων,[4] ὄντος τῆς ἐκβαλλούσης οἰκίας, ἐν ᾧ καὶ[5] τοὺς χρησμοὺς λέγει τοὺς δοθέντας αὐτῷ περὶ τῶν πλείστων.

6. Περὶ δὲ τῆς φύσεως τῶν τόπων καὶ τούτων καὶ τῶν Μεσσηνιακῶν ταῦτα μὲν ἀποδεκτέον, λέγοντος Εὐριπίδου· τὴν γὰρ Λακωνικήν φησιν ἔχειν

πολὺν μὲν ἄροτον, ἐκπονεῖν δ' οὐ ῥᾴδιον·
κοίλη γάρ, ὄρεσι περίδρομος, τραχεῖά τε
δυσείσβολός τε πολεμίοις·

[1] The passage τοὺς δὲ Προκλείδας . . . πλείστων, which, down to πλείστων, filled ten lines of A, is corrupt. There is a lacuna of from 11 to 16 letters at the end of each line. The other MSS. are helpful only in supplying A's third, fourth, and fifth lacunae (see Kramer's notes *ad loc.* II. 163). There is virtual agreement on the text except Παυσανίαν . . . πλείστων, where Jones adopts the reading of Ed. Meyer (*Forsch. zur. alt. Gesch.* 1892, I. 233 and *Hermes*, 1907, 135). Meyer's restoration is based on Jacob's new collation of the passage, which verifies that of Kramer in his *Praefatio*, p. 62. The various editors, including Kramer and Meineke, read οἰκείας (before ἐν τῇ φυγῇ) instead of οἰκίας, and λέγειν instead of λέγει, but with no MS. authority. See also B. Niese in *Nachr. von der königl. Gesellsch. der Wissensch. zu Göttingen*, 1906, 138; K. J. Neumann in *Sybels hist. Zeitsch. N. F.* 1906, 55; Wilamowitz in *Homerische Untersuch.* 272; and Cobet in *Miscell. Critica* 175.

called Eurysthenidae and Procleidae; instead, the respective descendants are called Agidae, after Agis the son of Eurysthenes, and Eurypontidae, after Eurypon the son of Procles; for Agis and Eurypon reigned in an honourable way, whereas Eurysthenes and Procles welcomed foreigners and through these maintained their overlordship; and hence they were not even honoured with the title of "archegetae,"[1] an honour which is always paid to founders; and further, Pausanias,[2] after he was banished because of the hatred of the Eurypontidae, the other royal house, and when he was in exile, prepared a discourse on the laws of Lycurgus, who belonged to the house that banished him,[3] in which he also tells the oracles that were given out to Lycurgus concerning most of the laws.

6. Concerning the nature of the regions, both Laconia and Messenia, one should accept what Euripides says in the following passages: He says that Laconia has "much arable land but is not easy to cultivate, for it is hollow,[4] surrounded by mountains, rugged, and difficult for enemies to invade";

[1] *i.e.* the original, or independent, founders of a new race or state.

[2] A member of the house of the Agidae, and king of Sparta, 408–394 B.C. (Diod. Sic. 13. 75 and 14. 89).

[3] He was the sixth in descent from Procles (10. 4. 18).

[4] *i.e.* "low-lying." Cp. Homer's "Hollow Lacedaemon" (*Iliad* 2. 581).

---

[2] βασιλεῦσαι, Cobet; others δυναστεῦσαι.

[3] Or μίσει.

[4] Meineke and others read: λόγ[ον κατὰ τοῦ Λυκούρ]γου, νόμων (note punctuation).

[5] Others ἐκβαλλούσῃ[ς (MSS.), or ἐκβαλούσῃ[ς, αὐτὸν αἴτιον καὶ] κτλ.

τὴν δὲ Μεσσηνιακὴν

> καλλίκαρπον
> κατάρρυτόν τε μυρίοισι νάμασι,
> καὶ βουσὶ καὶ ποίμναισιν εὐβοτωτάτην,
> οὔτ' ἐν πνοαῖσι χείματος δυσχείμερον
> οὔτ' αὖ τεθρίπποις ἡλίου θερμὴν ἄγαν·

καὶ ὑποβὰς τῶν πάλων φησίν, ὧν οἱ Ἡρακλεῖδαι περὶ τῆς χώρας ἐποιήσαντο, τὸν μὲν πρότερον γενέσθαι

> γαίας Λακαίνης κύριον, φαύλου χθονός·

τὸν δὲ δεύτερον τῆς Μεσσήνης,

> ἀρετὴν ἐχούσης μείζον' ἢ λόγῳ φράσαι,

οἵαν καὶ ὁ Τυρταῖος φράζει. τὴν δὲ Λακωνικὴν καὶ τὴν Μεσσηνίαν ὁρίζειν, αὐτοῦ φήσαντος,

> Παμισὸν εἰς θάλασσαν ἐξορμώμενον,

οὐ συγχωρητέον, ὃς διὰ μέσης ῥεῖ τῆς Μεσσηνίας, οὐδαμοῦ τῆς νῦν Λακωνικῆς ἁπτόμενος. οὐκ εὖ δὲ οὐδ' ὅτι, τῆς Μεσσηνίας ὁμοίως ἐπιθαλαττιαίας οὔσης τῇ Λακωνικῇ, φησὶν αὐτὴν πρόσω ναυτίλοισιν εἶναι. ἀλλ' οὐδὲ τὴν Ἦλιν εὖ διορίζει,

> πρόσω δὲ βάντι ποταμὸν Ἦλις, ἡ Διὸς
> γείτων, κάθηται.[1]

C 367 εἴτε [2] γὰρ τὴν νῦν Ἠλείαν βούλεται λέγειν, ἥτις ὁμορεῖ τῇ Μεσσηνίᾳ, ταύτης οὐ προσάπτεται ὁ Παμισός, ὥσπερ γε οὐδὲ [3] τῆς Λακωνικῆς· εἴρηται γὰρ ὅτι διὰ μέσης ῥεῖ τῆς Μεσσηνίας· εἴτε τὴν παλαιὰν τὴν Κοίλην καλουμένην, πολὺ μᾶλλον

and that Messenia is "a land of fair fruitage and watered by innumerable streams, abounding in pasturage for cattle and sheep, being neither very wintry in the blasts of winter nor yet made too hot by the chariot of Helios";[1] and a little below, in speaking of the lots which the Heracleidae cast for the country, he says that the first lot conferred "lordships over the land of Laconia, a poor country," and the second over Messenia, "whose fertility is greater than words can express"; and Tyrtaeus speaks of it in the same manner. But one should not admit that the boundary between Laconia and Messenia is formed, as Euripides says, "by the Pamisus, which rushes into the sea," for it flows through the middle of Messenia, nowhere touching the present Laconia. Neither is he right when he says that to mariners Messenia is far away, for Messenia like Laconia lies on the sea; and he does not give the right boundary of Elis either, "and far away, after one crosses the river, lies Elis, the neighbour of Zeus;" for if, on the one hand, he means the present Eleian country, which borders on Messenia, the Pamisus does not touch this country, any more than it does Laconia, for, as I have said, it flows through the middle of Messenia; or if, on the other hand, he means the old Coelê

[1] *Frag.* 1083 (Nauck).

---

[1] κάθηται, Meineke emends to καλεῖται.

[2] The passage εἴτε γὰρ . . . ἡ Ἦλις is corrupt (see C. Müller's *Ind. Var. Lect.* p. 995 and Kramer). On the several lacunae see Müller (*Ind. Var. Lect.*) or Kramer. The editors agree upon the above restorations with the exception of Λεπρεατῶν.

[3] οὐδέ, Casaubon inserts; so the later editors.

ἐκπίπτει τῆς ἀληθείας· διαβάντι γὰρ τὸν Παμισὸν ἔστι πολλὴ τῆς Μεσσηνίας, εἶθ' ἡ τῶν Λεπρεατῶν[1] ἅπασα καὶ Μακιστίων,[2] ἣν Τριφυλίαν ἐκάλουν, εἶθ' ἡ Πισᾶτις καὶ ἡ Ὀλυμπία, εἶτα μετὰ τριακοσίους σταδίους ἡ Ἦλις.

7. Γραφόντων δὲ τῶν μὲν Λακεδαίμονα κητώεσσαν, τῶν δὲ καιετάεσσαν, ζητοῦσι, τὴν κητώεσσαν τίνα δέχεσθαι χρή, εἴτε ἀπὸ τῶν κητῶν, εἴτε μεγάλην, ὅπερ δοκεῖ πιθανώτερον εἶναι· τήν τε καιετάεσσαν οἱ μὲν καλαμινθώδη δέχονται, οἱ δέ, ὅτι οἱ ἀπὸ τῶν σεισμῶν ῥωχμοὶ καιετοὶ λέγονται, καὶ ὁ καιέτας τὸ δεσμωτήριον ἐντεῦθεν τὸ παρὰ Λακεδαιμονίοις, σπήλαιόν τι· ἔνιοι δὲ κώους μᾶλλον τὰ τοιαῦτα κοιλώματα λέγεσθαί φασιν, ἀφ' οὗ καὶ τὸ

φηρσὶν ὀρεσκῴοισιν.

εὔσειστος δ' ἡ Λακωνική· καὶ δὴ τοῦ Ταϋγέτου κορυφάς τινας ἀπορραγῆναί τινες μνημονεύουσιν. εἰσὶ δὲ λατομίαι λίθου πολυτελοῦς τοῦ μὲν Ταιναρίου ἐν Ταινάρῳ παλαιαί, νεωστὶ δὲ καὶ ἐν τῷ Ταϋγέτῳ μέταλλον ἀνέῳξάν τινες εὐμέγεθες, χορηγὸν ἔχοντες τὴν τῶν Ῥωμαίων πολυτέλειαν.

[1] [Λεπρεατ]ῶν Müller-Dübner (in Latin translation) from conj. of Meineke. Kramer conj. [Ἐπει]ῶν; Curtius [Καυκών]ων.

[2] Μακιστίων, Jones, for Μεσσαίων, from conj. of Meineke. Groskurd conj. Μεσσηνίων, Kramer and Curtius Μινυῶν.

---

[1] See 8. 3. 2.

[2] *i.e.* in Homer's text, *Iliad* 2. 581 and *Odyssey* 4. 1.

[3] The usual meaning of Ketê is "deep-sea monsters," or more specifically the "cetaceans," but Strabo obviously speaks of the word in the sense of "ravines" or "clefts" (see Buttman, *Lexilogus s.v.*, and Goebel, *Lexilogus s.v.*).

Elis,[1] he deviates much further from the truth; for after one crosses the Pamisus there is still a large part of Messenia to traverse, and then the whole of the territories of the Lepreatae and the Macistii, which they used to call Triphylia; and then come Pisatis and Olympia, and then, three hundred stadia farther on, Elis.

7. Since some critics write[2] Lacedaemon "Ketoessan" and others "Kaietaessan," the question is asked, how should we interpret "Ketoessa," whether as derived from "Ketê,"[3] or as meaning "large,"[4] which seems to be more plausible. And as for "Kaietaessan," some interpret it as meaning "Kalaminthodê,"[5] whereas others say that the clefts caused by earthquakes are called "Kaietoi," and that from "Kaietoi" is derived "Kaietas," the word among the Lacedaemonians for their "prison," which is a sort of cavern. But some prefer to call such cavernous places "Kooi," and whence, they add, comes the expression "'oreskoioi' monsters."[6] Laconia is subject to earthquakes, and in fact some writers record that certain peaks of Taÿgetus have been broken away. And there are quarries of very costly marble—the old quarries of Taenarian marble on Taenarum; and recently some men have opened a large quarry in Taÿgetus, being supported in their undertaking by the extravagance of the Romans.

[4] The meaning given to the word in the scholia to Homer, and one which seems more closely associated with the usual meaning, "deep-sea monster."

[5] *i.e.* "abounding in mint."

[6] *Iliad* 1. 268, where Homer refers to the Centaurs, which, according to the above interpretation, are "monsters that live in mountain-caverns."

8. Ὅτι δὲ Λακεδαίμων ὁμωνύμως λέγεται καὶ ἡ χώρα καὶ ἡ πόλις, δηλοῖ καὶ Ὅμηρος (λέγω δὲ χώραν σὺν τῇ Μεσσηνίᾳ)· περὶ μὲν δὴ τῶν τόξων ὅταν λέγῃ·

> καλά, τά οἱ ξεῖνος Λακεδαίμονι δῶκε τυχήσας
> Ἴφιτος Εὐρυτίδης·

εἶτ' ἐπενέγκῃ·[1]

> τὼ δ' ἐν Μεσσήνῃ ξυμβλήτην ἀλλήλοιιν
> οἴκῳ ἐν Ὀρτιλόχοιο·

τὴν χώραν λέγει, ἧς μέρος ἦν καὶ ἡ Μεσσηνία· οὐ διήνεγκεν οὖν αὐτῷ καὶ οὕτως εἰπεῖν·

> ξεῖνος[2] Λακεδαίμονι δῶκε τυχήσας,

καὶ

> τὼ δ' ἐν Μεσσήνῃ ξυμβλήτην·

ὅτι γὰρ αἱ Φηραί εἰσιν ὁ τοῦ Ὀρτιλόχου οἶκος, δῆλον·

> ἐς Φηρὰς δ' ἵκοντο Διοκλῆος ποτὶ δῶμα,
> υἱέος Ὀρτιλόχοιο,

ὅ τε Τηλέμαχος καὶ ὁ Πεισίστρατος· αἱ δὲ Φηραὶ τῆς Μεσσηνίας εἰσίν. ὅταν δ' ἐκ τῶν Φηρῶν ὁρμηθέντας τοὺς περὶ Τηλέμαχον πανημερίους φῇ σείειν ζυγόν, εἶτ' εἴπῃ,

> δύσετό τ' ἠέλιος,
> οἱ δ' ἷξον κοίλην Λακεδαίμονα κητώεσσαν·
> πρὸς δ' ἄρα δώματ' ἔλων Μενελάου,

C 368 τὴν πόλιν δεῖ δέχεσθαι· εἰ δὲ μή, ἐκ Λακεδαίμονος εἰς Λακεδαίμονα φανεῖται λέγων τὴν ἄφιξιν· ἄλλως τε οὐ πιθανόν, μὴ ἐν Σπάρτῃ τὴν οἴκησιν

8. Homer makes it clear that both the country and the city are called by the same name, Lacedaemon (and when I say "country" I include Messenia with Laconia). For in speaking of the bows, when he says, "beautiful gifts which a friend had given him when he met him in Lacedaemon, even Iphitus the son of Eurytus,"[1] and then adds, "these twain met one another in Messenê in the home of Ortilochus,"[2] Homer means the country of which Messenia was a part. Accordingly it made no difference to him whether he said "a friend had given him when he met him in Lacedaemon" or "these twain met in Messenê." For, that Pherae is the home of Ortilochus, is clear from this passage: "and they" (Telemachus and Peisistratus) "went to Pherae, the home of Diocles, son of Ortilochus";[3] and Pherae is in Messenia. But when Homer says that, after Telemachus and his companions set out from Pherae, "they shook the yoke all day long,"[4] and then adds, "and the sun set, and they came to Hollow Lacedaemon 'Ketoessan,'[5] and then drove to the palace of Menelaüs,"[6] we must interpret him as meaning the city; otherwise it will be obvious that the poet speaks of their arrival at Lacedaemon from Lacedaemon! And, besides, it is not probable that

[1] *Odyssey* 21. 13. [2] *Odyssey* 21. 15.
[3] *Odyssey* 3. 488. [4] *Odyssey* 3. 486.
[5] See footnote 4, p 141. [6] *Odyssey* 4. 1–2.

---

[1] ἐπενέγκῃ, Corais, for ἐπήνεγκε; so the later editors.
[2] ξεῖνος, Xylander, for κοινῶς; so the later editors.

εἶναι τοῦ Μενελάου, οὐδέ,[1] μὴ οὔσης[2] ἐκεῖ, τὸν Τηλέμαχον λέγειν·

εἶμι γὰρ ἐς Σπάρτην τε καὶ εἰς Πύλον.

δοκεῖ ἀντιπίπτειν[3] τούτῳ τὸ τοῖς τῆς χώρας ἐπιθέτοις αὐτὸν χρῆσθαι,[4] εἰ μὴ νὴ Δία ποιητικῇ τις τοῦτο συγχωρήσει ἐξουσίᾳ, βέλτιον[5] γὰρ τὴν Μεσσήνην μετὰ τῆς Λακωνικῆς ἢ[6] Πύλου τῆς ὑπὸ τῷ Νέστορι, μηδὲ δὴ καθ' αὑτὴν τάττεσθαι ἐν τῷ Καταλόγῳ, μηδὲ κοινωνοῦσαν τῆς στρατείας.[7]

VI

1. Μετὰ δὲ Μαλέας ὁ Ἀργολικὸς ἐκδέχεται κόλπος καὶ ὁ Ἑρμιονικός· ὁ μὲν μέχρι τοῦ Σκυλλαίου πλέοντι ὡς πρὸς ἕω βλέπων καὶ πρὸς τὰς Κυκλάδας, ὁ δὲ ἑωθινώτερος τούτου μέχρι πρὸς Αἴγιναν καὶ τὴν Ἐπιδαυρίαν. τὰ μὲν δὴ πρῶτα τοῦ Ἀργολικοῦ Λάκωνες ἔχουσι, τὰ δὲ λοιπὰ Ἀργεῖοι· ἐν οἷς ἐστι τῶν μὲν Λακώνων τὸ Δήλιον, ἱερὸν Ἀπόλλωνος, ὁμώνυμον τῷ Βοιωτιακῷ, καὶ

[1] οὐδέ, Kramer inserts, from conj. of Pletho.

[2] μὴ οὔσης, Kramer, for μηνυούσης *Agh* and μηδ' οὔσης (*Blno*, and A *man. sec.*). So Meineke, Müller-Dübner and others.

[3] [δὲ ἀντι]πίπτειν, Madvig, for γὰρ συμπίπτειν *bno*; Meineke and Forbiger read δὲ συμπίπτειν.

[4] αὐ[τὸν χρῆσθαι], Kramer; Forbiger, αὐ[τὸν μὴ χρῆσθαι].

[5] A reads ἐξο . . . τιον, with a lacuna of about eight letters, but *bno* have ἐξουσίᾳ . . . τιον. Kramer conj. [βέλ]τιον, and Meineke so reads, but the earlier editors read [ἐναν]τίον.

[6] Meineke inserts καί (as in *bno*) instead of ἤ (Müller-Dübner).

the residence of Menelaüs was not at Sparta, nor yet, if it were not there, that Telemachus would say, "for I would go both to Sparta and to Pylus."[1] But the fact that Homer uses the epithets of the country[2] is in disagreement with this view[3] unless, indeed, one is willing to attribute this to poetic license—as one should do, for it were better for Messenê to be included with Laconia or with the Pylus that was subject to Nestor, and not to be set off by itself in the *Catalogue* as not even having a part in the expedition.

VI

1. After Maleae follows the Argolic Gulf, and then the Hermionic Gulf; the former stretches as far as Scyllaeum, facing approximately eastwards and towards the Cyclades, while the latter is more to the east than the former and extends as far as Aegina and Epidauria. Now the first places on the Argolic Gulf are occupied by Laconians, and the rest by the Argives. Among the places belonging to the Laconians is Delium, which is sacred to Apollo and bears the same name as the place in

[1] *Odyssey* 2. 359.

[2] In *Odyssey* 4. 1, and *Iliad* 2. 581 (*Catalogue of Ships*). But the epithets are omitted in *Odyssey* 21. 13.

[3] *i.e.* that Homer's *country* of Lacedaemon includes Messenia.

---

[7] A reads στρα . . . λεας with a lacuna of about twelve letters, but Μετὰ δὲ Μαλ (see next §) is supplied *man. sec.*

Μινώα φρούριον, ὁμώνυμος καὶ αὕτη τῇ Μεγαρικῇ, καὶ ἡ λιμηρὰ Ἐπίδαυρος, ὡς Ἀρτεμίδωρός φησιν. Ἀπολλόδωρος δὲ Κυθήρων πλησίον ἱστορεῖ ταύτην, εὐλίμενον δὲ οὖσαν βραχέως καὶ ἐπιτετμημένως λιμηρὰν εἰρῆσθαι, ὡς ἂν λιμενηράν, μεταβεβληκέναι δὲ τοὔνομα. ἔστι δὲ τραχὺς ὁ παράπλους εὐθὺς ἀπὸ Μαλεῶν ἀρξάμενος μέχρι πολλοῦ ὁ Λακωνικός, ἔχει δ' ὅμως ὑφόρμους καὶ λιμένας. ἡ λοιπὴ δ' ἐστὶ παραλία εὐλίμενος, νησίδιά τε πολλὰ πρόκειται αὐτῆς οὐκ ἄξια μνήμης.

2. Τῶν δ' Ἀργείων αἵ τε Πρασιαὶ καὶ τὸ Τημένιον, ἐν ᾧ τέθαπται Τήμενος, καὶ ἔτι πρότερον τὸ χωρίον, δι' οὗ ῥεῖ ποταμὸς ἡ Λέρνη καλουμένη, ὁμώνυμος τῇ λίμνῃ, ἐν ᾗ μεμύθευται τὰ περὶ τὴν Ὕδραν. τὸ δὲ Τημένιον ἀπέχει τοῦ Ἄργους ἓξ καὶ εἴκοσι σταδίους ὑπὲρ τῆς θαλάττης, ἀπὸ δὲ τοῦ Ἄργους εἰς τὸ Ἡραῖον τεσσαράκοντα, ἔνθεν δὲ εἰς Μυκήνας δέκα. μετὰ δὲ τὸ Τημένιον ἡ Ναυπλία, τὸ τῶν Ἀργείων ναύσταθμον· τὸ δ' ἔτυμον ἀπὸ τοῦ ταῖς ναυσὶ προσπλεῖσθαι. ἀπὸ τούτου δὲ πεπλάσθαι φασὶ τὸν Ναύπλιον καὶ τοὺς παῖδας αὐτοῦ παρὰ τοῖς νεωτέροις· οὐ γὰρ Ὅμηρον ἀμνημονῆσαι ἂν τούτων, τοῦ μὲν Παλαμήδους τοσαύτην σοφίαν καὶ σύνεσιν ἐπιδεδειγμένου, δολοφονηθέντος δὲ ἀδίκως, τοῦ δὲ Ναυπλίου τοσοῦτον ἀπεργασαμένου φθόρον ἀνθρώπων περὶ τὸν Καφηρέα. ἡ δὲ

---

1 The Boeotian Delium was on the site of the Dilesi of to-day. The site of the Laconian Delium is uncertain.

2 Limera: an epithet meaning "with the good harbour."

Boeotia;[1] and also Minoa, a stronghold, which has the same name as the place in Megaris; and Epidaurus Limera,[2] as Artemidorus says. But Apollodorus observes that this Epidaurus Limera is near Cythera, and that, because it has a good harbour, it was called "Limenera," which was abbreviated and contracted to "Limera," so that its name has been changed. Immediately after sailing from Maleae the Laconian coast is rugged for a considerable distance, but still it affords anchoring-places and harbours. The rest of the coast is well provided with harbours; and off the coast lie many small islands, but they are not worth mentioning.

2. But to the Argives belongs Prasiae, and also Temenium, where Temenus was buried, and, still before Temenium, the district through which flows the river Lernê, as it is called, bearing the same name as the marsh in which is laid the scene of the myth of the Hydra. Temenium lies above the sea at a distance of twenty-six stadia from Argos; and from Argos to Heraeum the distance is forty stadia, and thence to Mycenae ten. After Temenium comes Nauplia, the naval station of the Argives; and the name is derived from the fact that the place is accessible to ships.[3] And it is on the basis of this name, it is said, that the myth of Nauplius and his sons has been fabricated by the more recent writers of myth, for Homer would not have failed to mention these, if Palamedes had displayed such wisdom and sagacity, and if he was unjustly and treacherously murdered, and if Nauplius wrought destruction to so many men at Cape Caphereus. But in addition

[3] *i.e.* "Naus" (ship) + "pleō" (sail).

γενεαλογία πρὸς τῷ μυθώδει καὶ τοῖς χρόνοις διημάρτηται· δεδόσθω γὰρ Ποσειδῶνος εἶναι,
C 369 Ἀμυμώνης δὲ πῶς τὸν κατὰ τὰ Τρωικὰ ἔτι ζῶντα; ἐφεξῆς δὲ τῇ Ναυπλίᾳ τὰ σπήλαια καὶ οἱ ἐν αὐτοῖς οἰκοδομητοὶ λαβύρινθοι, Κυκλώπεια δ' ὀνομάζουσιν.

3. Εἶτ' ἄλλα χωρία, καὶ ἐφεξῆς ὁ Ἑρμιονικὸς κόλπος· καὶ γὰρ τοῦτον Ὁμήρου[1] τάξαντος ὑπὸ τῇ Ἀργείᾳ καὶ ἡμῖν οὐ παροπτέος ἐνέφηνεν[2] ὁ μερισμὸς τῆς περιοδείας οὗτος. ἄρχεται δ' ἀπὸ Ἀσίνης[3] πολίχνης· εἶθ' Ἑρμιόνη καὶ Τροιζήν· ἐν παράπλῳ δὲ πρόκειται καὶ Καλαυρία νῆσος, κύκλον ἔχουσα ἑκατὸν καὶ[4] τριάκοντα σταδίων, πορθμῷ δὲ τετρασταδίῳ διεστῶσα τῆς ἠπείρου.

4. Εἶθ' ὁ Σαρωνικὸς κόλπος· οἱ δὲ πόντον λέγουσιν, οἱ δὲ πόρον, καθ' ὃ καὶ πέλαγος λέγεται Σαρωνικόν· καλεῖται δὲ πᾶς ὁ συνάπτων πόρος ἀπὸ τῆς Ἑρμιονικῆς καὶ τῆς περὶ τὸν Ἰσθμὸν θαλάττης τῷ τε Μυρτῴῳ πελάγει καὶ τῷ Κρητικῷ. τοῦ δὲ Σαρωνικοῦ Ἐπίδαυρός τέ ἐστι καὶ ἡ προκειμένη νῆσος Αἴγινα· εἶτα Κεγχρεαί, τὸ τῶν Κορινθίων ἐπὶ τὰ πρὸς ἕω μέρη ναύσταθμον·

[1] A reads καὶ . . . ήρου, with lacuna of about ten letters, which Kramer supplies as above.

[2] The lacuna of about twelve letters in A is supplied by *bknol* as above.

[3] Ἀσίνης, added in marg. A, *man. sec.*; Ἀσιάνης, *man. sec.* Kramer would supply the lacuna in A (—ανῆς) thus: [Ἁλι]κῆς (see Pausanias 2. 36. 1).

[4] ἑκατὸν καί, Jones inserts (cp. 8. 6. 14, where the same insertion is made).

to its fabulous character the genealogy of Nauplius is also wholly incorrect in respect to the times involved; for, granting that he was the son of Poseidon, how could a man who was still alive at the time of the Trojan war have been the son of Amymonê?[1] Next after Nauplia one comes to the caverns and the labyrinths built in them, which are called Cyclopeian.[2]

3. Then come other places, and next after them the Hermionic Gulf; for, since Homer assigns this gulf also to Argeia, it is clear that I too should not overlook this section of the circuit. The gulf begins at the town of Asinê.[3] Then come Hermionê and Troezen; and, as one sails along the coast, one comes also to the island of Calauria, which has a circuit of one hundred and thirty stadia and is separated from the mainland by a strait four stadia wide.

4. Then comes the Saronic Gulf; but some call it a sea and others a strait; and because of this it is also called the Saronic Sea. Saronic Gulf is the name given to the whole of the strait, stretching from the Hermionic Sea and from the sea that is at the Isthmus, that connects with both the Myrtoan and Cretan Seas. To the Saronic Gulf belong both Epidaurus and the island of Aegina that lies off Epidaurus; then Cenchreae, the easterly naval station of the Corinthians; then, after sailing forty-

[1] Strabo confuses Nauplius, son of Poseidon and Amymonê and distant ancestor of Palamedes, with the Nauplius who was the father of Palamedes.

[2] Cp. 8. 6. 11.

[3] The Asinê in Argolis, not far from Nauplia, not the Messenian Asinê, of course (see Pauly-Wissowa).

εἶτα λιμὴν Σχοινοῦς πλεύσαντι τεσσαράκοντα καὶ πέντε σταδίους· ἀπὸ δὲ Μαλεῶν τοὺς πάντας περὶ χιλίους καὶ ὀκτακοσίους. κατὰ δὲ τὸν Σχοινοῦντα ὁ δίολκος, τὸ στενώτατον τοῦ Ἰσθμοῦ, περὶ ὃν τὸ τοῦ Ἰσθμίου Ποσειδῶνος ἱερόν· ἀλλὰ νῦν τὰ μὲν ὑπερκείσθω· ἔξω γάρ ἐστι τῆς Ἀργείας. ἀναλαβόντες δ' ἐφοδεύσωμεν πάλιν τὰ κατὰ τὴν Ἀργείαν.

5. Καὶ πρῶτον ποσαχῶς λέγεται παρὰ τῷ ποιητῇ τὸ Ἄργος καὶ καθ' αὑτὸ καὶ μετὰ τοῦ ἐπιθέτου, Ἀχαϊκὸν Ἄργος καλοῦντος ἢ Ἴασον ἢ ἵππιον ἢ Πελασγικὸν ἢ ἱππόβοτον. καὶ γὰρ ἡ πόλις Ἄργος λέγεται·

Ἄργος τε Σπάρτη τε·
οἵ δ' Ἄργος τ' εἶχον Τίρυνθά τε.

καὶ ἡ Πελοπόννησος,

ἡμετέρῳ ἐνὶ οἴκῳ ἐν Ἄργεϊ·

οὐ γὰρ ἡ πόλις γε ἦν οἶκος αὐτοῦ· καὶ ὅλη ἡ Ἑλλάς· Ἀργείους γοῦν καλεῖ πάντας, καθάπερ καὶ Δαναοὺς καὶ Ἀχαιούς. τὴν γοῦν ὁμωνυμίαν τοῖς ἐπιθέτοις διαστέλλεται, τὴν μὲν Θετταλίαν Πελασγικὸν Ἄργος καλῶν,

νῦν αὖ τούς, ὅσσοι τὸ Πελασγικὸν Ἄργος ἔναιον,

τὴν δὲ Πελοπόννησον,

εἰ δέ κεν Ἄργος ἱκοίμεθ' Ἀχαιικόν·
ἢ οὐκ Ἄργεος ἦεν Ἀχαιικοῦ;

σημαίνων ἐνταῦθα, ὅτι καὶ Ἀχαιοὶ ἰδίως ὠνο-

five stadia, one comes to Schoenus,[1] a harbour. From Maleae thither the total distance is about eighteen hundred stadia. Near Schoenus is the "Diolcus,"[2] the narrowest part of the Isthmus, where is the temple of the Isthmian Poseidon. However, let us for the present postpone the discussion of these places, for they lie outside of Argeia, and let us resume again our description of those in Argeia.

5. And in the first place let me mention in how many ways the term "Argos" is used by the poet, not only by itself, but also with epithets, when he calls Argos "Achaean," or "Iasian," or "hippian,"[3] or "Pelasgian," or "horse-pasturing."[4] For, in the first place, the city is called Argos: "Argos and Sparta,"[5] "and those who held Argos and Tiryns."[6] And, secondly, the Peloponnesus: "in our home in Argos,"[7] for the city of Argos was not his[8] home. And, thirdly, Greece as a whole; at any rate, he calls all Greeks Argives, just as he calls them Danaans and Achaeans. However, he differentiates identical names by epithets, calling Thessaly "Pelasgian Argos": "Now all, moreover, who dwelt in Pelasgian Argos";[9] and calling the Peloponnesus "Achaean Argos." "And if we should come to Achaean Argos,"[10] "Or was he not in Achaean Argos?"[11] And here he signifies that

[1] Now Kalamaki.

[2] See 8. 2. 1, and foot-note.

[3] But this epithet (ἵππιον, "land of horses") is not applied to Argos anywhere in the *Iliad* or the *Odyssey*. Pindar so uses it once, in *Isth.* 7 (6). 17.

[4] *e.g. Iliad* 2. 287.

[5] *Iliad* 4. 52.

[6] *Iliad* 2. 559.

[7] *Iliad* 1. 30.

[8] Agamemnon's.

[9] *Iliad* 2. 681.

[10] *Iliad* 9. 141.

[11] *Odyssey* 3. 251.

μάζοντο οἱ Πελοποννήσιοι κατ' ἄλλην σημασίαν. Ἴασόν τε Ἄργος τὴν Πελοπόννησον λέγει·

εἰ πάντες γ' ἐσίδοιεν ἀν' Ἴασον Ἄργος Ἀχαιοί

C 370 τὴν Πηνελόπην, ὅτι πλείους ἂν λάβοι μνηστῆρας·
οὐ γὰρ τοὺς ἐξ ὅλης τῆς Ἑλλάδος εἰκός, ἀλλὰ
τοὺς ἐγγύς. ἱππόβοτον δὲ καὶ ἵππιον κοινῶς
εἴρηκε.

6. Περὶ δὲ τῆς Ἑλλάδος καὶ Ἑλλήνων καὶ Πανελλήνων ἀντιλέγεται. Θουκυδίδης μὲν γὰρ τὸν ποιητὴν μηδαμοῦ βαρβάρους εἰπεῖν φησὶ διὰ τὸ μηδὲ Ἕλληνάς πω τὸ ἀντίπαλον εἰς ἓν ὄνομα ἀποκεκρίσθαι. καὶ Ἀπολλόδωρος δὲ μόνους τοὺς ἐν Θετταλίᾳ καλεῖσθαί φησιν Ἕλληνας·

Μυρμιδόνες δὲ καλεῦντο καὶ Ἕλληνες.

Ἡσίοδον μέντοι καὶ Ἀρχίλοχον ἤδη εἰδέναι καὶ Ἕλληνας λεγομένους τοὺς σύμπαντας καὶ Πανέλληνας, τὸν μὲν περὶ τῶν Προιτίδων λέγοντα, ὡς Πανέλληνες ἐμνήστευον αὐτάς, τὸν δὲ

ὡς Πανελλήνων ὀϊζὺς ἐς Θάσον συνέδραμεν.

ἄλλοι δ' ἀντιτιθέασιν, ὅτι ὁ ποιητὴς[1] καὶ βαρβάρους εἴρηκεν, εἰπών γε βαρβαροφώνους τοὺς Κᾶρας, καὶ Ἕλληνας τοὺς πάντας·

ἀνδρός, τοῦ κλέος εὐρὺ καθ' Ἑλλάδα καὶ μέσον
Ἄργος·

καὶ πάλιν·

εἰ δ' ἐθέλεις τραφθῆναι ἀν' Ἑλλάδα καὶ μέσον
Ἄργος.[2]

[1] ὁ ποιητής, Kramer proposes to insert in the lacuna of about fifteen letters in A between ἀντιτι and καί, thus supplementing the θεασιν ὅτι supplied by *man. sec.*

under a different designation the Peloponnesians were also called Achaeans in a special sense. And he calls the Peloponnesus "Iasian Argos": "If all the Achaeans throughout Iasian Argos could see" Penelope, she would have still more wooers; for it is not probable that he meant the Greeks from all Greece, but only those that were near. But the epithets "horse-pasturing" and "hippian" he uses in a general sense

6. But critics are in dispute in regard to the terms "Hellas," "Hellenes," and "Panhellenes." For Thucydides[1] says that the poet nowhere speaks of barbarians, "because the Hellenes had not as yet been designated by a common distinctive name opposed to that of the barbarians." And Apollodorus says that only the Greeks in Thessaly were called Hellenes: "and were called Myrmidons and Hellenes."[2] He says, however, that Hesiod and Archilochus already knew that all the Greeks were called, not only Hellenes, but also Panhellenes, for Hesiod, in speaking of the daughters of Proteus, says that the Panhellenes wooed them, and Archilochus says that "the woes of the Panhellenes centred upon Thasos." But others oppose this view, saying that the poet also speaks of barbarians, since he speaks of the Carians as men of barbarous speech,[3] and of all the Greeks as Hellenes, "the man whose fame is wide throughout Hellas and mid-Argos,"[4] and again, "If thou wishest to journey throughout Hellas and mid-Argos."[5]

[1] 1. 3. [2] *Iliad* 2. 684. [3] *Iliad* 2. 867. [4] *Odyssey* 1. 344. [5] *Odyssey* 15. 80.

---

[2] καὶ πάλιν . . . Ἄργος, omitted by BE*l*.

7. Ἡ μὲν οὖν πόλις ἡ τῶν Ἀργείων ἐν χωρίοις ἐπιπέδοις ἵδρυται τὸ πλέον, ἄκραν δ' ἔχει τὴν καλουμένην Λάρισαν, λόφον εὐερκῆ μετρίως, ἔχοντα ἱερὸν Διός· ῥεῖ δ' αὐτῆς πλησίον ὁ Ἴναχος, χαραδρώδης ποταμός, τὰς πηγὰς ἔχων ἐκ Λυρκείου τοῦ κατὰ τὴν Κυνουρίαν ὄρους τῆς Ἀρκαδίας.[1] περὶ δὲ τῶν μυθευομένων πηγῶν εἴρηται, διότι πλάσματα ποιητῶν ἐστί· πλάσμα δὲ καὶ τὸ Ἄργος ἄνυδρον,

θεοὶ δ' αὖ θέσαν Ἄργος ἔνυδρον,[2]

τῆς τε χώρας κοίλης οὔσης καὶ ποταμοῖς διαρρεομένης καὶ ἕλη καὶ λίμνας παρεχομένης, καὶ τῆς πόλεως εὐπορουμένης ὕδασι φρεάτων πολλῶν καὶ ἐπιπολαίων. αἰτιῶνται δὴ[3] τῆς ἀπάτης τὸ

καί κεν ἐλέγχιστος πολυδίψιον Ἄργος ἱκοίμην.

τοῦτο δ' ἤτοι ἀντὶ τοῦ πολυπόθητον κεῖται, ἢ χωρὶς τοῦ δ πολυίψιον, ὡς

πολύφθορόν τε δῶμα Πελοπιδῶν τόδε

φησὶ Σοφοκλῆς· τὸ γὰρ προϊάψαι καὶ ἰάψαι καὶ ἴψασθαι φθοράν τινα καὶ βλάβην σημαίνει·

[1] The words τοῦ κατὰ . . . Ἀρκαδίας are by Kramer regarded as an interpolation, and Meineke ejects them. C. Müller would emend Κυνουρίαν to συνορίαν.

[2] θεοὶ δ' αὖ θέσαν Ἄργος ἔνυδρον, Meineke, following conj. of Tyrwhitt, emends to Ἄργος ἄνυδρον ἐὸν Δαναοὶ θέσαν Ἄργος ἔνυδρον, the verse quoted by Strabo in § 8 following.

[3] δή, Meineke emends to δέ.

7. Now the city of the Argives[1] is for the most part situated in a plain, but it has for a citadel the place called Larisa, a hill that is fairly well fortified and contains a temple of Zeus. And near the city flows the Inachus, a torrential river that has its sources in Lyrceius, the mountain that is near Cynuria in Arcadia.[2] But concerning the sources of which mythology tells us, they are fabrications of poets, as I have already said.[3] And "waterless Argos" is also a fabrication ("but the gods made Argos well watered"),[4] since the country lies in a hollow, and is traversed by rivers, and contains marshes and lakes, and since the city is well supplied with waters of many wells whose water-level reaches the surface. So critics find the cause of the mistake in this verse: "And in utter shame would I return to *πολυδίψιον*[5] Argos."[6] *πολυδίψιον* either is used for *πολυπόθητον*,[7] or, omitting the *δ*, for *πολυΐψιον*,[8] in the sense of *πολύφθορον*,[9] as in the phrase of Sophocles, "and the *πολύφθορον* home of the Pelopidae there"; for the words *προϊάψαι* and *ἰάψαι* and *ἴψασθαι* signify a kind of destruction or

[1] Argos.

[2] It is Mt. Lycaeus, not Lyrceius, that is "near Cynuria in Arcadia." But Lycaeus (now Diophorti) is on the confines of Messenia and Arcadia. See critical note.

[3] 6. 2. 4.

[4] The authorship of these words is unknown.

[5] *i.e.* "very thirsty," though Strabo and Athenaeus (444 E) give the word a different interpretation.

[6] *Iliad* 4. 171.

[7] *i.e.* "much longed for."

[8] *i.e.* "very destructive."

[9] The word means either "very destructive" or "ruined by the deaths of many"—clearly the latter in the phrase here cited from the *Electra*, *l.* 10.

νῦν μὲν πειρᾶται, τάχα δ' ἴψεται υἷας Ἀχαιῶν·
κατὰ χρόα καλὸν ἰάψῃ·
Ἄϊδι προΐαψεν.

ἄλλως τε οὐ τὴν πόλιν λέγει τὸ Ἄργος (οὐ γὰρ ἐκεῖσε ἔμελλεν ἀφίξεσθαι), ἀλλὰ τὴν Πελοπόννησον, οὐ δήπου καὶ ταύτην διψηρὰν οὖσαν. καὶ σὺν τῷ δ δὲ ὑπερβατῶς δέχονταί τινες κατὰ συναλοιφὴν μετὰ τοῦ συνδέσμου τοῦ δέ· ἵν' ᾖ οὕτως,

καί κεν ἐλέγχιστος πολὺ δ' ἴψιον Ἄργος ἱκοίμην,

ἤγουν πολυίψιον[1] Ἄργοσδε ἱκοίμην ἀντὶ τοῦ εἰς Ἄργος.

C 371 8. Εἷς μὲν δὴ Ἴναχός ἐστιν ὁ διαρρέων τὴν Ἀργείαν· ἄλλος δὲ ποταμὸς Ἐρασῖνος ἐν τῇ Ἀργείᾳ ἐστίν· οὗτος δὲ τὰς ἀρχὰς ἐκ Στυμφάλου τῆς Ἀρκαδίας λαμβάνει καὶ τῆς ἐκεῖ λίμνης τῆς καλουμένης Στυμφαλίδος, ἐν ᾗ τὰς ὄρνεις μυθολογοῦσι τὰς ὑπὸ τοῦ Ἡρακλέους τοξεύμασι καὶ τυμπάνοις ἐξελαθείσας, ἃς[2] καὶ αὐτὰς καλοῦσι Στυμφαλίδας· δύντα δ' ὑπὸ γῆς φασὶ τὸν ποταμὸν τοῦτον ἐκπίπτειν εἰς τὴν Ἀργείαν καὶ ποιεῖν ἐπίρρυτον τὸ πεδίον· τὸν δ' Ἐρασῖνον καλοῦσι καὶ Ἀρσῖνον.[3] ῥεῖ δὲ καὶ ἄλλος ὁμώνυμος ἐκ τῆς Ἀρκαδίας εἰς τὸν κατὰ Βοῦραν

[1] Between ἱκοίμην and ψιον about ten letters have fallen out of the MSS. Instead of ἤγουν, which Kramer supplies, *no* has ἤτοι.

[2] ἅς, Corais inserts.

[3] The words τὸν . . . Ἀρσῖνον, Kramer suspects; Meineke ejects.

affliction: "Now he is merely making trial, but soon he will afflict[1] the sons of the Achaeans";[2] "mar[3] her fair flesh";[4] "untimely sent[5] to Hades."[6] And besides, Homer does not mean the city of Argos (for it was not thither that Agamemnon was about to return), but the Peloponnesus, which certainly is not a "thirsty" land either. Moreover some critics, retaining the δ, interpret the word by the figure *hyperbaton* and as a case of *synaloepha* with the connective δέ,[7] so that the verse would read thus: "And in utter shame would I return πολὺ δ' ἴψιον Ἄργος," that is to say, "would I return πολυίψιον Ἄργοσδε," where Ἄργοσδε stands for εἰς Ἄργος.

8. Now one of the rivers that flows through Argeia is the Inachus, but there is another river in Argeia, the Erasinus. The latter has its source in Stymphalus in Arcadia, that is, in the lake there which is called the Stymphalian Lake, which mythology makes the home of the birds that were driven out by the arrows and drums of Heracles; and the birds themselves are called Stymphalides. And they say that the Erasinus sinks beneath the ground and then issues forth in Argeia and waters the plain. The Erasinus is also called the Arsinus. And another river of the same name flows from Arcadia to the coast near Bura;

[1] ἴψεται, the primary meaning of which is "press hard," "oppress."

[2] *Iliad* 2. 193.

[3] ἰάψῃ. Primary meaning, "send on" or "drive on."

[4] *Odyssey* 2. 376.

[5] προΐαψεν.

[6] *Iliad* 1. 3.

[7] *i.e.* they take πολυδίψιον as an error for πολὺ δ' ἴψιον, and explain the error as due to the transposition (*hyperbaton*) of the δε in Ἄργοσδε and to the contraction into one word through the elision of the vowel ε (*synaloepha*).

αἰγιαλόν· ἄλλος δ' ἐστὶν ὁ Ἐρετρικός, καὶ ὁ ἐν τῇ Ἀττικῇ κατὰ Βραυρῶνα. δείκνυται δὲ καὶ Ἀμυμώνη τις κρήνη κατὰ Λέρνην. ἡ δὲ Λέρνη λίμνη τῆς Ἀργείας ἐστὶ καὶ τῆς Μυκηναίας, ἐν ᾗ τὴν Ὕδραν ἱστοροῦσι· διὰ δὲ τοὺς γινομένους καθαρμοὺς ἐν αὐτῇ παροιμία τις ἐξέπεσε, Λέρνη κακῶν. τὴν μὲν οὖν χώραν συγχωροῦσιν εὐυδρεῖν, αὐτὴν δὲ τὴν πόλιν ἐν ἀνύδρῳ[1] χωρίῳ μὲν κεῖσθαι, φρεάτων δ' εὐπορεῖν, ἃ ταῖς Δαναΐσιν ἀνάπτουσιν, ὡς ἐκείνων ἐξευρουσῶν· ἀφ' οὗ καὶ τὸ ἔπος εἰπεῖν τοῦτο·

> Ἄργος ἄνυδρον ἐὸν Δαναοὶ θέσαν Ἄργος ἔνυδρον·

τῶν δὲ φρεάτων τέτταρα καὶ ἱερὰ ἀποδειχθῆναι καὶ τιμᾶσθαι διαφερόντως, ἐν εὐπορίᾳ ὑδάτων ἀπορίαν εἰσάγοντες.

9. Τὴν δὲ ἀκρόπολιν τῶν Ἀργείων οἰκίσαι λέγεται Δαναός, ὃς τοσοῦτον τοὺς πρὸ αὐτοῦ δυναστεύοντας ἐν τοῖς τόποις ὑπερβαλέσθαι δοκεῖ, ὥστε κατ' Εὐριπίδην

> Πελασγιώτας ὠνομασμένους τὸ πρὶν
> Δαναοὺς καλεῖσθαι νόμον ἔθηκ' ἀν' Ἑλλάδα.

ἔστι δὲ καὶ τάφος αὐτοῦ κατὰ μέσην τὴν τῶν Ἀργείων ἀγοράν· καλεῖται δὲ Πάλινθος.[2] οἶμαι δ' ὅτι καὶ Πελασγιώτας καὶ Δαναούς, ὥσπερ καὶ Ἀργείους, ἡ δόξα τῆς πόλεως ταύτης ἀπ' αὐτῆς καὶ τοὺς ἄλλους Ἕλληνας καλεῖσθαι παρε-

[1] Between ἀνύδρῳ and κεῖσθαι A has a lacuna of about nine letters; B has χώρᾳ with χωρίῳ above *man. sec.* Kramer adds μέν.

[2] Πάλινθος, Meineke emends to πλίνθος, which is most tempting.

and there is another Erasinus in the territory of Eretria, and still another in Attica near Brauron. And a spring Amymonê is also pointed out near Lernê. And Lake Lernê, the scene of the story of the Hydra, lies in Argeia and the Mycenaean territory; and on account of the cleansings that take place in it there arose a proverb, "A Lernê of ills." Now writers agree that the country has plenty of water, and that, although the city itself lies in a waterless district, it has an abundance of wells. These wells they ascribe to the daughters of Danaüs, believing that they discovered them; and hence the utterance of this verse, "The daughters of Danaüs rendered Argos, which was waterless, Argos the well watered";[1] but they add that four of the wells not only were designated as sacred but are especially revered, thus introducing the false notion that there is a lack of water where there is an abundance of it.

9. The acropolis of the Argives is said to have been founded by Danaüs, who is reputed to have surpassed so much those who reigned in this region before him that, according to Euripides,[2] "throughout Greece he laid down a law that all people hitherto named Pelasgians should be called Danaans."[3] Moreover, his tomb is in the centre of the market-place of the Argives; and it is called Palinthus. And I think that it was the fame of this city that prepared the way, not only for the Pelasgians and the Danaans, as well as the Argives, to be named after it, but also for the rest of the Greeks; and

[1] Hesiod, *Frag.* 24 (Rzach). [2] *Frag.* 228. 7 (Nauck).
[3] Cp. 5. 2. 4.

σκευασεν· οὕτω δὲ καὶ Ἰασίδας καὶ Ἴασον Ἄργος καὶ Ἀπίαν καὶ Ἀπιδόνας οἱ νεώτεροί φασιν· Ὅμηρος δ' Ἀπιδόνας μὲν οὐ λέγει, ἀπίαν δὲ τὴν πόρρω μᾶλλον. ὅτι δ' Ἄργος τὴν Πελοπόννησον λέγει, προσλαβεῖν ἔστι καὶ τάδε,

> Ἀργείη δ' Ἑλένη·

καὶ

> ἔστι πόλις Ἐφύρη μυχῷ Ἄργεος,

καὶ

> μέσον Ἄργος,

καὶ

> πολλῇσιν νήσοισι καὶ Ἄργεϊ παντὶ ἀνάσσειν.

C 372 Ἄργος δὲ καὶ τὸ πεδίον λέγεται παρὰ τοῖς νεωτέροις, παρ' Ὁμήρῳ δ' οὐδ' ἅπαξ· μάλιστα δ' οἴονται Μακεδονικὸν καὶ Θετταλικὸν εἶναι.

10. Τῶν δ' ἀπογόνων τοῦ Δαναοῦ διαδεξαμένων τὴν ἐν Ἄργει δυναστείαν, ἐπιμιχθέντων δὲ τούτοις τῶν Ἀμυθαονιδῶν, ὡρμημένων ἐκ τῆς Πισάτιδος καὶ τῆς Τριφυλίας, οὐκ ἂν θαυμάσειέ τις, εἰ συγγενεῖς ὄντες οὕτω διείλοντο τὴν χώραν εἰς δύο βασιλείας τὸ πρῶτον, ὥστε τὰς ἡγεμονίδας[1] οὔσας ἐν αὐταῖς δύο πόλεις ἀποδειχθῆναι πλησίον ἀλλήλων ἱδρυμένας, ἐν ἐλάττοσιν ἢ πεντήκοντα σταδίοις, τό τε Ἄργος καὶ τὰς Μυκήνας, καὶ τὸ Ἡραῖον εἶναι κοινὸν ἱερὸν ἀμφοῖν[2] τὸ πρὸς ταῖς

[1] ἡγεμονίδας, Tzschucke, Kramer, and Müller-Dübner, following *Bl* (adding οὔσας), for ἡγεμονίας *aBl*. ἡγεμονικάς *no*, ἡγεμονευούσας (Pletho and Meineke), ἡγεμονίας *aBl*.

so, too, the more recent writers speak of "Iasidae," "Iasian Argos," "Apia," and "Apidones"; but Homer does not mention the "Apidones," though he uses the word "apia,"[1] rather of a "distant" land. To prove that by Argos the poet means the Peloponnesus, we can add the following examples: "Argive Helen,"[2] and "There is a city Ephyra in the inmost part of Argos,"[3] and "mid Argos,"[4] and "and that over many islands and all Argos he should be lord."[5] And in the more recent writers the plain, too, is called Argos, but not once in Homer. Yet they think that this is more especially a Macedonian or Thessalian usage.

10. After the descendants of Danaüs succeeded to the reign in Argos, and the Amythaonides, who were emigrants from Pisatis and Triphylia, became associated with these, one should not be surprised if, being kindred, they at first so divided the country into two kingdoms that the two cities in them which held the hegemony were designated as the capitals, though situated near one another, at a distance of less than fifty stadia, I mean Argos and Mycenae, and that the Heraeum[6] near Mycenae was a temple common to both. In this temple[7] are the images

[1] *Iliad* 1. 270, quoted by Strabo in 1. 1. 16.
[2] *Odyssey* 4. 296.
[3] *Iliad* 6. 152.
[4] *Odyssey* 1. 344.
[5] *Iliad* 2. 108.
[6] For a full account of the remarkable excavations at the Heraeum by the American School of Classical Studies, see Waldstein's *The Argive Heraeum*, 1902, 2 vols.
[7] The old temple was destroyed by fire in 423 B.C. (Thucydides 4. 133, Pausanias 2. 17) and the new one was built about 420 B.C. (Waldstein, *op. cit.*, p. 39).

---

[2] ἀμφοῖν, found here only in *no*, but in other MSS. after Μυκήναις.

Μυκήναις, ἐν ᾧ τὰ Πολυκλείτου ξόανα, τῇ μὲν τέχνῃ κάλλιστα τῶν πάντων, πολυτελείᾳ δὲ καὶ μεγέθει τῶν Φειδίου λειπόμενα. κατ' ἀρχὰς μὲν οὖν τὸ Ἄργος ἐπεκράτει μᾶλλον, εἶθ' αἱ Μυκῆναι, μείζονα ἐπίδοσιν λαβοῦσαι διὰ τὴν τῶν Πελοπιδῶν εἰς αὐτὰς μεθίδρυσιν· περιστάντων γὰρ εἰς τοὺς Ἀτρέως παῖδας ἁπάντων, Ἀγαμέμνων ὢν πρεσβύτερος, παραλαβὼν τὴν ἐξουσίαν, ἅμα τύχῃ τε καὶ ἀρετῇ πρὸς τοῖς οὖσι πολλὴν προσεκτήσατο τῆς χώρας· καὶ δὴ καὶ τὴν Λακωνικὴν[1] τῇ Μυκηναίᾳ προσέθηκε. Μενέλαος μὲν δὴ τὴν Λακωνικὴν ἔσχε, Μυκήνας δὲ καὶ τὰ μέχρι Κορίνθου καὶ Σικυῶνος καὶ τῆς Ἰώνων μὲν τότε καὶ Αἰγιαλέων καλουμένης, Ἀχαιῶν δὲ ὕστερον, Ἀγαμέμνων παρέλαβε. μετὰ δὲ τὰ Τρωικὰ τῆς Ἀγαμέμνονος ἀρχῆς καταλυθείσης, ταπεινωθῆναι συνέβη[2] Μυκήνας, καὶ μάλιστα μετὰ τὴν τῶν Ἡρακλειδῶν κάθοδον. κατασχόντες γὰρ οὗτοι τὴν Πελοπόννησον ἐξέβαλον τοὺς πρότερον κρατοῦντας, ὥσθ' οἱ τὸ Ἄργος ἔχοντες εἶχον καὶ τὰς Μυκήνας συντελούσας εἰς ἕν· χρόνοις δ' ὕστερον κατεσκάφησαν ὑπ' Ἀργείων, ὥστε νῦν μηδ' ἴχνος εὑρίσκεσθαι τῆς Μυκηναίων πόλεως. ὅπου δὲ Μυκῆναι τοιαῦτα πεπόνθασιν, οὐ δεῖ θαυμάζειν, οὐδ' εἴ τινες τῶν ὑπὸ τῷ Ἄργει καταλεγομένων

[1] Λακωνικήν, Xylander emends to Ἀργολικήν, following the tradition that Lacedaemon was presented to Menelaüs by his father-in-law Tyndareus; so Meineke.

[2] συνέβη, Pletho inserts; so Corais and Meineke.

---

[1] In particular the colossal image of Hera, which "is seated on a throne, is made of gold and ivory, and is a work

made by Polycleitus,[1] in execution the most beautiful in the world, but in costliness and size inferior to those by Pheidias. Now at the outset Argos was the more powerful, but later Mycenae waxed more powerful on account of the removal thereto of the Pelopidae; for, when everything fell to the sons of Atreus, Agamemnon, being the elder, assumed the supreme power, and by a combination of good fortune and valour acquired much of the country in addition to the possessions he already had; and indeed he also added Laconia to the territory of Mycenae. Now Menelaüs came into possession of Laconia, but Agamemnon received Mycenae and the regions as far as Corinth and Sicyon and the country which at that time was called the country of the Ionians and Aegialians but later the country of the Achaeans. But after the Trojan times, when the empire of Agememnon had been broken up, it came to pass that Mycenae was reduced, and particularly after the return of the Heracleidae; for when these had taken possession of the Peloponnesus they expelled its former masters, so that those who held Argos also held Mycenae as a component part of one whole. But in later times Mycenae was rased to the ground by the Argives, so that to-day not even a trace of the city of the Mycenaeans is to be found. And since Mycenae has suffered such a fate, one should not be surprised if also some of the cities which are catalogued as subject to Argos have now

of Polycleitus" (Pausanias 2. 17). According to E. L. Tilton's restoration (in Waldstein, *op. cit.*, Fig. 64, p. 127), the total height of the image including base and top of throne was about 8 metres and the seated figure of the goddess about 5⅓.

ἀφανεῖς νῦν εἰσίν. ὁ μὲν δὴ Κατάλογος ἔχει οὕτως·

οἳ δ' Ἄργος τ' εἶχον Τίρυνθά τε τειχιόεσσαν
Ἑρμιόνην τ' Ἀσίνην τε, βαθὺν κατὰ κόλπον ἐχούσας,
Τροιζῆν' Ἠιόνας τε καὶ ἀμπελόεντ' Ἐπίδαυρον,
οἵ τ' ἔχον Αἴγιναν Μάσητά τε, κοῦροι Ἀχαιῶν.

τούτων δὲ περὶ μὲν τοῦ Ἄργους εἴρηται, περὶ δὲ τῶν ἄλλων λεκτέον.

11. Τῇ μὲν οὖν Τίρυνθι ὁρμητηρίῳ χρήσασθαι
C 373 δοκεῖ Προῖτος καὶ τειχίσαι διὰ Κυκλώπων, οὓς ἑπτὰ μὲν εἶναι, καλεῖσθαι δὲ γαστερόχειρας,[1] τρεφομένους ἐκ τῆς τέχνης, ἥκειν δὲ μεταπέμπτους ἐκ Λυκίας· καὶ ἴσως τὰ σπήλαια τὰ περὶ τὴν Ναυπλίαν καὶ τὰ ἐν αὐτοῖς ἔργα τούτων ἐπώνυμά ἐστιν. ἡ δὲ ἀκρόπολις Λίκυμνα ἐπώνυμος Λικυμνίου, διέχει δὲ τῆς Ναυπλίας[2] περὶ δώδεκα σταδίους· ἔρημος δ' ἐστὶ κἀκείνη καὶ ἡ πλησίον Μιδέα, ἑτέρα οὖσα τῆς Βοιωτικῆς· ἐκείνη γάρ ἐστι Μίδεα,[3] ὡς Πρόνια, αὕτη δὲ Μιδέα, ὡς Τεγέα. ταύτῃ δ' ὅμορος Πρόσυμνα, . . . αὕτη[4]

[1] Corais inserts ὡς before τρεφομένους, following Eustathius (note on *Od.* 9. 183. p. 1622).

[2] Ναυπλίας *a*, Ναυπλίου A. Meineke reads *Ναυπλίους.

[3] Μίδεα (all MSS., and Eustathius, note on *Iliad* 2. 507, p. 270). Casaubon emends to Μίδεια ; so Meineke.

[4] Between Προσυ and αὕτη A has a lacuna of about nine or ten letters, except that *man. sec.* adds καί. In B καὶ . . . Ἥρας is omitted but added in margin *man. sec.* Kramer conjectures Πρόσυ[μνά ἐστι καὶ] αὕτη κτλ. Meineke conjectures [μνά ἐστι χώρα ἡ τὸ] omitting the αὕτη (*Vind. Strab.*), but in his text merely indicates a lacuna between Πρόσυμνα and αὕτη, not accepting the καί of the commonly adopted reading. Kramer's restoration may be right, but Jones conjectures χώρα or κώμη instead of his ἐστι.

disappeared. Now the *Catalogue* contains the following: "And those who held Argos, and Tiryns of the great walls, and Hermionê and Asinê that occupy a deep gulf, and Troezen and Eiones and vine-clad Epidaurus, and the youths of the Achaeans who held Aegina and Mases."[1] But of the cities just named I have already discussed Argos, and now I must discuss the others.

11. Now it seems that Tiryns was used as a base of operations by Proetus, and was walled by him through the aid of the Cyclopes, who were seven in number, and were called "Bellyhands" because they got their food from their handicraft, and they came by invitation from Lycia. And perhaps the caverns near Nauplia and the works therein are named after them.[2] The acropolis, Licymna, is named after Licymnius, and it is about twelve stadia distant from Nauplia; but it is deserted, and so is the neighbouring Midea, which is different from the Boeotian Midea; for the former is Mídea,[3] like Prónia,[4] while the latter is Midéa, like Tegéa. And bordering on Midea is Prosymna, . . .[5] this having a temple of

[1] *Iliad* 2. 559. [2] Cp. 8. 6. 2 (end).

[3] *i.e.* accented on the first syllable.

[4] The place and the name are still preserved in the modern Pronia near Nauplia.

[5] The text is corrupt (see critical note); and scholars, including Waldstein (*op. cit.*, p. 14), are still in doubt whether Strabo here refers to the same temple of Hera ("the common temple," "the Heraeum") previously mentioned or to an entirely different one. But the part of the clause that is unquestionably sound, together with other evidence, seems to prove that he is not referring to the Heraeum: (1) He says "*a* temple of Hera" and not "*the* temple" or "*the* Heraeum." (2) According to Pausanias (2. 17) Prosymna was the name of "the country *below* the Heraeum"; and therefore it did not include the Heraeum. (3) According to

ἱερὸν ἔχουσα Ἥρας· ἠρήμωσαν δὲ τὰς πλείστας οἱ Ἀργεῖοι ἀπειθούσας.[1] *οἱ δ' οἰκήτορες οἱ μὲν ἐκ τῆς Τίρυνθος ἀπῆλθον εἰς Ἐπίδαυρον, οἱ δὲ ε . . . εἰς τοὺς Ἁλιεῖς καλουμένους, οἱ δ' ἐκ τῆς Ἀσίνης (ἔστι δ' αὕτη κώμη τῆς Ἀργείας πλησίον Ναυπλίας) ὑπὸ Λακεδαιμονίων εἰς τὴν Μεσσηνίαν μετῳκίσθησαν ὅπου καὶ ἡ ὁμώνυμος τῇ Ἀργολικῇ Ἀσίνῃ πολίχνη. οἱ γὰρ Λακεδαιμόνιοι, φησὶν ὁ Θεόπομπος, πολλὴν κατακτησάμενοι τῆς ἀλλοτρίας εἰς ταύτην κατῴκιζον, οὓς ἂν ὑποδέξαιντο τῶν φυγόντων ἐπ' αὐτούς· καὶ οἱ*[2] *ἐκ τῆς Ναυπλίας ἐκεῖσε ἀνεχώρησαν.*

12. *Ἑρμιόνη δ' ἐστὶ τῶν οὐκ ἀσήμων πόλεων· ἧς τὴν παραλίαν ἔχουσιν Ἁλιεῖς λεγόμενοι θαλαττουργοί τινες ἄνδρες. παρ' Ἑρμιονεῦσι δὲ τεθρύληται τὴν εἰς Ἅιδου κατάβασιν σύντομον εἶναι· διόπερ οὐκ ἐντιθέασιν ἐνταῦθα τοῖς νεκροῖς ναῦλον.*

[1] In the passage *οἱ δ' οἰκήτορες κτλ.* there are six lacunae in A. The other MSS. are also corrupt, but their readings and corrections (see Kramer, note *ad loc.*, and C. Müller, *Ind. Var. Lect.* p. 997) assure the correctness of the above restorations (see Kramer's and Meineke's readings). The second lacuna Kramer, on the authority of B *man. sec.* supplies as follows: *οἱ δὲ ἐ[ξ Ἑρμιόνης] εἰς τοὺς Ἁλιεῖς*; but Curtius (cited by Kramer) and Meineke (*Vind. Strab.* 120), following conjecture of Ranke, rightly believe that Strabo wrote [*κ τῆς Μιδέας*].

[2] *καὶ οἱ*, supplied by *bkno*.

Stephanus Byzantinus, Prosymna was "a part of Argos," and its "founder" was "Prosymnaeus," which clearly indicates

Hera. But the Argives laid waste the most of the cities because of their disobedience; and of the inhabitants those from Tiryns migrated to Epidaurus, and those from . . .[1] to Halïeis, as it is called; but those from Asinê (this is a village in Argeia near Nauplia) were transferred by the Lacedaemonians to Messenia, where is a town that bears the same name as the Argolic Asinê; for the Lacedaemonians, says Theopompus, took possession of much territory that belonged to other peoples and settled there all who fled to them and were taken in. And the inhabitants of Nauplia also withdrew to Messenia.

12. Hermionê is one of the important cities; and its seaboard is held by the Halïeis,[2] as they are called, men who busy themselves on the sea. And it is commonly reported that the descent to Hades in the country of the Hermionians is a short cut; and this is why they do not put passage-money in the mouths of their dead.

[1] Either Hermionê or Midea (see critical note), but the latter seems correct.

[2] "Fishermen."

---

that it was an inhabited country. And since Strabo is now discussing only cities or towns (see last clause of § 10), one may infer that the country of Prosymna contained at least one town, for it was clearly "a large and wide tract" (Waldstein, *op. cit.*, p. 13, foot-note 1), perhaps even including "the site of such modern villages as Chonica, Anaphi, and Pasia" (*ibid.*, p. 14; see also map on p. 7). And one might further infer that the country even contained a town named Prosymna. In short, there seems to be no ground whatever for trying to identify the temple last mentioned with the Heraeum, though it is entirely possible that Strabo refers to some Prosymna, otherwise unknown, which had no connection with the Prosymna "below the Heraeum."

13. Δρυόπων δ' οἰκητήριόν φασι καὶ[1] τὴν Ἀσίνην, εἴτ' ἐκ τῶν περὶ Σπερχειὸν τόπων ὄντας αὐτοὺς Δρύοπος τοῦ Ἀρκάδος κατοικίσαντος ἐνταῦθα, ὡς Ἀριστοτέλης φησίν, εἴθ'[2] Ἡρακλέους ἐκ τῆς περὶ τὸν Παρνασσὸν Δωρίδος ἐξελάσαντος αὐτούς. τὸ δὲ Σκύλλαιον τὸ ἐν Ἑρμιόνῃ ὠνομάσθαι φασὶν ἀπὸ Σκύλλης τῆς Νίσου θυγατρός, ἥν ἐξ ἔρωτος προδοῦσαν Μίνῳ τὴν Νισαίαν καταποντωθῆναί φασιν ὑπ' αὐτοῦ, δεῦρο δ' ἐκκυμανθεῖσαν ταφῆς τυχεῖν. Ἠιόνες δὲ κώμη τις ἦν, ἣν ἐρημώσαντες Μυκηναῖοι ναύσταθμον ἐποίησαν, ἀφανισθεῖσα δ' ὕστερον οὐδὲ ναύσταθμόν ἐστιν.

14. Τροιζὴν δὲ ἱερά ἐστι Ποσειδῶνος, ἀφ' οὗ καὶ Ποσειδωνία ποτὲ ἐλέγετο, ὑπέρκειται δὲ τῆς θαλάττης εἰς πεντεκαίδεκα σταδίους, οὐδ' αὕτη ἄσημος πόλις. πρόκειται δὲ τοῦ λιμένος αὐτῆς, Πώγωνος τοὔνομα, Καλαυρία νησίδιον ὅσον ἑκατὸν καὶ[3] τριάκοντα σταδίων ἔχον τὸν κύκλον· ἐνταῦθα ἦν ἄσυλον Ποσειδῶνος ἱερόν, καί φασι τὸν θεὸν τοῦτον ἀλλάξασθαι πρὸς μὲν Λητὼ τὴν
C 374 Καλαυρίαν ἀντιδόντα Δῆλον, πρὸς Ἀπόλλωνα δὲ Ταίναρον ἀντιδόντα Πυθώ. Ἔφορος δὲ καὶ τὸν χρησμὸν λέγει·

Ἶσόν τοι Δῆλόν τε Καλαύρειάν τε νέμεσθαι,
Πυθώ τ' ἠγαθέην καὶ Ταίναρον ἠνεμόεντα.

ἦν δὲ καὶ Ἀμφικτυονία τις περὶ τὸ ἱερὸν τοῦτο

[1] καί is omitted by E, but Eustathius (note on *Iliad* 2. 560, p. 287) says: λέγει δὲ (ὁ γεώγραφος) καὶ ὅτι Ἀσίνη καὶ Ἑρμιὼν Δρυόπων οἰκητήριον.

[2] εἴθ', Kramer, for ἢ ὑφ' *Aghino*; omitted by BE*l*.

13. It is said that Asinê too[1] was a habitation of the Dryopians—whether, being inhabitants of the regions of the Spercheius, they were settled here by the Arcadian Dryops,[2] as Aristotle has said, or whether they were driven by Heracles out of the part of Doris that is near Parnassus. As for the Scyllaeum in Hermionê, they say that it was named after Scylla, the daughter of Nisus, who, they say, out of love for Minos betrayed Nisaea to him and was drowned in the sea by him, and was here cast ashore by the waves and buried. Eiones was a village, which was depopulated by the Mycenaeans and made into a naval station, but later it disappeared from sight and now is not even a naval station.

14. Troezen is sacred to Poseidon, after whom it was once called Poseidonia. It is situated fifteen stadia above the sea, and it too is an important city. Off its harbour, Pogon by name, lies Calauria, an isle with a circuit of about one hundred and thirty stadia. Here was an asylum sacred to Poseidon; and they say that this god made an exchange with Leto, giving her Delos for Calauria, and also with Apollo, giving him Pytho[3] for Taenarum. And Ephorus goes on to tell the oracle: "For thee it is the same thing to possess Delos or Calauria, most holy Pytho or windy Taenarum." And there was also a kind of Amphictyonic League connected with

[1] *i.e.* as well as Hermionê.
A fragment otherwise unknown. [3] Delphi.

[3] ἑκατὸν καί, Jones inserts (cp. same emendation in 8. 6. 3).

ἑπτὰ πόλεων, αἳ μετεῖχον τῆς θυσίας· ἦσαν δὲ Ἑρμιών, Ἐπίδαυρος, Αἴγινα, Ἀθῆναι, Πρασιεῖς, Ναυπλιεῖς, Ὀρχομενὸς ὁ Μινύειος· ὑπὲρ μὲν οὖν Ναυπλίων Ἀργεῖοι συνετέλουν, ὑπὲρ Πρασιέων δὲ Λακεδαιμόνιοι. οὕτω δ' ἐπεκράτησεν ἡ τιμὴ τοῦ θεοῦ τούτου παρὰ τοῖς Ἕλλησιν, ὥστε καὶ Μακεδόνες δυναστεύοντες ἤδη μέχρι δεῦρο ἐφύλαττόν πως τὴν ἀσυλίαν, καὶ τοὺς ἱκέτας ἀποσπᾶν ᾐδοῦντο τοὺς εἰς Καλαυρίαν καταφυγόντας· ὅπου γε οὐδὲ Δημοσθένη ἐθάρρησεν Ἀρχίας βιάσασθαι στρατιώτας ἔχων, ᾧ προσετέτακτο ὑπὸ Ἀντιπάτρου ζῶντα ἀγαγεῖν κἀκεῖνον καὶ τῶν ἄλλων ῥητόρων ὃν ἂν εὕρῃ τῶν ἐν ταῖς αἰτίαις ὄντων ταῖς παραπλησίοις, ἀλλὰ πείθειν ἐπειρᾶτο· οὐ μὴν ἔπεισέ γε, ἀλλ' ἔφθη φαρμάκῳ παραλύσας ἑαυτὸν τοῦ ζῆν· Τροιζὴν δὲ καὶ Πιτθεύς, οἱ Πέλοπος, ὁρμηθέντες ἐκ τῆς Πισάτιδος, ὁ μὲν τὴν πόλιν ὁμώνυμον ἑαυτοῦ κατέλιπεν, ὁ δὲ Πιτθεὺς ἐβασίλευσεν, ἐκεῖνον διαδεξάμενος. Ἄνθης δ' ὁ προκατέχων πλεύσας Ἁλικαρνασὸν ἔκτισεν· ἐροῦμεν δ' ἐν τοῖς Καρικοῖς περὶ τούτων[1] καὶ τοῖς Τρωικοῖς.

15. Ἡ Ἐπίδαυρος δ' ἐκαλεῖτο Ἐπίκαρος·[2] φησὶ γὰρ Ἀριστοτέλης κατασχεῖν αὐτὴν Κᾶρας, ὥσπερ καὶ Ἑρμιόνα· τῶν δὲ Ἡρακλειδῶν κατελθόντων, Ἴωνας αὐτοῖς συνοικῆσαι τοὺς ἐκ τῆς Ἀττικῆς Τετραπόλεως συνεπομένους εἰς Ἄργος.

[1] περὶ τούτων, the conjecture of Kramer for the lacuna, followed by —ον, of about eight letters in A.

[2] Ἐπίκαρος, Jones, for Ἐπίταυρος (see Müller's *Ind. Var. Lect.* p. 997, and especially Eustathius' note on *Iliad* 2. 567, p. 287), *a* having κα above ταυ.

this temple, a league of seven cities which shared in the sacrifice; they were Hermion,[1] Epidaurus, Aegina, Athens, Prasïeis, Nauplïeis, and Orchomenus Minyeius; however, the Argives paid dues for the Nauplians, and the Lacedaemonians for the Prasians. The worship of this god was so prevalent among the Greeks that even the Macedonians, whose power already extended as far as the temple, in a way preserved its inviolability, and were afraid to drag away the suppliants who fled for refuge to Calauria; indeed Archias, with soldiers, did not venture to do violence even to Demosthenes, although he had been ordered by Antipater to bring him alive, both him and all the other orators he could find that were under similar charges, but tried to persuade him; he could not persuade him, however, and Demosthenes forestalled him by killing himself with poison. Now Troezen and Pittheus, the sons of Pelops, came originally from Pisatis; and the former left behind him the city which was named after him, and the latter succeeded him and reigned as king. But Anthes, who previously had possession of the place, set sail and founded Halicarnassus; but concerning this I shall speak in my description of Caria and Troy.[2]

15. Epidaurus used to be called Epicarus, for Aristotle says that Carians took possession of it, as also of Hermionê, but that after the return of the Heracleidae the Ionians who had accompanied the Heracleidae from the Attic Tetrapolis[3] to Argos took up their abode with these Carians.[4] Epidaurus,

[1] The same as Hermionê. [2] 14. 2. 16.

[3] "Four-city," *i.e.* the northern part of Attica containing the four demes Marathon, Oenoê, Probalinthus and Tricorynthus. [4] A fragment otherwise unknown.

καὶ αὕτη δ' οὐκ ἄσημος ἡ πόλις, καὶ μάλιστα διὰ τὴν ἐπιφάνειαν τοῦ Ἀσκληπιοῦ θεραπεύειν νόσους παντοδαπὰς πεπιστευμένου, καὶ τὸ ἱερὸν πλῆρες ἔχοντος ἀεὶ τῶν τε καμνόντων καὶ τῶν ἀνακειμένων πινάκων, ἐν οἷς ἀναγεγραμμέναι τυγχάνουσιν αἱ θεραπεῖαι, καθάπερ ἐν Κῷ τε καὶ Τρίκκῃ. κεῖται δ' ἡ πόλις ἐν μυχῷ τοῦ Σαρωνικοῦ κόλπου, τὸν περίπλουν ἔχουσα σταδίων πεντεκαίδεκα, βλέπουσα πρὸς ἀνατολὰς θερινάς· περικλείεται δ' ὄρεσιν ὑψηλοῖς μέχρι πρὸς τὴν θάλατταν, ὥστ' ἐρυμνὴ κατεσκεύασται φυσικῶς πανταχόθεν.[1] μεταξὺ δὲ Τροιζῆνος καὶ Ἐπιδαύρου χωρίον ἦν ἐρυμνὸν Μέθανα καὶ χερρόνησος ὁμώνυμος τούτῳ· παρὰ Θουκυδίδῃ δὲ ἔν τισιν ἀντιγράφοις Μεθώνη φέρεται ὁμωνύμως[2] τῇ Μακεδονικῇ, ἐν ᾗ Φίλιππος ἐξεκόπη τὸν
C 375 ὀφθαλμὸν πολιορκῶν· διόπερ οἴεταί τινας ἐξαπατηθέντας ὁ Σκήψιος Δημήτριος τὴν ἐν τῇ Τροιζηνίᾳ[3] Μεθώνην ὑπονοεῖν, καθ' ἧς ἀράσασθαι λέγεται τοὺς ὑπ' Ἀγαμέμνονος πεμφθέντας ναυτολόγους, μηδέποτε παύσασθαι τοῦ[4] τειχοδομεῖν, οὐ τούτων, ἀλλὰ τῶν Μακεδόνων ἀνανευσάντων, ὥς φησι Θεόπομπος· τούτους δ' οὐκ εἰκός, ἐγγὺς ὄντας, ἀπειθῆσαι.

16. Αἴγινα δ' ἐστὶ μὲν καὶ τόπος τις τῆς Ἐπιδαυρίας, ἔστι δὲ καὶ νῆσος πρὸ τῆς ἠπείρου ταύτης, ἣν ἐν τοῖς ἀρτίως παρατεθεῖσιν ἔπεσι

[1] Here again (see Vol. III. p. 321, footnote 2), beginning with μεταξύ and ending with Κυλλήνη (8. 8. 1), A has lost a whole quaternion; (see Kramer, note *ad loc.*).

[2] ὁμωνύμως, Kramer, for ὁμώνυμος; so the later editors.

[3] Τροιζηνίᾳ, Meineke, for Τροιζῆνι.

too, is an important city, and particularly because of the fame of Asclepius, who is believed to cure diseases of every kind and always has his temple full of the sick, and also of the votive tablets on which the treatments are recorded, just as at Cos and Triccê. The city lies in the recess of the Saronic Gulf, has a circular coast of fifteen stadia, and faces the summer risings of the sun.[1] It is enclosed by high mountains which reach as far as the sea, so that on all sides it is naturally fitted for a stronghold. Between Troezen and Epidaurus there was a stronghold called Methana, and also a peninsula of the same name. In some copies of Thucydides the name is spelled "Methonê," the same as the Macedonian city in which Philip, in the siege, had his eye knocked out. And it is on this account, in the opinion of Demetrius of Scepsis, that some writers, being deceived, suppose that it was the Methonê in the territory of Troezen against which the men sent by Agamemnon to collect sailors are said to have uttered the imprecation that its citizens might never cease from their wall-building, since, in his opinion, it was not these citizens that refused, but those of the Macedonian city, as Theopompus says; and it is not likely, he adds, that these citizens who were near to Agamemnon disobeyed him.

16. Aegina is the name of a place in [a]Epidauria; and it is also the name of an island lying off this part of the mainland—the Aegina of which the poet

[1] North-east.

---

[a] τοῦ, Meineke inserts.

βούλεται φράζειν ὁ ποιητής· διὸ καὶ γράφουσί τινες

νῆσόν τ' Αἴγιναν,

ἀντὶ τοῦ

οἵ τ'[1] ἔχον Αἴγιναν,

διαστελλόμενοι τὴν ὁμωνυμίαν. ὅτι μὲν οὖν τῶν σφόδρα γνωρίμων ἐστὶν ἡ νῆσος, τί δεῖ λέγειν; ἐντεῦθεν γὰρ Αἰακός τε λέγεται καὶ οἱ ὑπ' αὐτόν.[2] αὕτη δ' ἐστὶν ἡ καὶ θαλαττοκρατήσασά ποτε καὶ περὶ πρωτείων ἀμφισβητήσασα πρὸς Ἀθηναίους ἐν τῇ περὶ Σαλαμῖνα ναυμαχίᾳ κατὰ τὰ Περσικά. λέγεται δὲ σταδίων ἑκατὸν ὀγδοήκοντα ὁ κύκλος τῆς νήσου, πόλιν δ' ὁμώνυμον ἔχει τετραμμένην πρὸς Λίβα· περιέχουσι δ' αὐτὴν ἥ τε Ἀττικὴ καὶ ἡ Μεγαρὶς καὶ τῆς Πελοποννήσου τὰ μέχρι Ἐπιδαύρου, σχεδόν τι ἑκατὸν σταδίους ἑκάστη διέχουσα· τὸ δὲ ἑωθινὸν μέρος καὶ τὸ νότιον πελάγει κλύζεται τῷ τε Μυρτῴῳ καὶ τῷ Κρητικῷ· νησίδια δὲ περίκειται πολλὰ μὲν πρὸς τῇ ἠπείρῳ, Βέλβινα δὲ πρὸς τὸ πέλαγος ἀνατείνουσα. ἡ δὲ χώρα αὐτῆς κατὰ βάθους μὲν γεώδης ἐστί, πετρώδης δ' ἐπιπολῆς, καὶ μάλιστα ἡ πεδιάς· διόπερ ψιλὴ πᾶσά ἐστι, κριθοφόρος δὲ ἱκανῶς. Μυρμιδόνας δὲ κληθῆναί φασιν, οὐχ ὡς ὁ μῦθος, τοὺς Αἰγινήτας, ὅτι λοιμοῦ μεγάλου συμπεσόντος οἱ μύρμηκες ἄνθρωποι γένοιντο κατ' εὐχὴν Αἰακοῦ, ἀλλ' ὅτι μυρμήκων τρόπον ὀρύττοντες τὴν γῆν ἐπισπείροιεν[3] ἐπὶ τὰς πέτρας, ὥστ' ἔχειν γε-

[1] οἵ τ' (as in 8. 6. 10), Corais, for οἱ δ'.
[2] ὑπ' αὐτόν, Meineke emends to ἀπ' αὐτοῦ.

means to speak in the verses just cited;[1] and it is on this account that some write "the island Aegina" instead of "who held Aegina,"[2] thus distinguishing between places of the same name. Now what need have I to say that the island is one of the most famous? for it is said that both Aeacus and his subjects were from there. And this is the island that was once actually mistress of the sea and disputed with the Athenians for the prize of valour in the sea-fight at Salamis at the time of the Persian War. The island is said to be one hundred and eighty stadia in circuit; and it has a city of the same name that faces south-west; and it is surrounded by Attica, Megaris, and the Peloponnesus as far as Epidaurus, being distant about one hundred stadia from each; and its eastern and southern sides are washed by the Myrtoan and Cretan Seas; and around it lie small islands, many of them near the mainland, though Belbina extends to the high sea. The country of Aegina is fertile at a depth below the surface, but rocky on the surface, and particularly the level part; and therefore the whole country is bare, although it is fairly productive of barley. It is said that the Aeginetans were called Myrmidons,—not as the myth has it, because, when a great famine occurred, the ants[3] became human beings in answer to a prayer of Aeacus, but because they excavated the earth after the manner of ants and spread the soil over the rocks, so as to have ground to till, and

[1] § 10. [2] *Iliad* 2. 562.

[3] The transliterated Greek word for "ants" is "myrmeces."

---

[3] ἐπισπείροιεν (B*kl* and Ald.), ἐπιφέροιεν (E*acghino* and the editors in general).

ωργεῖν, ἐν δὲ τοῖς ὀρύγμασιν οἰκεῖν φειδόμενοι πλίνθων. ὠνομάζετο δ' Οἰνώνη πάλαι ὁμωνύμως δυσὶ δήμοις τῆς Ἀττικῆς, τῷ τε πρὸς Ἐλευθεραῖς,

Οἰνώνῃ[1]
σύγχορτα ναίειν πεδία ταῖς δ' Ἐλευθεραῖς,

καὶ μιᾷ τῶν ἐκ τετραπόλεως τῆς περὶ Μαραθῶνα, καθ' ἧς ἡ παροιμία· Οἰνώνῃ τὴν χαράδραν.[2] ἐπῴκησαν δ' αὐτὴν Ἀργεῖοι καὶ Κρῆτες καὶ Ἐπιδαύριοι καὶ Δωριεῖς, ὕστερον δὲ κατεκληρούχησαν τὴν νῆσον Ἀθηναῖοι· ἀφελόμενοι δὲ
C 376 Λακεδαιμόνιοι τοὺς Ἀθηναίους τὴν νῆσον ἀπέδοσαν τοῖς ἀρχαίοις οἰκήτορσιν. ἀποίκους δ' ἔστειλαν Αἰγινῆται εἴς τε Κυδωνίαν τὴν ἐν Κρήτῃ καὶ εἰς Ὀμβρικούς. Ἔφορος δ' ἐν Αἰγίνῃ ἄργυρον πρῶτον κοπῆναί φησιν ὑπὸ Φείδωνος· ἐμπόριον γὰρ γενέσθαι, διὰ τὴν λυπρότητα τῆς χώρας τῶν ἀνθρώπων θαλαττουργούντων ἐμπορικῶς, ἀφ' οὗ τὸν ῥῶπον Αἰγιναίαν ἐμπολὴν λέγεσθαι.

17. Ὁ δὲ ποιητὴς ἔνια μὲν χωρία λέγει συνεχῶς, ὥσπερ καὶ κεῖται·

οἵ θ' Ὑρίην ἐνέμοντο καὶ Αὐλίδα,
οἳ δ' Ἄργος τ' εἶχον Τίρυνθά τε,
Ἑρμιόνην τ' Ἀσίνην τε,
Τροιζῆν' Ἠιόνας τε·

[1] Οἰνώνῃ, Tzschucke emends to Οἰνόῃ, Corais to Οἰνόης.
[2] Meineke relegates ὁμωνύμως . . . χαράδραν to the foot of the page as a gloss.

---

[1] On the demes and their number see 9. 1. 16 ff.
[2] The authorship of these words is unknown.
[3] See foot-note on 8. 6. 15.

because they lived in the dugouts, refraining from the use of soil for bricks. Long ago Aegina was called Oenonê, the same name as that of two demes[1] in Attica, one near Eleutherae, "to inhabit the plains that border on Oenonê and Eleutherae";[2] and another, one of the demes of the Marathonian Tetrapolis,[3] to which is applied the proverb, "To Oenonê —the torrent."[4] Aegina was colonised successively by the Argives, the Cretans, the Epidaurians, and the Dorians; but later the Athenians divided it by lot among settlers of their own; and then the Lacedaemonians took the island away from the Athenians and gave it back to its ancient settlers. And colonists were sent forth by the Aeginetans both to Cydonia in Crete and to the country of the Ombrici.[5] Ephorus says that silver was first coined in Aegina, by Pheidon; for the island, he adds, became a merchant-centre, since, on account of the poverty of the soil, the people employed themselves at sea as merchants, and hence, he adds, petty wares were called "Aeginetan merchandise."

17. The poet mentions some places in the order in which they are actually situated; "and these dwelt in Hyria and Aulis,"[6] "and those who held Argos and Tiryns, Hermionê and Asinê, Troezen and Eiones";[7]

[4] The whole passage, "the same name . . . torrent," is believed to be spurious, for "Oenonê" is well attested as a former name of Aegina, while the name of the two Attic demes was "Oenoê," not "Oenonê." Moreover, the proverb referred to "Oenoê," not "Oenonê." The inhabitants of Oenoê diverted the torrent "Charadra" for the purpose of irrigation. Much damage was the result, and hence the proverb came to be applied to people who were the authors of their own misfortunes.

[5] See 5. 2. 10. [6] *Iliad* 2. 496. [7] *Iliad* 2. 559.

ἄλλοτε δ', οὐχ ὡς ἔστι τῇ τάξει,

> Σχοῖνόν τε Σκῶλόν τε,
> Θέσπειαν Γραῖάν τε·

τά τ' ἐν ἠπείρῳ ταῖς νήσοις συμφράζει,

> οἵ ῥ' Ἰθάκην εἶχον,
> καὶ Κροκύλει' ἐνέμοντο·

τὰ γὰρ Κροκύλεια ἐν τοῖς Ἀκαρνᾶσιν. οὕτω δὲ καὶ νῦν τῇ Αἰγίνῃ τὸν Μάσητα συνῆψεν, ὄντα τῆς Ἀργολικῆς ἠπείρου. Θυρέας[1] δὲ Ὅμηρος μὲν οὐκ ὠνόμασεν, οἱ δ' ἄλλοι θρυλοῦσι· περὶ ὧν Ἀργείοις καὶ Λακεδαιμονίοις συνέστη ἀγών, τριακοσίοις πρὸς τριακοσίους· ἐνίκων δὲ Λακεδαιμόνιοι, στρατηγοῦντος Ὀθρυάδα· εἶναι δέ φησι τὸ χωρίον τοῦτο Θουκυδίδης ἐν τῇ Κυνουρίᾳ[2] κατὰ τὴν μεθορίαν τῆς Ἀργείας καὶ τῆς Λακωνικῆς. εἰσὶ δὲ καὶ Ὑσίαι, τόπος γνώριμος τῆς Ἀργολικῆς, καὶ Κεγχρεαί, αἳ κεῖνται ἐπὶ τῇ ὁδῷ τῇ ἐκ Τεγέας εἰς Ἄργος διὰ τοῦ Παρθενίου ὄρους καὶ τοῦ Κρεοπώλου.[3] Ὅμηρος δ' αὐτὰς οὐκ οἶδεν, οὐδὲ τὸ Λύρκειον,[4] οὐδ' Ὀρνεάς· κῶμαι δ' εἰσὶ τῆς Ἀργείας, ἡ μὲν ὁμώνυμος τῷ ὄρει τῷ πλησίον,[5] αἱ δὲ ταῖς Ὀρνεαῖς ταῖς μεταξὺ Κορίνθου καὶ Σικυῶνος ἱδρυμέναις.[6]

[1] Θυρέας, Xylander, for Θυραίας; so the later editors.

[2] Κυνουρίᾳ (*o* and the editors), for Κυνοσουρίᾳ.

[3] Κρεωπόλου B, Κρεεπολ *ag*, Κρεεπόλου *o*, Κρεσπώλου *c*. But Meineke relegates καὶ τοῦ Κρεοπώλου to the foot of the page. Some (see Kramer, note *ad loc.*) think that Strabo refers to Κρεῖον, the mountain near Argos mentioned by Callimachus.

but at other times not in their actual order: "Schoenus and Scolus, Thespeia and Graea";[1] and he mentions the places on the mainland at the same time with the islands: "those who held Ithaca and dwelt in Crocyleia,"[2] for Crocyleia is in the country of the Acarnanians. And so, also, he here[3] connects Mases with Aegina, although it is in Argolis on the mainland. Homer does not name Thyreae, although the others often speak of it; and it was concerning Thyreae that a contest arose between the Argives and the Lacedaemonians, three hundred against three hundred;[4] but the Lacedaemonians under the generalship of Othryadas won the victory. Thucydides says that this place is in Cynuria on the common border of Argeia and Laconia. And there are also Hysiae, a well-known place in Argolis, and Cenchreae, which lies on the road that leads from Tegea to Argos through Mt. Parthenius[5] and Creopolus,[6] but Homer does not know them. Nor yet does he know Lyrceium[7] nor Orneae, which are villages in Argeia, the former bearing the same name as the mountain near it and the latter the same as the Orneae which is situated between Corinth and Sicyon.

[1] *Iliad* 2. 497.
[2] *Iliad* 2. 632.
[3] *Iliad* 2. 562.
[4] So Herodotus 1. 82.
[5] So Pausanias 8. 6.
[6] See critical note.
[7] See critical note.

---

[4] Λύρκειον (conj. of Casaubon) Jones, for Λυκούργιον (see 6. 2. 4).

[5] πλησίον, Jones inserts after τῷ, filling the lacuna of about eight letters (Λυρκεί, Groskurd).

[6] The words οὐδὲ . . . ἱδρυμέναις are suspected by Kramer, and ejected by Meineke.

18. Τῶν δὴ[1] κατὰ Πελοπόννησον πόλεων ἐνδοξόταται γεγόνασι καὶ μέχρι νῦν εἰσὶν Ἄργος τε Σπάρτη τε, διὰ δὲ τὸ πολυθρύλητον ἥκιστα δεῖ μακρολογεῖν περὶ αὐτῶν· τὰ γὰρ ὑπὸ πάντων εἰρημένα λέγειν δόξομεν. τὸ παλαιὸν μὲν οὖν ηὐδοκίμει τὸ Ἄργος μᾶλλον, ὕστερον δὲ καὶ μέχρι παντὸς ὑπερεβάλοντο Λακεδαιμόνιοι καὶ διετέλεσαν τὴν αὐτονομίαν φυλάττοντες, πλὴν εἴ τί που μικρὸν προσπταίειν αὐτοὺς συνέβαινεν. Ἀργεῖοι δὲ Πύρρον μὲν οὐκ ἐδέξαντο, ἀλλὰ καὶ πρὸ τοῦ τείχους ἔπεσε, γραϊδίου τινός, ὡς ἔοικε,
C 377 κεραμίδα ἀφέντος ἄνωθεν ἐπὶ τὴν κεφαλήν, ὑπ᾽ ἄλλοις δ᾽ ἐγένοντο βασιλεῦσι· μετασχόντες δὲ τοῦ τῶν Ἀχαιῶν συστήματος σὺν ἐκείνοις εἰς τὴν τῶν Ῥωμαίων ἐξουσίαν ἦλθον, καὶ νῦν συνέστηκεν ἡ πόλις, δευτερεύουσα τῇ τάξει μετὰ τὴν Σπάρτην.

19. Ἑξῆς δὲ λέγωμεν περὶ τῶν ὑπὸ Μυκήναις καὶ τῷ Ἀγαμέμνονι τεταγμένων τόπων ἐν τῷ Καταλόγῳ τῶν νεῶν· ἔχει δ᾽ οὕτω τὰ ἔπη·

οἳ δὲ Μυκήνας εἶχον, ἐϋκτίμενον πτολίεθρον,
ἀφνειόν τε Κόρινθον ἐϋκτιμένας τε Κλεωνάς,
Ὀρνειάς τ᾽ ἐνέμοντο Ἀραιθυρέην τ᾽ ἐρατεινήν
καὶ Σικυῶν᾽, ὅθ᾽ ἄρ᾽ Ἄδρηστος πρῶτ᾽ ἐμβασίλευεν,
οἵ θ᾽ Ὑπερησίην τε καὶ αἰπεινὴν Γονόεσσαν
Πελλήνην τ᾽ εἶχον, ἠδ᾽ Αἴγιον ἀμφενέμοντο
Αἰγιαλόν τ᾽ ἀνὰ πάντα καὶ ἀμφ᾽ Ἑλίκην εὐρεῖαν.

αἱ μὲν οὖν Μυκῆναι νῦν οὐκέτ᾽ εἰσίν, ἔκτισε δ᾽ αὐτὰς Περσεύς, διεδέξατο δὲ Σθένελος, εἶτ᾽ Εὐρυσθεύς· οἱ δ᾽ αὐτοὶ καὶ τοῦ Ἄργους ἦρξαν. Εὐρυσθεὺς

[1] δή, Kramer, for δέ B (?), γοῦν *no*; so the later editors.

18. So then, of the cities in the Peloponnesus, Argos and Sparta prove to have been, and still are, the most famous; and, since they are much spoken of, there is all the less need for me to describe them at length, for if I did so I should seem to be repeating what has been said by all writers. Now in early times Argos was the more famous, but later and ever afterwards the Lacedaemonians excelled, and persisted in preserving their autonomy, except perhaps when they chanced to make some slight blunder.[1] Now the Argives did not, indeed, admit Pyrrhus into their city (in fact, he fell before the walls, when a certain old woman, as it seems, dropped a tile upon his head), but they became subject to other kings; and after they had joined the Achaean League they came, along with the Achaeans, under the dominion of Rome; and their city persists to this day second in rank after Sparta.

19. But let me speak next of the places which are named in the *Catalogue of Ships* as subject to Mycenae and Menelaüs. The words of the poet are as follows: "And those who held Mycenae, well-built fortress, and wealthy Corinth and well-built Cleonae, and dwelt in Orneiae and lovely Araethyreê and Sicyon, wherein Adrastus was king at the first; and those who held Hyperesiê and steep Gonoessa and Pellenê, and dwelt about Aegium and through all the Aegialus[2] and about broad Helicê."[3] Now Mycenae is no longer in existence, but it was founded by Perseus, and Perseus was succeeded by Sthenelus, and Sthenelus by Eurystheus; and the same men ruled over Argos also. Now

[1] For example, against the Roman praetors (see 8. 5. 5).
[2] "Shore-land."
[3] *Iliad* 2. 569 ff.

μὲν οὖν στρατεύσας εἰς Μαραθῶνα ἐπὶ τοὺς Ἡρακλέους παῖδας καὶ Ἰόλαον, βοηθησάντων Ἀθηναίων, ἱστορεῖται πεσεῖν ἐν τῇ μάχῃ, καὶ τὸ μὲν ἄλλο σῶμα Γαργηττοῖ ταφῆναι, τὴν δὲ κεφαλὴν χωρὶς ἐν Τρικορύνθῳ,[1] ἀποκόψαντος αὐτὴν Ἰολάου, περὶ τὴν κρήνην τὴν Μακαρίαν[2] ὑπὸ ἁμαξιτόν· καὶ ὁ τόπος καλεῖται Εὐρυσθέως κεφαλή. αἱ δὲ Μυκῆναι μετέπεσον εἰς τοὺς Πελοπίδας, ὁρμηθέντας ἐκ τῆς Πισάτιδος, εἶτ' εἰς τοὺς Ἡρακλείδας, καὶ τὸ Ἄργος ἔχοντας. μετὰ δὲ τὴν ἐν Σαλαμῖνι ναυμαχίαν Ἀργεῖοι μετὰ Κλεωναίων καὶ Τεγεατῶν ἐπελθόντες ἄρδην τὰς Μυκήνας ἀνεῖλον καὶ τὴν χώραν διενείμαντο. διὰ δὲ τὴν ἐγγύτητα τὰς δύο πόλεις ὡς μίαν οἱ τραγικοὶ συνωνύμως προσαγορεύουσιν, Εὐριπίδης δέ, καὶ ἐν τῷ αὐτῷ δράματι, τοτὲ μὲν Μυκήνας καλῶν, τοτὲ δ' Ἄργος τὴν αὐτὴν πόλιν, καθάπερ ἐν Ἰφιγενείᾳ καὶ Ὀρέστῃ. Κλεωναὶ δ' εἰσὶ πόλισμα ἐπὶ τῇ ὁδῷ κείμενον τῇ ἐξ Ἄργους εἰς Κόρινθον ἐπὶ λόφου περιοικουμένου πανταχόθεν καὶ τετειχισμένου καλῶς, ὥστ' οἰκείως εἰρῆσθαί μοι δοκεῖ τὸ ἐϋκτιμένας Κλεωνάς. ἐνταῦθα δὲ καὶ ἡ Νεμέα μεταξὺ Κλεωνῶν καὶ Φλιοῦντος καὶ τὸ ἄλσος, ἐν ᾧ καὶ τὰ Νέμεα συντελεῖν ἔθος τοῖς Ἀργείοις, καὶ τὰ περὶ τὸν Νεμεαῖον λέοντα μυθευόμενα, καὶ ἡ Βέμβινα κώμη· διέχουσι δ' αἱ Κλεωναὶ τοῦ μὲν Ἄργους σταδίους ἑκατὸν εἴκοσι, Κορίνθου δὲ ὀγδοήκοντα. καὶ ἡμεῖς ἀπὸ τοῦ Ἀκροκορίνθου κατωπτεύσαμεν τὸ κτίσμα.

[1] Τρικορύνθῳ, Meineke, for τῇ Κορίνθῳ (see notes on this word under 8. 7. 1 and 9. 1. 22).

[2] Μακαρίαν, Xylander, for Ἀκαρίαν; so the later editors.

Eurystheus made an expedition to Marathon against Iolaüs and the sons of Heracles, with the aid of the Athenians, as the story goes, and fell in the battle, and his body was buried at Gargettus, except his head, which was cut off by Iolaüs, and was buried separately at Tricorynthus near the spring Macaria below the wagon-road. And the place is called "Eurystheus' Head." Then Mycenae fell to the Pelopidae who had set out from Pisatis, and then to the Heracleidae, who also held Argos. But after the naval battle at Salamis the Argives, along with the Cleonaeans and Tegeatans, came over and utterly destroyed Mycenae, and divided the country among themselves. Because of the nearness of the two cities to one another the writers of tragedy speak of them synonymously as though they were one city; and Euripides, even in the same drama, calls the same city, at one time Mycenae, at another Argos, as, for example, in his *Iphigeneia*[1] and his *Orestes*.[2] Cleonae is a town situated by the road that leads from Argos to Corinth, on a hill which is surrounded by dwellings on all sides and is well fortified, so that in my opinion Homer's words, "well-built Cleonae," were appropriate. And here too, between Cleonae and Phlius, are Nemea and the sacred precinct in which the Argives are wont to celebrate the Nemean Games, and the scene of the myth of the Nemean lion, and the village Bembina. Cleonae is one hundred and twenty stadia distant from Argos, and eighty from Corinth. I myself have beheld the settlement from Acrocorinthus.

[1] *Iphigeneia in Tauris*, 508, 510 *et seq.*
[2] *Orestes* 98, 101, 1246.

C 378 20. Ὁ δὲ Κόρινθος ἀφνειὸς μὲν λέγεται διὰ τὸ ἐμπόριον, ἐπὶ τῷ Ἰσθμῷ κείμενος καὶ δυεῖν λιμένων[1] κύριος, ὧν ὁ μὲν τῆς Ἀσίας, ὁ δὲ τῆς Ἰταλίας ἐγγύς[2] ἐστι· [3] καὶ ῥᾳδίας ποιεῖ τὰς ἑκατέρωθεν ἀμοιβὰς τῶν φορτίων πρὸς ἀλλήλους τοῖς τοσοῦτον ἀφεστῶσιν. ἦν δ' ὥσπερ ὁ πορθμὸς οὐκ εὔπλους ὁ κατὰ τὴν Σικελίαν τὸ παλαιόν, οὕτω καὶ τὰ πελάγη, καὶ μάλιστα τὸ ὑπὲρ Μαλεῶν διὰ τὰς ἀντιπνοίας· ἀφ' οὗ καὶ παροιμιάζονται·

Μαλέας δὲ κάμψας ἐπιλάθου τῶν οἴκαδε.

ἀγαπητὸν οὖν ἑκατέροις ἦν τοῖς τε ἐκ τῆς Ἰταλίας καὶ ἐκ τῆς Ἀσίας ἐμπόροις ἀφεῖσι τὸν ἐπὶ[4] Μαλέας πλοῦν,[5] κατάγεσθαι τὸν φόρτον αὐτόθι· καὶ πεζῇ δὲ[6] τῶν ἐκκομιζομένων ἐκ τῆς Πελοποννήσου καὶ τῶν εἰσαγομένων ἔπιπτε τὰ τέλη τοῖς τὰ κλεῖθρα ἔχουσι. διέμεινε δὲ τοῦτο καὶ εἰς ὕστερον μέχρι παντός, τοῖς δ' ὕστερον καὶ πλείω προσεγίνετο πλεονεκτήματα· καὶ γὰρ ὁ Ἰσθμικὸς ἀγὼν ἐκεῖ συντελούμενος ὄχλους ἐπήγετο. καὶ οἱ Βακχιάδαι τυραννήσαντες, πλούσιοι καὶ πολλοὶ καὶ γένος λαμπροί, διακόσια ἔτη σχεδόν τι κατέσχον τὴν ἀρχὴν καὶ τὸ ἐμπόριον ἀδεῶς ἐκαρπώσαντο· τούτους δὲ Κύψελος καταλύσας αὐτὸς ἐτυράννησε, καὶ μέχρι τριγονίας ὁ οἶκος αὐτοῦ συνέμεινε· τοῦ δὲ περὶ τὸν οἶκον τοῦτον πλούτου μαρτύριον τὸ Ὀλυμπίασιν ἀνάθημα Κυψέλου, σφυρήλατος χρυσοῦς ἀνδριὰς εὐμεγέθης. Δη-

[1] ὤν, after λιμένων, Meineke inserts.
[2] εὐθύς, Jones, from conj. of Capps, for ἐγγύς.
[3] Before καί Meineke indicates a lacuna.
[4] ἐπί Meineke emends to περί, following conj. of Corais.

20. Corinth is called "wealthy" because of its commerce, since it is situated on the Isthmus and is master of two harbours, of which the one leads straight to Asia, and the other to Italy; and it makes easy the exchange of merchandise from both countries that are so far distant from each other. And just as in early times the Strait of Sicily was not easy to navigate, so also the high seas, and particularly the sea beyond Maleae, were not, on account of the contrary winds; and hence the proverb, "But when you double Maleae, forget your home." At any rate, it was a welcome alternative, for the merchants both from Italy and from Asia, to avoid the voyage to Maleae and to land their cargoes here. And also the duties on what by land was exported from the Peloponnesus and what was imported to it fell to those who held the keys. And to later times this remained ever so. But to the Corinthians of later times still greater advantages were added, for also the Isthmian Games, which were celebrated there, were wont to draw crowds of people. And the Bacchiadae, a rich and numerous and illustrious family, became tyrants of Corinth, and held their empire for nearly two hundred years, and without disturbance reaped the fruits of the commerce; and when Cypselus overthrew these, he himself became tyrant, and his house endured for three generations; and an evidence of the wealth of this house is the offering which Cypselus dedicated at Olympia, a huge statue of beaten gold.[1] Again, Demaratus,

[1] Also mentioned in 8. 3. 30.

[5] εἰς Κόρινθον, before κατάγεσθαι, Meineke ejects, placing the colon after αὐτόθι instead of after φόρτον.
[6] δέ, after πεζῇ, Meineke, for τε.

μαρατός τε, εἷς τῶν ἐν Κορίνθῳ δυναστευσάντων, φεύγων τὰς ἐκεῖ στάσεις, τοσοῦτον ἠνέγκατο πλοῦτον οἴκοθεν εἰς τὴν Τυρρηνίαν, ὥστε αὐτὸς μὲν ἦρξε τῆς δεξαμένης αὐτὸν πόλεως· ὁ δʼ υἱὸς αὐτοῦ καὶ Ῥωμαίων κατέστη βασιλεύς. τό τε τῆς Ἀφροδίτης ἱερὸν οὕτω πλούσιον ὑπῆρξεν, ὥστε πλείους ἢ χιλίας ἱεροδούλους ἐκέκτητο ἑταίρας, ἃς ἀνετίθεσαν τῇ θεῷ καὶ ἄνδρες καὶ γυναῖκες. καὶ διὰ ταύτας οὖν πολυωχλεῖτο ἡ πόλις καὶ ἐπλουτίζετο· οἱ γὰρ ναύκληροι ῥᾳδίως ἐξανηλίσκοντο, καὶ διὰ τοῦτο ἡ παροιμία φησίν·

οὐ παντὸς ἀνδρὸς ἐς Κόρινθον ἔσθʼ ὁ πλοῦς.

καὶ δὴ καὶ μνημονεύεταί τις ἑταίρα πρὸς τὴν ὀνειδίζουσαν, ὅτι οὐ φιλεργὸς εἴη οὐδʼ ἐρίων ἅπτοιτο, εἰπεῖν· "ἐγὼ μέντοι[1] ἡ τοιαύτη τρεῖς ἤδη καθεῖλον ἱστοὺς ἐν βραχεῖ χρόνῳ τούτῳ."

21. Τὴν δὲ τοποθεσίαν τῆς πόλεως, ἐξ ὧν
C 379 Ἱερώνυμός τε εἴρηκε καὶ Εὔδοξος καὶ ἄλλοι, καὶ αὐτοὶ δὲ εἴδομεν, νεωστὶ ἀναληφθείσης ὑπὸ τῶν Ῥωμαίων, τοιάνδε εἶναι συμβαίνει. ὄρος ὑψηλὸν ὅσον τριῶν ἥμισυ σταδίων ἔχον τὴν κάθετον, τὴν δʼ ἀνάβασιν καὶ τριάκοντα σταδίων, εἰς ὀξεῖαν τελευτᾷ κορυφήν· καλεῖται δὲ Ἀκροκόρινθος, οὗ τὸ μὲν πρὸς ἄρκτον μέρος ἐστὶ τὸ μάλιστα ὄρθιον, ὑφʼ ᾧ κεῖται ἡ πόλις ἐπὶ τραπεζώδους ἐπιπέδου

μέντοι, Corais, for μὲν τό; so the later editors.

---

[1] Tarquinii.
[2] Tarquinius Priscus (see 5. 2. 2).
[3] That is, "finished three webs." But there is a word-play in καθεῖλον ἱστούς which cannot be reproduced in

one of the men who had been in power at Corinth, fleeing from the seditions there, carried with him so much wealth from his home to Tyrrhenia that not only he himself became the ruler of the city[1] that admitted him, but his son was made king of the Romans.[2] And the temple of Aphroditê was so rich that it owned more than a thousand temple-slaves, courtesans, whom both men and women had dedicated to the goddess. And therefore it was also on account of these women that the city was crowded with people and grew rich; for instance, the ship-captains freely squandered their money, and hence the proverb, "Not for every man is the voyage to Corinth." Moreover, it is recorded that a certain courtesan said to the woman who reproached her with the charge that she did not like to work or touch wool: "Yet, such as I am, in this short time I have taken down three webs."[3]

21. The situation of the city, as described by Hieronymus[4] and Eudoxus[5] and others, and from what I myself saw after the recent restoration of the city by the Romans,[6] is about as follows: A lofty mountain with a perpendicular height of three stadia and one half, and an ascent of as much as thirty stadia, ends in a sharp peak; it is called Acrocorinthus, and its northern side is the steepest; and beneath it lies the city in a level, trapezium-

English. The words may also mean "lowered three masts," that is, "debauched three ship-captains."

[4] Apparently Hieronymus of Rhodes (see 14. 2. 13), who lived about 290–230 B.C.

[5] Eudoxus of Cnidus, the famous mathematician and astronomer, who flourished about 365 B.C.

[6] Cp. 8. 4. 8.

χωρίου πρὸς αὐτῇ τῇ ῥίζῃ τοῦ Ἀκροκορίνθου. αὐτῆς μὲν οὖν τῆς πόλεως ὁ κύκλος καὶ τεσσαράκοντα σταδίων ὑπῆρχεν· ἐτετείχιστο δ' ὅσον τῆς πόλεως γυμνὸν ἦν τοῦ ὄρους· συμπεριείληπτο δὲ τῷ περιβόλῳ τούτῳ καὶ τὸ ὄρος αὐτὸ ὁ Ἀκροκόρινθος, ᾗ δυνατὸν ἦν τειχισμὸν δέξασθαι, καὶ ἡμῖν ἀναβαίνουσιν ἦν δῆλα τὰ ἐρείπια τῆς σχοινίας· ὥσθ' ἡ πᾶσα περίμετρος ἐγίνετο περὶ πέντε καὶ ὀγδοήκοντα σταδίων. ἀπὸ δὲ τῶν ἄλλων μερῶν ἧττον ὄρθιόν ἐστι τὸ ὄρος, ἀνατέταται μέντοι καὶ ἐνθένδε ἱκανῶς, καὶ περίοπτόν ἐστιν. ἡ μὲν οὖν κορυφὴ ναΐδιον ἔχει Ἀφροδίτης, ὑπὸ δὲ τῇ κορυφῇ τὴν [1] Πειρήνην εἶναι συμβαίνει κρήνην, ἔκρυσιν μὲν οὐκ ἔχουσαν, μεστὴν δ' ἀεὶ διαυγοῦς καὶ ποτίμου ὕδατος. φασὶ δὲ καὶ ἐνθένδε καὶ ἐξ ἄλλων ὑπονόμων τινῶν φλεβίων συνθλίβεσθαι τὴν πρὸς τῇ ῥίζῃ τοῦ ὄρους κρήνην, ἐκρέουσαν εἰς τὴν πόλιν, ὥσθ' ἱκανῶς ἀπ' αὐτῆς ὑδρεύεσθαι. ἔστι δὲ καὶ φρεάτων εὐπορία κατὰ τὴν πόλιν, λέγουσι δὲ καὶ κατὰ τὸν Ἀκροκόρινθον· οὐ μὴν ἡμεῖς γε εἴδομεν. τοῦ δ' οὖν Εὐριπίδου φήσαντος οὕτως·

ἥκω περίκλυστον προλιποῦσ' Ἀκροκόρινθον,
ἱερὸν ὄχθον, πόλιν Ἀφροδίτας,

τὸ περίκλυστον ἤτοι κατὰ βάθους δεκτέον,[2] ἐπεὶ καὶ φρέατα καὶ ὑπόνομοι λιβάδες διήκουσι δι' αὐτοῦ, ἢ τὸ παλαιὸν ὑποληπτέον τὴν Πειρήνην ἐπιπολάζειν, καὶ κατάρρυτον ποιεῖν τὸ ὄρος.

[1] τε, before Πειρήνην, E omits; so Kramer and the later editors.

[2] δεκτέον, Casaubon, for λεκτέον. So the later editors.

shaped place[1] close to the very base of the Acrocorinthus. Now the circuit of the city itself used to be as much as forty stadia, and all of it that was unprotected by the mountain was enclosed by a wall; and even the mountain itself, the Acrocorinthus, used to be comprehended within the circuit of this wall wherever wall-building was possible, and when I went up the mountain the ruins of the encircling wall were plainly visible. And so the whole perimeter amounted to about eighty-five stadia. On its other sides the mountain is less steep, though here too it rises to a considerable height and is conspicuous all round. Now the summit has a small temple of Aphroditê; and below the summit is the spring Peirenê, which, although it has no overflow, is always full of transparent, potable water. And they say that the spring at the base of the mountain is the joint result of pressure from this and other subterranean veins of water—a spring which flows out into the city in such quantity that it affords a fairly large supply of water. And there is a good supply of wells throughout the city, as also, they say, on the Acrocorinthus; but I myself did not see the latter wells. At any rate, when Euripides says, "I am come, having left Acrocorinthus that is washed on all sides, the sacred hill-city of Aphroditê,"[2] one should take "washed on all sides" as meaning in the depths of the mountain, since wells and subterranean pools extend through it, or else should assume that in early times Peirenê was wont to rise over the surface and flow down the sides of the

[1] "This level is 200 feet above the plain, which lies between it and the Corinthian Gulf" (Tozer, *Selections*, p. 217).

[2] *Frag.* 1084 (Nauck).

ἐνταῦθα δέ φασι[1] πίνοντα τὸν Πήγασον ἁλῶναι ὑπὸ Βελλεροφόντου, πτηνὸν ἵππον ἐκ τοῦ τραχήλου τοῦ Μεδούσης ἀναπαλέντα κατὰ τὴν Γοργοτομίαν· τὸν δ' αὐτόν φασι καὶ τὴν Ἵππου κρήνην ἀναβαλεῖν ἐν τῷ Ἑλικῶνι, πλήξαντα τῷ ὄνυχι τὴν ὑποπεσοῦσαν[2] πέτραν. ὑπὸ δὲ τῇ Πειρήνῃ τὸ Σισύφειόν ἐστιν, ἱεροῦ τινὸς ἢ βασιλείου λευκοῦ λίθου[3] πεποιημένου διασῶζον ἐρείπια οὐκ ὀλίγα. ἀπὸ δὲ τῆς κορυφῆς πρὸς ἄρκτον μὲν ἀφορᾶται ὅ τε Παρνασσὸς καὶ ὁ Ἑλικών, ὄρη ὑψηλὰ καὶ νιφόβολα, καὶ ὁ Κρισαῖος κόλπος ὑποπεπτωκὼς ἀμφοτέροις, περιεχόμενος ὑπὸ τῆς Φωκίδος καὶ τῆς Βοιωτίδος[4] καὶ τῆς Μεγαρίδος καὶ τῆς ἀντιπόρθμου τῇ Φωκίδι Κορινθίας καὶ Σικυωνίας, πρὸς ἑσπέραν δέ·[5] ὑπέρκειται
C 380 δὲ τούτων ἁπάντων τὰ καλούμενα Ὄνεια ὄρη, διατείνοντα μέχρι Βοιωτίας καὶ Κιθαιρῶνος ἀπὸ τῶν Σκειρωνίδων πετρῶν, ἀπὸ τῆς παρὰ ταύτας ὁδοῦ πρὸς τὴν Ἀττικήν.

22. Ἀρχὴ δὲ τῆς παραλίας ἑκατέρας, τῆς μὲν

[1] φησι Bl.

[2] ὑποπεσοῦσαν, Meineke and others emend to ὑποῦσαν, which would mean "beneath *him*" (Pegasus). But ὑποπεσοῦσαν clearly implies "below *the mountain*" (cp. ὑποπεπτωκώς below, and in § 22, and similar uses of the verb *passim* in Strabo).

[3] λευκοῦ λίθου, Meineke (*Vind. Strab.* p. 124), for λευκῷ λίθῳ, but in his text he reads λευκῶν λίθων.

[4] Βοιωτίας, Meineke, for Βοιωτίδος.

[5] Meineke and Müller-Dübner place a colon after Σικυωνίας and indicate a lacuna after ἑσπέραν δέ. δέ is omitted by *gh*; and also by Groskurd, who reads after ἑσπέραν: [πρὸς ἕω] δὲ ὑπέρκειται τούτων κτλ.

mountain.[1] And here, they say, Pegasus, a winged horse which sprang from the neck of the Gorgon Medusa when her head was cut off, was caught while drinking by Bellerophon. And the same horse, it is said, caused Hippu-crenê [2] to spring up on Helicon when he struck with his hoof the rock that lay below that mountain. And at the foot of Peirenê is the Sisypheium, which preserves no inconsiderable ruins of a certain temple, or royal palace, made of white marble. And from the summit, looking towards the north, one can view Parnassus and Helicon—lofty, snow-clad mountains—and the Crisaean Gulf, which lies at the foot of the two mountains and is surrounded by Phocis, Boeotia, and Megaris, and by the parts of Corinthia and Sicyonia which lie across the gulf opposite to Phocis, that is, towards the west.[3] And above all these countries [4] lie the Oneian Mountains,[5] as they are called, which extend as far as Boeotia and Cithaeron from the Sceironian Rocks,[6] that is, from the road that leads along these rocks towards Attica.

22. The beginning of the seaboard on the two

[1] The Greek word περίκλυστον is translated above in its usual sense and as Strabo interpreted it, but Euripides obviously used it in the sense of "washed on *both* sides," that is, by the Corinthian and Saronic Gulfs (cf. Horace's "bimaris Corinthi," *Carmina*, 1. 7. 2).

[2] Also spelled "Hippocrenê," *i.e.* "Horse's Spring."

[3] From Acrocorinthus.

[4] *i.e.* towards the east.

[5] "Ass Mountains," but, as Tozer (*Selections*, p. 219) remarks, Strabo confuses these (they are south-east of Corinth) with Gerania, which lay on the confines of the territories of Corinth and Megara.

[6] On the Sceironian road between Megara and Corinth, see Pausanias, 1. 44. 10.

τὸ Λέχαιον, τῆς δὲ Κεγχρεαὶ κώμη καὶ λιμήν, ἀπέχων τῆς πόλεως ὅσον ἑβδομήκοντα σταδίους· τούτῳ μὲν οὖν χρῶνται πρὸς τοὺς ἐκ τῆς Ἀσίας, πρὸς δὲ τοὺς ἐκ τῆς Ἰταλίας τῷ Λεχαίῳ. τὸ δὲ Λέχαιον ὑποπέπτωκε τῇ πόλει κατοικίαν ἔχον οὐ πολλήν· σκέλη δὲ καθείλκυσται σταδίων περὶ δώδεκα ἑκατέρωθεν τῆς ὁδοῦ τῆς ἐπὶ[1] τὸ Λέχαιον. ἐντεῦθεν δὲ παρεκτείνουσα ἡ ἠϊὼν μέχρι Παγῶν τῆς Μεγαρίδος κλύζεται μὲν ὑπὸ τοῦ Κορινθιακοῦ κόλπου· κοίλη δ' ἐστί, καὶ ποιεῖ τὸν δίολκον πρὸς τὴν ἑτέραν ἠϊόνα τὴν κατὰ Σχοινοῦντα πλησίον ὄντα τῶν Κεγχρεῶν. ἐν δὲ τῷ μεταξὺ τοῦ Λεχαίου καὶ Παγῶν τὸ τῆς Ἀκραίας μαντεῖον Ἥρας ὑπῆρχε τὸ παλαιόν, καὶ αἱ Ὀλμιαί, τὸ ποιοῦν ἀκρωτήριον τὸν κόλπον ἐν ᾧ ἥ τε Οἰνόη καὶ Παγαί, τὸ μὲν τῶν Μεγαρέων φρούριον, ἡ δὲ Οἰνόη τῶν Κορινθίων. ἀπὸ δὲ[2] τῶν Κεγχρεῶν ὁ Σχοινοῦς, καθ' ὃν τὸ στενὸν τοῦ διόλκου· ἔπειθ' ἡ Κρομμυωνία. πρόκειται δὲ τῆς ἠϊόνος ταύτης ὅ τε Σαρωνικὸς κόλπος καὶ ὁ Ἐλευσινιακός, τρόπον τινὰ ὁ αὐτὸς ὤν, συνεχὴς τῷ Ἑρμιονικῷ. ἐπὶ δὲ τῷ Ἰσθμῷ καὶ το τοῦ Ἰσθμίου Ποσειδῶνος ἱερὸν ἄλσει πιτυώδει συνηρεφές, ὅπου τὸν ἀγῶνα τῶν Ἰσθμίων Κορίνθιοι συνετέλουν. ἡ δὲ Κρομμυὼν ἐστι κώμη τῆς Κορινθίας, πρότερον δὲ τῆς Μεγαρίδος, ἐν ᾗ μυθεύουσι τὰ περὶ τὴν Κρομμυωνίαν ὗν, ἣν μητέρα τοῦ Καλυδωνίου κάπρου φασί, καὶ τῶν Θησέως ἄθλων ἕνα τοῦτον παραδιδόασι τὴν τῆς ὑὸς ταύτης ἐξαίρεσιν. καὶ ἡ Τενέα δ' ἐστὶ

[1] ἐπί, Kramer, for περί (παρά *acgh*); so Meineke.
[2] δέ, after ἀπό, all editors insert.

sides is, on the one side, Lechaeum, and, on the other, Cenchreae, a village and a harbour distant about seventy stadia from Corinth. Now this latter they use for the trade from Asia, but Lechaeum for that from Italy. Lechaeum lies beneath the city, and does not contain many residences; but long walls about twelve stadia in length have been built on both sides of the road that leads to Lechaeum. The shore that extends from here to Pagae in Megaris is washed by the Corinthian Gulf; it is concave, and with the shore on the other side, at Schoenus, which is near Cenchreae, it forms the "Diolcus."[1] In the interval between Lechaeum and Pagae there used to be, in early times, the oracle of the Acraean Hera; and here, too, is Olmiae, the promontory that forms the gulf in which are situated Oenoê and Pagae, the latter a stronghold of the Megarians and Oenoê of the Corinthians. From Cenchreae one comes to Schoenus, where is the narrow part of the isthmus, I mean the "Diolcus"; and then one comes to Crommyonia. Off this shore lie the Saronic and Eleusinian Gulfs, which in a way are the same, and border on the Hermionic Gulf. On the Isthmus is also the temple of the Isthmian Poseidon, in the shade of a grove of pine-trees, where the Corinthians used to celebrate the Isthmian Games. Crommyon is a village in Corinthia, though in earlier times it was in Megaris; and in it is laid the scene of the myth of the Crommyonian sow, which, it is said, was the mother of the Caledonian boar; and, according to tradition, the destruction of this sow was one of the labours of Theseus. Tenea, also, is in Corinthia, and in

[1] See 8. 2. 1 and foot-note, and cp. 8. 6. 4.

κώμη τῆς Κορινθίας, ἐν ᾗ τοῦ Τενεάτου Ἀπόλλωνος ἱερόν· λέγεται δὲ καὶ Ἀρχίᾳ, τῷ στείλαντι τὴν εἰς Συρακούσας ἀποικίαν, τοὺς πλείστους τῶν ἐποίκων ἐντεῦθεν συνεπακολουθῆσαι, καὶ μετὰ ταῦτα εὐθηνεῖν μάλιστα τῶν ἄλλων τὴν κατοικίαν ταύτην, τὰ δ' ὕστατα καὶ καθ' αὑτοὺς πολιτεύεσθαι, προσθέσθαι τε τοῖς Ῥωμαίοις, ἀποστάντας Κορινθίων καὶ κατασκαφείσης τῆς πόλεως συμμεῖναι. φέρεται δὲ καὶ χρησμὸς ὁ δοθείς τινι τῶν ἐκ τῆς Ἀσίας[1] ἐρωτῶντι, εἰ λῷον εἴη μετοικεῖν εἰς Κόρινθον·

εὐδαίμων ὁ Κόρινθος,[2] ἐγὼ δ' εἴην Τενεάτης·

ὅπερ κατ' ἄγνοιάν τινες παρατρέπουσιν, ἐγὼ δ' εἴην Τεγεάτης. λέγεται δ' ἐνταῦθα ἐκθρέψαι Πόλυβος τὸν Οἰδίπουν. δοκεῖ δὲ καὶ συγγένειά τις εἶναι Τενεδίοις πρὸς τούτους ἀπὸ Τέννου τοῦ Κύκνου, καθάπερ εἴρηκεν Ἀριστοτέλης· καὶ ἡ τοῦ Ἀπόλλωνος δὲ τιμὴ παρ' ἀμφοτέροις ὁμοία οὖσα δίδωσιν οὐ μικρὰ σημεῖα.

C 381 23. Κορίνθιοι δ' ὑπὸ Φιλίππῳ ὄντες ἐκείνῳ τε συνεφιλονείκησαν, καὶ ἰδίᾳ πρὸς Ῥωμαίους ὑπεροπτικῶς εἶχον, ὥστε τινὲς καὶ τῶν πρέσβεων παριόντων τὴν οἰκίαν αὐτῶν ἐθάρρησαν καταντλῆσαι βόρβορον. ἀντὶ τούτων μὲν οὖν καὶ ἄλλων, ὧν ἐξήμαρτον, ἔτισαν δίκας αὐτίκα· πεμφθείσης γὰρ ἀξιολόγου στρατιᾶς, αὐτή τε κατέσκαπτο ὑπὸ Λευκίου Μομμίου, καὶ τἆλλα

[1] For Ἀσίας Corais conjectures Ἀσέας.
[2] Κορίνθος *Byk*, and Eustathius on *Iliad* 2. 607.

---

[1] This might be the country of Asia or the city of Asea

it is a temple of the Teneatan Apollo; and it is said that most of the colonists who accompanied Archias, the leader of the colonists to Syracuse, set out from there, and that afterwards Tenea prospered more than the other settlements, and finally even had a government of its own, and, revolting from the Corinthians, joined the Romans, and endured after the destruction of Corinth. And mention is also made of an oracle that was given to a certain man from Asia,[1] who enquired whether it was better to change his home to Corinth: "Blest is Corinth, but Tenea for me!" But in ignorance some pervert this as follows: "but Tegea for me!" And it is said that Polybus reared Oedipus here. And it seems, also, that there is a kinship between the peoples of Tenedos and Tenea, through Tennes[2] the son of Cycnus, as Aristotle says;[3] and the similarity in the worship of Apollo among the two peoples affords strong indications of such kinship.

23. The Corinthians, when they were subject to Philip, not only sided with him in his quarrel with the Romans, but individually behaved so contemptuously towards the Romans that certain persons ventured to pour down filth upon the Roman ambassadors when passing by their house. For this and other offences, however, they soon paid the penalty, for a considerable army was sent thither, and the city itself was rased to the ground by Leucius Mummius;[4] and the other countries as far

(in Arcadia), the name of which, according to Herodian (2. 479), was also spelled "Asia."

[2] For the story of King Tennes of Tenedos, see Pausanias 10. 14. 1 and Diodorus Siculus 5. 83.

[3] The quotation is a fragment otherwise unknown.

[4] Cf. 8. 4. 8 and foot-note.

μέχρι Μακεδονίας ὑπὸ Ῥωμαίοις ἐγένοντο,[1] ἐν ἄλλοις ἄλλων πεμπομένων στρατηγῶν· τὴν δὲ χώραν ἔσχον Σικυώνιοι τὴν πλείστην τῆς Κορινθίας. Πολύβιος δὲ τὰ συμβάντα περὶ τὴν ἅλωσιν ἐν οἴκτου μέρει λέγων προστίθησι καὶ τὴν στρατιωτικὴν ὀλιγωρίαν τὴν περὶ τὰ τῶν τεχνῶν ἔργα καὶ τὰ ἀναθήματα. φησὶ γὰρ ἰδεῖν παρὼν ἐρριμμένους πίνακας ἐπ' ἐδάφους, πεττεύοντας δὲ τοὺς στρατιώτας ἐπὶ τούτων. ὀνομάζει δ' αὐτῶν Ἀριστείδου γραφὴν τοῦ Διονύσου, ἐφ' οὗ τινὲς εἰρῆσθαί φασι τὸ οὐδὲν πρὸς τὸν Διόνυσον, καὶ τὸν Ἡρακλέα τὸν καταπονούμενον τῷ τῆς Δηιανείρας χιτῶνι. τοῦτον μὲν οὖν οὐχ ἑωράκαμεν ἡμεῖς, τὸν δὲ Διόνυσον ἀνακείμενον ἐν τῷ Δημητρείῳ τῷ ἐν Ῥώμῃ κάλλιστον ἔργον ἑωρῶμεν·[2] ἐμπρησθέντος δὲ τοῦ νεώ, συνηφανίσθη καὶ ἡ γραφὴ νεωστί. σχεδὸν δέ τι καὶ τῶν ἄλλων ἀναθημάτων τῶν ἐν Ῥώμῃ τὰ πλεῖστα καὶ ἄριστα ἐντεῦθεν ἀφῖχθαι· τινὰ δὲ καὶ αἱ κύκλῳ τῆς Ῥώμης πόλεις ἔσχον. μεγαλόφρων γὰρ ὢν μᾶλλον ἢ φιλότεχνος ὁ Μόμμιος, ὥς φασι, μετεδίδου ῥᾳδίως τοῖς δεηθεῖσι. Λεύκολλος δὲ κατασκευάσας τὸ τῆς Εὐτυχίας ἱερὸν καὶ

[1] ἐγένετο *klno*, and B *man. sec.*, and the editors before Kramer.

[2] ἑωράκαμεν *no*.

---

[1] According to Pliny (*Nat. Hist.* 35. 39), Aristeides of Thebes (fl. about 360 B.C.) was by some believed to be the inventor of painting in wax and in encaustic. See also *ibid.*, 35. 98 f.

[2] *i.e.* in speaking of the paintings of other artists. But the more natural meaning of the saying is, "That has

as Macedonia became subject to the Romans, different commanders being sent into different countries; but the Sicyonians obtained most of the Corinthian country. Polybius, who speaks in a tone of pity of the events connected with the capture of Corinth, goes on to speak of the disregard shown by the army for the works of art and votive offerings; for he says that he was present and saw paintings that had been flung to the ground and saw the soldiers playing dice on these. Among the paintings he names that of Dionysus by Aristeides,[1] to which, according to some writers, the saying, "Nothing in comparison with the Dionysus," referred;[2] and also the painting of Heracles in torture in the robe of Deianeira. Now I have not seen the latter, but I saw the Dionysus, a most beautiful work, on the walls of the temple of Ceres in Rome; but when recently the temple was burned,[3] the painting perished with it. And I may almost say that the most and best of the other dedicatory offerings at Rome came from there; and the cities in the neighbourhood of Rome also obtained some; for Mummius, being magnanimous rather than fond of art, as they say, readily shared with those who asked.[4] And when Leucullus built the Temple of Good Fortune

nothing to do with Dionysus"; and it appears, originally at least, to have been a protest of spectators against the omission of Dionysus and his satyrs, or of merely the dithyrambs, from a dramatic performance (see Tozer, *Selections*, p. 221).

[3] 31 B.C.

[4] According to Velleius Paterculus (1. 13. 4), Mummius told the men who were entrusted with taking these pictures and statues to Rome that, if they lost them, they would have to replace them with new ones!

στοάν τινα χρῆσιν ᾐτήσατο ὧν εἶχεν ἀνδριάντων ὁ Μόμμιος, ὡς κοσμήσων τὸ ἱερὸν μέχρι ἀναδείξεως, εἶτ' ἀποδώσων· οὐκ ἀπέδωκε δέ, ἀλλ' ἀνέθηκε, κελεύσας αἴρειν, εἰ βούλεται· πράως δ' ἤνεγκεν ἐκεῖνος, οὐ φροντίσας οὐδέν, ὥστ' ηὐδοκίμει τοῦ ἀναθέντος μᾶλλον. πολὺν δὲ χρόνον ἐρήμη μείνασα ἡ Κόρινθος, ἀνελήφθη πάλιν ὑπὸ Καίσαρος τοῦ Θεοῦ διὰ τὴν εὐφυΐαν, ἐποίκους πέμψαντος τοῦ ἀπελευθερικοῦ γένους πλείστους· οἳ τὰ ἐρείπια κινοῦντες καὶ τοὺς τάφους συνανασκάπτοντες εὕρισκον ὀστρακίνων τορευμάτων[1] πλήθη,[2] πολλὰ δὲ καὶ χαλκώματα· θαυμάζοντες δὲ τὴν κατασκευήν, οὐδένα τάφον ἀσκευώρητον εἴασαν, ὥστε εὐπορήσαντες τῶν τοιούτων καὶ διατιθέμενοι πολλοῦ Νεκροκορινθίων
C 382 ἐπλήρωσαν τὴν Ῥώμην· οὕτω γὰρ ἐκάλουν τὰ ἐκ τῶν τάφων ληφθέντα, καὶ μάλιστα τὰ ὀστράκινα. κατ' ἀρχὰς μὲν οὖν ἐτιμήθη σφόδρα ὁμοίως τοῖς χαλκώμασι τοῖς Κορινθιουργέσιν, εἶτ' ἐπαύσαντο τῆς σπουδῆς, ἐκλιπόντων τῶν ὀστράκων, καὶ οὐδὲ κατορθουμένων τῶν πλείστων. ἡ μὲν δὴ πόλις ἡ τῶν Κορινθίων μεγάλη τε καὶ πλουσία διὰ παντὸς ὑπῆρξεν, ἀνδρῶν τε ηὐπόρησεν ἀγαθῶν εἴς τε τὰ πολιτικὰ καὶ εἰς τὰς τέχνας τὰς δημιουργικάς· μάλιστα γὰρ καὶ ἐνταῦθα καὶ ἐν Σικυῶνι ηὐξήθη γραφική τε καὶ πλαστικὴ καὶ πᾶσα ἡ τοιαύτη δημιουργία. χώραν δ' ἔσχεν οὐκ εὔγεων σφόδρα, ἀλλὰ σκο-

[1] τορεύματα *acgh*; C. Müller conj. τροχηλάτων.
[2] παμπληθῆ *i*.

[1] From 146 to 44 B.C.

and a portico, he asked Mummius for the use of the statues which he had, saying that he would adorn the temple with them until the dedication and then give them back. However, he did not give them back, but dedicated them to the goddess, and then bade Mummius to take them away if he wished. But Mummius took it lightly, for he cared nothing about them, so that he gained more repute than the man who dedicated them. Now after Corinth had remained deserted for a long time,[1] it was restored again, because of its favourable position, by the deified Caesar, who colonised it with people that belonged for the most part to the freedmen class. And when these were removing the ruins and at the same time digging open the graves, they found numbers of terra-cotta reliefs, and also many bronze vessels. And since they admired the workmanship they left no grave unransacked; so that, well supplied with such things and disposing of them at a high price, they filled Rome with Corinthian "mortuaries," for thus they called the things taken from the graves, and in particular the earthenware. Now at the outset the earthenware was very highly prized, like the bronzes of Corinthian workmanship, but later they ceased to care much for them, since the supply of earthen vessels failed and most of them were not even well executed. The city of the Corinthians, then, was always great and wealthy, and it was well equipped with men skilled both in the affairs of state and in the craftsman's arts; for both here and in Sicyon the arts of painting and modelling and all such arts of the craftsman flourished most. The city had territory, however, that was not very fertile, but rifted and rough; and

λιάν τε καὶ τραχεῖαν, ἀφ' οὗ πάντες ὀφρυόεντα Κόρινθον εἰρήκασι, καὶ παροιμιάζονται·

Κόρινθος ὀφρυᾷ τε καὶ κοιλαίνεται.

24. Ὀρνεαὶ δ' εἰσὶν ἐπώνυμοι τῷ παραρρέοντι ποταμῷ, νῦν μὲν ἔρημοι, πρότερον δ' οἰκούμεναι καλῶς, ἱερὸν ἔχουσαι Πριάπου τιμώμενον, ἀφ' ὧν καὶ ὁ τὰ Πριάπεια ποιήσας Εὐφρόνιος[1] Ὀρνεάτην καλεῖ τὸν θεόν· κεῖνται δ' ὑπὲρ τοῦ πεδίου τοῦ Σικυωνίων, τὴν δὲ χώραν ἔσχον Ἀργεῖοι. Ἀραιθυρέα δ' ἐστὶν ἡ νῦν Φλιασία καλουμένη, πόλιν δ' εἶχεν ὁμώνυμον τῇ χώρᾳ πρὸς ὄρει Κηλώσσῃ· οἱ δ' ὕστερον ἀναστάντες ἐκεῖθεν πρὸ τριάκοντα σταδίων ἔκτισαν πόλιν, ἣν ἐκάλεσαν Φλιοῦντα· τῆς δὲ Κηλώσσης μέρος ὁ Καρνεάτης, ὅθεν λαμβάνει τὴν ἀρχὴν Ἀσωπὸς ὁ παραρρέων τὴν Σικυωνίαν[2] καὶ ποιῶν τὴν Ἀσωπίαν χώραν, μέρος οὖσαν τῆς Σικυωνίας. ἔστι δ' Ἀσωπὸς καὶ ὁ παρὰ Θήβας ῥέων καὶ Πλαταιὰς καὶ Τανάγραν, ἄλλος δ' ἐστὶν ἐν Ἡρακλείᾳ τῇ Τραχινίᾳ παρὰ κώμην ῥέων, ἣν Παρασωπίους ὀνομάζουσι, τέταρτος δ' ὁ ἐν Πάρῳ. κεῖται δ' ὁ Φλιοῦς ἐν μέσῳ Σικυωνίας, Ἀργείας, Κλεωνῶν καὶ Στυμφάλου, κύκλῳ περιεχόμενος· τιμᾶται δ' ἐν Φλιοῦντι καὶ Σικυῶνι τὸ τῆς Δίας ἱερόν· καλοῦσι δ' οὕτω τὴν Ἥβην.

[1] Εὐφρόνιος, Meineke emends to Εὐφορίων; Forbiger, Tardieu following. But see Pauly-Wissowa *s.vv.* "Euphorion," p. 1178, and "Euphronios," p. 1220.

from this fact all have called Corinth "beetling," and use the proverb, "Corinth is both beetle-browed and full of hollows."

24. Orneae is named after the river that flows past it. It is deserted now, although formerly it was well peopled, and had a temple of Priapus that was held in honour; and it was from Orneae that the Euphronius[1] who composed the *Priapeia* calls the god "Priapus the Orneatan." Orneae is situated above the plain of the Sicyonians, but the country was possessed by the Argives. Araethyrea is the country which is now called Phliasia; and near the mountain Celossa[2] it had a city of the same name as the country; but the inhabitants later emigrated from here, and at a distance of thirty stadia founded a city which they called Phlius. A part of the mountain Celossa is Mt. Carneates, whence the Asopus takes its beginning—the river that flows past Sicyonia, and forms the Asopian country, which is a part of Sicyonia. There is also an Asopus that flows past Thebes and Plataea and Tanagra, and there is another in the Trachinian Heracleia that flows past a village which they call Parasopii, and there is a fourth in Paros. Phlius is situated in the centre of a circle formed by Sicyonia, Argeia, Cleonae and Stymphalus. In Phlius and Sicyon the temple of Dia is held in honour; and Dia is their name for Hebê.

[1] The Alexandrian grammarian, who lived in the third century B.C.

[2] By Xenophon (*Hellenica*, 4. 7. 7) spelled "Celusa."

---

[2] Σικυωνίαν, Meineke, from conj. of Corais, emends to Σικυῶνα.

25. Τὴν δὲ Σικυῶνα πρότερον Μηκώνην ἐκάλουν, ἔτι δὲ πρότερον Αἰγιαλούς·[1] ἀνῴκισε[2] δ' αὐτὴν ἀπὸ θαλάττης ὅσον εἴκοσι σταδίοις, οἱ δὲ δώδεκά φασιν, ἐπὶ λόφον ἐρυμνὸν Δημήτριος·[3] τὸ δὲ παλαιὸν κτίσμα ἐπίνειόν ἐστιν ἔχον λιμένα. ὁρίζει δὲ τὴν Σικυωνίαν καὶ τὴν Κορινθίαν ποταμὸς Νεμέα. ἐτυραννήθη δὲ πλεῖστον χρόνον, ἀλλ' ἀεὶ τοὺς τυράννους ἐπιεικεῖς ἄνδρας ἔσχεν· Ἄρατον δ' ἐπιφανέστατον, ὃς καὶ τὴν πόλιν ἠλευθέρωσε, καὶ Ἀχαιῶν ἦρξε, παρ' ἑκόντων λαβὼν τὴν ἐξουσίαν, καὶ τὸ σύστημα ηὔξησε, προσθεὶς αὐτῷ τήν τε πατρίδα καὶ τὰς ἄλλας
C 383 πόλεις τὰς ἐγγύς. Ὑπερησίην δὲ καὶ τὰς ἑξῆς πόλεις, ἃς ὁ ποιητὴς λέγει, καὶ τὸν Αἰγιαλὸν τῶν Ἀχαιῶν ἤδη συμβέβηκεν εἶναι μέχρι Δύμης καὶ τῶν ὅρων τῆς Ἠλείας.

VII

1. Ταύτης δὲ τῆς χώρας τὸ μὲν παλαιὸν Ἴωνες ἐκράτουν, ἐξ Ἀθηναίων τὸ γένος ὄντες, ἐκαλεῖτο δὲ τὸ μὲν παλαιὸν Αἰγιάλεια, καὶ οἱ ἐνοικοῦντες Αἰγιαλεῖς, ὕστερον δ' ἀπ' ἐκείνων Ἰωνία, καθάπερ καὶ ἡ Ἀττική, ἀπὸ Ἴωνος τοῦ Ξούθου. φασὶ δὲ

[1] Αἰγιαλούς, Meineke emends to Αἰγιαλεῖς.
[2] ἀνῴκισε, Meineke, from conj. of Casaubon, for ἀνῳκίσθαι; so the editors in general.
[3] Δημήτριος, Meineke, from conj. of Casaubon, for Δήμητρος; so the editors in general.

---

[1] Spelled "Aegialeia" by Pausanias (2. 7).
[2] "The city built by Aegialeus on the plain was demolished by Demetrius the son of Antigonus (Poliorcetes), who founded

25. In earlier times Sicyon was called Meconê, and in still earlier times Aegiali,[1] but Demetrius rebuilt it upon a hill strongly fortified by nature about twenty stadia (others say twelve) from the sea;[2] and the old settlement, which has a harbour, is a naval station. The River Nemea forms the boundary between Sicyonia and Corinthia. Sicyon was ruled by tyrants most of the time, but its tyrants were always reasonable men, among whom the most illustrious was Aratus,[3] who not only set the city free,[4] but also ruled over the Achaeans, who voluntarily gave him the authority,[5] and he increased the league by adding to it both his native Sicyon and the other cities near it. But Hyperesia and the cities that come in their order after it, which the poet mentions,[6] and the Aegialus as far as Dymê and the boundaries of Eleia already belonged to the Achaeans.[7]

VII

1. In antiquity this country was under the mastery of the Ionians, who were sprung from the Athenians; and in antiquity it was called Aegialeia, and the inhabitants Aegialeians, but later it was called Ionia after the Ionians, just as Attica also was called Ionia[8] after Ion the son of Xuthus. They say that

the city of to-day near what was once the ancient acropolis" (Pausanias, 2. 7).

[3] Cf. Polybius, 4. 8. [4] 251 B.C.

[5] Strabo refers to the Achaean League (see 8. 7. 3).

[6] See 8. 7. 4 and the references.

[7] Again the Achaean League.

[8] See 8. 1. 2, and 9. 1. 5.

Δευκαλίωνος μὲν Ἕλληνα εἶναι, τοῦτον δὲ περὶ τὴν Φθίαν τῶν[1] μεταξὺ Πηνειοῦ καὶ Ἀσωποῦ δυναστεύοντα τῷ πρεσβυτάτῳ τῶν παίδων παραδοῦναι τὴν ἀρχήν, τοὺς δ' ἄλλους ἔξω διαπέμψαι, ζητήσοντας ἵδρυσιν ἕκαστον αὑτῷ· ὧν Δῶρος μὲν τοὺς περὶ Παρνασσὸν Δωριέας συνοικίσας κατέλιπεν ἐπωνύμους αὑτοῦ, Ξοῦθος δὲ τὴν Ἐρεχθέως θυγατέρα γήμας ᾤκισε τὴν Τετράπολιν τῆς Ἀττικῆς, Οἰνόην, Μαραθῶνα, Προβάλινθον καὶ Τρικόρυνθον.[2] τῶν δὲ τούτου παίδων Ἀχαιὸς μὲν φόνον ἀκούσιον πράξας ἔφυγεν εἰς Λακεδαίμονα, καὶ Ἀχαιοὺς τοὺς ἐκεῖ κληθῆναι παρεσκεύασεν, Ἴων δὲ τοὺς μετ' Εὐμόλπου νικήσας Θρᾷκας οὕτως ηὐδοκίμησεν, ὥστ' ἐπέτρεψαν αὐτῷ τὴν πολιτείαν Ἀθηναῖοι. ὁ δὲ πρῶτον μὲν εἰς τέτταρας φυλὰς διεῖλε τὸ πλῆθος, εἶτα εἰς τέτταρας βίους· τοὺς μὲν γὰρ γεωργοὺς ἀπέδειξε, τοὺς δὲ δημιουργούς, τοὺς δὲ ἱεροποιούς, τετάρτους δὲ τοὺς φύλακας· τοιαῦτα δὲ πλείω διατάξας τὴν χώραν ἐπώνυμον ἑαυτοῦ κατέλιπεν. οὕτω δὲ πολυανδρῆσαι τὴν χώραν τότε συνέπεσε, ὥστε καὶ ἀποικίαν τῶν Ἰώνων ἔστειλαν εἰς Πελοπόννησον Ἀθηναῖοι, καὶ τὴν χώραν, ἣν κατέσχον, ἐπώνυμον ἑαυτῶν ἐποίησαν Ἰωνίαν ἀντ' Αἰγιάλου[3] κληθεῖσαν, οἵ τε ἄνδρες ἀντὶ Αἰγιαλέων Ἴωνες προσηγορεύθησαν, εἰς δώδεκα πόλεις μερισθέντες. μετὰ δὲ τὴν Ἡρακλειδῶν κάθοδον ὑπ' Ἀχαιῶν ἐξελαθέντες ἐπανῆλθον πάλιν εἰς Ἀθήνας· ἐκεῖθεν δὲ μετὰ τῶν Κοδριδῶν ἔστειλαν τὴν Ἰωνικὴν

[1] τήν *ino.*

[2] Τρικόρυνθον, Meineke, for Τρικόρυθον; τρικόρινθον, *h.* See Τρικόρυνθος 9. 1. 22.

Hellen was the son of Deucalion, and that he was lord of the people between the Peneius and the Asopus in the region of Phthia and gave over his rule to the eldest of his sons, but that he sent the rest of them to different places outside, each to seek a settlement for himself. One of these sons, Dorus, united the Dorians about Parnassus into one state, and at his death left them named after himself; another, Xuthus, who had married the daughter of Erechtheus, founded the Tetrapolis of Attica, consisting of Oenoê, Marathon, Probalinthus, and Tricorynthus. One of the sons of Xuthus, Achaeus, who had committed involuntary manslaughter, fled to Lacedaemon and brought it about that the people there were called Achaeans; and Ion conquered the Thracians under Eumolpus, and thereby gained such high repute that the Athenians turned over their government to him. At first Ion divided the people into four tribes, but later into four occupations: some he designated as farmers, others as artisans, others as sacred officers, and a fourth group as the guards. And he made several regulations of this kind, and at his death left his own name to the country. But the country had then come to be so populous that the Athenians even sent forth a colony of Ionians to the Peloponnesus, and caused the country which they occupied to be called Ionia after themselves instead of Aegialus; and the men were divided into twelve cities and called Ionians instead of Aegialeians. But after the return of the Heracleidae they were driven out by the Achaeans and went back again to Athens; and from there they sent forth with the Codridae the Ionian colony to Asia, and these

[3] Αἰγιαλείας *Bk.*

ἀποικίαν εἰς τὴν Ἀσίαν, ἔκτισαν δὲ δώδεκα πόλεις ἐν τῇ παραλίᾳ τῆς Καρίας καὶ τῆς Λυδίας, εἰς τοσαῦτα μέρη διελόντες σφᾶς, ὅσα καὶ ἐν τῇ Πελοποννήσῳ κατεῖχον. οἱ δ' Ἀχαιοὶ Φθιῶται μὲν ἦσαν τὸ γένος, ᾤκησαν δ' ἐν Λακεδαίμονι, τῶν δ' Ἡρακλειδῶν ἐπικρατησάντων, ἀναληφθέντες ὑπὸ Τισαμενοῦ, τοῦ Ὀρέστου παιδός, ὡς προειρήκαμεν, τοῖς Ἴωσιν ἐπέθεντο, καὶ γενόμενοι κρείττους τοὺς μὲν ἐξέβαλον, αὐτοὶ δὲ κατέσχον τὴν γῆν, καὶ διεφύλαξαν τὸν αὐτὸν τῆς χώρας μερισ-
C 384 μόν, ὅνπερ καὶ παρέλαβον. οὕτω δ' ἴσχυσαν, ὥστε τὴν ἄλλην Πελοπόννησον ἐχόντων τῶν Ἡρακλειδῶν, ὧν ἀπέστησαν, ἀντεῖχον ὅμως πρὸς ἅπαντας, Ἀχαΐαν ὀνομάσαντες τὴν χώραν. ἀπὸ μὲν οὖν Τισαμενοῦ μέχρι Ὠγύγου βασιλευόμενοι διετέλουν· εἶτα δημοκρατηθέντες τοσοῦτον ηὐδοκίμησαν περὶ τὰς πολιτείας, ὥστε τοὺς Ἰταλιώτας μετὰ τὴν στάσιν τὴν πρὸς τοὺς Πυθαγορείους τὰ πλεῖστα τῶν νομίμων μετενέγκασθαι παρὰ τούτων συνέβη· μετὰ δὲ τὴν ἐν Λεύκτροις μάχην ἐπέτρεψαν Θηβαῖοι τούτοις τὴν δίαιταν περὶ τῶν ἀντιλεγομένων ταῖς πόλεσι πρὸς ἀλλήλας· ὕστερον δ' ὑπὸ Μακεδόνων λυθείσης τῆς κοινωνίας, ἀνέλαβον σφᾶς πάλιν κατὰ μικρόν· ἦρξαν δὲ Πύρρου στρατεύσαντος εἰς Ἰταλίαν τέτταρες συνιοῦσαι[1] πόλεις, ὧν ἦσαν Πάτραι καὶ

[1] συνιοῦσαι *no*, Corais, Meineke, for συνοῦσαι.

---

[1] 8. 5. 5. [2] The Greeks in Italy.

[3] The Pythagoreian Secret Order, which was composed of exclusive clubs at Crotona and other cities in Magna Graecia, was aristocratical in its tendencies, and in time seems to have become predominant in politics. This aroused the resentment of the people and resulted in the forcible

founded twelve cities on the seaboard of Caria and Lydia, thus dividing themselves into the same number of parts as the cities they had occupied in the Peloponnesus. Now the Achaeans were Phthiotae in race, but they lived in Lacedaemon; and when the Heracleidae prevailed, the Achaeans were won over by Tisamenus, the son of Orestes, as I have said before,[1] attacked the Ionians, and proving themselves more powerful than the Ionians drove them out and took possession of the land themselves; and they kept the division of the country the same as it was when they received it. And they were so powerful that, although the Heracleidae, from whom they had revolted, held the rest of the Peloponnesus, still they held out against one and all, and named the country Achaea. Now from Tisamenus to Ogyges they continued under the rule of kings; then, under a democratic government, they became so famous for their constitutions that the Italiotes,[2] after the uprising against the Pythagoreians,[3] actually borrowed most of their usages from the Achaeans.[4] And after the battle at Leuctra the Thebans turned over to them the arbitration of the disputes which the cities had with one another; and later, when their league was dissolved by the Macedonians, they gradually recovered themselves. When Pyrrhus made his expedition to Italy,[5] four cities came together and began a new league, among which were Patrae and Dymê;[6] and

suppression of the Order. At Crotona, for example, the people rose up against the "Three Hundred" during one of their meetings and burnt up the building and many of the assembled members.

[4] So Polybius, 2. 39. [5] 280 B.C.

[6] The other two were Tritaea and Pharae (Polybius, 2. 41).

Δύμη· εἶτα προσελάμβανόν τινας τῶν δώδεκα πλὴν Ὠλένου καὶ Ἑλίκης, τῆς μὲν οὐ συνελθούσης,[1] τῆς δ' ἀφανισθείσης ὑπὸ κύματος.

2. Ἐξαρθὲν γὰρ ὑπὸ σεισμοῦ τὸ πέλαγος κατέκλυσε καὶ αὐτὴν καὶ τὸ ἱερὸν τοῦ Ἑλικωνίου Ποσειδῶνος, ὃν[2] καὶ νῦν ἔτι τιμῶσιν Ἴωνες, καὶ θύουσιν ἐκεῖ τὰ Πανιώνια. μέμνηται δ', ὡς ὑπονοοῦσί τινες, ταύτης τῆς θυσίας Ὅμηρος, ὅταν φῇ·

> αὐτὰρ ὁ θυμὸν ἄϊσθε καὶ ἤρυγεν, ὡς ὅτε ταῦρος
> ἤρυγεν ἑλκόμενος Ἑλικώνιον ἀμφὶ ἄνακτα.

τεκμαίρονταί τε νεώτερον εἶναι τῆς Ἰωνικῆς ἀποικίας τὸν ποιητήν, μεμνημένον γε τῆς Πανιωνικῆς θυσίας, ἣν ἐν τῇ Πριηνέων χώρᾳ συντελοῦσιν Ἴωνες τῷ Ἑλικωνίῳ Ποσειδῶνι· ἐπεὶ καὶ αὐτοὶ οἱ Πριηνεῖς ἐξ Ἑλίκης εἶναι λέγονται, καὶ δὴ πρὸς τὴν θυσίαν ταύτην βασιλέα[3] καθιστᾶσιν ἄνδρα νέον Πριηνέα τὸν τῶν ἱερῶν ἐπιμελησόμενον. τεκμηριοῦνται δ' ἔτι μᾶλλον τὸ προκείμενον ἐκ τῶν περὶ τοῦ ταύρου πεφρασμένων· τότε γὰρ νομίζουσι καλλιερεῖν περὶ τὴν θυσίαν ταύτην Ἴωνες, ὅταν θυόμενος ὁ ταῦρος μυκήσηται. οἱ δ' ἀντιλέγοντες μεταφέρουσιν εἰς τὴν Ἑλίκην τὰ λεχθέντα τεκμήρια περὶ τοῦ ταύρου καὶ τῆς θυσίας, ὡς ἐκεῖ νενομισμένων τούτων καὶ τοῦ ποιητοῦ παραβάλλοντος τὰ ἐκεῖ συντελούμενα.

[1] For συνελθούσης Curtius (*Peloponnesos* I. 451) conjectures συνεστώσης ("was no longer in existence"), but cp. Polybius 2. 41.

[2] ὃν, Meineke inserts, from conjecture of Groskurd.

[3] βασιλέα is omitted by all MSS. except *Bkgt.*

then they began to add some of the twelve cities, except Olenus and Helicê, the former having refused to join and the latter having been wiped out by a wave from the sea.[1]

2. For the sea was raised by an earthquake and it submerged Helicê, and also the temple of the Heliconian Poseidon, whom the Ionians[2] worship even to this day, offering there[3] the Pan-Ionian sacrifices. And, as some suppose, Homer recalls this sacrifice when he says: "but he breathed out his spirit and bellowed, as when a dragged bull bellows round the altar of the Heliconian lord."[4] And they infer that the poet lived after the Ionian colonisation, since he mentions the Pan-Ionian sacrifice, which the Ionians perform in honour of the Heliconian Poseidon in the country of the Prienians; for the Prienians themselves are also said to be from Helicê; and indeed as king for this sacrifice they appoint a Prienian young man to superintend the sacred rites. But still more they base the supposition in question on what the poet says about the bull; for the Ionians believe that they obtain omens in connection with this sacrifice only when the bull bellows while being sacrificed. But the opponents of the supposition apply the above-mentioned inferences concerning the bull and the sacrifice to Helicê, on the ground that these were customary there and that the poet was merely comparing the rites that were celebrated there.

[1] So 1. 3. 18.

[2] In Asia Minor.

[3] At Panionium, on the promontory called Mycalê, according to Herodotus (1. 148); "in a desert place in the neighbourhood of what is called Mycalê," according to Diodorus Siculus, 15. 49.

[4] *Iliad* 20. 403.

κατεκλύσθη δ' ἡ Ἑλίκη δυσὶν ἔτεσι πρὸ τῶν Λευκτρικῶν. Ἐρατοσθένης δὲ καὶ αὐτὸς ἰδεῖν φησὶ τὸν τόπον, καὶ τοὺς πορθμέας λέγειν, ὡς ἐν τῷ πόρῳ ὀρθὸς ἑστήκει[1] Ποσειδῶν χάλκεος, ἔχων ἱππόκαμπον ἐν τῇ χειρί, κίνδυνον φέροντα τοῖς δικτυεῦσιν. Ἡρακλείδης δέ φησι κατ' αὐτὸν γενέσθαι τὸ πάθος νύκτωρ, δώδεκα σταδίους
C 385 διεχούσης τῆς πόλεως ἀπὸ θαλάσσης, καὶ τούτου τοῦ χωρίου παντὸς σὺν τῇ πόλει καλυφθέντος, δισχιλίους δὲ παρὰ τῶν Ἀχαιῶν πεμφθέντας ἀνελέσθαι μὲν τοὺς νεκροὺς μὴ δύνασθαι, τοῖς δ' ὁμόροις νεῖμαι τὴν χώραν· συμβῆναι δὲ τὸ πάθος κατὰ μῆνιν Ποσειδῶνος· τοὺς γὰρ ἐκ τῆς Ἑλίκης ἐκπεσόντας Ἴωνας αἰτεῖν πέμψαντας παρὰ τῶν Ἑλικέων μάλιστα μὲν τὸ βρέτας τοῦ Ποσειδῶνος, εἰ δὲ μή, τοῦ γε ἱεροῦ τὴν ἀφίδρυσιν· οὐ δόντων δέ, πέμψαι πρὸς τὸ κοινὸν τῶν Ἀχαιῶν· τῶν δὲ ψηφισαμένων, οὐδ' ὣς ὑπακοῦσαι· τῷ δ' ἑξῆς χειμῶνι συμβῆναι τὸ πάθος, τοὺς δ' Ἀχαιοὺς ὕστερον δοῦναι τὴν ἀφίδρυσιν τοῖς Ἴωσιν. Ἡσίοδος δὲ καὶ ἄλλης Ἑλίκης μέμνηται Θετταλικῆς.

3. Εἴκοσι μὲν δὴ ἔτη διετέλεσαν γραμματέα κοινὸν ἔχοντες καὶ στρατηγοὺς δύο κατ' ἐνιαυτὸν οἱ Ἀχαιοί, καὶ κοινοβούλιον εἰς ἕνα τόπον συνήγετο αὐτοῖς, ἐκαλεῖτο δὲ Ἀμάριον,[2] ἐν ᾧ τὰ

[1] For ἑστήκει Meineke conjectures ἕστηκε or ἑστήκοι.

[2] Ἀμάριον, Jones, for Ἀρνάριον (see Foucart, *Rev. Arch.* 32. 96 and Pauly-Wissowa, *s.v.* "Amarios"); likewise for Αἰνάριον in 8. 7. 5. Meineke, following the conjecture of Kramer, emends to Ἁμάριον in both places. Corais, following Schweighauser's conjecture (note on Polybius 5. 93), emends to Ὁμάριον; see also Polybius 2. 39 (Ζεὺς Ὁμόριος, or Ὁμάριος).

Helicê was submerged by the sea two years before the battle at Leuctra. And Eratosthenes says that he himself saw the place, and that the ferrymen say that there was a bronze Poseidon in the strait, standing erect, holding a hippo-campus in his hand, which was perilous for those who fished with nets. And Heracleides[1] says that the submersion took place by night in his time, and, although the city was twelve stadia distant from the sea, this whole district together with the city was hidden from sight; and two thousand men who had been sent by the Achaeans were unable to recover the dead bodies; and they divided the territory of Helicê among the neighbours; and the submersion was the result of the anger of Poseidon, for the Ionians who had been driven out of Helicê sent men to ask the inhabitants of Helicê particularly for the statue of Poseidon, or, if not that, for the model of the temple; and when the inhabitants refused to give either, the Ionians sent word to the general council of the Achaeans; but although the assembly voted favourably, yet even so the inhabitants of Helicê refused to obey; and the submersion resulted the following winter; but the Achaeans later gave the model of the temple to the Ionians. Hesiod[2] mentions still another Helicê, in Thessaly.

3. Now for twenty[3] years the Achaeans continued to have a general secretary and two generals, elected annually; and with them a common council was convened at one place (it was called Amarium),[4]

[1] Heracleides of Pontus (see *Dictionary*, Vol. I).

[2] *Shield of Heracles*, 381.

[3] Polybius (2. 43) says twenty-five.

[4] Amarium was the name of the sacred precinct of Zeus Amarius near Aegium, again mentioned in 8. 7. 5.

κοινὰ ἐχρημάτιζον καὶ οὗτοι καὶ Ἴωνες πρότερον· εἶτα ἔδοξεν ἕνα χειροτονεῖσθαι στρατηγόν. Ἄρατος δὲ στρατηγήσας ἀφείλετο Ἀντίγονον τὸν Ἀκροκόρινθον, καὶ τὴν πόλιν τοῖς Ἀχαιοῖς προσέθηκε, καθάπερ καὶ τὴν πατρίδα· προσελάβετο δὲ καὶ Μεγαρέας· καὶ τὰς παρ' ἑκάστοις τυραννίδας καταλύων Ἀχαιοὺς ἐποίει τοὺς ἐλευθερωθέντας·[1] . . . τὴν δὲ Πελοπόννησον ἠλευθέρωσε τῶν τυραννίδων, ὥστε καὶ Ἄργος καὶ Ἑρμιὼν καὶ Φλιοῦς καὶ Μεγαλόπολις,[2] ἡ μεγίστη τῶν ἐν Ἀρκαδίᾳ, προσετέθη τοῖς Ἀχαιοῖς, ὅτε δὴ καὶ πλεῖστον ηὔξηντο. ἦν δ' ὁ καιρός, ἡνίκα Ῥωμαῖοι Καρχηδονίους ἐκ τῆς Σικελίας ἐκβαλόντες ἐστράτευσαν ἐπὶ τοὺς περὶ τὸν Πάδον Γαλάτας. μέχρι δὲ τῆς Φιλοποίμενος στρατηγίας συμμείναντες ἱκανῶς οἱ Ἀχαιοὶ διελύθησαν κατ' ὀλίγον, ἤδη Ῥωμαίων ἐχόντων τὴν Ἑλλάδα σύμπασαν καὶ οὐ τὸν αὐτὸν τρόπον ἑκάστοις χρωμένων, ἀλλὰ τοὺς μὲν συνέχειν, τοὺς δὲ καταλύειν βουλομένων. εἶτα λέγει αἰτίαν τοῦ ἐμπλατύνεσθαι τοῖς περὶ Ἀχαιῶν λόγοις τὸ ἐπὶ τοσοῦτον αὐξηθέντας, ὡς καὶ Λακεδαιμονίους ὑπερβαλέσθαι, μὴ ἀξίως γνωρίζεσθαι.[3]

[1] After ἐλευθερωθέντας, *acghikn* add καὶ μετ' ὀλίγα or ὀλίγον. Kramer, Meineke and others indicate a lacuna.

[2] Μεγαλόπολις, *Bl* (cp. 8. 3. 12): Μεγάλη πόλις, other MSS.

[3] εἶτα . . . γνωρίζεσθαι, omitted in *Bnok*, but later added in the margin, Meineke ejects, indicating lacuna after βουλομένων. It seems clear (1) that the words are the work of an abbreviator and that Στράβων should be supplied as subject of λέγει, or else (2) that a lacuna after βουλομένων should be assumed and that Πολύβιος, whom Strabo seems now to be following rather closely, should be supplied (so think Casaubon and Groskurd). The former is more probable, for the extant text of Polybius (2. 37 ff.) contains no such state-

in which these, as did the Ionians before them, dealt with affairs of common interest; then they decided to elect only one general. And when Aratus was general he took the Acrocorinthus away from Antigonus[1] and added the city of Corinth to the Achaean League, just as he had added his native city; and he also took over the Megarians; and breaking up the tyrannies in the several cities he made the peoples who were thus set free members of the Achaean League. And he set the Peloponnesus free from its tyrannies, so that Argos, Hermion, Phlius, and Megalopolis, the largest city in Arcadia, were added to the League; and it was at this time that the League reached the height of its power. It was the time when the Romans, after their expulsion of the Carthaginians from Sicily,[2] made their expedition against the Galatae[3] who lived in the region of the Padus River. But although the Achaean League persisted rather firmly until the time of the generalship of Philopoemen, yet it was gradually dissolved, since by this time the Romans were in possession of the whole of Greece, and they did not deal with the several states in the same way, but wished to preserve some and to destroy others. Then he[4] tells the cause of his enlarging upon the subject of the Achaeans, saying that, although they increased in power to the point of surpassing even the Lacedaemonians, they are not as well known as they deserve to be.

[1] Antigonus Gonatas.
[2] 241 B.C.
[3] 224 B.C.
[4] See critical note.

---

ment, although in view of his lengthy and favourable discussion of the Achaeans one might by implication ascribe the thought to him.

4. Ἡ δὲ τάξις τῶν τόπων, οὓς κατῴκουν εἰς δώδεκα μέρη διῃρημένοι, τοιαύτη τίς ἐστι· μετὰ Σικυῶνα Πελλήνη κεῖται· εἶτα Αἴγειρα δευτέρα· τρίτη Αἰγαί, Ποσειδῶνος ἱερὸν ἔχουσα· τετάρτη Βοῦρα· μετ' αὐτὴν Ἑλίκη, εἰς ἣν κατεπεφεύγεισαν Ἴωνες, μάχῃ κρατηθέντες ὑπ' Ἀχαιῶν, καὶ τὸ τελευταῖον ἐξέπεσον ἐνθένδε· μετὰ δὲ Ἑλίκην
C 386 Αἴγιον καὶ Ῥύπες καὶ Πατρεῖς καὶ Φαρεῖς· εἶτ' Ὤλενος, παρ' ὃν Πεῖρος[1] ποταμὸς μέγας.[2] εἶτα Δύμη καὶ Τριταιεῖς. οἱ μὲν οὖν Ἴωνες κωμηδὸν ᾤκουν, οἱ δ' Ἀχαιοὶ πόλεις ἔκτισαν, ὧν εἰς τινας ὕστερον συνῴκισαν καὶ ἐκ τῶν ἄλλων μερίδων ἐνίας, καθάπερ τὰς Αἰγὰς εἰς Αἴγειραν (Αἰγαῖοι δ' ἐλέγοντο οἱ ἐνοικοῦντες), Ὤλενον δὲ εἰς Δύμην. δείκνυται δ' ἴχνη μεταξὺ Πατρῶν καὶ Δύμης τοῦ παλαιοῦ τῶν Ὠλενίων κτίσματος· αὐτοῦ δὲ καὶ τὸ τοῦ Ἀσκληπιοῦ ἱερὸν ἐπίσημον, ὃ[3] Δύμης μὲν ἀπέχει[4] τεσσαράκοντα σταδίους, Πατρῶν δὲ ὀγδοήκοντα. ὁμώνυμοι δ' εἰσὶ ταῖς μὲν Αἰγαῖς ταύταις αἱ ἐν Εὐβοίᾳ, τῷ δὲ Ὠλένῳ τὸ ἐν Αἰτωλίᾳ κτίσμα, καὶ αὐτὸ ἴχνη σῶζον μόνον. ὁ δὲ ποιητὴς τοῦ μὲν ἐν Ἀχαΐᾳ Ὠλένου οὐ μέμνηται, ὥσπερ οὐδ' ἄλλων πλειόνων τῶν περὶ τὸν Αἰγιαλὸν οἰκούντων, ἀλλὰ κοινότερον λέγει·

Αἰγιαλόν τ' ἀνὰ πάντα καὶ ἀμφ' Ἑλίκην εὐρεῖαν.

[1] Πεῖρος, Corais, from conj. of Causaubon, inserts; so the editors in general. See Herodotus 1. 145.
[2] Μέλας, after μέγας, Corais deletes. So the editors in general.
[3] ὅ, Kramer inserts; so the later editors.
[4] ἀπέχον B (?) and editors before Kramer.

4. The order of the places in which the Achaeans settled, after dividing the country into twelve parts, is as follows:[1] First after Sicyon lies Pellenê; then, second, Aegeira; third, Aegae, which has a temple of Poseidon; fourth, Bura; after Bura, Helicê, whither the Ionians fled for refuge after they were conquered in battle by the Achaeans, and whence at last they were expelled; and, after Helicê, Aegium and Rhypes and Patrae[2] and Pharae;[3] then Olenus, past which flows the Peirus, a large river; then Dymê and Tritaea.[4] Now the Ionians lived in villages, but the Achaeans founded cities; and to certain of these they later united others, transferring some from the other divisions, as, for example, Aegae to Aegeira (the inhabitants, however, were called Aegaeans), and Olenus to Dymê. Traces of the old settlement of the Olenians are shown between Patrae and Dymê; and here, too, is the notable temple of Asclepius, which is forty stadia distant from Dymê and eighty from Patrae. Of the same name as this Aegae is the Aegae in Euboea; and of the same name as Olenus is the settlement in Aetolia, this too preserving only traces of its former self. Now the poet does not mention the Olenus in Achaea, just as he does not mention several other inhabited places in the region of the Aegialus, although he speaks of them in a rather general way: "And through all the Aegialus and about broad Helicê."[5] But he mentions the

[1] Cp. the names and their order in Herodotus (1. 145), Polybius (2. 41) and Pausanias (7. 6).

[2] The Greek has "Patreis" ("the Patraeans").

[3] The Greek has "Phareis" ("the Pharaeans").

[4] The Greek has "Tritaeeis" ("the Tritaeans").

[5] *Iliad* 2. 575.

τοῦ δ' Αἰτωλικοῦ μέμνηται, ὅταν φῇ·

οἳ[1] Πλευρῶν' ἐνέμοντο καὶ Ὤλενον.

τὰς δ' Αἰγὰς ἀμφοτέρας λέγει, τὴν μὲν Ἀχαϊκήν,

οἱ δέ τοι εἰς Ἑλίκην τε καὶ Αἰγὰς δῶρ' ἀνάγουσι·

ὅταν δὲ φῇ·

Αἰγάς, ἔνθα τέ[2] οἱ κλυτὰ δώματα βένθεσι λίμνης·
ἔνθ' ἵππους ἔστησε Ποσειδάων·

βέλτιον δέχεσθαι τὰς ἐν Εὐβοίᾳ, ἀφ' ὧν εἰκὸς καὶ τὸ πέλαγος Αἰγαῖον λεχθῆναι· ἐκεῖ δὲ καὶ τῷ Ποσειδῶνι ἡ πραγματεία πεποίηται ἡ περὶ τὸν Τρωικὸν πόλεμον. πρὸς δὲ ταῖς Ἀχαϊκαῖς Αἰγαῖς ὁ Κρᾶθις ῥεῖ ποταμός, ἐκ δυεῖν ποταμῶν αὐξόμενος, ἀπὸ τοῦ κίρνασθαι τὴν ὀνομασίαν ἔχων· ἀφ' οὗ καὶ ὁ ἐν Ἰταλίᾳ Κρᾶθις.

5. Ἑκάστη δὲ τῶν δώδεκα μερίδων ἐκ δήμων συνειστήκει ἑπτὰ καὶ ὀκτώ· τοσοῦτον εὐανδρεῖν τὴν χώραν συνέβαινεν. ἔστι δ' ἡ Πελλήνη στάδια ἑξήκοντα τῆς θαλάττης ὑπερκειμένη, φρούριον ἐρυμνόν. ἔστι δὲ καὶ κώμη Πελλήνη, ὅθεν καὶ αἱ Πελληνικαὶ χλαῖναι, ἃς καὶ ἆθλα ἐτίθεσαν ἐν τοῖς ἀγῶσι· κεῖται δὲ μεταξὺ Αἰγίου[3] καὶ Πελλήνης· τὰ δὲ Πέλλανα ἕτερα τούτων ἐστί, Λακωνικὸν χωρίον, ὡς πρὸς τὴν Μεγαλοπολῖτιν νεῦον. Αἴγειρα δὲ ἐπὶ βουνοῦ κεῖται. Βοῦρα δ' ὑπέρκειται τῆς θαλάττης ἐν τετταράκοντά πως σταδίοις, ἣν ὑπὸ σεισμοῦ καταποθῆναι

[1] οἵ, omitted by *Bghikn*.

Aetolian Olenus, when he says: "those who dwelt in Pleuron and Olenus."[1] And he speaks of both places called Aegae: the Achaean Aegae, when he says, "yet they bring up gifts for thee into both Helicê and Aegae";[2] but when he says, "Aegae, where is his famous palace in the deeps of the mere,"[3] "where Poseidon halted his horses,"[4] it is better to take him as meaning the Aegae in Euboea, from which it is probable that also the Aegean Sea got its name; and here too the poet has placed the activities of Poseidon in connection with the Trojan War. Close to the Achaean Aegae flows the Crathis River, which is increased by the waters of two other rivers; and it gets its name from the fact that it is a mixture,[5] as does also the Crathis in Italy.

5. Each of the twelve divisions consisted of seven or eight communities, so populous was the country. Pellenê is situated sixty stadia above the sea, and it is a strong fortress. But there is also a village Pellenê, from which come the Pellenic cloaks, which they were also wont to set up as prizes at the games; it lies between Aegium and Pellenê. But Pellana is different from these two; it is a Laconian place, and its territory inclines, approximately, towards the territory of Megalopolis. Aegeira is situated on a hill. Bura, which was swallowed up in an earthquake, is situated above the sea at a distance of about forty stadia; and they say that it was

[1] *Iliad* 2. 639. [2] *Iliad* 8. 203.
[3] *Iliad* 13. 21. [4] *Iliad* 13. 34.
[5] Cp. Κρᾶθις and κραθῆναι.

---

[2] τέ, Kramer, for δέ; so the later editors.
[3] Αἰγαίου *cghi*, Αἰγῶν *no* and Corais, Αἰγίων (correction in B).

συνέβη. ἀπὸ δὲ τῆς ἐνταῦθα κρήνης Συβάριδος τὸν κατὰ τὴν Ἰταλίαν ποταμὸν ὀνομασθῆναί
C 387 φασιν. ἡ δ' Αἰγὰ (καὶ γὰρ οὕτω λέγουσι τὰς Αἰγὰς) νῦν μὲν οὐκ οἰκεῖται, τὴν δὲ πόλιν[1] ἔχουσιν Αἰγιεῖς. Αἴγιον δὲ ἱκανῶς οἰκεῖται· ἱστοροῦσι δ' ἐνταῦθα τὸν Δία ὑπ' αἰγὸς ἀνατραφῆναι, καθάπερ φησὶ καὶ Ἄρατος·

αἶξ ἱερή, τὴν μέν τε λόγος Διὶ μαζὸν ἐπισχεῖν·

ἐπιλέγει δὲ καὶ ὅτι

Ὠλενίην δέ μιν αἶγα Διὸς καλέουσ' ὑποφῆται·

δηλῶν τὸν τόπον, διότι πλησίον Ὠλένη. αὐτοῦ δὲ καὶ ἡ Κεραύνια,[2] ἐπὶ πέτρας ὑψηλῆς ἱδρυμένη. Αἰγιέων δ' ἐστὶ καὶ ταῦτα καὶ Ἑλίκη καὶ τὸ τοῦ Διὸς ἄλσος τὸ Ἀμάριον,[3] ὅπου συνῄεσαν οἱ Ἀχαιοὶ βουλευσόμενοι περὶ τῶν κοινῶν. ῥεῖ δὲ διὰ τῆς Αἰγιέων ὁ Σελινοῦς ποταμός, ὁμώνυμος τῷ τε ἐν Ἐφέσῳ παρὰ τὸ Ἀρτεμίσιον ῥέοντι, καὶ τῷ ἐν τῇ νῦν Ἠλείᾳ τῷ παραρρέοντι τὸ χωρίον, ὅ φησιν ὠνήσασθαι τῇ Ἀρτέμιδι Ξενοφῶν κατὰ χρησμόν· ἄλλος δὲ Σελινοῦς ὁ παρὰ τοῖς Ὑβλαίοις Μεγαρεῦσιν, οὓς ἀνέστησαν Καρχηδόνιοι. τῶν δὲ λοιπῶν πόλεων τῶν Ἀχαϊκῶν

[1] πόλιν, Pletho emends to χώραν; so most of the editors, including Meineke.

[2] Κεραύνια, Perizonius (note on Aelian *Var. Hist.* 13. 6) is almost certainly right in emending to Κερύνεια (Ceryneia), the city mentioned by Polybius (2. 41), Pausanias (7. 6) and others; and so read most of the editors (but cp. Groskurd's note).

[3] Ἀμάριον, Jones, for Αἰνάριον (see note on Ἀμάριον 8. 7. 3).

from the spring Sybaris in Bura that the river[1] in Italy got its name. Aega (for Aegae is also called thus) is now uninhabited, and the city[2] is in the possession of the people of Aegium. But Aegium has a considerable population. The story is told that Zeus was nursed by a goat there, just as Aratus says: "Sacred goat, which, in story, didst hold thy breast o'er Zeus";[3] and he goes on to say that "the interpreters call her the Olenian goat of Zeus,"[4] thus clearly indicating that the place is near Olenê. Here too is Ceraunia,[5] which is situated on a high rock. These places belong to Aegium, and so does Helicé, and Amarium, precinct of Zeus, where the Achaeans met to deliberate on affairs of common interest. And the Selinus River flows through the territory of Aegium; it bears the same name as the river that flows in Ephesus past the Artemisium, and also the river in the Eleia of to-day[6] that flows past the plot of land which Xenophon says he bought for Artemis in accordance with an oracle.[7] And there is another Selinus; it flows past the territory of the Hyblaean Megarians,[8] whom the Carthaginians forced to migrate. As for the remaining cities, or divisions, of the Achaeans,

[1] See 6. 1. 12–13.

[2] Others emend "city" to "country," but Strabo often speaks of cities thus, whether inhabited or not; and in giving the name of a city he often means to include all the surrounding territory which it possesses.

[3] *Phaenomena*, 163.

[4] *Ibid.*, 164.

[5] Ceraunia is almost certainly an error for "Ceryneia," the city mentioned by Polybius (2. 41), Pausanias (7. 6), and others.

[6] See 8. 3. 1.

[7] *Anabasis*, 5. 3. 8.

[8] Megara Hyblaea was on the eastern coast of Sicily, to the north of Syracuse.

εἴτε μερίδων Ῥύπες μὲν οὐκ οἰκοῦνται, τὴν δὲ χώραν Ῥυπίδα καλουμένην ἔσχον Αἰγιεῖς καὶ Φαρεῖς·[1] καὶ Αἰσχύλος δὲ λέγει που·

Βοῦράν θ' ἱερὰν καὶ κεραυνίας Ῥύπας.[2]

ἐκ δὲ τῶν Ῥυπῶν ἦν ὁ Μύσκελλος, ὁ Κρότωνος οἰκιστής· τῆς δὲ Ῥυπίδος καὶ τὸ Λεῦκτρον ἦν, δῆμος τῶν Ῥυπῶν. μετὰ δὲ τούτους Πάτραι, πόλις ἀξιόλογος· μεταξὺ δὲ τὸ Ῥίον καὶ τὸ Ἀντίρριον,[3] ἀπέχον Πατρῶν στάδια τεσσαράκοντα. Ῥωμαῖοι δὲ νεωστὶ μετὰ τὴν Ἀκτιακὴν νίκην ἵδρυσαν αὐτόθι τῆς στρατιᾶς μέρος ἀξιόλογον, καὶ διαφερόντως εὐανδρεῖ νῦν, ἀποικία Ῥωμαίων οὖσα· ἔχει δὲ ὕφορμον μέτριον. ἐφεξῆς δ' ἐστὶν ἡ Δύμη, πόλις ἀλίμενος, πασῶν δυσμικωτάτη, ἀφ' οὗ καὶ τοὔνομα· πρότερον δ' ἐκαλεῖτο Στράτος· διαιρεῖ δ' αὐτὴν ἀπὸ τῆς Ἠλείας κατὰ Βουπράσιον ὁ Λάρισος ποταμός, ῥέων ἐξ ὄρους· τοῦτο δ' οἱ μὲν Σκόλλιν καλοῦσιν, Ὅμηρος δὲ πέτρην Ὠλενίην. τοῦ δ' Ἀντιμάχου Καυκωνίδα τὴν Δύμην εἰπόντος, οἱ μὲν ἐδέξαντο ἀπὸ τῶν Καυκώνων ἐπιθέτως εἰρῆσθαι αὐτὸ μέχρι δεῦρο καθηκόντων, καθάπερ ἐπάνω προείπομεν· οἱ δ' ἀπὸ Καύκωνος ποταμοῦ τινός, ὡς αἱ Θῆβαι Διρκαῖαι καὶ Ἀσωπίδες, Ἄργος δ' Ἰνάχειον, Τροία δὲ Σιμουντίς. δέδεκται δ' οἰκήτορας καὶ ἡ Δύμη μικρὸν πρὸ ἡμῶν, ἀνθρώπους μιγάδας,
C 388 οὓς ἀπὸ τοῦ πειρατικοῦ πλήθους περιλιπεῖς ἔσχε

[1] Φαρεῖς, Pletho, for Φαριεῖς; so Corais, Meineke and others.

[2] καὶ Αἰσχύλος . . . Ῥύπας, Meineke relegates to foot of page; but see J. Partsch in *Berl. Phil. Woch.* 1902, 1411.

[3] καὶ τὸ Ἀντίρριον, Meineke ejects; Corais emends the καί to κατά ("opposite").

one of them, Rhypes, is uninhabited, and the territory called Rhypis was held by the people of Aegium and the people of Pharae. Aeschylus, too, says somewhere: "Sacred Bura and thunder-smitten Rhypes."[1] Myscellus, the founder of Croton, was from Rhypes. And Leuctrum too, a deme of Rhypes, belonged to the district of Rhypis. After Rhypes comes Patrae, a noteworthy city; between the two, however, is Rhium (also Antirrhium),[2] which is forty stadia distant from Patrae. And recently the Romans, after their victory at Actium, settled a considerable part of the army at Patrae; and it is exceptionally populous at present, since it is a Roman colony; and it has a fairly good anchoring-place. Next comes Dymê, a city without a harbour, the farthest of all towards the west, a fact from which it takes its name.[3] But in earlier times it was called Stratos. The boundary between it and the Eleian country, Buprasium, is formed by the Larisus River, which flows from a mountain. Some writers call this mountain Scollis, but Homer calls it the Olenian Rock. When Antimachus calls Dymê "Cauconian," some interpret "Cauconian" as an epithet derived from the Cauconians, since the Cauconians extended as far as Dymê, as I have already said above,[4] but others as derived from a River Caucon, just as Thebes is called "Dircaean" and "Asopian," Argos "Inacheian," and Troy "Simuntian." But shortly before my time Dymê received as colonists a mixed group of people whom Pompey still had left over from the

[1] *Frag.* 403 (Nauck). [2] See critical note.
[3] δύειν "to set," δύσμη "setting," "west."
[4] 8. 3. 11, 17.

Πομπήιος, καταλύσας τὰ λῃστήρια καὶ ἱδρύσας τοὺς μὲν ἐν Σόλοις τοῖς Κιλικίοις, τοὺς δ' ἄλλοθι καὶ δὴ καὶ ἐνταῦθα. ἡ δὲ Φάρα συνορεῖ μὲν τῇ Δυμαίᾳ, καλοῦνται δὲ οἱ μὲν ἐκ ταύτης τῆς Φάρας Φαρεῖς,[1] οἱ δ' ἐκ τῆς Μεσσηνιακῆς Φαραιᾶται·[2] ἔστι δ' ἐν τῇ Φαραϊκῇ Δίρκη κρήνη, ὁμώνυμος τῇ ἐν Θήβαις. ἡ δ' Ὤλενός ἐστι μὲν ἔρημος, κεῖται δὲ μεταξὺ Πατρῶν καὶ Δύμης· ἔχουσι δὲ Δυμαῖοι τὴν χώραν. εἶτ' Ἄραξος, τὸ ἀκρωτήριον τῆς Ἠλείας, ἀπὸ Ἰσθμοῦ στάδιοι χίλιοι τριάκοντα.[3]

VIII

1. Ἀρκαδία δ' ἐστὶν ἐν μέσῳ μὲν τῆς Πελοποννήσου, πλείστην δὲ χώραν ὀρεινὴν ἀποτέμνεται. μέγιστον δ' ὄρος ἐν αὐτῇ Κυλλήνη· τὴν γοῦν κάθετον οἱ μὲν εἴκοσι σταδίων φασίν, οἱ δ' ὅσον πεντεκαίδεκα. δοκεῖ δὲ παλαιότατα ἔθνη τῶν Ἑλλήνων εἶναι τὰ Ἀρκαδικά, Ἀζᾶνές τε καὶ Παρράσιοι καὶ ἄλλοι τοιοῦτοι. διὰ δὲ τὴν τῆς χώρας παντελῆ κάκωσιν οὐκ ἂν προσήκοι μακρολογεῖν περὶ αὐτῶν· αἵ τε γὰρ πόλεις ὑπὸ τῶν συνεχῶν πολέμων ἠφανίσθησαν, ἔνδοξοι γενόμεναι πρότερον, τήν τε χώραν οἱ γεωργήσαντες ἐκλελοίπασιν ἐξ ἐκείνων ἔτι τῶν χρόνων, ἐξ ὧν εἰς τὴν προσαγορευθεῖσαν Μεγάλην πόλιν[4]

[1] Φαρεῖς, Meineke, for Φαριεῖς.
[2] Φαραιᾶται, Meineke, for Φαρᾶται.

crowd of pirates, after he broke up all piracy and settled some of the pirates at Soli in Cilicia and others in other places—and in particular at Dymê. Phara borders on the territory of Dymê. The people of this Phara are called Phareis, but those of the Messenian city Pharaeatae; and in the territory of Phara is a spring Dircê which bears the same name as the spring at Thebes. But Olenus is deserted; it lies between Patrae and Dymê; and its territory is held by the people of Dymê. Then comes Araxus, the promontory of the Eleian country, one thousand and thirty stadia from the isthmus.

VIII

1. Arcadia lies in the middle of the Peloponnesus; and most of the country which it includes is mountainous. The greatest mountain in it is Cyllenê; at any rate some say that its perpendicular height is twenty stadia, though others say about fifteen. The Arcadian tribes—the Azanes, the Parrhasians, and other such peoples—are reputed to be the most ancient tribes of the Greeks. But on account of the complete devastation of the country it would be inappropriate to speak at length about these tribes; for the cities, which in earlier times had become famous, were wiped out by the continuous wars, and the tillers of the soil have been disappearing even since the times when most of the cities

[3] τριάκοντα (λ′), Meineke inserts, following conj. of Casaubon.
[4] Μεγαλόπολιν *Bl.*

αἱ πλεῖσται συνῳκίσθησαν. νυνὶ δὲ καὶ αὐτὴ ἡ Μεγάλη πόλις[1] τὸ τοῦ κωμικοῦ πέπονθε, καὶ

ἐρημία μεγάλη 'στὶν ἡ Μεγάλη πόλις·

βοσκήμασι δ' εἰσὶ νομαὶ δαψιλεῖς, καὶ μάλιστα ἵπποις καὶ ὄνοις τοῖς ἱπποβάτοις· ἔστι δὲ καὶ τὸ γένος τῶν ἵππων ἄριστον τὸ Ἀρκαδικόν, καθάπερ καὶ τὸ Ἀργολικὸν καὶ τὸ Ἐπιδαύριον. καὶ ἡ τῶν Αἰτωλῶν δὲ καὶ Ἀκαρνάνων ἐρημία πρὸς ἱπποτροφίαν εὐφυὴς γέγονεν, οὐχ ἧττον τῆς Θετταλίας.

2. Μαντίνειαν μὲν οὖν ἐποίησεν ἔνδοξον Ἐπαμεινώνδας, τῇ δευτέρᾳ νικήσας μάχῃ Λακεδαιμονίους, ἐν ᾗ καὶ αὐτὸς ἐτελεύτα· καὶ αὐτὴ δὲ καὶ Ὀρχόμενος καὶ Ἡραία καὶ Κλείτωρ καὶ Φενεὸς καὶ Στύμφαλος καὶ Μαίναλος καὶ Μεθύδριον καὶ Καφυεῖς καὶ Κύναιθα[2] ἢ οὐκέτ' εἰσίν, ἢ μόλις αὐτῶν ἴχνη φαίνεται καὶ σημεῖα. Τεγέα δ' ἔτι μετρίως συμμένει, καὶ τὸ ἱερὸν τῆς Ἀλέας[3] Ἀθηνᾶς· τιμᾶται δ' ἐπὶ μικρὸν καὶ τὸ τοῦ Λυκαίου Διὸς ἱερὸν κατὰ τὸ Λύκαιον κείμενον[4] ὄρος. τῶν δ' ὑπὸ τοῦ ποιητοῦ λεγομένων

Ῥίπην τε Στρατίην τε καὶ ἠνεμόεσσαν Ἐνίσπην

εὑρεῖν τε χαλεπόν, καὶ εὑροῦσιν οὐδὲν ὄφελος διὰ τὴν ἐρημίαν.

3. Ὄρη δ' ἐπιφανῆ πρὸς τῇ Κυλλήνῃ Φολόη

[1] Μεγαλόπολιν, MSS., but λη above λο added by first hand in A.

[2] Κύνηθα *Achino.*

were united into what was called the "Great City."[1] But now the Great City itself has suffered the fate described by the comic poet: "The Great City is a great desert."[2] But there are ample pastures for cattle, particularly for horses and asses that are used as stallions. And the Arcadian breed of horses, like the Argolic and the Epidaurian, is most excellent. And the deserted lands of the Aetolians and Acarnanians are also well adapted to horse-raising—no less so than Thessaly.

2. Now Mantineia was made famous by Epameinondas, who conquered the Lacedaemonians in the second battle, in which he himself lost his life. But Mantineia itself, as also Orchomenus, Heraea, Cleitor, Pheneus, Stymphalus, Maenalus, Methydrium, Caphyeis, and Cynaetha, no longer exist; or else traces or signs of them are scarcely to be seen. But Tegea still endures fairly well, and so does the temple of the Alean Athenê; and the temple of Zeus Lycaeus situated near Mt. Lycaeum is also honoured to a slight extent. But three of the cities mentioned by the poet, "Rhipê and Stratiê, and windy Enispê,"[3] are not only hard to find, but are of no use to any who find them, because they are deserted.

3. Famous mountains, in addition to Cyllenê, are

[1] Megalopolis.
[2] The authorship of these words is unknown.
[3] *Iliad* 2. 606.

---

[3] Ἀλέας, Corais, for Ἀλαίας; so the later editors.
[4] κείμενον is inserted by second hand in lacuna of about ten letters in A; and so read *no*; Meineke, following Kramer's conjecture, inserts μέγιστον; O. Meltzer (*Neue Jahrbücher* 111, 193), ἱδρύμενον.

C 389 τε καὶ Λύκαιον καὶ Μαίναλος καὶ τὸ Παρθένιον καλούμενον, καθῆκον ἐπὶ τὴν Ἀργείαν ἀπὸ τῆς Τεγεάτιδος.

4. Περὶ δὲ τοῦ Ἀλφειοῦ καὶ τοῦ Εὐρώτα τὸ συμβεβηκὸς παράδοξον εἴρηται καὶ τὸ περὶ Ἐρασῖνον τὸν ἐνδιδόντα ἐκ τῆς Στυμφαλίδος λίμνης εἰς τὴν Ἀργείαν νυνί, πρότερον δ' οὐκ ἔχοντα ἔκρυσιν, τῶν βερέθρων, ἃ καλοῦσιν οἱ Ἀρκάδες ζέρεθρα, τυφλῶν ὄντων καὶ μὴ δεχομένων ἀπέρασιν,[1] ὥστε τὴν τῶν Στυμφαλίων πόλιν νῦν μὲν καὶ πεντήκοντα[2] διέχειν σταδίους ἀπὸ τῆς λίμνης, τότε δ' ἐπ' αὐτῆς κεῖσθαι. τἀναντία δ' ὁ Λάδων ἔπαθε, τοῦ ῥεύματος ἐπισχεθέντος ποτὲ διὰ τὴν ἔμφραξιν τῶν πηγῶν· συμπεσόντα γὰρ τὰ περὶ Φενεὸν βέρεθρα ὑπὸ σεισμοῦ, δι' ὧν ἦν ἡ φορά, μονὴν ἐποίησε τοῦ ῥεύματος μέχρι τῶν κατὰ βάθους φλεβῶν τῆς πηγῆς. καὶ οἱ μὲν οὕτω λέγουσιν· Ἐρατοσθένης δέ φησι περὶ Φενεὸν μὲν τὸν Ἀνίαν[3] καλούμενον ποταμὸν λιμνάζειν τὰ πρὸ τῆς πόλεως, καταδύεσθαι δ' εἴς τινας ἠθμούς,[4] οὓς καλεῖσθαι ζέρεθρα· τούτων δ' ἐμφραχθέντων, ἔσθ' ὅτε ὑπερχεῖσθαι

[1] ἀπέκρυσιν *kno*, *man. sec.* B, Ald.

[2] For πεντήκοντα (ν') Tozer, following conj. of Leake and C. O. Müller, reads πέντε (ε'). But Jones conj. τέσσαρα (δ').

[3] For Ἀνίαν, Penzel and Groskurd conj. Ἀροάνιον; T. Birt (*Kritik und Hermeneutik*, in Müller's *Handb.* 1913, I, 3, p. 134), following E. Hiller (*Eratosthenes Carm. Rell.* p. 16), would emend to Ἀρύαν.

[4] Ἰσθμούς *Acghi*. Tzschucke conj. εἰσθμούς (see Hesychius *s.v.*).

---

[1] 6. 2. 9.

[2] *i.e.* "through a subterranean channel."

Pholoê, Lycaeum, Maenalus, and the Parthenium, as it is called, which extends from the territory of Tegea down to the Argive country.

4. I have already mentioned the marvellous circumstances pertaining to the Alpheius and the Eurotas,[1] and also to the Erasinus, which now flows underground from the Stymphalian Lake,[2] and issues forth into the Argive country, although in earlier times it had no outlet, since the "berethra,"[3] which the Arcadians call "zerethra," were stopped up and did not admit of the waters being carried off, so that the city of the Stymphalians[4] is now fifty stadia[5] distant from the lake, although then it was situated on the lake. But the contrary was the case with the Ladon, since its stream was once checked because of the blocking up of its sources; for the "berethra" near Pheneus, through which it flowed, fell in as the result of an earthquake and checked the stream as far down into the depths of the earth as the veins which supplied its source. Thus some writers tell it. But Eratosthenes says that near Pheneus the river Anias,[6] as it is called, makes a lake of the region in front of the city and flows down into sink-holes, which are called "zerethra"; and when these are stopped up the water sometimes overflows into the

[3] "Pits." [4] Stymphalus.

[5] It is incredible that Strabo wrote "fifty" here. Leake (*Morea*, III. 146), quoted approvingly by Tozer (*Selections*, 224), says that "five" must be right, which is "about the number of stades between the site of Stymphalus and the margin of the lake, on the average of the seasons." Palaeographically, however, it is far more likely that Strabo wrote "four" (see critical note).

[6] The river formed by the confluence of the Aroanius and the Olbius, according to Frazer (note on Pausanias, 8. 14. 3).

τὸ ὕδωρ εἰς τὰ πεδία, πάλιν δ' ἀναστομουμένων ἄθρουν ἐκ τῶν πεδίων ἐκπεσὸν εἰς τὸν Λάδωνα καὶ τὸν Ἀλφειὸν ἐμβάλλειν, ὥστε καὶ τῆς Ὀλυμπίας κλυσθῆναί ποτε τὴν περὶ τὸ ἱερὸν γῆν, τὴν δὲ λίμνην συσταλῆναι· τὸν Ἐρασῖνον δὲ παρὰ[1] Στύμφαλον ῥέοντα, ὑποδύντα ὑπὸ τὸ ὄρος, ἐν τῇ Ἀργείᾳ πάλιν ἀναφανῆναι· διὸ δὴ καὶ Ἰφικράτη, πολιορκοῦντα τὸν Στύμφαλον καὶ μηδὲν περαίνοντα, ἐπιχειρῆσαι τὴν κατάδυσιν ἀποφράξαι, σπόγγους πορισάμενον πολλούς, παύσασθαι δὲ διοσημίας γενομένης. περὶ Φενεὸν δ' ἐστὶ καὶ τὸ καλούμενον Στυγὸς ὕδωρ, λιβάδιον ὀλεθρίου ὕδατος νομιζόμενον ἱερόν. τοσαῦτα καὶ περὶ Ἀρκαδίας εἰρήσθω.

5. Πολυβίου δ' εἰρηκότος τὸ ἀπὸ Μαλεῶν ἐπὶ τὰς ἄρκτους μέχρι τοῦ Ἴστρου διάστημα περὶ μυρίους σταδίους, εὐθύνει τοῦτο ὁ Ἀρτεμίδωρος οὐκ ἀτόπως,[2] ἐπὶ μὲν Αἴγιον χιλίους καὶ [τετρακοσ]ίους εἶναι λέγων ἐκ Μαλεῶν ὁδόν, ἐνθένδε εἰς [Κίρραν πλοῦν] διακοσίων, ἐνθένδε διὰ Ἡρακλείας [εἰς Θαυμακοὺς] πεντακοσίων ὁδόν, εἶτα εἰς Λάρισαν [καὶ τὸν Πηνειὸν] τριακοσίων τετταράκοντα, εἶτα διὰ [τῶν Τεμπῶν ἐπὶ τὰς Πη]νειοῦ ἐκβολὰς διακοσίων τετταράκον[τα, εἶτα εἰς τὴν Θεσσα]λονίκειαν ἑξακοσίων ἑξήκοντα, ἐντεῦ[θεν ἐπ' Ἴστρον δι' Εἰδομ]ένης καὶ Στόβων καὶ Δαρδανίων τρισχι[λίους καὶ διακοσίο]υς· κατ' ἐκεῖνον δὴ συμβαίνει τὸ ἐκ [τοῦ Ἴστρου ἐπὶ τὰς Μαλ]έας

[1] παρά A; περί other MSS.

[2] The nine lacunae (indicated by brackets) in this passage are supplied in the editions of Müller-Dübner and Meineke.

plains, and when they are again opened up it rushes out of the plains all at once and empties into the Ladon and the Alpheius, so that even at Olympia the land around the temple was once inundated, while the lake was reduced; and the Erasinus, which flows past Stymphalus, sinks and flows beneath the mountain[1] and reappears in the Argive land; and it was on this account, also, that Iphicrates, when he was besieging Stymphalus and accomplishing nothing, tried to block up the sink with a large quantity of sponges with which he had supplied himself, but desisted when Zeus sent an omen from the sky. And near Pheneus is also the water of the Styx, as it is called—a small stream of deadly water which is held to be sacred. So much may be said concerning Arcadia.

5. Polybius[2] states that the distance from Maleae towards the north as far as the Ister is about ten thousand stadia, but Artemidorus corrects the statement in an appropriate manner by saying that from Maleae to Aegium is a journey of fourteen hundred stadia, and thence to Cyrrha a voyage of two hundred, and thence through Heracleia to Thaumaci a journey of five hundred, and then to Larisa and the Peneius three hundred and forty, and then through Tempê to the outlets of the Peneius two hundred and forty, and then to Thessaloniceia six hundred and sixty, and thence through Eidomenê and Stobi and Dardanii to the Ister three thousand two hundred. According to Artemidorus, therefore, the distance from the Ister to Maleae amounts to

[1] Apparently Mt. Chaon (see Pausanias, 2. 24).
[2] xxxiv. *Frag*. 12.

ἑξακισχιλίων πεντακοσίων τεσσαράκοντα.[1] αἴτιον δὲ τούτου, τὸ μὴ τὴν σύντομον καταμετρεῖν, ἀλλὰ τὴν τυχοῦσαν, ἣν ἐπορεύθη τῶν στρατηγῶν τις. οὐκ ἄτοπον δ' ἴσως καὶ τοὺς οἰκιστὰς προσθεῖναι τῶν τὴν Πελοπόννησον οἰκούντων, οὓς εἶπεν Ἔφορος, τοὺς μετὰ τὴν Ἡρακλειδῶν κάθοδον· Κορίνθου μὲν Ἀλήτην, Σικυῶνος δὲ Φάλκην, Ἀχαΐας δὲ Τισαμενόν, Ἤλιδος δ' Ὄξυλον, Μεσσήνης δὲ Κρεσφόντην, Λακεδαίμονος δ' Εὐρυσθένη καὶ Προκλῆ, Ἄργους δὲ Τήμενον κ[αὶ Κισσόν, τῶν δὲ [2]] περὶ τὴν Ἀκτὴν Ἀγαῖον[3] καὶ Δηιφόντην.

[1] τεσσαράκοντα (μ'), Jones inserts, thus making the total correct.

[2] This tenth lacuna is supplied by Kramer, who finds κισσον in the Epit.

[3] For Ἀγαῖον Meineke, following conj. of Corais and Kramer, reads Ἀγραῖον; but see Müller's *Ind. Var. Lect.* p. 998.

six thousand five hundred and forty stadia. The cause of this excess[1] is that he does not give the measurement of the shortest route, but of the chance route which one of the generals took. And it is not out of place, perhaps, to add also the colonisers, mentioned by Ephorus, of the peoples who settled in the Peloponnesus after the return of the Heracleidae: Aletes, the coloniser of Corinth, Phalces of Sicyon, Tisamenus of Achaea, Oxylus of Elis, Cresphontes of Messenê, Eurysthenes and Procles of Lacedaemon, Temenus and Cissus of Argos, and Agaeus and Deïphontes of the region about Actê.[2]

[1] *i.e.* in the estimate of Polybius, apparently, rather than in that of Artemidorus.

[2] The eastern coast of Argolis was called "Actê" ("Coast").

BOOK IX

Θ'

I

C 390 1. Περιωδευκόσι δὲ τὴν Πελοπόννησον, ἣν πρώτην ἔφαμεν καὶ ἐλαχίστην τῶν συντιθεισῶν τὴν Ἑλλάδα χερρονήσων, ἐφεξῆς ἂν εἴη τὰς συνεχεῖς ἐπελθεῖν. ἦν δὲ δευτέρα μὲν ἡ προστιθεῖσα τῇ Πελοποννήσῳ τὴν Μεγαρίδα, ὥστε τὸν Κρομμυῶν[α Μεγαρέων [1]] εἶναι, καὶ μὴ Κορινθίων·[2] τρίτη δὲ ἡ πρὸς ταύτῃ προσλαμβάνουσα τὴν Ἀττικὴν καὶ τὴν Βοιωτίαν καὶ τῆς Φωκίδος τι μέρος καὶ τῶν Ἐπικνημιδίων Λοκρῶν· περὶ τούτων [οὖν λεκτέον].[3] φησὶ δ' Εὔδοξος, εἴ τις νοήσειεν ἀπὸ τῶν Κεραυνίων ὀρῶν ἐπὶ Σούνιον, τὸ τῆς Ἀττικῆς ἄκρον, ἐπὶ τὰ πρὸς ἕω μέρη τεταμένην εὐθεῖαν, ἐν δεξιᾷ μὲν ἀπολείψειν τὴν Πελοπόννησον ὅλην πρὸς νότον, ἐν ἀριστερᾷ δὲ καὶ πρὸς τὴν ἄρκτον τὴν ἀπὸ τῶν Κεραυνίων ὀρῶν συνεχῆ παραλίαν μέχρι τοῦ Κρισαίου κόλπου καὶ τῆς Μεγαρίδος, καὶ συμπάσης τῆς Ἀττικῆς· νομίζει δ' οὐδ' ἂν [κοιλαίνεσθαι οὕτως [4]] τὴν ἠιόνα

[1] The lacuna of about nine letters in A is thus supplied by Kramer and Meineke. On this and the following lacunae see Kramer's notes and text, and Meineke's text.

[2] The words ὥστε . . . Κορινθίων appear in the MSS. after Λοκρῶν (following sentence). Meineke and others, following Du Theil, rightly transfer them as above.

[3] After λεκτέον *cbhkno* add νῦν, but the lacuna in A does not warrant so many letters.

BOOK IX

I

1. Now that I have completed my circuit of the Peloponnesus, which, as I have said,[1] was the first and the smallest of the peninsulas of which Greece consists, it will be next in order to traverse those that are continuous with it. The second peninsula is the one that adds Megaris to the Peloponnesus,[2] so that Crommyon belongs to the Megarians and not to the Corinthians; the third is the one which, in addition to the second, comprises Attica and Boeotia and a part of Phocis and of the Epicnemidian Locrians. I must therefore describe these two. Eudoxus[3] says that if one should imagine a straight line drawn in an easterly direction from the Ceraunian Mountains to Sunium, the promontory of Attica, it would leave on the right, towards the south, the whole of the Peloponnesus, and on the left, towards the north, the continuous coast-line from the Ceraunian Mountains to the Crisaean Gulf and Megaris, and the coast-line of all Attica. And he believes that the shore which

[1] 8. 1. 3.

[2] And therefore comprises both. The first peninsula includes the Isthmus, Crommyon being the first place beyond it, in Megaris.

[3] Eudoxus of Cnidus (fl. 350 B.C.).

---

[4] Thus Meineke supplies the lacuna of about sixteen letters. Kramer and Müller-Dübner, following Groskurd, insert σφόδρα instead of οὕτως.

τὴν ἀπὸ Σουνίου μέχρι [τοῦ Ἰσθμοῦ, ὥστε μεγάλην] ἔχειν ἐπιστροφήν, εἰ μὴ προσῆν τῇ [ᾐόνι ταύτῃ καὶ] τὰ συνεχῆ τῷ Ἰσθμῷ χωρία τὰ [ποιοῦντα τὸν κόλπον τὸν][1] Ἑρμιονικὸν καὶ τὴν Ἀκτήν· ὡς δ' αὔ[τως οὐδ' ἂν τὴν ἀπὸ τῶν Κεραυ]νίων[2] ἐπὶ τὸν Κορινθιακὸν κόλπον ἔχειν τινὰ τοσαύ[την ἐπιστρο]φήν,[3] ὥστε κοιλαίνεσθαι κολποειδῶς καθ' αὐ[τήν, εἰ μὴ τὸ[4]] Ῥίον καὶ τὸ Ἀντίρριον συναγόμενα εἰς στενὸν [παρεῖχε τὴν[5]] ἔμφασιν ταύτην· ὁμοίως δὲ καὶ τὰ περι[έχοντα[6]] τὸν μυχόν, εἰς ἃ καταλήγειν συμβαίνει τὴν ταύτῃ[7] θάλατταν.

2. Οὕτω δ' εἰρηκότος Εὐδόξου, μαθηματικοῦ
C 391 ἀνδρὸς καὶ σχημάτων ἐμπείρου καὶ κλιμάτων καὶ τοὺς τόπους τούτους εἰδότος, δεῖ νοεῖν τήνδε τὴν πλευρὰν τῆς Ἀττικῆς σὺν τῇ Μεγαρίδι τὴν ἀπὸ Σουνίου μέχρι Ἰσθμοῦ κοίλην μέν, ἀλλ' ἐπὶ μικρόν. ἐνταῦθα δ' ἐστὶ κατὰ μέσην που τὴν λεχθεῖσαν γραμμὴν ὁ Πειραιεύς, τὸ τῶν Ἀθηνῶν ἐπίνειον. διέχει γὰρ τοῦ μὲν Σχοινοῦντος τοῦ κατὰ τὸν Ἰσθμὸν περὶ τριακοσίους πεντήκοντα

[1] Thus Meineke supplies the lacuna of about twenty letters; Kramer and Müller-Dübner, *τεινόμενα ἐπὶ τὸν κόλπον*.

[2] Thus Meineke supplies the lacuna of about twenty-four letters; Groskurd and Müller-Dübner, [*τως τὴν ᾐόνα ἀπὸ τῶν Κεραυν*].

[3] Thus Groskurd and the later editors supply the lacuna of about nine letters.

[4] Thus Meineke supplies the lacuna of about eight letters; but *bno* have *ὅπου τό*, and so Kramer and Müller-Dübner.

[5] Thus Jones supplies the lacuna of about ten letters; *bno* have *ὥστε ποιεῖν τήν*; Müller-Dübner, *ποιεῖται τήν*; Meineke, *ἐποίει τήν*.

extends from Sunium to the Isthmus would not be so concave as to have a great bend, if to this shore were not added the districts continuous with the Isthmus which form the Hermionic Gulf and Actê; and, in the same way, he believes that the shore which extends from the Ceraunian Mountains to the Corinthian Gulf would not, viewed by itself alone, have so great a bend as to be concave like a gulf if Rhium and Antirrhium did not draw closely together and afford this appearance; and the same is true of the shores[1] that surround the recess of the gulf, where the sea in this region[2] comes to an end.

2. Since this is the description given by Eudoxus, a mathematician and an expert both in geometrical figures and in "climata,"[3] and acquainted with these places, one must conceive of this side of Attica together with Megaris—the side extending from Sunium to the Isthmus—as concave, though only slightly so. Now here, at about the centre of the aforesaid line, is the Peiraeus, the sea-port of Athens. It is distant from Schoenus, at the Isthmus, about three hundred and fifty stadia, and from

[1] Including the shore of the Isthmus.

[2] That is, the Corinthian Gulf, which Eudoxus and Strabo consider a part of the sea that extends eastward from the Sicilian Sea (cf. 8. 1. 3). Others, however, understand that Strabo refers to the recess of the Crisaean Gulf in the restricted sense, that is, the Gulf of Salona.

[3] For the meaning of "climata" see vol. i, p. 22, footnote 2.

---

[6] Thus Meineke supplies the lacuna of about six letters; Groskurd, Κρίσσαν καί, and so Müller-Dübner; Kramer conj. αὐτόν.

[7] Thus Meineke supplies the lacuna of about six letters; Groskurd, Müller-Dübner and others, Κρισσαίαν.

σταδίους, τοῦ δὲ Σουνίου τριάκοντα καὶ τριακοσίους· [τόσ]ον πώς ἐστι διάστημα καὶ τὸ ἐπὶ Πηγὰς ἀπὸ τοῦ Πει[ραιῶς], ὅσονπερ καὶ ἐπὶ Σχοινοῦντα· δέκα δ' ὅμως στα[δίοις] πλεονάζειν φασί. κάμψαντι δὲ τὸ Σούνιον πρὸς ἄρκτον μὲν ὁ πλοῦς, ἐκκλίνων [δὲ] πρὸς δύσιν.

3. Ἀκτὴ δ' ἐστὶν ἀμφιθάλαττος, στενὴ τὸ πρῶτον, εἶτ' εἰς τὴν μεσόγαιαν πλατύνεται, μηνοειδῆ δ' οὐδὲν ἧττον ἐπιστροφὴν λαμβάνει πρὸς Ὠρωπὸν τῆς Βοιωτίας, τὸ κυρτὸν ἔχουσαν πρὸς θαλάττῃ· τοῦτο δ' ἐστὶ τὸ δεύτερον πλευρὸν ἑῷον τῆς Ἀττικῆς. τὸ δὲ λοιπὸν ἤδη τὸ προσάρκτιόν ἐστι πλευρόν, ἀπὸ τῆς Ὠρωπίας ἐπὶ δύσιν παρατεῖνον μέχρι τῆς Μεγαρίδος, ἡ Ἀττικὴ ὀρεινή, πολυώνυμός τις, διείργουσα τὴν Βοιωτίαν ἀπὸ τῆς Ἀττικῆς· ὥσθ', ὅπερ εἶπον ἐν τοῖς πρόσθεν, ἰσθμὸν γίνεσθαι τὴν Βοιωτίαν, ἀμφιθάλαττον οὖσαν, τῆς τρίτης χερρονήσου τῆς λεχθείσης, ἀπολαμβάνοντα ἐντὸς τὰ πρὸς τῇ Πελοποννήσῳ, τήν τε Μεγαρίδα καὶ τὴν Ἀττικήν. διὰ δὲ τοῦτο καὶ Ἀκτήν φασι λεχθῆναι τὸ παλαιὸν καὶ Ἀκτικὴν τὴν νῦν Ἀττικὴν παρονομασθεῖσαν, ὅτι τοῖς ὄρεσιν ὑποπέπτωκε τὸ πλεῖστον μέρος αὐτῆς ἁλιτενὲς καὶ στενόν, μήκει δ' ἀξιολόγῳ κεχρημένον, προπεπτωκὸς μέχρι Σουνίου. ταύτας οὖν διέξιμεν ἀναλα[βόντες πάλιν ἐκ τῆς π]αραλίας,[1] ἀφ' ἧσπερ ἀπελίπομεν.

[1] Thus Meineke supplies the lacuna of about nineteen letters in A. A *man. sec.* and *bcghikno* read ἀναλαβόντες τὰς παραλίας.

Sunium three hundred and thirty. The distance from the Peiraeus to Pagae also is nearly the same as to Schoenus, though the former is said to exceed the latter by ten stadia. After doubling Sunium one's voyage is towards the north, but with an inclination towards the west.

3. Actê[1] is washed by two seas; it is narrow at first, and then it widens out into the interior,[2] though none the less it takes a crescent-like bend towards Oropus in Boeotia, with the convex side towards the sea; and this is the second, the eastern side of Attica. Then comes the remaining side, which faces the north and extends from the Oropian country towards the west as far as Megaris—I mean the mountainous part of Attica, which has many names and separates Boeotia from Attica; so that, as I have said before,[3] Boeotia, since it has a sea on either side, becomes an isthmus of the third peninsula above-mentioned, an isthmus comprising within it the parts that lie towards the Peloponnesus, that is, Megaris and Attica. And it is on this account, they say, that the country which is now, by a slight change of letters, called Attica, was in ancient times called Actê and Acticê,[4] because the greatest part of it lies below the mountains, stretches flat along the sea, is narrow, and has considerable length, projecting as far as Sunium. I shall therefore describe these sides, resuming again at that point of the seaboard where I left off.

[1] That is, Attica; not to be confused with the Actê in Argolis, mentioned in 9. 1. 1.

[2] *i.e.* the interior plain of Attica.

[3] 9. 1. 1, 8. 1. 3.

[4] *i.e.* Shore-land.

4. Μετὰ δὴ Κρομμυῶνα ὑπέρκεινται τῆς Ἀττικῆς[1] αἱ Σκειρωνίδες πέτραι, πάροδον οὐκ ἀπολείπουσαι πρὸς θαλάττῃ· ὑπὲρ αὐτῶν δ' ἐστὶν ἡ ὁδὸς ἡ ἐπὶ Μεγάρων καὶ τῆς Ἀττικῆς ἀπὸ τοῦ Ἰσθμοῦ· οὕτω δὲ σφόδρα πλησιάζει ταῖς πέτραις ἡ ὁδός, ὥστε πολλαχοῦ καὶ παράκρημνός ἐστι, διὰ τὸ ὑπερκείμενον ὄρος δύσβατόν τε καὶ ὑψηλόν· ἐνταῦθα δὲ μυθεύεται τὰ περὶ τοῦ Σκείρωνος καὶ τοῦ Πιτυοκάμπτου, τῶν ληιζομένων τὴν λεχθεῖσαν ὀρεινήν, οὓς καθεῖλε Θησεύς. ἀπὸ δὲ τῶν ἄκρων τούτων καταιγίζοντα σκαιὸν τὸν Ἀργέστην Σκείρωνα προσηγορεύκασιν Ἀθηναῖοι. μετὰ δὲ τὰς Σκειρωνίδας πέτρας ἄκρα πρόκειται Μινώα, ποιοῦσα τὸν ἐν τῇ Νισαίᾳ λιμένα. ἡ δὲ Νισαία ἐπίνειόν ἐστιν τῶν Μεγάρων, δεκαοκτὼ σταδίους
C 392 τῆς πόλεως διέχον, σκέλεσιν ἑκατέρωθεν συναπτόμενον πρὸς αὐτήν· ἐκαλεῖτο δὲ καὶ τοῦτο Μινώα.

5. Τὸ παλαιὸν μὲν οὖν Ἴωνες εἶχον τὴν χώραν ταύτην, οἵπερ καὶ τὴν Ἀττικήν, οὔπω τῶν Μεγάρων ἐκτισμένων· διόπερ οὐδ' ὁ ποιητὴς μέμνηται τῶν τόπων τούτων ἰδίως, ἀλλ' Ἀθηναίους καλῶν τοὺς ἐν τῇ Ἀττικῇ πάντας, συμπεριείληφε καὶ τούτους τῷ κοινῷ ὀνόματι, Ἀθηναίους νομίζων· ὡς ὅταν φῇ ἐν τῷ Καταλόγῳ·

οἳ δ' ἄρ' Ἀθήνας εἶχον, ἐϋκτίμενον πτολίεθρον,

δέχεσθαι δεῖ καὶ τοὺς νῦν Μεγαρέας, ὡς καὶ

[1] For Ἀττικῆς Tozer, following the conj. of Meineke, reads ἀκτῆς ("edge of the coast").

---

[1] "Pine-bender." His name was Sinis. For the story, see Pausanias, 2. 1. 3.

4. After Crommyon, and situated above Attica, are the Sceironian Rocks. They leave no room for a road along the sea, but the road from the Isthmus to Megara and Attica passes above them. However, the road approaches so close to the rocks that in many places it passes along the edge of precipices, because the mountain situated above them is both lofty and impracticable for roads. Here is the setting of the myth about Sceiron and the Pityocamptes,[1] the robbers who infested the abovementioned mountainous country and were killed by Theseus. And the Athenians have given the name Sceiron to the Argestes, the violent wind that blows down on the traveller's left[2] from the heights of this mountainous country. After the Sceironian Rocks one comes to Cape Minoa, which projects into the sea and forms the harbour at Nisaea. Nisaea is the naval station of the Megarians; it is eighteen stadia distant from the city and is joined to it on both sides by walls. The naval station, too, used to be called Minoa.

5. In early times this country was held by the same Ionians who held Attica. Megara, however, had not yet been founded; and therefore the poet does not specifically mention this region, but when he calls all the people of Attica Athenians he includes these too under the general name, considering them Athenians. Thus, when he says in the *Catalogue*, "And those who held Athens, well-built city,"[3] we must interpret him as meaning the people now called Megarians as well, and assume that these also

[2] That is, to one travelling from the Isthmus to Megaris and Attica.

[3] *Iliad* 2. 546.

τούτους[1] μετασχόντας τῆς στρατείας. σημεῖον δέ· ἡ γὰρ Ἀττικὴ τὸ παλαιὸν Ἰωνία καὶ Ἰὰς ἐκαλεῖτο, καὶ ὁ ποιητὴς ὅταν φῇ·

ἔνθα δὲ Βοιωτοὶ καὶ Ἰάονες,[2]

τοὺς Ἀθηναίους λέγει· ταύτης δ' ἦν μερὶς καὶ ἡ Μεγαρίς.

6. Καὶ δὴ καὶ[3] τῶν ὁρίων ἀμφισβητοῦντες πολλάκις οἵ τε Πελοποννήσιοι καὶ Ἴωνες, ἐν οἷς ἦν καὶ ἡ Κρομμυωνία, συνέβησαν καὶ στήλην ἔστησαν ἐπὶ τοῦ συνομολογηθέντος τόπου περὶ αὐτὸν τὸν Ἰσθμόν, ἐπιγραφὴν ἔχουσαν ἐπὶ μὲν τοῦ πρὸς τὴν Πελοπόννησον μέρους,

τάδ' ἐστὶ Πελοπόννησος, οὐκ Ἰωνία·

ἐπὶ δὲ τοῦ πρὸς Μέγαρα,

τάδ' οὐχὶ Πελοπόννησος, ἀλλ' Ἰωνία.

οἵ τε δὴ τὴν Ἀτθίδα συγγράψαντες, πολλὰ διαφωνοῦντες, τοῦτό γε ὁμολογοῦσιν, οἵ γε λόγου ἄξιοι, διότι[4] τῶν Πανδιονιδῶν τεσσάρων ὄντων, Αἰγέως τε καὶ Λύκου καὶ Πάλλαντος καὶ τετάρτου Νίσου, καὶ τῆς Ἀττικῆς εἰς τέτταρα μέρη διαιρεθείσης, ὁ Νίσος τὴν Μεγαρίδα λάχοι καὶ κτίσαι τὴν Νίσαιαν. Φιλόχορος μὲν οὖν ἀπὸ Ἰσθμοῦ μέχρι τοῦ Πυθίου διήκειν αὐτοῦ φησὶ τὴν ἀρχήν, Ἄνδρων δὲ μέχρι Ἐλευσῖνος καὶ τοῦ Θριασίου πεδίου. τὴν δ' εἰς τέτταρα μέρη διανομὴν ἄλλων ἄλλως εἰρηκότων, ἀρκεῖ ταῦτα παρὰ Σοφοκλέους

[1] αὐτούς *Bklno.*
[2] Ἰάονες, Xylander, for Ἴωνες; so the later editors.
[3] After καί *Bok* have περί.
[4] ὅτι *Bkno.*

had a part in the expedition. And the following is proof: In early times Attica was called Ionia and Ias; and when the poet says, "There the Boeotians and the Iaonians,"[1] he means the Athenians; and Megaris was a part of this Ionia.

6. Furthermore, since the Peloponnesians and Ionians were having frequent disputes about their boundaries, on which, among other places, Crommyonia was situated, they made an agreement and erected a pillar in the place agreed upon, near the Isthmus itself, with an inscription on the side facing the Peloponnesus reading: "This is Peloponnesus, not Ionia," and on the side facing Megara, "This is not Peloponnesus, but Ionia." And though the writers of the histories of *The Land of Atthis*[2] are at variance on many things, they all agree on this (at least all writers who are worth mentioning), that Pandion had four sons, Aegeus, Lycus, Pallas, and the fourth, Nisus, and that when Attica was divided into four parts, Nisus obtained Megaris as his portion and founded Nisaea. Now, according to Philochorus,[3] his rule extended from the Isthmus to the Pythium,[4] but according to Andron,[5] only as far as Eleusis and the Thriasian Plain. Although different writers have stated the division into four parts in different ways, it suffices to take the following from Sophocles:

[1] *Iliad* 13. 685.   [2] See Vol. II, p. 346, notes 1 and 2.

[3] Philochorus the Athenian (fl. about 300 B.C.) wrote a work entitled *Atthis*, in seventeen books. Only fragments remain.

[4] To what Pythium Philochorus refers is uncertain, but he seems to mean the temple of Pythian Apollo in the deme of Oenoê, about twelve miles north-west of Eleusis; or possibly the temple of Apollo which was situated between Eleusis and Athens on the site of the present monastery of Daphnê.

[5] See foot-note on 10. 4. 6.

λαβεῖν· φησὶ δ' ὁ Αἰγεύς, ὅτι[1] ὁ πατὴρ ὥρισεν ἐμοὶ μὲν ἀπελθεῖν εἰς ἀκτάς, τῆσδε γῆς πρεσβεῖα νείμας· τῷ δ' αὖ[2] Λύκῳ

τὸν ἀντίπλευρον κῆπον Εὐβοίας νεμεῖ,[3]
Νίσῳ δὲ τὴν ὅμαυλον[4] ἐξαιρεῖ χθόνα
Σκείρωνος ἀκτῆς, τῆς δὲ γῆς τὸ πρὸς νότον
ὁ σκληρὸς οὗτος καὶ γίγαντας ἐκτρέφων
εἴληχε Πάλλας.

ὅτι μὲν οὖν ἡ Μεγαρὶς τῆς Ἀττικῆς μέρος ἦν, τούτοις χρῶνται τεκμηρίοις.

7. Μετὰ δὲ τὴν τῶν Ἡρακλειδῶν κάθοδον καὶ τὸν τῆς χώρας μερισμόν, ὑπ' αὐτῶν καὶ τῶν
C 393 συγκατελθόντων αὐτοῖς Δωριέων ἐκπεσεῖν τῆς οἰκείας συνέβη πολλοὺς εἰς τὴν Ἀττικήν, ὧν ἦν καὶ ὁ τῆς Μεσσήνης βασιλεὺς Μέλανθος· οὗτος δὲ καὶ τῶν Ἀθηναίων ἐβασίλευσεν ἑκόντων, νικήσας ἐκ μονομαχίας τὸν τῶν Βοιωτῶν βασιλέα Ξάνθον. εὐανδρούσης δὲ τῆς Ἀττικῆς διὰ τοὺς φυγάδας, φοβηθέντες οἱ Ἡρακλεῖδαι, παροξυνόντων[5] αὐτοὺς μάλιστα τῶν ἐν Κορίνθῳ καὶ τῶν ἐν Μεσσήνῃ, τῶν μὲν διὰ τὴν γειτνίασιν, τῶν δέ, ὅτι Κόδρος τῆς Ἀττικῆς ἐβασίλευε τότε ὁ τοῦ Μελάνθου παῖς, ἐστράτευσαν ἐπὶ τὴν Ἀττικήν·

[1] In the unmetrical ὁ πατὴρ . . . Λύκῳ Strabo interweaves his own words with those of the poet. Jones conjectures that the poet wrote as follows:

ἐμοὶ μὲν ὥρισεν πατὴρ ἀκτὰς μολεῖν,
πρεσβεῖα νείμας τῆσδε γῆς· τῷ δ' αὖ Λύκῳ
κτλ.

For Meineke's conj. (followed by Nauck, *Frag.* 872) see *Vind. Strab.* p. 129.

Aegeus says that his father ordered him to depart to the shore-lands, assigning to him as the eldest the best portion of this land; then to Lycus "he assigns Euboea's garden that lies side by side therewith; and for Nisus he selects the neighbouring land of Sceiron's shore; and the southerly part of the land fell to this rugged Pallas, breeder of giants."[1] These, then, are the proofs which writers use to show that Megaris was a part of Attica.

7. But after the return of the Heracleidae and the partitioning of the country, it came to pass that many of the former inhabitants were driven out of their home-lands into Attica by the Heracleidae and the Dorians who came back with them. Among these was Melanthus, the king of Messenê. And he reigned also over the Athenians, by their consent, after his victory in single combat over Xanthus, the king of the Boeotians. But since Attica was now populous on account of the exiles, the Heracleidae became frightened, and at the instigation chiefly of the people of Corinth and the people of Messenê—of the former because of their proximity and of the latter because Codrus, the son of Melanthus, was at that time king of Attica—they made an expedition

[1] *Frag.* 872 (Nauck).

---

[2] τῷ δ' αὖ, Jones inserts. There is a lacuna in A with only the letter α before Λύκῳ. *acghino* have τῷ δέ. Meineke reads [εἶτ]α.

[3] νεμεῖ, Corais, for νέμων, the letters μων being supplied by second hand in A. So Meineke.

[4] ὄμαυλον E, ὄμαυδον A with λον written above in second hand. For other variants see C. Müller's *Ind. Var. Lect.* p. 999.

[5] παροξυνόντων *g*, for παροξυνάντων; so Corais and Meineke.

ἡττηθέντες δὲ μάχῃ τῆς μὲν ἄλλης ἐξέστησαν γῆς, τὴν Μεγαρικὴν δὲ κατέσχον καὶ τήν τε πόλιν ἔκτισαν τὰ Μέγαρα καὶ τοὺς ἀνθρώπους Δωριέας ἀντὶ Ἰώνων ἐποίησαν· ἠφάνισαν δὲ καὶ τὴν στήλην τὴν ὁρίζουσαν τούς τε Ἴωνας καὶ τοὺς Πελοποννησίους.

8. Πολλαῖς δὲ κέχρηται μεταβολαῖς ἡ τῶν Μεγαρέων πόλις, συμμένει δ' ὅμως μέχρι νῦν. ἔσχε δέ ποτε καὶ φιλοσόφων διατριβὰς τῶν προσαγορευθέντων Μεγαρικῶν, Εὐκλείδην διαδεξαμένων, ἄνδρα Σωκρατικόν, Μεγαρέα τὸ γένος· καθάπερ καὶ Φαίδωνα μὲν τὸν Ἠλεῖον οἱ Ἠλειακοὶ διεδέξαντο, καὶ τοῦτον Σωκρατικόν, ὧν ἦν καὶ Πύρρων, Μενέδημον δὲ τὸν Ἐρετριέα οἱ Ἐρετρικοί. ἔστι δ' ἡ χώρα τῶν Μεγαρέων παράλυπρος, καθάπερ καὶ ἡ Ἀττική, καὶ τὸ πλέον αὐτῆς ἐπέχει τὰ καλούμενα Ὄνεια ὄρη, ῥάχις τις μηκυνομένη μὲν ἀπὸ τῶν Σκειρωνίδων πετρῶν ἐπὶ τὴν Βοιωτίαν καὶ τὸν Κιθαιρῶνα, διείργουσα δὲ τὴν κατὰ Νίσαιαν θάλατταν ἀπὸ τῆς κατ[ὰ τὰς Παγάς],[1] Ἀλκυονίδος προσαγορευομένης.

9. Πρόκειται δ' ἀπὸ Νισαίας πλέοντι εἰς τὴν Ἀττικὴν πέντε νησία. εἶτα Σαλαμὶς ἑβδομήκοντά που σταδίων οὖσα τὸ μῆκος, οἱ δ' ὀγδοήκοντά φασιν· ἔχει δ' ὁμώνυμον πόλιν, τὴν μὲν ἀρχαίαν ἔρημον πρὸς Αἴγιναν τετραμμένην καὶ πρὸς νότον (καθάπερ καὶ Αἰσχύλος εἴρηκεν,

Αἴγινα δ' αὕτη πρὸς νότου κεῖται πνοάς),

τὴν δὲ νῦν ἐν κόλπῳ κειμένην ἐπὶ χερρονησοειδοῦς

[1] κατ[ὰ τὰς Παγάς], lacuna of about ten letters supplied by Kramer; Meineke and others following. A late hand in A writes κατὰ Κρίσαν, and so *kno* and, by correction, B.

against Attica. But being defeated in battle they retired from the whole of the land except the Megarian territory; this they occupied and not only founded the city Megara[1] but also made its population Dorians instead of Ionians. And they also destroyed the pillar which was the boundary between the Ionians and the Peloponnesians.

8. The city of the Megarians has experienced many changes, but nevertheless it has endured until the present time. It once even had schools of philosophers who were called the Megarian sect, these being the successors of Eucleides, the Socratic philosopher, a Megarian by birth, just as the Eleian sect, to which Pyrrhon belonged, were the successors of Phaedon the Eleian, who was also a Socratic philosopher, and just as the Eretrian sect were the successors of Menedemus the Eretrian. The country of the Megarians, like Attica, has rather poor soil, and the greater part of it is occupied by the Oneian Mountains, as they are called—a kind of ridge, which extends from the Sceironian Rocks to Boeotia and Cithaeron, and separates the sea at Nisaea from the Alcyonian Sea, as it is called, at Pagae.

9. On the voyage from Nisaea to Attica one comes to five small islands. Then to Salamis, which is about seventy stadia in length, though some say eighty. It contains a city of the same name; the ancient city, now deserted, faces towards Aegina and the south wind (just as Aeschylus has said, "And Aegina here lies towards the blasts of the south wind"),[2] but the city of to-day is situated on a

[1] Cf. 8. 1. 2.
[2] *Frag.* 404 (Nauck).

τόπου συνάπτοντος πρὸς τὴν Ἀττικήν. ἐκαλεῖτο δ' ἑτέροις ὀνόμασι τὸ παλαιόν· καὶ γὰρ Σκιρὰς καὶ Κυχρεία ἀπό τινων ἡρώων, ἀφ' οὗ μὲν Ἀθηνᾶ τε λέγεται Σκιρὰς καὶ τόπος Σκίρα ἐν τῇ Ἀττικῇ καὶ ἐπὶ Σκίρῳ[1] ἱεροποιΐα τις καὶ ὁ μὴν ὁ Σκιροφοριών· ἀφ' οὗ δὲ[2] καὶ Κυχρείδης ὄφις, ὅν φησιν Ἡσίοδος τραφέντα ὑπὸ Κυχρέως ἐξελαθῆναι ὑπὸ Εὐρυλόχου,[3] λυμαινόμενον τὴν νῆσον, ὑποδέξασθαι δὲ αὐτὸν τὴν Δήμητραν εἰς Ἐλευσῖνα καὶ γενέσθαι
C 394 ταύτης ἀμφίπολον. ὠνομάσθη δὲ καὶ Πιτυοῦσσα ἀπὸ τοῦ φυτοῦ· ἐπιφανὴς δὲ ἡ νῆσος ὑπῆρξε διά τε τοὺς Αἰακίδας ἐπάρξαντας[4] αὐτῆς, καὶ μάλιστα δι' Αἴαντα τὸν Τελαμώνιον, καὶ διὰ τὸ περὶ τὴν νῆσον ταύτην καταναυμαχηθῆναι Ξέρξην ὑπὸ τῶν Ἑλλήνων καὶ φυγεῖν εἰς τὴν οἰκείαν. συναπέλαυσαν δὲ καὶ Αἰγινῆται τῆς περὶ τὸν ἀγῶνα τοῦτον δόξης, γείτονές τε ὄντες καὶ ναυτικὸν ἀξιόλογον παρασχόμενοι. Βώκαρος δ' ἐστὶν ἐν Σαλαμῖνι[5] ποταμός, ὁ νῦν Βωκαλία καλούμενος.

10. Καὶ νῦν μὲν ἔχουσιν Ἀθηναῖοι τὴν νῆσον, τὸ δὲ παλαιὸν πρὸς Μεγαρέας ὑπῆρξεν αὐτοῖς ἔρις περὶ αὐτῆς· καί φασιν οἱ μὲν Πεισίστρατον,

[1] ἐπὶ Σκίρῳ, Kramer and later editors, following *gl* and *man. sec.* in A (ἐπισκίρῳ), for ἐπισκείρῳ A, ἐπισκίρωσιν *no*, ἐπισκίρωσις *o man. sec.*; ἔτι Σκίρα Corais.

[2] δέ, Corais, for δή; so the later editors.

[3] Εὐρυλόχου, Tzschucke, for Εὐρύκλου.

[4] ἐπάρξαντας, Meineke, from conj. of Corais and Kramer, for ὑπάρξαντας.

[5] Σαλαμῖνι, the editors (from Eustathius, note on *Iliad* 2. 637), for Ἐλευσῖνι.

gulf, on a peninsula-like place which borders on Attica. In early times it was called by different names, for example, "Sciras" and "Cychreia," after certain heroes. It is from one[1] of these heroes that Athena is called "Sciras," and that a place in Attica is called "Scira," and that a certain sacred rite is performed in honour of "Scirus,"[2] and that one of the months is called "Sciropliorion." And it is from the other hero that the serpent "Cychreides" took its name—the serpent which, according to Hesiod, was fostered by Cychreus and driven out by Eurylochus because it was damaging the island, and was welcomed to Eleusis by Demeter and made her attendant. And the island was also called Pityussa, from the tree.[3] But the fame of the island is due to the Aiacidae, who ruled over it, and particularly to Aias, the son of Telamon, and also to the fact that near this island Xerxes was defeated by the Greeks in a naval battle and fled to his home-land. And the Aeginetans also shared in the glory of this struggle, since they were neighbours and furnished a considerable fleet. And there is in Salamis a river Bocarus, which is now called Bocalia.

10. At the present time the island is held by the Athenians, although in early times there was strife between them and the Megarians for its possession. Some say that it was Peisistratus, others

[1] Scirus.

[2] Scirus founded the ancient sanctuary of Athena Sciras at Phalerum. After his death the Eleusinians buried him between Athens and Eleusis at a place which in his honour they called "Scira," or, according to Pausanias (1. 36. 4 *q.v.*) and others, "Scirum."

[3] "Pitys," "pine-tree."

οἱ δὲ Σόλωνα παρεγγράψαντα ἐν τῷ Νεῶν Καταλόγῳ μετὰ τὸ ἔπος τοῦτο,

Αἴας δ' ἐκ Σαλαμῖνος ἄγεν δυοκαίδεκα νῆας,

ἑξῆς τοῦτο,

στῆσε δ' ἄγων, ἵν' Ἀθηναίων ἵσταντο φάλαγγες,

μάρτυρι χρήσασθαι τῷ ποιητῇ τοῦ τὴν νῆσον ἐξ ἀρχῆς Ἀθηναίων ὑπάρξαι. οὐ παραδέχονται δὲ τοῦθ' οἱ κριτικοὶ διὰ τὸ πολλὰ τῶν ἐπῶν ἀντιμαρτυρεῖν αὐτοῖς. διὰ τί γὰρ ναυλοχῶν ἔσχατος φαίνεται ὁ Αἴας, οὐ μετ' Ἀθηναίων, ἀλλὰ μετὰ τῶν ὑπὸ Πρωτεσιλάῳ Θετταλῶν;

ἔνθ' ἔσαν Αἴαντός τε νέες καὶ Πρωτεσιλάου·

καὶ ἐν τῇ Ἐπιπωλήσει ὁ Ἀγαμέμνων

εὗρ' υἱὸν Πετεῶο Μενεσθῆα πλή[ξιππον
ἑστα]ότ',[1] ἀμφὶ δ' Ἀθηναῖοι, μήστωρες ἀϋτῆς.
αὐτὰρ ὁ πλησίον ἑστήκει πολύμητις Ὀδυσσεύς,
πὰρ δὲ Κεφαλλήνων ἀμφὶ στίχες.

ἐπὶ δὲ τὸν Αἴαντα καὶ τοὺς Σαλαμινίους πάλιν,

ἦλθε δ' ἐπ' Αἰάντεσσι·

καὶ παρ' αὐτοὺς

Ἰδομενεὺς δ' ἑτέρωθεν,

οὐ Μενεσθεύς. οἱ μὲν δὴ Ἀθηναῖοι τοιαύτην τινὰ σκήψασθαι[2] μαρτυρίαν παρ' Ὁμήρου δοκοῦσιν, οἱ δὲ Μεγαρεῖς ἀντιπαρῳδῆσαι οὕτως·

Αἴας δ' ἐκ Σαλαμῖνος ἄγεν νέας, ἔκ τε Πολίχνης
ἔκ τ' Αἰγειρούσσης Νισαίης τε Τριπόδων τε·

Solon, who inserted in the *Catalogue of Ships* immediately after the verse, "and Aias brought twelve ships from Salamis,"[1] the verse, "and, bringing them, halted them where the battalions of the Athenians were stationed," and then used the poet as a witness that the island had belonged to the Athenians from the beginning. But the critics do not accept this interpretation, because many of the verses bear witness to the contrary. For why is Aias found in the last place in the ship-camp, not with the Athenians, but with the Thessalians under Protesilaüs? "where were the ships of Aias and Protesilaüs."[2] And in the *Visitation* of the troops, Agamemnon "found Menestheus the charioteer, son of Peteos, standing still; and about him were the Athenians, masters of the battle-cry. And near by stood Odysseus of many wiles, and about him, at his side, the ranks of the Cephallenians."[3] And back again to Aias and the Salaminians, "he came to the Aïantes,"[4] and near them, "Idomeneus on the other side,"[5] not Menestheus. The Athenians, then, are reputed to have cited alleged testimony of this kind from Homer, and the Megarians to have replied with the following parody: "Aias brought ships from Salamis, from Polichnê, from Aegeirussa, from Nisaea, and from Tripodes"; these four are

[1] *Iliad* 2. 557.
[2] *Iliad* 13. 681.
[3] *Iliad* 4. 327.
[4] *Iliad* 4. 273.
[5] *Iliad* 3. 230.

---

[1] Thus *h* supplies the lacuna in A.
[2] χρήσασθαι *no*.

ἅ ἐστι χωρία Μεγαρικά, ὧν οἱ Τρίποδες Τριποδίσκιον λέγονται, καθ' ὃ ἡ νῦν ἀγορὰ τῶν Μεγάρων κεῖται.

C 395 11. Τινὲς δ' ἀπὸ τοῦ τὴν ἱέρειαν τῆς Πολιάδος Ἀθηνᾶς χλωροῦ τυροῦ, τοῦ μὲν ἐπιχωρίου μὴ ἅπτεσθαι, ξενικὸν δὲ μόνον προσφέρεσθαι, χρῆσθαι δὲ καὶ τῷ Σαλαμινίῳ, ξένην φασὶ τῆς Ἀττικῆς τὴν Σαλαμῖνα· οὐκ εὖ· καὶ γὰρ τὸν ἀπὸ τῶν ἄλλων νήσων τῶν ὁμολογουμένως τῇ Ἀττικῇ προσχώρων προσφέρεται, ξενικὸν πάντα τὸν διαπόντιον νοησάντων τῶν ἀρξάντων τοῦ ἔθους τούτου. ἔοικε δὲ τὸ παλαιὸν ἡ νῦν Σαλαμὶς καθ' αὑτὴν τάττεσθαι, τὰ δὲ Μέγαρα τῆς Ἀττικῆς ὑπάρξαι μέρος. ἐν δὲ τῇ παραλίᾳ τῇ κατὰ Σαλαμῖνα κεῖσθαι συμβαίνει τὰ ὅρια τῆς τε Μεγαρικῆς καὶ τῆς Ἀτθίδος, ὄρη δύο, ἃ καλοῦσι Κέρατα.

12. Εἶτ' Ἐλευσὶς[1] πόλις, ἐν ᾗ τὸ τῆς Δήμητρος ἱερὸν τῆς Ἐλευσινίας, καὶ ὁ μυστικὸς σηκός, ὃν κατεσκεύασεν Ἰκτῖνος, ὄχλον θεάτρου δέξασθαι δυνάμενον, ὃς καὶ τὸν Παρθενῶνα ἐποίησε τὸν ἐν ἀκροπόλει τῇ Ἀθηνᾷ, Περικλέους ἐπιστατοῦντος τῶν ἔργων· ἐν δὲ τοῖς δήμοις καταριθμεῖται ἡ πόλις.

13. Εἶτα τὸ Θριάσιον πεδίον καὶ ὁμώνυμος αἰγιαλὸς καὶ δῆμος· εἶθ' ἡ ἄκρα ἡ Ἀμφιάλη καὶ τὸ ὑπερκείμενον λατόμιον, καὶ ὁ εἰς Σαλαμῖνα πορθμὸς ὅσον διστάδιος, ὃν διαχοῦν ἐπειρᾶτο

[1] Ἐλευσίς *gk*, Corais, and Meineke, for Ἐλευσίν.

---

[1] Attica.

Megarian places, and, of these, Tripodes is called Tripodiscium, near which the present market-place of the Megarians is situated.

11. Some say that Salamis is foreign to Attica, citing the fact that the priestess of Athena Polias does not touch the fresh cheese made in Attica, but eats only that which is brought from a foreign country, yet uses, among others, that from Salamis. Wrongly, for she eats cheese brought from the other islands that are admittedly attached to Attica, since those who began this custom considered as "foreign" any cheese that was imported by sea. But it seems that in early times the present Salamis was a separate state, and that Megara was a part of Attica. And it is on the seaboard opposite Salamis that the boundaries between the Megarian country and Atthis[1] are situated—two mountains which are called Cerata.[2]

12. Then one comes to the city Eleusis, in which is the temple of the Eleusinian Demeter, and the mystic chapel which was built by Ictinus, a chapel which is large enough to admit a crowd of spectators. This Ictinus also built the Parthenon on the Acropolis in honour of Athena, Pericles superintending the work. Eleusis is numbered among the demes.

13. Then one comes to the Thriasian Plain, and the shore and deme bearing the same name. Then to Cape Amphialê and the quarry that lies above it, and to the passage to Salamis, about two stadia wide, across which Xerxes attempted to build a

[2] "Horns." Two horn-shaped peaks of a south-western spur of Cithaeron, and still called Kerata-Pyrgos or Keratopiko (Forbiger, *Handbuch der alten Geographie*, iii. 631, note 97).

Ξέρξης, ἔφθη δὲ ἡ ναυμαχία γενομένη καὶ φυγὴ τῶν Περσῶν. ἐνταῦθα δὲ καὶ αἱ Φαρμακοῦσσαι, δύο νησία, ὧν ἐν τῷ μείζονι Κίρκης τάφος δείκνυται.

14. Ὑπὲρ δὲ τῆς ἀκτῆς ταύτης ὄρος ἐστίν, ὃ καλεῖται Κορυδαλλός, καὶ ὁ δῆμος οἱ Κορυδαλλεῖς· εἶθ' ὁ Φώρων λιμὴν καὶ ἡ Ψυτταλία, νησίον ἔρημον πετρῶδες, ὅ τινες εἶπον λήμην[1] τοῦ Πειραιῶς· πλησίον δὲ καὶ ἡ Ἀταλάντη, ὁμώνυμος τῇ περὶ Εὔβοιαν καὶ Λοκρούς, καὶ ἄλλο νησίον, ὅμοιον τῇ Ψυτταλίᾳ καὶ τοῦτο· εἶθ' ὁ Πειραιεύς, καὶ αὐτὸς ἐν τοῖς δήμοις ταττόμενος, καὶ ἡ Μουνυχία.

15. Λόφος δ' ἐστὶν ἡ Μουνυχία χερρονησιάζων καὶ κοῖλος καὶ ὑπόνομος πολὺ μέρος φύσει τε καὶ ἐπίτηδες, ὥστ' οἰκήσεις δέχεσθαι, στομίῳ δὲ μικρῷ τὴν εἴσοδον ἔχων· ὑποπίπτουσι δ' αὐτῷ λιμένες τρεῖς. τὸ μὲν οὖν παλαιὸν ἐτετείχιστο καὶ συνῴκιστο ἡ Μουνυχία παραπλησίως, ὥσπερ ἡ τῶν Ῥοδίων πόλις, προσειληφυῖα τῷ περιβόλῳ τόν τε Πειραιᾶ καὶ τοὺς λιμένας πλήρεις νεωρίων, ἐν οἷς καὶ ἡ ὁπλοθήκη, Φίλωνος ἔργον· ἄξιόν τε

[1] λήμην, Corais, for λιμένα (but letters ένα written in *man. sec.* in A); so the later editors.

---

[1] So Ctesias, *Persica*, 26, but in the account of Herodotus (8. 97) it was after the naval battle that "he attempted to build a mole." In either case it is very improbable that he made a serious attempt to do so. See Smith and Laird, *Herodotus*, Books vii and viii, p. 381 (American Book Co.), note on χῶμα.

[2] Now called Lipsokutáli (see Frazer, note on Pausanias, 1. 36. 2).

mole,[1] but was forestalled by the naval battle and the flight of the Persians. Here, too, are the Pharmacussae, two small islands, on the larger of which is to be seen the tomb of Circê.

14. Above this shore is the mountain called Corydallus, and also the deme Corydalleis. Then one comes to the harbour Phoron, and to Psyttalia,[2] a small, deserted, rocky island, which some have called the eye-sore of the Peiraeus. And near by, too, is Atalanta, which bears the same name as the island near Euboea and the Locrians, and another island similar to Psyttalia. Then one comes to the Peiraeus, which also is classed among the demes, and to Munychia.

15. Munychia is a hill which forms a peninsula; and it is hollowed out and undermined[3] in many places, partly by nature and partly by the purpose of man, so that it admits of dwellings; and the entrance to it is by means of a narrow opening.[4] And beneath the hill lie three harbours. Now in early times Munychia was walled, and covered with habitations in a manner similar to the city of the Rhodians,[5] including within the circuit of its walls both the Peiraeus and the harbours, which were full of ship-houses, among which was the arsenal, the work of Philon. And the naval station was

[3] "Probably in part the result of quarrying, for numerous traces of quarries are visible on these hills at the present day" (Tozer, *Selections*, p. 228).

[4] *i.e.* the entrance by way of the narrow isthmus.

[5] "With broad straight streets, the houses of which rose one above another like the seats of a theatre. Under the auspices of Pericles, Peiraeus was laid out by the famous architect, Hippodamus of Miletus, who afterwards built the city of Rhodes" (Tozer, *l.c.*).

ἦν ναύσταθμον ταῖς τετρακοσίαις ναυσίν, ὧν οὐκ ἐλάττους ἔστελλον Ἀθηναῖοι. τῷ δὲ τείχει τούτῳ συνῆπτε τὰ καθειλκυσμένα ἐκ τοῦ ἄστεος σκέλη· ταῦτα δ' ἦν μακρὰ τείχη, τετταράκοντα σταδίων τὸ μῆκος, συνάπτοντα τὸ ἄστυ τῷ Πειραιεῖ. οἱ δὲ πολλοὶ πόλεμοι τὸ τεῖχος κατή-
C 396 ρειψαν καὶ τὸ τῆς Μουνυχίας ἔρυμα, τόν τε Πειραιᾶ συνέστειλαν εἰς ὀλίγην κατοικίαν, τὴν περὶ τοὺς λιμένας καὶ τὸ ἱερὸν τοῦ Διὸς τοῦ Σωτῆρος· τοῦ δὲ ἱεροῦ τὰ μὲν στοΐδια ἔχει πίνακας θαυμαστούς, ἔργα τῶν ἐπιφανῶν τεχνιτῶν, τὸ δ' ὕπαιθρον ἀνδριάντας. κατέσπασται δὲ καὶ τὰ μακρὰ τείχη, Λακεδαιμονίων μὲν καθελόντων πρότερον, Ῥωμαίων δ' ὕστερον, ἡνίκα Σύλλας ἐκ πολιορκίας εἷλε καὶ τὸν Πειραιᾶ καὶ τὸ ἄστυ.

16. Τὸ δ' ἄστυ αὐτὸ πέτρα ἐστὶν ἐν πεδίῳ περιοικουμένη κύκλῳ· ἐπὶ δὲ τῇ πέτρᾳ τὸ τῆς Ἀθηνᾶς ἱερόν, ὅ τε ἀρχαῖος νεὼς ὁ τῆς Πολιάδος, ἐν ᾧ ὁ ἄσβεστος λύχνος, καὶ ὁ Παρθενών, ὃν ἐποίησεν Ἰκτῖνος, ἐν ᾧ τὸ τοῦ Φειδίου ἔργον ἐλεφάντινον, ἡ Ἀθηνᾶ. ἀλλὰ γὰρ εἰς πλῆθος ἐμπίπτων τῶν περὶ τῆς πόλεως ταύτης ὑμνουμένων τε καὶ διαβοωμένων ὀκνῶ πλεονάζειν, μὴ συμβῇ τῆς προθέσεως ἐκπεσεῖν τὴν γραφήν. ἔπεισι γὰρ ὅ φησιν Ἡγησίας· "ὁρῶ τὴν ἀκρόπολιν καὶ τὸ περιττῆς τριαίνης ἐκεῖθι[1] σημεῖον· ὁρῶ τὴν Ἐλευσῖνα, καὶ τῶν ἱερῶν γέγονα μύστης·

[1] ἐκεῖθι, Meineke, for ἔχει τι, C. Müller approving.

---

[1] 86 B.C.

[2] The Erechtheium (see D'Ooge, *Acropolis of Athens*, Appendix iii).

sufficient for the four hundred ships, for no fewer than this the Athenians were wont to despatch on expeditions. With this wall were connected the "legs" that stretched down from the city; these were the long walls, forty stadia in length, which connected the city with the Peiraeus. But the numerous wars caused the ruin of the wall and of the fortress of Munychia, and reduced the Peiraeus to a small settlement, round the harbours and the temple of Zeus Soter. The small roofed colonnades of the temple have admirable paintings, the works of famous artists; and its open court has statues. The long walls, also, are torn down, having been destroyed at first by the Lacedaemonians, and later by the Romans, when Sulla took both the Peiraeus and the city by siege.[1]

16. The city itself is a rock situated in a plain and surrounded by dwellings. On the rock is the sacred precinct of Athena, comprising both the old temple of Athena Polias,[2] in which is the lamp that is never quenched,[3] and the Parthenon built by Ictinus, in which is the work in ivory by Pheidias, the Athena. However, if I once began to describe the multitude of things in this city that are lauded and proclaimed far and wide, I fear that I should go too far, and that my work would depart from the purpose I have in view. For the words of Hegesias[4] occur to me: "I see the acropolis, and the mark of the huge trident[5] there. I see Eleusis, and I have become an initiate into its sacred mysteries; yonder is the

[3] Cp. Pausanias 1. 26. 7.

[4] Hegesias of Magnesia (fl. about 250 B.C.) wrote a *History of Alexander the Great.* Only fragments remain.

[5] In the rock of the well in the Erechtheium.

ἐκεῖνο Λεωκόριον, τοῦτο Θησεῖον· οὐ δύναμαι δηλῶσαι καθ' ἓν ἕκαστον· ἡ γὰρ Ἀττικὴ θεῶν αὐτοῖς[1] [τέμενος[2]] καταλαβόντων καὶ τῶν προγόνων ἡρώων ἐστὶ κτῆμα."[3] οὗτος μὲν οὖν ἑνὸς ἐμνήσθη τῶν ἐν ἀκροπόλει σημείων· Πολέμων δ' ὁ περιηγητὴς τέτταρα βιβλία συνέγραψε περὶ τῶν ἀναθημάτων τῶν ἐν ἀκροπόλει. τὸ δ' ἀνάλογον συμβαίνει καὶ ἐπὶ τῶν ἄλλων τῆς πόλεως μερῶν καὶ τῆς χώρας· Ἐλευσῖνά τε εἰπὼν ἕνα τῶν ἑκατὸν ἑβδομήκοντα δήμων, πρὸς δὲ καὶ τεττάρων, ὥς φασιν, οὐδένα τῶν ἄλλων ὠνόμακεν.

17. Ἔχουσι δέ, κἂν εἰ μὴ πάντες, οἵ γε πολλοὶ μυθοποιίας συχνὰς καὶ ἱστορίας· καθάπερ Ἄφιδνα μὲν τὴν τῆς Ἑλένης ἁρπαγὴν ὑπὸ Θησέως καὶ τὴν ὑπὸ τῶν Διοσκούρων ἐκπόρθησιν αὐτῆς καὶ ἀνακομιδὴν τῆς ἀδελφῆς, Μαραθὼν δὲ τὸν Περσικὸν ἀγῶνα· Ῥαμνοῦς δὲ τὸ τῆς Νεμέσεως ξόανον, ὅ τινες μὲν Διοδότου φασὶν ἔργον, τινὲς δὲ Ἀγορακρίτου τοῦ Παρίου, καὶ μεγέθει καὶ κάλλει σφόδρα κατωρθωμένον καὶ ἐνάμιλλον τοῖς Φειδίου ἔργοις. οὕτω δὲ καὶ Δεκέλεια μέν, τὸ ὁρμητήριον τῶν Πελοποννησίων κατὰ τὸν Δεκελεικὸν πόλεμον, Φυλὴ δέ, ὅθεν ἐπήγαγε τὸν δῆμον Θρασύβουλος εἰς Πειραιᾶ, κἀκεῖθεν εἰς ἄστυ. οὕτω δὲ καὶ ἐπ' ἄλλων πλειόνων ἐστὶν ἱστορεῖν πολλά,

[1] αὐτοῖς, Jones, for αὑτοῖς, from conj. of Meineke.

[2] [τέμενος], Jones, from conj. of Professor Capps, inserts in lacuna of about eight letters in A; τόπον *g man. sec.*, *bno*; τὴν χώραν conj. Kramer; ἵδρυμα conj. Meineke.

Leocorium, here is the Theseium; I am unable to point them all out one by one; for Attica is the possession of the gods, who seized it as a sanctuary for themselves, and of the ancestral heroes." So this writer mentioned only one of the significant things on the acropolis; but Polemon the Periegete[1] wrote four books on the dedicatory offerings on the acropolis alone. Hegesias is proportionately brief in referring to the other parts of the city and to the country; and though he mentions Eleusis, one of the one hundred and seventy demes (or one hundred and seventy-four, as the number is given), he names none of the others.

17. Most of the demes, if not all, have numerous stories of a character both mythical and historical connected with them; Aphidna, for example, has the rape of Helen by Theseus, the sacking of the place by the Dioscuri and their recovery of their sister; Marathon has the Persian battle; Rhamnus has the statue of Nemesis, which by some is called the work of Diodotus and by others of Agoracritus the Parian, a work which both in grandeur and in beauty is a great success and rivals the works of Pheidias; and so with Deceleia, the base of operations of the Peloponnesians in the Deceleian War; and Phylê, whence Thrasybulus brought the popular party back to the Peiraeus and then to the city. And so, also, in the case of several other demes there are many historical incidents to

[1] A "Periegete" was a "Describer" of geographical and topographical details.

---

[3] ἐστὶ κτῆμα B; lacuna of about eleven letters in A; Meineke conj. ἐστὶν ἱερόν.

καὶ ἔτι[1] τὸ Λεωκόριον καὶ τὸ Θησεῖον μύθους[2] ἔχει καὶ τὸ Λύκειον, καὶ τὸ Ὀλυμπικόν ([ἔστι δὲ ταὐτ]ὸ[3] τὸ Ὀλύμπιον), ὅπερ ἡμιτελὲς κατέλιπε τελευτῶν ὁ ἀναθεὶς βασιλεύς· ὁμοίως δὲ καὶ ἡ Ἀκαδημία, καὶ οἱ κῆποι τῶν φιλοσόφων, καὶ τὸ Ὠιδεῖον, καὶ ἡ Ποικίλη στοά, καὶ τὰ ἱερὰ τὰ ἐν τῇ πόλ[ει θαυμαστὰ[4]] ἔχοντα τεχνιτῶν ἔργα.

C 397 18. Πολὺ δ' ἂν πλείων εἴη λόγος, εἰ τοὺς ἀρχηγέτας τοῦ κτίσματος ἐξετάζοι τις, ἀρξάμενος ἀπὸ Κέκροπος· οὐδὲ γὰρ ὁμοίως λέγουσιν ἅπαντες. τοῦτο δὲ καὶ ἀπὸ τῶν ὀνομάτων δῆλον· Ἀκτικὴν μὲν γὰρ ἀπὸ Ἀκταίωνός φασιν, Ἀτθίδα δὲ καὶ Ἀττικὴν ἀπὸ Ἀτθίδος τῆς Κραναοῦ, ἀφ' οὗ καὶ Κραναοὶ οἱ ἔνοικοι, Μοψοπίαν δὲ ἀπὸ Μοψόπου, Ἰωνίαν δὲ ἀπὸ Ἴωνος τοῦ Ξούθου, Ποσειδωνίαν δὲ καὶ Ἀθήνας ἀπὸ τῶν ἐπωνύμων θεῶν. εἴρηται δ' ὅτι κἀνταῦθα φαίνεται τὸ τῶν Πελασγῶν ἔθνος ἐπιδημῆσαν, καὶ διότι ὑπὸ τῶν Ἀττικῶν Πελαργοὶ προσηγορεύθησαν διὰ τὴν πλάνην.

19. Ὅσῳ δὲ πλέον ἐστὶ τὸ φιλείδημον[5] περὶ τὰ ἔνδοξα καὶ πλείους οἱ λαλήσαντές τι περὶ αὐτῶν, τοσῷδε μείζων ὁ ἔλεγχος, ἐὰν μὴ κρατῇ τις τῆς ἱστορίας· οἷον ἐν τῇ Συναγωγῇ τῶν ποταμῶν ὁ Καλλίμαχος γελᾶν φησίν, εἴ τις θαρρεῖ γράφειν τὰς τῶν Ἀθηναίων παρθένους

[1] ἔτι, Meineke, for εἰς.

[2] Θη[σεῖον μύθο]υς, lacuna of about nine letters in A supplied by Groskurd.

[3] [ἔστι δὲ ταὐτ]ό, lacuna of about ten letters supplied by Groskurd. So Müller-Dübner.

[4] πόλ[ει θαυμαστά], lacuna in A of about ten letters supplied by *hi*; so Müller-Dübner. ἅπαντα *no*; πλεῖστα Meineke.

[5] φιλείδημον, Jones, following Xylander, for φιλόδημον (cp. φιλείδημον in 1. 1. 23 and 1. 2. 28); others read φιλότιμον.

tell; and, further, the Leocorium and the Theseium have myths connected with them, and so has the Lyceium, and the Olympicum (the Olympium is the same thing), which the king[1] who dedicated it left half finished at his death. And in like manner also the Academia, and the gardens of the philosophers, and the Odeium, and the colonnade called "Poecilê,"[2] and the temples in the city containing marvellous works of different artists.

18. The account would be much longer if one should pass in review the early founders of the settlement, beginning with Cecrops; for all writers do not agree about them, as is shown even by the names. For instance, Acticê, they say, was derived from Actaeon; and Atthis and Attica from Atthis, the son of Cranaüs, after whom the inhabitants were also called Cranaï; and Mopsopia from Mopsopus; and Ionia from Ion, the son of Xuthus; and Poseidonia and Athens from the gods after whom they were named. As I have already said,[3] the race of the Pelasgi clearly sojourned here too, and on account of their wanderings were called "Pelargi" by the Attic people.[4]

19. The greater men's fondness for learning about things that are famous and the greater the number of men who have talked about them, the greater the censure, if one is not master of the historical facts. For example, in his *Collection of the Rivers*, Callimachus says that it makes him laugh if anyone makes bold to write that the Athenian virgins

[1] Antiochus Epiphanes, of the Seleucid Dynasty (reigned 175–164 B.C.). See Frazer, note on Pausanias 1. 18. 6.

[2] "Vari-coloured." The painting was done by Polygnotus, about the middle of the fifth century B.C.

[3] 5. 2. 4.

[4] *i.e.* "Storks" (see 5. 2. 4).

ἀφύσσεσθαι καθαρὸν γάνος Ἠριδανοῖο,

οὗ καὶ τὰ βοσκήματα ἀπόσχοιτ' ἄν. εἰσὶ μὲν νῦν αἱ πηγαὶ καθαροῦ καὶ ποτίμου ὕδατος, ὥς φασιν, ἐκτὸς τῶν Διοχάρους καλουμένων πυλῶν, πλησίον τοῦ Λυκείου· πρότερον δὲ καὶ κρήνη κατεσκεύαστό τις πλησίον πολλοῦ καὶ καλοῦ ὕδατος· εἰ δὲ μὴ νῦν, τί ἂν εἴη θαυμαστόν, εἰ πάλαι πολὺ καὶ καθαρὸν ἦν, ὥστε καὶ πότιμον[1] εἶναι, μετέβαλε δὲ ὕστερον; ἐν μὲν οὖν τοῖς καθ' ἕκαστα, τοσούτοις οὖσιν, οὐκ ἐνδέχεται διατρίβειν, οὐ μὴν οὐδὲ σιγῇ παρελθεῖν, ὥστε μηδ' ἐν κεφαλαίῳ μνησθῆναί τινων.

20. Τοσαῦτ' οὖν ἀπόχρη προσθήσειν,[2] ὅτι φησὶ Φιλόχορος πορθουμένης τῆς χώρας ἐκ θαλάττης μὲν ὑπὸ Καρῶν, ἐκ γῆς δὲ ὑπὸ Βοιωτῶν, οὓς ἐκάλουν Ἄονας, Κέκροπα πρῶτον εἰς δώδεκα πόλεις συνοικίσαι τὸ πλῆθος, ὧν ὀνόματα Κεκροπία, Τετράπολις, Ἐπακρία, Δεκέλεια, Ἐλευσίς, Ἄφιδνα (λέγουσι δὲ καὶ πληθυντικῶς Ἀφίδνας), Θόρικος, Βραυρών, Κύθηρος, Σφηττός, Κεφισιά,[3] πάλιν δ' ὕστερον εἰς μίαν πόλιν συναγαγεῖν λέγεται τὴν νῦν τὰς δώδεκα Θησεύς. ἐβασιλεύοντο μὲν οὖν[4] Ἀθηναῖοι πρότερον, εἶτ' εἰς δημοκρατίαν

[1] πότιμον, Xylander, for πόταμον; so the later editors.

[2] προσθήσειν, Corais and Meineke emend to προσθεῖσιν.

[3] After Κεφισιά *Bkno* add Φαληρός; Pletho, Ἀθῆναι. There is no sign of a lacuna in any MS.

[4] After οὖν Meineke inserts οἱ.

---

[1] Authorship unknown (see Schneider, *Callimachea, Frag.* 100 *e*).

[2] On the different views as to the position and course of the Eridanus at Athens, see Frazer note, on Pausanias I. 19. 5.

"draw pure liquid from the Eridanus,"[1] from which even cattle would hold aloof. Its sources are indeed existent now, with pure and potable water, as they say, outside the Gates of Diochares, as they are called, near the Lyceium;[2] but in earlier times there was also a fountain near by which was constructed by man, with abundant and excellent water; and even if the water is not so now, why should it be a thing to wonder at, if in early times the water was abundant and pure, and therefore also potable, but in later times underwent a change? However, it is not permitted me to linger over details, since they are so numerous, nor yet, on the other hand, to pass by them all in silence without even mentioning one or another of them in a summary way.

20. It suffices, then, to add thus much: According to Philochorus, when the country was being devastated, both from the sea by the Carians, and from the land by the Boeotians, who were called Aonians, Cecrops first settled the multitude in twelve cities, the names of which were Cecropia, Tetrapolis, Epacria, Deceleia, Eleusis, Aphidna (also called Aphidnae, in the plural), Thoricus, Brauron, Cytherus, Sphettus, Cephisia.[3] And at a later time Theseus is said to have united the twelve into one city, that of to-day. Now in earlier times the Athenians were ruled by kings; and then they

[3] Thus only eleven names are given in the most important MSS., though "Phalerus" appears after "Cephisia" in some (see critical note on opposite page). But it seems best to assume that Strabo either actually included Athens in his list or left us to infer that he meant Athens as one of the twelve.

μετέστησαν· τυράννων δ' ἐπιθεμένων αὐτοῖς, Πεισιστράτου καὶ τῶν παίδων, ὕστερόν τε ὀλιγαρχίας γενομένης, τῆς τε τῶν τετρακοσίων καὶ τῆς τῶν τριάκοντα τυράννων, οὓς ἐπέστησαν Λακεδαιμόνιοι, τούτους μὲν διεκρούσαντο ῥᾳδίως, ἐφύλαξαν δὲ τὴν δημοκρατίαν μέχρι τῆς Ῥωμαίων ἐπικρα-
C 398 τείας. καὶ γὰρ εἴ τι μικρὸν ὑπὸ τῶν Μακεδονικῶν βασιλέων παρελυπήθησαν, ὥσθ' ὑπακούειν αὐτῶν ἀναγκασθῆναι, τόν γε ὁλοσχερῆ τύπον τῆς πολιτείας τὸν αὐτὸν διετήρουν. ἔνιοι δέ φασι, καὶ βέλτιστα τότε αὐτοὺς πολιτεύσασθαι δεκαετῆ χρόνον, ὃν ἦρχε Μακεδόνων Κάσσανδρος.[1] οὗτος γὰρ ὁ ἀνὴρ πρὸς μὲν τὰ ἄλλα δοκεῖ τυραννικώτερος γενέσθαι, πρὸς Ἀθηναίους δὲ εὐγνωμόνησε, λαβὼν ὑπήκοον τὴν πόλιν· ἐπέστησε γὰρ τῶν πολιτῶν Δημήτριον τὸν Φαληρέα, τῶν Θεοφράστου τοῦ φιλοσόφου γνωρίμων, ὃς οὐ μόνον οὐ κατέλυσε τὴν δημοκρατίαν, ἀλλὰ καὶ ἐπηνώρθωσε. δηλοῖ δὲ τὰ ὑπομνήματα, ἃ συνέγραψε περὶ τῆς πολιτείας ταύτης ἐκεῖνος. ἀλλ' οὕτως ὁ φθόνος ἴσχυσε καὶ ἡ πρὸς ὀλίγους ἀπέχθεια, ὥστε μετὰ τὴν Κασσάνδρου τελευτὴν ἠναγκάσθη φυγεῖν εἰς Αἴγυπτον· τὰς δ' εἰκόνας αὐτοῦ πλείους ἢ τριακοσίας κατέσπασαν οἱ ἐπαναστάντες καὶ κατεχώνευσαν, ἔνιοι δὲ καὶ προστιθέασιν, ὅτι καὶ εἰς ἀμίδας. Ῥωμαῖοι δ' οὖν παραλαβόντες αὐτοὺς δημοκρατουμένους, ἐφύλαξαν τὴν αὐτονομίαν αὐτοῖς καὶ τὴν ἐλευθερίαν. ἐπιπεσὼν δ' ὁ Μιθριδατικὸς πόλεμος τυράννους αὐτοῖς κατέστησεν, οὓς ὁ βασιλεὺς ἐβούλετο· τὸν δ' ἰσχύσαντα μάλιστα, τὸν Ἀριστίωνα, καὶ ταύτην βιασάμενον

[1] Κάσσανδρος, Jones, for Κάσανδρος; and so elsewhere.

changed to a democracy; but tyrants assailed them, Peisistratus and his sons; and later an oligarchy arose, not only that of the four hundred, but also that of the thirty tyrants, who were set over them by the Lacedaemonians; of these they easily rid themselves, and preserved the democracy until the Roman conquest. For even though they were molested for a short time by the Macedonian kings, and were even forced to obey them, they at least kept the general type of their government the same. And some say that they were actually best governed at that time, during the ten years when Cassander reigned over the Macedonians. For although this man is reputed to have been rather tyrannical in his dealings with all others, yet he was kindly disposed towards the Athenians, once he had reduced the city to subjection; for he placed over the citizens Demetrius of Phalerum, one of the disciples of Theophrastus the philosopher, who not only did not destroy the democracy but even improved it, as is made clear in the *Memoirs* which Demetrius wrote concerning this government. But the envy and hatred felt for oligarchy was so strong that, after the death of Cassander, Demetrius was forced to flee to Egypt; and the statues of him, more than three hundred, were pulled down by the insurgents and melted, and some writers go on to say that they were made into chamber-pots. Be that as it may, the Romans, seeing that the Athenians had a democratic government when they took them over, preserved their autonomy and liberty. But when the Mithridatic War came on, tyrants were placed over them, whomever the king wished. The most powerful of these, Aristion, who violently oppressed the city, was

τὴν πόλιν, ἐκ πολιορκίας ἑλὼν Σύλλας, ὁ τῶν Ῥωμαίων ἡγεμών, ἐκόλασε, τῇ δὲ πόλει συγγνώμην ἔνειμε· καὶ μέχρι νῦν ἐν ἐλευθερίᾳ τέ ἐστι καὶ τιμῇ παρὰ τοῖς Ῥωμαίοις.

21. Μετὰ δὲ τὸν Πειραιᾶ Φαληρεῖς δῆμος ἐν τῇ ἐφεξῆς παραλίᾳ· εἶθ' Ἁλιμούσιοι, Αἰξωνεῖς, Ἀλαιεῖς,[1] οἱ Αἰξωνικοί, Ἀναγυράσιοι· εἶτα Θορεῖς[2] Λαμπτρεῖς,[3] Αἰγιλιεῖς,[4] Ἀναφλύστιοι, Ἀτηνεῖς[5] οὗτοι μὲν οἱ μέχρι τῆς ἄκρας τοῦ Σουνίου. μεταξὺ δὲ τῶν λεχθέντων δήμων μακρὰ[6] ἄκρα, πρώτη μετὰ τοὺς Αἰξωνέας, Ζωστήρ· εἶτ' ἄλλη μετὰ Θορέας, Ἀστυπάλαια, ὧν τῆς μὲν πρόκειται νῆσος Φάβρα, τῆς δ' Ἐλεοῦσσα· καὶ κατὰ τοὺς Αἰξωνέας δ' ἐστὶν Ὑδροῦσσα· περὶ δὲ Ἀνάφλυστόν ἐστι καὶ τὸ Πανεῖον, καὶ τὸ τῆς Κωλιάδος Ἀφροδίτης ἱερόν, εἰς ὃν τόπον ἐκκυμανθῆναι τὰ τελευταῖα τὰ ἐκ τῆς περὶ Σαλαμῖνα ναυμαχίας τῆς Περσικῆς ναυάγιά φασι, περὶ ὧν καὶ τὸν Ἀπόλλω προειπεῖν·

Κωλιάδες δὲ γυναῖκες ἐρέτμοισι φρύξουσι.[7]

πρόκειται δὲ καὶ τούτων τῶν τόπων Βέλβινα νῆσος οὐ πολὺ ἄπωθεν καὶ ὁ Πατρόκλου χάραξ· ἔρημοι δ' αἱ πλεῖσται τούτων.

22. Κάμψαντι δὲ τὴν κατὰ τὸ Σούνιον ἄκραν ἀξιόλογος δῆμος Σούνιον, εἶτα Θόρικος, εἶτα
C 399 Ποταμὸς δῆμος οὕτω καλούμενος, ἐξ οὗ οἱ ἄνδρες Ποτάμιοι, εἶτα Πρασία, Στειριά, Βραυ-

[1] Ἀλαιεῖς, Tzschucke, for Ἁλεεῖς; so the later editors.

[2] εἶθ' Ὀρεεῖς A; εἶθ' Ὡρεεῖς A *man. sec.*, BE*klno*: εἶτα Θορεῖς Tzschucke, Corais, Kramer; εἶτα Θοραιεῖς Meineke.

[3] Λαμπτρεῖς Kramer, for Λαμποιεῖς A (Λαμπυρεῖς *man. sec.*), BE*gklno*; so later editors.

punished by Sulla the Roman commander when he took this city by siege, though he pardoned the city itself; and to this day it is free and held in honour among the Romans.

21. After the Peiraeus comes the deme Phalereis, on the seaboard next to it; then Halimusii, Aexoneis, Alaeeis, Aexonici, and Anagyrasii. Then Thoreis, Lamptreis, Aegilieis, Anaphlystii, Ateneis. These are the demes as far as the cape of Sunium. Between the aforesaid demes is a long cape, the first cape after Aexoneis, Zoster; then another after Thoreis, I mean Astypalaea; off the former of these lies the island Phabra and off the latter the island Eleussa; and also opposite Aexonieis is Hydrussa. And in the neighbourhood of Anaphlystus is also the shrine of Pan, and the temple of Aphrodite Colias, at which place, they say, were cast forth by the waves the last wreckage of the ships after the Persian naval battle near Salamis, the wreckage concerning which Apollo predicted "the women of Colias will cook food with the oars." Off these places, too, is the island Belbina, at no great distance, and also the palisade of Patroclus. But most of these islands are uninhabited.

22. On doubling the cape of Sunium one comes to Sunium, a noteworthy deme; then to Thoricus; then to a deme called Potamus, whose inhabitants are called Potamii; then to Prasia, to Steiria, to

---

[4] Αἰγιλιεῖς Tzschucke, for Αἰγινεῖς; so the later editors.
[5] Ἀτηνεῖς, Loeper (*Ath. Mitth.* xvii, 1892, p. 335), for Ἀζηνιεῖς.
[6] *μακρά*, omitted by E*lnog* and Pletho; in A about twelve letters have disappeared between *μα* and *η μετά*.
[7] *φρύξουσι*, conj. of Kuhn, for *φρίξουσι* (cp. Herod. 8. 96).

ρών, ὅπου τὸ τῆς Βραυρωνίας Ἀρτέμιδος ἱερόν, [Ἁλαὶ Ἀραφη]νίδες[1], ὅπου τὸ τῆς Ταυροπόλου, Μυρρινοῦς, Προβάλινθος, Μαραθών, ὅπου Μιλτιάδης τὰς μετὰ Δάτιος τοῦ Πέρσου δυνάμεις ἄρδην διέφθειρεν, οὐ περιμείνας ὑστερίζοντας Λακεδαιμονίους διὰ τὴν πανσέληνον· ἐνταῦθα μεμυθεύκασι καὶ τὸν Μαραθώνιον ταῦρον, ὃν ἀνεῖλε Θησεύς. μετὰ δὲ Μαραθῶνα Τρικόρυνθος,[2] εἶτα Ῥαμνοῦς,[3] τὸ τῆς Νεμέσεως ἱερόν, εἶτα Ψαφὶς ἡ τῶν Ὠρωπίων· ἐνταῦθα δέ που καὶ τὸ Ἀμφιαράειόν ἐστι τετιμημένον ποτὲ μαντεῖον, ὅπου φυγόντα τὸν Ἀμφιάρεων, ὥς φησι Σοφοκλῆς,

> ἐδέξατο ῥαγεῖσα Θηβαία κόνις,
> αὐτοῖσιν ὅπλοις καὶ τετρωρίστῳ[4] δίφρῳ.

Ὠρωπὸς δ' ἐν ἀμφισβητησίμῳ γεγένηται πολλάκις· ἵδρυται γὰρ ἐν μεθορίῳ τῆς τε Ἀττικῆς καὶ τῆς Βοιωτίας. πρόκειται δὲ τῆς παραλίας ταύτης, πρὸ μὲν τοῦ Θορίκου[5] καὶ τοῦ Σουνίου, νῆσος Ἑλένη, τραχεῖα καὶ ἔρημος, παραμήκης ὅσον ἑξήκοντα σταδίων τὸ μῆκος· ἧς φασὶ μεμνῆσθαι τὸν ποιητήν, ἐν οἷς Ἀλέξανδρος λέγει πρὸς τὴν Ἑλένην·

> οὐδ' ὅτε σε πρῶτον Λακεδαίμονος ἐξ ἐρατεινῆς
> [ἔπλεον[6]] ἁρπάξας ἐν ποντοπόροισι νέεσσι,
> νήσῳ δ' ἐν Κρανάῃ ἐμίγην φιλότητι καὶ εὐνῇ.[7]

[1] [Ἁλαὶ Ἀραφη]νίδες, lacuna supplied by Xylander; so the later editors.

[2] Τρικόρυνθος A; Τρικόρυθος A *man. sec.*, and other MSS.

[3] After Ῥαμνοῦς Pletho and the later editors insert ὅπου.

[4] τετρωρίστῳ *Bcglkno*, for τετραορίστῳ other MSS. (τετραρίστῳ *hi*); so Meineke.

Brauron, where is the temple of the Artemis Brauronia, to Halae Araphenides, where is the temple of Artemis Tauropolus, to Myrrinus, to Probalinthus, and to Marathon, where Miltiades utterly destroyed the forces under Datis the Persian, without waiting for the Lacedaemonians, who came too late because they wanted the full moon. Here, too, is the scene of the myth of the Marathonian bull, which was slain by Theseus. After Marathon one comes to Tricorynthus; then to Rhamnus, the sanctuary of Nemesis; then to Psaphis, the land of the Oropians. In the neighbourhood of Psaphis is the Amphiaraeium, an oracle once held in honour, where in his flight Amphiaraüs, as Sophocles says, "with four-horse chariot, armour and all, was received by a cleft that was made[1] in the Theban dust."[2] Oropus has often been disputed territory; for it is situated on the common boundary of Attica and Boeotia. Off this coast are islands: off Thoricus and Sunium lies the island Helenê; it is rugged and deserted, and in its length of about sixty stadia extends parallel to the coast. This island, they say, is mentioned by the poet where Alexander[3] says to Helen: "Not even when first I snatched thee from lovely Lacedaemon and sailed with thee on the seafaring ships, and in the island Cranaë joined with thee in love and couch";[4] for he calls Cranaë[5] the

[1] By a thunderbolt of Zeus, to save the pious prophet from being slain. [2] *Frag.* 873 (Nauck).

[3] Paris. [4] *Iliad* 3. 443. [5] "Rough."

---

[5] Θορίκου, Tzschucke, from conj. of Casaubon, for Θορίου *a*BE, Θουρίου *l* (?), Ald.

[6] [ἔπλεον], lacuna supplied by Xylander; so the later editors. [7] φιλότητι καὶ εὐνῇ, omitted in A*cghlno*.

ταύτην γὰρ λέγει Κρανάην τὴν νῦν Ἑλένην ἀπὸ τοῦ ἐκεῖ γενέσθαι τὴν μῖξιν. μετὰ δὲ τὴν Ἑλένην ἡ Εὔβοια πρόκειται τῆς ἑξῆς παραλίας, ὁμοίως στενὴ καὶ μακρὰ καὶ κατὰ μῆκος τῇ ἠπείρῳ παραβεβλημένη, καθάπερ ἡ Ἑλένη. ἔστι δ' ἀπὸ τοῦ Σουνίου πρὸς τὸ νότιον τῆς Εὐβοίας ἄκρον, ὃ καλοῦσι Λευκὴν ἀκτήν, σταδίων τριακοσίων πλοῦς· ἀλλὰ περὶ Εὐβοίας μὲν εἰρήσεται ὕστερον,[1] τοὺς δ' ἐν τῇ μεσογαίᾳ δήμους τῆς Ἀττικῆς μακρὸν εἰπεῖν διὰ τὸ πλῆθος.

23. Τῶν δ' ὀρῶν τὰ μὲν ἐν ὀνόματι μάλιστά ἐστιν ὅ τε Ὑμηττὸς καὶ Βριλησσὸς καὶ Λυκαβηττός, ἔτι δὲ Πάρνης καὶ Κορυδαλλός. μαρμάρου δ' ἐστὶ τῆς τε Ὑμηττίας καὶ τῆς Πεντελικῆς[2] κάλλιστα μέταλλα πλησίον τῆς πόλεως· ὁ δ' Ὑμηττὸς καὶ μέλι ἄριστον ποιεῖ. τὰ δ' ἀργυρεῖα τὰ ἐν τῇ Ἀττικῇ κατ' ἀρχὰς μὲν ἦν ἀξιόλογα, νυνὶ δ' ἐκλείπει· καὶ δὴ καὶ οἱ ἐργαζόμενοι, τῆς μεταλλείας ἀσθενῶς ὑπακουούσης, τὴν παλαιὰν ἐκβολάδα καὶ σκωρίαν ἀναχωνεύοντες, εὕρισκον ἔτι ἐξ αὐτῆς ἀποκαθαιρόμενον ἀργύριον, τῶν ἀρχαίων ἀπείρως καμινευόντων. τοῦ δὲ μέλιτος
C 400 ἀρίστου τῶν πάντων ὄντος τοῦ Ἀττικοῦ, πολὺ βέλτιστόν φασι τὸ ἐν τοῖς ἀργυρείοις, ὃ καὶ ἀκάπνιστον καλοῦσιν ἀπὸ τοῦ τρόπου τῆς σκευασίας.

24. Ποταμοὶ δ' εἰσὶν ὁ μὲν Κηφισσὸς ἐκ

[1] εἰρήσεται ὕστερον, lacuna supplied by *bno*; μετ' ὀλίγον λέξομεν *i*.

island now called Helenê from the fact that the intercourse took place there. And after Helenê comes Euboea, which lies off the next stretch of coast; it likewise is narrow and long and in length lies parallel to the mainland, like Helenê. The voyage from Sunium to the southerly promontory of Euboea, which is called Leucê Actê, is three hundred stadia. However, I shall discuss Euboea later;[1] but as for the demes in the interior of Attica, it would be tedious to recount them because of their great number.

23. Of the mountains, those which are most famous are Hymettus, Brilessus, and Lycabettus; and also Parnes and Corydallus. Near the city are most excellent quarries of marble, the Hymettian and Pentelic. Hymettus also produces the best honey. The silver mines in Attica were originally valuable, but now they have failed. Moreover, those who worked them, when the mining yielded only meagre returns, melted again the old refuse, or dross, and were still able to extract from it pure silver, since the workmen of earlier times had been unskilful in heating the ore in furnaces. But though the Attic honey is the best in the world, that in the country of the silver mines is said to be much the best of all, the kind which is called *acapniston*,[2] from the mode of its preparation.

24. The rivers of Attica are the Cephissus, which

[1] 10. 1.

[2] "Unsmoked," *i.e.* the honey was taken from the hive without the use of smoke.

---

[2] Πεντελικῆς, Xylander, for ἑλικῆς; so later editors.

Τρινεμέων[1] τὰς ἀρχὰς ἔχων, ῥέων δὲ διὰ τοῦ πεδίου, ἐφ' οὗ καὶ ἡ γέφυρα καὶ οἱ γεφυρισμοί, διὰ δὲ τῶν σκελῶν τῶν ἀπὸ τοῦ ἄστεος εἰς τὸν Πειραιᾶ καθηκόντων, ἐκδίδωσιν εἰς τὸ Φαληρικόν, χειμαρρώδης τὸ πλέον, θέρους δὲ μειοῦται τελέως. ἔστι[2] δὲ τοιοῦτος μᾶλλον ὁ Ἰλισσός, ἐκ θατέρου μέρους τοῦ ἄστεος ῥέων εἰς τὴν αὐτὴν παραλίαν, ἐκ τῶν ὑπὲρ τῆς Ἄγρας καὶ τοῦ Λυκείου μερῶν, καὶ τῆς πηγῆς, ἣν ὕμνηκεν ἐν Φαίδρῳ Πλάτων. περὶ μὲν τῆς Ἀττικῆς ταῦτα.

II

1. Ἑξῆς δ' ἐστὶν ἡ Βοιωτία· περὶ ἧς λέγοντα καὶ περὶ τῶν συνεχῶν ἐθνῶν ἀνάμνησιν ποιήσασθαι χρὴ τοῦ σαφοῦς χάριν, ὧν εἴπομεν πρότερον. ἐλέγομεν δὲ τὴν ἀπὸ Σουνίου παραλίαν μέχρι Θετταλονικείας ἐπὶ τὰς ἄρκτους τετάσθαι, μικρὸν ἐκκλίνουσαν πρὸς δύσιν καὶ ἔχουσαν τὴν θάλασσαν πρὸς ἕω· τὰ δ' ὑπερ[κείμενα μέρη[3]] πρὸς δύσιν, ὡς ἂν ταινίας τινάς, διὰ τῆς [πάσης χώρας[4]] τεταμένας παραλλήλους· ὧν πρώτη ἐστὶν [ἡ Ἀττικὴ σὺν τῇ[5]] Μεγαρίδι, ὡς ἂν ταινία τις, τὸ

[1] Τρινεμέων, Kramer from conj. of Casaubon, for Τρινεμίων.
[2] ἔστι, Xylander, for ἔτι; so the later editors.
[3] ὑπερ[κείμενα μέρ]η: lacuna of about ten letters in A supplied by *bno* (κείμενα) and by Du Theil (μερ); Müller-Dübner and Meineke following.
[4] [πάσης χώρας]: lacuna of about ten letters in A supplied by Meineke. *bno* have χώρας ἑκάστης.
[5] Between ἐστίν and Μεγαρίδι, A has a lacuna of about twelve letters. Du Theil inserts as above, and so Müller-Dübner and Meineke.

has its source in the deme Trinemeis; it flows through the plain (hence the allusions to the "bridge" and the "bridge-railleries"[1]) and then through the legs of the walls which extend from the city to the Peiraeus; it empties into the Phaleric Gulf, being a torrential stream most of the time, although in summer it decreases and entirely gives out. And such is still more the case with the Ilissus, which flows from the other part of the city into the same coast, from the region above Agra[2] and the Lyceium, and from the fountain which is lauded by Plato in the *Phaedrus*.[3] So much for Attica.

II

1. Next in order is Boeotia; and when I discuss this country and the tribes that are continuous with it, I must, for the sake of clearness, call to mind what I have said before.[4] As I have said, the seaboard from Sunium to Thessaloniceia extends towards the north, slightly inclining towards the west and keeping the sea on the east; and that the parts above this seaboard lie towards the west—ribbon-like stretches of country extending parallel to one another through the whole country. The first of these parts is Attica together with Megaris—a ribbon-like stretch of country, having as its eastern

[1] Literally, the "gephyra" ("bridge") and "gephyrismi" ("bridge-isms"). It appears that on this bridge the Initiated, on their procession to Eleusis, engaged in mutual raillery of a wanton character (but see Pauly-Wissowa, *s.v.* Γεφυρισμοί).

[2] A suburb in the deme of Agrylê.

[3] 229 A. D.

[4] 2. 5. 21, 7. 7. 4, and 9. 1. 2.

μὲν ἑωθι[νὸν πλευρὸν ἔχουσ]α[1] τὴν ἀπὸ Σουνίου μέχρι Ὠρωποῦ καὶ [τῆς Βοιωτ]ίας,[2] τὸ δ' ἑσπέριον τόν τε Ἰσθμὸν καὶ τὴν [Ἀλκυονίδα θάλ]ατταν,[3] τὴν κατὰ Πηγὰς μέχρι τῶν [ὅρων τῆς Βοιωτί]ας[4] τῶν περὶ Κρέουσαν· τὰ δὲ λοιπὰ [τὴν ἀπὸ Σουνίου[5]] μέχρι Ἰσθμοῦ παραλίαν καὶ τὴν ὡς ἂν [παράλληλον αὐτῇ]ς[6] ὀρεινὴν τὴν διείργουσαν ἀπὸ τῆς [Βοιωτίας τὴν Ἀ]ττικήν·[7] δευτέρα δ' ἐστὶν ἡ Βοιωτία, ἀπὸ τῆς ἕω ἐπὶ δύσιν τεταμένη ταινία τις ἀπὸ τῆς κατ' Εὔβοιαν θαλάττης ἐπὶ θάλατταν τὴν κατὰ τὸν Κρισαῖον κόλπον, ἰσομήκης πως τῇ Ἀττικῇ ἢ καὶ ἐλάττων κατὰ μῆκος· ἀρετῇ μέντοι τῆς χώρας πάμπολυ διαφέρει.

2. Ἔφορος δὲ καὶ ταύτῃ κρείττω τὴν Βοιωτίαν ἀποφαίνει τῶν ὁμόρων ἐθνῶν, καὶ ὅτι μόνη τριθάλαττός ἐστι, καὶ λιμένων εὐπορεῖ πλειόνων, ἐπὶ μὲν τῷ Κρισαίῳ κόλπῳ καὶ τῷ Κορινθιακῷ τὰ ἐκ τῆς Ἰταλίας καὶ Σικελίας καὶ Λιβύης δεχομένη, ἐπὶ δὲ τῶν πρὸς Εὔβοιαν μερῶν ἐφ' ἑκάτερα τοῦ Εὐρίπου σχιζομένης τῆς παραλίας, τῇ μὲν ἐπὶ τὴν Αὐλίδα καὶ τὴν Ταναγρικήν, τῇ δ' ἐπὶ τὸν Σαλγανέα καὶ τὴν Ἀνθηδόνα, τῇ μὲν εἶναι συνεχῆ τὴν κατ' Αἴγυπτον καὶ Κύπρον καὶ τὰς νήσους θάλατταν, τῇ δὲ τὴν κατὰ Μακεδόνας

[1] ἑωθι[νὸν πλευρὸν ἔχου]σα: lacuna of about fourteen letters in A supplied by Du Theil; so Müller-Dübner and Meineke. *bno* have ἑωθινὸν μέρος ταινιοῦσα.

[2] [τῆς Βοιωτ]ίας: lacuna of about ten letters supplied by Du Theil. *bno* have τῆς ταύτῃ παραλίας.

[3] [Ἀλκυονίδα θάλ]ατταν: lacuna of about fourteen letters supplied by *bno*.

side the seaboard from Sunium to Oropus and Boeotia, and as its western side the Isthmus and the Alcyonian Sea, which extends from Pagae to the boundaries of Boeotia near Creusa, and as its remaining two sides, the seaboard from Sunium to the Isthmus and the mountainous country approximately parallel thereto which separates Attica from Boeotia. The second of these parts is Boeotia, extending ribbon-like from the east towards the west, from the Euboean Sea to the sea at the Crisaean Gulf; and it is about equal in length to Attica or perhaps less; in the fertility of its soil, however, it is far superior.

2. Ephorus declares that Boeotia is superior to the countries of the bordering tribes, not only in fertility of soil, but also because it alone has three seas and has a greater number of good harbours; in the Crisaean and Corinthian Gulfs it receives the products of Italy and Sicily and Libya, while in the part which faces Euboea, since its seaboard branches off on either side of the Euripus, on one side towards Aulis and the territory of Tanagra and on the other towards Salganeus and Anthedon, the sea stretches unbroken[1] in the one direction towards Egypt and Cyprus and the islands, and in the other direction

[1] *i.e.* unbroken by an isthmus or other obstacle.

---

[4] [ὅρων τῆς Βοιωτί]ας: lacuna of fourteen letters supplied by Kramer. τόπων (also suggested by Kramer), Meineke.

[5] [τὴν ἀπὸ Σουνίου]: lacuna of about twelve letters in A supplied by Du Theil; so Müller-Dübner.

[6] [παράλληλον αὐτῇ]ς: lacuna of thirteen letters in A supplied by Kramer; so Müller-Dübner.

[7] [Βοιωτίας τὴν 'Α]ττικήν: lacuna of about twelve letters supplied by Corais from conj. of Tzschucke; so Müller-Dübner and Meineke.

καὶ τὴν Προποντίδα καὶ τὸν Ἑλλήσποντον.
προστίθησι δέ, ὅτι καὶ τὴν Εὔβοιαν τρόπον τινὰ
μέρος αὐτῆς πεποίηκεν ὁ Εὔριπος, οὕτω στενὸς
ὢν καὶ γεφύρᾳ συνεζευγμένος πρὸς αὐτὴν διπλέ-
C 401 θρῳ. τὴν μὲν οὖν χώραν ἐπαινεῖ διὰ ταῦτα, καί
φησι πρὸς ἡγεμονίαν εὐφυῶς ἔχειν, ἀγωγῇ δὲ
καὶ παιδείᾳ μὴ χρησαμένους ἐπιμελεῖ[1] τοὺς ἀεὶ
προϊσταμένους αὐτῆς, εἰ καί[2] ποτε κατώρθωσαν,
ἐπὶ μικρὸν[3] τὸν χρόνον συμμεῖναι· καθάπερ
Ἐπαμεινώνδας ἔδειξε. τελευτήσαντος γὰρ ἐκείνου τὴν ἡγεμονίαν ἀποβαλεῖν εὐθὺς τοὺς Θηβαίους, γευσαμένους αὐτῆς μόνον· αἴτιον δὲ
εἶναι τὸ λόγων καὶ ὁμιλίας τῆς πρὸς ἀνθρώπους ὀλιγωρῆσαι, μόνης δ' ἐπιμεληθῆναι τῆς
κατὰ πόλεμον ἀρετῆς. ἔδει δὲ προσθεῖναι, διότι[4]
τοῦτο πρὸς Ἕλληνας χρήσιμόν ἐστιν, ἐπεὶ πρός
γε τοὺς βαρβάρους βία λόγου κρείττων ἐστί.
καὶ Ῥωμαῖοι δὲ τὸ παλαιὸν μέν, ἀγριωτέροις
ἔθνεσι πολεμοῦντες, οὐδὲν ἐδέοντο τῶν τοιούτων
παιδευμάτων, ἀφ' οὗ δὲ ἤρξαντο πρὸς ἡμερώτερα
ἔθνη καὶ φῦλα τὴν πραγματείαν ἔχειν, ἐπέθεντο[5]
καὶ ταύτῃ τῇ ἀγωγῇ καὶ κατέστησαν πάντων
κύριοι.

3. Ἡ δ' οὖν Βοιωτία πρότερον μὲν ὑπὸ βαρβάρων ᾠκεῖτο Ἀόνων καὶ Τεμμίκων, ἐκ τοῦ Σουνίου πεπλανημένων, καὶ Λελέγων καὶ Ὑάντων· εἶτα Φοίνικες ἔσχον οἱ μετὰ Κάδμου, ὃς τήν τε

[1] ἐπιμελεῖ, Madvig, for ἐπεὶ μηδέ; so Müller-Dübner. *no* omit altogether; Corais, ἐπιμελείᾳ.

[2] Corais and Meineke, from conj. of Pletho, insert τί before ποτέ.

[3] μακρόν *Bl.* [4] ὅτι *Blno.*

towards Macedonia and the regions of the Propontis and the Hellespont. And he adds that Euboea has, in a way, been made a part of Boeotia by the Euripus, since the Euripus is so narrow and is spanned by a bridge to Euripus only two plethra[1] long. Now he praises the country on account of these things; and he says that it is naturally well suited to hegemony, but that those who were from time to time its leaders neglected careful training and education, and therefore, although they at times achieved success, they maintained it only for a short time, as is shown in the case of Epameinondas; for after he died the Thebans immediately lost the hegemony, having had only a taste of it; and that the cause of this was the fact that they belittled the value of learning and of intercourse with mankind, and cared for the military virtues alone. Ephorus should have added that these things are particularly useful in dealing with Greeks, although force is stronger than reason in dealing with the barbarians. And the Romans too, in ancient times, when carrying on war with savage tribes, needed no training of this kind, but from the time that they began to have dealings with more civilised tribes and races, they applied themselves to this training also, and so established themselves as lords of all.

3. Be that as it may, Boeotia in earlier times was inhabited by barbarians, the Aones and the Temmices, who wandered thither from Sunium, and by the Leleges and the Hyantes. Then the Phoenicians occupied it, I mean the Phoenicians with Cadmus,

[1] 202 English feet.

[5] ἐπέθεντο, Xylander; so later editors.

Καδμείαν ἐτείχισε, καὶ ἀρχὴν τοῖς ἐκγόνοις ἀπέλιπεν. ἐκεῖνοι δὲ τὰς Θήβας τῇ Καδμείᾳ προσέκτισαν καὶ συνεφύλαξαν τὴν ἀρχήν, ἡγούμενοι τῶν πλείστων Βοιωτῶν ἕως τῆς τῶν Ἐπιγόνων στρατείας. κατὰ δὲ τούτους ὀλίγον χρόνον ἐκλιπόντες τὰς Θήβας ἐπανῆλθον πάλιν· ὡς δ' αὔτως ὑπὸ Θρᾳκῶν καὶ Πελασγῶν ἐκπεσόντες ἐν Θετταλίᾳ συνεστήσαντο τὴν ἀρχὴν μετὰ Ἀρναίων ἐπὶ πολὺν χρόνον, ὥστε καὶ Βοιωτοὺς κληθῆναι πάντας. εἶτ' ἀνέστρεψαν εἰς τὴν οἰκείαν, ἤδη τοῦ Αἰολικοῦ στόλου παρεσκευασμένου περὶ Αὐλίδα τῆς Βοιωτίας, ὃν ἔστελλον εἰς τὴν Ἀσίαν οἱ Ὀρέστου παῖδες. προσθέντες δὲ τῇ Βοιωτίᾳ τὴν Ὀρχομενίαν (οὐ γὰρ ἦσαν κοινῇ πρότερον, οὐδ' Ὅμηρος μετὰ Βοιωτῶν αὐτοὺς κατέλεξεν, ἀλλ' ἰδίᾳ, Μινύας προσαγορεύσας) μετ' ἐκείνων ἐξέβαλον τοὺς μὲν Πελασγοὺς εἰς Ἀθήνας, ἀφ' ὧν ἐκλήθη μέρος τι τῆς πόλεως Πελασγικόν, ᾤκησαν δὲ ὑπὸ τῷ Ὑμηττῷ, τοὺς δὲ Θρᾷκας ἐπὶ τὸν Παρνασσόν. Ὕαντες δὲ τῆς Φωκίδος Ὕαν πόλιν ᾤκισαν.

4. Φησὶ δ' Ἔφορος τοὺς μὲν Θρᾷκας, ποιησαμένους σπονδὰς πρὸς τοὺς Βοιωτούς, ἐπιθέσθαι νύκτωρ στρατοπεδεύουσιν ὀλιγωρότερον, ὡς εἰρήνης γεγονυίας· διακρουσαμένων δ' [1] αὐτούς, αἰτιωμένων τε ἅμα, ὅτι τὰς σπονδὰς παρέβαινον, μὴ
C 402 παραβῆναι φάσκειν ἐκείνους· συνθέσθαι γὰρ ἡμέρας, νύκτωρ δ' ἐπιθέσθαι· ἀφ' οὗ δὴ καὶ τὴν

[1] δ', Corais inserts; δέ *no.*

---

[1] The acropolis of Thebes. [2] *Iliad* 2. 511.

the man who fortified the Cadmeia[1] and left the dominion to his descendants. Those Phoenicians founded Thebes in addition to the Cadmeia, and preserved their dominion, commanding most of the Boeotians until the expedition of the Epigoni. On this occasion they left Thebes for a short time, but came back again. And, in the same way, when they were ejected by the Thracians and the Pelasgians, they established their government in Thessaly along with the Arnaei for a long time, so that they were all called Boeotians. Then they returned to the home-land, at the time when the Aeolian fleet, near Aulis in Boeotia, was now ready to set sail, I mean the fleet which the sons of Orestes were despatching to Asia. After adding the Orchomenian country to Boeotia (for in earlier times the Orchomenians were not a part of the Boeotian community, nor did Homer enumerate them with the Boeotians, but as a separate people, for he called them Minyae[2]), they, with the Orchomenians, drove out the Pelasgians to Athens (it was after these that a part of the city was named "Pelasgicon," though they took up their abode below Hymettus), and the Thracians to Parnassus; and the Hyantes founded a city Hyas in Phocis.

4. Ephorus says that the Thracians, after making a treaty with the Boeotians, attacked them by night when they, thinking that peace had been made, were encamping rather carelessly; and when the Boeotians frustrated the Thracians, at the same time making the charge that they were breaking the treaty, the Thracians asserted that they had not broken it, for the treaty said "by day," whereas they had made the attack by night; whence arose

παροιμίαν εἰρῆσθαι, Θρᾳκία παρεύρεσις. τοὺς δὲ Πελασγούς, μένοντος ἔτι τοῦ πολέμου, χρηστηριασομένους ἀπελθεῖν, ἀπελθεῖν δὲ καὶ τοὺς Βοιωτούς. τὸν μὲν οὖν τοῖς Πελασγοῖς δοθέντα χρησμὸν ἔφη μὴ ἔχειν εἰπεῖν, τοῖς δὲ Βοιωτοῖς ἀνελεῖν τὴν προφῆτιν ἀσεβήσαντας εὖ πράξειν· τοὺς δὲ θεωρούς, ὑπονοήσαντας χαριζομένην τοῖς Πελασγοῖς τὴν προφῆτιν κατὰ τὸ συγγενές (ἐπειδὴ[1] καὶ τὸ ἱερὸν Πελασγικὸν ἐξ ἀρχῆς ὑπῆρξεν) οὕτως ἀνελεῖν, ἁρπάσαντας τὴν ἄνθρωπον εἰς πυρὰν ἐμβαλεῖν, ἐνθυμηθέντας, εἴτε κακουργήσασαν, εἴτε μή, πρὸς ἀμφότερα ὀρθῶς ἔχειν, εἰ μὲν παρεχρηστηρίασε, κολασθείσης αὐτῆς, εἰ δ' οὐδὲν ἐκακούργησε, τὸ προσταχθὲν αὐτῶν πραξάντων. τοὺς δὲ περὶ τὸ ἱερὸν τὸ μὲν ἀκρίτους κτείνειν τοὺς πράξαντας, καὶ ταῦτ' ἐν ἱερῷ, μὴ δοκιμάσαι, καθιστάναι δ' εἰς κρίσιν, καλεῖν δ' ἐπὶ τὰς ἱερείας, ταύτας δὲ εἶναι τὰς προφήτιδας,[2] αἳ λοιπαὶ τριῶν οὐσῶν περιῆσαν· λεγόντων δ', ὡς οὐδαμοῦ νόμος εἴη δικάζειν γυναῖκας, προσελέσθαι καὶ ἄνδρας ἴσους ταῖς γυναιξὶ τὸν ἀριθμόν· τοὺς μὲν οὖν ἄνδρας ἀπογνῶναι, τὰς δὲ γυναῖκας καταγνῶναι, ἴσων δὲ τῶν ψήφων γενομένων, τὰς ἀπολυούσας νικῆσαι· ἐκ δὲ τούτων Βοιωτοῖς μόνοις ἄνδρας προθεσπίζειν ἐν Δωδώνῃ. τὰς μέντοι προφήτιδας, ἐξηγουμένας τὸ μαντεῖον[3] εἰπεῖν, ὅτι προστάττοι ὁ θεὸς τοῖς Βοιωτοῖς, τοὺς παρ' αὐτοῖς τρίποδας συλήσαντας

[1] ἐπεί Blk.

[2] After προφήτιδας a leaf has fallen out of A; but the loss is restored by a second hand (*a*).

[3] τοὐναντίον *abcg*.

the proverb, "Thracian pretense"; and the Pelasgians, when the war was still going on, went to consult the oracle, as did also the Boeotians. Now Ephorus is unable, he says, to tell the oracular response that was given to the Pelasgians, but the prophetess replied to the Boeotians that they would prosper if they committed sacrilege; and the messengers who were sent to consult the oracle, suspecting that the prophetess responded thus out of favour to the Pelasgians, because of her kinship with them (indeed, the temple also was from the beginning Pelasgian), seized the woman and threw her upon a burning pile, for they considered that, whether she had acted falsely or had not, they were right in either case, since, if she uttered a false oracle, she had her punishment, whereas, if she did not act falsely, they had only obeyed the order of the oracle. Now those in charge of the temple, he says, did not approve of putting to death without trial—and that too in the temple—the men who did this, and therefore they brought them to trial, and summoned them before the priestesses, who were also the prophetesses, being the two survivors of the three; but when the Boeotians said that it was nowhere lawful for women to act as judges, they chose an equal number of men in addition to the women. Now the men, he says, voted for acquittal, but the women for conviction, and since the votes cast were equal, those for acquittal prevailed; and in consequence of this prophecies are uttered at Dodona by men to Boeotians only; the prophetesses, however, explain the oracle to mean that the god ordered the Boeotians to steal the tripods[1] and

[1] *i.e.* steal the *dedicated* tripods, thus committing sacrilege.

ἕνα[1] εἰς Δωδώνην πέμπειν κατ' ἔτος· καὶ δὴ καὶ ποιεῖν τοῦτο· ἀεὶ γάρ τινα τῶν ἀνακειμένων τριπόδων νύκτωρ καθαιροῦντας καὶ κατακαλύπτοντας ἱματίοις, ὡς ἂν λάθρα, τριποδηφορεῖν εἰς Δωδώνην.

5. Μετὰ δὲ ταῦτα τὴν Αἰολικὴν ἀποικίαν συνέπραξαν τοῖς περὶ Πενθίλον, πλείστους ἐξ ἑαυτῶν συμπέμψαντες, ὥστε καὶ Βοιωτικὴν προσαγορευθῆναι. ὕστερον δὲ χρόνοις πολλοῖς ὁ Περσικὸς πόλεμος περὶ Πλαταιὰς γενόμενος διελυμήνατο τὴν χώραν. εἶτ' ἀνέλαβον σφᾶς πάλιν ἐπὶ τοσοῦτον, ὥστε καὶ τῆς τῶν Ἑλλήνων ἀρχῆς ἀμφισβητῆσαι Θηβαίους, δυσὶ μάχαις κρατήσαντας Λακεδαιμονίους. Ἐπαμεινώνδα δὲ πεσόντος ἐν τῇ μάχῃ, ταύτης μὲν τῆς ἐλπίδος διεσφάλησαν, ὑπὲρ δὲ τῶν Ἑλλήνων ὅμως ἐπολέμησαν πρὸς Φωκέας τοὺς τὸ ἱερὸν συλήσαντας
C 403 τὸ κοινόν. κακωθέντες δ' ὑπό τε τούτου τοῦ πολέμου, καὶ τῶν Μακεδόνων ἐπιθεμένων τοῖς Ἕλλησιν, ὑπὸ τῶν αὐτῶν τούτων καὶ ἀπέβαλον τὴν πόλιν κατασκαφεῖσαν καὶ ἀνέλαβον ἀνακτισθεῖσαν. ἐξ ἐκείνου δ' ἤδη πράττοντες ἐνδεέστερον ἀεὶ μέχρι εἰς ἡμᾶς οὐδὲ κώμης ἀξιολόγου τύπον σώζουσι· καὶ ἄλλαι δὲ πόλεις ἀνάλογον[2] πλὴν Τανάγρας καὶ Θεσπιῶν· αὗται δ' ἱκανῶς συμμένουσι πρὸς ἐκείνας κρινόμεναι.

6. Ἑξῆς δὲ τὴν περιήγησιν τῆς χώρας ποιητέον, ἀρξαμένους ἀπὸ τῆς πρὸς Εὔβοιαν παραλίας τῆς

[1] συλήσαντας, Groskurd, for συλλέγοντας, also adding ἕνα; Kramer approving.
[2] After ἀνάλογον *no* insert ἔχουσι.

---

[1] *i.e.* every year. [2] See 13. 1. 3.

take one of them to Dodona every year; and they actually do this, for they always[1] take down one of the dedicated tripods by night and cover it up with garments, and secretly, as it were, carry it to Dodona.

5. After this the Boeotians cooperated with Penthilus[2] and his followers in forming the Aeolian colony, sending with him most of their own people, so that it was also called a Boeotian colony. A long time afterwards the country was thoroughly devastated by the Persian war that took place near Plataeae. Then they recovered themselves to such an extent that the Thebans, having conquered the Lacedaemonians in two battles, laid claim to supremacy over the Greeks. But Epameinondas fell in the battle, and consequently they were disappointed in this hope; but still they went to war on behalf of the Greeks against the Phocians, who had robbed their common temple. And after suffering loss from this war, as also from the Macedonians when these attacked the Greeks,[3] they lost their city,[4] which was rased to the ground by these same people, and then received it back from them when rebuilt.[5] From that time on the Thebans have fared worse and worse down to our own time, and Thebes to-day does not preserve the character even of a respectable village; and the like is true of other Boeotian cities, except Tanagra and Thespiae, which, as compared with Thebes, have held out fairly well.

6. Next in order I must make a circuit of the country, beginning at that part of the coastline

[3] At the battle of Chaeroneia (338 B.C.).

[4] 335 B.C. [5] By Cassander (316 B.C.).

συνεχοῦς τῇ Ἀττικῇ. ἀρχὴ δ' ὁ Ὠρωπὸς καὶ ὁ Ἱερὸς Λιμήν, ὃν καλοῦσι Δελφίνιον, καθ' ὃν ἡ παλαιὰ Ἐρέτρια ἐν τῇ Εὐβοίᾳ, διάπλουν ἔχουσα ἑξήκοντα σταδίων. μετὰ δὲ τὸ Δελφίνιον ὁ Ὠρωπὸς ἐν εἴκοσι σταδίοις· κατὰ δὲ τοῦτόν ἐστιν ἡ νῦν Ἐρέτρια, διάπλους δ' ἐπ' αὐτὴν στάδιοι τετταράκοντα.

7. Εἶτα Δήλιον, τὸ ἱερὸν τοῦ Ἀπόλλωνος ἐκ Δήλου ἀφιδρυμένον, Ταναγραίων πολίχνιον, Αὐλίδος διέχον σταδίους τριάκοντα, ὅπου μάχῃ λειφθέντες Ἀθηναῖοι προτροπάδην ἔφυγον· ἐν δὲ τῇ φυγῇ πεσόντα ἀφ' ἵππου Ξενοφῶντα ἰδὼν κείμενον τὸν Γρύλλου Σωκράτης ὁ φιλόσοφος, στρατεύων πεζός, τοῦ ἵππου γεγονότος ἐκποδών, ἀνέλαβε τοῖς ὤμοις αὐτόν, καὶ ἔσωσεν ἐπὶ πολλοὺς σταδίους, ἕως ἐπαύσατο ἡ φυγή.

8. Εἶτα λιμὴν μέγας, ὃν καλοῦσι Βαθὺν λιμένα· εἶθ' ἡ Αὐλίς, πετρῶδες χωρίον[1] καὶ κώμη Ταναγραίων· λιμὴν δ' ἐστὶ πεντήκοντα πλοίοις, ὥστ' εἰκὸς τὸν ναύσταθμον τῶν Ἑλλήνων ἐν τῷ μεγάλῳ ὑπάρξαι λιμένι. καὶ ὁ Εὔριπος δ' ἐστὶ πλησίον ὁ Χαλκίδος, εἰς ὃν ἀπὸ Σουνίου στάδιοι ἑξακόσιοι[2] ἑβδομήκοντα· ἔστι δ' ἐπ' αὐτῷ γέφυρα

[1] πετρώδης χώρα *aghino*.

[2] ἑξακόσιοι (χ'), Jones, following conj. of Falconer; ἑπτακόσιοι, conj. Gosselin and Groskurd; πεντακόσιοι, conj. Kramer.

---

[1] Deep Harbour.

[2] In 411 B.C. Chalcis was joined to the mainland by a bridge. Moles were thrown out into the Euripus from each shore, high towers were built at the ends of the two moles, leaving a passage through for a single ship, and "wooden bridges were set over the channels" (Diodorus Siculus 13.

opposite Euboea which joins Attica. The beginning is Oropus, and the Sacred Harbour, which is called Delphinium, opposite which is the ancient Eretria in Euboea, the distance across being sixty stadia. After Delphinium, at a distance of twenty stadia, is Oropus; and opposite Oropus is the present Eretria, and to it the passage across the strait is forty stadia.

7. Then one comes to Delium, the sanctuary of Apollo, which is a reproduction of that in Delos. It is a small town of the Tanagraeans, thirty stadia distant from Aulis. It was to this place that the Athenians, after their defeat in battle, made their headlong flight; and in the flight Socrates the philosopher, who was serving on foot, since his horse had got away from him, saw Xenophon the son of Gryllus lying on the ground, having fallen from his horse, and took him up on his shoulders and carried him in safety for many stadia, until the flight ceased.

8. Then one comes to a large harbour, which is called Bathys Limen;[1] then to Aulis, a rocky place and a village of the Tanagraeans. Its harbour is large enough for only fifty boats; and therefore it is reasonable to suppose that the naval station of the Greeks was in the large harbour. And near by, also, is the Euripus at Chalcis, to which the distance from Sunium is six hundred and seventy stadia; and over it is a bridge two plethra long,[2] as I have

47). The plurals "bridges" and "channels" may be explained by the fact that there was a small rocky island in the middle of the strait between the two channels. In 334 B.C. they fortified the bridge with towers and gates and a wall, and included the Boeotian Mt. Canethus (Karababa?)

δίπλεθρος, ὡς εἴρηκα· πύργος δ' ἑκατέρωθεν ἐφέστηκεν, ὁ μὲν ἐκ τῆς Χαλκίδος, ὁ δ' ἐκ τῆς Βοιωτίας· διῳκοδόμηται δ' εἰς αὐτοὺς σῦριγξ. περὶ δὲ τῆς παλιρροίας τοῦ Εὐρίπου τοσοῦτον μόνον εἰπεῖν ἱκανόν, ὅτι ἑπτάκις μεταβάλλειν φασὶ καθ' ἡμέραν ἑκάστην καὶ νύκτα· τὴν δ' αἰτίαν ἐν ἄλλοις σκεπτέον.

9. Πλησίον δ' ἐστὶν ἐφ' ὕψους κείμενον χωρίον Σαλγανεύς, ἐπώνυμον τοῦ ταφέντος ἐπ' αὐτῷ Σαλγανέως, ἀνδρὸς Βοιωτίου, καθηγησαμένου τοῖς Πέρσαις εἰσπλέουσιν εἰς τὸν διάπλουν τοῦτον ἐκ τοῦ Μαλιακοῦ κόλπου, ὅν φασιν ἀναιρεθῆναι, πρὶν ἢ τῷ Εὐρίπῳ συνάπτειν, ὑπὸ τοῦ ναυάρχου Μεγαβάτου, νομισθέντα κακοῦργον, ὡς ἐξ ἀπάτης ἐμβαλόντα τὸν στόλον εἰς τυφλὸν τῆς θαλάσσης

---

as a bridgehead within the circuit of the city of Chalcis (Strabo 10. 1. 8). Chalcis was still joined to the continent by a bridge in 200 B.C. (Livy 28. 6), and Aemilius Paulus went to see it about 167 B.C. (Livy 45. 27). And there was still a bridge there in the time of Livy himself, although the tower mentioned by him (28. 6) was no longer there (note the tense of *claudebat*). Strabo's "two plethra" (202 feet) is accurate enough for the entire stretch across the strait, and he must have included the moles in his term "bridge." To-day the western channel is entirely closed, while the eastern is spanned by a swing-bridge about 85 feet long.

[1] 9. 2. 2.

[2] The usual interpretation of this clause, "a canal (σῦριγξ) has been constructed between (εἰς) the towers" seems impossible. The literal translation is, "a tube has been constructed across into them" (the towers). Bréquigny (quoted in the French trans., vol. iii, *Eclaircissemens* x) appears to be on the right track: "On y a pratique des σῦριγξ (*souterrains*) pour y communiquer" ("they have constructed sub-

said;[1] and a tower stands on each side, one on the side of Chalcis, and the other on the side of Boeotia; and tube-like passages have been constructed into the towers.[2] Concerning the refluent currents of the Euripus it is enough to say only thus much, that they are said to change seven times each day and night;[3] but the cause of the changes must be investigated elsewhere.

9. Near the Euripus, upon a height, is situated a place called Salganeus. It is named after Salganeus, a Boeotian, who was buried there—the man who guided the Persians when they sailed into this channel from the Maliac Gulf. It is said that he was put to death before they reached the Euripus by Megabates, the commander of the fleet, because he was considered a villain, on the ground that he had deceitfully rushed the fleet into a blind alley of

terranean passages so as to communicate with the towers"). Livy (28. 6) says: "The city has two fortresses, one threatening the sea, and the other in the middle of the city. Thence by a *cuniculum*" (literally, "rabbit-hole," and hence a "tube-like passage-way") "a road leads to the sea, and this road used to be shut off from the sea by a tower of five stories, a remarkable bulwark." Certainly σῦριγξ should mean an underground passage or else a roofed gallery of some sort above the ground (cf. the use of the word in Polybius 9. 41. 9 concerning the investment of Echinus by Philip, and in 15. 30. 6); and Strabo probably means that there was a protected passage across to the towers from both sides. See Leake's *Travels in Northern Greece*, II, 259; Grote's *Greece*, VIII, ch. 63; and the discussion by the French translators (*l. c.*), who believe that there were two passages for ships, one on each side of the strait.

[3] "They take place, not seven times in the twenty-four hours, as Strabo says, but at irregular intervals" (Tozer, *Selections*, p. 234). See the explanation of Admiral Mansell in Murray's *Greece*, pp. 387–388.

στενωπόν· αἰσθόμενον δὲ τὸν βάρβαρον τὴν περὶ αὐτὸν ἀπάτην μεταγνῶναί τε καὶ ταφῆς ἀξιῶσαι τὸν ἀναιτίως ἀποθανόντα.

C 404 10. Καὶ ἡ Γραῖα δ' ἐστὶ τόπος Ὠρωποῦ πλησίον καὶ τὸ ἱερὸν τοῦ Ἀμφιαράου καὶ τὸ Ναρκίσσου τοῦ Ἐρετριέως μνῆμα, ὃ καλεῖται Σιγηλοῦ,[1] ἐπειδὴ σιγῶσι παριόντες· τινὲς δὲ τῇ Τανάγρᾳ τὴν αὐτήν φασιν. ἡ Ποιμανδρὶς δ' ἐστὶν ἡ αὐτὴ τῇ Ταναγρικῇ·[2] καλοῦνται δὲ καὶ Γεφυραῖοι οἱ Ταναγραῖοι. ἐκ Κνωπίας δὲ τῆς Θηβαϊκῆς μεθιδρύθη κατὰ χρησμὸν δεῦρο τὸ Ἀμφιάρειον.

11. Καὶ ὁ Μυκαλησσὸς δὲ κώμη τῆς Ταναγραϊκῆς· κεῖται δὲ παρ' ὁδὸν τὴν ἐκ Θηβῶν[3] εἰς Χαλκίδα, καλοῦσι δὲ Βοιωτιακῶς Μυκαληττόν·[4] ὡς δ' αὔτως καὶ τὸ Ἅρμα τῆς Ταναγραϊκῆς, κώμη ἔρημος περὶ τὴν Μυκαληττόν,[5] ἀπὸ τοῦ Ἀμφιαράου ἅρματος λαβοῦσα τοὔνομα, ἑτέρα οὖσα τοῦ Ἅρματος τοῦ κατὰ τὴν Ἀττικήν, ὅ ἐστι περὶ Φυλήν, δῆμον τῆς Ἀττικῆς ὅμορον τῇ Τανάγρᾳ. ἐντεῦθεν δὲ ἡ παροιμία τὴν ἀρχὴν ἔσχεν ἡ λέγουσα· ὁπόταν[6] δι' Ἅρματος ἀστράψῃ· ἀστραπήν τινα σημειουμένων κατὰ χρησμὸν τῶν λεγομένων Πυθαϊστῶν, βλεπόντων ὡς ἐπὶ τὸ Ἅρμα, καὶ τότε πεμπόντων τὴν θυσίαν εἰς

[1] Σίγηλος κύριον ὄνομα Ναρκίσσου, σιγηλὸς δ' ὁ σιωπηλός (Eustathius, note on *Od.* 24. 465); οἱ τὸν σιγηλὸν ἥρω παριόντες (Alciphron *Epist.* 3. 58).

[2] Here MS. A resumes.

[3] τὴν ἐκ Θηβῶν, Meineke, for Θηβαίων.

[4] The words καλοῦσι . . . Μυκαληττόν, Meineke ejects.

[5] Μυκαληττόν, Meineke and others emend to Μυκαλησσόν.

[6] ὁπόταν (Eustathius, note on *Od.* 2. 498) for ὁπότε; so the later editors.

the sea, but that the barbarian, when he perceived that he himself was mistaken, not only repented, but deemed worthy of burial the man who had been put to death without cause.

10. Near Oropus is a place called Graea, and also the temple of Amphiaraüs, and the monument of Narcissus the Eretrian, which is called "Sigelus's,"[1] because people pass it in silence.[2] Some say that Graea is the same as Tanagra. The Poemandrian territory is the same as the Tanagraean;[3] and the Tanagraeans are also called Gephyraeans. The temple of Amphiaraüs was transferred hither in accordance with an oracle from the Theban Cnopia.

11. Also Mycalessus, a village, is in the Tanagraean territory. It is situated on the road that leads from Thebes to Chalcis; and in the Boeotian dialect it is called Mycalettus. And Harma is likewise in the Tanagraean territory; it is a deserted village near Mycalettus, and received its name from the chariot of Amphiaraüs, and is a different place from the Harma in Attica, which is near Phylë, a deme of Attica bordering on Tanagra.[4] Here originated the proverb, "when the lightning flashes through Harma"; for those who are called the Pythaistae look in the general direction of Harma, in accordance with an oracle, and note any flash of lightning in that direction, and then, when they see the

[1] *i.e.* "Silent's" (monument).

[2] For love of the indifferent Narcissus Echo died of a broken heart. Nemesis punished him by causing him to fall desperately in love with his own image which he saw in a fountain. He pined away and was changed to the flower which bears his name.

[3] "The people of Tanagra say that their founder was Poemander" (Pausanias 9. 10).

[4] Strabo means the Tanagraean *territory.*

Δελφούς, ὅταν ἀστράψαντα ἴδωσιν· ἐτήρουν δ' ἐπὶ τρεῖς μῆνας, καθ' ἕκαστον μῆνα ἐπὶ τρεῖς ἡμέρας καὶ νύκτας ἀπὸ τῆς ἐσχάρας τοῦ Ἀστραπαίου Διός· ἔστι δ' αὕτη ἐν τῷ τείχει μεταξὺ τοῦ Πυθίου καὶ τοῦ Ὀλυμπίου. περὶ δὲ τοῦ Ἅρματος τοῦ Βοιωτιακοῦ οἱ μὲν φασιν ἐκπεσόντος ἐκ τοῦ ἅρματος ἐν τῇ μάχῃ τοῦ Ἀμφιαράου κατὰ τὸν τόπον, ὅπου νῦν ἐστὶ τὸ ἱερὸν αὐτοῦ, τὸ ἅρμα ἔρημον ἐνεχθῆναι ἐπὶ[1] τὸν ὁμώνυμον τόπον· οἱ δὲ τοῦ Ἀδράστου συντριβῆναι τὸ ἅρμα φεύγοντός φασιν ἐνταῦθα, τὸν δὲ διὰ τοῦ Ἀρείονος σωθῆναι. Φιλόχορος δ' ὑπὸ τῶν κωμητῶν σωθῆναί φησιν αὐτόν, καὶ διὰ τοῦτο ἰσοπολιτείαν αὐτοῖς παρὰ τῶν Ἀργείων ὑπάρξαι.

12. Ἔστι δὲ τῷ ἐκ Θηβῶν εἰς Ἄργος[2] ἀπιόντι[3] ἐν ἀριστερᾷ ἡ Τάναγρα· κ . . .[4] ἐν δεξιᾷ κεῖται· καὶ ἡ Ὑρία[5] δὲ τῆς Ταναγραίας νῦν ἐστί, πρότερον δὲ τῆς Θηβαΐδος· ὅπου ὁ Ὑριεὺς[6] μεμύθευται καὶ ἡ τοῦ Ὠρίωνος γένεσις, ἥν φησι Πίνδαρος ἐν τοῖς διθυράμβοις· κεῖται δ' ἐγγὺς Αὐλίδος. ἔνιοι δὲ τὰς Ὑσίας Ὑρίην[7] λέγεσθαί

[1] περί Blk.

[2] On Ἄργος, which the editors in general consider corrupt, see C. Müller, *Ind. Var. Lect.*, p. 1000. Daebritz (*De Artemidoro Strabonis Auctore Capita Tria*) conj. εἰς Ἀθήνας ἰόντι.

[3] For ἀπιόντι, Meineke reads ἀνιόντι.

[4] Numerous efforts have been made to supply this lacuna of about fifteen letters, but all are mere guesswork (see C. Müller, *l. c.*, p. 1000). Daebritz (*l. c.*) conj. κ[αὶ ἡ τῶν Πλαταιέων].

[5] Ὑρία (Eustathius on *Od.* 2. 496) for Ὑρρία.

[6] Ὑρριεύς *acgh*. [7] Ὑρρίην, all MSS.

---

[1] See Dittenberger 611, note 3.

lightning flash, take the offering to Delphi.[1] They would keep watch for three months, for three days and nights each month, from the altar of Zeus Astrapaeus;[2] this altar is within the walls[3] between the Pythium and the Olympium.[4] In regard to the Harma in Boeotia, some say that Amphiaraüs fell in the battle out of his chariot[5] near the place where his temple now is, and that the chariot was drawn empty to the place which bears the same name; others say that the chariot of Adrastus, when he was in flight, was smashed to pieces there, but that Adrastus safely escaped on Areion.[6] But Philochorus[7] says that Adrastus was saved by the inhabitants of the village, and that on this account they obtained equal rights of citizenship from the Argives.

12. To anyone returning from Thebes to Argos,[8] Tanagra is on the left; and[9] . . . is situated on the right. And Hyria,[10] also, belongs to the Tanagraean territory now, though in earlier times it belonged to the Theban territory. Hyria is the scene of the myth of Hyrieus, and of the birth of Orion, of which Pindar speaks in his dithyrambs;[11] it is situated near Aulis. Some say that Hysiae is

[2] "Wielder of Lightning." [3] Of Athens.

[4] The temples of Pythian Apollo and Olympian Zeus.

[5] "Harma."

[6] "The fleet horse of Adrastus, of divine descent" (*Iliad* 23. 346).

[7] See foot-note on 9. 1. 6.

[8] If Strabo wrote "Argos," which is doubtful (see critical note), he must have been thinking of the route taken by Amphiaraüs, or Adrastus, back to the Peloponnesus.

[9] See critical note.

[10] The place mentioned in Homer, *Iliad* 2. 496.

[11] *Frag.* 73 (Bergk).

φασι, τῆς Παρασωπίας οὖσαν ὑπὸ τῷ Κιθαιρῶνι πλησίον Ἐρυθρῶν ἐν τῇ μεσογαίᾳ, ἄποικον Ὑριέων, κτίσμα δὲ Νυκτέως, τοῦ Ἀντιόπης πατρός. εἰσὶ δὲ καὶ ἐν τῇ Ἀργείᾳ Ὑσίαι κώμη, οἱ δ' ἐξ αὐτῆς Ὑσιᾶται λέγονται. τῶν δ' Ἐρυθρῶν τούτων ἄποικοι αἱ ἐν Ἰωνίᾳ[1] Ἐρυθραί. καὶ ὁ Ἑλεὼν[2] δ' ἐστὶ κώμη Ταναγρική, ἀπὸ τῶν ἑλῶν[3] ὠνομασμένη.

13. Μετὰ δὲ Σαλγανέα Ἀνθηδών, πόλις λιμένα ἔχουσα, ἐσχάτη τῆς Βοιωτιακῆς παραλίας τῆς
C 405 πρὸς Εὐβοίᾳ, καθάπερ καὶ ὁ ποιητὴς εἴρηκεν·

Ἀνθηδόνα τ' ἐσχατόωσαν.

εἰσὶ μέντοι ἔτι προϊόντι μικρὸν πολίχναι δύο τῶν Βοιωτῶν, Λάρυμνά τε, παρ' ἣν ὁ Κηφισσὸς[4] ἐκδίδωσι, καὶ ἔτι ἐπέκεινα Ἁλαί,[5] ὁμώνυμοι τοῖς Ἀττικοῖς δήμοις. κατὰ δὲ τὴν παραλίαν ταύτην κεῖσθαί φασιν Αἰγὰς τὰς ἐν Εὐβοίᾳ, ἐν αἷς τὸ τοῦ Ποσειδῶνος ἱερὸν τοῦ Αἰγαίου· ἐμνήσθημεν δ' αὐτοῦ καὶ πρότερον. δίαρμα δ' ἐστὶν ἀπὸ μὲν τῆς Ἀνθηδόνος εἰς Αἰγὰς ἑκατὸν εἴκοσι στάδιοι, ἀπὸ δὲ τῶν ἄλλων τόπων πολὺ ἐλάττους· κεῖται δ' ἐπὶ ὄρους ὑψηλοῦ τὸ ἱερόν, ἣν δέ ποτε καὶ πόλις· ἐγγὺς δὲ τῶν Αἰγῶν[6] καὶ αἱ Ὀρόβιαι.[7] ἐν δὲ τῇ Ἀνθηδονίᾳ Μεσσάπιον ὄρος

[1] Ἰωνίδι BE*l*.

[2] Ἑλεών, the later editors, for καὶ Αἰολέων A*cgh*, Ἐλαιών B*k*, ὁ Ἐλεών A *man. sec.*; ὁ Ἑλεών (Eustathius, note on *Od.* 2. 500).

[3] ἐλαιῶν B*h*.

[4] Κηφισός A.

[5] Ἁλαί, Palmer, for ἄλλαι; so the later editors.

[6] Αἰγῶν has fallen out of A, but is found in *bkno Epit.*

[7] Ὀρόβιαι, *Epit.*, for Ὀρόβαι.

called Hyria, belonging to the Parasopian country[1] below Cithaeron, near Erythrae, in the interior, and that it is a colony of the Hyrieans and was founded by Nycteus, the father of Antiopê. There is also a Hysiae in the Argive territory, a village; and its inhabitants are called Hysiatae. The Erythrae in Ionia is a colony of this Erythrae. And Heleon, also, is a village belonging to Tanagra, having been so named from the "hele."[2]

13. After Salganeus one comes to Anthedon, a city with a harbour; and it is the last city on that part of the Boeotian seaboard which is opposite to Euboea, as the poet says, "Anthedon at the extremity."[3] As one proceeds a little farther, however, there are still two small towns belonging to the Boeotians: Larymna, near which the Cephissus empties, and, still farther on, Halae, which bears the same name as the Attic demes.[4] Opposite this seaboard is situated, it is said, the Aegae[5] in Euboea, in which is the temple of the Aegaean Poseidon, which I have mentioned before.[6] The distance across the strait from Anthedon to Aegae is one hundred and twenty stadia, but from the other places it is much less. The temple is situated on a high mountain, where there was once a city. And Orobiae[7] also is near Aegae. In the Anthedonian territory is Mount

[1] *i.e.* the country along the Asopus River.

[2] "Marshes."

[3] *Iliad* 2. 508.

[4] *i.e. Halae* Aexonides and *Halae* Araphenides.

[5] See *Iliad* 13. 21, *Odyssey* 5. 381. Aegae was on the site of the modern Limni, or else a little to the south of it (see Pauly-Wissowa, *s.v.* "Aigai."

[6] 8. 7. 4.

[7] Destroyed by a tidal wave 426 B.C. (Thucydides 3. 89).

ἐστὶν ἀπὸ Μεσσάπου, ὃς εἰς τὴν Ἰαπυγίαν ἐλθὼν Μεσσαπίαν τὴν χώραν ἐκάλεσεν. ἐνταῦθα δὲ καὶ τὰ περὶ τὸν Γλαῦκον μυθεύεται τὸν Ἀνθηδόνιον, ὅν φασιν εἰς κῆτος μεταβαλεῖν.

14. Πλησίον δ' ἐστὶν Ἀνθηδόνος ἱεροπρεπὴς τόπος τῆς Βοιωτίας, ἴχνη πόλεως ἔχων, ὁ καλούμενος Ἶσος, συστέλλοντι τὴν πρώτην συλλαβήν. οἴονται δέ τινες δεῖν γράφειν

Ἰσόν[1] τε ζαθέην Ἀνθηδόνα τ' ἐσχατόωσαν,

ἐκτείνοντες τὴν πρώτην συλλαβὴν ποιητικῶς διὰ τὸ μέτρον, ἀντὶ τοῦ

Νῖσάν τε ζαθέην·

ἡ γὰρ Νῖσα οὐδαμοῦ φαίνεται τῆς Βοιωτίας, ὥς φησιν Ἀπολλόδωρος ἐν τοῖς Περὶ νεῶν· ὡς οὐκ ἂν εἴη,[2] εἰ μὴ τὴν Νῖσαν οὕτως εἴρηκεν· ἦν γὰρ [ὁμώνυμος πόλις ἐν[3]] Μεγαρικῇ, ἐκεῖθεν ἀπῳκισμένη [πρὸς τὴν ὑπώρειαν Κιθα]ιρῶνος,[4] ἐκλέλειπται δὲ νῦν. τινὲς δὲ γράφουσι

Κρεῦσάν τε ζαθέην,

τὴν νῦν Κρέουσαν δεχόμενοι, τὸ τῶν Θεσπιέων ἐπίνειον ἐν τῷ Κρισαίῳ ἱδρυμένον· ἄλλοι δὲ

Φαράς[5] τε ζαθέας.

[1] Ἶσαν, *man. prim.* Ac, *ghiklno.*

[2] The lacuna in [ὡς οὐκ ἂν ε]ἴη is supplied by *bkno.*

[3] The lacuna of about twelve letters in A between γάρ and Μεγαρικῇ is supplied by Jones, following the conj. of Kramer; *gbno* have ὁ [Ἶσος πόλις ἐν τῇ].

[4] The lacuna in [πρὸς τὴν ὑπώρειαν Κιθα]ιρῶνος is supplied by Groskurd.

[5] Φηράς, *aBcghikl*, but corrected in *a.*

Messapius,[1] named after Messapus, who, when he came into Iapygia, called the country Messapia.[2] Here, too, is the scene of the myth of Glaucus, the Anthedonian, who is said to have changed into a sea-monster.[3]

14. Near Anthedon, and belonging to Boeotia, is a place that is esteemed sacred, and contains traces of a city, Isus, as it is called, with the first syllable pronounced short. Some, however, think that the verse should be written, "sacred Isus and Anthedon at the extremity,"[4] lengthening the first syllable by poetic licence on account of the metre,[5] instead of "sacred Nisa,"[6] for Nisa is nowhere to be seen in Boeotia, as Apollodorus says in his work *On Ships*;[7] so that Nisa could not be the correct reading, unless by "Nisa" the poet means "Isus"; for there was a city Nisa bearing the same name in the territory of Megara, whose inhabitants emigrated to the foothills of Cithaeron, but it has now disappeared. Some, however, think that we should write "sacred Creusa," taking the poet to mean the Creusa of to-day, the naval station of the Thespians, which is situated in the Crisaean Gulf; but others think that we should read "sacred Pharae." Pharae is

[1] The modern Ktypa.

[2] See 6. 3. 1.

[3] On the change of Glaucus to a sea-deity, cf. Pausanias 9. 22 and Plato's *Republic* 611.

[4] *Iliad* 2. 508.

[5] *i.e.* they make the letter "I" long, and so indicate by using the circumflex accent instead of the acute; or he might mean that they lengthen the syllable by pronouncing the "s" as a double "s."

[6] The "i" in Nisa is long by nature.

[7] *i.e. On the* (Homeric) *Catalogue of Ships* (see 1. 2. 24).

ἔστι δὲ τῆς τετρακωμίας τῆς περὶ Τάναγραν, Ἑλεῶνος, Ἅρματος, Μυκαλησσοῦ, Φαρῶν,[1] γράφουσι δὲ καὶ τοῦτο·

Νῦσάν τε ζαθέην·

κώμη δ' ἐστὶ τοῦ Ἑλικῶνος ἡ Νῦσα. ἡ μὲν οὖν παραλία τοιαύτη τις ἡ πρὸς Εὔβοιαν.

15. Τὰ δ' ἑξῆς ἐν τῇ μεσογαίᾳ πεδία ἐστὶ κοῖλα πάντοθεν ἐκ τῶν ἄλλων μερῶν ὄρεσι περιεχόμενα, τοῖς Ἀττικοῖς μὲν πρὸς νότου, πρὸς ἄρκτου[2] δὲ τοῖς Φωκικοῖς· ἀπὸ δὲ τῆς ἑσπέρας ὁ Κιθαιρὼν λοξὸς ἐμπίπτει μικρὸν ὑπὲρ τῆς Κρισαίας θαλάττης, ἔχων τὴν ἀρχὴν συνεχῆ τοῖς Μεγαρικοῖς καὶ τοῖς Ἀττικοῖς ὄρεσιν, εἶτ' ἐπιστρέφων εἰς
C 406 τὰ πεδία, παυόμενος δὲ περὶ τὴν Θηβαίαν.

16. Τῶν δὲ[3] πεδίων τούτων τὰ μὲν λιμνάζει, ποταμῶν ἀναχεομένων εἰς αὐτά, τῶν δ' ἐμπιπτόντων, εἶτα ἐκρύσεις λαμβανόντων· τὰ δ'[4] ἀνέψυκται[5] καὶ γεωργεῖται παντοδαπῶς διὰ τὴν εὐκαρπίαν. ὑπάντρου δὲ καὶ σηραγγώδους οὔσης κατὰ βάθους τῆς γῆς, σεισμοὶ γενόμενοι πολλάκις ἐξαίσιοι τοὺς μὲν ἔφραξαν τῶν πόρων, τοὺς δὲ ἀνέῳξαν, τοὺς μὲν μέχρι τῆς ἐπιφανείας, τοὺς δὲ δι' ὑπονόμων· συμβαίνει δὴ καὶ τοῖς ὕδασι, τοῖς μὲν δι' ὑπονόμων φέρεσθαι τῶν ῥείθρων, τοῖς δ' ἐπιπολῆς, τοῖς τε λιμναίοις καὶ τοῖς ποταμίοις· ἐγχωσθέντων δὲ κατὰ βάθους τῶν πόρων, αὔξεσθαι τὰς λίμνας συμβαίνει μέχρι τῶν οἰκουμένων

[1] Φηρῶν, *Bchikl*, and *man. sec.* in *a*.
[2] νότου . . . ἄρκτον, B*kl*.
[3] δή BE*kl*.
[4] μέν (for δ') B*k*.
[5] τὰ δέ, B*k* insert before καί.

one of the "Four United Villages" in the neighbourhood of Tanagra, which are: Heleon, Harma, Mycalessus, and Pharae. And still others write as follows: "sacred Nysa." And Nysa is a village in Helicon.[1] Such, then, is the seaboard facing Euboea.

15. The plains in the interior, which come next in order, are hollows, and are surrounded everywhere on the remaining sides[2] by mountains; by the mountains of Attica on the south, and on the north by the mountains of Phocis; and, on the west, Cithaeron inclines, obliquely, a little above the Crisaean Sea; it begins contiguous with the mountains of Megara and Attica, and then bends into the plains, terminating in the neighbourhood of Thebes.

16. Some of these plains are marshy, since rivers spread out over them, though other rivers fall into them and later find a way out; other plains are dried up, and on account of their fertility are tilled in all kinds of ways. But since the depths of the earth are full of caverns and holes,[3] it has often happened that violent earthquakes have blocked up some of the passages, and also opened up others, some up to the surface of the earth and others through underground channels. The result for the waters, therefore, is that some of the streams flow through underground channels, whereas others flow on the surface of the earth, thus forming lakes and rivers. And when the channels in the depths of the earth are stopped up, it comes to pass that the lakes expand as far as the inhabited places, so that they

[1] The range of mountains in Boeotia between Lake Copais and the Corinthian Gulf.

[2] *i.e.* except the eastern side, on the Euboean Sea.

[3] Cf. 8. 8. 4.

τόπων, ὥστε καὶ πόλεις καταπίνεσθαι καὶ χώρας, ἀνοιχθέντων δὲ τῶν αὐτῶν ἢ ἄλλων ἀνακαλύπτεσθαι, καὶ τοὺς αὐτοὺς τόπους ποτὲ μὲν πλεῖσθαι, ποτὲ δὲ πεζεύεσθαι, καὶ τὰς αὐτὰς πόλεις ποτὲ μὲν ἐπὶ τῇ λίμνῃ, ποτὲ δὲ ἄπωθεν κεῖσθαι.

17. Διττῶς δὲ τοῦτο γίνεται·[1] καὶ[2] γὰρ μενουσῶν ἀκινήτων τῶν πόλεων, ὅταν ἡ αὔξησις τῶν ὑδάτων ἥττων ᾖ τῆς ὑπερχύσεως διὰ ὕψος τῶν οἰκήσεων, ἢ διὰ ἀπόστασιν, καὶ διὰ ἀνοικισμόν, ὅταν τῷ πλησιασμῷ κινδυνεύσαντες πολλάκις ἀπαλλαγὴν πορίσωνται τοῦ φόβου τὴν μετάληψιν τῶν χωρίων τῶν ἄπωθεν ἢ τῶν ἐν ὕψει. παρακολουθεῖ δὲ τοῖς οὕτως ἀνοικισθεῖσι τὸ τὴν αὐτὴν προσηγορίαν φυλάττουσιν, ἐτύμως πρότερον λεγομένοις ἀπὸ τοῦ συμβεβηκότος τοπικῶς, μηκ[έτι λέγεσθαι ἐτύμως·[3]] Πλαταιὰς γὰρ ἀπὸ τῆς πλάτης τῶν κωπῶν εἰρῆσθαι πιθανὸν καὶ Πλαταιέας τοὺς ἀπὸ κωπηλασίας ζῶντας, ἀλλὰ νῦν, ἄπωθεν τῆς λίμνης οἰκοῦντες, οὐκέτ' ἂν προσαγορεύοιντο ἐτύμως. Ἕλος τε καὶ Ἑλεὼν καὶ Εἰλέσιον ἐκλήθη διὰ τὸ ἐπὶ τοῖς ἕλεσιν ἱδρῦσθαι, νῦν δὲ οὐχ ὁμοίως ἔχει ταῦτα, ἢ ἀνοικισθέντων, ἢ τῆς λίμνης ἐπιπολὺ ταπεινωθείσης διὰ τὰς ὕστερον γενομένας ἐκρύσεις· καὶ γὰρ τοῦτο δυνατόν.

[1] δύναται *Bl.*

[2] ἢ *Bkl.*

[3] In lacuna of about thirteen letters in A between μὴ κ and Πλαταιάς *g man. sec.* and *no* read νῦν μηκέτ' ἔχουσιν ὡς πρότερον; A *man. sec.* has μὴ λέγεσθαι; Corais νῦν μηκέτι λέγεσθαι ἐτύμως, and so Jones, but omitting νῦν.

swallow up both cities and districts, and that when the same channels, or others, are opened up, these cities and districts are uncovered; and that the same regions at one time are traversed in boats and at another on foot, and the same cities at one time are situated on the lake[1] and at another far away from it.

17. One of two things has taken place: either the cities have remained unremoved, when the increase in the waters has been insufficient to overflow the dwellings because of their elevation, or else they have been abandoned and rebuilt elsewhere, when, being oftentimes endangered by their nearness to the lake, they have relieved themselves from fear by changing to districts farther away or higher up. And it follows that the cities thus rebuilt which have kept the same name, though at first called by names truly applying to them, derived from local circumstances, have names which no longer truly apply to them; for instance, it is probable that "Plataeae" was so called from the "blade"[2] of the oars, and "Plataeans" were those who made their living from rowing; but now, since they live far away from the lake, the name can no longer truly apply to them. Helos and Heleon and Heilesium were so called because they were situated near marshes;[3] but now the case is different with these places, since they have been rebuilt elsewhere, or else the lake has been greatly reduced because of outflows that later took place; for this is possible.

[1] Strabo is thinking primarily of Lake Copais. For a complete account of this lake, which is now completely drained, see Tozer, note on Pausanias 9. 24. 1.

[2] In Greek, "platē."

[3] Helos ("marsh"), Helê ("marshes").

18. Δηλοῖ δὲ καὶ ὁ Κηφισσὸς[1] τοῦτο μάλιστα, τὴν Κωπαΐδα λίμνην πληρῶν. αὐξομένης γὰρ αὐτῆς, ὥστε κινδυνεύειν καταποθῆναι τὰς Κώπας ἃς[2] ὅ τε ποιητὴς ὀνομάζει, καὶ ἀπ' αὐτῶν ἡ λίμνη τὴν ἐπωνυμίαν εἴληφε, χάσμα γενηθὲν πρὸς τῇ λίμνῃ πλησίον τῶν Κωπῶν ἀνέῳξεν ὑπὸ γῆς ῥεῖθρον ὅσον τριάκοντα σταδίων καὶ ἐδέξατο τὸν ποταμόν, εἶτα ἐξέρρηξεν εἰς τὴν ἐπιφάνειαν κατὰ Λάρυμναν τῆς Λοκρίδος τὴν ἄνω· καὶ γὰρ ἑτέρα ἐστίν, ἧς ἐμνήσθημεν,[3] ἡ Βοιωτιακὴ ἐπὶ τῇ θαλάττῃ, ᾗ προσέθεσαν Ῥωμαῖοι τὴν ἄνω.
C 407 καλεῖται δ' ὁ τόπος Ἀγχόη· ἔστι δὲ καὶ λίμνη ὁμώνυμος· ἐντεῦθεν δ' ἤδη ὁ Κηφισσὸς ἐκδίδωσιν ἐπὶ τὴν θάλατταν. τότε μὲν οὖν, παυσαμένης τῆς πλημμυρίδος, παῦλα καὶ τοῦ κινδύνου τοῖς παροικοῦσιν ὑπῆρξε, πλὴν τῶν ἤδη καταποθεισῶν πόλεων. πάλιν δ' ἐγχουμένων τῶν πόρων, ὁ μεταλλευτὴς Κράτης,[4] ἀνὴρ Χαλκιδεύς, ἀνακαθαίρειν τὰ ἐμφράγματα ἐπαύσατο, στασιασάντων τῶν Βοιωτῶν, καίπερ, ὡς αὐτὸς ἐν τῇ πρὸς Ἀλέξανδρον ἐπιστολῇ φησίν, ἀνεψυγμένων ἤδη πολλῶν, ἐν οἷς οἱ μὲν τὸν Ὀρχομενὸν οἰκεῖσθαι τὸν ἀρχαῖον ὑπελάμβανον, οἱ δ' Ἐλευσῖνα καὶ Ἀθήνας παρὰ

[1] Κηφισός B. [2] ἅς, Pletho inserts.
[3] [ἐμνήσθη]μεν, lacuna of about six letters supplied by Groskurd; ἧς εἴπομεν *gbkno*; ὡς εἴπομεν Corais.
[4] μεταλλευτὴς Κράτης, Frère (*Mém. de l'Ac.* 23, p. 142), for μ.. αλλεὺς τῆς Κρήτης; so the later editors.

[1] In Greek, "oars."
[2] *Iliad* 2. 502.
[3] See Tozer, *Selections*, p. 236, note 2.
[4] 9. 2. 13. [5] Lower Larymna.

18. This is best shown by the Cephissus, which fills Lake Copais; for when the lake had increased so much that Copae[1] was in danger of being swallowed up (Copae is named by the poet,[2] and from it the lake took its name), a rent in the earth, which was formed by the lake near Copae, opened up a subterranean channel[3] about thirty stadia in length and admitted the river; and then the river burst forth to the surface near Larymna in Locris; I mean the Upper Larymna, for there is another Larymna, which I have already mentioned,[4] the Boeotian Larymna[5] on the sea, to which the Romans annexed the Upper Larymna.[6] The place is called Anchoê;[7] and there is also a lake of the same name. And when it leaves this lake the Cephissus at last flows out to the sea. Now at that time, when the flooding of the lake ceased, there was also a cessation of danger to those who lived near it, except in the case of the cities which had already been swallowed up. And though the subterranean channels filled up again, Crates the mining engineer of Chalcis ceased clearing away the obstructions[8] because of party strife among the Boeotians, although, as he himself says in the letter to Alexander, many places had already been drained. Among these places, some writers suppose, was the ancient site of Orchomenus, and others, those of Eleusis and Athens on the

[6] According to Pausanias (9. 23. 4), "Lower Larymna anciently belonged to Opus," the Locrian city, but later "joined the Boeotian confederacy." For a complete account of the two Larymnas see Frazer, note on Pausanias 9. 23. 7.

[7] "Outflow" (Ἀγχόη).

[8] There seems to be an omission here. We should expect, "Crates . . . began to clear away the obstructions but ceased."

τὸν Τρίτωνα ποταμόν· λέγεται δ' οἰκίσαι[1] Κέκροπα, ἡνίκα τῆς Βοιωτίας ἐπῆρξε,[2] καλουμένης τότε Ὠγυγίας, ἀφανισθῆναι δὲ ταύτας ἐπικλυσθείσας ὕστερον. γενέσθαι δέ φασι καὶ κατὰ Ὀρχομενὸν χάσμα, καὶ δέξασθαι τὸν Μέλανα ποταμὸν τὸν ῥέοντα διὰ τῆς Ἁλιαρτίας καὶ ποιοῦντα ἐνταῦθα τὸ ἕλος τὸ φύον τὸν αὐλητικὸν κάλαμον. ἀλλ' οὗτος ἠφάνισται τελέως, εἴτε τοῦ χάσματος διαχέοντος αὐτὸν εἰς ἀδήλους πόρους, εἴτε τῶν περὶ Ἁλίαρτον ἑλῶν καὶ λιμνῶν προαναλισκόντων[3] αὐτόν, ἀφ' ὧν ποιήεντα καλεῖ τὸν τόπον ὁ ποιητής,

καὶ ποιήενθ' Ἁλίαρτον

λέγων.

19. Οὗτοι μὲν οὖν ἐκ τῶν Φωκικῶν ὀρῶν οἱ ποταμοὶ καταφέρονται, ὧν ὁ Κηφισσὸς ἐκ Λιλαίας, Φωκικῆς πόλεως, τὴν ἀρχὴν λαμβάνει, καθάπερ καὶ Ὅμηρός φησιν·

οἵ τε Λίλαιαν ἔχον πηγῇς ἔπι Κηφισσοῖο·

δι' Ἐλατείας δὲ ῥυείς, μεγίστης τῶν ἐν Φωκεῦσι πόλεων, καὶ διὰ Παραποταμίων καὶ Φανοτέων,[4] ὁμοίως Φωκικῶν πολισμάτων, εἰς Χαιρώνειαν τῆς Βοιωτίας πρόεισιν, εἶτα διὰ τῆς Ὀρχομενίας καὶ τῆς Κορωνειακῆς εἰς τὴν Κωπαΐδα λίμνην ἐξίησι· καὶ ὁ Περμησσὸς δὲ καὶ ὁ Ὀλμειός, ἐκ τοῦ Ἑλικῶνος συμβάλλοντες ἀλλήλοις, εἰς τὴν αὐτὴν

[1] δ' οἰκίσαι, lacuna of about seven letters in A supplied by Corais; καὶ κατά *bgno*.

[2] ἐπῆρξε, Corais, for ὑπῆρξε; so Meineke.

[3] προαναλισκόντων, Corais, for προσαναλισκόντων; so the later editors.

Triton River.[1] These cities, it is said, were founded by Cecrops, when he ruled over Boeotia, then called Ogygia, but were later wiped out by inundations. And it is said that a fissure in the earth opened up near Orchomenus, also, and that it admitted the Melas River, which flowed through the territory of Haliartus[2] and formed there the marsh which produces the reed that is used for flutes.[3] But this river has completely disappeared, either because it is dispersed by the fissure into invisible channels or because it is used up beforehand by the marshes and lakes in the neighbourhood of Haliartus, from which the poet calls the place "grassy," when he says, "and grassy Haliartus."[4]

19. Now these rivers flow down from the Phocian mountains, and among them the Cephissus, which takes its beginning at Lilaea, a Phocian city, as Homer says: "And those who held Lilaea, at the sources of Cephissus."[5] And flowing through Elateia, the largest of the cities of Phocis, and through Parapotamii and Phanoteus,[6] which are likewise Phocian towns, it goes on into Chaeroneia in Boeotia, and then through the territories of Orchomenus and Coroneia, and discharges into Lake Copais. And also the Permessus and the Olmeius, flowing from Helicon, meet one another and fall into the same

[1] On the Triton River, see Pausanias, 9. 33. 5.

[2] How could this be when the Melas lay on the northern side of the lake and Haliartus on the southern (Tozer, *op. cit.*, p. 237)?

[3] So Pliny 16. 66.

[4] *Iliad* 2. 503.

[5] *Iliad* 2. 523.

[6] The usual spelling is "Panopeus."

---

[4] Φανοτέων, Corais, for Φανητέων; so the later editors.

ἐμπίπτουσι λίμνην τὴν Κωπαΐδα τοῦ Ἁλιάρτου πλη[σίον· καὶ ἄλλα [1]] δὲ ῥεύματα εἰς αὐτὴν ἐμβάλλει. ἔστι μὲν οὖν μεγάλη, τὴν περίμετρον ἔχουσα ὀγδοήκοντα καὶ τριακοσίων σταδίων, αἱ δὲ ἐκρύσεις οὐδαμοῦ φαίνονται πλὴν τοῦ δεχομένου τὸν Κηφισσὸν χάσματος καὶ τῶν ἑλῶν.

20. [Τῶν δὲ περι]κειμένων [2] λιμνῶν ἐστὶν ἥ τε Τρεφία, καὶ ἡ Κηφισσίς·[3] μέμνηται καὶ Ὅμηρος·

ὅς ῥ' ἐν Ὕλῃ ναίεσκε μέγα πλούτοιο μεμηλώς,
λίμνῃ κεκλιμένος Κηφισσίδι.

οὐ γὰρ λίμνην τὴν Κωπαΐδα βούλεται λέγειν, ὡς οἴονταί τινες, ἀλλὰ τὴν Ὑλικὴν προσαγορευομένην (τῇ προσῳδίᾳ ὡς λυρικήν) ἀπὸ τῆς πλησίον κώμης,[4] ἣν καλοῦσιν Ὕλας (ὡς λύρας καὶ θύρας), οὐδὲ Ὕδην, ὡς ἔνιοι γράφουσιν,

ὅς ῥ' ἐν Ὕδῃ ναίεσκεν.

ἡ μὲν γάρ ἐστιν ἐν Λυδίᾳ

C 408 Τμώλῳ ὕπο νιφόεντι, Ὕδης ἐν πίονι δήμῳ,

ἡ δὲ Βοιωτιακή· ἐπιφέρει γοῦν τῷ

λίμνῃ κεκλιμένος Κηφισσίδι

τὸ

πὰρ δέ οἱ ἄλλοι
ναῖον Βοιωτοί.

ἡ μὲν γάρ ἐστι μεγάλη, καὶ οὐκ ἐν τῇ Θηβαΐδι, ἡ δὲ [5] μικρά, ἐκεῖθεν δι' ὑπονόμων πληρουμένη,

[1] The lacuna of about fourteen letters between πλη and δέ is supplied by Meineke. Groskurd and Müller-Dübner add πλείω after ἄλλα. *bkno* have πλησίον· καὶ τὰ τούτου.

Lake Copais near Haliartus; and also other streams empty into it. Now it is a large lake, having a circuit of three hundred and eighty stadia, but its outlets are nowhere to be seen, except for the fissure which admits the Cephissus, and for the marshes.

20. Among the neighbouring lakes are Lake Trephia[1] and the Cephissian Lake, which is also mentioned by Homer: "Who dwelt in Hylê, strongly intent upon wealth, on the shore of the Cephissian Lake."[2] For he does not mean Lake Copais, as some think, but Lake Hylicê (accented on the last syllable like *lyricé*), which is named after the village near by that is called Hýlê (accented like *lýra* and *thýra*), not Hydê, as some write, "who dwelt in Hydê." For Hydê is in Lydia, "below snowy Tmolus in the fertile land of Hydê,"[3] whereas Hylê is in Boeotia; at any rate, the poet appends to the words, "on the shore of the Cephissian Lake," the words, "and near him dwelt the rest of the Boeotians." For Lake Copais is large, and not in the territory of Thebes; whereas the other is small, and is filled from Lake Copais through subterranean

[1] Otherwise unknown. [2] *Iliad* 5. 708.
[3] *Iliad* 20. 385.

---

[2] The lacuna of about nine letters before κειμένων is supplied by Groskurd; so Kramer, Meineke, and Müller-Dübner.

[3] A reads ἡ K . . ., inserting ἧς in first hand; *abcghikno*, ἡ Κωπαΐς. From conj. of Falconer, Meineke and Müller-Dübner read as above, though Falconer and Corais read δέ instead of ἧς.

[4] πόλεως, BE*kl*.

[5] ἡ δέ, for καί, Casaubon; so the later editors.

κειμένη μεταξὺ Θηβῶν καὶ Ἀνθηδόνος. Ὅμηρος δ' ἑνικῶς ἐκφέρει, τοτὲ μὲν ἐκτείνων τὴν πρώτην συλλαβήν, ὡς ἐν τῷ Καταλόγῳ,

ἠδ' Ὕλην καὶ Πετεῶνα,

ποιητικῶς· τοτὲ δὲ συστέλλων·

ὅς ῥ' ἐν Ὕλῃ ναίεσκε,

Τυχίος[1]

σκυτοτόμων ὄχ' ἄριστος, Ὕλῃ ἔνι οἰκία ναίων·

οὐδ' ἐνταῦθα εὖ γραφόντων τινῶν Ὕδῃ ἔνι· οὐ γὰρ ὁ Αἴας ἐκ Λυδίας τὸ σάκος μετεπέμπετο.

21. Αὗται δ' αἱ[2] λίμναι τὴν τάξιν τῶν ἐφεξῆς τόπω[ν σημήναιντ' ἄν, ὥστε τῷ[3]] λόγῳ περιληφθῆναι σαφῶς, ὅτι ὁ ποιητὴς ἀτάκτως χρῆται[4] τοῖς ὀνόμασι τῶν τόπων τῶν τε [ἀξίων μνήμης καὶ τῶν μή·[5]]· χαλεπὸν δ' ἐν τοσούτοις, καὶ ἀσήμοις τοῖς πλείστοις καὶ ἐν μεσογαίᾳ, μηδαμοῦ τῇ τάξει διαπεσεῖν· ἡ παραλία δ' ἔχει τι πλεονέκτημα πρὸς τοῦτο· καὶ γνωριμώτεροι οἱ τόποι, καὶ ἡ θάλαττα τό γε ἑξῆς ὑπαγορεύει βέλτιον· διόπερ καὶ ἡμεῖς ἐκεῖθεν πειρώμ[εθα τὰς ἀρχὰς λαβεῖν,[6]] ἐνταῦθα δ' ἐάσαντες τοῦτο τῷ π[οιητῇ ἀκολουθοῦντες ποιήσομεν τὴν[7]] διαρίθμησιν προστιθέντες ὅ τι ἂν χρήσιμον ᾖ [ληφθὲν ἐξ ἄλλω]ν[8] ἡμῖν, ὑπ' ἐκείνου

[1] Τυχίος, Meineke omits.

[2] [Αὗται δ' αἱ], lacuna supplied by Groskurd; so the later editors.

[3] τόπω[ν σημήναιντ' ἄν, ὥστε τῷ], lacuna supplied by Groskurd; so Müller-Dübner. ὑπογράφουσιν ὥστε, Meineke.

[4] [ποιητὴς ἀτάκτως χρῆται], lacuna supplied by Groskurd; so later editors.

[5] [ἀξίων μνήμης καὶ τῶν μή], lacuna supplied by Groskurd; so Müller-Dübner. ἀξιολόγων κτλ., Meineke.

channels; and it is situated between Thebes and Anthedon. Homer, however, uses the word in the singular number, at one time making the first syllable long, as in the *Catalogue*, "and Hȳlê and Peteôn," [1] by poetic licence, and at another making it short, "who dwelt in Hy̆lê," and "Tychius . . . , by far the best of leather-workers, who had his home in Hy̆lê." [2] And certain critics are not correct in writing Hydê here, either; for Aias was not sending to fetch his shield from Lydia.

21. These lakes suggest the order of the places that come next after them, so that nominally their positions are clearly determined, because the poet observes no order in naming the places, whether those that are worthy of mention or those that are not. But it is difficult, in naming so many places, most of them insignificant and situated in the interior, to avoid error in every case in the matter of their order. The seaboard, however, has a certain advantage with regard to this: the places there are better known; and, too, the sea more readily suggests the order of places. Therefore I, too, shall try to take my beginnings from the seaboard, although at present I shall disregard this intention, and following the poet shall make my enumeration of the places, adding everything taken from other writers, but omitted by him, that may be useful to

[1] *Iliad* 2. 500. [2] *Iliad* 7. 221.

[6] πειρώμ[εθα τὰς ἀρχὰς λαβεῖν], lacuna supplied by Groskurd; so Müller-Dübner. [εθα περιοδεύειν], Meineke.

[7] π[οιητῇ ἀκολουθοῦντες ποιήσομεν τὴν], lacuna supplied by Groskurd; so Müller-Dübner and Meineke.

[8] [ληφθὲν ἐξ ἄλλω]ν, lacuna supplied by Groskurd; so Müller-Dübner. [πρὸς τὴν ὑπόθεσι]ν, Meineke.

δὲ παραλειφθέν.[1] ἄρχεται δ' ἀπὸ τῆς Ὑρίης καὶ τῆς Αὐλίδος, περὶ ὧν εἰρήκαμεν.

22. Σχοῖνος δ' ἐστὶ χώρα τῆς Θηβαϊκῆς κατὰ τὴν ὁδὸν τὴν ἐπὶ Ἀνθηδόνος, διέχουσα τῶν Θηβῶν ὅσον πεντήκοντα σταδίους· ῥεῖ δὲ καὶ ποταμὸς δι' αὐτῆς Σχοινοῦς.

23. Σκῶλος δ' ἐστὶ κώμη τῆς Παρασωπίας ὑπὸ τῷ Κιθαιρῶνι, δυσοίκητος τόπος καὶ τραχύς, ἀφ' οὗ καὶ ἡ παροιμία·

εἰς Σκῶλον μήτ' αὐτὸς ἴναι, μήτ' ἄλλῳ ἕπεσθαι.

καὶ τὸν Πενθέα δὲ ἐνθένδε καταγόμενον διασπασθῆναί φασιν. ἦν δὲ καὶ τῶν περὶ Ὄλυνθον πόλεων ὁμώνυμος αὐτῇ Σκῶλος. εἴρηται δ' ὅτι Παρασώπιοι καὶ κώμη τις καλεῖται ἐν Ἡρακλείᾳ τῇ Τραχινίᾳ, παρ' ἣν ῥεῖ Ἀσωπὸς ποταμός, καὶ ὅτι ἐν Σικυωνίᾳ[2] ἄλλος ἐστὶν Ἀσωπὸς καὶ ἡ χώρα Ἀσωπία, δι' ἧς ῥεῖ· εἰσὶ δὲ[3] καὶ ἄλλοι ποταμοὶ ὁμώνυμοι τῷ ποταμῷ τούτῳ.

24. Ὁ Ἐτεωνὸς δὲ Σκάρφη[4] μετωνομάσθη, καὶ αὕτη δὲ τῆς Παρασωπίας. ὁ γὰρ Ἀσωπὸς καὶ ὁ Ἰσμηνὸς διὰ τοῦ πεδίου ῥέουσι τοῦ πρὸ τῶν Θηβῶν. ἔστι δὲ καὶ ἡ Δίρκη κρήνη καὶ Πότνιαι,[5]
C 409 ἐφ' ὧν μυθεύεται τὰ περὶ τὸν Ποτνιέα Γλαῦκον τὸν διασπασθέντα ὑπὸ τῶν Ποτνιάδων ἵππων τῆς πόλεως πλησίον. καὶ ὁ Κιθαιρὼν δὲ οὐκ ἄπωθεν τῶν Θηβῶν τελευτᾷ· παρ' αὐτὸν δὲ ὁ

[1] παραλειφθέν, Corais, for παραληφθέν; so the later editors.
[2] Σικυωνίᾳ, Corais, for Σικυῶνι; so the later editors.
[3] εἰσὶ δέ, Corais, for ῥέουσι; so the later editors; Meineke, however, relegates εἰσὶ δὲ . . . τούτῳ to the foot of the page.
[4] Σκάρφη, Xylander, for Σκάφλαι; so the later editors.

us. He begins at Hyria and Aulis, concerning which I have already spoken.[1]

22. Schoenus[2] is a district of the Theban territory on the road that leads from Thebes to Anthedon, and is about fifty stadia distant from Thebes; and there is also a river Schoenus which flows through it.

23. Scolus is a village in the Parasopian[3] country at the foot of Mount Cithaeron, a place that is rugged and hardly habitable; whence the proverb, "neither go to Scolus thyself nor follow another thither." And this is also said to be the place from which Pentheus was brought when he was torn to pieces.[4] And there was another Scolus among the cities in the neighbourhood of Olynthus bearing the same name as this village. And, as I have already said,[5] there is also in the Trachinian Heracleia a village called Parasopii, past which flows a River Asopus; and in Sicyonia there is another Asopus River, and also the country Asopia, through which that Asopus flows; and there are also other rivers which bear this name.

24. The name "Eteonus"[6] was changed to "Scarphê," and Scarphê too is in Parasopia; for the Asopus and the Ismenus flow through the plain which is in front of Thebes. And there is the spring called Dircê; and also Potniae, where is the scene of the myth of Glaucus of Potniae, who was torn to pieces by the Potnian mares near the city. Cithaeron, also, ends not far from Thebes. The

[1] 9. 2. 8 and 9. 2. 12.

[2] *Iliad* 2. 497.

[3] *i.e.* along the Asopus River.

[4] *i.e.* by the Bacchic women.

[5] 8. 6. 24.

[6] See 7. 3. 6.

[5] Πότνιαι, all editors, for Πότνια.

Ἀσωπὸς ῥεῖ, τὴν ὑπώρειαν αὐτοῦ κλύζων καὶ ποιῶν τοὺς Παρασωπίους εἰς κατοικίας πλείους διῃρημένους· ἅπαντας δ' ὑπὸ Θηβαίοις ὄντας, ἕτεροι δ' ἐν τῇ Πλαταιέων φασὶ τόν τε Σκῶλον καὶ τὸν Ἐτεωνὸν καὶ τὰς Ἐρυθράς· καὶ γὰρ παραρρεῖ[1] Πλαταιὰς καὶ παρὰ Τάναγραν ἐκδίδωσιν· ἐν δὲ τῇ Θηβαίων εἰσὶ καὶ αἱ Θεράπναι καὶ ὁ Τευμησσός, ὃν ἐκόσμησεν Ἀντίμαχος διὰ πολλῶν ἐπῶν, τὰς μὴ προσούσας ἀρετὰς διαριθμούμενος·

ἔστι τις ἠνεμόεις ὀλίγος λόφος·

γνώριμα δὲ τὰ ἔπη.

25. Θέσπειαν δὲ λέγει τὰς νῦν Θεσπίας, πολλῶν ὀνομάτων τῶν μὲν ἀμφοτέρως λεγομένων καὶ ἑνικῶς καὶ πληθυντικῶς, καθάπερ καὶ ἀρρενικῶς καὶ θηλυκῶς, τῶν δ' ὁποτέρως. ἔστι δὲ πόλις πρὸς τῷ Ἑλικῶνι, νοτιωτέρα αὐτοῦ, ἐπικειμένη δὲ τῷ Κρισαίῳ κόλπῳ καὶ αὐτὴ καὶ ὁ Ἑλικών· ἐπίνειον δ' ἔχουσιν αἱ Θεσπιαὶ[2] Κρέουσαν, ἣν καὶ Κρεουσίδα[3] καλοῦσιν. ἐν δὲ τῇ Θεσπιέων[4] ἐστὶ καὶ ἡ Ἄσκρη κατὰ τὸ πρὸς Ἑλικῶνα μέρος, ἡ τοῦ Ἡσιόδου πατρίς· ἐν δεξιᾷ γάρ ἐστι τοῦ Ἑλικῶνος, ἐφ' ὑψηλοῦ καὶ τραχέος τόπου κειμένη, ἀπέχουσα τῶν Θεσπιῶν ὅσον τετταράκοντα σταδίους, ἣν καὶ κεκωμῴδηκεν αὐτὸς ἐν ἔπεσι

[1] παραρρεῖ, Du Theil, for παρά; so the later editors.
[2] Θεσπιαί (see Θεσπιάς above), for Θεσπειαί.
[3] Κρεουσίδα, conj. of Kramer, for Κρεουσίαν. So spelled by Xenophon, *Hellenica* 5. 4. 16, and Pausanias 9. 32. 1.

Asopus flows past it, washing its foothills and causing the division of the Parasopii into several settlements; and all the settlements are subject to Thebes, though another set of writers say that Scolus, Eteonus, and Erythrae are in the territory of the Plataeans, for the river flows past Plataea, also, and empties near Tanagra. And in the territory of Thebes are also Therapnae and Teumessus, which latter Antimachus has adorned with praise in many verses,[1] although he enumerates goodly attributes which do not belong to it, as, for instance, "there is a windy little hill"; but the verses are well known.

25. The "Thespiae" of to-day is by Antimachus spelled "Thespeia"; for there are many names of places which are used in both ways, both in the singular and in the plural, just as there are many which are used both in the masculine and in the feminine, whereas there are others which are used in either one or the other number only. Thespiae is a city near Mt. Helicon, lying somewhat to the south of it; and both it and Helicon are situated on the Crisaean Gulf. It has a sea-port Creusa, also called Creusis. In the Thespian territory, in the part lying towards Helicon, is Ascrê, the native city of Hesiod; it is situated on the right of Helicon,[2] on a high and rugged place, and is about forty stadia distant from Thespiae. This city Hesiod himself has satirised in verses which allude to his father,

[1] In his epic poem entitled *Thebais*.
[2] *i.e.* as viewed from Thespiae.

[4] Θεσπιέων (see Θεσπιάς above), Meineke, for Θεσπειέων.

περὶ[1] τοῦ πατρός,[2] ὅτι ἐκ Κύμης τῆς Αἰολίδος μ[ετῴκησε πρό]τερον,[3] λέγων

νάσσατο δ' ἄγχ' Ἑλικῶνος ὀϊζυρῇ ἐνὶ κώμῃ,[4]
Ἄσκρῃ, χεῖμα κακῇ, θέρει ἀργαλέῃ, οὐδέ ποτ' ἐσθλῇ.[5]

ὁ δὲ Ἑλικὼν συνεχής ἐστι τῇ Φωκίδι ἐκ τῶν πρὸς ἄρκτον αὐτοῦ[6] μερῶν· μικρὰ δὲ καὶ ἐκ τῶν πρὸς ἑσπέραν κατὰ τὸν ὕστατον λιμένα τῆς Φωκίδος, ὃν καλοῦσιν ἀπὸ τοῦ συμβεβηκότος Μυχόν· ὑπέρκειται γὰρ κατὰ τοῦτον μάλιστα τὸν λιμένα τοῦ Κρισαίου[7] κόλπου καὶ ὁ Ἑλικὼν καὶ ἡ Ἄσκρη καὶ ἔτι αἱ Θεσπιαὶ καὶ τὸ ἐπίνειον αὐτῆς ἡ Κρέουσα. τοῦτο δὲ καὶ κοιλότατον νομίζεται τὸ μέρος τοῦ Κρισαίου κόλπου καὶ ἁπλῶς τοῦ Κορινθιακοῦ· στάδιοι δ' εἰσὶ τῆς [παραλίας[8]] τῆς ἀπὸ τοῦ Μυχοῦ τοῦ λιμένος εἰς Κρέουσαν ἐνενήκοντα· ἐντεῦθεν δὲ ἑκατὸν εἴκοσι ἕως τῆς ἄκρας, ἣν [Ὀλμιὰς[9]] καλοῦσιν· ἐν δὲ τῷ κοιλοτάτῳ τοῦ κόλπου τοῦ [Κρισαίου συμβέβηκε[10]] τὰς Πηγὰς κεῖσθαι καὶ τὴν Οἰνόην, πε[ρὶ ὧν εἰ]ρήκαμεν.[11] ὁ μὲν οὖν Ἑλικὼν οὐ πολὺ διεστηκὼς τοῦ[12]

[1] ἐ[ν ἔπεσι περί], lacuna of about eleven letters in A supplied by Jones, following Müller-Dübner, who insert τοῖς before ἔπεσι. Kramer conj. ἔ[πη ποιησάμενος κατά]. Meineke reads ἐ[πιλαβόμενος]. *bcghi* have ἐκεῖνος περί and *no* περί only.

[2] *bkno* add λέγων after πατρός.

[3] μ[ετῴκησε πρό]τερον, lacuna of about ten letters in A supplied by Jones. Cp. ὁ πατὴρ αὐτοῦ (*i.e.* Ἡσιόδου) Δῖος μετῴκησεν εἰς Βοιωτούς (13. 3. 6). Kramer conj. μ[ετανέστη πρό] (Müller-Dübner so read); and Meineke reads μ[ετέστη θρασύ]τερον.

[4] [ἐνὶ κώμῃ], lacuna supplied in *h man. sec.*

[5] [ἐσθλῇ], lacuna supplied in *h man. sec.*

because at an earlier time his father changed his abode to this place from the Aeolian Cymê, saying: "And he settled near Helicon in a wretched village, Ascrê, which is bad in winter, oppressive in summer, and pleasant at no time."[1] Helicon is contiguous to Phocis in its northerly parts, and to a slight extent also in its westerly parts, in the region of the last harbour belonging to Phocis, the harbour which, from the fact in the case, is called Mychus;[2] for, speaking generally, it is above this harbour of the Crisaean Gulf that Helicon and Ascrê, and also Thespiae and its sea-port Creusa, are situated. This is also considered the deepest recess of the Crisaean Gulf, and in general of the Corinthian Gulf. The length of the coast-line from the harbour Mychus to Creusa is ninety stadia; and the length from Creusa as far as the promontory called Holmiae is one hundred and twenty; and hence Pagae and Oenoê, of which I have already spoken,[3] are situated in the deepest recess of the gulf. Now Helicon, not far

[1] *Works and Days* 639–40.

[2] *i.e.* "Mychus," "Recess," of what is now Gulf Zalitza.

[3] 8. 6. 22.

---

[6] *αὐτοῦ*, conj. of Palmer for *αὐτῆς* B*klno*, *αὐτῇ* *acghi*. So Corais, Kramer, Müller-Dübner, and Meineke.

[7] Κρισσαίου BE*l*.

[8] [*παραλίας*], lacuna of seven or eight letters in A supplied by *bknop*.

[9] Ὀλμιάς, conj. of Palmer for lacuna of about six letters; so later editors.

[10] [Κρισαίου συμ]βέβηκε, lacuna of about ten letters supplied by Kramer; so the later editors. *τού[του συμ]βέβηκε bkno*.

[11] *πε[ρὶ ὧν εἰ]ρήκαμεν*, lacuna of about six letters supplied by Groskurd; so the later editors. *bkno* have ἧς instead of ὧν.

[12] B*kl* add Κορινθιακοῦ before Παρνασσοῦ; Pletho Φωκικοῦ.

Παρνασσοῦ ἐνάμιλλός ἐστιν ἐκείνῳ κατά τε ὕψος
C 410 καὶ περίμετρον· ἄμφω γὰρ χιονόβολα τὰ ὄρη καὶ πετρώδη, περιγράφεται δ' οὐ πολλῇ χώρᾳ. ἐνταῦθα δ' ἐστὶ τό τε τῶν Μουσῶν ἱερὸν καὶ ἡ Ἵππου κρήνη καὶ τὸ τῶν Λειβηθρίδων νυμφῶν ἄντρον· ἐξ οὗ τεκμαίροιτ' ἄν τις Θρᾷκας εἶναι τοὺς τὸν Ἑλικῶνα ταῖς Μούσαις καθιερώσαντας, οἳ καὶ τὴν Πιερίδα[1] καὶ τὸ Λείβηθρον καὶ τὴν Πίμπλειαν[2] ταῖς αὐταῖς θεαῖς ἀνέδειξαν. ἐκαλοῦντο δὲ Πίερες· ἐκλιπόντων δ' ἐκείνων, Μακεδόνες νῦν ἔχουσι τὰ χωρία ταῦτα. εἴρηται δ' ὅτι τὴν Βοιωτίαν ταύτην ἐπῴκησάν ποτε Θρᾷκες, βιασάμενοι τοὺς Βοιωτούς, καὶ Πελασγοὶ καὶ ἄλλοι βάρβαροι. αἱ δὲ Θεσπιαὶ πρότερον μὲν ἐγνωρίζοντο διὰ τὸν Ἔρωτα τὸν Πραξιτέλους, ὃν ἔγλυψε μὲν ἐκεῖνος, ἀνέθηκε δὲ Γλυκέρα ἡ ἑταίρα Θεσπιεῦσιν, ἐκεῖθεν οὖσα τὸ γένος, λαβοῦσα δῶρον παρὰ τοῦ τεχνίτου. πρότερον μὲν οὖν ὀψόμενοι τὸν Ἔρωτά τινες ἀνέβαινον ἐπὶ τὴν Θέσπειαν,[3] ἄλλως οὐκ οὖσαν ἀξιοθέατον, νυνὶ δὲ μόνη συνέστηκε τῶν Βοιωτιακῶν πόλεων καὶ Τάναγρα· τῶν δ' ἄλλων ἐρείπια καὶ ὀνόματα λέλειπται.

26. [Μετ]ὰ[4] δὲ Θεσπιὰς καταλέγει Γραῖαν καὶ Μυκα[λησσόν, περ]ὶ[5] ὧν εἰρήκαμεν· ὡς δ' αὕτως καὶ περὶ τῶν [ἄλλων·

[1] Πιερίαν *Bkno*. [2] Πίπλειαν *Acghino*.
[3] Θέσπειαν, Du Theil, for θέαν; so Kramer and Meineke.
[4] [Μετ]ά, lacuna supplied by *i*; so the later editors. But *bkno* have ταῖς δὲ Θεσπίαις.

distant from Parnassus, rivals it both in height and in circuit; for both mountains are rocky and covered with snow, and their circuit comprises no large extent of territory.[1] Here are the temple of the Muses and Hippu-crenê[2] and the cave of the nymphs called the Leibethrides; and from this fact one might infer that those who consecrated Helicon to the Muses were Thracians, the same who dedicated Pieris and Leibethrum and Pimpleia to the same goddesses.[3] The Thracians used to be called Pieres, but, now that they have disappeared, the Macedonians hold these places. It has been said[4] that Thracians once settled in this part of Boeotia, having overpowered the Boeotians, as did also Pelasgians and other barbarians. Now in earlier times Thespiae was well known because of the Eros of Praxiteles, which was sculptured by him and dedicated by Glycera the courtesan (she had received it as a gift from the artist) to the Thespians, since she was a native of the place. Now in earlier times travellers would go up to Thespeia, a city otherwise not worth seeing, to see the Eros; and at present it and Tanagra are the only Boeotian cities that still endure; but of all the rest only ruins and names are left.

26. After Thespiae Homer names Graea and Mycalessus, concerning which I have already spoken.[5] He likewise says concerning the rest:[6] "And those

[1] *i.e.* they descend sharply and without foothills to the plains.
[2] See 8. 6. 21.
[3] Cp. 10. 3. 17.
[4] 9. 2. 3.
[5] 9. 2 10, 11.
[6] 9. 2. 11, 12, 17, 20.

---

[5] Μυκα[λησσόν, περ]ί, lacuna supplied by later MSS.; so the later editors.

οἵ τ'[1]] ἀμφ' Ἅρμ' ἐνέμοντο καὶ Εἰλέσιον καὶ Ἐρυθράς,
[οἵ τ' Ἐλεῶν'[2]] εἶχον ἠδ' Ὕλην καὶ Πετεῶνα.

Πετεὼν δὲ κώμη τῆς Θηβαΐδος ἐγγὺς τῆς ἐπ' Ἀνθηδόνα ὁδοῦ, ἡ δ' Ὠκαλέη μέση Ἁλιάρτου καὶ Ἀλαλκομενίου ἑκατέρου τριάκοντα σταδίους ἀπέχουσα· παραρρεῖ δ' αὐτὴν ποτάμιον ὁμώνυμον. Μεδεὼν δ' ὁ μὲν Φωκικὸς ἐν τῷ Κρισαίῳ[3] κόλπῳ, διέχων Βοιωτίας σταδίους ἑκατὸν ἑξήκοντα, ὁ δὲ Βοιωτιακὸς ἀπ' ἐκείνου κέκληται, πλησίον δ' ἐστὶν Ὀγχηστοῦ ὑπὸ τῷ Φοινικίῳ ὄρει, ἀφ' οὗ καὶ μετωνόμασται Φοινικίς· τῆς δὲ Θηβαίας καὶ τοῦτο λέγεται, [ὑπ' ἐνίων[4]] δὲ τῆς Ἁλιαρτίας καὶ Μεδεὼν καὶ Ὠκαλέα.[5]

27. Εἶτά φησι

Κώπας Εὔτρησίν τε πολυτρήρωνά τε Θίσβην.

περὶ μὲν οὖν Κωπῶν εἴρηται. προσάρκτιος δέ ἐστιν ἐπὶ τῇ Κωπαΐδι λίμνῃ, αἱ δ' ἄλλαι κύκλῳ εἰσὶν αἵδε· Ἀκραιφίαι, Φοινικίς, Ὀγχηστός, Ἁλίαρτος, Ὠκαλέα,[6] Ἀλαλκομεναί, Τιλφούσιον, Κορώνεια. καὶ τό γε παλαιὸν οὐκ ἦν τῆς λίμνης
C 411 κοινὸν ὄνομα, ἀλλὰ καθ' ἑκάστην πρὸς αὐτῇ κατοικίαν ἐκείνης ἐπώνυμος ἐλέγετο, Κωπαῒς μὲν τῶν Κωπῶν, Ἁλιαρτὶς[7] δὲ Ἁλιάρτου, καὶ οὕτως ἐπὶ τῶν ἄλλων, ὕστερον δ' ἡ πᾶσα Κωπαῒς ἐλέχθη

[1] [ἄλλων· οἵ τ'], lacuna of about six letters supplied by later MSS.; so the later editors.

[2] [οἵ τ' Ἐλεῶν'], lacuna of about eight letters supplied by Hopper; so the later editors.

[3] Κρισσαίῳ BE*l*.

[4] [ὑπ' ἐνί]ων, lacuna of about four letters supplied by Meineke; Kramer conj. ὑφ' ἑτέρων; *bkno* read Πετεών.

who lived about Harma and Eilesium and Erythrae, and those who held Eleon and Hylê and Peteon."[1] Peteon is a village in the Theban territory near the road to Anthedon. Ocaleê is midway between Haliartus and Alalcomenium, thirty stadia distant from each; and a rivulet bearing the same name flows past it. The Phocian Medeon is on the Crisaean Gulf, at a distance of one hundred and sixty stadia from Boeotia, whereas the Boeotian Medeon, which was named after it, is near Onchestus at the base of the mountain Phoenicius; and from this fact its name has been changed to Phoenicis. This mountain is also called a part of the Theban territory; but by some both Medeon and Ocalea are called a part of the territory of Haliartus.

27. Homer then goes on to say: "Copae, and Eutresis, and Thisbê abounding in doves."[2] Concerning Copae I have already spoken.[3] It lies towards the north on Lake Copais; and the others around the lake are these: Acraephiae, Phoenicis, Onchestus, Haliartus, Ocalea, Alalcomenae, Tilphusium, Coroneia. In early times, at least, the lake had no common name, but was called by different names corresponding to the several settlements lying on it, as, for instance, Copais from Copae, Haliartis from Haliartus, and so in the case of the rest of the settlements; but later the whole lake was called Copais, this name prevailing over

[1] *Iliad* 2. 499. [2] *Iliad* 2. 502. [3] 9. 2. 18.

[5] Ὠκαλέα, Corais, for Ὤκαλαι; so Meineke.
[6] Ὠκαλέα, Corais, for Ὤκαλαι; so Meineke.
[7] Ἁλιαρτίς, for Ἁλίαρτος, conj. Kramer; so Meineke reads.

κατ' ἐπικράτειαν· κοιλότατον γὰρ τοῦτο τὸ χωρίον. Πίνδαρος δὲ καὶ Κηφισσίδα καλεῖ ταύτην· παρατίθησι γοῦν τὴν Τιλφῶσσαν κρήνην ὑπὸ τῷ Τιλφωσσίῳ ὄρει ῥέουσαν πλησίον Ἁλιάρτου καὶ Ἀλαλκομενῶν, ἐφ' ᾗ τὸ Τειρεσίου μνῆμα· αὐτοῦ δὲ καὶ τὸ τοῦ Τιλφωσσίου Ἀπόλλωνος ἱερόν.

28. Ὁ δὲ ποιητὴς ἐφεξῆς ταῖς Κώπαις Εὔτρησιν τίθησι, κωμίον Θεσπιέων· ἐνταῦθά φασι Ζῆθον καὶ Ἀμφίονα οἰκῆσαι, πρὶν βασιλεῦσαι Θηβῶν. ἡ δὲ Θίσβη Θίσβαι νῦν λέγονται, οἰκεῖται δὲ μικρὸν ὑπὲρ τῆς θαλάττης ὅμορον Θεσπιεῦσι τὸ χωρίον καὶ τῇ Κορωνειακῇ, ὑποπεπτωκὸς ἐκ τοῦ νοτίου μέρους τῷ Ἑλικῶνι καὶ αὐτό· ἐπίνειον δ' ἔχει πετρῶδες περιστερῶν μεστόν, ἐφ' οὗ φησὶν ὁ ποιητὴς "πολυτρήρωνά τε Θίσβην·" πλοῦς δ' ἐστὶν ἐνθένδε εἰς Σικυῶνα σταδίων ἑκατὸν ἑξήκοντα.

29. Ἑξῆς δὲ Κορώνειαν καταλέγει καὶ Ἁλίαρτον καὶ Πλαταιὰς καὶ Γλίσσαντα. ἡ μὲν οὖν Κορώνεια ἐγγὺς τοῦ Ἑλικῶνός ἐστιν ἐφ' ὕψους ἱδρυμένη, κατελάβοντο δ' αὐτὴν ἐπανιόντες ἐκ τῆς Θετταλικῆς Ἄρνης οἱ Βοιωτοὶ μετὰ τὰ Τρωικά, ὅτε περ καὶ τὸν Ὀρχομενὸν ἔσχον· κρατήσαντες δὲ τῆς Κορωνείας ἐν τῷ πρὸ αὐτῆς πεδίῳ τὸ τῆς Ἰτωνίας[1] Ἀθηνᾶς ἱερὸν ἱδρύσαντο, ὁμώνυμον τῷ Θετταλικῷ, καὶ τὸν παραρρέοντα ποταμὸν Κουάριον[2] προσηγόρευσαν ὁμοφώνως τῷ ἐκεῖ. Ἀλκαῖος δὲ καλεῖ Κωράλιον, λέγων·

[1] Ἰτωνίας, for Ἰωνίας, conj. Pletho; so later editors read.

all others; for the region of Copae forms the deepest recess of the lake. Pindar calls this lake Cephissis;[1] at any rate, he places near it the spring Tilphossa, which flows at the foot of Mount Tilphossius near Haliartus and Alalcomenae, near which latter is the tomb of Teiresias; and here, too, is the temple of the Tilphossian Apollo.

28. Next in order after Copae Homer names Eutresis, a small village of the Thespians, where Zethus and Amphion are said to have lived before they reigned over Thebes. Thisbê is now called Thisbae; the place is inhabited and is situated slightly above the sea, bordering on the territory of the Thespians and on that of Coroneia; and it, too, lies at the foot of Helicon on the south; and it has a sea-port situated on a rocky place, which abounds in doves, in reference to which the poet says, "Thisbê abounding in doves." From here to Sicyon is a voyage of one hundred and sixty stadia.

29. Next Homer names Coroneia, Haliartus, Plataeae, and Glissas. Now Coroneia is situated on a height near Helicon. The Boeotians took possession of it on their return from the Thessalian Arnê after the Trojan War, at which time they also occupied Orchomenus. And when they got the mastery of Coroneia, they built in the plain before the city the temple of the Itonian Athena, bearing the same name as the Thessalian temple; and they called the river which flowed past it Cuarius, giving it the same name as the Thessalian river. But Alcaeus calls it Coralius, when he says, "Athena,

[1] Cp. 9. 2. 20.

[2] Κουάριον, for Κουάλιον, conj. Palmer; so later editors read.

[1] [ὦ 'ν]ασσ' 'Αθανάα πολε[μηδόκος],
ἅ ποι[2] Κορωνείας[3] ἐπὶ λαΐω[4]
ναύω πάροιθεν [ἀμφι]βαίνεις[5]
Κωραλίω ποταμῶ παρ' ὄχθαις.

ἐνταῦθα δὲ καὶ τὰ Παμβοιώτια συνετέλουν· συγκαθίδρυται δὲ τῇ 'Αθηνᾷ ὁ Ἅιδης κατά τινα, ὥς φασι, μυστικὴν αἰτίαν. οἱ μὲν οὖν ἐν τῇ Κορωνείᾳ Κορώνιοι λέγονται, οἱ δ' ἐν τῇ Μεσσηνιακῇ Κορωναεῖς.[6]

30. Ἁλίαρτος δὲ νῦν οὐκέτι ἐστί, κατασκαφεῖσα ἐν τῷ πρὸς Περσέα πολέμῳ, τὴν χώραν δ' ἔχουσιν 'Αθηναῖοι δόντων Ῥωμαίων. ἔκειτο δὲ ἐν στενῷ χωρίῳ μεταξὺ ὑπερκειμένου ὄρους καὶ τῆς Κωπαΐδος λίμνης πλησίον τοῦ Περμησσοῦ καὶ τοῦ 'Ολμειοῦ[7] καὶ τοῦ ἕλους τοῦ φύοντος τὸν αὐλητικὸν κάλαμον.

31. Πλαταιαὶ δέ, ἃς ἑνικῶς εἶπεν ὁ ποιητής,
C 412 ὑπὸ τῷ Κιθαιρῶνί εἰσι μεταξὺ αὐτοῦ καὶ Θηβῶν κατὰ τὴν ὁδὸν τὴν εἰς 'Αθήνας καὶ Μέγαρα ἐπὶ τῶν ὅρων τῶν τῆς 'Αττικῆς καὶ τῆς Μεγαρίδος.[8] αἱ[9] γὰρ 'Ελευθεραὶ πλησίον, ἃς οἱ μὲν τῆς 'Αττικῆς, οἱ δὲ τῆς Βοιωτίας φασίν. εἴρηται δ' ὅτι παραρρεῖ τὰς Πλαταιὰς ὁ 'Ασωπός. ἐνταῦθα Μαρδόνιον[10] καὶ τὰς τριάκοντα μυριάδας Περσῶν αἱ τῶν Ἑλλήνων δυνάμεις ἄρδην ἠφάνισαν·

[1] [ὦ 'ν]ασσ' 'Αθανάα πολε[μηδόκος] : so read the later editors, following Welcker, inserting ὦ 'ν before ασσ' and supplying the lacuna of about seven letters after πολε.

[2] ἅ ποι, Welcker, for ἀπό ; so later editors.

[3] Κορωνείας, Welcker, for Κοιρωνίας ; so later editors.

[4] λαΐω, Welcker, for [ἐπι]δευω[ν αυω] ; so later editors.

[5] [ἀμφι]βαίνεις, lacuna of about seven letters supplied by Welcker ; so later editors.

warrior queen, who dost keep watch o'er the cornfields of Coroneia before thy temple on the banks of the Coralius River." Here, too, the Pamboeotian Festival used to be celebrated. And for some mystic reason, as they say, a statue of Hades[1] was dedicated along with that of Athena. Now the people in Coroneia are called Coronii, whereas those in the Messenian Coroneia are called Coronaeis.

30. Haliartus is no longer in existence, having been rased to the ground in the war against Perseus; and the country is held by the Athenians, a gift from the Romans. It was situated in a narrow place, between the mountain situated above it and Lake Copais, near the Permessus and Olmeius Rivers and the marsh that produces the flute-reed.

31. Plataeae, which Homer[2] speaks of in the singular number, is at the foot of Cithaeron, between it and Thebes, along the road that leads to Athens and Megara, on the confines of Attica and Megaris; for Eleutherae is near by, which some say belongs to Attica, others to Boeotia. I have already said[3] that the Asopus flows past Plataeae. Here it was that the forces of the Greeks completely wiped out Mardonius and his three hundred thousand Persians;

[1] P. Foucart (see *Bulletin de la Correspondance Hellénique*, 1885, ix. 433), on the basis of a Boeotian inscription, conjectures that "Hades" should be corrected to "Ares."

[2] *Iliad* 2. 504.

[3] 8. 6. 24.

---

[6] Κορωνεῖς BE*l*.

[7] 'Ολμειοῦ E, 'Ολμίου *Acghilno*.

[8] Μεγαρίδος, Du Theil, Corais, Groskurd, and Meineke, following conj. of Pletho, emend to Βοιωτίας.

[9] αἱ, Meineke inserts, following conj. of Kramer; others, εἰσί.

[10] Μαρδόνιον, the later editors, for Μαρδώνιον.

ἱδρύσαντό τε Ἐλευθερίου Διὸς ἱερὸν καὶ ἀγῶνα γυμνικὸν στεφανίτην ἀπέδειξαν, Ἐλευθέρια προσαγορεύσαντες· ταφή τε δείκνυται δημοσία τῶν τελευτησάντων ἐν τῇ μάχῃ. ἔστι δὲ καὶ ἐν τῇ Σικυωνίᾳ δῆμος Πλαταιαί, ὅθενπερ ἦν Μνασάλκης ὁ ποιητής·

Μνασάλκεος τὸ μνᾶμα τῶ Πλαταιάδα.

Γλίσσαντα δὲ λέγει κατοικίαν ἐν τῷ Ὑπάτῳ ὄρει, ὅ ἐστιν ἐν τῇ Θηβαϊκῇ πλησίον Τευμησσοῦ καὶ τῆς Καδμείας. τὰ δὲ[1] γεώλοφα καλεῖται Δρί[α οἷς ὑποπ]ίπτει[2] τὸ Ἀόνιον[3] καλούμενον πεδίον, ὃ διατείνει [μέχρις Θηβῶν[4]] ἀπὸ τοῦ Ὑπάτου ὄρους.

32. Τὸ δ' οὕτω ῥηθέν,

οἵ θ' Ὑποθήβας εἶχον,

οἱ μὲν δέχονται πολείδιόν τι Ὑποθήβας καλούμενον, οἱ δὲ τὰς Ποτνίας· τὰς γὰρ Θήβας ἐκλελεῖφθαι διὰ τὴν τῶν Ἐπιγόνων στρατείαν καὶ μὴ μετασχεῖν τοῦ Τρωικοῦ πολέμου· οἱ δὲ μετασχεῖν μέν, οἰκεῖν δὲ ὑπὸ τῇ Καδμείᾳ τότε ἐν τοῖς ἐπιπέδοις χωρίοις, μετὰ τὴν τῶν Ἐπιγόνων ἄφοδον τὴν Καδμείαν ἀδυνατοῦντας ἀνακτίσαι· ἐπεὶ δὲ ἡ Καδμεία ἐκαλεῖτο Θῆβαι, Ὑποθήβας εἰπεῖν ἀντὶ τοῦ ὑπὸ τῇ Καδμείᾳ οἰκοῦντας τὸν ποιητὴν τοὺς τότε Θηβαίους.

33. Ὀγχηστὸς δ' ἐστὶν ὅπου τὸ Ἀμφικτυονικὸν

[1] τὰ δέ, Jones inserts.

[2] Δρί[α οἷς ὑποπ]ίπτει, lacuna of about six letters supplied by Groskurd. Meineke ejects γεώλοφα . . . δρι from the text, and reads ᾧ instead of οἷς. See Δαυνίας . . . Δρίον 6. 3. 9.

and they built a temple of Zeus Eleutherius, and instituted the athletic games in which the victor received a crown, calling them the Eleutheria. And tombs of those who died in the battle, erected at public expense, are still to be seen. In Sicyonia, also, there is a deme called Plataeae, the home of Mnasalces the poet:[1] "The tomb of Mnasalces the Plataean." Homer speaks of Glissas, a settlement in the mountain Hypatus, which is in the Theban country near Teumessus and Cadmeia. The hillocks below which lies the Aonian Plain, as it is called, which extends from the Hypatus mountain to Thebes, are called "Dria."[2]

32. In these words of the poet, "and those who held Hypothebes,"[3] some take him to mean some little city called Hypothebes, others Potniae; for Thebes, the latter say, was deserted because of the expedition of the Epigoni and had no part in the Trojan War. The former, however, say that the Thebans indeed had a part in the war, but that they were living in the level districts below Cadmeia[4] at that time, since they were unable to rebuild Cadmeia; and since Cadmeia was called Thebes, they add, the poet called the Thebans of that time "Hypothebans" instead of "people who live below Cadmeia."

33. Onchestus is where the Amphictyonic Council

[1] Of his works only sixteen epigrams are now extant.
[2] *i.e.* "Thickets."
[3] *Iliad* 2. 505.
[4] The acropolis of Thebes.

---

[3] Ἀόνιον, Corais, for ὄνιον *Aghi*, Ἰόνιον *bkno*; so the later editors.

[4] [μέχρις Θηβῶν], lacuna of about twelve letters supplied by C. Müller (*Ind. Var. Lect.*, p. 1001); others, εἰς τὴν Καδμείαν.

συνήγετο ἐν τῇ Ἁλιαρτίᾳ πρὸς τῇ Κωπαΐδι λίμνῃ καὶ τῷ Τηνερικῷ πεδίῳ, ἐν ὕψει κείμενος ψιλός, ἔχων Ποσειδῶνος ἱερόν, καὶ αὐτὸ ψιλόν. οἱ δὲ ποιηταὶ κοσμοῦσιν, ἄλση καλοῦντες τὰ ἱερὰ πάντα, κἂν ᾖ ψιλά· τοιοῦτόν ἐστι καὶ τὸ τοῦ Πινδάρου περὶ τοῦ Ἀπόλλωνος λεγόμενον·

[κι]νηθεὶς[1] ἐπήει
γᾶν τε καὶ θάλασσαν, καὶ σκοπιαῖσιν μεγάλαις
ὀρέων ὕπερ ἔστα,
καὶ μύλους δινάσατο[2] βαλλό[μενος[3]] κρηπῖδας
ἀλσέων.

οὐκ εὖ δ' ὁ Ἀλκαῖος, ὥσπερ τὸ τοῦ ποταμοῦ ὄνομα παρέτρεψε τοῦ Κουαρίου, οὕτω καὶ τοῦ Ὀγχηστοῦ κατέψευσται πρὸς ταῖς ἐσχατιαῖς τοῦ
C413 Ἑλικῶνος αὐτὸν τιθείς· ὁ δ' ἐστὶν ἄπωθεν ἱκανῶς τούτου τοῦ ὄρους.

34. Τὸ δὲ Τηνερικὸν πεδίον ἀπὸ Τηνέρου προσηγόρευται· μυθεύεται δ' Ἀπόλλωνος υἱὸς ἐκ Μελίας, προφήτης τοῦ μαντείου κατὰ τὸ Πτῷον ὄρος, ὅ φησιν εἶναι τρικόρυφον ὁ αὐτὸς ποιητής·

καί ποτε τὸν τρικάρανον Πτώου κευθμῶνα
κατέσχεθε·

καὶ τὸν Τήνερον καλεῖ

ναοπόλον μάντιν δαπέδοισιν ὁμοκλέα.

ὑπέρκειται δὲ τὸ Πτῷον τοῦ Τηνερικοῦ πεδίου καὶ τῆς Κωπαΐδος λίμνης πρὸς Ἀκραιφίῳ· Θηβαίων δ' ἦν τό τε μαντεῖον καὶ τὸ ὄρος· τὸ

[1] [κι]νηθείς, lacuna of about two letters Jones supplies, following conj. of Meineke, who, in his text, reads δινηθείς. Bergk (*Frag.* 101) reads περιδιναθείς.

used to convene, in the territory of Haliartus near Lake Copais and the Teneric Plain; it is situated on a height, is bare of trees, and has a sacred precinct of Poseidon, which is also bare of trees. But the poets embellish things, calling all sacred precincts "sacred groves," even if they are bare of trees. Such, also, is the saying of Pindar concerning Apollo: "stirred, he traversed both land and sea, and halted on great lookouts above mountains, and whirled great stones, laying foundations of sacred groves."[1] But Alcaeus is wrong, for just as he perverted the name of the River Cuarius, so he falsified the position of Onchestus, placing it near the extremities of Helicon, although it is at quite a distance from this mountain.

34. The Teneric Plain is named after Tenerus. In myth he was the son of Apollo by Melia, and was a prophet of the oracle on the Ptoüs Mountain, which the same poet calls three-peaked: "and once he took possession of the three-peaked hollow of Ptoüs."[2] And he calls Tenerus "temple-minister, prophet, called by the same name as the plains." The Ptoüs lies above the Teneric Plain and Lake Copais near Acraephium. Both the oracle and the mountain belonged to the Thebans. And Acraephium

[1] *i.e.* foundations of *temples*. This fragment from Pindar is otherwise unknown (see Bergk, *Frag.* 101).

[2] Bergk, *Frag.* 102.

---

[2] μύλους δινάσατο, C. Müller (*Ind. Var. Lect.* p. 1001), for μυχοὺς δινάσσατο (δεινάσατο *Acghi*). Müller-Dübner and Bergk read μυχοὺς δινάσσατο, forcing the verb to mean "shake." Of other readings suggested only that of Emperius, μυχοὺς δ' ἐνάσσατο ("took up his abode in"), is at all tempting.

[3] βαλλό[μενος], lacuna supplied by Meineke.

δ' Ἀκραίφιον καὶ αὐτὸ κεῖται ἐν ὕψει. φασὶ δὲ τοῦτο καλεῖσθαι Ἄρνην ὑπὸ τοῦ ποιητοῦ, ὁμώνυμον τῇ Θετταλικῇ.

35. Οἱ δέ φασι καὶ τὴν Ἄρνην ὑπὸ τῆς λίμνης καταποθῆναι καὶ τὴν Μίδειαν. Ζηνόδοτος δέ, γράφων

οἳ δὲ πολυστάφυλον Ἄσκρην ἔχον,

οὐκ ἔοικεν ἐντυχόντι τοῖς ὑπὸ Ἡσιόδου περὶ τῆς πατρίδος λεχθεῖσι καὶ τοῖς ὑπ' Εὐδόξου, πολὺ χείρω λέγοντος περὶ τῆς Ἄσκρης. πῶς γὰρ ἄν τις πολυστάφυλον τὴν τοιαύτην ὑπὸ τοῦ ποιητοῦ λέγεσθαι πιστεύσειεν; οὐκ εὖ δὲ οὐδὲ[1] οἱ Τάρνην ἀντὶ τῆς Ἄρνης γράφοντες· οὐδὲ γὰρ μία δείκνυται Τάρνη παρὰ τοῖς Βοιωτοῖς, ἐν δὲ Λυδοῖς ἐστίν, ἧς καὶ Ὅμηρος μέμνηται·

Ἰδομενεὺς δ' ἄρα Φαῖστον ἐνήρατο Μῄονος[2] υἱόν
Βώρου, ὃς ἐκ Τάρνης ἐριβώλακος εἰληλούθει.

λοιπαὶ δ' εἰσὶ τῶν μὲν περικειμένων τῇ λίμνῃ αἵ τε Ἀλαλκομεναὶ καὶ τὸ Τιλφώσσιον,[3] τῶν δ' ἄλλων Χαιρώνεια καὶ Λεβάδεια καὶ Λεῦκτρα, περὶ ὧν ἄξιον μνησθῆναι.

36. Ἀλαλκομενῶν τοίνυν μέμνηται ὁ ποιητής, ἀλλ' οὐκ ἐν Καταλόγῳ·

Ἥρη τ' Ἀργείη καὶ Ἀλαλκομενηὶς Ἀθήνη.

ἔχει δ' ἀρχαῖον ἱερὸν Ἀθηνᾶς σφόδρα τιμώμενον, καί φασί γε τὴν θεὸν γεγενῆσθαι ἐνθάδε, καθάπερ καὶ τὴν Ἥραν ἐν Ἄργει, καὶ διὰ τοῦτο

[1] οὐδέ, Meineke, for οὔτε.

itself also lies on a height. They say that this is called Arnê by the poet, the same name as the Thessalian city.

35. Some say that Arnê too was swallowed up by the lake, as well as Mideia.[1] Zenodotus, who writes "and those who possessed Ascrê[2] rich in vineyards," seems not to have read the statements of Hesiod concerning his native land, nor those of Eudoxus, who says much worse things concerning Ascrê. For how could anyone believe that such a place was called "rich in vineyards" by the poet? Wrong, also, are those who write "Tarnê" instead of "Arnê"; for not a single place named Tarnê is pointed out among the Boeotians, though there is one among the Lydians, and this the poet mentions: "Idomeneus then slew Phaestus, son of Borus the Maeonian, who came from fertile Tarnê." The remaining Boeotian cities concerning which it is worth while to make mention are: of those situated round the lake, Alalcomenae and Tilphossium, and, of the rest, Chaeroneia, Lebadeia, and Leuctra.

36. Now as for Alalcomenae, the poet mentions it, but not in the *Catalogue*: "Argive Hera and Alalcomenian Athena."[3] It has an ancient temple of Athena which is held in great honour; and they say, at least, that the goddess was born there, just as Hera was born in Argos, and that it was because of

[1] Cf. 1. 3. 18.
[2] *i.e.* Zenodotus emended Homer's "Arnê" (*Iliad* 2. 507) to "Ascrê."
[3] *Iliad* 4. 8.

---

[2] Μηΐονος, Du Theil, for τέκτονος; so most later editors.
[3] Τισφώσιον *Ach.*

τὸν ποιητήν, ὡς ἀπὸ πατρίδων τούτων, ἀμφοτέρας οὕτως ὀνομάσαι. διὰ τοῦτο δ' ἴσως οὐδ' ἐν τῷ Καταλόγῳ μέμνηται τῶν ἐνταῦθα ἀνδρῶν, ἐπειδή, ἱεροὶ ὄντες, παρεῖντο τῆς στρατείας. καὶ γὰρ καὶ ἀπόρθητος ἀεὶ διετέλεσεν ἡ πόλις, οὔτε μεγάλη οὖσα, οὔτ' ἐν εὐερκεῖ χωρίῳ κειμένη, ἀλλ' ἐν πεδίῳ· τὴν δὲ θεὸν σεβόμενοι πάντες ἀπείχοντο πάσης βίας, ὥστε καὶ Θηβαῖοι κατὰ τὴν τῶν Ἐπιγόνων στρατείαν, ἐκλιπόντες τὴν πόλιν, ἐκεῖσε λέγονται καταφεύγειν καὶ εἰς τὸ ὑπερκείμενον ὄρος ἐρυμνὸν τὸ Τιλφώσσιον, ὑφ' ᾧ Τιλφῶσσα κρήνη καὶ τὸ τοῦ Τειρεσίου μνῆμα, ἐκεῖ τελευτήσαντος κατὰ τὴν φυγήν.

C 414 37. Χαιρώνεια δ' ἐστὶν Ὀρχομενοῦ πλησίον, ὅπου Φίλιππος ὁ Ἀμύντου μάχῃ μεγάλῃ νικήσας Ἀθηναίους τε καὶ Βοιωτοὺς καὶ Κορινθίους κατέστη τῆς Ἑλλάδος κύριος· δείκνυται δὲ κἀνταῦθα ταφὴ τῶν πεσόντων ἐν τῇ μάχῃ δημοσία· περὶ δὲ τοὺς τόπους τοὺς αὐτοὺς καὶ Ῥωμαῖοι τὰς Μιθριδάτου δυνάμεις πολλῶν μυριάδων κατηγωνίσαντο, ὥστ' ὀλίγους ἐπὶ θάλατταν σωθέντας φυγεῖν ἐν ταῖς ναυσί, τοὺς δ' ἄλλους τοὺς μὲν ἀπολέσθαι, τοὺς δὲ καὶ ἁλῶναι.

38. Λεβάδεια δ' ἐστὶν ὅπου Διὸς Τροφωνίου μαντεῖον ἵδρυται, χάσματος ὑπονόμου κατάβασιν ἔχον, καταβαίνει δ' αὐτὸς ὁ χρηστηριαζόμενος· κεῖται δὲ μεταξὺ τοῦ Ἑλικῶνος καὶ τῆς Χαιρωνείας, Κορωνείας πλησίον.

---

[1] 338 B.C.

this that the poet named them both in this way, as natives of these places. And it was because of this, perhaps, that he did not mention in the *Catalogue* the men of Alalcomenae, since, being sacred, they were excused from the expedition. And in fact the city always continued unravaged, although it was neither large nor situated in a secure position, but in a plain. But all peoples, since they revered the goddess, held aloof from any violence towards the inhabitants, so that when the Thebans, at the time of the expedition of the Epigonoi, left their city, they are said to have fled for refuge to Alalcomenae, and to Tilphossius, the mountain, a natural stronghold that lies above it; and at the base of this mountain is a spring called Tilphossa, and the monument of Teiresias, who died there at the time of the flight.

37. Chaeroneia is near Orchomenus. It was here that Philip the son of Amyntas conquered the Athenians, Boeotians, and Corinthians in a great battle,[1] and set himself up as lord of Greece. And here, too, are to be seen tombs of those who fell in the battle, tombs erected at public expense. And it was in the same region that the Romans so completely defeated the forces of Mithridates, many tens of thousands in number, that only a few escaped in safety to the sea and fled in their ships, whereas the rest either perished or were taken captive.

38. At Lebadeia is situated an oracle of Trophonian Zeus. The oracle has a descent into the earth consisting of an underground chasm; and the person who consults the oracle descends into it himself. It is situated between Mt. Helicon and Chaeroneia, near Coroneia.

39. Τὰ δὲ Λεῦκτρά ἐστιν ὅπου Λακεδαιμονίους μεγάλῃ μάχῃ νικήσας Ἐπαμεινώνδας ἀρχὴν εὕρετο τῆς καταλύσεως αὐτῶν· οὐκέτι γὰρ ἐξ ἐκείνου τὴν τῶν Ἑλλήνων ἡγεμονίαν ἀναλαβεῖν ἴσχυσαν ἣν εἶχον πρότερον, καὶ μάλιστ᾽ ἐπειδὴ καὶ τῇ δευτέρᾳ συμβολῇ τῇ περὶ Μαντίνειαν κακῶς ἔπραξαν. τὸ μέντοι μὴ ὑφ᾽ ἑτέροις[1] εἶναι, καίπερ οὕτως ἐπταικόσι, συνέμεινε μέχρι τῆς Ῥωμαίων ἐπικρατείας· καὶ παρὰ τούτοις δὲ τιμώμενοι διατελοῦσι διὰ τὴν τῆς πολιτείας ἀρετήν. δείκνυται δὲ ὁ τόπος οὗτος κατὰ τὴν ἐκ Πλαταιῶν εἰς Θεσπιὰς ὁδόν.

40. Ἑξῆς δ᾽ ὁ ποιητὴς μέμνηται τοῦ τῶν Ὀρχομενίων καταλόγου, χωρίζων αὐτοὺς ἀπὸ τοῦ Βοιωτιακοῦ ἔθνους. καλεῖ δὲ Μινύειον τὸν Ὀρχομενὸν ἀπὸ ἔθνους τοῦ Μινυῶν· ἐντεῦθεν δὲ ἀποικῆσαί τινας τῶν Μινυῶν εἰς Ἰωλκόν φασιν, ὅθεν τοὺς Ἀργοναύτας Μινύας λεχθῆναι. φαίνεται δὲ τὸ παλαιὸν καὶ πλουσία τις γεγονυῖα πόλις καὶ δυναμένη μέγα· τοῦ μὲν οὖν πλούτου μάρτυς καὶ Ὅμηρος· διαριθμούμενος γὰρ τοὺς τόπους τοὺς πολυχρηματήσαντάς[2] φησιν·

οὐδ᾽ ὅσ᾽ ἐς Ὀρχομενὸν ποτινίσσεται, οὐδ᾽ ὅσα Θήβας
Αἰγυπτίας·

τῆς δυνάμεως δέ, ὅτι Θηβαῖοι δασμὸν ἐτέλουν τοῖς Ὀρχομενίοις καὶ Ἐργίνῳ τῷ τυραννοῦντι αὐτῶν, ὃν ὑφ᾽ Ἡρακλέους καταλυθῆναί φασιν. Ἐτεοκλῆς δέ, τῶν βασιλευσάντων ἐν Ὀρχομενῷ

[1] ἑτέραν *acghi*.

39. Leuctra is the place where Epameinondas defeated the Lacedaemonians in a great battle and found a beginning of his overthrow of them; for after that time they were never again able to regain the hegemony of the Greeks which they formerly held, and especially because they also fared badly in the second clash near Mantineia. However, although they had suffered such reverses, they continued to avoid being subject to others until the Roman conquest. And among the Romans, also, they have continued to be held in honour because of the excellence of their government. This place is to be seen on the road that leads from Plataeae to Thespiae.

40. Next the poet gives the catalogue of the Orchomenians, whom he separates from the Boeotian tribe. He calls Orchomenus "Minyeian," after the tribe of the Minyae. They say that some of the Minyae emigrated from here to Iolcus, and that from this fact the Argonauts were called Minyae. Clearly it was in early times both a rich and very powerful city. Now to its wealth Homer also is a witness, for when enumerating the places that abounded in wealth he says: "Nor yet all that comes to Orchomenus[1] nor all that comes to Egyptian Thebes."[2] And of its power there is this proof, that the Thebans were wont to pay tribute to the Orchomenians and to Erginus their tyrant, who is said to have been put to death by Heracles. Eteocles, one of those who reigned as king at Orchomenus, who founded a

[1] On the wealth of Orchomenus, see Pausanias 8. 33.
[2] *Iliad* 9. 381.

---

[2] πολυχρηματήσαντας, Corais, for πολυχρηματίσαντας; so Meineke.

τις, Χαρίτων ἱερὸν ἱδρυσάμενος, πρῶτος ἀμφότερα ἐμφαίνει, καὶ πλοῦτον καὶ δύναμιν· ὅς, εἴτ' ἐν τῷ λαμβάνειν χάριτας εἴτ' ἐν τῷ διδόναι
C 415 κατορθῶν εἴτε καὶ ἀμφότερα, τὰς θεὰς ἐτίμησε ταύτας. [1]ἀνάγκη γὰρ πρὸς εὐεργεσίαν εὐφυῆ γενόμενον ἐκεῖνον πρὸς τὴν τῶν θεῶν τούτων ὁρμῆσαι τιμήν, ὥστε ταύτην μὲν ἐκέκτητο ἤδη τὴν δύναμιν. ἀλλὰ πρὸς ταύτῃ καὶ χρημάτων ἔδει· οὔτε γὰρ μὴ ἔχων τις πολλὰ διδοίη ἂν πολλά, οὔτε μὴ[2] λαμβάνων πολλὰ οὐκ ἂν ἔχοι πολλά· εἰ δ' ἀμφότερα συνέχει, τὴν ἀμοιβὴν ἔχει.[3] τὸ γὰρ κενούμενον ἅμα καὶ πληρούμενον πρὸς τὴν χρείαν ἀεὶ πλῆρές ἐστιν, ὁ δὲ διδοὺς μέν, μὴ λαμβάνων δέ, οὐδ' ἂν ἐπὶ θάτερα κατορθοίη· παύσεται γὰρ διδούς, ἐπιλείποντος τοῦ ταμείου,[4] παύσονται δὲ καὶ οἱ διδόντες τῷ λαμβάνοντι μόνον, χαριζομένῳ δὲ μηδέν, ὥστ' οὐδ' οὗτος ἑτέρως ἂν κατορθοίη. ὅμοια δὲ καὶ περὶ δυνάμεως λέγοιτ' ἄν. χωρὶς δὲ τοῦ κοινοῦ λόγου, διότι

τὰ χρήματ' ἀνθρώποισι τιμιώτατα,
δύναμίν τε πλείστην τῶν ἐν ἀνθρώποις ἔχει,

καὶ ἐκ τῶν καθ' ἕκαστα σκοπεῖν δεῖ. μάλιστα γὰρ τοὺς βασιλέας δύνασθαί φαμεν· διόπερ καὶ δυνάστας προσαγορεύομεν. δύνανται δ' ἄγοντες ἐφ' ἃ βούλονται τὰ πλήθη διὰ πειθοῦς ἢ βίας. πείθουσι μὲν οὖν δι' εὐεργεσίας μάλιστα· οὐ γὰρ ἥ γε διὰ τῶν λόγων ἐστὶ βασιλική, ἀλλ' αὕτη

[1] ἀνάγκη γὰρ . . . ὁ πλεῖστα κεκτημένος appears to be a gloss, as Kramer notes. Meineke ejects.

[2] μή, Tyrwhitt inserts.

[3] ἔχοι A.

temple of the Graces, was the first to display both wealth and power; for he honoured these goddesses either because he was successful in receiving graces,[1] or in giving them, or both. For necessarily, when he had become naturally inclined to kindly deeds, he began doing honour to these goddesses; and therefore he already possessed this power; but in addition he also had to have money, for neither could anyone give much if he did not have much, nor could anyone have much if he did not receive much. But if he has both together, he has the reciprocal giving and receiving; for the vessel that is at the same time being emptied and filled is always full for use; but he who gives and does not receive could not succeed in either, for he will stop giving because his treasury fails; also the givers will stop giving to him who receives only and grants no favours; and therefore he could not succeed in either way. And like things might be said concerning power. Apart from the common saying, "money is the most valuable thing to men, and it has the most power of all things among men," we should look into the subject in detail. We say that kings have the greatest power; and on this account we call them potentates. They are potent in leading the multitudes whither they wish, through persuasion or force. Generally they persuade through kindness, for persuasion through words is not kingly; indeed, this belongs to the

[1] *i.e.* favours.

---

[4] After ταμείου, the last word on the page, a whole sheet has been lost from A, and A resumes at Ἑσπερίων καὶ τῶν in 9. 3. 1. But the missing part is supplied by the second hand.

μὲν ῥητορική, βασιλικὴν δὲ πειθὼ λέγομεν, ὅταν εὐεργεσίαις φέρωσι καὶ διάγωσιν[1] ἐφ' ἃ βούλονται· πείθουσι μὲν δὴ δι' εὐεργεσιῶν, βιάζονται δὲ διὰ τῶν ὅπλων. ταῦτα δ' ἄμφω χρημάτων ὤνιά ἐστι· καὶ γὰρ στρατιὰν ἔχει πλείστην ὁ τρέφειν δυνάμενος, καὶ εὐεργετεῖν δύναται πλεῖστον ὁ πλεῖστα κεκτημένος.

Λέγουσι δὲ τὸ χωρίον, ὅπερ ἡ λίμνη κατέχει νῦν ἡ Κωπαΐς, ἀνεψύχθαι πρότερον, καὶ γεωργεῖσθαι παντοδαπῶς ὑπὸ τοῖς Ὀρχομενίοις ὄν,[2] πλησίον οἰκοῦσι· καὶ τοῦτ' οὖν τεκμήριον τοῦ πλούτου τιθέασι.

41. Τὴν δ' Ἀσπληδόνα χωρὶς τῆς πρώτης συλλαβῆς ἐκάλουν τινές· εἶτ' Εὐδείελος μετωνομάσθη καὶ αὐτὴ καὶ ἡ χώρα, τάχα τι ἰδίωμα προσφερομένη ἐκ τοῦ δειλινοῦ κλίματος οἰκεῖον τοῖς κατοικοῦσι, καὶ μάλιστα τὸ εὐχείμερον.[3] ψυχρότατα μὲν γὰρ τὰ ἄκρα τῆς ἡμέρας ἐστί, τούτων δὲ τὸ δειλινὸν τοῦ ἑωθινοῦ ψυχρότερον· εἰς ἐπίτασιν γὰρ ἄγει πλησίαζον τῇ νυκτί, τὸ δ' εἰς ἄνεσιν ἀφιστάμενον τῆς νυκτός. ἴαμα δὲ τοῦ ψύχους ὁ ἥλιος· τὸν οὖν ἡλιαζόμενον πλεῖστον ἐν τῷ ψυχροτάτῳ καιρῷ εὐχειμερώτατον.

[1] διάγωσιν, Meineke emends to ἄγωσιν.

[2] ὄν, Meineke, for ὤν.

[3] ψυχρότατα . . . εὐχειμερώτατον, apparently a gloss; ejected by Meineke.

---

[1] *Deilinou klimatos*: apparently a false etymology of "Eudeielos," based on the fact that the effect of the sun's heat is greatest in the *deilê* (evening). But the most likely meaning of *eudeielos* is "sunny," the word being used of places exposed to the hot sun (*e.g.* see Pindar, *O.* 3. 111 and

orator, whereas we call it kingly persuasion when kings win and attract men whither they wish by kindly deeds. They persuade men, it is true, through kindly deeds, but they force them by means of arms. Both these things may be bought with money; for he has the largest army who is able to support the largest, and he who possesses the most means is also able to show the most kindness.

They say that the place now occupied by Lake Copais was formerly dry ground, and that it was tilled in all kinds of ways when it was subject to the Orchomenians, who lived near it. And this fact, accordingly, is adduced as an evidence of their wealth.

41. Aspledon was by some called Spledon, without the first syllable. Then the name, both of it and of the country, was changed to Eudeielos, perhaps because, from its "evening" inclination,[1] it offered a special advantage peculiar to its inhabitants, especially the mildness of its winters; for the two ends of the day are coldest; and of these the evening is colder than the morning, for as night approaches the cold is more intense, and as night retires it abates. But the sun is a means of mitigating the cold. The place, therefore, that is warmed most by the sun at the coldest time is mildest in winter. Eudeielos is twenty

Gildersleeve's note thereon), and having a southerly rather than an "evening" (westerly) inclination, as is the case with Aspledon (Buttmann *Lexilogus*, *s.v.* Δείλη §§ 7–9, *q.v.*). Butcher and Lang, and Murray, in their translations of the *Odyssey* (*e.g.* 9. 21), translate the word "clear-seen," and Cunliffe (*Lexicon Homeric Dialect*), "bright, shining," as though used for εὔδηλος. Certainly Strabo, as the context shows, is thinking of the *position* of the place and of the *sun's heat* (see 10. 2. 12, where he discusses "*eudeielos* Ithaca" at length).

διέχει δὲ τοῦ Ὀρχομενοῦ στάδια εἴκοσι· μεταξὺ δ' ὁ Μέλας ποταμός.

C 416 42. Ὑπέρκειται δ' Ὀρχομενίας ὁ Πανοπεύς, Φωκικὴ πόλις, καὶ Ὑάμπολις· τούτοις δ' ὁμορεῖ Ὀποῦς, ἡ τῶν Λοκρῶν μητρόπολις τῶν Ἐπικνημιδίων. πρότερον μὲν οὖν οἰκεῖσθαι τὸν Ὀρχομενόν φασιν ἐπὶ πεδίῳ, ἐπιπολαζόντων δὲ τῶν ὑδάτων, ἀνοικισθῆναι πρὸς τὸ Ἀκόντιον ὄρος, παρατεῖνον ἐπὶ ἑξήκοντα σταδίους μέχρι Παραποταμίων τῶν ἐν τῇ Φωκίδι. ἱστοροῦσι δὲ τοὺς ἐν τῷ Πόντῳ καλουμένους Ἀχαιοὺς ἀποίκους Ὀρχομενίων εἶναι τῶν μετὰ Ἰαλμένου πλανηθέντων ἐκεῖσε μετὰ τὴν τῆς Τροίας ἅλωσιν. καὶ περὶ Κάρυστον δ' ἦν τις Ὀρχομενός. εὖ γὰρ τὴν τοιαύτην ὕλην ὑποβεβλήκασιν ἡμῖν οἱ τὰ περὶ τῶν Νεῶν συγγράψαντες, οἷς ἀκολουθοῦμεν, ὅταν οἰκεῖα λέγωσι πρὸς τὴν ἡμετέραν ὑπόθεσιν.

III

1. Μετὰ δὲ τὴν Βοιωτίαν καὶ τὸν Ὀρχομενὸν ἡ Φωκίς ἐστι πρὸς ἄρκτον παραβεβλημένη τῇ Βοιωτίᾳ παραπλησίως ἀπὸ θαλάττης εἰς θάλατταν, τό γε παλαιόν. ὁ γὰρ Δαφνοῦς ἦν τότε τῆς Φωκίδος,[1] σχίζων ἐφ' ἑκάτερα τὴν Λοκρίδα καὶ μέσος ταττόμενος τοῦ τε Ὀπουντίου κόλπου καὶ τῆς τῶν Ἐπικνημιδίων παραλίας· νῦν δὲ Λοκρῶν ἐστὶν ἡ χώρα (τὸ δὲ πόλισμα κατέσκαπται), ὥστ' οὐδ' ἐκεῖ[2] καθήκει[3] οὐκέτι μέχρι τῆς πρὸς

[1] Φωκίδος, the editors, for Λοκρίδος; Φωκίδος appears *man. sec.* in B and between the lines in *n*.

[2] *Eacl* and B *man. prim.* read οὐ δοκεῖ instead of οὐδ' ἐκεῖ.

stadia distant from Orchomenus. And the River Melas is between them.

42. Above the Orchomenian territory lies Panopeus, a Phocian city, and also Hyampolis. And bordering on these is Opus, the metropolis of the Epicnemidian Locrians. Now in earlier times Orchomenus was situated on a plain, they say, but when the waters overflowed, the inhabitants migrated up to the mountain Acontius, which extends for a distance of sixty stadia to Parapotamii in Phocis. And they relate that the Achaeans in Pontus, as they are called, are a colony of Orchomenians who wandered there with Ialmenus after the capture of Troy. There was also an Orchomenus in the neighbourhood of Carystus. Those who have written concerning the *Ships*[1] have supplied us well with such materials, and are the writers we follow when they say things appropriate to the purpose of our work.

III

1. After Boeotia and Orchomenus one comes to Phocis; it stretches towards the north alongside Boeotia, nearly from sea to sea; it did so in early times, at least, for in those times Daphnus belonged to Phocis, splitting Locris into two parts and being placed by geographers midway between the Opuntian Gulf and the coast of the Epicnemidians. The country now belongs to the Locrians (the town has been rased to the ground), so that even here Phocis

[1] *i.e.* Homer's *Catalogue of Ships.*

---

[3] καθήκειν, Meineke emends to καθήκει.

Εὐβοίᾳ θαλάττης ἡ Φωκίς, τῷ δὲ Κρισαίῳ[1] κόλπῳ συνῆπται. αὐτὴ γὰρ ἡ Κρῖσα[2] τῆς Φωκίδος ἐστὶν ἐπ' αὐτῆς ἱδρυμένη τῆς θαλάττης καὶ Κίρρα καὶ Ἀντίκυρα[3] καὶ τὰ ὑπὲρ αὐτῶν ἐν τῇ μεσογαίᾳ συνεχῆ κείμενα χωρία πρὸς τῷ Παρνασσῷ, Δελφοί τε καὶ Κίρφις καὶ Δαυλὶς καὶ αὐτὸς ὁ Παρνασσός,[4] τῆς τε Φωκίδος ὢν καὶ ἀφορίζων τὸ ἑσπέριον πλευρόν. ὃν τρόπον δ' ἡ Φωκὶς τῇ Βοιωτίᾳ παράκειται, τοῦτον καὶ ἡ Λοκρὶς τῇ Φωκίδι ἑκατέρα. διττὴ γάρ ἐστι, διῃρημένη ὑπὸ τοῦ Παρνασσοῦ δίχα· ἡ μὲν ἐκ τοῦ ἑσπερίου μέρους παρακειμένη τῷ Παρνασσῷ καὶ μέρος αὐτοῦ νεμομένη, καθήκουσα δ' ἐπὶ τὸν Κρισαῖον κόλπον, ἡ δ' ἐκ τοῦ πρὸς ἕω τελευτῶσα ἐπὶ τὴν πρὸς Εὐβοίᾳ θάλατταν. καλοῦνται δ' οἱ μὲν ἑσπέριοι Λοκροὶ καὶ Ὀζόλαι, ἔχουσί τε ἐπὶ τῇ δημοσίᾳ σφραγῖδι τὸν ἕσπερον ἀστέρα ἐγκεχαραγμένον· οἱ δ' ἕτεροι δίχα πως καὶ αὐτοὶ διῃρημένοι, οἱ μὲν Ὀπούντιοι ἀπὸ τῆς μητροπόλεως, ὅμοροι Φωκεῦσι καὶ Βοιωτοῖς, οἱ δ' Ἐπικνημίδιοι ἀπὸ ὄρους Κνημῖδος, προσεχεῖς Οἰταίοις τε καὶ Μαλιεῦσιν. ἐν μέσῳ δὲ ἀμφοῖν τῶν τε Ἑσπερίων καὶ τῶν ἑτέρων Παρνασσός, παραμήκης εἰς τὸ προσάρκτιον μέρος ἐκτεινόμενος
C 417 ἀπὸ τῶν περὶ Δελφοὺς τόπων μέχρι τῆς συμβολῆς τῶν τε Οἰταίων ὀρῶν καὶ τῶν Αἰτωλικῶν καὶ τῶν ἀνὰ μέσον Δωριέων. πάλιν γὰρ ὥσπερ ἡ Λοκρὶς διττὴ οὖσα[5] τοῖς Φωκεῦσι παραβέ-

[1] Κρισαίῳ, Kramer and later editors, for Κρισσαίῳ.

[2] Κρῖσα, Kramer and later editors, for Κρίσσα.

[3] Ἀντίκυρα (as in 9. 3. 4 and 9. 5. 10), Kramer, for Ἀντίκιρρα; so later editors.

[4] Παρνασός, *aBl*; so in later instances.

no longer extends as far as the Euboean Sea, though it does border on the Crisaean Gulf. For Crisa itself belongs to Phocis, being situated by the sea itself, and so do Cirrha and Anticyra and the places which lie in the interior and contiguous to them near Parnassus—I mean Delphi, Cirphis, and Daulis—and Parnassus itself, which belongs to Phocis and forms its boundary on its western side. In the same way as Phocis lies alongside Boeotia, so also Locris lies alongside Phocis on either side; for Locris is double, being divided into two parts by Parnassus, the part on the western side lying alongside Parnassus and occupying a part of it, and extending to the Crisaean Gulf, whereas the part on the side towards the east ends at the Euboean Sea. The Westerners[1] are called Locrians and Ozolae; and they have the star Hesperus engraved on their public seal. The other division of inhabitants is itself also divided, in a way, into two parts: the Opuntians, named after their metropolis, whose territory borders on Phocis and Boeotia, and the Epicnemidians, named after a mountain called Cnemis, who are next to the Oetaeans and Malians. In the middle between both, I mean the Westerners and the other division, is Parnassus, extending lengthwise into the northerly part of the country, from the region of Delphi as far as the junction of the Oetaean and the Aetolian mountains, and the country of the Dorians which lies in the middle between them. For again, just as Locris, being double, lies alongside Phocis, so also the country of

[1] In Greek, the "Hesperioi."

[5] ἡ Λο[κρὶς διττὴ οὖ]σα, lacuna of about ten letters in A supplied by Corais from conj. of Casaubon.

βληται, οὕτω καὶ ἡ τῶν Οἰταίων[1] μετὰ τῆς Αἰτωλίας καί τινων ἀνὰ μέσον τόπων τῆς Δωρικῆς[2] τετραπόλεως τῇ Λοκρίδι ἑκατέρᾳ καὶ Παρνασσῷ[3] καὶ τοῖς Δωριεῦσιν. ὑπὲρ τούτων δ' ἤδη οἱ Θετταλοὶ[4] καὶ τῶν Αἰτωλῶν οἱ προσάρκτιοι καὶ Ἀκαρνᾶνες καί τινα[5] τῶν Ἠπειρωτικῶν ἐθνῶν καὶ τῶν Μακεδονικῶν· δεῖ δέ,[6] ὅπερ ἔφαμεν καὶ πρότερον, παραλλήλους ὥσπερ ταινίας[7] τινὰς τεταμένας ἀπὸ τῆς ἑσπέρας ἐπὶ τὰς ἀνατολὰς[8] νοῆσαι τὰς λεχθείσας χώρας. ἱεροπρεπὴς δ' ἐστὶ πᾶς ὁ Παρνασσός, ἔχων ἄντρα τε καὶ ἄλλα χωρία τιμώμενά τε καὶ ἁγιστευόμενα· ὧν ἐστι γνωριμώτατόν τε καὶ κάλλιστον τὸ Κωρύκιον, νυμφῶν ἄντρον ὁμώνυμον τῷ Κιλικίῳ. τῶν δὲ πλευρῶν τοῦ Παρνασσοῦ τὸ μὲν ἑσπέριον νέμονται Λοκροί τε οἱ Ὀζόλαι καί τινες τῶν Δωριέων καὶ Αἰτωλοὶ κατὰ τὸν Κόρακα προσαγορευόμενον Αἰτωλικὸν ὄρος· τὸ δὲ[9] Φωκεῖς καὶ Δωριεῖς οἱ πλείους, ἔχοντες τὴν Τετράπολιν περικειμένην πως τῷ Παρνασσῷ, πλεονάζουσαν δὲ τοῖς πρὸς ἕω. αἱ μὲν οὖν κατὰ τὸ μῆκος πλευραὶ τῶν[10] λεχθεισῶν χωρῶν τε καὶ ταινιῶν

[1] [καὶ ἡ τῶν Οἰταίων], lacuna of about fourteen letters supplied by Jones from conj. of Kramer: [καὶ ἡ πᾶσα Οἰταία], Meineke.

[2] τ[όπων τῆς Δω]ρικῆς, lacuna of about ten letters supplied by Kramer from conj. of Du Theil.

[3] [καὶ Παρνασ]σῷ, lacuna of about ten letters in A supplied by *bkno*.

[4] [οἱ Θετταλοί], lacuna of about ten letters supplied by Groskurd.

[5] Ἀκαρν[ᾶνες καί τινα], lacuna of about eight letters supplied by Corais (see Kramer's note *ad loc.*).

[6] [δεῖ δέ], lacuna of about six letters supplied by Corais.

the Oetaeans together with Aetolia and with certain places of the Dorian Tetrapolis, which lie in the middle between them, lie alongside either part of Locris and alongside Parnassus and the country of the Dorians. Immediately above these are the Thessalians, the northerly Aetolians, the Acarnanians, and some of the Epeirote and Macedonian tribes. As I was saying before,[1] one should think of the above-mentioned countries as ribbon-like stretches, so to speak, extending parallel to one another from the west towards the east. The whole of Parnassus is esteemed as sacred, since it has caves and other places that are held in honour and deemed holy. Of these the best known and most beautiful is Corycium, a cave of the nymphs bearing the same name as that in Cilicia. Of the sides of Parnassus, the western is occupied by the Ozolian Locrians and by some of the Dorians and by the Aetolians who live near the Aetolian mountain called Corax; whereas the other side is occupied by Phocians and by the majority of the Dorians, who occupy the Tetrapolis, which in a general way lies round Parnassus, but widens out in its parts that face the east. Now the long sides of each of the above-mentioned countries and ribbon-

[1] 9. 2. 1.

---

[7] ὥσ[περ ταινίας], lacuna of about nine letters supplied by Corais. ὥσπερ τινάς *bkno*.

[8] ἀ[νατολάς], lacuna of about seven letters supplied by Corais. ἄρκτους *bkno*.

[9] Following the Epitome Xylander added πρὸς ἕω after τὸ δέ. So later editors before Kramer.

[10] πλευ[ραὶ τῶν], lacuna of about seven letters supplied by *bkno*.

ἑκάστης παράλληλοι[1] ἅπασαί εἰσιν, ἡ μὲν οὖσα προσάρκτιος, ἡ δὲ πρὸς νότον·[2] αἱ δὲ λοιπαὶ ἑσπέριοι ταῖς ἑῴαις οὐκ εἰσι παράλληλοι· οὐδὲ[3] ἡ παραλία ἑκατέρα, ἥ τε τοῦ Κρισαίου κόλπου μέχρι[4] Ἀκτίου, καὶ ἡ πρὸς Εὔβοιαν μέχρι τῆς Θεσσαλονικείας[5] παράλληλοι ἀλλήλαις εἰσίν, εἰς ἃς τελευτᾷ ταῦτα τὰ[6] ἔθνη· ἀλλ' οὕτω δέχεσθαι δεῖ τὰ σχήματα τούτων τῶν χωρίων,[7] ὡς ἂν ἐν τριγώνῳ παρὰ τὴν βάσιν γεγραμμένων[8] γραμμῶν πλειόνων· τὰ γὰρ ἀποληφθέντα σχήματα παράλληλα[9] μὲν ἀλλήλοις ἔσται, καὶ τὰς κατὰ μῆκος ἐναντίον[10] πλευρὰς ἕξει παραλλήλους, τὰς δὲ κατὰ πλάτος οὐκέτι.[11] ὁ μὲν οὖν ὁλοσχερὴς τύπος οὗτος τῆς λοιπῆς καὶ ἐφεξῆς περιοδείας, τὰ καθ' ἕκαστα δ' ἑξῆς λέγωμεν, ἀπὸ τῆς Φωκίδος ἀρξάμενοι.

2. Ταύτης δ' ἐπιφανέσταται δύο πόλεις Δελφοί τε καὶ Ἐλάτεια· Δελφοὶ μὲν διὰ τὸ ἱερὸν τοῦ Πυθίου Ἀπόλλωνος καὶ τὸ μαντεῖον ἀρχαῖον ὄν, εἴ γε Ἀγαμέμνων ἀπ' αὐτοῦ χρηστηριάσασθαι

[1] παρ[άλληλοι], lacuna of about seven letters restored by Kramer from conj. of Du Theil. παραμήκεις *bkno*.

[2] ἡ [δὲ πρὸς νότον], lacuna of about ten letters supplied by Meineke from conj. of Kramer. ἡ δὲ ἑσπέριος *bkno*. ἡ δὲ νότιος Corais from conj. of Du Theil.

[3] π[αράλληλοι οὐ]δέ, lacuna of about eight letters supplied by Kramer from conj. of Du Theil. παραμήκεις *bkno*.

[4] Κρι[σαίου κόλπου μέ]χρι, lacuna of about twelve letters supplied by Kramer. *bkno* omit κόλπου.

[5] [Θεσσαλονικείας], lacuna of about twelve letters supplied by Corais.

like stretches are all parallel, one side being towards the north and the other towards the south; but as for the remaining sides, the western are not parallel to the eastern; neither are the two coast-lines, where the countries of these tribes end, I mean that of the Crisaean Gulf as far as Actium and that facing Euboea as far as Thessaloniceia, parallel to one another. But one should conceive of the geometrical figures of these regions as though several lines were drawn in a triangle parallel to the base, for the figures thus marked off will be parallel to one another, and they will have their opposite long sides parallel, but as for the short sides this is no longer the case. This, then, is my rough sketch of the country that remains to be traversed and is next in order. Let me now describe each separate part in order, beginning with Phocis.

2. Of Phocis two cities are the most famous, Delphi and Elateia. Delphi, because of the temple of the Pythian Apollo, and because of the oracle, which is ancient, since Agamemnon is said by the

---

[6] τελ[ευτᾷ ταῦτα τά], lacuna of about twelve letters supplied by Kramer from conj. of Du Theil.

[7] [τούτων τῶν χω]ρίων, lacuna of about ten letters supplied by Kramer from conj. of Du Theil. τῶν τοιούτων χωρίων *bkno*.

[8] [βάσιν γεγραμμένων], lacuna of about sixteen letters supplied by Jones. [βάσιν τεταμένων] Kramer, Meineke, Müller-Dübner and others.

[9] ἀποληφ[θέντα σχήματα πα]ράλληλα, lacuna of about thirteen letters supplied by Kramer. The MSS., however, read ἀπολειφθ. Corais supplies χωρία instead of σχήματα.

[10] [κατὰ μῆκος έναν]τίον, lacuna of about fourteen letters supplied by Kramer from conj. of Groskurd.

[11] τ[ὰς δὲ κατὰ πλάτος οὐ]κέτι, lacuna of about fourteen letters supplied by Kramer. τ[ὰς δὲ λοιπὰς οὐ]κέτι Corais.

λέγεται ὑπὸ τοῦ ποιητοῦ· ὁ γὰρ κιθαρῳδὸς ᾄδων εἰσάγεται

νεῖκος Ὀδυσσῆος καὶ Πηλειδέω Ἀχιλῆος,[1]
ὥς ποτε δηρίσαντο·—ἄναξ δ' ἀνδρῶν Ἀγαμέμνων
χαῖρε νόῳ.
C 418 ὣς γὰρ οἱ χρείων μυθήσατο Φοῖβος Ἀπόλλων
Πυθοῖ·

Δελφοὶ μὲν δὴ διὰ ταῦτα, Ἐλάτεια δέ, ὅτι πασῶν μεγίστη τῶν ἐνταῦθα πόλεων καὶ ἐπικαιριωτάτη διὰ τὸ ἐπικεῖσθαι τοῖς στενοῖς καὶ τὸν ἔχοντα ταύτην ἔχειν τὰς εἰσβολὰς τὰς εἰς τὴν Φωκίδα καὶ τὴν Βοιωτίαν. ὄρη γάρ ἐστιν Οἰταῖα πρῶτον, ἔπειτα τὰ τῶν Λοκρῶν καὶ τῶν Φωκέων, οὐ πανταχοῦ στρατοπέδοις βάσιμα τοῖς ἐκ Θετταλίας ἐμβάλλουσιν,[2] ἀλλ' ἔχει παρόδους στενὰς μέν, ἀφωρισμένας δέ, ἃς αἱ παρακείμεναι πόλεις φρουροῦσιν· ἁλουσῶν δ' ἐκείνων κρατεῖσθαι συμβαίνει καὶ τὰς παρόδους. ἐπεὶ δ' ἡ τοῦ ἱεροῦ ἐπιφάνεια τοῦ ἐν Δελφοῖς ἔχει πρεσβεῖον, καὶ ἅμα ἡ θέσις τῶν χωρίων ἀρχὴν ὑπαγορεύει φυσικήν (ταῦτα γάρ ἐστι τὰ ἑσπεριώτατα μέρη τῆς Φωκίδος), ἐντεῦθεν ἀρκτέον.

3. Εἴρηται δ', ὅτι καὶ ὁ Παρνασσὸς ἐπὶ[3] τῶν ἑσπερίων ὅρων[4] ἵδρυται τῆς Φωκίδος. τούτου δὴ τὸ μὲν πρὸς δύσιν πλευρὸν οἱ Λοκροὶ κατέχουσιν οἱ Ὀζόλαι, τὸ δὲ νότιον οἱ Δελφοί, πετρῶδες χωρίον, θεατροειδές, κατὰ κορυφὴν ἔχον τὸ μαντεῖον

[1] Ἀχιλῆος, editors before Kramer, for ἄνακτος.
[2] εἰσβάλλουσιν BEl and *man. sec.* A.

poet to have had an oracle given him from there; for the minstrel is introduced as singing "the quarrel of Odysseus and Achilles, son of Peleus, how once they strove . . ., and Agamemnon, lord of men, rejoiced at heart . . ., for thus Phoebus Apollo, in giving response to him at Pytho, had told him that it should be."[1] Delphi, I say, is famous because of these things, but Elateia, because it is the largest of all the cities there, and has the most advantageous position, because it is situated in the narrow passes and because he who holds this city holds the passes leading into Phocis and Boeotia. For, first, there are the Oetaean Mountains; and then those of the Locrians and Phocians, which are not everywhere passable to invaders from Thessaly, but have passes, both narrow and separated from one another, which are guarded by the adjacent cities; and the result is, that when these cities are captured, their captors master the passes also. But since the fame of the temple at Delphi has the priority of age, and since at the same time the position of its places suggests a natural beginning (for these are the most westerly parts of Phocis), I should begin my description there.

3. As I have already said, Parnassus is situated on the western boundaries of Phocis. Of this mountain, then, the side towards the west is occupied by the Ozolian Locrians, whereas the southern is occupied by Delphi, a rocky place, theatre-like, having the

[1] *Odyssey* 8. 75.

---

[3] μέχρι A*cghino*, but ἐπί on margin of A, *man. sec.*
[4] ὅρων, Kramer, for ὀρῶν AE*cghilno*, μερῶν B.

καὶ τὴν πόλιν, σταδίων ἑκκαίδεκα κύκλον πληροῦσαν. ὑπέρκειται δ' αὐτῆς ἡ Λυκώρεια, ἐφ' οὗ τόπου πρότερον ἵδρυντο οἱ Δελφοὶ ὑπὲρ τοῦ ἱεροῦ· νῦν δ' ἐπ' αὐτῷ οἰκοῦσι περὶ τὴν κρήνην τὴν Κασταλίαν. πρόκειται δὲ τῆς πόλεως ἡ Κίρφις ἐκ τοῦ νοτίου μέρους, ὄρος ἀπότομον, νάπην ἀπολιπὸν μεταξύ, δι' ἧς ὁ Πλεῖστος διαρρεῖ ποταμός. ὑποπέπτωκε δὲ τῇ Κίρφει πόλις ἀρχαία Κίρρα, ἐπὶ τῇ θαλάττῃ ἱδρυμένη, ἀφ' ἧς ἀνάβασις εἰς Δελφοὺς ὀγδοήκοντά που σταδίων· ἵδρυται δ' ἀπαντικρὺ Σικυῶνος. πρόκειται δὲ τῆς Κίρρας τὸ Κρισαῖον πεδίον εὔδαιμον· πάλιν γὰρ[1] ἐφεξῆς ἐστὶν ἄλλη πόλις, Κρῖσα,[2] ἀφ' ἧς ὁ κόλπος Κρισαῖος· εἶτα Ἀντίκυρα, ὁμώνυμος τῇ κατὰ τὸν Μαλιακὸν κόλπον καὶ τὴν Οἴτην. καὶ δή φασιν ἐκεῖ τὸν ἐλλέβορον φύεσθαι τὸν ἀστεῖον, ἐνταῦθα δὲ σκευάζεσθαι βέλτιον, καὶ διὰ τοῦτο ἀποδημεῖν δεῦρο πολλούς, καθάρσεως καὶ θεραπείας χάριν· γίνεσθαι γάρ τι σησαμοειδὲς φάρμακον ἐν τῇ Φωκικῇ, μεθ' οὗ σκευάζεσθαι τὸν Οἰταῖον ἐλλέβορον.

4. Αὕτη μὲν οὖν συμμένει, ἡ δὲ Κίρρα καὶ ἡ Κρῖσα[3] κατεσπάσθησαν, ἡ μὲν [πρότερον ὑπὸ Κρισαίων, αὐτὴ δ' ἡ Κρῖσα[4]] ὕστερον ὑπ' Εὐρυλόχου τοῦ Θετταλοῦ κατὰ τὸν Κρισαῖον πόλεμον· εὐτυχήσαντες γὰρ οἱ Κρισαῖοι διὰ τὰ ἐκ τῆς Σικελίας καὶ τῆς Ἰταλίας τέλη,

[1] Instead of γάρ BE*kl* read δ'.
[2] Κρίσσα MSS. and editors before Kramer.
[3] Κρίσσα B*kl*.

oracle and the city on its summit, and filling a circuit of sixteen stadia. Situated above Delphi is Lycoreia, on which place, above the temple, the Delphians were established in earlier times. But now they live close to the temple, round the Castalian fountain. Situated in front of the city, toward the south, is Cirphis, a precipitous mountain, which leaves in the intervening space a ravine, through which flows the Pleistus River. Below Cirphis lies Cirrha, an ancient city, situated by the sea; and from it there is an ascent to Delphi of about eighty stadia. It is situated opposite Sicyon. In front of Cirrha lies the fertile Crisaean Plain; for again one comes next in order to another city, Crisa, from which the Crisaean Gulf is named. Then to Anticyra, bearing the same name as the city on the Maliac Gulf near Oeta. And, in truth, they say that it is in the latter region that the hellebore of fine quality is produced, though that produced in the former is better prepared, and on this account many people resort thither to be purged and cured; for in the Phocian Anticyra, they add, grows a sesame-like medicinal plant with which the Oetaean hellebore is prepared.

4. Now Anticyra still endures, but Cirrha and Crisa have been destroyed, the former earlier, by the Crisaeans, and Crisa itself later, by Eurylochus the Thessalian, at the time of the Crisaean War.[1] For the Crisaeans, already prosperous because of the duties levied on importations from Sicily and Italy,

[1] About 595 B.C.

[4] πρότερον ὑπὸ Κρισαίων, αὐτὴ δ' ἡ Κρῖσα, lacuna supplied by Corais, following Pletho and marginal note in *n*.

C 419 πικρῶς ἐτελώνουν τοὺς ἐπὶ τὸ ἱερὸν ἀφικνουμένους καὶ παρὰ τὰ προστάγματα τῶν Ἀμφικτυόνων. τὰ δ' αὐτὰ καὶ τοῖς Ἀμφισσεῦσι συνέβη· Λοκρῶν δ' εἰσὶν οὗτοι τῶν Ὀζολῶν. ἐπελθόντες γὰρ καὶ οὗτοι τήν τε Κρῖσαν ἀνέλαβον, καὶ τὸ πεδίον τὸ ὑπὸ τῶν Ἀμφικτυόνων ἀνιερωθὲν αὖθις κατεγεώργουν, καὶ χείρους ἦσαν περὶ τοὺς ξένους τῶν πάλαι Κρισαίων. καὶ τούτους οὖν ἐτιμωρήσαντο οἱ Ἀμφικτύονες, καὶ τῷ θεῷ τὴν χώραν ἀπέδοσαν. ὠλιγώρηται δ' ἱκανῶς καὶ τὸ ἱερόν, πρότερον δ' ὑπερβαλλόντως ἐτιμήθη·[1] δηλοῦσι δ' οἵ τε θησαυροί, οὓς καὶ δῆμοι καὶ δυνάσται κατεσκεύασαν, εἰς οὓς καὶ χρήματα ἀνετίθεντο καθιερωμένα καὶ ἔργα τῶν ἀρίστων δημιουργῶν, καὶ ὁ ἀγὼν ὁ Πυθικὸς καὶ τὸ πλῆθος τῶν ἱστορουμένων χρησμῶν.

5. Φασὶ δ' εἶναι τὸ μαντεῖον ἄντρον κοῖλον κατὰ βάθους, οὐ μάλα εὐρύστομον, ἀναφέρεσθαι δ' ἐξ αὐτοῦ πνεῦμα ἐνθουσιαστικόν, ὑπερκεῖσθαι δὲ τοῦ στομίου τρίποδα ὑψηλόν, ἐφ' ὃν τὴν Πυθίαν ἀναβαίνουσαν, δεχομένην τὸ πνεῦμα, ἀποθεσπίζειν ἔμμετρά τε καὶ ἄμετρα· ἐντείνειν δὲ καὶ ταῦτα εἰς μέτρον ποιητάς τινας ὑπουργοῦντας τῷ ἱερῷ. πρώτην δὲ Φημονοην γενέσθαι φασὶ Πυθίαν, κεκλῆσθαι δὲ καὶ τὴν προφῆτιν οὕτω καὶ τὴν πόλιν ἀπὸ τοῦ πυθέσθαι, ἐκτετάσθαι δὲ τὴν πρώτην συλλαβήν, ὡς ἐπὶ τοῦ ἀθανάτου καὶ

[1] ἐτιμήθη, Meineke inserts, following conj. of Casaubon.

---

[1] Of Apollo at Delphi.

[2] *i.e.* "Pȳthia" and "Pȳtho."

[3] "To inquire of the oracle." Other mythologers more plausibly derived the two names from the verb pȳthesthai,

proceeded to impose harsh taxes on those who came to visit the temple,[1] even contrary to the decrees of the Amphictyons. And the same thing also happened in the case of the Amphissians, who belonged to the Ozolian Locrians. For these too, coming over, not only restored Crisa and proceeded to put under cultivation again the plain which had been consecrated by the Amphictyons, but were worse in their dealings with foreigners than the Crisaeans of old had been. Accordingly, the Amphictyons punished these too, and gave the territory back to the god. The temple, too, has been much neglected, though in earlier times it was held in exceedingly great honour. Clear proofs of this are the treasure-houses, built both by peoples and by potentates, in which they deposited not only money which they had dedicated to the god, but also works of the best artists; and also the Pythian Games, and the great number of the recorded oracles.

5. They say that the seat of the oracle is a cave that is hollowed out deep down in the earth, with a rather narrow mouth, from which arises breath that inspires a divine frenzy; and that over the mouth is placed a high tripod, mounting which the Pythian priestess receives the breath and then utters oracles in both verse and prose, though the latter too are put into verse by poets who are in the service of the temple. They say that the first to become Pythian priestess was Phemonoê; and that both the prophetess and the city were so called[2] from the word "pȳthésthai,"[3] though the first syllable was

"to rot" (note the length of the vowel), because the serpent Python, slain by Apollo, "rotted" at the place.

ἀκαμάτου καὶ διακόνου. ἡ μὲν οὖν ἐπίνοια αὕτη τῆς τε τῶν πόλεων κτίσεως καὶ τῆς τῶν κοινῶν ἱερῶν ἐκτιμήσεως. καὶ γὰρ κατὰ πόλεις συνῄεσαν καὶ κατὰ ἔθνος, φυσικῶς κοινωνικοὶ ὄντες, καὶ ἅμα τῆς παρ' ἀλλήλων χρείας χάριν, καὶ εἰς τὰ ἱερὰ τὰ κοινὰ ἀπήντων διὰ τὰς αὐτὰς αἰτίας, ἑορτὰς καὶ πανηγύρεις συντελοῦντες. φιλικὸν γὰρ πᾶν τὸ τοιοῦτον, ἀπὸ τῶν ὁμοτραπέζων ἀρξάμενον καὶ ὁμοσπόνδων καὶ ὁμοροφίων. ὅσῳ δὲ πλεῖον [1] καὶ ἐκ πλειόνων ἐπεδήμει, τοσῷδε μεῖζον καὶ τὸ ὄφελος ἐνομίζετο.[2]

6. Ἡ μὲν οὖν ἐπὶ τὸ πλεῖον τιμὴ τῷ ἱερῷ τούτῳ διὰ τὸ χρηστήριον συνέβη, δόξαντι ἀψευδεστάτῳ τῶν πάντων ὑπάρξαι, προσέλαβε δέ [3] τι καὶ ἡ θέσις τοῦ τόπου. τῆς γὰρ Ἑλλάδος ἐν μέσῳ πώς ἐστι τῆς συμπάσης, τῆς τε ἐντὸς Ἰσθμοῦ καὶ τῆς ἐκτός, ἐνομίσθη δὲ καὶ τῆς οἰκουμένης, καὶ ἐκάλεσαν τῆς γῆς ὀμφαλόν, προσπλάσαντες καὶ μῦθον, ὅν φησι Πίνδαρος, ὅτι συμπέσοιεν ἐνταῦθα οἱ ἀετοὶ οἱ ἀφεθέντες ὑπὸ τοῦ Διός, ὁ μὲν ἀπὸ τῆς
C 420 δύσεως, ὁ δ' ἀπὸ τῆς ἀνατολῆς, οἱ δὲ κόρακάς φασι. δείκνυται δὲ καὶ ὀμφαλός τις ἐν τῷ ναῷ τεταινιωμένος καὶ ἐπ' αὐτῷ αἱ δύο εἰκόνες τοῦ μύθου.

7. Τοιαύτης δὲ τῆς εὐκαιρίας οὔσης τῆς περὶ τοὺς Δελφούς, συνῄεσάν τε ῥᾳδίως ἐκεῖσε,

[1] πλεῖον, Tzschucke, for πλείων.
[2] ἡ μὲν οὖν . . . ἐνομίζετο, Meineke, following Kramer, ejects.
[3] προσελάβετο *Bkl.*

---

[1] But in "diakonos" it is the second syllable that is long; and Homer does not use the word. For the uses of the first two with long *a* see (e.g.) *Iliad* 6. 108 and 5. 4.

lengthened, as in *ăthanatos*, *ăkamatos*, and *diăkonos*.[1] Now the following is the idea which leads to the founding of cities and to the holding of common sanctuaries in high esteem: men came together by cities and by tribes, because they naturally tend to hold things in common, and at the same time because of their need of one another; and they met at the sacred places that were common to them for the same reasons, holding festivals and general assemblies; for everything of this kind tends to friendship, beginning with eating at the same table, drinking libations together, and lodging under the same roof; and the greater the number of the sojourners and the greater the number of the places whence they came, the greater was thought to be the use of their coming together.

6. Now although the greatest share of honour was paid to this temple because of its oracle, since of all oracles in the world it had the repute of being the most truthful, yet the position of the place added something. For it is almost in the centre of Greece taken as a whole, between the country inside the Isthmus and that outside it; and it was also believed to be in the centre of the inhabited world, and people called it the navel of the earth, in addition fabricating a myth, which is told by Pindar, that the two eagles (some say crows) which had been set free by Zeus met there, one coming from the west and the other from the east. There is also a kind of navel to be seen in the temple; it is draped with fillets, and on it are the two likenesses of the birds of the myth.

7. Such being the advantages of the site of Delphi, the people easily came together there, and

μάλιστα δ' οἱ ἐγγύθεν, καὶ δὴ καὶ τὸ Ἀμφικτυονικὸν σύστημα ἐκ τούτων συνετάχθη, περί τε τῶν κοινῶν βουλευσόμενον καὶ τοῦ ἱεροῦ τὴν ἐπιμέλειαν ἔξον κοινοτέραν, ἅτε καὶ χρημάτων ἀποκειμένων πολλῶν καὶ ἀναθημάτων, φυλακῆς καὶ ἁγιστείας δεομένων μεγάλης. τὰ πάλαι μὲν οὖν ἀγνοεῖται, Ἀκρίσιος δὲ τῶν μνημονευομένων πρῶτος διατάξαι δοκεῖ τὰ περὶ τοὺς Ἀμφικτύονας καὶ πόλεις ἀφορίσαι τὰς μετεχούσας τοῦ συνεδρίου καὶ ψῆφον ἑκάστῃ δοῦναι, τῇ μὲν καθ' αὑτήν, τῇ δὲ μεθ' ἑτέρας ἢ μετὰ πλειόνων, ἀποδεῖξαι δὲ καὶ τὰς Ἀμφικτυονικὰς δίκας, ὅσαι πόλεσι πρὸς πόλεις εἰσίν· ὕστερον δ' ἄλλαι πλείους διατάξεις γεγόνασιν, ἕως κατελύθη καὶ τοῦτο τὸ σύνταγμα, καθάπερ τὸ τῶν Ἀχαιῶν. αἱ μὲν οὖν πρῶται δυοκαίδεκα συνελθεῖν λέγονται πόλεις· ἑκάστη δ' ἔπεμπε Πυλαγόραν, δὶς κατ' ἔτος οὔσης τῆς συνόδου, ἔαρός τε καὶ μετοπώρου· ὕστερον δὲ καὶ πλείους προσῆλθον[1] πόλεις. τὴν δὲ σύνοδον Πυλαίαν ἐκάλουν, τὴν μὲν ἐαρινήν, τὴν δὲ μετοπωρινήν, ἐπειδὴ ἐν Πύλαις συνήγοντο, ἃς καὶ Θερμοπύλας καλοῦσιν· ἔθυον δὲ τῇ Δήμητρι οἱ Πυλαγόραι. τὸ μὲν οὖν ἐξ ἀρχῆς τοῖς ἐγγὺς μετῆν καὶ τούτων καὶ τοῦ μαντείου, ὕστερον δὲ καὶ οἱ πόρρωθεν ἀφικνοῦντο καὶ ἐχρῶντο τῷ μαντείῳ καὶ ἔπεμπον δῶρα καὶ θησαυροὺς κατεσκεύαζον, καθάπερ Κροῖσος καὶ ὁ πατὴρ Ἀλυάττης καὶ Ἰταλιωτῶν τινὲς καὶ Σικελοί.

8. Ἐπίφθονος δ' ὢν ὁ πλοῦτος δυσφύλακτός

[1] προσῆλθον A, συνῆλθον A *man. sec.* and other MSS.

---

[1] See 8. 7. 3. [2] *i.e.* Pylae—assemblyman

especially those who lived near it. And indeed the Amphictyonic League was organised from the latter, both to deliberate concerning common affairs and to keep the superintendence of the temple more in common, because much money and many votive offerings were deposited there, requiring great vigilance and holiness. Now the facts of olden times are unknown, but among the names recorded Acrisius is reputed to have been the first to administer the Amphictyony and to determine the cities that were to have a part in the council and to give a vote to each city, to one city separately or to another jointly with a second or with several, and also to proclaim the Amphictyonic Rights—all the rights that cities have in their dealings with cities. Later there were several other administrations, until this organisation, like that of the Achaeans,[1] was dissolved. Now the first cities which came together are said to have been twelve, and each sent a Pylagoras,[2] the assembly convening twice a year, in spring and in late autumn; but later still more cities were added. They called the assembly Pylaea, both that of spring and that of late autumn, since they convened at Pylae, which is also called Thermopylae; and the Pylagorae sacrificed to Demeter. Now although at the outset only the people who lived near by had a share both in these things and in the oracle, later the people living at a distance also came and consulted the oracle and sent gifts and built treasure-houses, as, for instance, Croesus, and his father Alyattes, and some of the Italiotes,[3] and the Sicilians.

8. But wealth inspires envy, and is therefore

[3] Greeks living in Italy.

ἐστι, κἂν ἱερὸς ᾖ. νυνί γέ τοι πενέστατόν ἐστι τὸ ἐν Δελφοῖς ἱερὸν χρημάτων γε[1] χάριν, τῶν δ'[2] ἀναθημάτων τὰ μὲν ἦρται, τὰ δὲ πλείω μένει. πρότερον δὲ πολυχρήματον ἦν τὸ ἱερόν, καθάπερ Ὅμηρός τε εἴρηκεν,

οὐδ' ὅσα λάϊνος οὐδὸς ἀφήτορος ἐντὸς ἐέργει
Φοίβου Ἀπόλλωνος Πυθοῖ ἐνὶ πετρηέσσῃ,

καὶ οἱ θησαυροὶ δηλοῦσι καὶ ἡ σύλησις ἡ γενηθεῖσα ὑπὸ τῶν Φωκέων, ἐξ ἧς ὁ Φωκικὸς καὶ ἱερὸς καλούμενος ἐξήφθη πόλεμος. αὕτη μὲν οὖν ἡ σύλησις γεγένηται κατὰ Φίλιππον τὸν Ἀμύντου,
C 421 προτέραν δ' ἄλλην ἐπινοοῦσιν[3] ἀρχαίαν, ἣ τὸν ὑφ' Ὁμήρου λεγόμενον πλοῦτον ἐξεφόρησεν· οὐδὲ γὰρ ἴχνος αὐτοῦ σωθῆναι πρὸς τοὺς ὕστερον χρόνους, ἐν οἷς οἱ περὶ Ὀνόμαρχον καὶ Φάϋλλον ἐσύλησαν τὸ ἱερόν, ἀλλὰ τὰ μὲν [τότε[4]] ἀπενεχθέντα νεώτερα ἐκείνων εἶναι τῶν χρημάτων· ἀποκεῖσθαι γὰρ ἐν θησαυροῖς ἀπὸ λαφύρων ἀνατεθέντα, ἐπιγραφὰς σώζοντα, ἐν αἷς καὶ οἱ ἀναθέντες· Γύγου γὰρ καὶ Κροίσου καὶ Συβαριτῶν καὶ Σπινητῶν τῶν περὶ τὸν Ἀδρίαν, καὶ οὕτως ἐπὶ τῶν ἄλλων. οἷς [οὐκ ἂν προσ]ήκοι[5] τὰ

[1] γε, Meineke, for δέ. Corais deletes δέ.

[2] δ', after τῶν, Corais inserts; so the later editors.

[3] ἐπινοοῦσιν, Jones restores, for ὑπονοοῦσιν, Groskurd and later editors.

[4] [τότε], lacuna of about four letters in A, supplied by Müller-Dübner, following conj. of Kramer. ὑπὸ τούτων Corais.

[5] οἷς [οὐκ ἂν προσ]ήκοι, Jones, for οὔτ (οὐ *bno*) . . . ήκοι,

difficult to guard, even if it is sacred. At present, certainly, the temple at Delphi is very poor, at least so far as money is concerned; but as for the votive offerings, although some of them have been carried off, most of them still remain. In earlier times the temple was very wealthy, as Homer states: "nor yet all the things which the stone threshold of the archer Phoebus Apollo enclosed in rocky Pytho."[1] The treasure-houses[2] clearly indicate its wealth, and also the plundering done by the Phocians, which kindled the Phocian War, or Sacred War, as it is called. Now this plundering took place in the time of Philip, the son of Amyntas, although writers have a notion of another and earlier plundering, in ancient times, in which the wealth mentioned by Homer was carried out of the temple. For, they add, not so much as a trace of it was saved down to those later times in which Onomarchus and his army, and Phaÿllus and his army,[3] robbed the temple; but the wealth then carried away was more recent than that mentioned by Homer; for there were deposited in treasure-houses offerings dedicated from spoils of war, preserving inscriptions on which were included the names of those who dedicated them; for instance, Gyges, Croesus, the Sybarites, and the Spinetae[4] who lived near the Adriatic, and so with the rest. And it would not

[1] *Iliad* 9. 404. [2] See vol. ii, page 314, note 2.

[3] 352 B.C. Both were Phocian generals. For an account of their robberies see Diodorus Siculus 16. 31–61.

[4] See 5. 1. 7.

---

where there is a lacuna of about ten letters. *οὔτ[ε τούτοις ἂν προσ]ήκοι* conj. Kramer. *οἷς [οὐ προσ]ῆκε*, reading of Corais. Meineke leaves lacuna.

παλαιὰ χρήματα ἀναμεμῖχθαι, ὡς[1] καὶ ἄλλοι τόποι διασημαίνουσιν ὑπὸ τούτων σκευωρηθέντες τῶν ἀνδρῶν. ἔνιοι δὲ τὸν ἀφήτορα δεξάμενοι λέγεσθαι θησαυρόν, ἀφήτορος δ' οὐδὸν κατὰ γῆς θησαυρισμόν, ἐν τῷ ναῷ κατωρύχθαι φασὶ τὸν πλοῦτον ἐκεῖνον, καὶ τοὺς περὶ τὸν Ὀνόμαρχον ἐπιχειρήσαντας ἀνασκάπτειν νύκτωρ, σεισμῶν γενομένων μεγάλων, ἔξω τοῦ ναοῦ φυγεῖν καὶ παύσασθαι τῆς ἀνασκαφῆς, ἐμβαλεῖν δὲ καὶ τοῖς ἄλλοις φόβον τῆς τοιαύτης ἐπιχειρήσεως.

9. Τῶν δὲ ναῶν[2] τὸν μὲν πτέρινον εἰς τοὺς μύθους τακτέον, τὸν δὲ δεύτερον Τροφωνίου καὶ Ἀγαμήδους ἔργον φασί, τὸν δὲ νῦν Ἀμφικτύονες κατεσκεύασαν. δείκνυται δ' ἐν τῷ τεμένει τάφος Νεοπτολέμου κατὰ χρησμὸν γενόμενος, Μαχαιρέως, Δελφοῦ ἀνδρός, ἀνελόντος αὐτόν, ὡς μὲν ὁ μῦθος, δίκας αἰτοῦντα τὸν θεὸν τοῦ πατρῴου φόνου, ὡς δὲ τὸ εἰκός, ἐπιθέμενον τῷ ἱερῷ. τοῦ δὲ Μαχαιρέως ἀπόγονον Βράγχον φασὶ τὸν προστατήσαντα τοῦ ἐν Διδύμοις ἱεροῦ.

10. Ἀγὼν δὲ ὁ μὲν ἀρχαῖος ἐν Δελφοῖς κιθαρῳδῶν ἐγενήθη, παιᾶνα ᾳδόντων εἰς τὸν θεόν· ἔθηκαν δὲ Δελφοί· μετὰ δὲ τὸν Κρισαῖον πόλεμον οἱ Ἀμφικτύονες ἱππικὸν καὶ γυμνικὸν ἐπ' Εὐρυλόχου διέταξαν στεφανίτην καὶ Πύθια ἐκάλεσαν.

[1] ὡς, Groskurd inserts; so the later editors. See Kramer's note *ad loc.*

[2] ναῶν, Casaubon, for νώτων A(ὤτων *man. sec.*)*cghi*; so the later editors. Word omitted by B*no*.

---

[1] The Greek word translated "archer" in the above citation from Homer.

[2] Achilles.

be reasonable to suppose that the treasures of olden times were mixed up with these, as indeed is clearly indicated by other places that were ransacked by these men. Some, however, taking "aphetor"[1] to mean "treasure-house," and "threshold of the aphetor" to mean "underground repository of the treasure-house," say that that wealth was buried in the temple, and that Onomarchus and his army attempted to dig it up by night, but since great earthquakes took place they fled outside the temple and stopped their digging, and that their experience inspired all others with fear of making a similar attempt.

9. Of the temples, the one "with wings" must be placed among the myths; the second is said to be the work of Trophonius and Agamedes; and the present temple was built by the Amphictyons. In the sacred precinct is to be seen the tomb of Neoptolemus, which was made in accordance with an oracle, Machaereus, a Delphian, having slain him because, according to the myth, he was asking the god for redress for the murder of his father;[2] but according to all probability it was because he had attacked the temple. Branchus, who presided over the temple at Didyma, is called a descendant of Machaereus.

10. As for the contests at Delphi, there was one in early times between citharoedes, who sang a paean in honour of the god; it was instituted by the Delphians. But after the Crisaean war, in the time of Eurylochus,[3] the Amphictyons instituted equestrian and gymnastic contests in which the prize was a crown, and called them Pythian Games.

[3] On the time, compare 9. 3. 4 and foot-note.

προσέθεσαν δὲ τοῖς κιθαρῳδοῖς αὐλητάς τε καὶ κιθαριστὰς χωρὶς ᾠδῆς, ἀποδώσοντάς τι μέλος, ὃ καλεῖται νόμος Πυθικός. πέντε δ' αὐτοῦ μέρη ἐστίν, ἄγκρουσις, ἄμπειρα, κατακελευσμός, ἴαμβοι καὶ δάκτυλοι, σύριγγες. ἐμελοποίησε μὲν οὖν Τιμοσθένης, ὁ ναύαρχος τοῦ δευτέρου Πτολεμαίου ὁ καὶ τοὺς λιμένας συντάξας ἐν δέκα βίβλοις. βούλεται δὲ τὸν ἀγῶνα τοῦ Ἀπόλλωνος τὸν πρὸς τὸν δράκοντα διὰ τοῦ μέλους ὑμνεῖν, ἀνάκρουσιν μὲν τὸ προοίμιον δηλῶν, ἄμπειραν δὲ τὴν πρώτην κατάπειραν τοῦ ἀγῶνος, κατακελευσμὸν δὲ αὐτὸν τὸν ἀγῶνα, ἴαμβον δὲ καὶ δάκτυλον τὸν ἐπιπαιανισμὸν[1] τὸν [γινόμενον[2]] ἐπὶ τῇ νίκῃ μετὰ τοιούτων
C 422 ῥυθμῶν, ὧν ὁ μὲν ὕμνοις ἐστὶν οἰκεῖος, ὁ δ' ἴαμβος κακισμοῖς, ὡς καὶ τὸ ἰαμβίζειν, σύριγγας δὲ τὴν ἔκλειψιν τοῦ θηρίου μιμουμένων ὡς ἂν καταστρέφοντος εἰς ἐσχάτους τινὰς συριγμούς.

11. Ἔφορος δ', ᾧ τὸ πλεῖστον προσχρώμεθα διὰ τὴν περὶ ταῦτα ἐπιμέλειαν, καθάπερ καὶ Πολύβιος μαρτυρῶν τυγχάνει, ἀνὴρ ἀξιόλογος, δοκεῖ μοι τἀναντία ποιεῖν ἔσθ' ὅτε τῇ προαιρέσει

[1] ἐπιπαιανισμόν, Corais, for ἐπιπαιωνισμόν.
[2] [γινόμενον], lacuna in A supplied by *man. sec.*, with ὄντα written above. Word omitted by *Bckl.*

---

[1] The citharoedes *sang* to the accompaniment of the cithara, and their contests must have had no connection with those of the flute-players and the citharists, whose performance (of the Pythian Nome) was a purely instrumental affair.

[2] If the text of this sentence is correct, Strabo must be referring to the melody played as the Pythian Nome in his own time or in that of some authority whom he is quoting, earlier compositions perhaps having been superseded by that

And to the citharoedes[1] they added both flute-players and citharists who played without singing, who were to render a certain melody which is called the Pythian Nome. There are five parts of it: *angkrousis, ampeira, katakeleusmos, iambi* and *dactyli*, and *syringes*. Now the melody was composed by Timosthenes, the admiral of the second Ptolemy, who also compiled *The Harbours*, a work in ten books;[2] and through this melody he means to celebrate the contest between Apollo and the dragon, setting forth the prelude as *anakrousis*, the first onset of the contest as *ampeira*, the contest itself as *katakeleusmos*, the triumph following the victory as *iambus* and *dactylus*, the rhythms being in two measures, one of which, the dactyl, is appropriate to hymns of praise, whereas the other, the iamb, is suited to reproaches (compare the word "iambize"), and the expiration of the dragon as *syringes*, since with *syringes*[3] players imitated the dragon as breathing its last in hissings.[4]

11. Ephorus, whom I am using more than any other authority because, as Polybius, a noteworthy writer, testifies, he exercises great care in such matters, seems to me sometimes to do the opposite

of Timosthenes (fl. about 270 B.C.). But since the invention of the Pythian Nome has been ascribed to Sacadas (Pollux 4. 77), who was victorious with the flute at the Pythian Games about three hundred years before the time of Timosthenes (Pausanias 6. 14. 9 and 10. 7. 4), Guhrauer (*Jahrb. für Class. Philol.*, Suppl. 8, 1875–1876, pp. 311–351) makes a strong argument for a lacuna in the Greek text, and for making Strabo say that the melody was composed by Sacadas and later merely described by Timosthenes in one of his numerous works. Cp. also H. Riemann, *Handb. der Musikgeschichte* 1919, vol. i, pp. 63–65.

[3] "Pipes." [4] "Pipings."

καὶ ταῖς ἐξ ἀρχῆς ὑποσχέσεσιν. ἐπιτιμήσας γοῦν τοῖς φιλομυθοῦσιν ἐν τῇ τῆς ἱστορίας γραφῇ καὶ τὴν ἀλήθειαν ἐπαινέσας προστίθησι τῷ περὶ τοῦ μαντείου τούτου λόγῳ σεμνήν τινα ὑπόσχεσιν, ὡς πανταχοῦ μὲν ἄριστον νομίζει τἀληθές, μάλιστα δὲ κατὰ τὴν ὑπόθεσιν ταύτην. ἄτοπον γάρ, εἰ περὶ μὲν τῶν ἄλλων τὸν τοιοῦτον ἀεὶ τρόπον διώκομεν, φησί, περὶ δὲ τοῦ μαντείου λέγοντες, ὃ πάντων ἐστὶν ἀψευδέστατον, τοῖς οὕτως ἀπίστοις καὶ ψευδέσι χρησόμεθα λόγοις. ταῦτα δ' εἰπὼν ἐπιφέρει παραχρῆμα, ὅτι ὑπολαμβάνουσι κατασκευάσαι τὸ μαντεῖον Ἀπόλλωνα μετὰ Θέμιδος, ὠφελῆσαι βουλόμενον τὸ γένος ἡμῶν· εἶτα τὴν ὠφέλειαν εἰπών, ὅτι εἰς ἡμερότητα προὐκαλεῖτο καὶ ἐσωφρόνιζε, τοῖς μὲν χρηστηριάζων καὶ τὰ μὲν προστάττων, τὰ δ' ἀπαγορεύων, τοὺς δ' οὐδ' ὅλως προσιέμενος. ταῦτα δὲ[1] διοικεῖν νομίζουσι, φησίν, αὐτόν, οἱ μὲν αὐτὸν τὸν θεὸν σωματοειδῆ γινόμενον, οἱ δ' ἀνθρώποις ἔννοιαν παραδιδόντα τῆς ἑαυτοῦ βουλήσεως.

12. Ὑποβὰς δέ, περὶ τῶν Δελφῶν, οἵτινές εἰσι, διαλεγόμενος, φησὶ τὸ παλαιὸν Παρνασσίους[2] τινὰς αὐτόχθονας καλουμένους οἰκεῖν τὸν Παρνασσόν· καθ' ὃν χρόνον Ἀπόλλωνα, τὴν γῆν ἐπιόντα, ἡμεροῦν τοὺς ἀνθρώπους ἀπό τε τῶν ἡμέρων καρπῶν καὶ τῶν βίων, ἐξ Ἀθηνῶν δ' ὁρμηθέντα ἐπὶ Δελφοὺς ταύτην ἰέναι τὴν ὁδόν,

of what he intended, and at the outset promised, to do. At any rate, after censuring those who love to insert myths in the text of their histories, and after praising the truth, he adds to his account of this oracle a kind of solemn promise, saying that he regards the truth as best in all cases, but particularly on this subject; for it is absurd, he says, if we always follow such a method in dealing with every other subject, and yet, when speaking of the oracle which is the most truthful of all, go on to use the accounts that are so untrustworthy and false. Yet, though he says this, he adds forthwith that historians take it for granted that Apollo, with Themis, devised the oracle because he wished to help our race; and then, speaking of the helpfulness of it, he says that Apollo challenged men to gentleness and inculcated self-control by giving out oracles to some, commanding them to do certain things and forbidding them to do other things, and by absolutely refusing admittance to other consultants. Men believe that Apollo directs all this, he says, some believing that the god himself assumes a bodily form, others that he transmits to human beings a knowledge of his own will.

12. A little further on, when discussing who the Delphians were, he says that in olden times certain Parnassians who were called indigenous inhabited Parnassus; and that at this time Apollo, visiting the land, civilised the people by introducing cultivated fruits and cultured modes of life; and that when he set out from Athens to Delphi he went by the road

---

[1] δέ, Corais brackets; Meineke deletes.

[2] Παρνασσίους, Kramer, for Παρνασίους.

ᾗ νῦν Ἀθηναῖοι τὴν Πυθιάδα πέμπουσι· γενόμενον δὲ κατὰ Πανοπέας Τιτυὸν καταλῦσαι, ἔχοντα τὸν τόπον, βίαιον ἄνδρα καὶ παράνομον· τοὺς δὲ Παρνασσίους, συμμίξαντας αὐτῷ, καὶ ἄλλον μηνῦσαι χαλεπὸν ἄνδρα, Πύθωνα τοὔνομα, ἐπίκλησιν δὲ Δράκοντα, κατατοξεύοντος δ' ἐπικελεύειν ἵε παιάν, ἀφ' οὗ τὸν παιωνισμὸν οὕτως ἐξ ἔθους παραδοθῆναι τοῖς μέλλουσι συμπίπτειν εἰς παράταξιν· ἐμπρησθῆναι δὲ καὶ σκηνὴν τότε τοῦ Πύθωνος ὑπὸ τῶν Δελφῶν, καθάπερ καὶ νῦν ἔτι καὶ ἀεὶ ὑπόμνημα ποιουμένους τῶν τότε γενομένων. τί δ' ἂν εἴη μυθωδέστερον ἢ Ἀπόλλων
C 423 τοξεύων καὶ κολάζων Τιτυοὺς καὶ Πύθωνας καὶ ὁδεύων ἐξ Ἀθηνῶν εἰς Δελφοὺς καὶ γῆν πᾶσαν ἐπιών ; εἰ δὲ ταῦτα μὴ ὑπελάμβανε μύθους εἶναι, τί ἐχρῆν τὴν μυθευομένην Θέμιν γυναῖκα καλεῖν, τὸν δὲ μυθευόμενον Δράκοντα ἄνθρωπον, πλὴν εἰ συγχεῖν ἐβούλετο τόν τε τῆς ἱστορίας καὶ τὸν τοῦ μύθου τύπον ;[1] παραπλήσια τούτοις ἐστὶ[2] καὶ τὰ περὶ τῶν Αἰτωλῶν εἰρημένα. φήσας γὰρ ἀπορθήτους αὐτοὺς ἐκ παντὸς τοῦ χρόνου, τοτὲ μὲν Αἰολέας φησὶν ἐκεῖ[3] οἰκῆσαι[4] τοὺς κατέχοντας βαρβάρους ἐκβαλόντας, τοτὲ δ' Αἰτωλὸν μετὰ

[1] τύπον, Corais, for τόπον, from conj. of Tyrwhitt; so the later editors.

[2] ἐστί, Jones inserts, from conj. of Kramer. The lacuna of about twelve letters in A before καί is partially supplied by the second hand with τούτοις.

[3] ἐκεῖ, Jones inserts.

which the Athenians now take when they conduct the Pythias;[1] and that when he arrived at the land of the Panopaeans he destroyed Tityus, a violent and lawless man who ruled there; and that the Parnassians joined him and informed him of another cruel man named Python and known as the Dragon, and that when Apollo shot at him with his arrows the Parnassians shouted "Hie Paean"[2] to encourage him (the origin, Ephorus adds, of the singing of the Paean which has been handed down as a custom for armies just before the clash of battle); and that the tent of Python was burnt by the Delphians at that time, just as they still burn it to this day in remembrance of what took place at that time. But what could be more mythical than Apollo shooting with arrows and punishing Tityuses and Pythons, and travelling from Athens to Delphi and visiting the whole earth? But if Ephorus did not take these stories for myths, by what right did he call the mythological Themis a woman, and the mythological Dragon a human being—unless he wished to confound the two types, history and myth? Similar to these statements are also those concerning the Aetolians; for after saying that from all time their country had been unravaged, he at one time says that Aeolians took up their abode there, having ejected the barbarians who were in possession of it, and at another time that Aetolus together with the

[1] A sacred mission despatched from Athens to Pytho (Delphi). See 9. 2. 11.

[2] A shout addressed to Apollo in his capacity as Paean (Healer).

---

[4] οἰκίσας A.

τῶν ἐξ Ἤλιδος Ἐπειῶν, καταλυθῆναι δ' ὑπ' Αἰολέων[1] τῶν ἐχθρῶν· τούτους δ' ὑπ' Ἀλκμαίωνος καὶ Διομήδους. ἀλλ' ἐπάνειμι ἐπὶ τοὺς Φωκέας.

13. Ἐξ ἀρχῆς[2] γὰρ ἐν τῇ παραλίᾳ μετὰ τὴν Ἀντίκυραν πολίχνιόν ἐστιν Ὀπισθομάραθος·[3] εἶτ' ἄκρα Φαρύγιον, ἔχουσα ὕφορμον· εἶθ' ὁ λιμὴν ὕστατος ὁ προσαγορευθεὶς Μυχὸς ἀπὸ τοῦ συμβεβηκότος, ὑπὸ τῷ Ἑλικῶνι καὶ τῇ Ἄσκρῃ κείμενος. οὐδ' αἱ Ἀβαὶ δὲ τὸ μαντεῖον ἄπωθεν τῶν τόπων τούτων ἐστίν, οὐδ' ἡ Ἄμβρυσος, [οὐδ' ἡ Με]δεὼν[4] ὁμώνυμος τῇ Βοιωτιακῇ. ἔτι δὲ μᾶλλον ἐν τῇ μεσογαίᾳ μετὰ Δελφοὺς ὡς πρὸς τὴν ἕω Δαυλὶς πολίχνιον, ὅπου Τηρέα τὸν Θρᾷκά φασι δυναστεῦσαι (καὶ τὰ περὶ Φιλομήλαν καὶ Πρόκνην ἐκεῖ μυθεύουσι, Θουκυδίδης δ' ἐν Μεγάροις φησί)·[5] τοὔνομα δὲ τῷ τόπῳ γεγονέναι ἀπὸ τοῦ δάσους· δαυλοὺς γὰρ καλοῦσι τὰ δάση. Ὅμηρος μὲν οὖν Δαυλίδα εἶπεν, οἱ δ' ὕστερον Δαυλίαν. καὶ τὸ

Κυπάρισσον δ' ἔχον

[1] , καταλυθῆναι δ' ὑπ' Αἰολέων, lacuna of about twenty-two letters supplied by Jones. Kramer conj. κρατηθῆναι δὴ ὑπὸ τούτων (see his discussion in note *ad loc.*). Groskurd rashly emends Αἰολέας to Κουρῆτας, and inserts τὴν χώραν after φησίν. For other quotations from Ephorus bearing on this passage, see 7. 7. 7, 8. 3. 33, 10. 2. 25, 10. 3. 1–6.

[2] ἐξ ἀρχῆς, Corais and Meineke emend to ἑξῆς.

Epeii from Elis took up their abode there, but were overthrown by the Aeolians, their foes, and that these latter were destroyed by Alcmaeon and Diomedes. But I return to the Phocians.

13. On the sea-coast after Anticyra, one comes first to a town called Opisthomarathus; then to a cape called Pharygium, where there is an anchoring-place; then to the harbour that is last, which, from the fact in the case, is called Mychus;[1] and it lies below Helicon and Ascrê. And the oracle of Abae is not far from this region, nor Ambrysus, nor Medeon,[2] which bears the same name as the Boeotian Medeon. Still farther in the interior, after Delphi, approximately towards the east, is a town Daulis, where Tereus the Thracian is said to have held sway (the scene of the mythical story of Philomela and Procnê is laid there, though Thucydides[3] says at Megara). The place got its name from the thickets, for they call thickets "dauli." Now Homer called it Daulis, but later writers call it Daulia. And "Cyparissus," in the words "held Cyparissus,"[4] is

[1] Inmost recess.

[2] On the site of Medeon see Frazer's Pausanias, note on 36. 6.

[3] But Thucydides (2. 29) says: "In that country (Daulia) Itys suffered at the hands of Philomela and Procnê." Eustathius (note on *Iliad* 2. 520) repeats without correction Strabo's erroneous reference.

[4] *Iliad* 2. 519.

---

[3] Ὀπισθομάραθος *Agino*; other MSS. ὄπισθεν ὁ Μάραθος.

[4] [οὐδ' ἡ Με]δεών, lacuna of about six letters in A, supplied by Kramer.

[5] Θουκυδίδης . . . φησί, Meineke ejects.

δέχονται διττῶς, οἱ μὲν ὁμωνύμως [τῷ φυ]τῷ,[1] οἱ δε παρωνύμως κώμην ὑπὸ τῇ Λυκωρείᾳ.

14. Πανοπεὺς δ' ὁ νῦν Φανοτεύς, ὅμορος τοῖς περὶ Λεβάδειαν τόποις, ἡ τοῦ Ἐπειοῦ πατρίς. καὶ τὰ περὶ τὸν Τιτυὸν δὲ ἐνταῦθα μυθεύουσιν. Ὅμηρος δέ φησιν, ὅτι οἱ Φαίηκες τὸν Ῥαδάμανθυν εἰς Εὔβοιαν

ἤγαγον, ὀψόμενον Τιτυὸν γαιήιον υἱόν·

καὶ Ἐλάριόν τι σπήλαιον ἀπὸ τῆς Τιτυοῦ μητρὸς Ἐλάρας δείκνυται κατὰ τὴν νῆσον καὶ ἡρῷον τοῦ Τιτυοῦ καὶ τιμαί τινες. πλησίον δὲ Λεβαδείας καὶ ἡ Τραχίν, ὁμώνυμος τῇ Οἰταίᾳ, Φωκικὴ πολίχνη· οἱ δ' ἐνοικοῦντες Τραχίνιοι λέγονται.

15. Ἡ δὲ Ἀνεμώρεια ὠνόμασται ἀπὸ τοῦ συμβαίνοντος πάθους· καταιγίζει γὰρ εἰς αὐτὴν ὁ καλούμενος Κατοπτήριος χῶρος, κρημνός τις ἀπὸ τοῦ Παρνασσοῦ διήκων· ὅριον δ' ἦν ὁ τόπος οὗτος Δελφῶν τε καὶ Φωκέων, ἡνίκα ἀπέστησαν τοὺς Δελφοὺς ἀπὸ τοῦ κοινοῦ συστήματος τῶν Φωκέων Λακεδαιμόνιοι καὶ ἐπέτρεψαν καθ' αὑτοὺς
C 424 πολιτεύεσθαι· τινὲς δὲ Ἀνεμώλειαν καλοῦσιν. εἶθ' Ὑάμπολις (Ὕα μετὰ ταῦτα ἐκλήθη ὑπό

[1] There is a lacuna of about ten letters in A between ὁμωνύμως and τῷ, οἱ δέ, but the second hand supplies τῷ φυ. Groskurd proposes the insertion of μόνον before τῷ φυτῷ.

---

[1] Cyparissus is the word for cypress-tree.

[2] As the text stands, the meaning is obscure. The scholiast on Ven. A, *Iliad* 2. 519, says that Cyparissus was named after Cyparissus the brother of Orchomenus, or after the cypress-trees that grew in it; and the scholiast on Ven. B *ibid.*, "Cyparissus, the present Apollonias, named after

interpreted by writers in two ways, by some as bearing the same name as the tree,[1] and by others, by a slight change in the spelling, as a village below Lycoreia.[2]

14. Panopeus, the Phanoteus of to-day, borders on the region of Lebadeia, and is the native land of Epeius. And the scene of the myth of Tityus is laid here. Homer says that the Phaeacians "led" Rhadamanthys into Euboea "to see Tityus, son of the Earth."[3] And a cave called Elarium is to be seen in the island, named after Elara the mother of Tityus; and also a hero-temple of Tityus, and certain honours which are paid to him. Near Lebadeia, also, is Trachin, a Phocian town, which bears the same name as the Oetaean city; and its inhabitants are called Trachinians.

15. Anemoreia[4] has been named from a circumstance connected with it: squalls of wind sweep down upon it from Catopterius,[5] as it is called, a beetling cliff extending from Parnassus. This place was a boundary between Delphi and the Phocians when the Lacedaemonians caused the Delphians to revolt from the common organisation of the Phocians,[6] and permitted them to form a separate State of their own. Some, however, call the place Anemoleia. And then one comes to Hyampolis (later called Hya by some), to which,

Cyparissus." Pausanias (10. 36. 3) says: "In earlier times the name of the city was Cyparissus, and Homer, in his list of the Phocians, purposely used this name, though the city was even then called Anticyra" (see Frazer, note *ad loc.*). On the position of Lycoreia, see 9. 3. 3.

[3] *Od.* 7. 324.

[4] "Wind-swept."

[5] "The Look-out."

[6] About 457 B.C. (see Thucydides 1. 107–108).

τινων), εἰς ἣν ἐκ Βοιωτίας ἐκπεσεῖν ἔφαμεν τοὺς Ὕαντας· ἔστι δʼ ἐν τῇ μεσογαίᾳ μάλιστα καὶ αὕτη, πλησίον τῶν Παραποταμίων, ἑτέρα οὖσα τῆς ἐν τῷ Παρνασσῷ Ὑαμπείας, καὶ Ἐλάτεια, ἡ μεγίστη πόλις τῶν Φωκικῶν, ἣν Ὅμηρος μὲν οὐκ οἶδε· νεωτέρα γάρ ἐστι τῆς ἡλικίας ἐκείνης·[1] ἐπικαιρίως δʼ ἵδρυται πρὸς τὰς ἐκ τῆς Θετταλίας[2] εἰσβολάς. δηλοῖ δὲ τὴν εὐφυίαν ταύτην καὶ Δημοσθένης, φράζων τὸν θόρυβον τὸν γενηθέντα Ἀθήνησιν αἰφνιδίως, ἐπειδὴ ἧκέ τις ἀπαγγέλλων ὡς τοὺς πρυτάνεις, ὡς Ἐλάτεια κατείληπται.

16. Παραποτάμιοι δʼ εἰσὶ κατοικία τις ἐπὶ τῷ Κηφισσῷ ἱδρυμένη πλησίον Φανοτεῦσι καὶ Χαιρωνεῦσι καὶ Ἐλατείᾳ. φησὶ δὲ Θεόπομπος τὸν τόπον τοῦτον διέχειν τῆς μὲν Χαιρωνείας ὅσον τετταράκοντα σταδίους, διορίζειν δὲ τοὺς Ἀμβρυσέας καὶ Πανοπέας καὶ Δαυλιέας· κεῖσθαι δʼ ἐπὶ τῆς ἐμβολῆς τῆς ἐκ Βοιωτίας εἰς Φωκέας ἐν λόφῳ μετρίως ὑψηλῷ, μεταξὺ τοῦ τε Παρνασσοῦ καὶ τοῦ [Ἁδυλίου ὄ]ρους[3] πενταστάδιον σχεδόν τι ἀπολειπόντων ἀν[ὰ μέσον χω]ρίον,[4] διαιρεῖν δὲ τὸν Κηφισσόν, στενὴν ἑκατέρωθεν διδόντα πάροδον, τὰς μὲν ἀρχὰς ἐκ Λιλαίας ἔχοντα Φωκικῆς πόλεως (καθάπερ καὶ Ὅμηρός φησιν,

οἵ τε Λίλαιαν ἔχον πηγῇς ἔπι Κηφισσοῖο),

εἰς δὲ τὴν Κωπαΐδα λίμνην ἐκδιδόντα· τὸ δὲ Ἁδύλιον[5] παρατείνειν ἐφʼ ἑξήκοντα σταδίους

[1] ἐκείνου Bno.

[2] Θετταλίας, *man. sec.* in *n*, for θαλάττης; so the later editors.

[3] [Ἁδυλίου ὄ]ρους, lacuna of about seven letters supplied by Kramer. Ἡδυλίου, Politus on Eustathius, II. 567.

as I have said,[1] the Hyantes were banished from Boeotia. This city is very far inland, near Parapotamii, and is not the same as Hyampeia on Parnassus; also far inland is Elateia, the largest city of the Phocians, which is unknown by Homer, for it is more recent than the Homeric age, and it is advantageously situated in that it commands the passes from Thessaly. Demosthenes[2] clearly indicates the natural advantage of its position when he speaks of the commotion that suddenly took place at Athens when a messenger came to the Prytanes with the report that Elateia had been captured.[3]

16. Parapotamii is a settlement on the Cephissus River near Phanoteus and Chaeroneia and Elateia. Theopompus says that this place is distant from Chaeroneia about forty stadia and marks the boundary of the territories of the Ambryseans, the Panopeans and the Daulians; and that it lies on a moderately high hill at the pass which leads from Boeotia into Phocis, between the mountains Parnassus and Hadylius, between which is left a tract of about five stadia divided by the Cephissus River, which affords a narrow pass on each side. The river, he continues, has its beginnings in the Phocian city Lilaea (just as Homer says, "and those who held Lilaea, at the fountains of Cephissus"),[4] and empties into Lake Copais; and the mountain Hadylius extends over a

[1] 9. 2. 3. Cf. 10. 3. 4.
[2] *On the Crown*, 168.
[3] By Philip in 338 B.C.
[4] *Iliad* 2. 523.

[4] *ἀν[ὰ μέσον χω]ρίον* (*ρίων* A, *δρίων* B*ikno*), lacuna of about six letters, supplied by Meineke, following conj. of Kramer.

[5] Ἀδύλιον, Kramer (Ἡδύλιον, Politus), for Δαύλιον; so the later editors.

μέχρι τοῦ Ἀκοντίου,[1] ἐφ' ᾧ κεῖται ὁ Ὀρχομενός. καὶ Ἡσίοδος δ' ἐπὶ πλέον περὶ τοῦ ποταμοῦ λέγει καὶ τῆς ῥύσεως, ὡς δι' ὅλης ῥέοι τῆς Φωκίδος σκολιῶς καὶ δρακοντοειδῶς·

> παρὲκ Πανοπῆα[2] διὰ Γλήχωνά τ' ἐρυμνὴν
> καί τε[3] δι' Ὀρχομενοῦ εἱλιγμένος εἶσι, δράκων ὥς.

τὰ δὲ στενὰ τὰ περὶ τοὺς Παραποταμίους[4] ἢ τὴν Παραποταμίαν (λέγεται γὰρ ἀμφοτέρως) περιμάχητα ὑπῆρξεν ἐν τ[ῷ Φωκικῷ πολέ]μῳ,[5] μίαν ἐχόντων ταύτην ἐμβολὴν [εἰς τὴν Φωκίδα[6]]. ἔστι δὲ Κηφισσὸς ὅ τε Φωκικὸς καὶ ὁ Ἀθήνησι καὶ ὁ ἐν Σαλαμῖνι, τέταρτος δὲ καὶ πέμπτος ὁ ἐν Σικυῶνι καὶ ὁ ἐν Σκύρῳ, ἕκτος δὲ ὁ ἐν Ἄργει, τὰς πηγὰς ἔχων ἐκ Λυρκείου·[7] ἐν Ἀπολλωνίᾳ δὲ τῇ πρὸς Ἐπιδάμνῳ πηγή ἐστι κατὰ τὸ γυμνάσιον, ἣν καλοῦσι Κηφισσόν.

17. Δαφνοῦς δὲ νῦν μὲν κατέσκαπται· ἦν δέ ποτε τῆς Φωκίδος πόλις ἁπτομένη τῆς Εὐβοϊκῆς θαλάττης, διαιροῦσα τοὺς Ἐπικνημιδίους Λοκρούς, τοὺς μὲν ἐπὶ τὸ πρὸς Βοιω[τίαν μέρος, τοὺς δὲ πρὸς[8]] Φωκίδα τὴν ἀπὸ θαλάττης καθήκ[ουσαν
C 425 τότε ἐπὶ θάλατταν[9]]. τεκμήριον δὲ τὸ ἐν αὐτῷ

[1] Ἀκοντίου, Palmer, for Ὑφαντείου, Kramer approving.

[2] Πανοπῆα, Meineke, for Πανοπη *Ag*, Πανοπίδα *Bkno* and editors before Kramer.

[3] τε, Corais, for δέ; so later editors.

[4] Παραποταμίους, *man. sec.* in *n*, for ποταμούς; so the editors.

[5] τ[ῷ Φωκικῷ πολέ]μῳ, lacuna of about thirteen letters supplied by Groskurd.

distance of sixty stadia as far as the mountain Acontius,[1] where Orchomenus is situated. And Hesiod, too, describes at considerable length the river and the course of its flow, saying that it flows through the whole of Phocis in a winding and serpentine course; "like a dragon it goes in tortuous courses out past Panopeus and through strong Glechon and through Orchomenus."[2] The narrow pass in the neighbourhood of Parapotamii, or Parapotamia (for the name is spelled both ways), was an object of contention in the Phocian war, since the enemy had here their only entrance into Phocis. There are, besides the Phocian Cephissus, the one at Athens, the one in Salamis, a fourth and a fifth in Sicyon and in Scyros, and a sixth in Argos, which has its sources in Mt. Lyrceius; and at Apollonia near Epidamnus there is a fountain near the gymnasium which is called Cephissus.

17. Daphnus is now rased to the ground. It was at one time a city of Phocis, bordering on the Euboean Sea; it divided the Epicnemidian Locrians into two parts, one part in the direction of Boeotia, and the other facing Phocis, which at that time reached from sea to sea. And evidence of this

[1] Cf. 9. 2. 42.

[2] A fragment otherwise unknown (*Frag.* 37, Rzach).

---

[6] [εἰς τὴν Φωκίδα], lacuna of about fifteen letters supplied by Meineke, following conj. of Kramer.

[7] ἔκτος . . . Λυρκείου, ejected by Meineke (cp. 6. 2. 4, 8. 6. 7).

[8] Βοιω[τίαν μέρος, τοὺς δὲ πρός], lacuna of about eighteen letters supplied by Groskurd; so the later editors.

[9] καθήκ[ουσαν τότε ἐπὶ θάλατταν], lacuna of about eighteen letters supplied by Groskurd; so the later editors.

Σχεδιεῖον, ὅ φασιν εἶναι τάφον Σχεδίου. [εἴρη]ται[1] δὲ ὁ Δαφνοῦς ἐφ' ἑκάτερα τὴν Λοκρίδα [σχίσαι, ὥστε[2]] μηδαμοῦ ἅπτεσθαι ἀλλήλων τούς τ' Ἐπικνημι[δίους καὶ το]ὺς[3] Ὀπουντίους· ὕστερον δὲ προσωρίσθη τοῖς [Ὀπουντίοις ὁ τόπος.[4]] περὶ μὲν δὴ τῆς Φωκίδος ἀπόχρη.

IV

1. Ἐφεξῆς δ' ἐστὶν ἡ Λοκρίς, ὥστε περὶ ταύτης λεκτέον. διῄρηται δὲ δίχα· τὸ μὲν γὰρ αὐτῆς ἐστιν οἱ πρὸς Εὔβοιαν Λοκροί, [οὓς ἐλέ]γομεν[5] σχίζεσθαί ποτε ἐφ' ἑκάτερα τοῦ Δαφνοῦντος· ἐπεκαλοῦντο δ' οἱ μὲν Ὀπούντιοι ἀπὸ τῆς μητροπόλεως, οἱ δ' Ἐπικνημίδιοι ἀπὸ ὄρους τινὸς Κνημῖδος· τὸ δὲ λοιπὸν οἱ ἑσπέριοί εἰσι Λοκροί, οἱ δ' αὐτοὶ καὶ Ὀζόλαι καλοῦνται. χωρίζει δ' αὐτοὺς ἀπὸ τῶν Ὀπουντίων καὶ τῶν Ἐπικνημιδίων ὅ τε Παρνασσὸς μεταξὺ ἱδρυμένος καὶ ἡ τῶν Δωριέων τετράπολις. ἀρκτέον δ' ἀπὸ τῶν Ὀπουντίων.

2. Ἐφεξῆς τοίνυν ταῖς Ἁλαῖς,[6] εἰς ἃς κατέληξεν[7] ἡ Βοιωτιακὴ παραλία ἡ πρὸς Εὐβοίᾳ,

[1] [εἴρη]ται, lacuna of about four letters supplied by Kramer; so the later editors.

[2] [σχίσαι, ὥστ]ε, lacuna of about eighteen letters supplied by Groskurd; so the later editors.

[3] Ἐπικνημι[δίους καὶ το]ύς, lacuna of about ten letters supplied by Groskurd; so the later editors.

[4] [Ὀπουντίοις ὁ τόπος], lacuna of about twelve letters supplied by Kramer from conj. of Groskurd.

is the Schedieium in Daphnus, which, they say, is the tomb of Schedius; but as I have said,[1] Daphnus "split"[2] Locris on either side, so that the Epicnemidian and Opuntian Locrians nowhere bordered on one another; but in later times the place was included within the boundaries of the Opuntians. Concerning Phocis, however, I have said enough.

IV

1. LOCRIS comes next in order, and therefore I must describe this country. It is divided into two parts: one part is that which is inhabited by the Locrians and faces Euboea; and, as I was saying, it was once split into two parts, one on either side of Daphnus. The Opuntians were named after their metropolis,[3] and the Epicnemidians after a mountain called Cnemis. The rest of Locris is inhabited by the Western Locrians, who are also called Ozolian Locrians. They are separated from the Opuntians and the Epicnemidians by Parnassus, which is situated between them, and by the Tetrapolis of the Dorians. But I must begin with the Opuntians.

2. Next, then, after Halae,[4] where that part of the Boeotian coast which faces Euboea terminates,

[1] 9. 3. 1.

[2] The Greek word for "split" is "schidzo," which Strabo connects etymologically with "Schedius" (see *Iliad* 2. 517).

[3] Opus.

[4] See 9. 2. 13.

---

[5] [οὓς ἐλέ]γομεν, lacuna of about six letters supplied by Kramer; so the later editors.

[6] Ἁλαῖς, Holstenius, for ἄλλαις; so the later editors.

[7] κατέληξεν, Meineke emends to κατέληγεν.

τὸν Ὀπούντιον κόλπον κεῖσθαι συμβαίνει. ὁ δ' Ὀποῦς ἐστὶ μητρόπολις, καθάπερ καὶ τὸ ἐπίγραμμα δηλοῖ τὸ ἐπὶ τῇ πρώτῃ τῶν πέντε στηλῶν τῶν περὶ Θερμοπύλας ἐπιγεγραμμένον πρὸς τῷ πολυανδρίῳ·

τούσδε ποθεῖ φθιμένους ὑπὲρ Ἑλλάδος ἀντία Μήδων,
μητρόπολις Λοκρῶν εὐθυνόμων Ὀπόεις.[1]

ἀπέχει δὲ τῆς θαλάττης περὶ πεντεκαίδεκα σταδίους, τοῦ δ' ἐπινείου[2] καὶ ἑξήκοντα. Κῦνος δ' ἐστὶ τὸ ἐπίνειον, ἄκρα τερματίζουσα τὸν Ὀπούντιον κόλπον σταδίων ὄντα περὶ τετταράκοντα· μεταξὺ δὲ Ὀποῦντος καὶ Κύνου πεδίον εὔδαιμον· κεῖται δὲ κατὰ Αἰδηψὸν τῆς Εὐβοίας, ὅπου τὰ θερμὰ τὰ Ἡρακλέους, πορθμῷ διειργόμενος σταδίων ἑξήκοντα καὶ ἑκατόν. ἐν δὲ τῷ Κύνῳ Δευκαλίωνά φασιν οἰκῆσαι,[3] καὶ τῆς Πύρρας αὐτόθι δείκνυται σῆμα, τοῦ δὲ Δευκαλίωνος Ἀθήνησι. διέχει δὲ τῆς Κνημῖδος ὁ Κῦνος ὅσον πεντήκοντα σταδίους. καὶ ἡ Ἀταλάντη δὲ νῆσος κατὰ Ὀποῦντα ἵδρυται, ὁμώνυμος τῇ πρὸ τῆς Ἀττικῆς. λέγεσθαι δ' Ὀπουντίους τινὰς καὶ ἐν τῇ Ἠλείᾳ φασίν, ὧν οὐκ ἄξιον μεμνῆσθαι, πλὴν ὅτι συγγένειαν αὐτῶν ἐξανανεοῦνται τοῖς Ὀπουντίοις ὑπάρχουσαν. ὅτι δ' ἐξ Ὀποῦντος ἦν ὁ Πάτροκλος, λέγει Ὅμηρος, καὶ διότι φόνον ἀκούσιον πράξας ἔφυγεν εἰς Πηλέα, ὁ δὲ πατὴρ Μενοίτιος ἔμεινεν ἐν τῇ πατρίδι· ἐκεῖσε γάρ φησιν ὁ Ἀχιλλεὺς ὑπο-

[1] Ὀπίοις A, Ὀπόεις *Bkh.* For variants of εὐθυνόμων Ὀπόεις see Müller, *Ind. Var. Lect.*

[2] δὲ Πηνειοῦ *Ahnop.*

lies the Opuntian Gulf. Opus is the metropolis, as is clearly indicated by the inscription on the first of the five pillars in the neighbourhood of Thermopylae, near the Polyandrium:[1] "Opöeis, metropolis of the Locrians of righteous laws, mourns for these who perished in defence of Greece against the Medes." It is about fifteen stadia distant from the sea, and sixty from the sea-port. Cynus is the sea-port, a cape which forms the end of the Opuntian Gulf, the gulf being about forty stadia in extent. Between Opus and Cynus is a fertile plain; and Cynus lies opposite Aedepsus in Euboea, where are the hot waters of Heracles, and is separated from it by a strait one hundred and sixty stadia[2] wide. Deucalion is said to have lived in Cynus; and the grave of Pyrrha is to be seen there, though that of Deucalion is to be seen at Athens. Cynus is about fifty stadia distant from Mount Cnemis. The island Atalanta is also situated opposite Opus, and bears the same name as the island in front of Attica. It is said that a certain people in Eleia are also called Opuntians, but it is not worth while to mention them, except to say that they are reviving a kinship which exists between them and the Opuntians. Now Homer says that Patroclus was from Opus,[3] and that after committing an involuntary murder he fled to Peleus, but that his father Menoetius remained in his native land; for thither Achilles says that he promised Menoetius to bring

[1] A polyandrium is a place where many heroes are buried.
[2] An error. The actual distance is about half this.
[3] *Iliad* 23. 85.

---

[8] οἰκεῖσθαι *Bklno*, ᾠκῆσθαι, Tzschucke.

σχέσθαι τῷ Μενοιτίῳ κατάξειν τὸν Πάτροκλον ἐκ τῆς στρατείας ἐπανελθόντα. οὐ μὴν ἐβασίλευέ γε ἐκεῖνος τῶν Ὀπουντίων, ἀλλ' Αἴας ὁ Λοκρός, πατρίδος ὤν, ὥς φασι, Ναρύκου.[1] Αἰάνην δ' ὀνομάζουσι τὸν ἀναιρεθέντα ὑπὸ τοῦ Πατρόκλου, ἀφ' οὗ καὶ τέμενος Αἰάνειον δείκνυται καὶ κρήνη τις Αἰανίς.

C 426 3. Ἑξῆς μετὰ τὸν Κῦνον Ἀλόπη ἐστὶ καὶ ὁ Δαφνοῦς, ὃν ἔφαμεν κατεσπάσθαι· λιμὴν δ' ἐστὶν αὐτόθι διέχων Κύνου περὶ ἐνενήκοντα σταδίους, Ἐλατείας δὲ πεζεύοντι εἰς τὴν μεσόγαιαν ἑκατὸν εἴκοσι. ἤδη δ' ἐστὶ ταῦτα τοῦ Μαλιακοῦ κόλπου· μετὰ γὰρ τὸν Ὀπούντιον συνεχής ἐστιν οὗτος.

4. Μετὰ δὲ Δαφνοῦντα Κνημῖδες, χωρίον ἐρυμνόν, ὅσον σταδίους εἴκοσι πλεύσαντι· καθ' ὃ τὸ Κήναιον ἐκ τῆς Εὐβοίας ἀντίκειται, ἄκρα βλέπουσα πρὸς ἑσπέραν καὶ τὸν Μαλιέα κόλπον, πορθμῷ διειργομένη σχεδὸν εἰκοσασταδίῳ. ταῦτα δ' ἤδη τῶν Ἐπικνημιδίων ἐστὶ Λοκρῶν. ἐνταῦθα καὶ αἱ Λιχάδες καλούμεναι τρεῖς νῆσοι πρόκεινται, ἀπὸ Λίχα τοὔνομα ἔχουσαι· καὶ ἄλλαι δ' εἰσὶν ἐν τῷ λεχθέντι παράπλῳ, ἃς ἑκόντες παραλείπομεν. μετὰ δὲ εἴκοσι σταδίους ἀπὸ Κνημίδων λιμήν, ὑπὲρ οὗ κεῖται τὸ Θρόνιον ἐν σταδίοις τοῖς ἴσοις κατὰ τὴν μεσόγαιαν. εἶθ' ὁ Βοάγριος ποταμὸς ἐκδίδωσιν ὁ παραρρέων τὸ Θρόνιον, Μάνην δ' ἐπονομάζουσιν αὐτόν· ἔστι δὲ χειμάρρους, ὥστ' ἀβρόχοις ἐμβαίνειν τοῖς ποσίν, ἄλλοτε δὲ καὶ δίπλεθρον ἴσχειν πλάτος. μετὰ δὲ ταῦτα Σκάρφεια, σταδίοις ὑπερκειμένη τῆς θαλάττης δέκα,

[1] φασι, Ναρύκου, Tzschucke, for φασιν, Ἀρύκου.

back Patroclus when Patroclus should return from the expedition. However, Menoetius was not king of the Opuntians, but Aias the Locrian, whose native land, as they say, was Narycus. They call the man who was slain by Patroclus "Aeanes"; and both a sacred precinct, the Aeaneium, and a spring, Aeanis, named after him, are to be seen.

3. Next after Cynus, one comes to Alopê and to Daphnus, which latter, as I said, is rased to the ground;[1] and here there is a harbour which is about ninety stadia distant from Cynus, and one hundred and twenty stadia from Elateia, for one going on foot into the interior. We have now reached the Maliac Gulf, which is continuous with the Opuntian Gulf.

4. After Daphnus one comes to Cnemides, a natural stronghold, about twenty stadia by sea; and opposite it, in Euboea, lies Cenaeum, a cape facing the west and the Maliac Gulf, and separated from it by a strait about twenty stadia in width. At this point we have now reached the territory of the Epicnemidian Locrians. Here, too, lying off the coast, are the three Lichades Islands, as they are called, named after Lichas; and there are also other islands along the coast, but I am purposely omitting them. After twenty stadia from Cnemides one comes to a harbour, above which, at an equal distance in the interior, lies Thronium. Then one comes to the Boagrius River, which flows past Thronium and empties into the sea. They also call it Manes. It is a winter-stream, so that at times one can cross it dry-shod, though at other times it has a breadth of two plethra. After this one comes to Scarpheia, which is situated ten stadia above the

[1] 9. 3. 1.

διέχουσα μὲν[1] τοῦ Θρονίου τριάκοντα, ἐλάττοσι δὲ μικρῷ [τοῦ λιμένος αὐτοῦ. ἔπειτα[2]] Νίκαιά ἐστι καὶ αἱ Θερμοπύλαι.

5. Τῶν δὲ λοιπῶν πόλεων τῶν μὲν ἄλλων οὐκ ἄξιον μεμνῆσθαι, ὧν δ' Ὅμηρος μέμνηται, Καλλίαρος μὲν οὐκέτι οἰκεῖται, [εὐήροτον δὲ νῦν ἐσ]τὶ[3] πεδίον, καλοῦσι δ'[4] οὕτως ἀπὸ τοῦ [συμβεβηκότος· καὶ Βῆσσα δ'[5]] οὐκ ἔστι, δρυμώδης τις τόπος· οὐδ' [αἱ Αὐγειαί, ὧν τὴν χώ]ραν[6] ἔχουσι Σκαρφιεῖς· ταύτην μὲν οὖν τὴν Βῆσσαν ἐν τοῖς δυσὶ γραπτέον σῖγμα (ἀπὸ γὰρ τοῦ δρυμώδους ὠνόμασται ὁμωνύμως, ὥσπερ καὶ Νάπη ἐν τῷ Μηθύμνης πεδίῳ, ἣν Ἑλλάνικος ἀγνοῶν [7] Λάπην ὀνομάζει), τὸν δ' ἐν τῇ Ἀττικῇ δῆμον, ἀφ' οὗ Βησαιεῖς οἱ δημόται λέγονται, ἐν τῷ ἑνὶ σῖγμα.[8]

6. Ἡ δὲ Τάρφη[9] κεῖται ἐφ' ὕψους, διέχουσα Θρονίου[10] σταδίους εἴκοσι, χώραν δ' εὔκαρπόν τε καὶ εὔδενδρον ἔχει· ἤδη γὰρ καὶ αὕτη ἀπὸ τοῦ δάσους ὠνόμασται. καλεῖται δὲ νῦν Φαρύγαι· ἵδρυται δ' αὐτόθι Ἥρας Φαρυγαίας ἱερόν, ἀπὸ

[1] μέν, Jones, for δέ, following conj. of Kramer.

[2] [τοῦ λιμένος αὐτοῦ. ἔπειτα], lacuna of about sixteen letters in A supplied by the second hand (ἔπειτα) and by Groskurd.

[3] [εὐήροτον δὲ νῦν ἐσ]τί, lacuna of about fourteen letters supplied by Du Theil (see Eustathius on *Iliad* 2. 532); so Meineke.

[4] καλοῦσι δ', Meineke, for καλοῦσιν.

[5] [συμβεβηκότος· καὶ Βῆσσα δ'], lacuna of about eighteen letters supplied by Du Theil; so Meineke.

[6] [αἱ Αὐγειαί, ὧν τὴν χώ]ραν, lacuna of about eighteen letters supplied by Meineke.

[7] Before Λάπην A leaves a space for about five letters.

[8] After σῖγμα *Bkno* add γράφουσιν.

sea, thirty stadia distant from Thronium, and slightly less from the harbour itself. Then one comes to Nicaea and Thermopylae.

5. As for the remaining cities, it is not worth while to mention any of them except those which are mentioned by Homer. Calliarus is no longer inhabited, but is now a beautifully-tilled plain, and they so call it from what is the fact in the case.[1] Bessa, too, does not exist; it is a wooded place. Neither does Augeiae, whose territory is held by the Scarphians. Now this Bessa should be written with a double *s* (for it is named from its being a wooded place, being spelled the same way—like Napê[2] in the plain of Methymnê, which Hellanicus ignorantly names Lapê), whereas the deme in Attica, whose inhabitants are accordingly called Besaeeis, should be written with one *s*.

6. Tarphê is situated on a height, at a distance of twenty stadia from Thronium; its territory is both fruitful and well-wooded, for already[3] this place had been named from its being thickly wooded. But it is now called Pharygae; and here is situated a temple of Pharygaean Hera, so called from the

[1] *i.e.* from καλός (beautiful) and ἀρόω (till). Eustathius (note on *Iliad* 2. 531) says: "Calliarus, they say, was named after Calliarus, son of Hodoedocus and Laonomê; others say that it was named Calliara, in the neuter gender, because the land there was beautifully tilled."

[2] Both "bessa" and "napê" mean "wooded glen."

[3] *i.e.* in the time of Homer, who names Tarphê (cp. "tarphos," "thicket") and Thronium together, *Iliad* 2. 533.

---

[9] Τάρφη, for Σκάρφη (see Σκάρφεια 9. 4. 4), Kramer, following Tzschucke; so the later editors.

[10] Θρονίου, Groskurd inserts; so the later editors.

τῆς ἐν Φαρύγαις τῆς Ἀργείας· καὶ δὴ καὶ ἄποικοί φασιν εἶναι Ἀργείων.

7. Τῶν γε μὴν Ἑσπερίων Λοκρῶν Ὅμηρος οὐ μέμνηται, ἢ οὐ ῥητῶς γε, ἀλλὰ μόνον τῷ δοκεῖν ἀντιδιαστέλλεσθαι τούτοις ἐκείνους, περὶ ὧν εἰρήκαμεν,

Λοκρῶν, οἳ ναίουσι πέρην ἱερῆς Εὐβοίης,

ὡς καὶ ἑτέρων ὄντων· ἀλλ' οὐδ' ὑπὸ[1] ἄλλων τεθρύληνται πολλῶν· πόλεις δ' ἔσχον Ἄμφισσάν τε καὶ Ναύπακτον, ὧν ἡ Ναύπακτος συμμένει τοῦ Ἀντιρρίου πλησίον, ὠνόμασται δ' ἀπὸ τῆς
C 427 ναυπηγίας τῆς ἐκεῖ γενομένης, εἴτε τῶν Ἡρακλειδῶν ἐκεῖ ναυπηγησαμένων τὸν στόλον, εἴθ' (ὥς φησιν Ἔφορος) Λοκρῶν ἔτι πρότερον παρασκευασάντων· ἔστι δὲ νῦν Αἰτωλῶν, Φιλίππου προσκρίναντος.

8. Αὐτοῦ δὲ καὶ ἡ Χαλκίς, ἧς μέμνηται καὶ ὁ ποιητὴς ἐν τῷ Αἰτωλικῷ καταλόγῳ, ὑποκάτω Καλυδῶνος· αὐτοῦ δὲ καὶ ὁ Ταφιασσὸς λόφος, ἐν ᾧ τὸ τοῦ Νέσσου μνῆμα καὶ τῶν ἄλλων Κενταύρων, ὧν ἀπὸ τῆς σηπεδόνος φασὶ τὸ ὑπὸ τῇ ῥίζῃ τοῦ λόφου προχεόμενον δυσῶδες καὶ θρόμβους ἔχον ὕδωρ ῥεῖν· διὰ δὲ τοῦτο καὶ Ὀζόλας καλεῖσθαι τὸ ἔθνος. καὶ ἡ Μολύκρεια δ' ἐστὶ κατὰ τὸ Ἀντίρριον, Αἰτωλικὸν πολίχνιον. ἡ δ' Ἄμφισσα ἐπὶ τοῖς ἄκροις ἵδρυται τοῦ Κρισαίου πεδίου, κατέσπασαν δ' αὐτὴν οἱ Ἀμφικτύονες, καθάπερ εἰρήκαμεν· καὶ Οἰάνθεια δὲ καὶ

[1] οὐδ' ὑπό, Müller-Dübner, following conj. of Kramer, for οὐδ' ὑπὸ τῶν *Bl*, οὔ ποτε other MSS.

Hera in the Argive Pharygae; and, indeed, they say that they are colonists of the Argives.

7. However, Homer does not mention the Western Locrians, or at least not in express words, but only in that he seems by contrast to distinguish these from those other Locrians of whom I have already spoken, when he says, "of the Locrians who dwell opposite sacred Euboea," implying that there was a different set of Locrians. But they have not been much talked about by many others either. The cities they held were Amphissa and Naupactus; of these, Naupactus survives, near Antirrhium, and it was named from the shipbuilding[1] that was once carried on there, whether it was because the Heracleidae built their fleet there, or (as Ephorus says) because the Locrians had built ships there even before that time. It now belongs to the Aetolians, having been adjudged to them by Philip.

8. Here, also, is Chalcis, which the poet mentions in the Aetolian *Catalogue*;[2] it is below Calydon. Here, also, is the hill Taphiassus, on which are the tombs of Nessus and the other Centaurs, from whose putrefied bodies, they say, flows forth at the base of the hill the water which is malodorous and clotted; and it is on this account, they add, that the tribe is also called Ozolian.[3] Molycreia, an Aetolian town, is also near Antirrhium. The site of Amphissa is on the edge of the Crisaean Plain; it was rased to the ground by the Amphictyons, as I have said.[4] And

[1] "Naus" (ship) and "pactos" (put together, built), the Doric spelling of the verbal πηκτός.

[2] *Iliad* 2. 640.

[3] *i.e.* Ozolian Locrians, as well as Western (see 9. 4. 1). The authorities quoted by Strabo derive "Ozolian" from "ozein" (to smell).

[4] 9. 3. 4.

Εὐπάλιον Λοκρῶν εἰσίν. ὁ δὲ πᾶς παράπλους ὁ Λοκρικὸς μικρὸν ὑπερβάλλει τῶν διακοσίων σταδίων.

9. Ἀλόπην δὲ καὶ ἐνταῦθα καὶ ἐν τοῖς Ἐπικνημιδίοις ὀνομάζουσι καὶ ἐν τῇ Φθιώτιδι· οὗτοι μὲν οὖν ἄποικοι τῶν Ἐπικνημιδίων εἰσίν, οἱ δ' Ἐπιζεφύριοι τούτων.

10. Τοῖς δὲ Λοκροῖς τοῖς μὲν Ἑσπερίοις συνεχεῖς εἰσὶν Αἰτωλοί, τοῖς δ' Ἐπικνημιδίοις Αἰνιᾶνες συνεχεῖς οἱ τὴν Οἴτην ἔχοντες, καὶ μέσοι Δωριεῖς. οὗτοι μὲν οὖν εἰσὶν οἱ τὴν τετράπολιν οἰκήσαντες, ἥν φασιν εἶναι μητρόπολιν τῶν ἁπάντων Δωριέων, πόλεις δ' ἔσχον Ἐρινεόν, Βοῖον, Πίνδον, Κυτίνιον· ὑπέρκειται δ' ἡ Πίνδος τοῦ Ἐρινεοῦ, παραρρεῖ δ' αὐτὴν ὁμώνυμος ποταμός, ἐμβάλλων εἰς τὸν Κηφισσὸν οὐ πολὺ τῆς Λιλαίας ἄπωθεν· τινὲς δ' Ἀκύφαντα λέγουσι τὴν Πίνδον. τούτων ὁ βασιλεὺς Αἰγίμιος,[1] ἐκπεσὼν τῆς ἀρχῆς, κατήχθη πάλιν, ὡς ἱστοροῦσιν, ὑφ' Ἡρακλέους· ἀπεμνημόνευσεν οὖν αὐτῷ τὴν χάριν τελευτήσαντι περὶ τὴν Οἴτην· Ὕλλον γὰρ εἰσεποιήσατο τὸν πρεσβύτατον τῶν ἐκείνου παίδων, καὶ διεδέξατο ἐκεῖνος τὴν ἀρχὴν καὶ οἱ ἀπόγονοι. ἐντεῦθεν ὁρμηθεῖσι τοῖς Ἡρακλείδαις ὑπῆρξεν ἡ εἰς Πελοπόννησον κάθοδος.

11. Τέως μὲν οὖν ἦσαν ἐν ἀξιώματι αἱ πόλεις, καίπερ οὖσαι μικραὶ καὶ λυπρόχωροι, ἔπειτ' ὠλιγωρήθησαν· ἐν δὲ τῷ Φωκικῷ πολέμῳ καὶ τῇ

[1] Αἰγίμιος, Kramer, for Αἰπάλιος; so the later editors.

---

[1] He means, apparently, the Ozolian Locrians.

both Oeantheia and Eupalium belong to the Locrians. The whole voyage along the Locrian coast slightly exceeds two hundred stadia in length.

9. There is a place named Alopê, not only here and among the Epicnemidian Locrians, but also in Phthiotis. Now these[1] are colonists of the Epicnemidian Locrians, but the Epizephyrian Locrians are colonists of these.[2]

10. The Aetolians border on the western Locrians; and the Aenianians who inhabit Mount Oeta border on the Epicnemidian Locrians; and in the middle between them are Dorians.[3] Now these Dorians are the people who inhabited the Tetrapolis, which, they say, was the metropolis of all the Dorians; and the cities they held were Erineus, Boeum, Pindus and Cytinium. Pindus is situated above Erineus; and a river bearing the same name flows past it, emptying into the Cephissus not very far from Lilaea. By some, however, Pindus is called Acyphas. The king of these Dorians was Aegimius, who was driven from his throne, but was brought back again, as the story goes, by Heracles; accordingly, Aegimius requited the favour to Heracles after the latter's death on Oeta; for he adopted Hyllus, the eldest of the sons of Heracles; and Hyllus and his descendants became his successors on the throne. From here it was that the Heracleidae set out on their return to the Peloponnesus.

11. Now for a time the cities in question were held in respect, although they were small and had poor soil, but afterwards they were lightly esteemed. During the Phocian War and the domination of the

[2] Again he appears to mean the Ozolian Locrians.
[3] See 9. 3. 1.

Μακεδόνων ἐπικρατείᾳ καὶ Αἰτωλῶν καὶ Ἀθαμάνων θαυμαστόν, εἰ καὶ ἴχνος αὐτῶν εἰς Ῥωμαίους ἦλθε. τὰ δ' αὐτὰ πεπόνθασι καὶ Αἰνιᾶνες· καὶ γὰρ τούτους ἐξέφθειραν Αἰτωλοί τε καὶ Ἀθαμᾶνες, Αἰτωλοὶ μὲν μετὰ Ἀκαρνάνων πολεμοῦντες καὶ μέγα δυνάμενοι, Ἀθαμᾶνες δ' ὕστατοι τῶν Ἠπειρωτῶν εἰς ἀξίωμα προαχθέντες, ἤδη τῶν ἄλλων ἀπειρηκότων, καὶ μετ' Ἀμυνάνδρου τοῦ βασιλέως
C 428 δύναμιν κατασκευασάμενοι. οὗτοι δὲ τὴν Οἴτην διακατεῖχον.

12. Τὸ δ' ὄρος διατείνει ἀπὸ Θερμοπυλῶν καὶ τῆς ἀνατολῆς μέχρι πρὸς τὸν κόλπον τὸν Ἀμβρακικὸν καὶ τὴν ἑσπέραν· τρόπον δέ τινα καὶ πρὸς ὀρθὰς τέμνει τὴν ἀπὸ τοῦ Παρνασσοῦ μέχρι Πίνδου καὶ τῶν ὑπερκειμένων βαρβάρων ὀρεινὴν τὸ ὄρος τοῦτο. τούτου δὴ τὸ μὲν πρὸς Θερμοπύλας νενευκὸς μέρος Οἴτη καλεῖται, σταδίων διακοσίων τὸ μῆκος, τραχὺ καὶ ὑψηλόν, ὑψηλότατον δὲ κατὰ τὰς Θερμοπύλας· κορυφοῦται γὰρ ἐνταῦθα καὶ τελευτᾷ πρὸς ὀξεῖς καὶ ἀποτόμους μέχρι τῆς θαλάττης κρημνούς, ὀλίγην δ' ἀπολείπει πάροδον τοῖς ἀπὸ τῆς παραλίας ἐμβάλλουσιν εἰς τοὺς Λοκροὺς ἐκ τῆς Θετταλίας.

13. Τὴν μὲν οὖν πάροδον Πύλας καλοῦσι καὶ Στενὰ καὶ Θερμοπύλας· ἔστι γὰρ καὶ θερμὰ πλησίον ὕδατα, τιμώμενα ὡς Ἡρακλέους ἱερά· τὸ δ' ὑπερκείμενον ὄρος Καλλίδρομον· τινὲς δὲ καὶ τὸ λοιπὸν τὸ δι' Αἰτωλίας καὶ τῆς Ἀκαρνανίας διῆκον μέχρι τοῦ Ἀμβρακικοῦ κόλπου Καλλίδρομον προσαγορεύουσι. πρὸς δὲ ταῖς Θερμοπύλαις ἐστὶ φρούρια ἐντὸς τῶν Στενῶν, Νίκαια μὲν ἐπὶ θάλατ-

Macedonians, Aetolians, and Athamanians—it is marvellous that even a trace of them passed to the Romans. And the Aenianians had the same experience, for they too were destroyed by the Aetolians and the Athamanians: by the Aetolians, when they waged war in conjunction with the Acarnanians, and were very powerful, and by the Athamanians, when they attained to distinction (the last of the Epeirotes to do so, the other peoples having by this time been worn out) and under their king Amynander had acquired power. These Athamanians kept possession of Oeta.

12. This mountain extends from Thermopylae in the east to the Ambracian Gulf in the west; and, in a way, it cuts at right angles the mountainous country which extends from Parnassus to Pindus and to the barbarians who are situated beyond Pindus. Of this mountain, the part which verges towards Thermopylae is called Oeta; its length is two hundred stadia, and it is rugged and high; but it is highest at Thermopylae, for there it rises into a peak, and ends at the sea in sharp and abrupt precipices, though it leaves a narrow pass for invasions from Thessaly into the country of the Locrians.

13. Now the pass is called not only "Pylae" and "Narrows," but also "Thermopylae,"[1] for there are hot waters near it that are held in honour as sacred to Heracles; and the mountain that lies above it is called Callidromus, but by some the remaining part of the mountain, which extends through Aetolia and Acarnania to the Ambracian Gulf, is also called Callidromus. Near Thermopylae, inside the narrows, are forts—Nicaea, towards the sea of the

[1] "Hot-gates."

ταν Λοκρῶν, Τειχιοῦς δὲ καὶ Ἡράκλεια ὑπὲρ αὐτῆς, ἡ Τραχὶν καλουμένη πρότερον, Λακεδαιμονίων κτίσμα· διέχει δὲ τῆς ἀρχαίας Τραχῖνος περὶ ἓξ σταδίους ἡ Ἡράκλεια· ἑξῆς δὲ ἡ Ῥοδουντία, χωρίον ἐρυμνόν.

14. Ποιεῖ δὲ δυσείσβολα τὰ χωρία ταῦτα ἥ τε τραχύτης καὶ τὸ πλῆθος τῶν ὑδάτων φάραγγας ποιούντων, ἃς διέξεισι. πρὸς γὰρ τῷ Σπερχειῷ τῷ παραρρέοντι τὴν Ἀντίκυραν[1] καὶ ὁ Δύρας[2] ἐστίν, ὅν φασιν ἐπιχειρῆσαι τὴν Ἡρακλέους σβέσαι πυράν· καὶ ἄλλος Μέλας, διέχων Τραχῖνος εἰς πέντε σταδίους. πρὸς δὲ μεσημβρίαν τῆς Τραχῖνός φησιν Ἡρόδοτος εἶναι βαθεῖαν διασφάγα, δι' ἧς Ἀσωπός, ὁμώνυμος τοῖς εἰρημένοις Ἀσωποῖς, εἰς τὴν θάλατταν ἐκπίπτει τὴν ἐκτὸς[3] Πυλῶν, παραλαβὼν καὶ τὸν Φοίνικα ἐκ τῆς μεσημβρίας συμβάλλοντα[4] αὐτῷ, ὁμώνυμον τῷ ἥρωι, οὗ καὶ τάφος πλησίον δείκνυται· στάδιοι δ' εἰσὶν ἐπὶ Θερμοπύλας ἀπὸ τοῦ Ἀσωποῦ πεντεκαίδεκα.

15. Τότε μὲν οὖν ἦν ἐνδοξότατα τὰ χωρία ταῦτα, ἡνίκα τῶν κλείθρων ἐκυρίευε τῶν περὶ τὰ Στενά, καὶ τοῖς ἔξω τῶν Στενῶν πρὸς τοὺς ἐντὸς ἦσαν ἀγῶνες πρωτείων, καθάπερ καὶ πέδας ἐκάλει Φίλιππος τῆς Ἑλλάδος τὴν Χαλκίδα καὶ τὴν Κόρινθον, πρὸς τὰς ἐκ τῆς Μακεδονίας ἀφορμὰς βλέπων· ἐπιδέσμους δ' οἱ ὕστερον προσηγόρευον ταύτας τε καὶ ἔτι τὴν Δημητριάδα· καὶ γὰρ αὕτη

[1] Ἀντίκυραν, Kramer, for Ἀντίκιρραν; so the later editors.
[2] ὁ Δύρας, Hopper, for Ὀλύρας *man. sec.* in A, Ὄλυρος A, ὁ Λύρος *cghi*, ὁ Λύρας *Bkl*; so later editors.
[3] ἐκτός, Groskurd, for ἐντός; so Meineke.
[4] συμβάντα *Bkl*.

Locrians, and above it, Teichius and Heracleia, the latter in earlier times having been called Trachin, a settlement of Lacedaemonians. Heracleia is about six stadia distant from the old Trachin. Next one comes to Rhoduntia, a natural stronghold.

14. These places are rendered difficult of access both by the ruggedness of the country and by the number of streams of water which here form ravines through which they flow. For besides the Spercheius, which flows past Anticyra, there is the Dyras River, which, they say, tried to quench the funeral pyre of Heracles, and also another[1] Melas, which is five stadia distant from Trachin. To the south of Trachin, according to Herodotus,[2] there is a deep gorge through which the Asopus, bearing the same name as the aforesaid Asopus Rivers,[3] empties into the sea outside Pylae after receiving the Phoenix River, which meets it from the south and bears the name of the hero Phoenix, whose tomb is to be seen near it. The distance from the Asopus to Thermopylae is fifteen stadia.

15. Now at that time these places were at the height of their fame when they held the mastery over the keys of the Narrows, and when there were struggles for the primacy between the peoples outside the Narrows and those inside them; for instance, Philip used to call Chalcis and Corinth "the fetters of Greece," having Macedonia in view as his base of operations;[4] and the men of later times called, not only these, but also the city Demetrias "shackles,"

[1] See Vol. III, Book 7, *Frag.* 52.

[2] 7. 198, 200.

[3] 8. 6. 24 and 9. 2. 23.

[4] *i.e.* by holding these places he could control Greece even from distant Macedonia.

παρόδων ἦν κυρία τῶν περὶ τὰ Τέμπη, τό τε
C 429 Πήλιον ἔχουσα καὶ τὴν Ὄσσαν. ὕστερον δὲ πάντων ὑπὸ μίαν ἐξουσίαν ὑπηγμένων, ἅπαντ᾽ ἀτελεύεται[1] πᾶσι καὶ ἀνέῳγε.

16. Περὶ δὲ τὰ Στενὰ ταῦτα οἱ περὶ Λεωνίδαν μετὰ ὀλίγων τῶν ὁμόρων τοῖς τόποις ἀντέσχον πρὸς τὰς τοσαύτας τῶν Περσῶν δυνάμεις, μέχρι περιελθόντες δι᾽ ἀτραπῶν τὰ ὄρη κατέκοψαν αὐτοὺς οἱ βάρβαροι. καὶ νῦν τὸ πολυάνδριον ἐκείνων ἔστι καὶ στῆλαι καὶ ἡ θρυλουμένη ἐπιγραφὴ τῇ Λακεδαιμονίων στήλῃ, οὕτως[2] ἔχουσα·

ὦ ξέν᾽, ἀπάγγειλον Λακεδαιμονίοις, ὅτι τῇδε
κείμεθα τοῖς κείνων πειθόμενοι νομίμοις.

17. Ἔστι δὲ καὶ λιμὴν μέγας αὐτόθι καὶ Δήμητρος ἱερόν, ἐν ᾧ κατὰ πᾶσαν Πυλαίαν θυσίαν ἐτέλουν οἱ Ἀμφικτύονες. ἐκ δὲ τοῦ λιμένος εἰς Ἡράκλειαν τὴν Τραχῖνα πεζῇ στάδιοι τετταράκοντα, πλοῦς δ᾽ ἐπὶ τὸ Κήναιον ἑβδομήκοντα. ἔξω δὲ Πυλῶν εὐθὺς ὁ Σπερχειὸς ἐκδίδωσιν. ἐπὶ δὲ Πύλας ἀπὸ Εὐρίπου στάδιοι πεντακόσιοι τριάκοντα. καὶ ἡ μὲν Λοκρὶς τέλος ἔχει, τὰ δ᾽ ἔξω Θετταλῶν ἐστι τὰ πρὸς ἕω καὶ τὸν Μαλιακὸν κόλπον, τὰ δὲ πρὸς δύσιν Αἰτωλῶν καὶ Ἀκαρνάνων. Ἀθαμᾶνες δὲ καὶ αὐτοὶ ἐκλελοίπασι.

18. Μέγιστον δὴ καὶ παλαιότατον τῶν Θετταλῶν σύστημα, ὧν τὰ μὲν Ὅμηρος εἴρηκε, τὰ δ᾽ ἄλλοι πλείους. Αἰτωλοὺς δ᾽ Ὅμηρος μὲν ἀεὶ ἑνὶ ὀνόματι λέγει, πόλεις, οὐκ ἔθνη τάττων ὑπ᾽ αὐτοῖς,

[1] ἅπαντ᾽ ἀτελεύεται, Meineke, for πάντα τελευτᾷ.
[2] The words from οὕτως to ὁ δὲ ποιητής (9. 5. 4) have fallen out in A, but are restored by the second hand.

for Demetrias commanded the passes round Tempê, since it held both Pelion and Ossa. But later, now that all peoples have been brought into subjection to a single power, everything is free from toll and open to all mankind.

16. It was at these Narrows that Leonidas and his men, with a few who came from the neighbourhood thereof, held out against all those forces of the Persians, until the barbarians, coming around the mountains through by-paths, cut them down. And to-day their Polyandrium[1] is to be seen, and pillars, and the oft-quoted inscription on the pillar of the Lacedaemonians, which is as follows: "Stranger, report to the Lacedaemonians that we lie here in obedience to their laws."

17. There is also a large harbour here, and a temple of Demeter, in which at the time of every Pylaean assembly the Amphictyons performed sacrificial rites. From the harbour to Heracleian Trachin the distance on foot is forty stadia, and by boat to Cenaeum seventy stadia. The Spercheius empties immediately outside Pylae. The distance to Pylae from the Euripus is five hundred and thirty stadia. And whereas Locris ends at Pylae, the parts outside Pylae towards the east and the Maliac Gulf belong to the Thessalians, and the parts towards the west belong to the Aetolians and the Acarnanians. As for the Athamanians, they are now extinct.

18. Now the largest and most ancient composite part of the Greeks is that of the Thessalians, who have been described partly by Homer and partly by several others. The Aetolians Homer always speaks of under one name, classing cities, not tribes, under

[1] See 9. 4. 2 and foot-note.

πλὴν εἰ τοὺς Κουρῆτας, οὓς ἐν μέρει τακτέον Αἰτωλικῶν. ἀπὸ Θετταλῶν δ' ἀρκτέον, τὰ μὲν σφόδρα παλαιὰ καὶ μυθώδη, καὶ οὐχ ὁμολογούμενα τὰ πολλά, ἐῶντες, καθάπερ καὶ ἐν τοῖς ἄλλοις ἐποιήσαμεν, τὰ δὲ φαινόμενα ἡμῖν καίρια λέγοντες.

V

1. Ἔστι δ' αὐτῆς πρὸς θαλάττῃ μὲν ἡ ἀπὸ Θερμοπυλῶν μέχρι τῆς ἐκβολῆς τοῦ Πηνειοῦ καὶ τῶν ἄκρων τοῦ Πηλίου παραλία βλέπουσα πρὸς ἕω καὶ πρὸς τὰ ἄκρα τῆς Εὐβοίας τὰ βόρεια. ἔχουσι δὲ τὰ μὲν πρὸς Εὐβοίᾳ καὶ Θερμοπύλαις Μαλιεῖς καὶ οἱ Φθιῶται Ἀχαιοί, τὰ δὲ πρὸς τῷ Πηλίῳ Μάγνητες. αὕτη μὲν οὖν ἡ πλευρὰ τῆς Θετταλίας ἑῴα λεγέσθω καὶ παραλία. ἑκατέρωθεν δ' ἀπὸ μὲν Πηλίου καὶ Πηνειοῦ πρὸς τὴν μεσόγαιαν Μακεδόνες παράκεινται μέχρι Παιονίας [1] καὶ τῶν Ἠπειρωτικῶν ἐθνῶν· ἀπὸ δὲ τῶν Θερμοπυλῶν τὰ παράλληλα τοῖς Μακεδόσιν ὄρη τὰ Οἰταῖα καὶ Αἰτωλικά, τοῖς Δωριεῦσι καὶ τῷ Παρνασσῷ συνάπτοντα· καλείσθω δὲ τὸ μὲν πρὸς τοῖς Μακεδόσι πλευρὸν ἀρκτικόν, τὸ δ' ἕτερον νότιον. λοιπὸν δ' ἐστὶ τὸ ἑσπέριον, ὃ περικλείουσιν Αἰτωλοὶ καὶ Ἀκαρνᾶνες καὶ Ἀμφίλοχοι καὶ τῶν Ἠπειρωτῶν

[1] Groskurd, Du Theil and other scholars wrongly regard Παιονίας as an error (see *Frags.* 10, 11, and 12 *a* on pp. 329 ff. in Vol. III).

---

[1] Cf. 10. 3. 1.
[2] Cf. *Frag.* 12, on page 330 in Vol. III.

them, except the Curetes, who in part should be classified as Aetolians.[1] But I must begin with Thessaly, omitting such things as are very old and mythical and for the most part not agreed upon, as I have already done in all other cases, and telling such things as seem to me appropriate to my purpose.

V

1. Thessaly comprises, first, on the sea, the coast which extends from Thermopylae to the outlet of the Peneius River[2] and the extremities of Pelion, and faces the east and the northern extremities of Euboea. The parts that are near Euboea and Thermopylae are held by the Malians and the Achaean Phthiotae, and the parts near Pelion by the Magnetans. Let this side of Thessaly, then, be called the eastern or coastal side. As for the two sides[3] of Thessaly: on one side, beginning at Pelion and the Peneius,[4] Macedonia stretches towards the interior as far as Paeonia and the Epeirote tribes, and on the other side, beginning at Thermopylae, the Oetaean and Aetolian mountains lie parallel to Macedonia, bordering on the country of the Dorians and on Parnassus.[5] Let the former side, which borders on Macedonia, be called the northern side, and the latter the southern side. There remains the western side, which is surrounded by the Aetolians and Acarnanians and Amphilochians, and, of the Epeirotes, the

[3] *i.e.* the northern and southern boundaries.

[4] The *mouth* of the Peneius.

[5] On the boundaries of Macedonia, see *Frags.* 10, 11, 12*a* and 13 on pp. 329–30 in Vol. III.

C 430 Ἀθαμᾶνες καὶ Μολοττοὶ καὶ ἡ τῶν Αἰθίκων ποτὲ λεγομένη γῆ καὶ ἁπλῶς ἡ περὶ Πίνδον. [ἡ δὲ χώρα πάσης Θετταλίας ἐστὶ πεδιὰς[1]] πλὴν τοῦ Πηλίου καὶ τῆς Ὄσσης. ταῦτ' ἐξῆρται μὲν ἱκανῶς· οὐ μήν γε πολλὴν περιλαμβάνει κύκλῳ χώραν, ἀλλ' εἰς τὰ πεδία τελευτᾷ.

2. Ταῦτα δ' ἐστὶ τὰ μέσα τῆς Θετταλίας, εὐδαιμονεστάτη χώρα, πλὴν ὅση ποταμόκλυστός ἐστιν. ὁ γὰρ Πηνειὸς διὰ μέσης ῥέων καὶ πολλοὺς δεχόμενος ποταμοὺς ὑπερχεῖται πολλάκις· τὸ δὲ παλαιὸν καὶ ἐλιμνάζετο, ὡς λόγος, τὸ πεδίον, ἔκ τε τῶν ἄλλων μερῶν ὄρεσι περιειργόμενον, καὶ τῆς παραλίας μετεωρότερα τῶν πεδίων ἐχούσης τὰ χωρία. ὑπὸ δὲ σεισμῶν ῥήγματος γενομένου κατὰ[2] τὰ νῦν καλούμενα Τέμπη καὶ τὴν Ὄσσαν ἀποσχίσαντος ἀπὸ τοῦ Ὀλύμπου, διεξέπεσε ταύτῃ πρὸς θάλατταν ὁ Πηνειὸς καὶ ἀνέψυξε τὴν χώραν ταύτην. ὑπολείπεται δ' ὅμως ἥ τε Νεσσωνὶς λίμνη μεγάλη καὶ ἡ Βοιβηίς, ἐλάττων ἐκείνης καὶ πλησιεστέρα τῇ παραλίᾳ.

3. Τοιαύτη δ' οὖσα εἰς τέτταρα μέρη διῄρητο· ἐκαλεῖτο δὲ τὸ μὲν Φθιῶτις, τὸ δ' Ἑστιαιῶτις, τὸ δὲ Θετταλιῶτις, τὸ δὲ Πελασγιῶτις. ἔχει δ' ἡ μὲν Φθιῶτις τὰ νότια τὰ παρὰ τὴν Οἴτην ἀπὸ τοῦ Μαλιακοῦ κόλπου καὶ Πυλαϊκοῦ μέχρι τῆς Δολοπίας καὶ τῆς Πίνδου διατείνοντα, πλατυνό-

[1] The words ἡ δὲ . . . πεδιάς are supplied by Jones. Cp. Plato's *Laws* 625 D: τὴν γὰρ τῆς χώρας πάσης Κρήτης φύσιν ὁρᾶτε ὡς οὐκ ἔστι, καθάπερ ἡ τῶν Θετταλῶν, πεδιάς. Others only indicate a lacuna, except Groskurd, who fills the lacuna with too many words.

[2] κατά, Corais inserts. So the later editors.

Athamanians and Molossians and what was once called the land of the Aethices, or, in a word, the land about Pindus.[1] The land of Thessaly, as a whole, is a plain, except Pelion and Ossa. These mountains rise to a considerable height; they do not, however, enclose much territory in their circuits, but end in the plains.

2. These plains are the middle parts of Thessaly, a country most blest, except so much of it as is subject to inundations by rivers. For the Peneius, which flows through the middle of it and receives many rivers, often overflows; and in olden times the plain formed a lake, according to report, being hemmed in by mountains on all sides except in the region of the sea-coast; and there too the region was more elevated than the plains. But when a cleft was made by earthquakes at Tempê, as it is now called, and split off Ossa from Olympus, the Peneius poured out through it towards the sea and drained the country in question. But there remains, nevertheless, Lake Nessonis, which is a large lake, and Lake Boebeïs, which is smaller than the former and nearer to the sea-coast.

3. Such being its nature, Thessaly was divided into four parts. One part was called Phthiotis, another Hestiaeotis,[2] another Thessaliotis, and another Pelasgiotis. Phthiotis occupies the southern parts which extend alongside Oeta from the Maliac, or Pylaïc, Gulf as far as Dolopia and Pindus, and widen out

[1] In 7. 7. 1 and 7. 7. 8 Strabo classes the Amphilochians as Epeirotes.

[2] "Hestiaeotis" is the Attic spelling, and "Histiaeotis" the Ionic and Doric spelling, according to Stephanus Byzantinus, *s.v.* Ἱστίαιαν.

μενα δὲ μέχρι Φαρσάλου[1] καὶ τῶν πεδίων τῶν Θετταλικῶν· ἡ δ' Ἑστιαιῶτις τὰ ἑσπέρια καὶ τὰ μεταξὺ Πίνδου καὶ τῆς ἄνω Μακεδονίας· τὰ δὲ λοιπὰ οἵ τε ὑπὸ τῇ Ἑστιαιώτιδι νεμόμενοι τὰ πεδία, καλούμενοι δὲ Πελασγιῶται,[2] συνάπτοντες ἤδη τοῖς κάτω Μακεδόσι, καὶ οἱ Θετταλιῶται[3] ἐφεξῆς τὰ μέχρι Μαγνητικῆς παραλίας ἐκπληροῦντες χωρία. κἀνταῦθα δ' ἐνδόξων ὀνομάτων ἔσται ἀρίθμησις καὶ ἄλλως καὶ[4] διὰ τὴν Ὁμήρου ποίησιν· τῶν δὲ πόλεων ὀλίγαι σώζουσι τὸ πάτριον ἀξίωμα, μάλιστα δὲ Λάρισα.[5]

4. Ὁ δὲ ποιητὴς εἰς δέκα μέρη καὶ δυναστείας διελὼν τὴν σύμπασαν γῆν, ἣν νῦν Θετταλίαν προσαγορεύομεν, προσλαβὼν τινα καὶ τῆς Οἰταίας καὶ τῆς Λοκρικῆς, ὡς δ' αὔτως καὶ τῆς ὑπὸ Μακεδόσιν νῦν τεταγμένης, ὑπογράφει τι κοινὸν καὶ πάσῃ χώρᾳ συμβαῖνον, τὸ μεταβάλλεσθαι καὶ τὰ ὅλα καὶ τὰ καθ' ἕκαστα παρὰ τὰς τῶν ἐπικρατούντων δυνάμεις.

5. Πρώτους δὴ καταλέγει τοὺς ὑπ' Ἀχιλλεῖ,[6] τοὺς τὸ νότιον πλευρὸν κατέχοντας καὶ πα-

[1] Φαρσάλου, Kramer, for Φαρσαλίου. So the later editors.

[2] Θετταλιῶται *acghi*.

[3] Θετταλιῶται, Müller-Dübner insert, from conj. of Buttmann and Groskurd.

[4] καί, Casaubon inserts. So the later editors.

as far as Pharsalus and the Thessalian plains. Hestiaeotis occupies the western parts and the parts between Pindus and Upper Macedonia.[1] The remaining parts of Thessaly are held, first, by the people who live in the plains below Hestiaeotis (they are called Pelasgiotae and their country borders on Lower Macedonia), and, secondly, by the Thessaliotae next in order, who fill out the districts extending as far as the Magnetan sea-coast. Here, too, there will be an enumeration of famous names of cities, and especially because of the poetry of Homer; only a few of the cities preserve their ancient dignity, but Larisa most of all.

4. The poet, after dividing into ten parts, or dynasties,[2] the whole of the country which we now call Thessaly, and after adding certain parts both of the Oetaean and the Locrian countries, and likewise certain parts of the country now classed under Macedonia, intimates a fact which is common to, and true of, all countries, that whole regions and their several parts undergo changes in proportion to the power of those who hold sway.

5. Now the first peoples he names in the *Catalogue* are those under Achilles, who occupied the southern

[1] See *Frag.* 12 in Vol. III, page 331.

[2] The dynasties of Achilles, Protesilaüs, Eumelus, Philoctetes, Podaleirus, Eurypylus, Polypoetes, Guneus, Prothoüs, and Phoenix, all of whom are mentioned in *Iliad* 2. 685–756, except Phoenix, who in 9. 484 is "lord over the Dolopians" and in 16. 196 is "ruler of the fourth company" of the Myrmidons.

---

[5] Λάρισα, Kramer, for Λάρισσα. So the later editors.

[6] καί, before τούς, omitted by *Bk* and the later editors.

ρακειμένους τῇ τε Οἴτῃ καὶ τοῖς Ἐπικνημιδίοις Λοκροῖς,

ὅσσοι τὸ Πελασγικὸν Ἄργος ἔναιον
οἵ τ' Ἄλον οἵ τ' Ἀλόπην οἵ τε Τρηχῖν' ἐνέμοντο
οἵ τ' εἶχον Φθίην ἠδ' Ἑλλάδα καλλιγύναικα,
Μυρμιδόνες δὲ καλεῦντο καὶ Ἕλληνες καὶ Ἀχαιοί.

C 431 συζεύγνυσι δὲ τούτοις καὶ τοὺς ὑπὸ τῷ Φοίνικι καὶ κοινὸν ἀμφοῖν ποιεῖ τὸν στόλον. ὁ μὲν οὖν ποιητὴς οὐδαμοῦ μέμνηται Δολοπικῆς στρατιᾶς[1] κατὰ τοὺς περὶ Ἴλιον ἀγῶνας· οὐδὲ γὰρ αὐτῶν τὸν ἡγεμόνα Φοίνικα πεποίηκεν εἰς τοὺς κινδύνους ἐξιόντα, καθάπερ τὸν Νέστορα· ἄλλοι δ' εἰρήκασι, καθάπερ καὶ Πίνδαρος μνησθεὶς τοῦ Φοίνικος·

ὃς Δολόπων ἄγαγε θρασὺν ὅμιλον σφενδονᾶσαι,
ἱπποδάμων Δαναῶν βέλεσι πρόσφορον.

τοῦτο δὴ καὶ παρὰ τῷ ποιητῇ κατὰ τὸ σιωπώμενον, ὡς εἰώθασι λέγειν οἱ γραμματικοί, συνυπακουστέον. γελοῖον γὰρ τὸ τὸν βασιλέα μετέχειν τῆς στρατείας

(ναῖον δ' ἐσχατιὴν Φθίης Δολόπεσσιν ἀνάσσων),[2]

τοὺς δ' ὑπηκόους μὴ παρεῖναι· οὐδὲ γὰρ συστρατεύειν ἂν τῷ Ἀχιλλεῖ δόξειεν, ἀλλὰ μόνον ὀλίγων[3] ἐπιστάτης καὶ ῥήτωρ ἕπεσθαι, εἰ δ' ἄρα,

[1] στρατιᾶς, Corais, for στρατείας. So the later editors.
[2] This verse is ejected by Meineke.

side and were situated alongside Oeta and the Epicnemidian Locrians, "all who dwelt in the Pelasgian Argos and those who inhabited Alus and Alopê and Trachin, and those who held Phthia and also Hellas the land of fair women, and were called Myrmidons and Hellenes and Achaeans."[1] With these he joins also the subjects of Phoenix, and makes the expedition common to both leaders. It is true that the poet nowhere mentions the Dolopian army in connection with the battles round Ilium, for he does not represent their leader Phoenix as going forth into the perils of battle either, any more than he does Nestor; yet others so state, as Pindar, for instance, who mentions Phoenix and then says, "who led a throng of Dolopians, bold in the use of the sling and bringing aid to the missiles of the Danaans, tamers of horses."[2] This, in fact, is the interpretation which we must give to the Homeric passage according to the principle of silence, as the grammarians are wont to call it, for it would be ridiculous if the king Phoenix shared in the expedition ("I dwelt in the farthermost part of Phthia, being lord over the Dolopians")[3] without his subjects being present; for if they were not present, he would not have been regarded as sharing in the expedition with Achilles, but only as following him in the capacity of a chief over a few men and as a speaker, perhaps as a

[1] *Iliad* 2. 681. [2] *Frag.* 183 (Bergk).
[3] *Iliad* 9. 484; possibly an interpolation.

---

[3] ὀλίγων ἐστί, Meineke ejects, but Jones retains ὀλίγων.

σύμβουλος. τὰ δ' ἔπη βούλεται καὶ τοῦτο δηλοῦν· τοιοῦτον γὰρ τὸ

μύθων τε ῥητῆρ' ἔμεναι πρηκτῆρά τε ἔργων.

[δῆλος οὖν[1]] ταὐτὰ[2] λέγων, ὡς[3] εἴρηται, τό τε ὑπὸ τῷ Ἀχιλλεῖ [καὶ τῷ Φοίνικι·[4]] αὐτὰ δὲ λεχθέντα περὶ τῶν ὑπ' [Ἀχιλλεῖ ἐν ἀντι]λογίᾳ[5] ἐστί. τό τε Ἄργος τὸ Πελασγικὸν καὶ πόλιν δέχονται Θετταλικὴν[6] περὶ Λάρισαν ἱδρυμένην ποτέ, νῦν δ' οὐκέτι οὖσαν· οἱ δ' οὐ πόλιν, ἀλλὰ τὸ τῶν Θετταλῶν πεδίον, οὕτως ὀνοματικῶς λεγόμενον, θεμένου τοὔνομα Ἄβαντος, ἐξ Ἄργους δεῦρ' ἀποικήσαντος.

6. Φθίαν τε οἱ μὲν τὴν αὐτὴν εἶναι τῇ Ἑλλάδι καὶ Ἀχαΐᾳ, ταύτας δ' εἶναι διατεμνομένης τῆς συμπάσης Θετταλίας θάτερον μέρος τὸ νότιον· οἱ δὲ διαιροῦσιν. ἔοικε δ' ὁ ποιητὴς δύο ποιεῖν τήν τε Φθίαν καὶ τὴν Ἑλλάδα, ὅταν οὕτως φῇ·

οἵ τ' εἶχον Φθίην ἠδ' Ἑλλάδα,

ὡς δυεῖν οὐσῶν· καὶ ὅταν οὕτως φῇ·

ἔπειτ' ἀπάνευθε δι' Ἑλλάδος εὐρυχόροιο,
Φθίην δ' ἐξικόμην,

καὶ ὅτι

πολλαὶ Ἀχαιίδες εἰσὶν ἀν' Ἑλλάδα τε Φθίην τε.

ὁ μὲν οὖν ποιητὴς δύο ποιεῖ, πότερον δὲ πόλεις ἢ

[1] [δῆλος οὖν], lacuna of about seven letters supplied by Kramer, who places a period after λέγων.
[2] ταὐτά, Jones, for ταῦτα, following conj. of Kramer.
[3] ὡς, Jones inserts, following conj. of Müller-Dübner.

counsellor. Homer's verses[1] on this subject mean also to make this clear, for such is the import of the words, "to be a speaker of words and a doer of deeds."[2] Clearly, therefore, he means, as I have already said, that the forces under Achilles and Phoenix are the same. But the aforesaid statements concerning the places subject to Achilles are themselves under controversy. Some take the Pelasgian Argos as a Thessalian city once situated in the neighbourhood of Larisa but now no longer existent; but others take it, not as a city, but as the plain of the Thessalians, which is referred to by this name because Abas, who brought a colony there from Argos, so named it.

6. As for Phthia, some say that it is the same as Hellas and Achaea, and that these constitute the other, the southern, of the two parts into which Thessaly as a whole was divided; but others distinguish between Hellas and Achaea. The poet seems to make Phthia and Hellas two different things when he says, "and those who held Phthia and Hellas,"[3] as though there were two, and when he says, "And then (I fled) far away through spacious Hellas, and I came to Phthia,"[4] and, "There are many Achaean women throughout Hellas and Phthia."[5] So the poet makes them two, but he does not make it plain whether

[1] *i.e.* concerning Phoenix. [2] *Iliad* 9. 443.
[3] *Iliad* 2. 683. [4] *Iliad* 9. 478.
[5] *Iliad* 9. 395.

---

[4] [καὶ τῷ Φοίνικι], lacuna of about seven letters supplied by Kramer. So the later editors.

[5] ὑπ' ['Αχιλλεῖ ἐν ἀντι]λογίᾳ, lacuna supplied by A *man. sec.* (ἐν ἀντι) and by Groskurd ('Αχιλλεῖ).

[6] Θετταλικήν, Tzschucke, for Θετταλονικήν. So the later editors.

χώρας, οὐ δηλοῖ. οἱ δ' ὕστερον τὴν Ἑλλάδα οἱ μὲν εἰπόντες χώραν διατετάσθαι φασὶν εἰς τὰς Θήβας τὰς Φθιώτιδας ἀπὸ Παλαιφαρσάλου· ἐν δὲ τῇ χώρᾳ ταύτῃ καὶ τὸ Θετίδιόν ἐστι πλησίον τῶν Φαρσάλων ἀμφοῖν, τῆς τε παλαιᾶς καὶ τῆς νέας, κἀκ τοῦ Θετιδίου τεκμαιρόμενοι τῆς ὑπὸ τῷ Ἀχιλλεῖ μέρος εἶναι καὶ τήνδε τὴν χώραν· οἱ δ' εἰπόντες πόλιν, Φαρσάλιοι μὲν δεικνύουσιν ἀπὸ ἑξήκοντα σταδίων τῆς ἑαυτῶν πόλεως κατεσκαμ-
C 432 μένην πόλιν, ἣν πεπιστεύκασιν εἶναι τὴν Ἑλλάδα καὶ δύο κρήνας πλησίον, Μεσσηίδα καὶ Ὑπέρειαν, Μελιταιεῖς δ' ἄπωθεν ἑαυτῶν ὅσον δέκα σταδίους ᾠκῆσθαι[1] τὴν Ἑλλάδα πέραν τοῦ Ἐνιπέως, ἡνίκα ἡ ἑαυτῶν πόλις Πύρρα ὠνομάζετο, ἐκ δὲ τῆς Ἑλλάδος, ἐν ταπεινῷ χωρίῳ κειμένης, εἰς τὴν ἑαυτῶν[2] μετοικῆσαι τοὺς Ἕλληνας· μαρτύριον δ' εἶναι τὸν ἐν τῇ ἀγορᾷ τῇ σφετέρᾳ τάφον τοῦ Ἕλληνος, τοῦ Δευκαλίωνος υἱοῦ καὶ Πύρρας. ἱστορεῖται γὰρ ὁ Δευκαλίων τῆς Φθιώτιδος ἄρξαι καὶ ἁπλῶς τῆς Θετταλίας. ὁ δ' Ἐνιπεὺς ἀπὸ τῆς Ὄθρυος παρὰ Φάρσαλον ῥυεὶς εἰς τὸν Ἀπιδανὸν παραβάλλει, ὁ δ' εἰς τὸν Πηνειόν. περὶ μὲν Ἑλλήνων ταῦτα.

7. Φθῖοι δὲ καλοῦνται οἵ τε ὑπ' Ἀχιλλεῖ καὶ ὑπὸ Πρωτεσιλάῳ καὶ Φιλοκτήτῃ· ὁ δὲ ποιητὴς τούτου μάρτυς. εἰπὼν γὰρ ἐν τῷ καταλόγῳ τῶν ὑπ' Ἀχιλλεῖ·

οἵ τ' εἶχον Φθίην,

ἐν τῇ ἐπὶ ναυσὶ μάχῃ τούτους μὲν ὑπομένοντας ἐν ταῖς ναυσὶ πεποίηκε μετὰ τοῦ Ἀχιλλέως καὶ

[1] οἰκεῖσθαι Acghi. [2] αὐτῶν Bklno.

they are cities or countries. As for later authorities, some, speaking of Hellas as a country, say that it stretches from Palaepharsalus[1] to Phthiotic Thebes. In this country also is the Thetideium,[2] near both Pharsaluses, both the old and the new; and they infer from the Thetideium that this country too is a part of that which was subject to Achilles. As for those, however, who speak of Hellas as a city, the Pharsalians point out at a distance of sixty stadia from their own city a city in ruins which they believe to be Hellas, and also two springs near it, Messeïs and Hypereia, whereas the Melitaeans say that Hellas was situated about ten stadia distant from themselves on the other side of the Enipeus, at the time when their own city was named Pyrrha, and that it was from Hellas, which was situated in a low-lying district, that the Hellenes migrated to their own city; and they cite as bearing witness to this the tomb of Hellen, son of Deucalion and Pyrrha, situated in their market-place. For it is related that Deucalion ruled over Phthia, and, in a word, over Thessaly. The Enipeus, flowing from Othrys past Pharsalus, turns aside into the Apidanus, and the latter into the Peneius. Thus much, then, concerning the Hellenes.

7. "Phthians" is the name given to those who were subject to Achilles and Protesilaüs and Philoctetes. And the poet is witness to this, for after mentioning in the *Catalogue* those who were subject to Achilles "and those who held Phthia,"[3] he represents these, in the battle at the ships, as staying behind with Achilles in their ships and as being

[1] Old Pharsalus.
[2] Temple of Thetis, mother of Achilles.
[3] *Iliad* 2. 683.

καθ' ἡσυχίαν ὄντας, τοὺς δ' ὑπὸ Φιλοκτήτῃ μαχομένους ἔχοντας Μέδον[τα κοσμήτορα [1]] καὶ τοὺς ὑπὸ Πρωτεσιλάῳ ὑπὸ [2] Ποδάρκους κοσμηθέντας περὶ [3] ὧν κοινῶς μὲν οὕτω φησίν·

> ἔνθα δὲ Βοιωτοὶ καὶ Ἰάονες ἑλκεχίτωνες,
> Λοκροὶ καὶ Φθῖοι καὶ φαιδιμόεντες Ἐπειοί·

ἰδίως δέ·

> πρὸ Φθίων δὲ Μέδων τε μενεπτόλεμός τε Ποδάρκης.
> οἱ μὲν πρὸ Φθίων μεγαθύμων θωρηχθέντες
> ναῦφιν ἀμυνόμενοι μετὰ Βοιωτῶν [4] ἐμάχοντο.

τάχα δὲ καὶ οἱ σὺν Εὐρυπύλῳ Φθῖοι ἐλέγοντο, ὅμοροι τούτοις ὄντες·[5] νῦν μέντοι Μαγνησίας νομίζουσι τῆς τε ὑπ' Εὐρυπύλῳ τὰ περὶ Ὀρμένιον [6] καὶ τὴν ὑπὸ Φιλοκτήτῃ πᾶσαν· τὴν δ' ὑπὸ Πρωτεσιλάῳ [7] τῆς Φθίας ἀπὸ Δολοπίας καὶ τῆς Πίνδου [8] μέχρι τῆς Μαγνητικῆς θαλάττης· μέχρι δὲ τῆς ὑπὸ Πρωτεσιλάῳ πόλεως Ἀντρῶνος, ἣ νῦν πληθυντικῶς λέγεται, τὸ πλάτος ἀφορίζεται τῆς ὑπὸ Πηλεῖ καὶ Ἀχιλλεῖ γῆς, ἀπὸ τῆς Τραχινίας καὶ τῆς Οἰταίας ἀρξαμένοις· τὸ δ' αὐτὸ σχεδόν τι μῆκός ἐστι τοῦ Μαλιακοῦ κόλπου.

[1] Μέδον[τα κοσμήτορα], lacuna of about thirteen letters supplied by Jones, instead of Kramer's ἡγεμόνα. See *Iliad* 2. 727.

[2] ὑπό, Jones inserts.

[3] [κοσμηθέντας πε]ρί, lacuna of about eleven letters supplied by Jones (see *Iliad* 2. 704).

[4] [μετὰ Βοιω]τῶν, lacuna of about ten letters supplied by Tzschucke from *Iliad* 13. 700.

[5] μένοντες *Acghik*.

[6] Ὀρμένιον, Xylander, for Ὄρμενον. So the later editors.

inactive, but those who were subject to Philoctetes as taking part in the battle, having Medon as "marshal,"[1] and those who were subject to Protesilaüs as "marshalled by Podarces."[2] Concerning these, speaking in a general way, he says, "And there the Boeotians and Ionians with trailing tunics, the Locrians and Phthians and illustrious Epeians";[3] and, in a specific way, "and in front of the Phthians was Medon, and also Podarces steadfast in war. These in their armour, in front of the great-hearted Phthians, were fighting along with the Boeotians in defence of the ships."[4] Perhaps the men with Eurypylus also were called Phthians, since their country indeed bordered on Phthia. Now, however, historians regard as belonging to Magnesia, not only the region round Ormenium, which belonged to the country that was subject to Eurypylus, but also the whole of the country that was subject to Philoctetes; but they regard the country that was subject to Protesilaüs as a part of Phthia, extending from Dolopia and Pindus as far as the Magnetan Sea; whereas the land subject to Peleus and Achilles, beginning at the Trachinian and Oetaean countries, is defined as extending in breadth as far as Antron, the city subject to Protesilaüs, the name of which is now spelled in the plural number. And the Maliac Gulf has about the same length.

[1] *Iliad* 2. 727. [2] *Iliad* 2. 704. [3] *Iliad* 13. 685.
[4] *Iliad* 13. 693, 699. Cf. 2. 727 and 2. 704.

---

[7] Πρωτεσιλάῳ, Kramer inserts from conj. of Du Theil. So the later editors.

[8] τῆς Πίνδου, Du Theil, for τοῦ πεδίου. So the later editors.

8. Περὶ Ἅλου δὲ καὶ Ἀλόπης διαποροῦσι, μὴ οὐ τούτους λέγει τοὺς τόπους, οἳ νῦν ἐν τῷ Φθιωτικῷ τέλει φέρονται, ἀλλὰ τοὺς ἐν Λοκροῖς, μέχρι δεῦρο ἐπικρατοῦντος τοῦ Ἀχιλλέως, ὥσπερ καὶ μέχρι Τραχῖνος καὶ τῆς Οἰταίας. ἔστι γὰρ καὶ Ἅλος καὶ Ἁλιοῦς ἐν τῇ παραλίᾳ τῶν Λοκρῶν, καθάπερ καὶ Ἀλόπη. οἱ δὲ τὸν Ἁλιοῦντα ἀντὶ Ἀλόπης τιθέασι καὶ γράφουσιν οὕτως·

> οἵ θ' Ἅλον οἵ θ' Ἁλιοῦνθ' οἵ τε Τρηχῖν' ἐνέμοντο.

C 433 ὁ δὲ Φθιωτικὸς Ἅλος ὑπὸ τῷ πέρατι κεῖται τῆς Ὄθρυος, ὄρους πρὸς ἄρκτον κειμένου τῇ Φθιώτιδι, ὁμόρου δὲ τῷ Τυφρηστῷ[1] καὶ τοῖς Δόλοψιν, [κἀκεῖθεν[2]] παρατείνοντος εἰς τὰ πλησίον τοῦ Μαλιακοῦ κόλπου. ἀπέχει δὲ Ἰτώνου περὶ ἑξήκοντα σταδίους ὁ Ἅλος ἢ ἡ Ἅλος (λέγεται γὰρ ἀμφοτέρως). ᾤκισε δὲ ὁ Ἀθάμας τὴν Ἅλον, ἀφανισθεῖσαν δὲ[3] συνῴκισαν Φαρσάλιοι[4] χρόνοις ὕστερον. ὑπέρκειται δὲ τοῦ Κροκίου πεδίου· ῥεῖ δὲ ποταμὸς Ἄμφρυσος[5] πρὸς τῷ τείχει. ὑπὸ δὲ τῷ Κροκίῳ Θῆβαί εἰσιν αἱ Φθιώτιδες, καὶ ἡ Ἅλος[6] δὲ Φθιῶτις καλεῖται καὶ[7] Ἀχαϊκή, συνάπτουσα τοῖς Μαλιεῦσιν, ὥσπερ καὶ οἱ τῆς Ὄθρυος πρόποδες. καθάπερ δὲ ἡ Φυλάκη ἡ

[1] Τεφρηστῷ *Acghino*; Τυμφρηστῷ *bk* and editors before Kramer.

[2] [κἀκεῖθεν], lacuna of about eight letters supplied by Pletho on the basis of *Echl.* Meineke writes κἀνθένδε.

[3] δέ, Meineke inserts.

[4] συν[ῴκισαν Φαρσάλιοι], lacuna of about fifteen letters supplied by Kramer. So the later editors.

[5] Ἄμφρυσος, Xylander, for Ἄμφυσσος. So the later editors.

8. But as regards Halus and Alopê, historians are thoroughly in doubt, suspecting that the poet does not mean the places so named which now are classed in the Phthiotic domain, but those among the Locrians, since the dominion of Achilles extended thus far, just as it also extended as far as Trachin and the Oetaean country; for there is both a Halus and a Halius on the seaboard of the Locrians, just as there is also an Alopê. Some substitute Halius for Alopê and write as follows: "and those who dwelt in Halus and in Halius and in Trachin."[1] The Phthiotic Halus is situated below the end of Othrys, a mountain situated to the north of Phthiotis, bordering on Mount Typhrestus and the country of the Dolopians, and extending from there to the region of the Maliac Gulf. Halus (either feminine or masculine, for the name is used in both genders) is about sixty stadia distant from Itonus.[2] It was Athamas who founded Halus, but in later times, after it had been wiped out, the Pharsalians colonised the place. It is situated above the Crocian Plain; and the Amphrysus River flows close to its walls. Below the Crocian Plain lies Phthiotic Thebes. Halus is called both Phthiotic and Achaean Halus, and it borders on the country of the Malians, as do also the spurs of Othrys Mountain. And just as the Phylacê, which was

[1] *Iliad* 2. 682.

[2] On Halus, see Rawlinson's note on "Alus," Herodotus, 7. 173.

---

[6] Instead of ἡ Ἅλος *Bkno* read ἡ χώρα.

[7] ἡ, after καί, Casaubon omits. So in general the later editors.

ὑπὸ Πρωτεσιλάῳ τῆς Φθιώτιδός ἐστι τῆς προσχώρου τοῖς Μαλιεῦσιν, οὕτω καὶ ἡ Ἅλος· διέχει δὲ Θηβῶν περὶ ἑκατὸν σταδίους, ἐν μέσῳ δ' ἐστὶ Φαρσάλου καὶ Φθιωτῶν· Φίλιππος μέντοι Φαρσαλίοις προσένειμεν, ἀφελόμενος τῶν Φθιωτῶν. οὕτω δὲ συμβαίνει τοὺς ὅρους καὶ τὰς συντάξεις τῶν τε ἐθνῶν καὶ τῶν τόπων ἀλλάττεσθαι ἀεί, καθάπερ εἴπομεν. οὕτω καὶ Σοφοκλῆς τὴν Τραχινίαν Φθιῶτιν εἴρηκεν. Ἀρτεμίδωρος δὲ τὴν Ἅλον ἐν τῇ παραλίᾳ τίθησι, ἔξω μὲν τοῦ Μαλιακοῦ κόλπου κειμένην, Φθιῶτιν δέ· προϊὼν γὰρ ἐνθένδε ὡς ἐπὶ τὸν Πηνειὸν μετὰ τὸν Ἀντρῶνα τίθησι Πτελεόν, εἶτα τὸν Ἅλον ἀπὸ τοῦ Πτελεοῦ διέχοντα ἑκατὸν καὶ δέκα σταδίους. περὶ δὲ τῆς Τραχῖνος εἴρηται, ὁποία τις, καὶ ὁ ποιητὴς κατονομάζει.

9. Τοῦ δὲ Σπερχειοῦ μεμνημενος πολλάκις, ὡς ἐπιχωρίου ποταμοῦ, τὰς πηγὰς ἔχοντος ἐκ Τυφρηστοῦ,[1] Δρυοπικοῦ ὄρους τοῦ καλουμένου [2] . . . πρότερον, ἐκδιδόντος δὲ πλησίον Θερμοπυλῶν μεταξὺ αὐτῶν καὶ Λαμίας, δηλοῖ, ὅτι καὶ τὰ ἐντὸς πυλῶν ὅσα τοῦ Μαλιακοῦ κόλπου, και τὰ ἐκτὸς ὑπ' ἐκείνῳ ἦν· ἀπέχει δὲ Λαμίας ὁ Σπερχειὸς περὶ τριάκοντα σταδίους ὑπερκειμένης πεδίου τινὸς καθήκοντος ἐπὶ τὸν Μαλιακὸν κόλ-

[1] Τυφρηστοῦ, Kramer, for Τρυφῆς τοῦ *man. prim.*, Τρυφησσός A *man. sec.*, Τυμφρηστοῦ A (in margin) BEno*p* and editors before Kramer.

[2] The lacuna of about five letters between καλουμένου and *ότερον*, except πρ, has not been supplied with certainty. Groskurd would write Τυμφρηστοῦ; Tzschucke conj. Τεφρηστοῦ; Jones conj. Τέφρα or Τύφρα (see Stephanus and *Etymol. Magnum*, *s.v.* Τυφρηστός).

subject to Protesilaüs, is in that part of Phthiotis which lies next to the country of the Malians, so also is Halus; it is about one hundred stadia distant from Thebes, and it is midway between Pharsalus and the Phthiotae. However, Philip took it away from the Phthiotae and assigned it to the Pharsalians. And so it comes to pass, as I have said before,[1] that the boundaries and the political organisations of tribes and places are always undergoing changes. So, also, Sophocles speaks of Trachinia as belonging to Phthiotis. And Artemidorus places Halus on the seaboard, as situated outside the Maliac Gulf, indeed, but as belonging to Phthiotis; for proceeding thence in the direction of the Peneius, he places Pteleum after Antron, and then Halus at a distance of one hundred and ten stadia from Pteleum. As for Trachin, I have already described it,[2] and the poet mentions it by name.

9. Since the poet often[3] mentions the Spercheius as a river of this country,[4] and since it has its sources in Typhrestus, the Dryopian mountain which in earlier times was called . . .,[5] and empties near Thermopylae and between it and Lamia, he plainly indicates that both the region inside the Gates, I mean in so far as it belonged to the Maliac Gulf, and the region outside the Gates, were subject to Achilles. The Spercheius is about thirty stadia distant from Lamia, which is situated above a certain plain that extends down to the Maliac Gulf. And

[1] 9. 5. 4. Cf. 3. 4. 19, 4. 1. 1, and 8. 3 10.
[2] 9. 4. 13 ff.
[3] Three times only, *Iliad* 16. 174, 176 and 23. 144.
[4] *i.e.* of Achilles' domain.
[5] See critical note.

που· ὅτι δ' ὁ Σπερχειὸς ἐπιχώριος, ἔκ τε τοῦ τρέφειν ἐκείνῳ τὴν κόμην φάσκειν καὶ τοῦ τὸν Μενέσθιον, ἕνα τῶν λοχαγῶν αὐτοῦ, Σπερχειοῦ λέγεσθαι παῖδα καὶ τῆς ἀδελφῆς τῆς Ἀχιλλέως. Μυρμιδόνας δ' εἰκὸς καλεῖσθαι πάντας τοὺς ὑπὸ τῷ Ἀχιλλεῖ καὶ τῷ Πατρόκλῳ, οἳ συνηκολούθησαν ἐξ Αἰγίνης φεύγοντι τῷ Πηλεῖ. Ἀχαιοὶ δ' ἐκαλοῦντο οἱ Φθιῶται πάντες.

10. Διαριθμοῦνται δὲ τὰς ὑπὸ τῷ Φθιωτικῷ τέλει τῷ ὑπ' Ἀχιλλεῖ κατοικίας ἀπὸ[1] Μαλιέων ἀρξάμενοι πλείους μέν, ἐν δ' αὐταῖς Θήβας τὰς Φθιώτιδας, Ἐχῖνον,[2] Λαμίαν,[3] περὶ ἣν ὁ Λαμιακὸς συνέστη πόλεμος Μακεδόσι καὶ Ἀντιπάτρῳ πρὸς Ἀθηναίους· ἐν ᾧ Λεωσθένης τε
C 434 ἔπεσε τῶν Ἀθηναίων στρατηγός, καὶ Λεοννάτος[4] ὁ Ἀλεξάνδρου τοῦ βασιλέως ἑταῖρος· [ἔτι δὲ Ναρθάκιον[5]], Ἐρινεόν, Κορώνειαν, ὁμώνυμον τῇ Βοιωτικῇ, Μελίταιαν,[6] Θαυμακούς, Προέρναν, Φάρσαλον, Ἐρέτριαν, ὁμώνυμον τῇ Εὐβοϊκῇ, Παραχελῳίτας, καὶ τούτους ὁμωνύμους τοῖς Αἰτωλικοῖς· καὶ γὰρ ἐνταῦθά ἐστιν Ἀχελῷος ποταμὸς πλησίον Λαμίας, παρ' ὃν οἰκοῦσιν οἱ Παραχελῳῖται. παρέτεινε δ' ἡ χώρα αὕτη πρὸς ἄρκτον μὲν τῇ τῶν Ἀσκληπιαδῶν τῶν μάλιστα προσεσπερίων, καὶ τῇ Εὐρυπύλου κα[ὶ ἔτι τῇ[7]]

[1] ἀπό, Corais inserts; so the later editors.
[2] Ἐχίναν *Bkl*; ἔχειν ἀνδαμίαν *Acghion.*
[3] See preceding note.
[4] καὶ Λεοννάτος, Corais inserts; so the later editors.
[5] [ἔτι δὲ Ναρθάκ]ιον, lacuna of about thirteen letters supplied by Meineke; only [Ναρθάκ]ιον, Du Theil.
[6] Μελίταιαν, Xylander, for Μελιτεία A, Μελιτείαν other MSS.

he plainly indicates that the Spercheius was a river of this country, not only by the assertion of Achilles that he "fostered the growth of his hair as an offering to Spercheius,"[1] but also by the fact that Menesthius, one of his commanders, was called the son of Spercheius and the sister of Achilles.[2] And it is reasonable to suppose that all the people, the subjects of Achilles and Patroclus, who had accompanied Peleus in his flight from Aegina, were called Myrmidons. And all the Phthiotae were called Achaeans.

10. Historians enumerate the settlements in the Phthiotic domain that was subject to Achilles, and they begin with the Malians. They name several, and among them Phthiotic Thebes, Echinus, Lamia (near which the Lamian War arose between the Macedonians, under Antipater, and the Athenians, and in this war Leosthenes, a general of the Athenians, fell, and also Leonnatus, the comrade of king Alexander), and also Narthacium, Erineus, Coroneia (bearing the same name as the Boeotian city), Melitaea, Thaumaci, Proerna, Pharsalus, Eretria (bearing the same name as the Euboean city), and Paracheloïtae (this, too, bearing the same name as the Aetolian city), for here too, near Lamia, is a river Acheloüs, on whose banks live the Paracheloïtae. This country bordered, in its stretch towards the north, on the country of the most westerly of the Asclepiadae, and on the country of Eurypylus,

[1] *Iliad* 23. 142. [2] *Iliad* 16. 173–175.

---

[7] κα[ὶ ἔτι τῇ], lacuna of about eight letters supplied by Müller-Dübner and Meineke, from conj. of Kramer.

Πρωτεσιλάου, ταῖς πρὸς ἕω κεκλιμέναις, πρὸς νότον δὲ τῇ Οἰταίᾳ, εἰς τετταρεσκαίδεκα δήμους διῃρημένῃ,[1] Ἡράκλειάν τε καὶ τὴν Δρυοπίδα, τετράπολιν γεγονυῖάν ποτε, καθάπερ καὶ τὴν Δωρίδα, μητρόπολιν δὲ τῶν ἐν Πελοποννήσῳ Δρυόπων νομιζομένην. τῆς δ' Οἰταίας καὶ ὁ Ἀκύφας ἐστὶ καὶ Παρασωπιὰς καὶ Οἰνειάδαι καὶ Ἀντίκυρα,[2] ὁμώνυμος τῇ ἐν Λοκροῖς τοῖς Ἑσπερίοις. λέγω δὲ τὰς διατάξεις ταύτας οὐκ ἀεὶ μεμενηκυίας τὰς αὐτάς, ἀλλὰ ποικίλως μεταβεβλημένας· αἱ δ' ἐπισημόταται μάλιστα ἄξιαι μνήμης εἰσί.

11. Τοὺς δὲ Δόλοπας φράζει καὶ ὁ ποιητὴς ἱκανῶς, ὅτι ἐπὶ ταῖς ἐσχατιαῖς εἰσὶ τῆς Φθίας, καὶ ὅτι ὑπὸ τῷ αὐτῷ ἡγεμόνι ἦσαν τῷ Πηλεῖ οὗτοί τε καὶ οἱ Φθιῶται· ἔναιον γάρ, φησίν, ἐσχατιὴν Φθίης[3] Δολόπεσσιν ἀνάσσων, δόντος τοῦ Πηλέως. γειτνιᾷ δὲ τῇ Πίνδῳ καὶ τοῖς περὶ αὐτὴν χωρίοις, Θετταλικοῖς οὖσι τοῖς πλείστοις. διὰ γὰρ τὴν ἐπιφάνειάν τε καὶ τὴν ἐπικράτειαν τῶν Θετταλῶν καὶ τῶν Μακεδόνων οἱ πλησιάζοντες αὐτοῖς μάλιστα τῶν Ἠπειρωτῶν, οἱ μὲν ἑκόντες, οἱ δ' ἄκοντες, μέρη καθίσταντο Θετταλῶν ἢ Μακεδόνων, καθάπερ Ἀθαμᾶνες καὶ Αἴθικες

[1] διῃρημένῃ, Mannert, for διῃρημένη; so later editors.
[2] Ἀντίκιρρα *Bcghlno*.
[3] ἢ Φοίνιξ, after Φθίης, suspected by Kramer; ejected by Meineke.

---

[1] The Trachinian Heracleia (see 9. 4. 13 and 9. 2. 23) was in the Oetaean country (9. 3. 14), and, in the above passage, the same appears to have been true of Dryopis. But something seems to have fallen out of the MSS. after "demes"; and it is not clear whether Strabo means to include Heracleia

and also on that of Protesilaüs, these countries inclining towards the east; and in its stretch towards the south, on the Oetaean country, which was divided into fourteen demes, and also Heracleia and Dryopis,[1] Dryopis having at one time been a tetrapolis, like Doris,[2] and regarded as the metropolis of the Dryopians who lived in the Peloponnesus. To the Oetaean country belong also Acyphas,[3] Parasopias,[4] Oeneiadae, and Anticyra, which bears the same name as the city among the Western Locrians. But I am speaking of these divisions of the country, not as having always remained the same, but as having undergone various changes. However, only the most significant divisions are particularly worthy of mention.

11. As for the Dolopians, the poet himself says clearly enough that they were situated in the farthermost parts of Phthia, and that both these and the Phthiotae were under the same leader, Peleus; for "I dwelt," he says, "in the farthermost part of Phthia, being lord over the Dolopians, whom Peleus gave me."[5] The country borders on Pindus, and on the region round Pindus, most of which belongs to the Thessalians. For both on account of the fame and of the predominance of the Thessalians and the Macedonians, the countries of those Epeirotes who were their nearest neighbours were made, some willingly and the others unwillingly, parts of Thessaly or Macedonia; for instance, the Athamanes,

and Dryopis in the fourteen demes or to name them as additional parts of the Oetaean country.

[2] See 9. 3. 1 and 9. 4. 10. [3] The city Pindus (9. 4. 10).

[4] The same as Parasopii (9. 2. 23).

[5] *Iliad* 9. 483–484 (Phoenix speaking).

καὶ Τάλαρες Θετταλῶν, Ὀρέσται δὲ καὶ Πελαγόνες καὶ Ἐλιμιῶται Μακεδόνων.

12. Ἡ δὲ Πίνδος ὄρος ἐστὶ μέγα, πρὸς ἄρκτον μὲν τὴν Μακεδόνων, πρὸς ἑσπέραν δὲ Περραιβοὺς μετανάστας ἀνθρώπους ἔχον,[1] πρὸς δὲ μεσημβρίαν Δόλοπας, πρὸς ἕω δὲ τὴν Ἑστιαιῶτιν·[2] αὕτη δ' ἐστὶ τῆς Θετταλίας. ἐπ' αὐτῇ δὲ τῇ Πίνδῳ ᾤκουν Τάλαρες, Μολοττικὸν φῦλον, τῶν περὶ τὸν Τόμαρον[3] ἀπόσπασμα, καὶ Αἴθικες, εἰς[4] οὓς ἐξελαθῆναί φησιν ὑπὸ Πειρίθου τοὺς Κενταύρους ὁ ποιητής· ἐκλελοιπέναι δὲ νῦν ἱστοροῦνται. τὴν δ' ἔκλειψιν διττῶς ἀκουστέον· ἢ γὰρ ἀφανισθέντων τῶν ἀνθρώπων καὶ τῆς χώρας τελέως ἠρη-
C 435 μωμένης, ἢ τοῦ ὀνόματος τοῦ ἐθνικοῦ μηκέτι ὄντος, μηδὲ τοῦ συστήματος διαμένοντος τοιούτου. ὅταν οὖν ἄσημον τελέως ᾖ τὸ λειπόμενον νυνὶ σύστημα, οὐκ ἄξιον μνήμης τίθεμεν οὔτ' αὐτὸ οὔτε τοὔνομα τὸ μεταληφθέν, ὅταν δ' ἔχῃ τοῦ μεμνῆσθαι δικαίαν πρόφασιν, λέγειν ἀναγκαῖον τὴν μεταβολήν.

13. Λοιπὸν δ' εἰπεῖν τῆς παραλίας τὴν τάξιν τῆς ὑπὸ τῷ Ἀχιλλεῖ, ἀπὸ Θερμοπυλῶν ἀρξαμένους· τὴν γὰρ Λοκρικὴν καὶ [τὴν Οἰταία]ν[5]

[1] ἔχον, Kramer, for ἔχουσα B(*man. sec.*)*kno*.

[2] πρὸς ἕω δὲ τὴν Ἑστιαιῶτιν, inserted by Pletho; so Corais, Müller-Dübner and Meineke.

[3] Τόμαρον *n* (*man. sec.*) for Ἴσμαρον *Acghino*, Ἴμαρον B*Ekl*; so later editors.

[4] εἰς omitted by MSS., but added later in B*n*; so Corais and later editors.

the Aethices, and the Talares were made parts of Thessaly, and the Orestae, the Pelagonians, and the Elimiotae of Macedonia.

12. The Pindus Mountain is large, having the country of the Macedonians on the north, the Perrhaebian immigrants on the west, the Dolopians on the south, and Hestiaeotis[1] on the east; and this last is a part of Thessaly. The Talares, a Molossian tribe, a branch of those who lived in the neighbourhood of Mount Tomarus, lived on Mount Pindus itself, as did also the Aethices, amongst whom, the poet says, the Centaurs were driven[2] by Peirithoüs; but history now tells us that they are "extinct." The term "extinct" is to be taken in one of two meanings; either the people vanished and their country has become utterly deserted, or else merely their ethnic name no longer exists and their political organisation no longer remains what it was. When, therefore, any present political organisation that survives from an earlier time is utterly insignificant, I hold that it is not worth mentioning, either itself or the new name it has taken; but when it affords a fair pretext for being mentioned, I must needs give an account of the change.

13. It remains for me to tell the order of the places on the coast that were subject to Achilles, beginning at Thermopylae; for I have already spoken of the Locrian and the Oetaean countries.

[1] See 9. 5. 2 and note on "Hestiaeotis."
[2] From Pelion (*Iliad* 2. 744).

---

[5] [τὴν Οἰταία]ν, lacuna of about ten letters supplied by Meineke. [τὴν μεσόγαια]ν, Groskurd and Müller-Dübner.

εἰρήκαμεν. αἱ τοίνυν Θερμοπύλαι τοῦ μὲν Κηναίου διεστήκασιν ἑβδομηκονтаσταδίῳ πορθμῷ, παραπλέοντι δ' ἔξω Πυλῶν τοῦ Σπερχειοῦ ὡς σταδίους δέκα·[1] ἔνθεν δ' εἰς Φάλαρα εἴκοσι· τῶν δὲ Φαλάρων ἀπὸ θαλάσσης ὑπέρκειται πεντήκοντα σταδίους ἡ τῶν [Λαμιέων πόλι]ς.[2] εἶθ' ἑξῆς παραπλεύσαντι σταδίοις ἑκατὸν ὁ Ἐχῖνος ὑπέρκειται. τῆς δ' ἑξῆς παραλίας ἐν μεσογείῳ ἐστὶν ἡ Κρεμαστὴ Λάρισα, εἴκοσι σταδίους αὐτῆς διέχουσα, ἡ δ' αὐτὴ καὶ Πελασγία λεγομένη Λάρισα.[3]

14. Εἶτα Μυόννησος νησίον, εἶτ' Ἀντρών· ἦν δὲ αὕτη ὑπὸ Πρωτεσιλάῳ. τοσαῦτα μὲν περὶ τῆς ὑπὸ τῷ Ἀχιλλεῖ μερίδος. ἐπεὶ δ' ὁ ποιητὴς εἰς πολλὰ καὶ γνώριμα μέρη διε[λὼν δι]ὰ [4] τὸ ὀνομάζειν τούς τε ἡγεμόνας καὶ τὰς ὑπ' αὐτοῖς πόλεις τὸν σύμπαντα τῆς Θετταλίας κύκλον διέταξεν, [ἡμεῖς ἀκολ]ουθοῦντες [5] τούτῳ πάλιν, ὥσπερ ἐν τοῖς ἐπάνω, προσεκπληρώσομεν τὴν λοιπὴν περιοδείαν τῆς χώρας. καταλέγει τοίνυν ἐφεξῆς τοῖς ὑπ' Ἀχιλλεῖ τοὺς ὑπὸ Πρωτεσιλάῳ· οὗτοι δ' εἰσὶν οἱ καὶ ἐφεξῆς ὄντες τῇ ὑπὸ τῷ Ἀχιλλεῖ παραλίᾳ μέχρι Ἀντρῶνος. ὁριζομένη τοίνυν τῆς ἐφεξῆς ἐστὶν ἡ ὑπὸ τῷ Πρωτεσιλάῳ, ἔξω μὲν οὖσα τοῦ Μαλιακοῦ κόλπου, ἔτι δ' ἐντὸς

[1] δέκα (ι') "ten," seems to be an error for ἑβδομήκοντα (ο'), "seventy," as Kramer suggests. Cp. 9. 4. 14, 9. 4. 17, and Herod. 7. 198–200.

[2] [Λαμιέων πόλι]ς, lacuna of about ten letters supplied by Groskurd; so the later editors. See Müller, *Ind. Var. Lect.* p. 1004.

[3] Λάρισα A, *man. prim.*, and the editors, for Λάρισσα.

[4] διε[λὼν δι]ά, lacuna of about four letters supplied by Groskurd; so the later editors.

Thermopylae, then, is separated from Cenaeum by a strait seventy stadia wide; but, to one sailing along the coast beyond Pylae, it is about ten[1] stadia from the Spercheius; and thence to Phalara twenty stadia; and above Phalara, fifty stadia from the sea, is situated the city of the Lamians; and then next, after sailing a hundred stadia along the coast, one comes to Echinus, which is situated above the sea; and in the interior from the next stretch of coast, twenty stadia distant from it, is Larisa Cremastê (it is also called Larisa Pelasgia).

14. Then one comes to Myonnesus, a small island; and then to Antron, which was subject to Protesilaüs. So much, then, for the portion that was subject to Achilles. But since the poet, through naming both the leaders and the cities subject to them, has divided Thessaly into numerous well-known parts and arranged in order the whole circuit of it, I, following him again, as above, shall go on to complete the remainder of my geographical description of the country. Now he enumerates next in order after those who were subject to Achilles those who were subject to Protesilaüs; and these are also the people who come next in order after the stretch of coast which was subject to Achilles as far as Antron. Therefore, the territory that was subject to Protesilaüs is in the boundaries of the country that comes next in order, that is, it lies outside the Maliac Gulf, but still inside Phthiotis, though not

[1] See critical note.

---

[5] [ἡμεῖς ἀκολ]ουθοῦντες, lacuna of about nine letters supplied by Groskurd; so the later editors.

τῆς Φθιώτιδος, οὐ μὴν τῆς [ὑπὸ τῷ Ἀχιλλεῖ.[1]] ἡ μὲν οὖν Φυλάκη ἐγγὺς Θηβῶν ἐστὶ τῶν Φθιωτίδων, αἵπερ εἰσὶ καὶ αὐταὶ ὑπὸ τῷ Πρωτεσιλάῳ· καὶ Ἅλος δὲ καὶ Λάρισα[2] ἡ Κρεμαστὴ καὶ τὸ Δημήτριον ὑπ' ἐκείνῳ, πᾶσαι πρὸς ἕω τῆς Ὄθρυος. τὸ δὲ Δημήτριον Δήμητρος εἴρηκε τέμενος καὶ ἐκάλεσε Πύρασον. ἦν δὲ πόλις εὐλίμενος ἡ Πύρασος, ἐν δυσὶ σταδίοις ἔχουσα Δήμητρος ἄλσος καὶ ἱερὸν ἅγιον, διέχουσα Θηβῶν σταδίους εἴκοσι. ὑπέρκεινται δὲ Πυράσου μὲν αἱ Θῆβαι, τῶν Θηβῶν δὲ ἐν τῇ μεσογαίᾳ τὸ Κρόκιον πεδίον πρὸς τῷ καταλήγοντι τῆς Ὄθρυος, δι' οὗ ὁ Ἄμφρυσος ῥεῖ. τούτου δ' ὑπέρκειται ὁ Ἴτωνος, ὅπου τὸ τῆς Ἰτωνίας ἱερόν, ἀφ' οὗ καὶ τὸ ἐν τῇ Βοιωτίᾳ, καὶ ὁ Κουάριος ποταμός· εἴρηται δὲ π[ερὶ τούτου καὶ[3]] τῆς Ἄρνης ἐν τοῖς Βοιωτιακοῖς. ταῦτα δ' ἐστὶ τῆς Θετταλιώτιδος μιᾶς τῶν τεττάρων μερίδων τῆς συμπάσης Θετταλίας, ἧς[4] καὶ τὰ ὑπ' Εὐρυπύλῳ, καὶ ὁ Φύλλ[ος, ὅπου Ἀπόλλω]νος[5] τοῦ Φυλλίου[6] ἱερόν, καὶ Ἴχναι, ὅπου ἡ Θέμις Ἰχναία τιμᾶται. καὶ Κίερος δ' εἰς αὐτὴν συντελεῖ[7] καὶ [τἄλλα μέχρι[8]] τῆς Ἀθαμανίας. κατὰ δὲ τὸν Ἀντρῶνα ἕρμα[9] ὕφαλον ἐν τῷ πρὸς Εὐβοίᾳ ἐστὶ πόρῳ, καλού-

[1] [ὑπὸ τῷ Ἀχιλλεῖ], lacuna of about twelve letters supplied by Falconer; so Kramer, Müller-Dübner and Meineke.

[2] Λάρισα, the editors, for Λάρισσα.

[3] π[ερὶ τούτου καί], lacuna of about ten letters in A supplied by Kramer. Corais adds a second περί before τῆς.

[4] Casaubon inserts ἦν after ἧς.

[5] Φύλλ[ος ὅπου Ἀπόλλω]νος, lacuna of about ten letters supplied by *bkno*, except that they have ἔνθα instead of ὅπου, Kramer's emendation.

[6] Φυλλίου, Meineke, for Φυλαίου A, Φυλλαίου other MSS.

inside the part of Phthiotis[1] that was subject to Achilles. Now Phylacê is near Phthiotic Thebes, which itself is subject to Protesilaüs. And Halus, also, and Larisa Cremastê, and Demetrium, are subject to him, all being situated to the east of the Othrys Mountain. Demetrium he speaks of as "sacred precinct of Demeter,"[2] and calls it "Pyrasus." Pyrasus was a city with a good harbour; at a distance of two stadia it had a sacred precinct and a holy temple, and was twenty stadia distant from Thebes. Thebes is situated above Pyrasus, but the Crocian Plain is situated in the interior back of Thebes near the end of Othrys; and it is through this plain that the Amphrysus flows. Above this river are the Itonus, where is the temple of the Itonian,[3] after which the temple in Boeotia is named, and the Cuarius Rivers. But I have already spoken of this river and of Arnê in my description of Boeotia.[4] These places are in Thessaliotis, one of the four portions of all Thessaly, in which were not only the regions that were subject to Eurypylus, but also Phyllus, where is the temple of Phyllian Apollo, and Ichnae, where the Ichnaean Themis is held in honour. Cierus, also, was tributary to it, and so was the rest of that region as far as Athamania. Near Antron, in the Euboean strait, is a submarine reef

[1] Cf. 9. 5. 10.
[2] *Iliad* 2. 696.
[3] *i.e.* Ĭtonian Athena.
[4] 9. 2. 3, 29, 33, 34.

[7] συντελεῖ καί, Corais, for συντελεῖται; so the later editors.
[8] [τἆλλα μέχρι], lacuna of about eight letters supplied by Meineke, following conj. of Kramer.
[9] ἕρμα, Casaubon, for ἑρμ (A *man. prim.*), αιον with ἔρυμα above (A *man. sec.*), ἑρμαῖον *ghi*, ἔρυμα BE*lno*; so the later editors

μενον ὄνος Ἀντρῶνος· εἶτα Πτελεὸν καὶ ὁ Ἅλος· εἶτα τὸ τῆς Δήμητρος ἱερὸν καὶ ὁ Πύρασος κατεσκαμμένος, ὑπὲρ αὐτὸν δὲ αἱ Θῆβαι· εἶτα ἄκρα Πύρρα καὶ δύο νησία [1] πλησίον, ὧν τὸ μὲν Πύρρα, τὸ δὲ Δευκαλίων καλεῖται. ἐνταῦθα δὲ καὶ ἡ Φθιῶτίς πως τελευτᾷ.

C 436 15. Ἑξῆς δὲ τοὺς ὑπὸ τῷ Εὐμήλῳ καταλέγει, τὴν συνεχῆ παραλίαν, ἥπερ ἐστὶν [2] ἤδη Μαγνησίας καὶ τῆς Πελασγιώτιδος γῆς. Φεραὶ μὲν οὖν εἰσὶ πέρας τῶν Πελασγικῶν πεδίων πρὸς τὴν Μαγνησίαν, ἃ παρατείνει μέχρι τοῦ Πηλίου σταδίους ἑκατὸν ἑξήκοντα. ἐπίνειον δὲ τῶν Φερῶν Παγασαί, διέχον ἐννενήκοντα σταδίους αὐτῶν, Ἰωλκοῦ δὲ εἴκοσι. ἡ δ' Ἰωλκὸς κατέσκαπται μὲν ἐκ παλαιοῦ, ἐντεῦθεν δ' ἔστειλε τὸν Ἰάσονα καὶ τὴν Ἀργὼ Πελίας· ἀπὸ δὲ τῆς ναυπηγίας τῆς Ἀργοῦς καὶ Παγασὰς λέγεσθαι μυθεύουσι τὸν τόπον, οἱ δὲ πιθανώτερον ἡγοῦνται τοὔνομα τῷ τόπῳ τεθῆναι τοῦτο ἀπὸ τῶν πηγῶν, αἳ πολλαί τε καὶ δαψιλεῖς ῥέουσι· πλησίον δὲ καὶ Ἀφέται, ὡς ἂν ἀφετήριόν τι τῶν Ἀργοναυτῶν. τῆς δὲ Δημητριάδος ἑπτὰ σταδίους ὑπέρκειται τῆς θαλάττης Ἰωλκός. ἔκτισε δὲ Δημήτριος ὁ Πολιορκητὴς ἐπώνυμον ἑαυτοῦ τὴν Δημητριάδα μεταξὺ Νηλίας καὶ Παγασῶν ἐπὶ θαλάττῃ, τὰς πλησίον πολίχνας εἰς αὐτὴν συνοικίσας, Νηλίαν τε καὶ Παγασὰς καὶ Ὀρμένιον,

[1] νησίδια *Bklno.*

[2] ἥπερ ἐστίν, Tzschucke, for ἔπεστιν; so Müller-Dübner, and Meineke.

---

[1] The Greek word is a compound of "nau(s)" ("ship")

called "Ass of Antron"; and then one comes to Pteleum and Halus; and then to the temple of Demeter; and to Pyrasus, which has been rased to the ground; and, above it, to Thebes; and then to Cape Pyrrha, and to two isles near it, one of which is called Pyrrha and the other Deucalion. And it is somewhere here that Phthiotis ends.

15. Next the poet enumerates the peoples that were subject to Eumelus, that is, the adjacent sea-coast, which from this point on belongs to Magnesia and the land of Pelasgiotis. Now Pherae is at the end of the Pelasgian plains on the side towards Magnesia; and these plains extend as far as Pelion, one hundred and sixty stadia. The sea-port of Pherae is Pagasae, which is ninety stadia distant from Pherae and twenty from Iolcus. Iolcus has indeed been rased to the ground from early times, but it was from there that Pelias despatched Jason and the Argo. It was from the construction here of the ship[1] Argo, according to mythology, that the place was called Pagasae, though some believe, more plausibly, that this name was given the place from its fountains,[2] which are both numerous and of abundant flow. Near by is Aphetae also, so named as being the "apheterium"[3] of the Argonauts. Iolcus is situated above the sea seven stadia from Demetrias. Demetrias, which is on the sea between Nelia and Pagasae, was founded by Demetrius Poliorcetes, who named it after himself, settling in it the inhabitants of the near-by towns, Nelia and Pagasae and Ormenium,

and "pagia" ("construction"), "pagia" being the Doric spelling.

[2] In Greek (Doric spelling), "pagae."

[3] *i.e.* "starting-place."

ἔτι δὲ Ῥιζοῦντα, Σηπιάδα, Ὀλιζῶνα, Βοίβην, Ἰωλκόν, αἳ δὴ νῦν εἰσὶ κῶμαι τῆς Δημητριάδος. καὶ δὴ καὶ ναύσταθμον ἦν τοῦτο καὶ βασίλειον μέχρι πολλοῦ τοῖς βασιλεῦσι τῶν Μακεδόνων, ἐπεκράτει δὲ καὶ τῶν Τεμπῶν καὶ τῶν ὀρῶν ἀμφοῖν, ὥσπερ[1] εἴρηται, τοῦ τε Πηλίου καὶ τῆς Ὄσσης· νῦν δὲ συνέσταλται μέν, τῶν δ' ἐν τῇ Μαγνησίᾳ πασῶν ὅμως διαφέρει. ἡ δὲ Βοιβηὶς λίμνη πλησιάζει μὲν ταῖς Φεραῖς, συνάπτει δὲ καὶ τοῖς ἀπολήγουσι τοῦ Πηλίου πέρασι καὶ τῆς Μαγνησίας· Βοίβη δὲ χωρίον ἐπὶ τῇ λίμνῃ κείμενον. καθάπερ δὲ τὴν Ἰωλκὸν αὐξηθεῖσαν ἐπὶ πλέον κατέλυσαν αἱ στάσεις καὶ αἱ τυραννίδες, οὕτως καὶ τὰς Φερὰς συνέστειλαν ἐξαρθείσας ποτὲ καὶ συγκαταλυθείσας τοῖς τυράννοις. πλησίον δὲ τῆς Δημητριάδος ὁ Ἄναυρος[2] ῥεῖ, καλεῖται δὲ καὶ ὁ[3] συνεχὴς αἰγιαλὸς Ἰωλκός· ἐνταῦθα δὲ καὶ τὴν Πυλαϊκὴν[4] πανήγυριν συνετέλουν. ὁ δ' Ἀρτεμίδωρος ἀπωτέρω τῆς Δημητριάδος τίθησι τὸν Παγασιτικὸν κόλπον εἰς τοὺς ὑπὸ Φιλοκτήτῃ τόπους· ἐν δὲ τῷ κόλπῳ φησὶν εἶναι τὴν Κικύνηθον νῆσον καὶ πολίχνην ὁμώνυμον.

16. Ἑξῆς δ' αἱ ὑπὸ Φιλοκτήτῃ πόλεις καταλέγονται. ἡ μὲν οὖν Μηθώνη[5] ἑτέρα ἐστὶ τῆς Θρᾳκίας Μεθώνης, ἣν κατέσκαψε Φίλιππος·

[1] ὥσπερ, Corais, for ὧνπερ; so the later editors.

[2] ὁ Ἄναυρος, Casaubon, for ὁ ναῦρος; so the later editors.

[3] ὁ, before συνεχής, Casaubon inserts; so the other editors before Kramer.

and also Rhizus, Sepias, Olizon, Boebê, and Iolcus, which are now villages belonging to Demetrias. Furthermore, for a long time this was both a naval station and a royal residence for the kings of the Macedonians; and it held the mastery over both Tempê and the two mountains, Pelion and Ossa, as I have already said.[1] At present it is reduced in power, but still it surpasses all the cities in Magnesia. Lake Boebeïs is near Pherae, and also borders on the foothills of Pelion and the frontiers of Magnesia; and Boebê is a place situated on the lake. Just as seditions and tyrannies destroyed Iolcus after its power had been greatly increased, so they reduced Pherae also, which had once been raised to greatness by its tyrants and was then destroyed along with them. Near Demetrias flows the Anaurus River; and the adjoining shore is also called Iolcus. Here, too, they used to hold the Pylaic Festal Assembly.[2] Artemidorus places the Pagasitic Gulf in the region subject to Philoctetes, farther away from Demetrias; and he says that the island Cicynethos and a town bearing the same name are in the gulf.

16. The poet next enumerates the cities subject to Philoctetes. Now Mēthonē is different from the Thracian Mĕthonē, which was rased to the ground

[1] 9. 4. 15.

[2] No other reference to a "Pylaic" Assembly in Iolcus has been found. It could hardly be identified with the "Pylaean (Amphictyonic) Assembly" (9. 3. 7). Groskurd emends "Pylaic" to "Peliac" (*i.e.* held in honour of Pelias), which is probably right.

---

[4] [Πυλαϊκ]ήν, lacuna supplied in A by second hand. Groskurd writes Πελιακήν; and Meineke (*Vind. Strab.* 153) conj. Δημητριακήν, citing Diod. Sic. 20. 102.

[5] Μηθώνη, Meineke, for Μεθώνη.

ἐμνήσθημεν δὲ καὶ πρότερον τῆς τῶν ὀνομάτων τούτων καὶ τῶν ἐν Πελοποννήσῳ τινῶν[1] τροπῆς· τἆλλα δὲ διηρίθμηται,[2] ἥ τε Θαυμακία καὶ ὁ Ὀλιζὼν[3] καὶ ἡ Μελίβοια, ἃ τῆς ἑξῆς παραλίας ἐστίν. πρόκεινται δὲ τῶν Μαγνήτων νῆσοι συχναὶ μέν, αἱ δ' ἐν ὀνόματι Σκίαθός τε καὶ Πεπάρηθος καὶ Ἰκός, Ἁλόννησός τε καὶ Σκῦρος, ὁμωνύμους ἔχουσαι πόλεις. μάλιστα δ' ἐστὶν ἐν ὀνόματι Σκῦρος διὰ τὴν Λυκομήδους πρὸς Ἀχιλ-
C 437 λέα οἰκειότητα καὶ τὴν Νεοπτολέμου τοῦ Ἀχιλλέως ἐνταῦθα γένεσίν τε καὶ ἐκτροφήν. ὕστερον δὲ Φίλιππος αὐξηθείς, ὁρῶν Ἀθηναίους ἐπικρατοῦντας τῆς θαλάττης καὶ τῶν νήσων ἄρχοντας καὶ τούτων καὶ τῶν ἄλλων, ἐποίησε τὰς πλησίον ἑαυτῷ μάλιστα ἐνδόξους. πολεμῶν γὰρ περὶ τῆς ἡγεμονίας ἐπεχείρει πρώτοις ἀεὶ τοῖς ἐγγύθεν, καὶ καθάπερ αὐτῆς τῆς Μαγνήτιδος τὰ πολλὰ μέρη Μακεδονίαν ἐποίησε καὶ τῆς Θρᾴκης καὶ τῆς ἄλλης τῆς κύκλῳ γῆς, οὕτω καὶ τὰς πρὸ τῆς Μαγνησίας νήσους ἀφῃρεῖτο, καὶ τὰς ὑπ' οὐδενὸς γνωριζομένας πρότερον περιμαχήτους καὶ γνωρίμους ἐποίει. τὴν δ' οὖν Σκῦρον καὶ μάλιστα μὲν αἱ ἀρχαιολογίαι συνιστῶσιν, ἀλλὰ καὶ τὰ τοιαῦτα θρυλεῖσθαι ποιεῖ, οἷον αἱ τῶν αἰγῶν ἀρεταὶ τῶν Σκυρίων, καὶ τὰ μέταλλα τῆς ποικίλης λίθου τῆς Σκυρίας, καθάπερ τῆς Καρυ-

[1] [τινῶν], lacuna of about four letters supplied by Jones. Kramer, Müller-Dübner, and others, [μετα]τροπῆς; Meineke conj. τόπων. For the use of τροπή with the same meaning see *e.g.* Eustath. on *Iliad* 2. 729, Steph. Byz. *s. v.* Ἰθώμη, and Hesych. *s. v.* τροπή.

[2] δι-, Kramer inserts; so the later editors.

by Philip. I have mentioned heretofore the change of the names of these places, and of certain places in the Peloponnesus.[1] And the other places enumerated by the poet are Thaumacia and Olizon and Meliboea, which are on the next stretch of sea-coast. Off the country of the Magnetans lie numerous islands, but the only notable ones are Sciathos, Peparethos, and Icos, and also Halonnesos and Scyros, all having cities of the same name. But Scyros is the most notable, because of the family-relation between Lycomedes and Achilles, and of the birth and nurture there of Neoptolemus the son of Achilles. In later times, when Philip had waxed powerful and saw that the Athenians dominated the sea and ruled over the islands, both these and the rest, he caused the islands that were near him to be most famous; for, since he was fighting for the hegemony, he always attacked those places which were close to him, and, just as he added to Macedonia most parts of the Magnetan country and of Thrace and of the rest of the land all round, so he also seized the islands off Magnesia and made those which were previously well-known to nobody objects of contention and hence well-known. Now Scyros is chiefly commended by the place it occupies in the ancient legends, but there are other things which cause it to be widely mentioned, as, for instance, the excellence of the Scyrian goats, and the quarries of the Scyrian variegated marble, which is comparable to the Carys-

[1] See 8. 4. 3–4, 8. 5. 3 and 8. 6. 15.

---

[3] [ὁ 'Ολιζ]ών, lacuna of about four letters supplied by Corais.

στίας καὶ τῆς Δοκιμαίας,[1] ἢ[2] Συνναδικῆς, καὶ τῆς[3] Ἱεραπολιτικῆς. μονολίθους γὰρ κίονας καὶ πλάκας μεγάλας ὁρᾶν ἔστιν ἐν τῇ Ῥώμῃ τῆς ποικίλης λιθίας, ἀφ' ἧς ἡ πόλις κοσμεῖται δημοσίᾳ τε καὶ ἰδίᾳ· πεποίηκέ τε τὰ λευκόλιθα οὐ πολλοῦ ἄξια.

17. Ὁ δ' οὖν ποιητὴς μέχρι δεῦρο προελθὼν τῆς Μαγνητικῆς παραλίας ἐπάνεισιν ἐπὶ τὴν ἄνω Θετταλίαν· καὶ γὰρ τὰ παρατείνοντα τῇ Φθιώτιδι,[4] ἀρξάμενος ἀπὸ τῆς Δολοπίας καὶ τῆς Πίνδου, [μέχρι τῆς[5]] κάτω Θετταλίας διέξεισιν·

οἳ δ' εἶχον Τρίκκην καὶ Ἰθώμην κλωμακόεσσαν.

ταῦτα τὰ χωρία ἐστὶ μὲν τῆς Ἱστιαιώτιδος, ἐκαλεῖτο δ', ὥς φασι, πρότερον Δωρίς· κατασχόντων δὲ τῶν Περραιβῶν αὐτήν, οἳ καὶ τῆς Εὐβοίας τὴν Ἱστιαιῶτιν κατεστρέψαντο καὶ τοὺς ἀνθρώπους εἰς τὴν ἤπειρον ἀνέσπασαν, διὰ τὸ πλῆθος τῶν ἐποικησάντων Ἱστιαίων τὴν χώραν ἀπ' ἐκείνων οὕτως ἐκάλεσαν. καλοῦσι δὲ καὶ [αὐτὴν καὶ[6]] τὴν Δολοπίαν τὴν ἄνω Θετταλίαν, ἐπ' εὐθείας οὖσα[ν τῇ ἄνω[7]] Μακεδονίᾳ, καθάπερ καὶ τὴν κάτω τῇ κάτω. ἔστι δ' ἡ μὲν Τρίκκη, ὅπου τὸ ἱερὸν τοῦ Ἀσκληπιοῦ τὸ ἀρχαιότατον καὶ ἐπιφανέστατον,

[1] Δοκιμαίας, C. Müller (approving conj. of Reinesius, *Ind. Var. Lect.* p. 1005), for Δευκαλλίοι A, Δευκαλίας *klno*, Δευκολλίας *Bm*; Λευκολλείας Tzschucke, Λευκολλείου Corais, Λευκαδίας Tyrwhitt.

[2] ἤ, Jones, for καὶ τῆς, from conj. of C. Müller (ἤτοι).

[3] καὶ τῆς, Jones inserts, from conj. of C. Müller.

[4] Φ[θιώτιδι], lacuna supplied by Corais; so the later editors.

[5] [μέχρι τῆς], lacuna supplied by Corais; so the later editors.

tian marble,[1] and to the Docimaean or Synnadic,[2] and to the Hierapolitic.[3] For at Rome are to be seen monolithic columns and great slabs of the variegated marble; and with this marble the city is being adorned both at public and at private expense; and it has caused the quarries of white marble[4] to be of little worth.

17. However, the poet, after proceeding thus far on the Magnetan sea-coast, returns to Upper Thessaly; for, beginning at Dolopia and Pindus, he recounts the parts that stretch alongside Phthiotis, as far as Lower Thessaly: "And those who held Triccê and rocky Ithomê."[5] These places belong in fact to Histiaeotis,[6] though in earlier times Histiaeotis was called Doris, as they say; but when the Perrhaebians took possession of it, who had already subdued Histiaeotis in Euboea and had forced its inhabitants to migrate to the mainland, they called the country Histiaeotis after these Histiaeans, because of the large number of these people who settled there. They call Histiaeotis and Dolopia Upper Thessaly, which is in a straight line with Upper Macedonia, as is Lower Thessaly with Lower Macedonia. Now Triccê, where is the earliest and most famous temple of Asclepius, borders on the country

[1] See 10. 1. 6. [2] See 12. 8. 14. [3] See 13. 4. 14.

[4] But the Greek might mean, instead of "quarries of white marble," simply "white marble" in general.

[5] *Iliad* 2. 729. [6] See 9. 5. 3 and foot-note.

---

[6] [αὐτὴν καί], lacuna supplied by Du Theil; so the later editors.

[7] οὖσα[ν τῇ ἄνω], lacuna supplied by Du Theil; so the later editors.

ὅμορος [1] τοῖς τε Δόλοψιν καὶ τοῖς περὶ τὴν Πίνδον τόποις. τὴν δ' Ἰθώμην ὁμωνύμως τῇ Μεσσηνιακῇ λεγομένην οὔ φασι δεῖν οὕτως ἐκφέρειν, ἀλλὰ τὴν πρώτην συλλαβὴν ἀφαιρεῖν· οὕτω γὰρ καλεῖσθαι πρότερον, νῦν δὲ Ἰθώμη [2] μετωνομάσθαι, χωρίον ἐρυμνὸν καὶ τῷ ὄντι κλωμακόεν, ἱδρυμένον μεταξὺ τεττάρων φρουρίων, ὥσπερ ἐν τετραπλεύρῳ κειμένων, Τρίκκης τε καὶ Μητροπόλεως καὶ Πελινναίου καὶ Γόμφων. τῆς δὲ δὴ Μητροπολιτῶν ἐστὶ χώρας ἡ Ἰθώμη. ἡ δὲ Μητρόπολις πρότερον μὲν ἐκ τριῶν συνῴκιστο πολιχνίων ἀσήμων, ὕστερον δὲ καὶ πλείους προσελήφθησαν, ὧν ἦν καὶ ἡ Ἰθώμη. Καλλίμαχος μὲν οὖν φησὶν ἐν τοῖς
C 438 ἰάμβοις τὰς Ἀφροδίτας (ἡ θεὸς γὰρ οὐ μία) τὴν Καστνιῆτιν ὑπερβάλλεσθαι πάσας τῷ φρονεῖν, ὅτι μόνη παραδέχεται τὴν τῶν ὑῶν θυσίαν. καὶ μὴν πολυίστωρ, εἴ τις ἄλλος, καὶ πάντα τὸν βίον, ὡς αὐτὸς εἴρηκεν, ὁ ταῦτα μυθεῖσθαι [3] βουλόμενος· οἱ δ' ὕστερον ἤλεγξαν οὐ μίαν Ἀφροδίτην μόνον, ἀλλὰ καὶ πλείους ἀποδεδεγμένας τὸ ἔθος τοῦτο· ὧν εἶναι καὶ τὴν ἐν τῇ Μητροπόλει· ταύτῃ δὲ μίαν τῶν συνοικισθεισῶν εἰς αὐτὴν πόλεων παραδοῦναι τὸ ἔθος Ὀνθούριον.[4] ἔστι δὲ καὶ Φαρκαδὼν ἐν τῇ Ἱστιαιώτιδι, καὶ ῥεῖ δι' αὐτῶν ὁ Πηνειὸς

[1] ὅμορος, Palmer, for ὅμορον; so the later editors.

[2] Ἰθώμη *Bno*, Θαμαί *Eaghil*, Ἰθώμην *k* and Eustathius; but Kramer conj. Θούμαιον from Steph. Byz. *s. v.* Ἰθώμη; but see *Etym. Magnum s. v.* Θώμη.

[3] Meineke suspects μυθεῖσθαι; C. Müller conj. ἀληθεύεσθαι for μυθεῖσθαι; Capps conj. μάλιστα. Kramer conj. τοιαῦτα for ὁ ταῦτα.

[4] Ὀνθούριον, Meineke (following Steph. Byz. *s. v.*), for ὀνούριον (ὀμούριον B, ὀμίριον editors before Corais).

of the Dolopians and the regions round Pindus. Ithomê, which is called by the same name as the Messenian city, ought not, they say, to be pronounced in this way, but without the first syllable;[1] for thus, they add, it was called in earlier times, though now its name has been changed to Ithomê. It is a stronghold and is in reality a heap of stones;[2] and it is situated between four strongholds, which lie in a square, as it were: Triccê, Metropolis, Pelinnaeum, and Gomphi. But Ithomê belongs to the territory of the Metropolitans. Metropolis in earlier times was a joint settlement composed of three insignificant towns; but later several others were added to it, among which was Ithomê. Now Callimachus, in his *Iambics*, says that, "of all the Aphroditês (for there was not merely one goddess of this name), Aphroditê Castnietis surpasses all in wisdom, since she alone accepts the sacrifice of swine."[3] And surely he was very learned, if any other man was, and all his life, as he himself states, wished to recount these things.[4] But the writers of later times have discovered that not merely one Aphroditê, but several, have accepted this rite; and that among these was the Aphroditê at Metropolis, and that one of the cities included in the settlement transmitted to it the Onthurian rite.[5] Pharcadon, also, is in Histiaeotis; and the Peneius and the

[1] *i.e.* Thomê. [2] "Thomos" means "heap of stones."

[3] *Frag.* 82 b, Schneider.

[4] The text is probably corrupt. We should expect either "wished to tell the truth about matters of this sort," or, as Professor Capps suggests, "preferred this branch of learning."

[5] "Onthurium" was a "Thessalian city near Arnê" (Stephanus Byzantinus, *s.v.*).

καὶ ὁ Κουράλιος· ὧν ὁ Κουράλιος, ῥυεὶς παρὰ τὸ τῆς Ἰτωνίας Ἀθηνᾶς ἱερόν, εἰς τὸν Πηνειὸν ἐξίησιν. αὐτὸς δ' ὁ Πηνειὸς ἄρχεται μὲν ἐκ Πίνδου, καθάπερ εἴρηται· ἐν ἀριστερᾷ δ' ἀφεὶς Τρίκκην τε καὶ Πελινναῖον[1] καὶ Φαρκαδόνα φέρεται παρά τε Ἄτρακα καὶ Λάρισαν,[2] καὶ τοὺς ἐν τῇ Θετταλιώτιδι δεξάμενος ποταμοὺς πρόεισι διὰ τῶν Τεμπῶν ἐπὶ τὰς ἐκβολάς. τὴν δ' Οἰχαλίαν πόλιν Εὐρύτου λεγομένην ἔν τε τοῖς τόποις τούτοις ἱστοροῦσι καὶ ἐν Εὐβοίᾳ καὶ ἐν Ἀρκαδίᾳ, καὶ μετονομάζουσιν ἄλλως, ὃ καὶ ἐν τοῖς Πελοποννησιακοῖς εἴρηται. περὶ δὲ τούτων ζητοῦσι, καὶ μάλιστα, τίς ἦν ἡ ὑπὸ Ἡρακλέους ἁλοῦσα, καὶ περὶ τίνος συνέγραψεν ὁ ποιήσας τὴν Οἰχαλίας ἅλωσιν. ταῦτα μὲν δὴ τὰ χωρία τοῖς Ἀσκληπιάδαις ὑπέταξεν.

18. Ἑξῆς δὲ λέγει τὴν ὑπ' Εὐρυπύλῳ·

οἳ δ' ἔχον Ὀρμένιον οἵ τε κρήνην Ὑπέρειαν
οἵ τ' ἔχον Ἀστέριον Τιτάνοιό τε λευκὰ κάρηνα.

τὸ μὲν οὖν Ὀρμένιον[3] νῦν Ὀρμίνιον καλεῖται, ἔστι δ' ὑπὸ τῷ Πηλίῳ κώμη κατὰ τὸν Παγασιτικὸν κόλπον τῶν συνῳκισμένων εἰς τὴν Δημητριάδα πόλεων, ὡς εἴρηται. ἀνάγκη δὲ καὶ τὴν Βοιβηίδα λίμνην εἶναι πλησίον, ἐπειδὴ καὶ ἡ Βοίβη τῶν περιοικίδων ἦν τῆς Δημητριάδος καὶ αὐτὸ τὸ Ὀρμένιον. τὸ μὲν οὖν Ὀρμένιον ἀπέχει

[1] Πεληνναῖον A*cgh*, Πελινναίην *l*.
[2] Λάρισσα, MSS. except A.
[3] Ὀρμένιον, Kramer, for ὄρμενον A(μενον written by *man. sec.* in A)*ghno*; Ὀρμίνιον BE*kl*, and Eustathius, note on *Il.* 2. 734.

Curalius flow through its territory. Of these rivers, the Curalius flows past the temple of the Itonian Athena and empties into the Peneius; but the Peneius itself rises in Pindus, as I have already said,[1] and after leaving Triccê and Pelinnaeum and Pharcadon on the left flows past both Atrax and Larisa, and after receiving the rivers in Thessaliotis flows on through Tempê to its outlet. Historians place the Oechalia which is called the "city of Eurytus"[2] not only in this region, but also in Euboea and in Arcadia; and they give its name in different ways, as I have already said in my description of the Peloponnesus.[3] They inquire concerning these, and particularly in regard to what Oechalia it was that was captured by Heracles,[4] and concerning what Oechalia was meant by the poet who wrote *The Capture of Oechalia*.[5] These places, then, were classed by Homer as subject to the Asclepiadae.

18. Next he speaks of the country subject to Eurypylus: "and those who held Ormenium and the fountain Hypereia, and those who held Asterium and the white summits of Titanus."[6] Now at the present time Ormenium is called Orminium; it is a village situated at the foot of Pelion near the Pagasitic Gulf, one of the cities included in the settlement of Demetrias, as I have said.[7] And Lake Boebeïs, also, must be near, since Boebê, as well as Ormenium itself, was one of the dependencies of Demetrias. Now Ormenium is distant by land twenty-seven

[1] *Frags.* 14, 15, 15*a*, Vol. III, pp. 335, 337.
[2] *Iliad* 2. 596.
[3] See 9. 5. 16 and foot-note.
[4] Cf. 10. 1. 10.
[5] See 14. 1. 18.
[6] *Iliad* 2. 734.
[7] 9. 5. 15.

τῆς Δημητριάδος πεζῇ σταδίους ἑπτὰ καὶ εἴκοσι, ὁ δὲ τῆς Ἰωλκοῦ τόπος ἐν ὁδῷ κείμενος τῆς μὲν Δημητριάδος ἑπτὰ σταδίους διέστηκε, τοῦ δ' Ὀρμενίου τοὺς λοιποὺς σταδίους εἴκοσι. φησὶ δ' ὁ Σκήψιος ἐκ τοῦ Ὀρμενίου τὸν Φοίνικα εἶναι, καὶ φεύγειν αὐτὸν ἐνθένδε παρὰ τοῦ πατρὸς Ἀμύντορος Ὀρμενίδαο εἰς τὴν Φθίαν ἐς Πηλῆα ἄνακτα· ἐκτίσθαι γὰρ ὑπὸ Ὀρμένου τὸ χωρίον τοῦτο τοῦ Κερκάφου[1] τοῦ Αἰόλου· παῖδας δὲ τοῦ Ὀρμένου
C 439 γενέσθαι τόν τε Ἀμύντορα καὶ Εὐαίμονα, ὧν τοῦ μὲν εἶναι Φοίνικα, τοῦ δ' Εὐρύπυλον· φυλαχθῆναι δὲ τῷ Εὐρυπύλῳ τὴν διαδοχὴν κοινήν, ἅτε[2] ἀπελθόντος τοῦ Φοίνικος ἐκ τῆς οἰκείας· καὶ δὴ καὶ γράφει οὕτως·

οἷον ὅτε πρῶτον λίπον Ὀρμένιον πολύμηλον,

ἀντὶ τοῦ

λίπον Ἑλλάδα καλλιγύναικα.

Κράτης δὲ Φωκέα ποιεῖ τὸν Φοίνικα, τεκμαιρόμενος ἐκ τοῦ κράνους τοῦ Μέγητος, ᾧ ἐχρήσατο ὁ Ὀδυσσεὺς κατὰ τὴν νυκτεγερσίαν, περὶ οὗ φησὶν ὁ ποιητής, ὅτι

ἐξ Ἐλεῶνος Ἀμύντορος Ὀρμενίδαο
ἐξέλετ' Αὐτόλυκος, πυκινὸν δόμον ἀντιτορήσας.

τόν τε γὰρ Ἐλεῶνα ἐν τῷ Παρνασσῷ πολίχνιον εἶναι, τόν τε Ὀρμενίδην Ἀμύντορα οὐκ ἄλλον τινὰ λέγεσθαι ἢ τὸν τοῦ Φοίνικος πατέρα, καὶ τὸν Αὐτόλυκον οἰκοῦντα ἐν τῷ Παρνασσῷ τοιχωρυχεῖν τὰ τῶν γειτόνων, ὅπερ κοινόν ἐστι τοιχωρύχου παντός, οὐ τὰ τῶν πόρρωθεν. ὁ δὲ

stadia from Demetrias, whereas the site of Iolcus, which is situated on the road, is distant seven stadia from Demetrias and the remaining twenty stadia from Ormenium. The Scepsian[1] says that Phoenix was from Ormenium, and that he fled thence from his father Amyntor the son of Ormenus into Phthia to Peleus the king; for this place, he adds, was founded by Ormenus the son of Cercaphus the son of Aeolus; and he says that both Amyntor and Euaemon were sons of Ormenus, and that Phoenix was son of the former and Eurypylus of the latter, but that the succession to the throne, to which both had equal right, was kept for Eurypylus, inasmuch as Phoenix had gone away from his home-land. Furthermore, the Scepsian writes thus, "as when first I left Ormenium rich in flocks," instead of "I left Hellas, land of fair women."[2] But Crates makes Phoenix a Phocian, judging this from the helmet of Meges, which Odysseus used at the time of his night-spying, concerning which the poet says, "Autolycus filched it from Eleon, from Amyntor the son of Ormenus, having broken into his close-built home."[3] For Eleon, he says, is a town of Parnassus; and Amyntor, son of Ormenus, means no other than the father of Phoenix; and Autolycus, who lived on Parnassus, must have broken into the house of a neighbour (as is the way of any housebreaker), and not into that of people far away. But the Scepsian

1 Demetrius of Scepsis. 2 *Iliad* 9. 447.
3 *Iliad* 10. 266.

1 Κερφίου A *man. prim.*, Κεκάφου A *man. sec.* and other MSS., and Eustathius.
2 ἄν, after ἄτε, Jones deletes; ὡς ἄν A *man. sec.*, *Bklno*; ὅτε ἄν *chi.*

Σκήψιός φησι μήτε Ἐλεῶνα μηδένα τόπον τοῦ Παρνασσοῦ δείκνυσθαι, ἀλλὰ Νεῶνα, καὶ ταύτην οἰκισθεῖσαν μετὰ τὰ Τρωικά, μήτ' ἐκ γειτόνων τὰς τοιχωρυχίας γίνεσθαι μόνον. καὶ ἄλλα δ' ἐστίν, ἃ λέγοι τις ἄν, ἀλλ' οὖν ὀκνῶ διατρίβειν ἐπὶ πλέον. ἄλλοι δὲ γράφουσιν ἐξ Ἑλεῶνος· Ταναγρικὴ δέ ἐστιν αὕτη· καὶ μᾶλλον ἐλέγχοι ἀτόπως ἂν λεγόμενον τό

φεῦγον ἔπειτ' ἀπάνευθε δι' Ἑλλάδος,
Φθίην δ' ἐξικόμην.

ἡ δ' Ὑπέρεια κρήνη ἐν μέσῃ ἐστὶ τῇ Φεραίων πόλει Εὐμήλου οὔσῃ·[1] ἄτοπον τοίνυν [δοῦναι Εὐρυπύ]λῳ.[2] Τίτανος δ' ἀπὸ τοῦ συμβεβηκότος ὠνομάσθη· λευκόγεων γάρ ἐστι τὸ χωρίον Ἄρνης πλησίον καὶ [τῶν Ἀφε]τῶν·[3] καὶ τὸ Ἀστέριον δ' οὐκ ἄπωθεν τούτων ἐστί.

19. Συνεχεῖς δὲ τῇ μερίδι ταύτῃ λέγονται οἱ ὑπὸ τῷ Πολυποίτῃ·

οἳ δ' Ἄργισσαν ἔχον καὶ Γυρτώνην ἐνέμοντο,
Ὄρθην Ἠλώνην τε πόλιν τ' Ὀλοοσσόνα λευκήν.

ταύτην τὴν χώραν πρότερον μὲν ᾤκουν Περραιβοί, τὸ πρὸς θαλάττῃ μέρος νεμόμενοι καὶ τῷ Πηνειῷ μέχρι τῆς ἐκβολῆς αὐτοῦ καὶ Γυρτῶνος, πόλεως Περραιβίδος. εἶτα ταπεινώσαντες ἐκείνους καὶ ἀπώσαντες[4] εἰς τὴν ἐν τῇ μεσογαίᾳ ποταμίαν,[5]

[1] Εὐμήλου οὔσῃ, Kramer, for μεταλαιούσῃ; so Meineke. ὑπ' Εὐμήλῳ οὔσῃ Du Theil, μεγάλῃ οὔσῃ conj. Casaubon, μεσογαίᾳ οὔσῃ Politus, μεταλλευούσῃ Toup, ἔτι μενούσῃ Corais.

[2] [δοῦναι Εὐρυπύ]λῳ, lacuna supplied by Du Theil, who,

says that there is no place called Eleon to be seen on Parnassus, though there is a place called Neon, founded in fact after the Trojan War, and also that housebreakings are not confined to neighbours only. And there are other arguments which one might give, but I hesitate to spend further time on this subject. Others write "from Heleon,"[1] but Heleon is a place in Tanagria, and this reading would increase the absurdity of the statement, "Then I fled afar off through Hellas and came to Phthia."[2] The fountain Hypereia is in the middle of the city of the Pheraeans, which belonged to Eumelus. It is absurd, therefore, to assign the fountain to Eurypylus. Titanus[3] was named from the fact in the case there; for the region near Arnê and Aphetae has white soil. Asterium, also, is not far from these.

19. Continuous with this portion of Thessaly is the country of those who are called the subjects of Polypoetes: "And those who held Argissa and dwelt in Gyrtonê, Orthê, and Elonê and the white city Oloosson."[4] In earlier times the Perrhaebians inhabited this country, dwelling in the part near the sea and near the Peneius, extending as far as its outlet and Gyrton, a Perrhaebian city. Then the Lapiths humbled the Perrhaebians and thrust them back into the river-country in the interior, and seized

[1] Instead of "from Eleon."
[2] *Iliad* 9. 478.
[3] "White earth."
[4] *Iliad* 2. 738.

however, inserts also αὐτὴν after δοῦναι, omitted by Kramer and Meineke.

[3] [τῶν 'Αφε]τῶν, lacuna of about six letters supplied by Groskurd; so the later editors.

[4] καὶ ἀπώσαντες, Corais inserts.

[5] εἰς . . . ποταμίαν, Meineke ejects.

Λαπίθαι κατέσχον αὐτὰ τὰ χωρία, Ἰξίων καὶ ὁ υἱὸς Πειρίθους, ὃς καὶ τὸ Πήλιον κατεκτήσατο, βιασάμενος τοὺς κατασχόντας Κενταύρους, ἄγριόν τι φῦλον.[1] τούτους μὲν οὖν

ἐκ Πηλίου ὦσε καὶ Αἰθίκεσσι πέλασσε,

C 440 τοῖς δὲ Λαπίθαις τὰ πεδία παρέδωκε· τινὰ δ' αὐτῶν καὶ οἱ Περραιβοὶ κατεῖχον, τὰ πρὸς τῷ Ὀλύμπῳ· ἔστι δ' ὅπου καὶ ὅλοι ἀναμὶξ τοῖς Λαπίθαις ᾤκουν. ἡ μὲν οὖν Ἄργισσα,[2] ἡ νῦν Ἄργουρα,[3] ἐπὶ τῷ Πηνειῷ κεῖται· ὑπέρκειται δ' αὐτῆς Ἄτραξ ἐν τετταράκοντα σταδίοις, τῷ ποταμῷ πλησιάζουσα καὶ αὕτη· τὴν δ' ἀνὰ μέσον ποταμίαν εἶχον Περραιβοί. Ὄρθην δέ τινες τὴν ἀκρόπολιν τῶν Φαλανναίων εἰρήκασιν· ἡ δὲ Φάλαννα Περραιβικὴ πόλις πρὸς τῷ Πηνειῷ πλησίον τῶν Τεμπῶν. οἱ μὲν οὖν Περραιβοὶ καταδυνασθέντες ὑπὸ τῶν Λαπιθῶν εἰς τὴν ὀρεινὴν ἀπανέστησαν οἱ πλείους τὴν περὶ Πίνδον καὶ Ἀθαμᾶνας καὶ Δόλοπας, τὴν δὲ χώραν καὶ τοὺς ὑπολειφθέντας τῶν Περραιβῶν κατέσχον Λαρισαῖοι,[4] πλησίον μὲν οἰκοῦντες τοῦ Πηνειοῦ, γειτνιῶντες δ' ἐκείνοις, νεμόμενοι δὲ τὰ εὐδαιμονέστατα μέρη τῶν πεδίων, πλὴν εἴ τι σφόδρα κοῖλον πρὸς τῇ λίμνῃ τῇ Νεσσωνίδι, εἰς ἣν ὑπερκλύζων ὁ ποταμὸς ἀφῃρεῖτό τι τῆς ἀροσίμου τοὺς Λαρισαίους· ἀλλ' ὕστερον παραχώμασιν ἐπηνώρθωσαν Λαρισαῖοι. οὗτοι δ' οὖν κατεῖχον τέως τὴν Περραιβίαν καὶ φόρους ἐπράττοντο, ἕως

[1] *acghno* add ὄν; also A *man. prim.*

[2] Ἄργισσα (*Iliad* 2. 738), the editors, for Ἄργισα B, Ἄργεισα A, with ισ over ει in *man. sec.*

their country—I mean the Lapiths Ixion and his son Peirithoüs, the latter of whom also took possession of Pelion, forcing out the Centaurs, a wild folk, who had seized it. Now these "he thrust from Pelion and made them draw near to the Aethices,"[1] and he gave over the plains to the Lapiths, though the Perrhaebians kept possession of some of them, those near Olympus, and also in some places lived completely intermingled with the Lapiths. Now Argissa, the present Argura, is situated on the Peneius; and forty stadia above it lies Atrax, which also is close to the river; and the Perrhaebians held the river-country between the two places. Some have called Orthê the acropolis of the Phalannaeans; and Phalanna is a Perrhaebian city close to the Peneius near Tempê. Now the Perrhaebians, being overpowered by the Lapiths, for the most part emigrated to the mountainous country about Pindus and to the countries of the Athamanians and Dolopians, but their country and all Perrhaebians who were left behind there were seized by the Larisaeans, who lived near the Peneius and were their neighbours and dwelt in the most fertile parts of the plains, though not in the very low region near the lake called Nessonis, into which the river, when it overflowed, would carry away a portion of the arable soil belonging to the Larisaeans. Later, however, they corrected this by means of embankments. The Larisaeans, then, kept possession of Perrhaebia and exacted tribute until Philip established himself as

[1] *Iliad* 2. 744.

[3] Ἄργουρα, Xylander, for Ἄργουσα; so the later editors.
[2] Λαρισαῖοι, Kramer, for Λαρισσαῖοι; so the later editors.

Φίλιππος κατέστη κύριος τῶν τόπων. Λάρισα δ' ἐστὶ καὶ ἐν τῇ Ὄσσῃ χωρίον· καὶ ἡ Κρεμαστή, ὑπό τινων δὲ Πελασγία[1] λεγομένη· καὶ ἐν τῇ Κρήτῃ πόλις ἡ νῦν εἰς Ἱεράπυτναν συνοικισθεῖσα, ἀφ' ἧς καὶ τὸ ὑποκείμενον πεδίον νῦν[2] Λαρίσιον[3] καλεῖται· καὶ ἐν Πελοποννήσῳ ἥ τε τῶν Ἀργείων ἄκρα καὶ ὁ τὴν Ἠλείαν ἀπὸ Δύμης διορίζων Λάρισος[4] ποταμός. Θεόπομπος δὲ καὶ πόλιν λέγει ἐν τῇ αὐτῇ μεθορίᾳ κειμένην Λάρισαν· καὶ ἐν τῇ Ἀσίᾳ ἥ τε Φρικωνὶς ἡ περὶ τὴν Κύμην καὶ ἡ κατὰ Ἁμαξιτὸν τῆς Τρῳάδος· καὶ ἡ Ἐφεσία Λάρισά ἐστι καὶ ἡ ἐν Συρίᾳ, τῆς δὲ Μιτυλήνης ἀπὸ πεντήκοντα σταδίων εἰσὶ Λαρισαῖαι πέτραι κατὰ τὴν ἐπὶ Μηθύμνης ὁδόν· καὶ ἐν τῇ Ἀττικῇ[5] δ' ἐστὶ Λάρισα· καὶ τῶν Τράλλεων διέχουσα κώμη τριάκοντα σταδίους ὑπὲρ τῆς πόλεως ἐπὶ Καΰστρου πεδίον διὰ τῆς Μεσωγίδος ἰόντων κατὰ τὸ τῆς Ἰσοδρόμης Μητρὸς ἱερόν, ὁμοίαν τὴν θέσιν καὶ τὴν ἀρετὴν ἔχουσα τῇ Κρεμαστῇ Λαρίσῃ· καὶ γὰρ εὔυδρος καὶ ἀμπελόφυτος· ἴσως δὲ καὶ ὁ Λαρίσιος Ζεὺς ἐκεῖθεν ἐπωνόμασται· καὶ ἐν τοῖς ἀριστεροῖς δὲ τοῦ Πόντου κώμη τις καλεῖται Λάρισα μεταξὺ Ναυ[λόχου[6]] . . . .[7] πλησίον τῶν ἄκρων τοῦ Αἵμου. καὶ Ὀλοοσσὼν[8] δέ, λευκὴ προσαγορευθεῖσα ἀπὸ τοῦ λευκάργιλος εἶναι, καὶ Ἠλώνη,

[1] Πελασγία, Xylander, for πλάγια; so the later editors.
[2] πεδίον ἐστὶ ὃ νῦν Aghino.
[3] Λαρίσιον, Kramer, for Λαρίσσιον; so the later editors.
[4] Λάρισος, Kramer, for Λαρίσσος; so the later editors.
[5] On Ἀττικῇ, see C. Müller. *Ind. Var. Lect.* p. 1005.
[6] Ναυλό[χου], lacuna supplied by Kramer; so the later editors.

lord over the region. Larisa is also the name of a place on Ossa; another is Larisa Cremastê, by some called Pelasgia;[1] and in Crete is a city Larisa, now joined to Hierapytna, whence the plain that lies below is now called Larisian Plain; and, in the Peloponnesus both Larisa, the citadel of the Argives, and the Larisus River, which is the boundary between the Eleian country and Dymê. Theopompus speaks of another city Larisa situated on the same common boundary; and in Asia is a Larisa Phryconis near Cymê; and also the Larisa near Hamaxitis in the Troad; and there is the Ephesian Larisa, and the Larisa in Syria; and there are Larisaean Rocks fifty stadia from Mitylenê on the road to Methymnê; and there is a Larisa in Attica; and a village Larisa thirty stadia distant from Tralleis, above the city, on the road which runs through Mesogis towards the Caÿster Plain near the temple of the Isodromian Mother,[2] which in its topographical position and its goodly attributes is like Larisa Cremastê, for it has an abundance of water and of vineyards; and perhaps the Larisaean Zeus received his epithet from this place; and also on the left of the Pontus is a village called Larisa, between Naulochus and . . . ,[3] near the end of Mount Haemus. And Oloosson, called "white" from the fact that its soil is a white clay,

[1] See 9. 5. 13.

[2] *i.e.* Cybelê.

[3] "Odessa" seems to be the lost word.

---

[7] It is almost certain that the remainder of the lacuna (about eight letters) should be supplied with καὶ Ὀδησσοῦ.

[8] Ὀλοσσών *Aghilno*, Meineke. See Ὀλοοσσόνα at beginning of 9. 5. 19.

Περραιβικαὶ πόλεις, καὶ Γόννος. ἡ δ' Ἠλώνη μετέβαλε τοὔνομα, Λειμώνη μετονομασθεῖσα· κατέσκαπται δὲ νῦν· ἄμφω δ' ὑπὸ τῷ Ὀλύμπῳ
C 441 κεῖνται, οὐ πολὺ ἄπωθεν τοῦ Εὐρώπου[1] ποταμοῦ, ὃν ὁ ποιητὴς Τιταρήσιον καλεῖ.

20. Λέγει δὲ καὶ περὶ τούτου καὶ περὶ τῶν Περραιβῶν ἐν τοῖς ἑξῆς ὁ ποιητής, ὅταν φῇ·

Γουνεὺς δ' ἐκ Κύφου ἦγε δύω καὶ εἴκοσι νῆας.
τῷ δ' Ἐνιῆνες ἕποντο μενεπτόλεμοί τε Περαιβοί,
οἳ περὶ Δωδώνην δυσχείμερον οἰκί' ἔθεντο,
οἵ τ' ἀμφ' ἱμερτὸν Τιταρήσιον ἔργ' ἐνέμοντο.

λέγει μὲν οὖν τούτους τοὺς τόπους τῶν Περραιβῶν, ἀπὸ μέρους τῆς Ἑστιαιώτιδος[2] ἐπειληχότας·[3] ἦσαν δὲ καὶ αἱ[4] ὑπὸ τῷ Πολυποίτῃ ἐκ μέρους Περραιβικαί, τοῖς μέντοι Λαπίθαις προσένειμε διὰ τὸ ἀναμὶξ οἰκεῖν καὶ τὰ μὲν πεδία κατέχειν τοὺς Λαπίθας καὶ τὸ ἐνταῦθα Περραιβικὸν ὑπὸ τούτοις τετάχθαι ὡς ἐπὶ πλέον, τὰ δ' ὀρεινότερα χωρία πρὸς τῷ Ὀλύμπῳ καὶ τοῖς Τέμπεσι τοὺς Περραιβούς, καθάπερ τὸν Κύφον καὶ τὴν Δωδώνην καὶ τὰ περὶ τὸν Τιταρήσιον, ὃς ἐξ ὄρους Τιταρίου[5] συμφυοῦς τῷ Ὀλύμπῳ ῥέων εἰς τὰ πλησίον τῶν Τεμπῶν χωρία τῆς Περραιβίας αὐτοῦ που τὰς συμβολὰς ποιεῖται πρὸς τὸν Πηνειόν. τὸ μὲν οὖν τοῦ Πηνειοῦ καθαρόν ἐστιν

[1] Εὐρώπου, Kramer, for Εὐρώτου; so the later editors.
[2] Ἱστιαιώτιδος *l*, Ald., Corais.
[3] ἐπειληχότας, conj. of Meineke, for ἐπειληφότας; ἐπειληφότων, Groskurd.
[4] αἱ, after καί, Corais inserts.
[5] Κιταρίου *Agi*.

and Elonê, and Gonnus are Perrhaebian cities. But Elonê changed its name to Leimonê, and is now in ruins. Both are situated below Olympus, not very far from the Europus River, which the poet calls the Titaresius.[1]

20. The poet next mentions both Titaresius and the Perrhaebians, when he says, "And Guneus led from Cyphus twenty-two ships. And there followed him the Enienians,[2] and the Perrhaebians steadfast in war, who had established their homes round wintry Dodona,[3] and dwelt in the fields about lovely Titaresius."[4] Now he speaks of these places as belonging to the Perrhaebians, places which fell into their possession as a part of Hestiaeotis.[5] And also the cities subject to Polypoetes were in part Perrhaebian. However, he assigned them to the Lapiths because the two peoples lived intermingled with one another,[6] and also because, although the Lapiths held possession of the plains and the Perrhaebian element there were for the most part subject to the Lapiths, the Perrhaebians held possession of the more mountainous parts near Olympus and Tempê, as, for example, Cyphus, and Dodona, and the region about the Titaresius; this river rises in the Titarius Mountain, which connects with Olympus, and flows into the territory of Perrhaebia which is near Tempê, and somewhere in that neighbourhood unites with the Peneius. Now the water of the Peneius is pure,

[1] *Iliad* 2. 751.

[2] The Homeric spelling of "Aenianians" (9. 4. 11.)

[3] The Thessalian Dodona mentioned in *Frags.* 1, 1*a*, 1*b*, 1*c*, Vol. III, pp. 321, 323.

[4] *Iliad* 2. 748.

[5] The Perrhaebians had seized Hestiaeotis (9. 5. 17).

[6] See 9. 5. 19.

ὕδωρ, τὸ δὲ τοῦ Τιταρησίου λιπαρὸν ἔκ τινος ὕλης, ὥστ᾽ οὐ συμμίσγεται,

ἀλλά τέ μιν καθύπερθεν ἐπιτρέχει ἠΰτ᾽ ἔλαιον.

διὰ δὲ τὸ ἀναμὶξ οἰκεῖν Σιμωνίδης Περραιβοὺς καὶ Λαπίθας καλεῖ τοὺς Πελασγιώτας ἅπαντας, τοὺς τὰ ἑῷα κατέχοντας τὰ περὶ Γυρτῶνα καὶ τὰς ἐκβολὰς τοῦ Πηνειοῦ καὶ Ὄσσαν καὶ Πήλιον καὶ τὰ περὶ Δημητριάδα καὶ τὰ ἐν τῷ πεδίῳ, Λάρισαν, Κραννῶνα, Σκοτοῦσσαν, Μόψιον, Ἄτρακα, καὶ τὰ περὶ τὴν Νεσσωνίδα λίμνην καὶ τὴν Βοιβηίδα· ὧν ὁ ποιητὴς ὀλίγων μέμνηται διὰ τὸ μὴ οἰκισθῆναί πω τἆλλα ἢ φαύλως οἰκισθῆναι διὰ τοὺς κατακλυσμοὺς ἄλλοτ᾽ ἄλλους γινομένους· ἐπεὶ οὐδὲ τῆς Νεσσωνίδος μέμνηται λίμνης, ἀλλὰ τῆς Βοιβηίδος μόνον, πολὺ ἐλάττονος οὔσης· ταύτης δὲ μόνης μενούσης, ἐκείνης δέ, ὡς εἰκός, τοτὲ μὲν πληρουμένης ἀτάκτως, τοτὲ δ᾽ ἐκλειπομένης. τῆς δὲ Σκοτούσσης ἐμνήσθημεν καὶ ἐν τοῖς περὶ Δωδώνης λόγοις καὶ τοῦ μαντείου τοῦ ἐν Θετταλίᾳ, διότι περὶ τοῦτον ὑπῆρξε τὸν τόπον. ἔστι δ᾽ ἐν τῇ Σκοτούσσῃ χωρίον τι Κυνὸς Κεφαλαὶ καλούμενον, περὶ ὃ Ῥωμαῖοι μετ᾽ Αἰτωλῶν καὶ Τίτος Κοΐντιος ἐνίκων μάχῃ μεγάλῃ Φίλιππον τὸν Δημητρίου, Μακεδόνων βασιλέα.

21. Πέπονθε δέ τι τοιοῦτο[1] καὶ ἡ Μαγνῆτις· κατηριθμημένων γὰρ ἤδη πολλῶν αὐτῆς τόπων,
C 442 οὐδένας τούτων ὠνόμακε Μάγνητας Ὅμηρος, ἀλλ᾽

[1] τοιοῦτο, Meineke, for τοιοῦτον.

[1] *Iliad* 2. 754. [2] 7. 7. 12

but that of the Titaresius is oily, because of some substance or other, so that it does not mingle with that of the Peneius, "but runs over it on the top like oil."[1] Because of the fact that the two peoples lived intermingled, Simonides uses the terms Perrhaebians and Lapiths of all the Pelasgiotes who occupy the region about Gyrton and the outlets of the Peneius and Mount Ossa and Mount Pelion, and the region about Demetrias, and the region in the plain, I mean Larisa, Crannon, Scotussa, Mopsium, Atrax, and the region about Lake Nessonis and Lake Boebeïs. Of these places the poet mentions only a few, because the rest of them had not yet been settled, or else were only wretched settlements, on account of the inundations which took place at various times. Indeed, he does not mention Lake Nessonis either, but Lake Boebeïs only (though it is much smaller), because the latter alone persisted, whereas the former, in all probability, was at times filled at irregular intervals and at times gave out altogether. Scotussa I have already mentioned in my account of Dodona and of the oracle in Thessaly, saying that originally it was near this place.[2] In the territory of Scotussa there is a place called Cynoscephalae,[3] near which Titus Quintius[4] and the Romans, along with the Aetolians, in a great battle[5] conquered Philip the son of Demetrius, king of the Macedonians.

21. Magnetis, also, has been treated by Homer in about the same way. For although he has already enumerated many of the places in Magnetis, none of these are called Magnetan by him except those two

[3] "Dogs' Heads," a low range of hills.
[4] Titus Quintius Flamininus. [5] 197 B.C.

ἐκείνους μόνους, οὓς τυφλῶς καὶ οὐ γνωρίμως διασαφεῖ,

> οἳ περὶ Πηνειὸν καὶ Πήλιον εἰνοσίφυλλον
> ναίεσκον.

ἀλλὰ μὴν περὶ τὸν Πηνειὸν καὶ τὸ Πήλιον οἰκοῦσι καὶ οἱ τὴν Γυρτῶνα ἔχοντες, οὓς ἤδη κατέλεξε, καὶ τὸ Ὀρμένιον καὶ ἄλλοι πλείους, καὶ ἔτι ἀπωτέρω τοῦ Πηλίου ὅμως Μάγνητες ἦσαν, ἀρξάμενοι ἀπὸ τῶν ὑπ' Εὐμήλῳ, κατά γε τοὺς ὕστερον ἀνθρώπους. ἐοίκασιν οὖν διὰ τὰς συνεχεῖς μεταστάσεις καὶ ἐξαλλάξεις τῶν πολιτειῶν καὶ ἐπιμίξεις συγχεῖν καὶ τὰ ὀνόματα καὶ τὰ ἔθνη, ὥστε τοῖς νῦν ἔσθ' ὅτε ἀπορίαν παρέχειν,[1] καθάπερ τοῦτο τὸ πρῶτον μὲν ἐπὶ Κραννῶνος καὶ τῆς Γυρτῶνος γεγένηται. τοὺς μὲν γὰρ Γυρτωνίους Φλεγύας πρότερον ἐκάλουν ἀπὸ Φλεγύου τοῦ Ἰξίονος ἀδελφοῦ, τοὺς δὲ Κραννωνίους Ἐφύρους, ὥστε διαπορεῖν, ὅταν φῇ ὁ ποιητής·

> τὼ μὲν ἄρ' ἐκ Θρήκης Ἐφύρους μέτα θωρήσσεσθον
> ἠὲ μετὰ Φλεγύας μεγαλήτορας,

τίνας ποτὲ βούλεται λέγειν.

22. Ἔπειτα τοῦτο καὶ ἐπὶ τῶν Περραιβῶν καὶ τῶν Αἰνιάνων[2] συνέβη. Ὅμηρος μὲν γὰρ συνέζευξεν αὐτούς, ὡς πλησίον ἀλλήλων οἰκοῦντας· καὶ δὴ καὶ λέγεται ὑπὸ τῶν ὕστερον ἐπὶ χρόνον

[1] παρέχειν, Pletho, for παρεῖχεν A, παρεῖχε *a* and other MSS.

[2] Αἰνιάνων, Pletho, for Ἀθαμάνων; so the later editors.

places, and even these are designated by him in a dim and indistinct way:[1] "who dwelt about Peneius and Pelion with its shaking foliage."[2] Assuredly, however, about the Peneius and Pelion lived those who held Gyrton, whom he had already named,[3] as also those who held Ormenium,[4] and several other Perrhaebian peoples; and yet farther away from Pelion there were still Magnetans, beginning with those subject to Eumelus, at least according to the writers of later times. These writers, however, on account of the continual migrations, changes of political administrations, and intermixture of tribes, seem to have confused both the names and the tribes, so that they sometimes present difficult questions for the writers of to-day. For example, this has proved true, in the first place, in the case of Crannon and Gyrton; for in earlier times the Gyrtonians were called "Phlegyae," from Phlegyas, the brother of Ixion, and the Crannonians "Ephyri," so that it is a difficult question who can be meant by the poet when he says, "Verily these twain, going forth from Thrace, arm themselves to pursue the Ephyri, or to pursue the great-hearted Phlegyae."[5]

22. Again, the same thing is true in the case of the Perrhaebians and Aenianians. For Homer[6] connected the two, as living near one another; and in fact we are told by the writers of later times that for a long

Homer nowhere specifically names either the Magnetans or their country except in *Iliad* 2. 756, where he says, "Prothoüs, son of Tenthredon, was the leader of the Magnetans."

[2] *Iliad* 2. 757. [3] *Iliad* 2. 738. [4] *Iliad* 2. 734.

[5] Some modern scholars question the authenticity of this passage. See Leaf's note *ad loc.*

[6] *Iliad* 2. 749.

συχνὸν ἡ οἴκησις τῶν Αἰνιάνων[1] ἐν τῷ Δωτίῳ γενέσθαι πεδίῳ, τοῦτο δ' ἐστὶ πλησίον τῆς ἄρτι λεχθείσης Περραιβίας καὶ τῆς Ὄσσης καὶ ἔτι τῆς Βοιβηίδος λίμνης ἐν μέσῃ μέν πως τῇ Θετταλίᾳ, λόφοις δὲ ἰδίοις[2] περικλειόμενον· περὶ οὗ Ἡσίοδος οὕτως εἴρηκεν·

ἢ οἵη Διδύμους ἱεροὺς ναίουσα κολωνοὺς
Δωτίῳ ἐν πεδίῳ πολυβότρυος ἄντ' Ἀμύροιο
νίψατο Βοιβιάδος λίμνης πόδα παρθένος ἀδμής.

οἱ μὲν οὖν Αἰνιᾶνες[3] οἱ πλείους εἰς τὴν Οἴτην ἐξηλάθησαν ὑπὸ τῶν Λαπιθῶν, κἀνταῦθα δὲ ἐδυνάστευσαν ἀφελόμενοι τῶν τε Δωριέων τινὰ μέρη καὶ τῶν Μαλιέων μέχρι Ἡρακλείας καὶ Ἐχίνου, τινὲς δ' αὐτῶν ἔμειναν περὶ Κύφον, Περραιβικὸν ὄρος ὁμώνυμον κατοικίαν ἔχον. οἱ δὲ Περραιβοί, τινὲς μὲν συσταλέντες περὶ τὰ ἑσπέρια τοῦ Ὀλύμπου μέρη κατέμενον αὐτόθι, πρόσχωροι ὄντες Μακεδόσι, τὸ δὲ πολὺ μέρος εἰς τὰ περὶ τὴν Ἀθαμανίαν ὄρη καὶ τὴν Πίνδον ἐξέπεσε· νυνὶ δὲ μικρὸν ἢ οὐδὲν αὐτῶν ἴχνος σώζεται· τοὺς δ' οὖν ὑπὸ τοῦ ποιητοῦ λεχθέντας Μάγνητας ὑστάτους ἐν τῷ Θετταλικῷ καταλόγῳ
C 443 νομιστέον τοὺς ἐντὸς τῶν Τεμπῶν ἀπὸ τοῦ Πηνειοῦ καὶ τῆς Ὄσσης ἕως Πηλίου, Μακεδόνων τοῖς Πιεριώταις ὁμόρους, τοῖς ἔχουσι τὴν τοῦ Πηνειοῦ περαίαν μέχρι τῆς θαλάττης. τὸ μὲν οὖν Ὁμόλιον ἢ τὴν Ὁμόλην (λέγεται γὰρ ἀμφοτέρως) ἀποδοτέον

[1] Αἰνιάνων, Pletho, for Ἀθαμάνων; so the later editors.
[2] For δὲ ἰδίοις, Meineke conj. διδύμοις.

time the habitation of the Aenianians was in the Dotian Plain. This plain is near the Perrhaebia just mentioned above, and Ossa and Lake Boebeïs; and while it is situated in the middle of Thessaly, yet it is enclosed all round by hills of its own. Concerning this plain Hesiod has spoken thus: "Or as the unwedded virgin[1] who, dwelling on the holy Didyman Hills, in the Dotian Plain, in front of Amyrus, bathed her foot in Lake Boebeïs."[2] Now as for the Aenianians, most of them were driven into Oeta by the Lapiths; and there too they became predominant, having taken away certain parts of the country from the Dorians and the Malians as far as Heracleia and Echinus, although some remained in the neighbourhood of Cyphus, a Perrhaebian mountain which had a settlement of the same name. As for the Perrhaebians, some of them drew together round the western parts of Olympus and stayed there, being neighbours to the Macedonians, but the greater part of them were driven out of their country into the mountains round Athamania and Pindus. But to-day little or no trace of them is preserved. At any rate, the Magnetans mentioned last by the poet in the Thessalian *Catalogue* should be regarded as those inside Tempê, extending from the Peneius and Ossa as far as Pelion, and bordering on the Pieriotae in Macedonia, who held the country on the far side of the Peneius as far as the sea. Now Homolium, or Homolê (for it is spelled both ways), should be

[1] Coronis, mother of Asclepius.
[2] *Frag.* 122 (Rzach): again quoted in 14. 1. 40.

---

[3] Αἰνίανες, Pletho, for Ἀθάμανες; so the later editors.

αὐτοῖς· εἴρηται δ' ἐν τοῖς Μακεδονικοῖς, ὅτι ἐστὶ πρὸς τῇ Ὄσσῃ κατὰ τὴν ἀρχὴν τῆς[1] τοῦ Πηνειοῦ διὰ τῶν Τεμπῶν διεκβολῆς. εἰ δὲ καὶ μέχρι τῆς παραλίας προϊτέον τῆς ἐγγυτάτω τοῦ Ὁμολίου, λόγον ἔχει, ὥστε[2] τὸν Ῥιζοῦντα προσνέμειν καὶ Ἐρυμνὰς ἐν τῇ ὑπὸ Φιλοκτήτῃ παραλίᾳ κειμένας καὶ τῇ ὑπὸ Εὐμήλῳ. τοῦτο μὲν οὖν ἐν ἀσαφεῖ κείσθω. καὶ ἡ τάξις δὲ τῶν ἐφεξῆς τόπων μέχρι Πηνειοῦ οὐ διαφανῶς λέγεται, ἀδόξων δ' ὄντων τῶν τόπων, οὐδ' ἡμῖν περὶ πολλοῦ θετέον. ἡ μέντοι Σηπιὰς ἀκτὴ καὶ τετραγῴδηται μετὰ ταῦτα καὶ ἐξύμνηται διὰ τὸν ἐνταῦθα ἀφανισμὸν τοῦ Περσικοῦ στόλου· ἔστι δ' αὕτη μὲν ἀκτὴ πετρώδης, μεταξὺ δ' αὐτῆς καὶ Κασθαναίας κώμης ὑπὸ τῷ Πηλίῳ κειμένης αἰγιαλός ἐστιν, ἐν ᾧ ὁ Ξέρξου στόλος ναυλοχῶν, ἀπηλιώτου πολλοῦ πνεύσαντος, ὁ μὲν εὐθὺς αὐτοῦ πρὸς τὸ ξηρὸν ἐξώκειλε καὶ διελύθη παραχρῆμα, ὁ δ' εἰς Ἰπνούς,[3] τόπον τραχὺν τῶν περὶ τὸ Πήλιον, παρενεχθείς, ὁ δ' εἰς Μελίβοιαν, ὁ δ' εἰς τὴν Κασθαναίαν διεφθάρη. τραχὺς δ' ἐστὶν ὁ παράπλους πᾶς ὁ τοῦ Πηλίου,[4] ὅσον σταδίων ὀγδοήκοντα· τοσοῦτος δ' ἐστὶ καὶ τοιοῦτος καὶ ὁ τῆς Ὄσσης. μεταξὺ δὲ κόλπος σταδίων πλειόνων ἢ διακοσίων, ἐν ᾧ ἡ Μελίβοια. ὁ δὲ πᾶς ἀπὸ Δημητριάδος ἐγκολπίζοντι ἐπὶ τὸν Πηνειὸν μείζων τῶν χιλίων, ἀπὸ δὲ Σπερχειοῦ

[1] τῆς, transferred here from position after διά.

[2] Meineke inserts καί after ὥστε.

[3] Ἰπνούς, Kramer and Meineke (see Herod. 7. 188) for Ἰπνοῦν ABE*ghis*, Ὑπνοῦν *lm*, Ἰπνοῦντα *ckno*; Ἰπνοῦντα correction in B, and so Corais.

[4] Πηλίου, Palmer, for Πηνειοῦ; so later editors.

assigned to the Magnetans; as I have said in my description of Macedonia,[1] it is close to Ossa, situated where the Peneius begins to discharge its waters through Tempê. And if one were to proceed as far as the sea-coast nearest to Homolium, there is reason for assigning to them Rhizus and Erymnae, which were situated on that part of the sea-coast which was subject to Philoctetes and on that which was subject to Eumelus. However, let this question remain undecided. And also the order of the places next thereafter as far as the Peneius is not plainly told by the poet; but since these places are without repute, neither should I myself regard the matter as of great importance. Cape Sepias, however, was afterwards celebrated both in tragedies and in hymns on account of the total destruction there of the Persian fleet. Sepias itself is a rocky cape, but between it and Casthanaea, a village situated at the foot of Pelion, is a beach where the fleet of Xerxes was lying in wait when, a violent east wind bursting forth, some of the ships were immediately driven high and dry on the beach and broken to pieces on the spot, and the others were carried along the coast to Ipni, one of the rugged places in the region of Pelion, or to Meliboea, or to Casthanaea, and destroyed. The whole voyage along the coast of Pelion is rough, a distance of about eighty stadia; and that along the coast of Ossa is equally long and rough. Between the two mountains is a gulf more than two hundred stadia in circuit, on which is Meliboea. The whole voyage along the coast from Demetrias to the Peneius, following the sinuosities of the gulfs, is more than one thousand stadia in length, and from the Sperchius eight hun-

[1] *Frag.* 16*b* (see also 16*c*), Vol. III., p 337.

καὶ ἄλλων ὀκτακοσίων, ἀπὸ δὲ Εὐρίπου δισχιλίων τριακοσίων[1] πεντήκοντα. Ἱερώνυμος δὲ τῆς πεδιάδος Θετταλίας καὶ Μαγνήτιδος τὸν κύκλον τρισχιλίων ἀποφαίνεται σταδίων· ᾠκῆσθαι δ' ὑπὸ Πελασγῶν· ἐξελαθῆναι δὲ τούτους εἰς τὴν Ἰταλίαν[2] ὑπὸ Λαπιθῶν· εἶναι δὲ τὸ νῦν καλούμενον Πελασγικὸν πεδίον, ἐν ᾧ Λάρισα[3] καὶ Γυρτώνη[4] καὶ Φεραὶ καὶ Μόψιον καὶ Βοιβηὶς καὶ Ὄσσα καὶ Ὁμόλη καὶ Πήλιον καὶ Μαγνῆτις· Μόψιον δ' ὠνόμασται οὐκ ἀπὸ Μόψου τοῦ Μαντοῦς τῆς[5] Τειρεσίου, ἀλλ' ἀπὸ τοῦ Λαπίθου τοῦ συμπλεύσαντος τοῖς Ἀργοναύταις· ἄλλος δ' ἐστὶ Μόψοπος,[6] ἀφ' οὗ ἡ Ἀττικὴ Μοψοπία.

23. Τὰ καθ' ἕκαστα μὲν ταῦτα περὶ Θετταλίας, καθ' ὅλου δ', ὅτι Πυρραία πρότερον ἐκαλεῖτο ἀπὸ Πύρρας τῆς Δευκαλίωνος γυναικός, Αἱμονία δὲ ἀπὸ Αἵμονος, Θετταλία δὲ ἀπὸ Θετταλοῦ τοῦ Αἵμονος. ἔνιοι δέ, διελόντες δίχα, τὴν μὲν πρὸς νότον λαχεῖν φασὶ Δευκαλίωνι, καὶ καλέσαι Πανδώραν ἀπὸ τῆς μητρός, τὴν δ' ἑτέραν Αἵμονι,
C 444 ἀφ' οὗ Αἱμονίαν λεχθῆναι· μετωνομάσθαι δὲ τὴν μὲν Ἑλλάδα ἀπὸ Ἕλληνος τοῦ Δευκαλίωνος, τὴν δὲ Θετταλίαν ἀπὸ τοῦ υἱοῦ Αἵμονος· τινὲς δὲ ἀπὸ Ἐφύρας τῆς Θεσπρωτίδος ἀπογόνους Ἀντίφου

[1] ὀκτακοσίων, editors before Kramer; see his note.

[2] Ἰταλίαν, Kramer, instead of Αἰτωλίαν (BE*lno* and editors before Kramer). A has αἰτω in *man. sec.* above; and *ch* have both.

[3] ἐν ᾧ Λάρισα, Politus, for ἐν Λαρίσσῃ; so the editors.

dred more, and from the Euripus two thousand three hundred and fifty. Hieronymus[1] declares that the plain-country of Thessaly and Magnetis is three thousand stadia in circuit, and that it was inhabited by Pelasgians, and that these were driven out into Italy by the Lapiths, and that the present Pelasgian Plain, as it is called, is that in which are situated Larisa, Gyrtonê, Pherae, Mopsium, Boebeïs, Ossa, Homolê, Pelion, and Magnetis. Mopsium is named, not after Mopsus, the son of Manto the daughter of Teiresias, but after Mopsus the Lapith who sailed with the Argonauts. But Mopsopus, after whom the Attic Mopsopia is named, is a different person.[2]

23. So much, then, for the several parts of Thessaly. But speaking of it as a whole, I may say that in earlier times it was called Pyrrhaea, after Pyrrha the wife of Deucalion, and Haemonia after Haemon, and Thessaly after Thessalus the son of Haemon. But some writers, dividing it into two parts, say that Deucalion obtained the portion towards the south and called it Pandora after his mother, and that the other part fell to Haemon, after whom it was called Haemonia, but that the former name was changed to Hellas, after Hellen the son of Deucalion, and the latter to Thessaly, after the son of Haemon. Some, however, say that descendants of Antiphus and

[1] Apparently Hieronymus of Rhodes (see note on 8. 6. 21).
[2] See 9. 1. 18.

---

[4] Instead of Γυρτώνη BE*klno* have Φεραῖς.
[5] Μαντοῦς τῆς, Tzschucke, from conj. of Kuhn, for *μάντεως τοῦ*; so the later editors.
[6] All MSS., except *no*, have Μόψος; see *Μοψοόπου* 9. 1. 18.

καὶ Φειδίππου,[1] τῶν Θετταλοῦ τοῦ Ἡρακλέους, ἐπελθόντας ἀπὸ Θετταλοῦ, τοῦ ἑαυτῶν προγόνου, τὴν χώραν ὀνομάσαι. εἴρηται δὲ καὶ Νεσσωνὶς ὀνομασθῆναί ποτε ἀπὸ Νέσσωνος τοῦ Θετταλοῦ, καθάπερ καὶ ἡ λίμνη.

[1] Φειδίππου, Lipsius, for Φιλίππου; so the editors.

Pheidippus, the sons of Thessalus the son of Heracles, invaded the country from Thesprotian Ephyra and named it after Thessalus, their own ancestor. And it has been said that the country too was once named Nessonis, like the lake, after Nesson the son of Thessalus.

A PARTIAL DICTIONARY OF PROPER NAMES[1]

A

Acarnanians, the, 5, 17, 183, 229, 345, 393, 395
Achaean League, the, 185, 215, 357
Achaeans, the, 133, 135, 137, 161, 167, 169, 185, 207, 209, 211, 215, 217, 219, 223, 341, 401, 413
Acheloüs River, the, 17, 43, 77
Achilles, domain of, 349, 379, 399, 403, 405, 407, 409, 411, 413, 417, 419, 427
Acidon River, the, 65, 67, 79
Acrocorinthus, 119, 187, 191, 193, 217
Actium, victory of Romans at, 225, 347
Aegialus, the, 185, 207, 209, 219
Aegina, 149, 153, 177, 179, 181, 183, 251, 413
Aegium, 185, 219, 223, 225, 233
Aeolians, the, 367, 369
Aeolic dialect, the, 5
Aeschylus, the tragic poet, on Cypros and Paphos, 37; on Bura and Rhypes, 225; on Aegina, 251
Aethices, the, 397, 417, 439
Aetolians, the, 5, 17, 91, 229, 345, 367, 385, 387, 389, 393, 395
Aetolus, 101, 103
Agamedes, designer of temple at Delphi, 361
Agamemnon, 109, 111, 115, 167, 177, 255, 347, 349
Agis, son of Eurysthenes, 135, 139
Agoracritus, the Parian sculptor (fl. 440–428 B.C., favourite pupil of Pheidias), by some thought to have made the statue of Nemesis at Rhamnus, 263
Agrippa (see *Dictionary* in vol. ii), put to death Bogus, king of the Maurusians, at Methonê, 111
Aias, 253, 255, 381
Alalcomenae, 323, 331, 333
Alcaeus (see *Dictionary* in vol. i), on the Coralius River, 323, 325; wrong on the site of Onchestus, 329
Alcman of Sardis (fl. about 625 B.C.), the founder of Dorian lyric poetry, 37
Alopê, 381, 387, 401, 409
Alpheius River, the, 21, 33, 47, 53, 61, 65, 73, 81, 85, 87, 99, 101, 231, 233
Amarium, where the Achaean League convened, 215, 223
Ambracian Gulf, the, 11, 13, 389
Amphiaraüs, 273, 293, 295
Amphictyonic Council, the, 327
Amphictyonic League, the, 173, 357
Amphictyonic Rights, the, 357
Amphictyons, the, 353, 361, 385, 393
Andron, author of a work on the *Land of Atthis;* on the limits of Megaris, 247
Anthedon, 279, 297, 299, 311, 313, 321
Anticyra, 343, 351, 369, 391, 415
Antigonus Gonatas, Acrocorinthus wrested from, by Aratus, 217
Antimachus of Colophon, author of an epic poem entitled *Thebaïs* and an elegiac poem entitled *Lydê*, 55; *apocopê* in, 131; calls Dymê "Cauconian," 225; spells "Thespiae" "Thespeia," 315
Antirrhium, 17, 19, 241, 385
Antony, Marcus, the triumvir, 111
Antron, 407, 411, 419, 421
Aphroditê, temples of, 49; her temple at Corinth, 191, 193; temple of Aphroditê Colias, 271

[1] A complete index will appear in the last volume.

A PARTIAL DICTIONARY OF PROPER NAMES

B

C

A PARTIAL DICTIONARY OF PROPER NAMES

A PARTIAL DICTIONARY OF PROPER NAMES

R

MACEDONIA,
EPEIRUS, THESSALIA
0 50 100 200 300 Stadia
Epidamnus (Dyrrachium)
PARTHINI
Via Egnatia
Apsus F.
Apollonia
Byllis
BYLLIONES
Oricum
Ceraunii M.
Panormus
CHAONES
Phoenice
Onchesmus
Phalacrum Pr.
Posidium Pr.
Cassiope
Buthrotum
Corcyra
CORCYRA I.
SICULUM sive AUSONIUM MARE
Leucimna Pr.
Sybota Ins.
Thyamis F.
THESPROTI
Pandosia
Chimerium Pr.
Cichyrus olim Ephyra
Glycys Port.
Bucheton
CASSOPAEI
Batiae
Ambracia
Nicopolis
Comarus Portus
Ambracius Sinus
Actium
Neritus
Leucas
LEUCAS I.
ACARNANIA
Palaerus
Alyzia
Stratus
AMPHILOCHIA
Argos Amphilochicum
AETOLIA
Dodona
MOLOSSI
Hellopia
ATINTANES
Lychnidus
Lychnitis L.
Lydrea
Heraclea Lyncestis
LYNCESTIS
Lyncestarum M.
AGRIANES
Bryanium?
Alcomenae?
DEUROPES
Stymbara?
PELAGONIA (ORESTIA)
Stobi
Erigon F.
Argos Oresticum
ORESTIS
ELIMEIA
TYMPHAEA
Tymphe M.
Oxynia
Europus
Aeginium
Oechalia
Tricca
Pelinna
Gomphi
Ithome
Metropolis
DOLOPES
ATHAMANES
THESSALIA
Achelous F.
Acheron F.
Aous s. Aeas F.
Sesarethii sive Desarethii
ENCHELEAE
BRYGI
MACEDONIA SUPERIOR
EORDAEA

THRACIA
Orbelus M.
Parorbelia
Garescus?
Callipolis?
Orthopolis?
Philippopolis?
Doberus?
Idomene
Gortynium
Nestus F.
Drabescus
Crenides (Philippi)
Bisaltae
Odones
Neapolis
Datum
Odomantes
Scotussa
Bergae
Heracleia
Sithones
Myrcinus
Amphipolis
Phagres
Galepsus
Apollonia
Arethusa
Strymonicus Sinus
Caprus I.
Thasos I.
Pella
Thessaloniceia (Therma)
Mygdones
Bolbe Palus
Apollonia
Stageirus
Cissus
Alorus
Methone
Pydna
Enea
Crusis
Chalcidenses
Acanthius Sinus
Acanthus
Olophyxus
Mecyberna
Dium
Thyssus
Cleonae
Acrathoi
Athos M.
Olynthus
Potidaea
Singus
Singiticus Sinus
Nymphaeum Pr.
Dium
Ibi Haliacmon sec Strabonem
Thermaeus Sinus
Toronaeus Sinus
Aphytis
Sane
Pallene
Phlegra
Mende
Scione
Cophus Port.
Derris Pr.
Canastraeum Pr.
Mare Thracicum
Libethria
Peneius F.
Erymnae
Homole
Phalanna
Gyrton
Ossa M.
Atrax
Larissa
Rhizus
Meliboea
Castanaea
Ipnus
Pelion M.
Mare Aegaeum
Crannon
Pelasgiotis
Pherae
Cynoscephalae
Scotussa
Pagasae
Iolcus
Demetrias
Pyrrha Pr.
Methone
Pharsalus
Thebae
Pagasiticus Sinus
Cicynethus I.
Sepias
Proerna
Narthacium
Thaumaci
Eretria
Phylace
Itonus
Halus
Coroneia
Melitaea
Phthiotis
Aphetae
Olizon
Sciathus
Peparethus
Posidium Pr.
Pteleum
Antrones
Larissa Cremaste
Echinus
Alope
Orcus
Hestiaeotis
Lamia
Phalara
Maliacus Sinus
Anticyra
Nicaea
Scarphea
Cnemis
Thronium
Alope
Cenaeum Pr.
Cerinthus
Orobiae
Cynus
Aegae
Thermopylae
Heracleia
Scyrus I.

Molossi
Pandosia
Cassopaei
Ambracia
Nicopolis
Ambracicus Sinus
Actium
Anactorium
Neritus
Leucas
LEUCAS I.
(Ithaca Homerica?)
Taphus
Taphiae s. Teleboides I.
Apollinis T.
Leucates Pr.
(Crocyleia I.?)
Aegilips I.?
Asteris I.
Neritum M.
Ithaca I.
Artemita I.
Neium M.
Alalcomenae
Same, Samus
CEPHALLENIA (SAME, SAMUS I.)
Cranii
Pronesus
Dolichium I.
Echinades I.
Stratus
Argos
Agraei
DOLOPES
Therma
Vetus Aetolia
Lysimacheia
Trichonium
Calydon
Pleuron
Oeniadae
Chalcis
Antirrhium Pr.
Rhium Pr.
Naupactus
Drepanum Pr.
Eupalium
Alope
Oeantheia
Cirrha
Cirphis
Delphi
Amphissa
LOCRI OZOLAE HESPERII
Marathus
Anticyra
Haliartus
Thisbe
Creusis
Thessaliotis
Pharsalus
Thaumaci
Theba
Eretria
Pagaseticus Sinus
Halus
Phthiotis
Melitaea
Coroneia
Pteleum
Antrones
Larissa
Lamia
Echinus
ANIANES
DRYOPES
Typhrestus M.
Oechalia?
Anticyra
Trachis
Heraclea
Maliacus Sinus
Thermopylae
Scarpheia
Lichades I.
Cnemis
Thronium
Alope
Cynus
Elateia
Doris
Tetrapolis
PHOCIS
Daulis
Panopeus
Orchomenus
Chaeroneia
Coroneia
Cyparissus
Sinus Crissaeus sive Corinthius
Mychus Portus
Olmiae Pr.
Aegeirusa
Lechaeum
Isthmus
Corinth
Araxus Pr.
Dyme
Olenus
Patrae
Rhypes
Aegium
Helice
Cerynia
Bura
Aegae
Aegeira
Pellene
Pharae
Tritaea
Hyrmine?
Buprasium
Cyllene?
Chelonatas Pr.
Myrtuntium
Elis
Pylus
Lampeia
Psophis
Cleitor
Pheneus
Cyllene M.
Stymphalus
Sicyon
Phlius
Cleonae
Nemea
Orneae
Mycenae
Heraeum
Midea
Tiryns
Nauplia
Argos
Temenium
ZACYNTHUS I.
Zacynthus
Elison, Elisa F.
PISATIS
(Jardanes F.)
Alpheius F.
Pheia Pr.
Olympia
Ichthys Pr.
Dyspontium
Thryon
Heraea
Phrixa
ARCADIA
Orchomenus
Methydrium
Mantineia
Cenchreae
Maenalus
Tegea
Samicum
Pylus
Macistus
Lepreum
Phigalia
Lycaeus M.
Megalopolis
Nedon
Cyparisseeis F.
Cyparissia
Dorium
Andania
Oechalia
Ithome M.
Messene
Strophades I.
Platamodes Pr.
MESSENIA
Erana
Thuria
Prote I.
Pylus ad Coryphasium
Sphagia s. Sphacteria I.
Rhium
Corone
(Aepeia Hom.?)
Methone
(Pedasus)
(Aepeia?)
Asine
(Antheia?)
Acritas Pr.
Messeniacus Sinus
Charadra
Gerena (Enope)
Cardamyle
Leuctrum
Thalamae
Sparta
Amyclae
Pharis, Pharae
Cynuria
Argolicus Sinus
Helos
Acraeae
Gythium
Las
Asopus
Oetylus
(Boetylus)
Laconicus Sin.
(Messa)
Thyrides Pr.
Psamathus
Taenarum Pr.
Cythera I.
Cythera
MARE SICULUM
HELLAS
PELOPONNESUS
Stadia
0 100 200 300

GRÆCIÆ FIGURA
sec. Strabonem.
Thessaloniceia
Ceraunii M.
Sinus Ambracicus
Ægium
Thermopylæ
Isthmus
Chelonatas Pr.
Megalopolitis
Athenæ
Sunium Pr.
Maleæ Pr.
Parallelus Rhodum Transiens.
Stadia
0 500 1000 1500
DELOS I.
Delos
Cynthus M.
Inopus
1 STADIUM
CRETA
Stadia
0 100 200
MARE CRETICUM
MARE LIBYCUM
Corycus Pr.
Phalasarna
Dictynnæum
Cydonia
Aptera
Albi M.
Ida M.
Gortyna
Cnossos
Dia I.
Heracleium
Chersonesus
Lyttus
Minoa
Phœnix
Phæstus
Matalum
Lissen
Leben
Prasus
Hierapytna
Criumetopon Pr.
Samonium Pr.
Halonnesos I.?
Icos I.?
Sciathos I.
Peparethos I.
Peparethos
Cerinthus
Chalcis
Eretria
Oropus
Thebæ
Tanagra
Platææ
Marathon
Rhamnus
Aphidna
Styra
Caphereus Pr.
Geræstus
Carystus
Geræstus Pr.
ATTICA
Athenæ
Salamis I.
Peiræeus
Megara
Eleusis
Brauron
Prasiæ
Potamus
Thoricus
Sunium
Sunium Pr.
Helena I.
Ægina
Ægina I.
Saronicus S.
Salaminius Sinus
Methana
Trœzen
Calauria I.
Scyllæum Pr.
Hermionicus Sinus
Belbina I.
Andros
Tenos
Gyaros
Ceos
Iulis
Coressia
Carthaea
Pœëessa
Cythnos
Syros
Rhenea
Myconos
Delos
Melantii Scopuli
CYCLADES I.
Seriphos
Paros
Naxos
Oliaros
Siphnos
Prepesinthos
Cimolos
Melos
Amorgos
Ios
Sicinos
Pholegandros
Lagusa
Thera
Therasia
Anaphe
T. Apollonis
SPORADES I.
MARE ÆGÆUM
MARE MYRTOUM
MARE CRETICUM

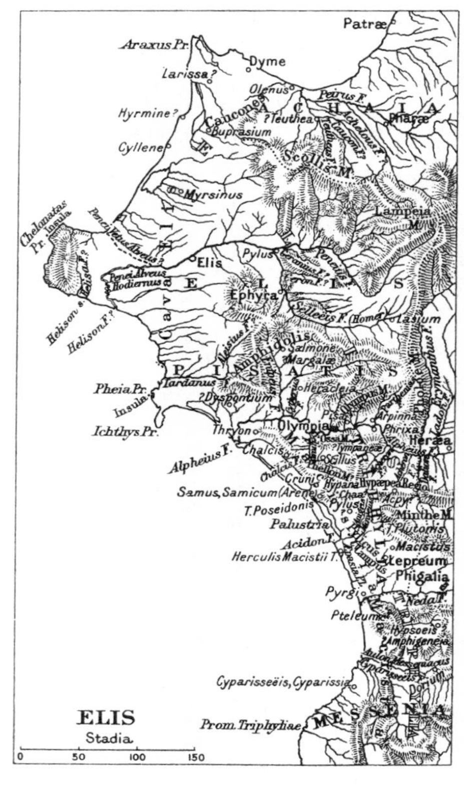

Patræ
Araxus Pr.
Dyme
Larissa?
Olenus
Peirus F.
A C H A I A
Pharæ
Hyrmine?
Caucones
?Teuthea
Buprasium
Cyllene
Scollis M.
Myrsinus
Lampeia M.
Chelonatas Pr.
Insula
Elis
Pylus
Penei Alveus Hodiernus
E L I S
Ephyra
Selleeis F. (Homer)
Lasium
Helison F.?
Amphidolis
Salmone
Margalæ
P I S A T I S
Pheia Pr.
Insula
Iardanus
?Dyspontium
Heracleia
Ichthys Pr.
Thryon
Olympia
Arpinna
Phrixa
Heræa
Erymanthus F.
Alpheius F.
Chalcis
Scillus
Hypana
Hypaepea Regio
Samus, Samicum (Arene)
T. Poseidonis
Pylus
Aepy
Palustria
Minthe M.
T. Plutonis
Acidon F.
Macistus
Herculis Macistii T.
Lepreum
Phigalia
Pyrgi
Neda F.
Pteleum
Hypsoeis
?Amphigeneia
Cyparisseëis, Cyparissia
Dorium
Prom. Triphyliae
M E S S E N I A
ELIS
Stadia
0
50
100
150

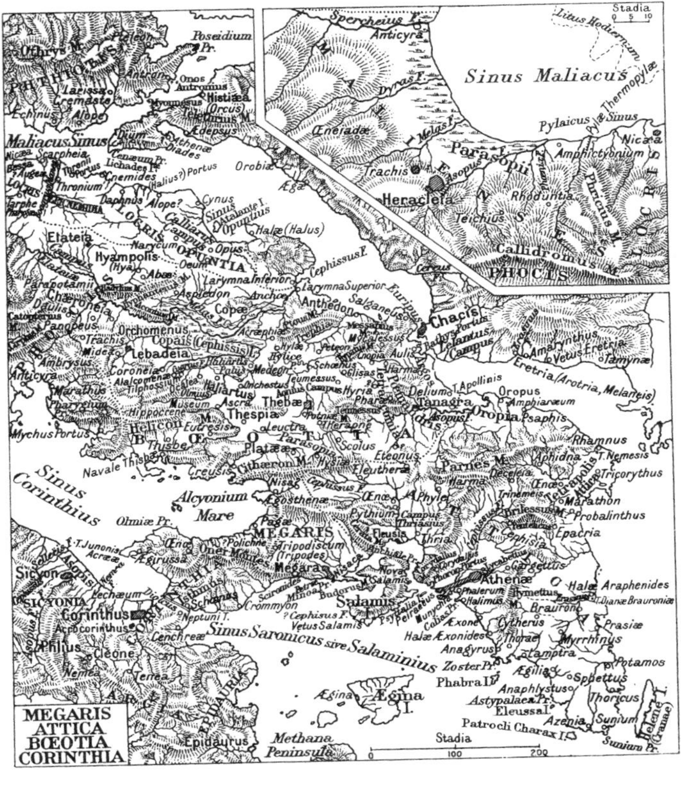
MEGARIS
ATTICA
BŒOTIA
CORINTHIA
Sinus Maliacus
Sinus Corinthius
Alcyonium Mare
Sinus Saronicus sive Salaminius
Athenæ
Thebæ
Megara
Corinthus
Chalcis
Eretria
Marathon
Plataeæ
Thespiæ
Tanagra
Oropus
Eleusis
Salamis
Ægina
Sicyon
Heraclea
Trachis
Callidromus M.
Stadia